Lecture Notes in Computer Science   8734

Commenced Publication in 1973
Founding and Former Series Editors:
Gerhard Goos, Juris Hartmanis, and Jan van Leeuwen

Borzoo Bonakdarpour   Scott A. Smolka (Eds.)

Runtime Verification

5th International Conference, RV 2014
Toronto, ON, Canada, September 22-25, 2014
Proceedings

 Springer

Volume Editors

Borzoo Bonakdarpour
McMaster University
Department of Computing and Software
1280 Main Street West, Hamilton
ON L8S 4L7, Canada
E-mail: borzoo@mcmaster.ca

Scott A. Smolka
State University of New York at Stony Brook
Department of Computer Science
1423 Computer Science, Stony Brook
NY 11794-4400, USA
E-mail: sas@cs.sunysb.edu

ISSN 0302-9743　　　　　　　　　　　e-ISSN 1611-3349
ISBN 978-3-319-11163-6　　　　　　　e-ISBN 978-3-319-11164-3
DOI 10.1007/978-3-319-11164-3
Springer Cham Heidelberg New York Dordrecht London

Library of Congress Control Number: 2014947359

LNCS Sublibrary: SL 2 – Programming and Software Engineering

Typesetting: Camera-ready by author, data conversion by Scientific Publishing Services, Chennai, India

Printed on acid-free paper

Springer is part of Springer Science+Business Media (www.springer.com)

Preface

The 14th International Conference on Runtime Verification (RV 2014) was held September 22–25, 2014, at the Fields Institute for Research in Mathematical Sciences on the campus of University of Toronto, Canada. The conference program included invited talks, tutorials, peer-reviewed presentations, and tool demonstrations.

RV started in 2001 as an annual workshop and turned into a conference in 2010. The workshops were organized as satellite events to an established forum, including CAV and ETAPS. The proceedings for RV from 2001 to 2005 were published in the *Electronic Notes in Theoretical Computer Science*. Since 2006, the RV proceedings have been published in Springer's *Lecture Notes in Computer Science*.

RV 2014 was attended by researchers and practitioners from all around the world. The conference program included papers on a wide variety of subjects, such as theoretical aspects of runtime verification, testing, tracing, bug finding, monitoring distributed systems, timed systems, and cyber-physical systems.

We are extremely pleased to have had three excellent invited speakers:

- Jeannette Wing, Vice President and Head of Microsoft Research International, is a leading figure in computer science research, particularly in formal methods, security, and privacy.
- Kevin Driscoll is a fellow at Honeywell Labs with 40 years, experience in safety and security critical systems.
- Assaf Schuster is Professor of Computer Science at the Technion, Israel, and has made significant contributions to monitoring distributed data streams and big data technology.

The conference also included two exciting tutorials:

- Vijay K. Garg (UT-Austin) and Neeraj Mittal (UT-Dallas) gave a tutorial on lattice-theoretic approaches to monitoring distributed systems.
- David Basin (ETH-Zurich) and Felix Klaedtke (NEC Labs, Europe) gave the second tutorial on runtime monitoring and enforcement of security policies.

We would like to extend our deep thanks to the authors of all submitted papers, to the members of the Program Committee, and to the external reviewers for their outstanding job in thoroughly evaluating all submitted papers. RV 2014 received 70 submissions: 57 regular papers, three tool papers, and 10 short papers. Most regular papers were reviewed by five Program Committee members. Tool and short papers were reviewed by three members of the Program Committee, who in the end decided to accept 18 are regular papers, 2 are tool papers, 7 short papers. Most paper discussions were conducted through the EasyChair conference manager. Four papers were discussed over a live conference call.

We would also like to thank the Fields Institute for its generous monetary contribution to the conference, as well as sharing its facility to hold the conference free of charge. We highly appreciate EasyChair for its free service to manage submissions.

Finally, our special thanks go to the incomparable chair of the Steering Committee, Klaus Havelund, for his invaluable help during all stages of organizing RV 2014.

July 2014   Borzoo Bonakdarpour
                                                        Scott A. Smolka

Organization

General Chair

Sebastian Fischmeister   University of Waterloo, Canada

Program Chairs

Borzoo Bonakdarpour   McMaster University, Canada
Scott Smolka   Stony Brook University, USA

Tools Track Chair

Ezio Bartocci   TU Wien, Austria

Runtime Monitoring Competition Chairs

Ezio Bartocci   TU Wien, Austria
Borzoo Bonakdarpour   McMaster University, Canada
Ylies Falcone   Université Joseph Fourier, France

Tutorials and Proceedings Chair

Nadia Polikarpova   ETH Zurich, Switzerland

Publicity Chair

Ylies Falcone   Université Joseph Fourier, France

Local Arrangements Chair

Patrick Lam   University of Waterloo, Canada

Program Committee

Gul Agha   University of Illinois at Urbana-Champaign, USA
Thomas Ball   Microsoft Research, USA
Howard Barringer   The University of Manchester, UK
Ezio Bartocci   TU Wien, Austria
David Basin   ETH Zurich, Switzerland

Saddek Bensalem	CEA-Leti, France
Borzoo Bonakdarpour (Co-chair)	McMaster University, Canada
Ivona Brandic	TU Wien, Austria
Marsha Chechik	University of Toronto, Canada
Michael Clarkson	George Washington University, USA
Laura Dillon	Michigan State University, USA
Shlomi Dolev	Ben-Gurion University, Israel
Alastair Donaldson	Imperial College London, UK
Dawson Engler	Stanford University, USA
Ylies Falcone	Université Joseph Fourier, France
Vijay Garg	University of Texas at Austin, USA
Steve Goddard	University of Nebraska-Lincoln, USA
Ganesh Gopalakrishnan	University of Utah, USA
Wolfgang Grieskamp	Google, USA
Radu Grosu	TU Wien, Austria
Klaus Havelund	NASA/JPL, USA
Mats Heimdahl	University of Minnesota, USA
Gerard Holzmann	NASA/JPL, USA
Taylor Johnson	UT-Arlington, USA
Daniel Keren	Haifa University, Israel
Sandeep Kulkarni	Michigan State University, USA
Marta Kwiatkowska	University of Oxford, USA
Insup Lee	University of Pennsylvania, USA
Axel Legay	IRISA/Inria, Rennes, France
Martin Leucker	University of Lübeck, Germany
Leonardo Mariani	University of Milano Bicocca, Italy
Patrick Meredith	University of Illinois at Urbana-Champaign, USA
David Naumann	Stevens Institute of Technology, USA
Samaneh Navabpour	University of Waterloo, Canada
Doron Peled	Bar-Ilan University, Israel
Mauro Pezzè	University of Lugano, Switzerland
Lee Pike	Galois, Inc., USA
Nadia Polikarpova	ETH Zurich, Switzerland
Zvonimir Rakamaric	University of Utah, USA
Grigore Rosu	University of Illinois at Urbana-Champaign, USA
Andrey Rybalchenko	TUM, Germany
Andre Schiper	EPFL, Switzerland
Scott Smolka (Co-chair)	Stony Brook University, USA
Oleg Sokolsky	University of Pennsylvania, USA
Scott Stoller	Stony Brook University, USA
Serdar Tasiran	Koç University, Turkey
Michael W. Whalen	University of Minnesota, USA
Lenore Zuck	University of Illinois at Chicago, USA

Additional Reviewers

Abdellatif, Takoua
Alglave, Jade
Arusoaie, Andrei
Avni, Hillel
Bak, Stanley
Balasubramanian, Bharath
Bardsley, Ethel
Binun, Alexander
Blankenburg, Martin
Chang, Yen-Jung
Charalambides, Minas
Chauhan, Himanshu
Chen, Yu-Fang
Chiang, Wei-Fan Chiang
Chong, Nathan
Chudnov, Andrey
Ciobaca, Stefan
Combaz, Jaques
Creswick, Rogan
Decker, Normann
Estler, Hans-Christian
Farokhi, Soodeh
Feng, Lu
Fernandez, Jean-Claude
Griffith, Dennis
Haran, Arvind
Hicks, Michael
Huang, Jeff
Ivanov, Radoslav
Jaber, Mohamad
Jovanovic, Aleksandra
Kahil, Ramzi Martin
Kandl, Susanne
Kim, Chang Hwan Peter
Klaedtke, Felix
Korthikanti, Vijay Anand
Kuru, Ismail
Kühn, Franziska

Liew, Dan
Lucanin, Drazen
Margaria, Tiziana
Marinovic, Srdjan
Matar, Hassan Salehe
Melnychenko, Oleksandr
Meng, Wenrui
Mutlu, Erdal
Mutluergil, Suha Orhun
Müller, Peter
Nizol, Matthew
Ozkan, Burcu Kulahcioglu
Paoletti, Nicola
Park, Junkil
Pastore, Fabrizio
Porter, Joseph
Ratasich, Denise
Reger, Giles
Rydeheard, David
Santoro, Mauro
Scheffel, Torben
Sedwards, Sean
Selyunin, Konstantin
Sharma, Subodh
Sridhar, Meera
Stümpel, Annette
Thoma, Daniel
Thomson, Paul
Ujma, Mateusz
Wang, Shaohui
Weimer, James
Weiss, Gera
Wickerson, John
Wiltsche, Clemens
Winwood, Simon
Xu, Meng
Zalinescu, Eugen

Invited Talks

Murphy Strikes Again
Kevin Driscoll (Honeywell Labs, USA)

An objective of a conference keynote is to provide some rationale and motivation for the conference: Why are we here? For this conference: Why do Runtime Verification? It must be for applications critical enough to warrant this additional expense to ensure that the application performs adequately in the presence of faults – design faults and hardware faults. There is an interesting link between the latter and the former. In critical applications, there often is a higher density of faults in the fault-tolerance software than there is in the rest of the software! Three reasons for this are: (1) The higher density of complex conditional branches in this type of software. (2) The lack of understanding of all possible failure scenarios leading to vague or incomplete requirements. (3) This software is the last to be tested... when the funding and schedule are exhausted. My boss once said that "All system failures are caused by design faults." This is because, regardless of the requirements, critical systems should be designed to never fail. It is extremely rare for a critical system to fail in a way that was anticipated by the designers (e.g., redundancy exhaustion). NASA's C. Michael Holloway observed: "To a first approximation, we can say that accidents are almost always the result of incorrect estimates of the likelihood of one or more things." This keynote will explore the factors that lead to designers underestimating the possibility/probabilities of certain failures. Examples of rare, but actually occurring, failures will be given. These will include Byzantine faults, component transmogrification, "evaporating" software, and exhaustively tested software that still failed. The well known Murphy's Law states that: "If anything can go wrong, it will go wrong." For critical systems, the following should added: "And, if anything can't go wrong, it will go wrong anyway."

Monitoring Big, Distributed, Streaming Data
Assaf Schuster (Technion, Israel)

More and more tasks require efficient processing of continuous queries over scalable, distributed data streams. Examples include optimizing systems using their operational log history, mining sentiments using sets of crawlers, and data fusion over heterogeneous sensor networks. However, distributed mining and/or monitoring of global behaviors can be prohibitively difficult. The naïve solution which sends all data to a central location mandates extremely high communication volume, thus incurring unbearable overheads in terms of resources and energy. Furthermore, such solutions require expensive powerful central platform, while data transmission may violate privacy rules. An attempt to enhance the naïve solution by periodically polling aggregates is bound to fail, exposing a vicious tradeoff between communication and latency. Given a continuous global query, the solution proposed in the talk is to generate filters, called safe zones, to be applied locally at each data stream. Essentially, the safe zones represent geometric constraints which, until violated by at least one of the sources, guarantee that a global property holds. In other words, the safe zones allow for constructive quiescence: There is no need for any of the data sources to transmit anything as long as all constraints are held with the local data confined to the local safe zone. The typically-rare violations are handled immediately, thus the latency for discovering global conditions is negligible. The safe zones approach makes the overall system implementation, as well as its operation, much simpler and cheaper. The saving, in terms of communication volume, can reach many orders of magnitude. The talk will describe a general approach for compiling efficient safe zones for many tasks and system configurations.

Formal Methods: An Industrial Perspective
Jeannette Wing (Carnegie Mellon University and Microsoft Research, USA)

Formal methods research has made tremendous progress since the 1980s when a proof using a theorem prover was worthy of a Ph.D. thesis and a bug in a VLSI textbook was found using a model checker. Now, with advances in theorem proving, model checking, satisfiability modulo theories (SMT) solvers, and program analysis, the engines of formal methods are more sophisticated and are applicable and scalable: to a wide range of domains, from biology to mathematics; to a wide range of systems, from asynchronous systems to spreadsheets; and for a wide range of properties, from security to program termination. In this talk, I will present a few Microsoft Research stories of advances in formal methods and their application to Microsoft products and services. Formal methods use, however, is not routine—yet—in industrial practice. So, I will close with outstanding challenges and new directions for research in formal methods.

Invited Tutorials

A Lattice-Theoretic Approach to Monitoring Distributed Computations

Vijay K. Garg (UT Austin, USA)
Neeraj Mittal (UT Dallas, USA)

Reasoning about distributed programs is hard because the non-deterministic interleaving of concurrent activities in the system dramatically increases the number of possible executions of the program. This non-determinism also makes it difficult to test or verify the correctness of a distributed program before deployment. Continuous monitoring of a running system is a complementary approach for increasing the dependability of a distributed program after deployment.

An execution of a distributed system, also referred to as a distributed computation, can be modeled as a partially ordered set (poset) of events ordered by the happened-before relation. The set of all consistent global states of the computation correspond to the lattice of all down-sets of the poset. The problem of runtime monitoring can be viewed as evaluating a predicate on this lattice. In this tutorial, we will give a survey of algorithms and their limitations for evaluating global predicates in distributed systems. The algorithms exploit lattice-theoretic properties of predicates for efficiency. For example, if the given predicate B is meet-closed and join-closed, then we can compute a subcomputation (called slice) which exactly captures all the consistent global states that satisfy B. We will describe centralized and distributed algorithms to compute such a slice. We also show how slices can be used to detect temporal logic predicates in a distributed computation.

Runtime Monitoring and Enforcement of Security Policies

David Basin (ETH Zurich, Switzerland)
Felix Klaedtke (NEC Europe Ltd., Switzerland)

Many kinds of digitally stored data should only be used in restricted ways. The intended usage may be stipulated by government regulations, corporate privacy policies, preferences of the data owner, etc. Such policies cover not only who may access which data, but also how the data may or must not be used after access. An example of such a usage restriction is that "collected data must be deleted after 30 days and not accessed or forwarded to third parties."

In this tutorial, we present different methods and results for monitoring and enforcing such policies along with their underlying foundations. We show how temporal logical can be used not only to formalize such regulations, but to synthesize efficient monitors from specifications. These monitors can then be used either online or offline to check whether the behavior of system agents, i.e., users and processes, is policy compliant. A particular focus here will be on the use of metric first-order temporal logic as a policy language, its algorithmic realization in the MonPoly tool, and our experience using this tool.

We will also consider the question of when and how can such policies be enforced by execution monitoring. We will review Schneider's seminal work on policy enforcement as well as its limitations. We will show how to overcome the limitations of Schneider's setting by distinguishing between system actions that are controllable by an enforcement mechanism and those actions that are only observable, that is, the enforcement mechanism sees them but cannot prevent their execution. For this refined setting, we give necessary and sufficient conditions on when a security policy is enforceable. Furthermore for different specification languages, we investigate the problem of deciding whether a given policy is enforceable and synthesizing an enforcement mechanism from an enforceable policy.

Table of Contents

Runtime Verification of Real-Time and Embedded Systems

Testing and Bug Finding

Inference and Learning

First International Competition
on Software for Runtime Verification

Ezio Bartocci[1], Borzoo Bonakdarpour[2], and Yliès Falcone[3]

[1] Vienna University of Technology, Austria
ezio.bartocci@tuwien.ac.at
[2] McMaster University, Canada
borzoo@mcmaster.ca
[3] Université Grenoble-Alpes, Laboratoire d'Informatique de Grenoble, France
ylies.falcone@ujf-grenoble.fr

Abstract. We report on the process of organizing the First International Competition on Software for Runtime Verification (CSRV). The report describes the format, participating teams and evaluation process. The competition was held as a satellite event of the 14th International Conference on Runtime Verification (RV'14). The Competition was organized in three tracks: offline monitoring, online monitoring of C programs, and online monitoring of Java programs.

1 Introduction

Runtime Verification (RV) is a lightweight yet powerful formal specification-based technique for offline analysis (e.g., for testing) as well as runtime monitoring of software. RV is based on extracting information from a running system and checking if the observed behavior satisfies or violates the properties of interest. During the last decade, many important tools and techniques have been developed and successfully employed. However, due to lack of standard benchmark suites as well as scientific evaluation methods to validate and test new techniques, we believe our community is in pressing need to have an organized venue whose goal is to provide mechanisms for comparing different aspects of existing tools and techniques.

For these reasons, inspired by the success of similar events in other areas of computer-aided verification (e.g., SV-COMP, SAT, SMT), we organized the First International Competition on Software for Runtime Verification (CSRV 2014) with the aim to foster the process of comparison and evaluation of software runtime verification tools. The aim of CSRV'14 was the following:

- To stimulate the development of new efficient and practical runtime verification tools and the maintenance of the already developed ones.
- To produce benchmark suites for runtime verification tools, by sharing case studies and programs that researchers and developers can use in the future to test and to validate their prototypes.
- To discuss the metrics employed for comparing the tools.

B. Bonakdarpour and S.A. Smolka (Eds.): RV 2014, LNCS 8734, pp. 1–9, 2014.

- To compare different aspects of the tools running with different benchmarks and evaluating them using different criteria.
- To enhance the visibility of presented tools among different communities (verification, software engineering, distributed computing and cyber security) involved in software monitoring.

CSRV'14 was held in September 2014, in Toronto, Canada, as a satellite event of the 14th International conference on Runtime Verification (RV'14). The event was organized in three tracks: (1) offline monitoring, (2) online monitoring of C programs, and (3) online monitoring of Java programs. The competition included three phases for each track:

1. collection of benchmarks,
2. training and monitor submissions,
3. evaluation.

This report presents the procedures, rules, and participating teams of CSRV'14. The final results of the competition are planned to be announced during the RV'14 conference.

2   Format of the Competition

In this section we describe in detail the phases of the competition.

2.1   Declaration of Intent and Submission of Benchmarks and Specifications

The competition was announced in relevant mailing lists starting from October 2013. Potential participants were requested to declare their intent for participating in CSRV by December 15, 2013. For each of the three main tracks (offline, C and Java), the tools participating in the competition listed in alphabetical order in Tables 1, 2, and 3, respectively.

Subsequently, participants were asked to prepare benchmark/specification sets. These were collected in a shared repository[1]. The deadline was June 1st, 2014. The benchmarks were collected and classified into a hierarchy of folders representing the competition tracks and participating teams.

Online monitoring of Java and C programs tracks. In the case of Java and C tracks, each benchmark contribution was required to be structured as follows:

- *Program package* containing the program source code, a script to compile it, a script to run the executable, and an English description of the functionality of the program.
- *Specification package* is a collection of files, each containing a property that contains a formal representation of it, informal explanation and the expected verdict (the evaluation of the property on the program), instrumentation information, and an English description.

---

[1] https://bitbucket.org/borzoob/csrv14

Table 1. Tools participating in online monitoring of C programs track

Tool	Ref.	Contact person	Affiliation
RiTHM	[11]	B. Bonakdarpour	McMaster Univ. and U. Waterloo, Canada
E-ACSL	[7]	J. Signoles	CEA LIST, France
RTC		P. Pirkelbauer	University of Alabama at Birmingham, USA

Table 2. Tools participating in online monitoring of Java programs track

Tool	Ref.	Contact person	Affiliation
LARVA	[4]	C. Colombo	University of Malta, Malta
jUnitRV	[5]	N. Decker	ISP, University of Lübeck, Germany
jUnitRV (MMT)	[6]	N. Decker	ISP, University of Lübeck, Germany
JavaMop	[10]	G. Rosu	U. of Illinois at Urbana Champaign, USA
prMj4	[12]	E. Bodden	TU Darmstadt, Germany
QEA	[1]	G. Reger	University of Manchester, UK

Table 3. Tools participating in the offline monitoring track

Tool	Ref.	Contact person	Affiliation
ZOT+SOLOIS	[3]	D. Bianculli	Politecnico di Milano, Italy
		S. Krstic	University of Luxembourg, Luxembourg
LogFire	[9]	K. Havelund	NASA JPL, USA
RiTHM2	[11]	B. Bonakdarpour	McMaster Univ. and U. Waterloo, Canada
MonPoly	[2]	E. Zalinescu	ETH Zurich, Switzerland
STePr		N. Decker	ISP, University of Lübeck, Germany
Breach	[8]	A. Donzé	University of California, Berkeley, USA
QEA	[1]	G. Reger	University of Manchester, England

The instrumentation information maps the events referred in the properties to concrete program events. A property consists of a formally defined object (e.g., an automaton, logical formula, etc), an informal description, and whether the program satisfies the property (i.e., the expected verdict). Instrumentation is a mapping from concrete events (in the program) to abstract events (in the specification). For instance, if one considers the HasNext property on iterators, the mapping should indicate that the hasNext event in the property refers to a call to the hasNext() method on an Iterator object. We allow for several concrete events to be associated to one abstract event.

Offline monitoring track. In the case of offline track, each benchmark contribution should consist of:

- a *trace* in either XML, CSV, or JSON format
- a *specification package*, which consists of a collection of files, each containing the formal representation of a property, informal explanation and the expected verdict (the evaluation of the property on the program), instrumentation information, and a brief English description.

Below we present some examples, where **an_event_name** ranges over the set of possible event names, **a_field_name** ranges over the set of possible field names, **a_value** ranges over the set of possible runtime values.

```
JSON format:
an_event_name
a_field_name = a_value
a_field_name = a_value

an_event_name
a_field_name = a_value
a_field_name = a_value

CSV format:
an_event_name, a_field_name = a_value, a_field_name = a_value
an_event_name, a_field_name = a_value, a_field_name = a_value

XML format
<log>

  <event>
   <name>an_event_name</name>
   <field>
     <name>a_field_name</name>
     <value>a_value</value>
   </field>
   <field>
     <name>a_field_name</name>
     <value>a_value</value>
   </field>
  </event>
  <event>
   <name>EVR</name>
   <field>
     <name>a_field_name</name>
     <value>a_value</value>
   </field>
   <field>
     <name>a_field_name</name>
     <value>a_value</value>
   </field>
  </event>

</log>
```

2.2 Training Phase and Monitor Collection phase

After a sanity check of the benchmarks performed by the organisers, the training phase started on June 18, 2014. During this phase, all participants are supposed to train their tools with all the available benchmarks in the repository. This phase was scheduled to be completed by July 20, 2014, when the participants will submit the monitored versions of benchmarks. In this phase, a contribution consists of a the source of a program and a list of pairs of program and property identifier. That is, a contribution is related to a program and contains monitors for the properties of this program. Each monitor is related to one property. A monitor consists of two scripts, one for building the (monitored version of) program, one for running the monitored version of the program.

2.3 Benchmark Evaluation Phase

The competition experiments for evaluation will be performed on DataMill (http://datamill.uwaterloo.ca), a distributed infrastructure for computer performance experimentation targeted at scientists that are interested in performance evaluation. DataMill aims to allow the user to easily produce robust and reproducible results at low cost. DataMill executes experiments on real hardware and incorporates results from existing research on how to setup experiments and hidden factors.

Each participant will have the possibility to setup and try directly their tool using DataMill. The final evaluation will be performed by the competition organizers. In the next section, we present in detail the algorithm to calculate the final score for each tool.

3 Evaluation - Calculating Scores

Let us consider one of the three competition tracks (Java, C, and offline). Let N be the number of tools participating in the considered track and L be the total number of benchmarks provided by all teams. The total number of experiments for the track will be $N \times L$. Then, for each tool T_i ($1 \leq i \leq N$) w.r.t. each benchmark B_j ($1 \leq j \leq L$), we assign three different scores: the correctness score $C_{i,j}$, the overhead score $O_{i,j}$, and the memory utilization score $M_{i,j}$. In case of online monitoring, let E_j be the execution time of benchmark B_j (without monitor). Note, in the following, for simplicity of notation, we assume that all participants of a track want to compete on benchmark B_j. Participants can of course decide not to qualify on a benchmark of their track. In this case, the following score definitions can be adapted easily.

3.1 Correctness Score

The correctness score $C_{i,j}$ for a tool T_i running a benchmark B_j is calculated as follows:

- $C_{i,j} = 0$, if the property associated with benchmark B_j cannot be expressed in the specification language of T_i.
- $C_{i,j} = -10$, if the property can be expressed, but the monitored program crashes.
- $C_{i,j} = -5$, if, in case of online monitoring, the property can be expressed and no verdict is reported after $10 \times E_j$.
- $C_{i,j} = -5$, if, in case of offline monitoring, the property can be expressed, but the monitor crashes.
- $C_{i,j} = -5$, if the property can be expressed, the tool does not crash, and the verification verdict is incorrect.
- $C_{i,j} = 10$, if the tool does not crash, it allows to express the property of interest, and it provides the correct verification verdict.

Note that in case of a negative correctness score there is no evaluation w.r.t the overhead and memory utilization scores for the pair (T_i, B_j).

3.2 Overhead Score

The overhead score $O_{i,j}$ for a tool T_i running a benchmark B_j is related to the timing performance of the tool for detecting the (unique) verdict. For all benchmarks, a fixed total number of points O is allocated when evaluating the tools on a benchmark. Thus, the scoring method for overhead ensures that

$$\sum_{i=1}^{N} \sum_{j=1}^{L} O_{i,j} = O.$$

The overhead score is calculated as follows. First, we compute the *overhead index* $o_{i,j}$, for tool T_i running a benchmark B_j, where the larger overhead index, the better.

- In the case of offline monitoring, for the overhead, we consider the elapsed time till the property under scrutiny is either found to be satisfied or violated. If monitoring (with tool T_i) of the trace of benchmark B_j executes in time V_i, then we define the overhead as

$$o_{i,j} = \begin{cases} \dfrac{1}{V_i} & \text{if } C_{i,j} > 0 \\ 0 & \text{otherwise} \end{cases}$$

- In the case of online monitoring (C or Java), the overhead associated with monitoring is a measure of how much longer a program takes to execute due to runtime monitoring. If the monitored program (with monitor from tool T_i) executes in $V_{i,j}$ time units, we define the overhead index as

$$o_{i,j} = \begin{cases} \dfrac{\sqrt[N]{\prod_{l=1}^{N} V_{l,j}}}{V_{i,j}} & \text{if } C_{i,j} > 0 \\ 0 & \text{otherwise} \end{cases}$$

In other words, the overhead index for tool T_i evaluated on benchmark B_j is the geometric mean of the overheads of the monitored programs with all tools over the overhead of the monitored program with tool T_i.

Then, the overhead score $O_{i,j}$ for a tool T_i w.r.t benchmark B_j is defined as follows:

$$O_{i,j} = O \times \frac{o_{i,j}}{\sum_{l=1}^{N} o_{l,j}}.$$

For each tool, the overhead score is a harmonization of the overhead index so that the sum of overhead scores is equal to O.

3.3　Memory Utilization Score

The memory utilization score $M_{i,j}$ is calculated similarly to the overhead score. For all benchmarks, a fixed total number of points O is allocated when evaluating the tools on a benchmark. Thus the scoring method for memory utilization ensures that

$$\sum_{i=1}^{N} \sum_{j=1}^{L} M_{i,j} = M.$$

First, we measure the memory utilization index $m_{i,j}$ for tool T_i running a benchmark B_j, where the larger memory utilization index, the better.

- In the case of offline monitoring, we consider the maximum memory allocated during the tool execution. If monitoring (with tool T_i) of the trace of benchmark B_j uses a quantity of memory D_i, then we define the overhead as

$$m_{i,j} = \begin{cases} \dfrac{1}{D_i} & \text{if } C_{i,j} > 0 \\ 0 & \text{otherwise} \end{cases}$$

  That is, the memory utilization index for tool T_i evaluated on benchmark B_j is the geometric mean of the memory utilizations of the monitored programs with all tools over the memory utilization of the monitored program with tool T_i.

- In the case of online monitoring (C or Java tracks), memory utilization associated with monitoring is a measure of the extra memory the monitored program needs (due to runtime monitoring). If the monitored program uses D_i, we define the memory utilization as

$$m_{i,j} = \begin{cases} \dfrac{\sqrt[N]{\prod_{l=1}^{N} D_{l,i}}}{D_{i,j}} & \text{if } C_{i,j} > 0 \\ 0 & \text{otherwise} \end{cases}$$

Then, the memory utilization score $M_{i,j}$ for a tool T_i w.r.t. a benchmark B_j is defined as follows:

$$M_{i,j} = M \times \frac{m_{i,j}}{\sum_{l=1}^{N} m_{l,j}}.$$

3.4   Final Score

The final score F_i for tool T_i is then computed as follows:

$$F_i = \sum_{j=1}^{L} S_{i,j}$$

where:

$$S_{i,j} = \begin{cases} C_{i,j} & \text{if } C_{i,j} \leq 0, \\ C_{i,j} + O_{i,j} + M_{i,j} & \text{otherwise.} \end{cases}$$

4   Concluding Remarks

This report was written during the training phase. Once this phase is complete, the organizers will evaluate all the submitted monitors using the formula proposed in Section 3. The results of the competition is expected to be announced during the RV 2014 conference in Toronto, Canada. This report is published to assist future organizers of CSRV to build on the efforts made to organize CSRV 2014.

References

1. Barringer, H., Falcone, Y., Havelund, K., Reger, G., Rydeheard, D.: Quantified Event Automata: Towards Expressive and Efficient Runtime Monitors. In: Giannakopoulou, D., Méry, D. (eds.) FM 2012. LNCS, vol. 7436, pp. 68–84. Springer, Heidelberg (2012)
2. Basin, D., Harvan, M., Klaedtke, F., Zălinescu, E.: MONPOLY: Monitoring Usage-control Policies. In: Khurshid, S., Sen, K. (eds.) RV 2011. LNCS, vol. 7186, pp. 360–364. Springer, Heidelberg (2012)
3. Bianculli, D., Ghezzi, C., San Pietro, P.: The Tale of SOLOIST: A Specification Language for Service Compositions Interactions. In: Păsăreanu, C.S., Salaün, G. (eds.) FACS 2012. LNCS, vol. 7684, pp. 55–72. Springer, Heidelberg (2013)
4. Colombo, C., Pace, G.J., Schneider, G.: Larva — safer monitoring of real-time java programs (tool paper). In: Proceedings of the 2009 Seventh IEEE International Conference on Software Engineering and Formal Methods, SEFM 2009, pp. 33–37. IEEE Computer Society, Washington, DC (2009), http://dx.doi.org/10.1109/SEFM.2009.13
5. Decker, N., Leucker, M., Thoma, D.: jUnit^{rv}-adding runtime verification to junit. In: Brat, G., Rungta, N., Venet, A. (eds.) NFM 2013. LNCS, vol. 7871, pp. 459–464. Springer, Heidelberg (2013)
6. Decker, N., Leucker, M., Thoma, D.: Monitoring Modulo Theories. In: Ábrahám, E., Havelund, K. (eds.) TACAS 2014. LNCS, vol. 8413, pp. 341–356. Springer, Heidelberg (2014)
7. Delahaye, M., Kosmatov, N., Signoles, J.: Common specification language for static and dynamic analysis of c programs. In: Proceedings of SAC 2013: the 28th Annual ACM Symposium on Applied Computing, pp. 1230–1235. ACM (2013)

8. Donzé, A.: Breach, a toolbox for verification and parameter synthesis of hybrid systems. In: Touili, T., Cook, B., Jackson, P. (eds.) CAV 2010. LNCS, vol. 6174, pp. 167–170. Springer, Heidelberg (2010), http://dx.doi.org/10.1007/978-3-642-14295-6_17
9. Havelund, K.: Rule-based Runtime Verification Revisited. International Journal on Software Tools for Technology Transfer (STTT) (to appear, 2014)
10. Jin, D., Meredith, P.O., Lee, C., Roşu, G.: JavaMOP: Efficient Parametric Runtime Monitoring Framework. In: Proceedings of ICSE 2012: THE 34th International Conference on Software Engineering, Zurich, Switzerland, June 2-9, pp. 1427–1430. IEEE Press (2012)
11. Navabpour, S., Joshi, Y., Wu, C.W.W., Berkovich, S., Medhat, R., Bonakdarpour, B., Fischmeister, S.: RiTHM: a tool for enabling time-triggered runtime verification for c programs. In: ACM Symposium on the Foundations of Software Engineering (FSE), pp. 603–606 (2013)
12. Parzonska, M.: A Library-Based Approach to Efficient Parametric Runtime Monitoring of Java Programs. Master's thesis, TU Darmstadt, Germany (2013)

Multiple Ways to Fail: Generalizing a Monitor's Verdict for the Classification of Execution Traces[*]

Simon Varvaressos, Kim Lavoie, Sébastien Gaboury, and Sylvain Hallé

Laboratoire d'informatique formelle,
Département d'informatique et de mathématique,
Université du Québec à Chicoutimi, Canada
shalle@acm.org

Abstract. This paper introduces a new approach at classifying event traces, generalizing a monitor's classical two- or three-valued outcome. Given the specification of a system's behaviour expressed as a Linear Temporal Logic formula, we produce from the evaluation of the formula on a given trace a data structure called a trace hologram. When interpreted as equivalence classes, we show how manipulations on these holograms cluster event traces into various natural categories, depending on the precise way in which each group of traces violate the specification.

1 Introduction

Management systems called bug trackers have been developed to help file, categorize, prioritize and analyze bug reports of a system under development. Yet, while bug reports may in some cases be filed automatically, their management from that point on is still mostly qualitative and manual. Existing schemes for classifying bugs only provide a handful of coarse classification schemes have been proposed in past literature, allowing bug reports to be clustered by e.g. "severity" (low, medium, high) [1] or type (e.g. system bugs, code bugs, etc.) [4]. Moreover, assessing each bug report to these categories almost always requires human intervention, as is the task of determining whether two reports are actually occurrences of the same bug. On the other hand, various runtime monitoring can techniques detect the occurrence of bugs [3], but, most of the time, only produce a Boolean verdict which is of limited use for classification.

This paper presents a novel technique for classifying execution traces using an extension of Linear Temporal Logic (LTL). The evaluation of an LTL formula on a given trace can be used to produce a data structure we call a *trace hologram*. This hologram is a generalized verdict of the formula and may be used as a label, with traces producing the same hologram belonging to the same category. However, different traces are likely to have different holograms, so we introduce a number of systematic rules to merge different traces in the same category.

Our proposed approach distinguishes itself from past works by being the first to be fully automatable, based on a formal specification, parameterizable in various ways, and expressed directly in terms of the system's execution traces.

---

[*] The author gratefully acknowledges the financial support of the Natural Sciences and Engineering Research Council of Canada (NSERC).

B. Bonakdarpour and S.A. Smolka (Eds.): RV 2014, LNCS 8734, pp. 10–14, 2014.

2 Traces and Temporal Specifications

The general problem of classifying bugs can be seen as devising a function $\kappa : \Sigma^* \to C$ that associates to every trace of events from the alphabet Σ a "category" taken from some set C. For the purpose of bug tracking, one is interested in avoiding filing separate entries for traces that belong to the same category, as they are intuitively taken to be two instances of the "same" bug. For some category $c \in C$, we will denote as $[\![c]\!]_\kappa$ the set $S \subset \Sigma^*$ such that $\sigma \in S$ if and only if $\kappa(\sigma) = c$, i.e. the set of all traces in category c.

Strictly speaking, a formula in the First-Order Linear Temporal Logic LTL-FO$^+$ [2] induces one such function $\kappa_\downarrow$ with $C = \{\top, \bot, ?\}$, where:

$$\kappa_\downarrow(\overline{\sigma}) = \begin{cases} \top, & \text{if } \overline{\sigma} \models \varphi \\ \bot, & \text{if } \overline{\sigma} \not\models \varphi \\ ?, & \text{otherwise.} \end{cases}$$

The value "?" stands for "inconclusive". It is required, since the evaluation of an LTL-FO$^+$ formula on a finite trace may sometimes return neither true nor false; for example, this is the case for the expression $\mathbf{G}\,a$ evaluated on any finite trace where a has never occurred.

At the other end of the spectrum, if we take $C = \Sigma^*$, the function $\kappa_\uparrow(\overline{\sigma}) = \overline{\sigma}$ is a much finer partition where each trace stands alone in its own category. Neither of these two extremes is particularly useful: $\kappa_\downarrow$ merely distinguishes between "buggy" and "non-buggy" traces, while $\kappa_\uparrow$ will treat any trace as a different bug. Clearly, a meaningful classification κ is a partition that should lie somewhere in between. In the following, we shall elicit two properties that a logic-based classification of traces should exhibit.

First, the function κ must be a sub-partition of $\kappa_\downarrow$; that is, it should not mix buggy and non-buggy traces in the same category.

Property 1. For every category $c \in C$, exactly one of these statements is true: $[\![c]\!]_\kappa \subseteq [\![\top]\!]_{\kappa_\downarrow}$, or $[\![c]\!]_\kappa \subseteq [\![\bot]\!]_{\kappa_\downarrow}$, or $[\![c]\!]_\kappa \subseteq [\![?]\!]_{\kappa_\downarrow}$.

This first requirement imposes that the classification not be too coarse.

The second desirable property bounds the precision of κ in the opposite way, stating that the classification should not be too fine. As an extreme example, consider the specification $\varphi = \bot$; it would not make sense for κ to send some traces in a category c, and some other traces in another category c', as this makes an arbitrary distinction that is finer than the specification itself. In other words, different categories should reveal actually different ways of making the specification true or false.

This can be formalized as follows. Let $\pi \in \Pi$ be some path expression, $\overline{\sigma}, \overline{\sigma}' \in \Sigma^*$ two traces that are identical, except that at their i-th event, $\overline{\sigma}_i(\pi) \neq \overline{\sigma}'_i(\pi)$. These two traces are said to be (π, i)-different. A formula φ is said to be π-invariant if, for any pair of (π, i)-different traces $\overline{\sigma}, \overline{\sigma}'$, $\overline{\sigma} \models \varphi$ if and only if $\overline{\sigma}' \models \varphi$. A meaningful classification of traces should not arbitrarily separate traces that the formula φ itself does not discriminate.

Property 2. For every $\pi \in \Pi$, if φ is π-invariant and $\overline{\sigma}, \overline{\sigma}'$ are two (π, i)-different traces, then $\kappa(\overline{\sigma}) = \kappa(\overline{\sigma}')$.

The evaluation of an LTL-FO$^+$ formula φ on a trace $\overline{\sigma}$ induces a tree by repeatedly applying its associated rules. Figure 1 shows such a tree for the formula $\mathbf{G}\,(a \to \mathbf{X}b)$, evaluated on the trace *cab*. Ultimately, only Boolean conditions on individual events remain, and the value of each subformula can then be obtained by combining and propagating values towards the top of the tree.

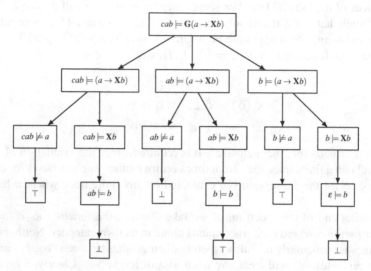

Fig. 1. Evaluating an LTL-FO$^+$ formula on a trace induces a tree

From this representation, one can extract a simplified tree whose nodes are simply labelled by the top-level operator that is being evaluated. Each operator is accompanied by a symbol indicating the truth value of the sub-expression it represents. We shall call such a representation a *trace hologram*. The tree structure contains the "complete" information about how a particular formula is evaluated on a given trace. Moreover, provided that n-ary operators are evaluated in a fixed order, this structure is uniquely defined for a given formula and a given trace.

As a first classification, we take κ to be the function that associates each trace to its hologram. It is then possible to demonstrate that it fulfils the properties described earlier.

Theorem 1. *Given some LTL-FO$^+$ formula φ, if two traces $\overline{\sigma}, \overline{\sigma}' \in \Sigma^*$ have the same hologram, then $\overline{\sigma} \models \varphi$ if and only if $\overline{\sigma}' \models \varphi$.*

Theorem 2. *Let c be a category of $\kappa_\uparrow^\varphi$. Let κ' be a classification function, such that there exists two distinct categories c' and c'' such that $[\![c]\!] = [\![c']\!] \cup [\![c'']\!]$. Suppose in addition that both $[\![c']\!]$ and $[\![c'']\!]$ are not empty. Then κ' violates either Property 1 or 2.*

In other words, it is possible do show that no categorization finer than $\kappa_\uparrow^\varphi$ is possible. This result shows that function $\kappa_\uparrow^\varphi$, although it does not partition Σ^* into arbitrarily small classes, is still probably too fine for most practical purposes; modulo π-invariance, all traces yield different holograms and are considered as different bugs: one is therefore interested in a coarser categorization.

3 Natural Generalizations of κ

We now briefly describe a number of *generalizations* of $\kappa_{\uparrow}^{\varphi}$. The construction of these generalizations follows the same principle: delete nodes, branches or labels from a hologram according to some systematic pattern. This has for effect that some holograms that were different before deletion can become identical after, thereby creating the clustering of categories sought after. The space of possible generalizations of κ is potentially infinite since deletion rules can be applied in all combinations and many of them are parameterizable.

The first deletion pattern is the fail-fast deletion. It consists of deleting all children of a temporal operator node that no longer have an influence on its truth value. Figure 2 shows the procedure for the **G** operator; φ is an arbitrary subformula, and the symbols $\star_i$ represent its truth value for each event, with the additional condition that $\star_i \neq \perp$ for $1 \leq i < n$. The box φ_n hence represents the first child node that evaluates to $\perp$. One can see in Figure 2b that all nodes following φ_n are deleted. Intuitively, this represents the fact that, once the n-th event has φ evaluate to $\perp$, then **G** φ itself evaluates to $\perp$, no matter how φ evaluates on the subsequent events since one does not care what follows a violation.

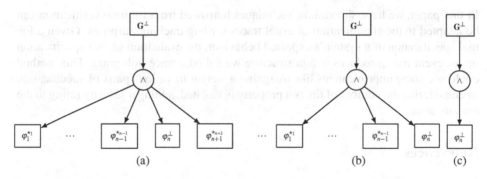

(a)   (b)   (c)

Fig. 2. Two deletion patterns for the **G** operator. (a) Original hologram (b) After fail-fast deletion (c) After polarity deletion.

Fail-fast deletion applies only to temporal operators. As an extension of that rule, one may only keep nodes that are sufficient to decide on the value of an expression. For example, if the expression $\varphi \wedge \psi$ evaluates to $\perp$ because φ evaluates to $\perp$, then it is not necessary to conserve ψ, since its truth value has no effect on the result (and dually for the $\vee$ operator). Similarly, if the formula **G** φ evaluates to $\perp$ because the n-th event of a trace $\bar{\sigma}$ does not satisfy φ, it is not necessary to conserve nodes describing how φ

evaluates to $\top$ on the $n - 1$ previous events: the knowledge that $\overline{\sigma}^n \not\models \varphi$ is sufficient to decide on the value of $\mathbf{G}\,\varphi$.

More generally, it is not necessary to keep nodes of a hologram whose *polarity* (i.e. their truth value) does not contribute to the final result of the global formula. This is the polarity deletion. When applied to temporal operators, this deletion rule expresses the fact that two traces where the same violating sequence of events occurs are considered the same, even if this sequence is preceded by a varying number of events irrelevant to the violation.

In a way, applying polarity deletion only keeps the "Boolean structure" of a failure, but disregards the relative positioning of events that cause it. When applied to first-order quantifiers, the rule expresses the fact that what distinguishes a trace are the values that make the formula fail, and not those that fulfill it.

Finally, a further simplification regarding values is to remove them from quantifiers and/or equalities. Used in isolation, value removal only discards values of variables, but still keeps the subtrees associated to each; hence, it assimilates traces that differ only in their offending parameter values, but still distinguishes *how many* such values they contain.

A simple deletion rule, truncation, consists of trimming from the hologram all nodes beyond a certain depth n. An extreme case is $n = 1$, which deletes all but the root of the hologram. For other values of n, truncation is such that one does not distinguish traces up to a certain level of abstraction.

4   Conclusion and Future Work

In this paper, we have shown how techniques borrowed from runtime verification can be adapted to the classification of event traces for bug tracking purposes. Given a formal specification of a system's expected behaviour, the evaluation of that specification on an event trace produces a data structure we called a trace hologram. This method could see some improvements like assigning a weight to various parts of specification or considering the number of times a property is violated, adding a severity rating to the classification.

References

1. Carstensen, P.H., Sørensen, C., Tuikkar, T.: Let's talk about bugs!! Scandinavian Journal of Information Systems 7(6) (1995)
2. Hallé, S., Villemaire, R.: Runtime enforcement of web service message contracts with data. IEEE Trans. Services Computing 5(2), 192–206 (2012)
3. Leucker, M., Schallhart, C.: A brief account of runtime verification. J. Log. Algebr. Program. 78(5), 293–303 (2009)
4. Wiszniewski, H.K.B., Mork, H.: Classification of software defects in parallel programs. Technical Report 2, Faculty of Electronics, Technical University of Gdansk, Poland (1994)

Two Generalisations of Roşu and Chen's Trace Slicing Algorithm A

Clemens Ballarin

aicas GmbH,
Haid-und-Neu-Straße 18,
76131 Karlsruhe, Germany
ballarin@aicas.com

Abstract. Roşu and Chen's trace analysis algorithm identifies activity streams in a monitored application based on data (such as memory locations) and groups events accordingly into slices. It can be generalised to assign several such activity streams to the same slice, even if data is unrelated. This is useful for monitoring scheduling algorithms, which linearise activity streams that are not necessarily related. The algorithm can be generalised further to impose constraints on the generated slices such that, for example, each trace relates a high-priority activity to a low-priority activity. There are no limitations on constraints other than that constraint solvers efficient enough for runtime analysis need to be available.

Keywords: Asynchronous events, constraint solving, runtime monitoring, scheduling, trace slicing.

1 Introduction

Slicing separates a stream of monitored events into parts, called *slices*, that can be analysed independently of each other. In Roşu and Chen's Algorithm A [11] the separation is based on the data contained in the events. Events that share a piece of data — for example, the address of an object in memory — are identified as related and are put into the same slice. The algorithm is motivated by the observation that activities in a program that operate on separate sets of objects are usually not related. For example, when an iterator is created in a Java program, and the task is to monitor that the underlying collection is not modified while an iterator is used, operations on iterators created from other collections are irrelevant and these events need not (and should not) be put into the slice corresponding to that iterator.

There are monitoring scenarios where it is desirable that events triggered by activities not related directly to each other in the above sense are put into the same slice. An example are scheduling algorithms, which ensure that concurrent activities are executed in an appropriate order — for example, based on priority. Algorithm A is not directly applicable to such scenarios, but it can be extended in a straightforward manner to make it applicable. How this can be done is the subject of the present work.

B. Bonakdarpour and S.A. Smolka (Eds.): RV 2014, LNCS 8734, pp. 15–30, 2014.

1.1   Fixed-Priority Scheduling

Fixed-priority scheduling is the most commonly used scheme for scheduling activities in realtime systems [5]. In order to schedule m concurrent activities (for example, threads) on $n < m$ executors (for example, CPUs) each activity is assigned a priority and only the n activities of highest priority are executed. Activities with lower priorities can only make progress when higher-priority activities are blocked.

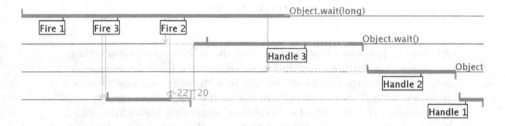

Fig. 1. Firing and Handling of Asynchronous Events on a Multicore System

Fig. 1 shows an execution trace of a Java program running on the realtime-capable JamaicaVM [1] on VxWorks 6.9. The application is based on the Real-Time Specification for Java (RTSJ) [13] and contains threads communicating through *asynchronous events*. The trace was obtained with JamaicaVM's built-in monitoring facilities. It shows four threads running on two CPUs. The first thread, which runs on its own CPU, fires three asynchronous events 1, 2 and 3, and is then suspended in the Java method `wait(long)`. The other three threads share the other CPU and act as handlers. The box labelled "Fire 1" marks the point in time where 1 is fired. A short while later, the corresponding handler, which is the lowest priority thread, is woken up and starts its activity. Concurrently, the first thread now fires 3. This asynchronous event has higher priority than 1 and is handled by the second thread. In order to do so, this thread now apparently needs to enter a lock currently held by the handler of 1, which is of lower priority. This situation is known as *priority inversion*. To prevent a deadlock the priority of the thread holding the lock is temporarily raised. Then, that handler can proceed, the priority is lowered, and 3 is handled. Afterwards, asynchonous event 2, which has been fired in the meantime, is handled, and eventually the handler of 1 resumes and completes its task.

The boxes labelled "Fire x" and "Handle y" in the diagram represent monitor events in the application's execution trace, and they will be abbreviated as $f(x)$ and $h(y)$, where x and y denote asynchronous events.[1] For scheduling to be correct, whenever several asynchronous events are pending simultaneously, the

---

[1] Events in the execution trace should not be confused with asynchronous events of the RTSJ. When the meaning of "event" is not clear from the context the term "monitor event" will be used for referring to an event in a trace.

higher-priority asynchronous events need to be handled first. That is, for two asynchronous events x and y with priority$(x) >$ priority(y) whenever $f(x)$ is observed then there may either be no $f(y)$ until $h(x)$ or otherwise $h(x)$ must come before $h(y)$.

Such properties can, for example, be expressed with linear temporal logic and monitored with automata [8]. In a scenario with m asynchronous events, rather than constructing a monitor for m asynchronous events, using monitors for pairs of asynchronous events in combination with slicing is more practical.

1.2 Overview of the Paper

Roşu and Chen's algorithm processes a trace of events and computes mappings from event parameters to data. Each mapping yields a slice. The mappings are partial functions and will be called parameter instantiations. In this paper, it will first be shown that the correctness proof of Algorithm A is even valid when generalised from partial functions to semilattices (Sect. 2). Then the algorithm will be extended so it can combine events from multiple activity streams into one slice, and it becomes applicable to monitoring scheduling algorithms (Sect. 3). The extended algorithm yields two slices for each pair of asynchronous events, while according to priorities only one slice is useful. It will then be shown how this can be addressed by generalising the algorithm further with constraint solving techniques (Sect. 4).

2 Algorithm A Revisited

Roşu and Chen's algorithm computes a set of partial functions, which are parameter instantiations, and a slice for each instantiation. In this section the algorithm and its correctness proof are shown to be valid if instantiations are generalised to an arbitrary semilattice. The exposition of semilattices and partial functions follows Jacobson's textbook on basic algebra [7].

2.1 Partial Orders and Upper Semilattices

Lattices are partial orders in which least upper bounds and greatest lower bounds exist. The notions of least upper bound and greatest lower bound are dual, and a lattice can be seen as comprising two semilattices. The semilattice formed by least upper bounds is sufficient for understanding Algorithm A.

Definition 1. *A partially ordered set is a tuple $(S, \leq)$ where S is a set and $\leq$ is a binary relation on S satisfying reflexivity, antisymmetry and transitivity.*

Let $A \subseteq S$. An element $u \in S$ in an *upper bound* of A if $x \leq u$ for every $x \in A$. It is a *least upper bound* of A if it is an upper bound of A and $u \leq v$ for every upper bound v of A. If a least upper bound exists for A it is unique. The least upper bound of A is denoted as $\bigvee A$. If $\bigvee A \in A$ then the least upper bound of A is also called the *greatest* element of A and denoted $\max A$.

Definition 2. *An* (upper or join) *semilattice is a partially ordered set* $(L, \leq)$ *in which any two elements have a least upper bound.*

The least upper bound of x and y is denoted as $x \vee y$ ("x join y"). By induction, any non-empty finite set of elements of a semilattice has a least upper bound. The least upper bound of $x_1, x_2, \ldots, x_n$ is denoted as $x_1 \vee x_2 \vee \cdots \vee x_n$. A partially ordered set for which every subset A has a least upper bound is called a *complete (upper) semilattice*. The following properties of the join operation of semilattices are generally known to hold for lattices (with both meet and join), but proofs [7, Chap. 8] already apply to semilattices.

Lemma 1. *The join operation* $\vee$ *of a semilattice satisfies commutativity, associativity and idempotence. The order relation and the join operation have these relationships:*

1. *$x \leq y$ if, and only if $x \vee y = y$.*
2. *If $x \leq z$ and $y \leq z$ then $x \vee y \leq z$.*
3. *If $x \leq y$ then $x \vee z \leq y \vee z$ (monotonicity).*

For a finite semilattice every non-empty subset A has a least upper bound. Likewise for a complete semilattice. If A coincides with the underlying set L of the semilattice then $\bigvee A$ is the greatest element of L. $\bigvee L$ is called the *top* element of L and denoted $\top$. Conversely, let A be the empty set $\varnothing$. Any $u \in L$ is an upper bound of $\varnothing$. If a least upper bound exists for $\varnothing$ it is called the *bottom* element of L, and $\bigvee \varnothing$ is denoted by $\bot$. Unlike top, not all semilattices have a bottom element. By definition, complete semilattices have a bottom element, and finite semilattices with bottom element are complete.

Definition 3. *A subset M of a semilattice L is called a* sublattice *(more precisely, an* upper subsemilattice, *but the former will be used throughout for brevity) if it is closed under the operation* $\vee$.

It is evident that M is a semilattice relative to the induced join operation of the sublattice. A sublattice of a complete lattice is complete if it contains a bottom element (which need not coincide with the bottom element of L).

Let $a \in L$ be fixed. The subset of elements $x \in M$ such that $x \leq a$ is either empty or, by Lemma 1.2, a sublattice of M (and of L). We denote this set by $M[a]$. This observation implies

Lemma 2. *If M is a sublattice of L, $a \in L$ and $M[a]$ is non-empty then its least upper bound is an element of $M[a]$ — that is, $\max M[a]$ exists.*

Additional Results. Roşu and Chen lift the binary join operation to sets: for $M, N \subseteq L$ let

$$M \vee N = \{x \vee y \mid x \in M \text{ and } y \in N\}.$$

If M and N are sublattices of L then $M \vee N$ is a sublattice of L as well. If $\bot \in M$ and $\bot \in N$ then $\bot \in M \vee N$. (In fact, this condition holds for any $x \in L$.)

Lemma 3 ([11, Proposition 8.3]). *Let L be a complete semilattice, let Θ be a sublattice of L, $\perp \in \Theta$ and $\theta \in L$, and let $\theta_1, \theta_2 \in \{\theta\} \vee \Theta$ such that $\theta_1 = \bigvee \Theta[\theta_2]$. Then $\theta_1 = \theta_2$.*

Proof. In the original proof it is shown that $\{\theta' \in \Theta \mid \theta_2 = \theta \vee \theta'\}$ has a greatest element q and $q = \theta_1$. It follows that $\theta_2 = \theta \vee \theta_1 = \theta_1$. The original proof applies, which can be shown by step-by-step inspection. $\square$

2.2   Partial Functions

Roşu and Chen's original algorithm operates on partial functions. These do not form a semilattice, but they can be made one by adding an additional element that will be called the "inconsistent function".

Let S and T be non-empty sets. Functions are sets of tuples $(s, t) \in S \times T$. The set of partial functions from S to T is denoted by $S \rightharpoonup T$, the set of (total) functions as $S \to T$. Let be $\alpha \in S \rightharpoonup T$. The set of elements s such that there is a t with $(s, t) \in \alpha$ is the *domain* of α, written $\mathrm{Dom}\,\alpha$. If α is total, its domain coincides with S. For a partial function, the domain is allowed to be the empty set. In this case, α is called the *empty function* and is denoted as $\perp$.

The subset relation is a partial order on sets. The set of partial functions $S \rightharpoonup T$ is partially ordered by the subset relation as well. Let $\alpha, \beta \in S \rightharpoonup T$. If $\alpha \subseteq \beta$ then $\mathrm{Dom}\,\alpha \subseteq \mathrm{Dom}\,\beta$ and α and β agree on $\mathrm{Dom}\,\alpha$. If additionally $\alpha \subseteq \gamma$ and $\beta \subseteq \gamma$ for some total function γ, then α and β may be viewed as providing partial information towards γ and β being more informative than α. In the sequel, this order relation on partial functions will be denoted as $\sqsubseteq$.

Let α and β again be arbitrary partial functions $\in S \rightharpoonup T$. They are said to be *compatible* if $\alpha(s) = \beta(s)$ for any $s \in \mathrm{Dom}\,\alpha \cap \mathrm{Dom}\,\beta$. It is evident that a least upper bound of α and β exists in $S \rightharpoonup T$ if, and only if α and β are compatible. In particular, $S \rightharpoonup T$ is not a semilattice. This can be rectified by introducing the "inconsistent function" $\top$ and declaring $\alpha \sqsubseteq \top$ for any $\alpha \in (S \rightharpoonup T) \cup \{\top\}$. The latter set will be denoted as $S \overset{\top}{\rightharpoonup} T$.

These considerations show

Lemma 4. *$(S \overset{\top}{\rightharpoonup} T, \sqsubseteq)$ is a semilattice with bottom.*

The bottom element is the empty function and the top element is the "inconsistent function". The least upper bound $\alpha \sqcup \beta$ of two partial functions α and β is either $\{(s, t) \mid (s, t) \in \alpha$ or $(s, t) \subset \beta\}$ if α and β are consistent or, otherwise, $\top$. The least upper bound of a set of partial functions A is denoted as $\bigsqcup A$.

Injective functions will be needed later. The set of injective partial functions will be denoted by $S \rightharpoonup_i T$ and its extension by the inconsistent function as $S \overset{\top}{\rightharpoonup}_i T$. The latter is a sublattice of $S \overset{\top}{\rightharpoonup} T$. Let α and $\beta \in S \overset{\top}{\rightharpoonup}_i T$. The least upper bound of α and β is $\alpha \sqcup \beta$ if that is injective or $\top$ otherwise. It is denoted as $\alpha \sqcup_i \beta$. The least upper bound of $A \subseteq S \overset{\top}{\rightharpoonup}_i T$ is $\bigsqcup_i A$.

2.3 Traces and Slices

A trace is either a sequence of base events or a sequence of events with data. Let $\mathcal{E}$ be the set of base events, X a set of variables and V a set of values (representing the data). Roşu and Chen model events with data as follows. For each $e \in \mathcal{E}$, $X_e \subseteq X$ is the set of *parameters of e*. An *event with data* consists of a base event e and a parameter instantiation $\theta \in X \rightharpoonup V$ such that $\mathrm{Dom}\,\theta = X_e$. We denote the set of events with data as $\mathcal{E}\langle X \rightharpoonup V\rangle$. The sets $\mathcal{E}^*$ and $\mathcal{E}\langle X \rightharpoonup V\rangle^*$ are the sets of sequences of events; they include the empty sequence ε.

Definition 4. *For a trace $\tau \in \mathcal{E}\langle X \rightharpoonup V\rangle^*$ and a parameter instantiation θ, the slice $\tau\!\restriction_\theta$ is the subsequence of base events e such that $e\langle\theta'\rangle \in \tau$ and $\theta' \sqsubseteq \theta$.*

That is, $\tau\!\restriction_\theta$ contains all events of τ whose instantiation is less informative than or equal to θ.

Since a trace is finite, the sets $\mathcal{E}$ and V can be assumed to be finite, and since each base event has only a finite number of parameters, a finite set X of parameters is sufficient as well. Consequently, the set of partial functions $X \rightharpoonup V$ is finite, and $X \overset{\top}{\rightharpoonup} V$ is a complete semilattice. Its bottom element is the empty function $\bot$.

Lemma 5 (Lookup [11, Proposition 14]). *Let τ be a trace with data, and let Θ be a sublattice of $X \overset{\top}{\rightharpoonup} V$ such that $\{\theta' \mid e\langle\theta'\rangle \in \tau\} \subseteq \Theta$ and $\bot \in \Theta$. Let $\theta \in X \overset{\top}{\rightharpoonup} V$. Then $\tau\!\restriction_{\bigsqcup\Theta[\theta]} = \tau\!\restriction_\theta$.*

Proof. The least upper bound $\bigsqcup\Theta[\theta]$ exists by Lemma 2 and is an element of $\Theta[\theta]$. Consider an arbitrary event $e\langle\theta'\rangle \in \tau$. By the premises $\theta' \in \Theta$. It is sufficient to show that $\theta' \sqsubseteq \bigsqcup\Theta[\theta]$ if, and only if, $\theta' \sqsubseteq \theta$. Let $\theta' \sqsubseteq \bigsqcup\Theta[\theta]$; θ is an upper bound of $\Theta[\theta]$ and so $\theta' \sqsubseteq \bigsqcup\Theta[\theta] \sqsubseteq \theta$. Conversely, let $\theta' \sqsubseteq \theta$. Then $\theta' \sqsubseteq \theta_0$ for any upper bound θ_0 of $\Theta[\theta]$ and in particular for $\bigsqcup\Theta[\theta]$. $\square$

2.4 The Algorithm

Roşu and Chen's slicing algorithm reads a sequence of events with data and computes sequences of *base events*. The algorithm is shown in Fig. 2. The input is a trace $\tau \in \mathcal{E}\langle X \rightharpoonup V\rangle^*$, which is processed sequentially. The computation yields a set of parameter instantiations $\Theta \subseteq X \overset{\top}{\rightharpoonup} V$ and a map $\mathbb{T} \in (X \overset{\top}{\rightharpoonup} V) \rightharpoonup \mathcal{E}^*$. The latter is the table of slices computed by the algorithm.

Apart from notational details, the only difference to the original version [11, Fig. 2] is the inclusion of the "inconsistent function" $\top$ in Θ and $\mathrm{Dom}\,\mathbb{T}$. This modification ensures that these sets are semilattices and serves simplifying the correctness argument. Semilattice replaces Roşu and Chen's notion of a closed set of partial functions. Implementations can either exclude $\top$ right away (as done in the original version) or drop the additional trace when returning the result.

Algorithm A

Input $\tau \in \mathcal{E}\langle X \rightarrow V\rangle^*$

Output $\mathbb{T} \in (X \xrightarrow{\top} V) \rightharpoonup \mathcal{E}^*$ and $\Theta \subseteq X \xrightarrow{\top} V$

1: $\mathbb{T} \leftarrow \{\bot \mapsto \varepsilon, \top \mapsto \varepsilon\}; \Theta \leftarrow \{\bot, \top\}$
2: **for each** $e\langle\theta\rangle \in \tau$ **do**
3:     **for each** $\theta' \in \{\theta\} \sqcup \Theta$ **do**
4:         $\mathbb{T}(\theta') \leftarrow \mathbb{T}(\bigsqcup \Theta[\theta'])e$
5:     **end for**
6:     $\Theta \leftarrow \{\bot, \theta\} \sqcup \Theta$
7: **end for**

Fig. 2. Roşu and Chen's Original Algorithm

Algorithm A with Patterns

Input $P \subseteq A(X)$ and $\tau \in A(V)^*$

Output $\mathbb{T} \in (X \xrightarrow{\top} V) \rightharpoonup A(V)^*$ and $\Theta \subseteq X \xrightarrow{\top} V$

1: $\mathbb{T} \leftarrow \{\bot \mapsto \varepsilon, \top \mapsto \varepsilon\}; \Theta \leftarrow \{\bot, \top\}$
2: **for each** $q \in \tau$ **do**
3:     $\Sigma \leftarrow \{\mathrm{mgm}_i(p, q) \mid p \in P\}$
4:     **for each** $\theta' \in \Sigma \sqcup_i \Theta$ **do**
5:         $\mathbb{T}(\theta') \leftarrow \mathbb{T}(\bigsqcup_i \Theta[\theta'])q$
6:     **end for**
7:     $\Theta \leftarrow \Theta \cup (\Sigma \sqcup_i \Theta)$
8: **end for**

Fig. 3. Data Interpretation Based on Patterns

Algorithm A with Constraints

Input $c \in C$, $P \subseteq A(X)$ and $\tau \in A(V)^*$

Output $\mathbb{T} \in C \rightharpoonup A(V)^*$ and $\Theta \subseteq C$

1: $\mathbb{T} \leftarrow \{c \mapsto \varepsilon, \top \mapsto \varepsilon\}; \Theta \leftarrow \{c, \top\}$
2: **for each** $q \in \tau$ **do**
3:     $\Sigma \leftarrow \{true.\mathrm{mgm}(p, q) \mid p \in P\}$
4:     **for each** $\theta' \in \Sigma \wedge \Theta$ **do**
5:         $\mathbb{T}(\theta') \leftarrow \mathbb{T}(\bigwedge \Theta[\theta'])q$
6:     **end for**
7:     $\Theta \leftarrow \Theta \cup (\Sigma \wedge \Theta)$
8: **end for**

Fig. 4. Trace Slicing with Constraints

Theorem 1 (Slicing [11, Theorem 1]). *Let $\tau \in \mathcal{E}\langle X \rightharpoonup V \rangle^*$ be a trace where $\mathcal{E}$, X and V are sets of events, parameters and values, respectively, and let $\mathbb{T}$ and Θ be the result of processing τ with Algorithm A. Then these conditions hold:*

$$\mathrm{Dom}\,\mathbb{T} = \Theta \tag{1}$$

$$\{\theta \mid e\langle\theta\rangle \in \tau\} \subseteq \Theta \tag{2}$$

$$\mathbb{T}(\theta) = \tau\!\restriction_\theta \text{ for any } \theta \in \Theta \tag{3}$$

$$\tau\!\restriction_\theta = \mathbb{T}(\bigsqcup \Theta[\theta]) \text{ for any } \theta \in X \overset{\top}{\rightharpoonup} V \tag{4}$$

The proof follows Roşu and Chen's proof.

Proof. All arguments are by induction on the outer loop. Let $\mathbb{T}$ and Θ denote the states of the variables $\mathbb{T}$ and Θ at the beginning of the body of the outer loop and $\mathbb{T}'$ and Θ' the states at the end, and let $e\langle\theta\rangle$ be the processed event.

First, Θ is a semilattice with bottom element $\bot$: the set is initialised to $\{\bot, \top\}$, which is a sublattice of $X \overset{\top}{\rightharpoonup} V$, in line 1, and it remains one when updated to $\{\bot, \theta\} \sqcup \Theta$ in line 6 since the join operation on sets preserves sublattices. Moreover, Θ is complete.

Equation (1) is also immediate from how $\mathbb{T}$ and Θ are updated. In particular, the inner loop defines $\mathbb{T}$ at $\{\theta\} \sqcup \Theta$ (if not defined already) and so

$$\mathrm{Dom}\,\mathbb{T}' = \mathrm{Dom}\,\mathbb{T} \cup \{\theta\} \sqcup \Theta = \Theta \cup \{\theta\} \sqcup \Theta = \{\bot, \theta\} \sqcup \Theta = \Theta'$$

by the induction hypothesis and the definition of the join operator on sets.

Condition (2) is again immediate from the updates in lines 1 and 6.

The sequence in which the elements of $\{\theta\}\sqcup\Theta$ are processed by the inner loop (lines 3 to 5) is not specified, and in particular an event e must not be added to the same slice twice. In fact, the outcome of the loop is invariant under the processing sequence, and it is sufficient to show that the order of two elements $\theta_1, \theta_2 \in \{\theta\} \sqcup \Theta$ that are processed consecutively in the loop does not matter. This is a consequence of Lemma 3.

For (3) the induction hypothesis is $\mathbb{T}(\theta_0) = \tau\!\restriction_{\theta_0}$ for any $\theta_0 \in \Theta$. Let $\theta' \in \Theta'$. The event e is added to the slice $\mathbb{T}(\theta')$ if, and only if, $\theta' \in \{\theta\} \sqcup \Theta$. This is equivalent to $\theta \sqsubseteq \theta'$ since $\theta' \in \Theta' = \Theta \cup (\{\theta\} \sqcup \Theta)$, and the assignment in line 4 updates the correct slot. It remains to be shown that, if e is added to a slot, the table lookup retrieves the correct prefix: $\mathbb{T}(\bigsqcup \Theta[\theta']) = \tau\!\restriction_{\bigsqcup\Theta[\theta']} = \tau\!\restriction_{\theta'}$. This follows from the induction hypothesis and Lemma 5.

Equation (4) follows from (3) and Lemma 5. $\qquad\qquad\qquad\square$

3   Combining Multiple Activity Streams into One Slice

Let us now return to the monitoring problem of Sect. 1.1, where asynchronous events are fired and handled in an application. Firing and handling are traced as $f(x)$ and $h(x)$, respectively. In order to monitor whether for each pair of asynchronous events x and y the order of the recorded fire and handle monitor events adheres to the scheduling policy, slices for each pair of events are extracted from the trace. Consider, for example,

$$\tau = f(2)h(2)f(1)f(2)h(2)f(3)h(3)h(1)$$

with three asynchronous events 1, 2 and 3, and priority(3) > priority(2) > priority(1). Slicing should yield a trace for each pair of asynchronous events:

$$\tau_{2,1} = f(2)h(2)f(1)f(2)h(2)h(1)$$
$$\tau_{3,1} = f(1)f(3)h(3)h(1)$$
$$\tau_{3,2} = f(2)h(2)f(2)h(2)f(3)h(3)$$

Each slice can then be processed individually — for example, by an instance of a suitable parametric automaton where x represents the high-priority and y the low-priority asynchronous event.

This example illustrates the main challenge when combining multiple activity streams into one slice. Distinct instances of $f(x)$ and $f(y)$ need to be put in the same slice. Algorithm A is not designed to support this. In fact, this is a limitation of the trace model.

3.1   Events and Event Patterns

The modified trace model uses terminology from term algebra [2], but it is only a subtle generalisation of the original model. Like in Sect. 2.3, X and V denote the sets of parameters (variables) and values, respectively, of the base events. A *term* is either a parameter or a value. $T = X \cup V$ denotes the set of terms. Base events are now symbols that can be applied to a fixed number of terms. Let $e \in \mathcal{E}$. Then $\alpha_e \in \mathbb{N}$ is the *arity* of e. Let $\alpha_e = k$ and $t_1, \ldots, t_k \in T$. Then $e(t_1, \ldots, t_k)$ is an *atom*; if $k = 0$ then the atom is denoted as e. If $t_1, \ldots, t_k \in V$ then $e(t_1, \ldots, t_k)$ is a *ground atom*. The set of atoms is denoted as $A(X, V)$, the set of ground atoms as $A(V)$. Atoms are also called *patterns*, and ground atoms now represent events with data. $A(X)$ is the set of patterns that contain no values.

An instantiation is again a partial function $\theta \in X \rightharpoonup V$. The result of its application to a term t is denoted as $\theta(t)$ and is defined as $\theta(t)$ if $t \in \mathrm{Dom}\,\theta$. Otherwise, it is t. In particular, a value is mapped to itself. Instantiations are lifted to atoms: $\sigma(e(t_1, \ldots, t_k)) = e(\sigma(t_1), \ldots, \sigma(t_k))$.

Instantiations are no longer considered part of the trace but are inferred by matching events against patterns. A pattern $p \in A(X, V)$ *matches* an event $q \in A(V)$ if there is an instantiation $\theta \in X \rightharpoonup V$ such that $\theta(p) = q$, and θ is a *matcher* of p and q. A minimal (or most general) matcher of p and q maps exactly the variables that occur in p to the corresponding values in q. If a matcher exists for p and q the minimal matcher is unique. It is denoted as $\mathrm{mgm}(p, q)$. We define $\mathrm{mgm}(p, q) = \top$ if p does not match q. If the minimal matcher is injective, $\mathrm{mgm}_i(p, q)$ is defined as $\mathrm{mgm}(p, q)$. Otherwise $\mathrm{mgm}_i(p, q) = \top$.

3.2   Slicing Based on Patterns

A slice of a trace $\tau \in A(V)^*$ is a subsequence of events that match an element of a given set $P \subseteq A(X)$ of patterns.

Definition 5 (Slice with Patterns). *For a set of patterns $P \subseteq A(X)$, a trace $\tau \in A(V)$ and a parameter instantiation θ, the slice $\tau|_\theta$ is defined as follows. Either $\theta = \top$. Then $\tau|_\theta$ is the full sequence τ. Otherwise, it is the subsequence of events $q \in \tau$ such that there exists a pattern $p \in P$ and $\theta(p) = q$.*

The modified slicing algorithm is shown in Fig. 3. It takes the set P of patterns as an additional argument. The inner loop iterates over parameter instantiations θ' that extend minimal matchers of these patterns and the processed event q. Only instantiations that are injective are considered.

Lemma 6 (Lookup with Patterns). *Let $P \subseteq A(X)$ and $\tau \in A(V)^*$, and let Θ be a sublattice of $X \xrightarrow{\top}_i V$ such that $\{\mathrm{mgm}_i(p,q) \mid p \in P, q \in \tau\} \subseteq \Theta$ and $\bot, \top \in \Theta$. Let $\theta \in X \xrightarrow{\top}_i V$. Then $\tau|_{\bigsqcup_i \Theta[\theta]} = \tau|_\theta$.*

Proof. Let $q \in \tau|_\theta$. Either $\theta = \top$, and so $\bigsqcup_i \Theta[\theta] = \top$ and $q \in \tau|_{\bigsqcup_i \Theta[\theta]}$. Otherwise there is a $p \in P$ with $\theta(p) = q$. Then $\mathrm{mgm}_i(p,q) \sqsubseteq \theta$ and $\mathrm{mgm}_i(p,q) \in \Theta$. Therefore $\mathrm{mgm}_i(p,q) \sqsubseteq \bigsqcup_i \Theta[\theta]$ and $(\bigsqcup_i \Theta[\theta])(p) = q$. This implies $q \in \tau|_{\bigsqcup_i \Theta[\theta]}$. Conversely, let $q \in \bigsqcup_i \Theta[\theta]$. Either $\bigsqcup_i \Theta[\theta] = \top$ and so $\theta = \top$ or there is a $p \in P$ such that $(\bigsqcup_i \Theta[\theta])(p) = q$. From $\bigsqcup_i \Theta[\theta] \sqsubseteq \theta$ follows $\theta(p) = q$ and $q \in \tau|_\theta$. $\square$

Theorem 2 (Slicing with Patterns). *Let $P \subseteq A(X)$ and $\tau \in A(V)^*$, and let $\mathbb{T}$ and Θ be the result of processing P and τ with Algorithm A with Patterns. Then these conditions hold:*

$$\mathrm{Dom}\,\mathbb{T} = \Theta \tag{5}$$

$$\{\mathrm{mgm}_i(p,q) \mid p \in P \text{ and } q \in \tau\} \subseteq \Theta \tag{6}$$

$$\mathbb{T}(\theta) = \tau|_\theta \text{ for any } \theta \in \Theta \tag{7}$$

$$\tau|_\theta = \mathbb{T}(\bigsqcup_i \Theta[\theta]) \text{ for any } \theta \in X \xrightarrow{\top}_i V \tag{8}$$

The conditions are direct analogues of those of Theorem 1 except (6), which says that traces for all minimal matchers of patterns and events are computed.

Proof. The argument that Θ is a semilattice is more involved than for Theorem 1 since a set of matchers is processed in each iteration of the outer loop. It is easy to see that $\Theta \subseteq X \xrightarrow{\top}_i V$ throughout the computation. Further, in line 7, Θ is updated to $\Theta \cup (\Sigma \sqcup_i \Theta) = (\{\bot, \top\} \cup \Sigma) \sqcup_i \Theta$. The set $\{\bot, \top\} \cup \Sigma$ is a semilattice where the elements of Σ are not comparable. Let σ_1 and σ_2 be two distinct elements of Σ. They are matchers of distinct patterns with the same event q. Since these patterns only contain variables, $\sigma_1 \sqcup \sigma_2$ is not injective, and so $\sigma_1 \sqcup_i \sigma_2 = \top$. By induction, Θ is a sublattice of $X \xrightarrow{\top}_i V$.

Since the proof of Theorem 1 applies to semilattices in general, most of the reasoning is directly applicable to slicing with patterns. The exception is (7) because the definition of slice has changed. The induction hypothesis is $\mathbb{T}(\theta_0) = \tau|_{\theta_0}$ for any $\theta_0 \in \Theta$, and let q again be the processed event. Consider $\theta' \in \Theta' = \Theta \cup (\Sigma \sqcup_i \Theta)$ where $\Sigma = \{\mathrm{mgm}_i(p, q) \mid p \in P\}$. The event q is added to the slice $\mathbb{T}(\theta')$ if, and only if, $\theta' \in \Sigma \sqcup_i \Theta$. There are two cases. Either $\theta' \in \Sigma \sqcup_i \Theta$. Then there is a pattern $p \in P$ and $\theta' \in \{\mathrm{mgm}_i(p, q)\} \sqcup_i \Theta$, and so $\theta'(p) = q$ and $q \in \tau q|_{\theta'}$. Otherwise, $\theta' \notin \Sigma \sqcup_i \Theta$ but $\theta' \in \Theta$. If there were a $p \in P$ such that $\theta'(p) = q$ then, by the minimality of the elements of Σ, $\theta' \in \Sigma \sqcup_i \Theta$. So $q \notin \tau q|_{\theta'}$. Therefore the assignment in line 5 updates the correct slot. By the induction hypothesis and Lemma 6 the table lookup in the same line retrieves the correct prefix: $\mathbb{T}(\sqcup_i \Theta[\theta']) = \tau|_{\sqcup_i \Theta[\theta']} = \tau|_{\theta'}$. □

3.3   Examples

It is illustrative to inspect the working of the algorithm. We return to the scheduling example from the beginning of the section. Let $P = \{f(x), f(y), h(x), h(y)\}$ and let

$$\tau = f(2)h(2)f(1)f(2)h(2)f(3)h(3)h(1)$$

be the monitored trace. After processing the first two events, the set of instantiations Θ is $\{\bot, \{x \mapsto 2\}, \{y \mapsto 2\}, \top\}$ and $\mathbb{T}$ contains four slices:

$$\mathbb{T}(\bot) = \varepsilon, \quad \mathbb{T}(\{x \mapsto 2\}) = \mathbb{T}(\{y \mapsto 2\}) = \mathbb{T}(\top) = f(2)h(2)$$

When the next event, $f(1)$, is processed the set of instantiations is duplicated, and $f(1)$ is added to all slices of instantiations that contain a mapping to 1 (and of $\top$). The full result of processing τ is shown in Table 1. The third group of slices, containing mappings to 3, is added when $f(3)$ is processed. One can see that indeed the expected slices are computed. For example, $\tau_{2,1} = \mathbb{T}(\{x \mapsto 2, y \mapsto 1\})$.

Slices for instantiations that map only one parameter to a value, for example for $\{x \mapsto 2\}$, appear to be redundant but are required so they can be cloned whenever a monitor event for a new asynchronous event arrives. On the other hand, having two instantiations for each pair of asynchronous events, such as $\{x \mapsto 1, y \mapsto 2\}$ in addition to $\{x \mapsto 2, y \mapsto 1\}$ is redundant. It is desirable to only compute slices for instantiations with $\mathrm{priority}(x) > \mathrm{priority}(y)$. This will be the subject of the following section.

A trace processed by the original Algorithm A is also amenable for processing by Algorithm A with Patterns. For each base event $e \in \mathcal{E}$ let the set P of patterns contain one $f(x_1, \ldots, x_k)$ such that $X_e = \{x_1, \ldots, x_k\}$ and $x_1, \ldots, x_{l_0}$ is the intended order of parameters. Since each event q is matched by exactly one pattern $p \in P$ the set of instantiations Σ computed in line 3 is singleton and the algorithm is schematically reduced to the original version. The remaining difference is that the former operates on parameter instantiations that are injective. The author believes that this is not a fundamental limitation. It appears that in typical applications of the original algorithm, only injective parameter instantiations are relevant.

Table 1. Slices for $\tau = f(2)h(2)f(1)f(2)h(2)f(3)h(3)h(1)$

θ	$\bot$	ε
$x \mapsto 2$	$f(2)\ h(2)$	$f(2)\ h(2)$
$y \mapsto 2$	$f(2)\ h(2)$	$f(2)\ h(2)$
$\top$	$f(2)\ h(2)\ f(1)\ f(2)\ h(2)\ f(3)\ h(3)\ h(1)$	
$x \mapsto 1$	$f(1)$	$h(1)$
$y \mapsto 1$	$f(1)$	$h(1)$
$x \mapsto 1, y \mapsto 2$	$f(2)\ h(2)\ f(1)\ f(2)\ h(2)$	$h(1)$
$x \mapsto 2, y \mapsto 1$	$f(2)\ h(2)\ f(1)\ f(2)\ h(2)$	$h(1)$
$y \mapsto 3$		$f(3)\ h(3)$
$x \mapsto 3$		$f(3)\ h(3)$
$x \mapsto 1, y \mapsto 3$	$f(1)$	$f(3)\ h(3)\ h(1)$
$x \mapsto 2, y \mapsto 3$	$f(2)\ h(2)$	$f(2)\ h(2)\ f(3)\ h(3)$
$x \mapsto 3, y \mapsto 1$	$f(1)$	$f(3)\ h(3)\ h(1)$
$x \mapsto 3, y \mapsto 2$	$f(2)\ h(2)$	$f(2)\ h(2)\ f(3)\ h(3)$
θ		$\mathbb{T}(\theta)$

4 Adding Constraints

The slicing algorithm with patterns computes slices for all combinations of asynchronous events (see Table 1), while only slices for events with $x > y$ or, more precisely, priority(x) > priority(y) are meaningful for the subsequent analysis. It is easy to filter out the undesired slices before passing them on to analysis. But it is even possible to avoid generating these slices right away by imposing constraints on the parameter instantiation.

4.1 Constraint Solving

Constraint solving is an established technique from the problem solving domain, and efficient solvers exist for many arithmetic and finite domains. The following introduction follows Marriott and Stuckey's textbook [10].

A *constraint domain* defines the language of constraints and the set of values over which they range. Constraints involve variables. The set of variables and values are X and V, respectively, sharing the notation for instances from the previous sections. A *constraint* c is of the form $\gamma_1 \wedge \cdots \wedge \gamma_n$, where the γ_i are *primitive constraints*. The latter are predicate symbols applied to expressions. The set of expressions is defined by the constraint domain. It includes variables and values.

A *valuation* maps variables to values (the notion is identical to the that of instantiations from the previous section). If a constraint evaluates to *true* under a valuation it is said to have a *solution*. The empty conjunction of primitive constraints, for which any valuation is a solution, is denoted by *true*, the constraint that has no solution as *false*.

Let c_1 and c_2 be constraints. The conjunction $c_1 \wedge c_2$ is the conjunction of the primitive constraints of c_1 and c_2. The constraint c_1 *implies* c_2 if $\theta(c_1) = true$ implies $\theta(c_2) = true$ for all valuations θ such that $\text{Dom}\,\theta$ contains the variables that occur in c_1 and c_2. Implication is denoted by $c_1 \to c_2$. If $c_1 \to c_2$ and $c_2 \to c_1$ then c_1 and c_2 are *equivalent*. In the sequel, equivalent constraints are considered equal. It is also assumed that equations of the form $x = v$ for $x \in X$ and $v \in V$ can be expressed as constraints, and that implication and equivalence are computable — that is, a complete solver exists. For $\theta \in X \rightharpoonup V$ we denote the extension of a constraint c by the equational constraints given by the mappings of θ as $c.\theta$. For the "inconsistent function", $c.\top = false$.

The set C of constraints for a constraint domain is partially ordered by implication. It is also partially ordered by reverse implication. The latter is an upper semilattice where $c_1 \wedge c_2$ is the least upper bound of c_1 and c_2. The least upper bound of a set $C' \subseteq C$ of constraints is denoted by $\bigwedge C'$. The top element is *false* and the bottom element *true*.[2]

4.2   Slicing with Constraints

Slicing with constraints involves an *initial constraint* c, which is taken into account while matching patterns to events. For example, the constraints $x > y$ (or priority$(x) >$ priority(y)) expresses the priority condition for the scheduling example, where $\{f(x), f(y), h(x), h(y)\}$ is the set of patterns. This constraint already entails injectivity of parameter instantiations. Explicit references to injectivity can be pulled out of the algorithm by requiring the initial constraint to imply injectivity of instantiations.

Definition 6 (Slice with Constraints). *For an initial constraint $c \in C$, a set of patterns $P \subseteq A(X)$, a trace $\tau \in A(V)$ and a constraint θ, the slice $\tau|_\theta$ is defined as follows. Either $\theta = false$. Then $\tau|_\theta$ is the full sequence τ. Otherwise, it is the subsequence of events $q \in \tau$ such that there exists a pattern $p \in P$ and $\theta \to c.\text{mgm}(p, q)$.*

The modified slicing algorithm is shown in Fig. 4. It takes the initial constraint c as an additional argument. The inner loop iterates over constraints θ' that imply c.

Lemma 7 (Lookup with Constraints). *Let $\tau \in A(V)^*$, $c \in C$ and let Θ be a sublattice of C such that $\{c.\text{mgm}(p, q) \mid p \in P, q \in \tau\} \subseteq \Theta$ and $c, \top \in \Theta$. Let $\theta \in C$ with $\theta \to c$. Then $\tau|_{\bigsqcup \Theta[\theta]} = \tau|_\theta$.*

Proof. Let $q \in \tau|_\theta$. Either $\theta = false$, and so $\bigwedge \Theta[\theta] = false$ and $q \in \tau|_{\bigwedge \Theta[\theta]}$. Otherwise there is a $p \in P$ with $\theta \to c.\text{mgm}(p, q)$ and $c.\text{mgm}(p, q) \in \Theta$, and so $\bigwedge \Theta[\theta] \to c.\text{mgm}(p, q)$. This implies $q \in \tau|_{\bigwedge \Theta[\theta]}$. Conversely, let $q \in \bigwedge \Theta[\theta]$. Either $\bigwedge \Theta[\theta] = false$ and so $\theta = false$ or there is a $p \in P$ such that $\bigwedge \Theta[\theta] \to c.\text{mgm}(p, q)$. From $\theta \to \bigwedge \Theta[\theta]$ follows $\theta \to c.\text{mgm}(p, q)$ and $q \in \tau|_\theta$.

---

[2] Logic-inclined readers might find it more intuitive to interpret C as a lower semilattice with top *true* and bottom *false*. For consistency with the previous versions of the algorithm this has not been done here.

Definition and lemma differ from their counterparts from Sect. 3 only in notation, and the proof of the lemma is a literal translation of the version for patterns.

Theorem 3 (Slicing with Constraints). *Let $c \in C$ and $P \subseteq A(X)$ such that $c \wedge (x = y) \to false$ for any two distinct variables $x, y \in X$. Let $\tau \in A(V)^*$ and let $\mathbb{T}$ and Θ be the result of processing τ with Algorithm A with Constraints. Then these conditions hold:*

$$\text{Dom}\,\mathbb{T} = \Theta \tag{9}$$

$$\{c.\text{mgm}(p, q) \mid p \in P \text{ and } q \in \tau\} \subseteq \Theta \tag{10}$$

$$\mathbb{T}(\theta) = \tau|_\theta \text{ for any } \theta \in \Theta \tag{11}$$

$$\tau|_\theta = \mathbb{T}(\bigwedge \Theta[\theta]) \text{ for any } \theta \in C \text{ with } \theta \to c \tag{12}$$

Proof. It is sufficient to observe that Θ is maintained during the computation to be a sublattice of C with bottom element c and top element *false*. Then the arguments for Theorem 2 apply. □

4.3 Experiments

Algorithm A with Constraints was implemented in Java. The implementation is generic in the constraint domain and enables experiments with different constraint solvers. It can read traces generated by JamaicaVM, but it is not designed for online monitoring. The implementation is a fairly direct rendering of the pseudocode from Fig. 4 and has not been optimised in any way.

Two solvers were provided. The first is a wrapper for the semilattice $X \xrightarrow{\top}_i V$. The second supports the primitive constraints $x \leq y$ and $x \neq y$. The order constraints are maintained as a directed graph, and whenever there is a a $x \neq y$ such that x and y are in the same strongly connected component the collection of primitive constraints has no solution (is inconsistent).

Configuring Algorithm A with Constraints with the solver for injective functions and the initial constraint $c = true$ yields Algorithm A with Patterns. Hence the former is a generalisation of the latter. The slices shown in Table 1 were obtained with this configuration of the implementation. When switching to the solver for order constraints and inequality, and with the initial constraint $x > y$, the result is the same, except that the slices for $\{x \mapsto 1, y \mapsto 2\}$, $\{x \mapsto 1, y \mapsto 3\}$ and $\{x \mapsto 2, y \mapsto 3\}$ disappear as expected. The implementation was tested on a number of traces including the example from Roşu and Chen [11, Table 1] and yielded the expected results.

5 Conclusions

This work was inspired by work by Boden and Stolz [4,12]. The idea pursued initially was to use a combination of alternating automata and constraint solvers for imposing priority constraints on the monitors. While this seemed to work in principle, the solution was fairly complicated, and an extension to time — for example, timed automata [9] —, which is indispensable for monitoring realtime systems, would have complicated things even further. The combination of constraint solvers with a slicing algorithm is much cleaner. It enables using any monitoring technology.

An extension to the Algorithms B and C, which are versions of A optimised for use in practice, has not yet been investigated. Neither have we experimented with efficient finite-domain solvers, which seem most appropriate for handling priority constraints. The main requirement for efficiency, namely that the table T of slices can be updated in parallel in the inner loop of the algorithm, is also met by the two variants of A presented here.

Solutions to monitoring events with data differ in the trade-off between monitoring speed and expressiveness. Quantified event automata [3] share some features of this work — for example, the use of pattern matching to categorise events — but go beyond beyond its specification capabilities by allowing existential quantification of data. Both extensions can monitor properties not amenable to the original algorithm. Temporal data logic [6] is a monitoring formalism based on the combination of a temporal logic for specifying the order of events with a logic for reasoning about the data. Like with our constraint-based extension of Roşu and Chen's algorithm a reasoning specialist — in this case an SMT solver — is used for analysing the data.

The distinctive contribution of this work is that Roşu and Chen's algorithm itself is applicable to a wider range of monitoring problems than it was designed for. Whether an integration of the algorithm with constraint solvers performs better in practice than filtering out unwanted slices generated by the version for patterns remains to be seen. The main result is theoretical: a deeper understanding of Roşu and Chen's algorithm, which opens the field for new applications.

Acknowledgements. The work was funded in part by the European Union within the 7th Framework Programme, Project JUNIPER, Grant Agreement 318763, and as Artemis Joint Undertaking, Project CONCERTO, Grant Agreement 333053. Quantified event automata were brought to the attention of the author by two of the anonymous reviewers.

References

1. aicas GmbH, Karlsruhe, Germany: JamaicaVM 6.3 User Manual (2014)
2. Baader, F., Nipkow, T.: Term Rewriting and All That. Cambridge University Press (1998)
3. Barringer, H., Falcone, Y., Havelund, K., Reger, G., Rydeheard, D.: Quantified event automata: Towards expressive and efficient runtime monitors. In: Giannakopoulou, D., Méry, D. (eds.) FM 2012. LNCS, vol. 7436, pp. 68–84. Springer, Heidelberg (2012)
4. Bodden, E.: J-LO A tool for runtime-checking of temporal assertions. Diplomarbeit, RWTH Aachen (2005)

5. Burns, A., Wellings, A.: Real-Time Systems and Programming Languages, 3rd edn. Addison Wesley (2001)
6. Decker, N., Leucker, M., Thoma, D.: Monitoring modulo theories. In: Ábrahám, E., Havelund, K. (eds.) TACAS 2014. LNCS, vol. 8413, pp. 341–356. Springer, Heidelberg (2014)
7. Jacobson, N.: Basic Algebra I, 2nd edn. Freeman (1985)
8. Leucker, M., Schallhart, C.: A brief account of runtime verification. The Journal of Logic and Algebraic Programming 78(5), 293–303 (2009)
9. Maler, O., Nickovic, D., Pnueli, A.: From MITL to timed automata. In: Asarin, E., Bouyer, P. (eds.) FORMATS 2006. LNCS, vol. 4202, pp. 274–289. Springer, Heidelberg (2006)
10. Marriott, K., Stuckey, P.J.: Programming with Constraints. MIT Press (1998)
11. Roşu, G., Chen, F.: Semantics and algorithms for parametric monitoring. Logical Methods in Computer Science 8(1:9), 1–47 (2012)
12. Stolz, V.: Temporal assertions for sequential and concurrent programs. Ph.D. thesis, RWTH Aachen, also Technical Report AIB-2007-15 (2006)
13. Wellings, A.: Concurrent and Real-Time Programming in Java. Wiley (2004)

Scalable Offline Monitoring*

David Basin[1], Germano Caronni[2], Sarah Ereth[3], Matúš Harvan[4],
Felix Klaedtke[5], and Heiko Mantel[3]

[1] Institute of Information Security, ETH Zurich, Switzerland
[2] Google Inc., Switzerland
[3] Department of Computer Science, TU Darmstadt, Germany
[4] ABB Corporate Research, Switzerland
[5] NEC Europe Ltd., Heidelberg, Germany

Abstract. We propose an approach to monitoring IT systems offline,
where system actions are logged in a distributed file system and subsequently checked for compliance against policies formulated in an expressive temporal logic. The novelty of our approach is that monitoring is
parallelized so that it scales to large logs. Our technical contributions comprise a formal framework for slicing logs, an algorithmic realization based
on MapReduce, and a high-performance implementation. We evaluate our
approach analytically and experimentally, proving the soundness and completeness of our slicing techniques and demonstrating its practical feasibility and efficiency on real-world logs with 400 GB of relevant data.

1 Introduction

Data owners, such as individuals and companies, are increasingly concerned
that their private data, collected and shared by IT systems, is used only for
the purposes for which it was collected. Conversely, those parties responsible
for collecting and managing such data must increasingly follow regulations on
how it is processed. For example, US hospitals must follow the US Health Insur-
ance Portability and Accountability Act (HIPAA) and financial services must
conform to the Sarbanes-Oxley Act (SOX), and these laws even stipulate the
use of mechanisms in IT system for monitoring system behavior. Although various monitoring approaches have been developed for different expressive policy
specification languages, such as [9, 10, 13, 15, 18], they do not scale to checking
compliance of large-scale IT systems like cloud-based services and systems that
process machine-generated data. These systems typically log terabytes or even
petabytes of system actions each day. Existing monitoring approaches fail to
cope with such enormous quantities of logged data.

In this paper, we propose a scalable approach to offline monitoring, where
system components log their actions and monitors inspect the logs to identify

---

* This work was partly done while Matúš Harvan was at ETH Zurich and Google Inc.
and Felix Klaedtke was at ETH Zurich. The Center for Advanced Security Research
Darmstadt (www.cased.de), the Zurich Information Security and Privacy Center
(www.zisc.ethz.ch), and Google Inc. supported this work.

B. Bonakdarpour and S.A. Smolka (Eds.): RV 2014, LNCS 8734, pp. 31–47, 2014.

policy violations. Given a policy, our solution works by decomposing the logs into small parts, called slices, that can be independently analyzed. We can therefore parallelize and distribute the monitoring process over multiple computers.

One of the main challenges is to generate the slices without weakening the guarantees provided by monitoring. In particular, the slices must be *sound* and *complete* for the given policy and logged data. That means that only actual violations are reported and every violation is reported by at least one monitor. Furthermore, slicing should be effective, i.e., producing the slices should be fast and the slices should be small. We provide a framework for obtaining slices with these properties. In particular, our framework lays the foundations for slicing logs, where logs are represented as temporal structures and policies are given as formulas in metric first-order temporal logic (MFOTL) [8, 9]. Although we use temporal structures for representing logs and MFOTL as a policy specification language, the underlying principles of our slicing framework are general and apply to other representations of logs and other logic-based policy languages.

Within our theoretical slicing framework, we define orthogonal methods to generate sound and complete slices. The first method constructs slices for checking system compliance for specific entities, such as all users whose login name starts with the letter "A." Note that it is not sufficient to consider just the actions of these users to check their compliance; other users' actions might also be relevant and must also be included in a slice to be sound. The second method checks system compliance during a specific time period, such as a particular week. In addition to these two basic methods for slicing with respect to data and time, we describe slicing by filtering, which discards parts of a slice to speed up monitoring. Finally, we show that slicing is compositional. We can therefore obtain new, more powerful slicing methods by composing existing methods.

We demonstrate how to employ the MapReduce framework [12] to parallelize and distribute the slicing and monitoring tasks. We propose algorithms, for both slicing and filtering. Moreover, we explain how to flexibly combine slicing and filtering. As required by MapReduce, we define map and reduce functions that constitute the backbone of the algorithmic realization of our slicing framework. The map function realizes slicing and the reduce function realizes monitoring. MapReduce runs in its map phase and in its reduce phase multiple instances of the respective function in parallel, where each instance is responsible for a part of the logged data. Splitting and parallelizing the workload this way enables monitoring to scale in the high-performance implementation of our approach.

We deploy and evaluate our monitoring solution in a real-world setting, where we check the compliance of more than 35,000 computers, producing approximately 1 TB of log data each day. The policies considered concern the updating of system configurations and access to sensitive resources. We successfully monitor the relevant actions logged by these computers. The log consist of several billion log entries from a two year period, requiring 0.4 TB of storage. The monitoring takes just a few hours, using only 1,000 machines in a MapReduce cluster.

Overall, we see our contributions as follows. First, we provide a framework for splitting logs into slices for monitoring. Second, we give a scalable algorithmic realization of our framework for monitoring large logs in an offline setting. Both our framework and our algorithmic realization support compositional slicing. Finally, with our case study, we show that the approach is effective and scales well. In particular, our deployment and the evaluation demonstrate the feasibility of checking compliance in large-scale IT systems.

We proceed as follows. In Section 2, we give background on MFOTL and monitoring. In Section 3, we describe our approach to slicing and monitoring, including its algorithmic realization in MapReduce. In Section 4, we experimentally evaluate our approach. We discuss related work in Section 5 before drawing conclusions in Section 6. Additional details, including proofs and pseudo code omitted due to space restrictions, are given in the full version of this paper, which is available from the authors or their webpages.

2 Preliminaries

In this section, we explain how we use MFOTL to represent system requirements, and how we monitor a single stream of logged system actions.

Specification Language. We give just a brief overview of MFOTL; further details can be found in the paper's full version. MFOTL is similar to propositional real-time logics like MTL [2]. However, as it is a first-order logic, MFOTL's syntax is defined with respect to a signature. Furthermore, instead of timed words, its models are temporal structures $(\bar{\mathcal{D}}, \bar{\tau})$, where $\bar{\mathcal{D}} = (\mathcal{D}_0, \mathcal{D}_1, \dots)$ is a sequence of structures and $\bar{\tau} = (\tau_0, \tau_1, \dots)$ is a sequence of natural numbers. As is usual, a structure $\mathcal{D}$ over a signature $\mathcal{S}$ (without function symbols) consists of a domain $|\mathcal{D}| \neq \emptyset$ and interpretations $c^{\mathcal{D}} \in |\mathcal{D}|$ and $r^{\mathcal{D}} \subseteq |\mathcal{D}|^{\iota(r)}$, for each constant symbol c and predicate symbol r of the signature $\mathcal{S}$, where $\iota(r)$ denotes r's arity.

The formulas over the signature $\mathcal{S}$ are given by the grammar

$$\varphi ::= t_1 \approx t_2 \,|\, t_1 \prec t_2 \,|\, r(t_1, \dots, t_{\iota(r)}) \,|\, \neg \varphi \,|\, \varphi \vee \varphi \,|\, \exists x.\, \varphi \,|\, \bullet_I \varphi \,|\, \bigcirc_I \varphi \,|\, \varphi \, \mathsf{S}_I \, \varphi \,|\, \varphi \, \mathsf{U}_I \, \varphi \,,$$

where $t_1, t_2, \dots$ are variables or constant symbols of $\mathcal{S}$, r a predicate symbol of S, x a variable, and I an interval $[a, b) \subseteq \mathbb{N}$. The temporal operators $\bullet_I$ ("previous"), $\bigcirc_I$ ("next"), S_I ("since"), and U_I ("until") require the satisfaction of a formula within a particular time interval in the past or future. An operator's subscript I specifies this time interval. MFOTL's satisfaction relation $\models$ is defined as expected for (i) a time point $i \in \mathbb{N}$, (ii) a valuation v interpreting the variables, and (iii) a temporal structure $(\bar{\mathcal{D}}, \bar{\tau})$. We call the indices of the τ_is and $\mathcal{D}_i$s *time points* and the τ_is *timestamps*. In particular, τ_i is the timestamp at time point $i \in \mathbb{N}$.

We use standard terminology and syntactic sugar, see e.g., [3,14]. For instance, we use terms like *free variable* and *atomic formula*, and abbreviations such as $\blacklozenge_I \varphi := true \, \mathsf{S}_I \, \varphi$ ("once"), $\Diamond_I \varphi := true \, \mathsf{U}_I \, \varphi$ ("eventually"), $\blacksquare_I \varphi := \neg \blacklozenge_I \neg \varphi$ ("historically"), and $\square_I \varphi := \neg \Diamond_I \neg \varphi$ ("always"), where $true := \exists x.\, x \approx x$. Intuitively, the formula $\blacklozenge_I \varphi$ states that φ holds at some time point in the past within the time window I and $\blacksquare_I \varphi$ states that φ holds at all time points in the past within the time window I. The corresponding future operators are $\Diamond_I$ and $\square_I$. We also use non-metric operators like $\square \varphi := \square_{[0,\infty)} \varphi$. To omit parentheses, we use the standard conventions about the binding strength of logical connectives, e.g., Boolean operators bind stronger than temporal ones and unary operators bind stronger than binary ones.

Throughout the paper, we make the following assumptions when not stated otherwise. First, formulas and temporal structures are over the signature S consisting of the sets C and R of constant and predicate symbols, and the function ι assigns an arity to each predicate symbol. Second, the set of variables is V. Third, the structures' domain is $\mathbb{D}$ and constant symbols are interpreted identically in all structures. The set of all these temporal structures is $\mathbf{T}$. Finally, without loss of generality, variables are quantified at most once in a formula and quantified variables are disjoint from the formula's free variables.

Monitoring. We use MFOTL to check the policy compliance of a stream of system actions as follows [8]. Policies are given as MFOTL formulas of the form $\square\,\psi$. For illustration, consider the policy stating that SSH connections must last no longer than 24 hours. This can be formalized in MFOTL as

$$\square\,\forall c.\,\forall s.\,ssh\_login(c, s) \rightarrow \Diamond_{[0,25)}\,ssh\_logout(c, s)\,, \qquad (P0)$$

where we assume that time units are in hours and the signature consists of the two binary predicate symbols ssh_login and ssh_logout. We also assume that the system actions are logged. In particular, the ith entry in the stream of logged actions consists of the performed actions and a timestamp τ_i that records the time when the actions occurred. For checking compliance with respect to the formula $(P0)$, we assume that the logged actions are the logins and logouts, with the parameters specifying the computer's name and the session identifier.

The corresponding temporal structure $(\bar{\mathcal{D}}, \bar{\tau})$ for such a stream of logged SSH login and logout actions is as follows. The domain of $\bar{\mathcal{D}}$ contains all possible computer names and session identifiers. The ith structure in $\bar{\mathcal{D}}$ contains the relations $ssh\_login^{\mathcal{D}i}$ and $ssh\_logout^{\mathcal{D}i}$, where (1) $(c, s) \in ssh\_login^{\mathcal{D}i}$ iff there is a logged login action in the ith entry of the stream with the parameter values c and s, and (2) $(c, s) \in ssh\_logout^{\mathcal{D}i}$ iff there is a logged logout action in the ith entry of the stream with the parameter values c and s. The ith timestamp in $\bar{\tau}$ is simply the timestamp τ_i of the ith log entry. This generalizes straightforwardly to an arbitrary stream of logged actions, where the kind of actions correspond to the predicate symbols specified by the temporal structure's signature and the actions' parameter values are elements from the temporal structure's domain.

In practice, we can only monitor finite prefixes of temporal structures to detect policy violations. However, to ease our exposition, we require that temporal structures, and thus also logs, describe infinite streams of system actions. We use the monitoring tool MONPOLY [7] to check whether a stream of system actions complies with a policy formalized in MFOTL. It implements the monitoring algorithm in [9]. MONPOLY iteratively processes the temporal structure $(\bar{\mathcal{D}}, \bar{\tau})$ representing a stream of logged actions, either offline or online, and outputs the policy violations. Formally, for a formula $\square\,\psi$, a *policy violation* is a pair (v, τ) of a valuation v and a timestamp τ such that $(\bar{\mathcal{D}}, \bar{\tau}, v, i) \models \neg\psi$, for some time point i with $\tau_i = \tau$. The formula ψ may contain free variables and the valuation v interprets these variables. As MONPOLY searches for all combinations of timepoints and interpretations of the free variables for which a given stream of logged actions violates the policy, in practice we drop the outer universal quantifications in the policy's MFOTL formalization to obtain additional information about the violations. For instance, if we remove the universal quantification over s in the formula $(P0)$, then the valuation v in each policy violation (v, τ) specifies a session identifier of an SSH connection that lasted 25 hours or more.

In general, we assume that the subformula ψ of $\square\,\psi$ formalizing the given policy is *bounded*, i.e., the interval I of every temporal operator U_I occurring in ψ is finite. Since ψ is bounded, the monitor only needs to process a finite prefix of $(\bar{\mathcal{D}}, \bar{\tau}) \in \mathbf{T}$ when determining the valuations satisfying $\neg\psi$ at any given time point. To effectively determine all these valuations, we also assume here that predicate symbols have finite interpretations in $(\bar{\mathcal{D}}, \bar{\tau})$, that is, the relation $r^{\mathcal{D}_j}$ is finite, for every predicate symbol r and every $j \in \mathbb{N}$. Furthermore, we require that $\neg\psi$ can be rewritten to a formula that is temporal safe-range [9], a generalization of the standard notion of safe-range database queries [1]. In our SSH example, the rewritten formula of $(P0)$ without the outermost temporal operator and quantifiers is $ssh\_login(c, s) \wedge \neg \lozenge_{[0,25)}\, ssh\_logout(c, s)$.

3 Log Slicing

In Section 3.1, we present the logical foundation of our slicing framework. A slicer splits the temporal structure to be monitored into *slices*. We introduce the notions of soundness and completeness for individual slices relative to sets of possible violations, called *restrictions*. We show that soundness and completeness of each individual slice in a set are sufficient to find all violations of a given policy, provided that the restrictions are chosen appropriately. We also show that slicing is compositional. In Section 3.2, we present concrete instances of slicers and in Section 3.3, we present an algorithmic realization of our slicing framework.

3.1 Slicing Foundations

Slices. Slicing entails splitting a temporal structure, which represents a stream of logged actions, into multiple temporal structures. Each such temporal structure contains only a subset of the logged actions. Formally, a slice is defined as follows.

Definition 1. *Let $s\colon [0, \ell) \to \mathbb{N}$ be a strictly increasing function, with $\ell \in \mathbb{N} \cup \{\infty\}$. The temporal structure $(\bar{\mathcal{D}}', \bar{\tau}') \in \mathbf{T}$ is a slice of $(\bar{\mathcal{D}}, \bar{\tau}) \in \mathbf{T}$ (with respect to the function s) if $\tau'_i = \tau_{s(i)}$ and $r^{\mathcal{D}'_i} \subseteq r^{\mathcal{D}_{s(i)}}$, for all $i \in [0, \ell)$ and all $r \in R$.*

Recall that the logged system actions at a time point $i \in \mathbb{N}$ are represented as the elements in $\mathcal{D}_i$'s relations $r^{\mathcal{D}_i}$, with $r \in R$. The function s determines which time points of the temporal structure $(\bar{\mathcal{D}}, \bar{\tau})$ are in the slice $(\bar{\mathcal{D}}', \bar{\tau}')$. For the time points present in the slice, some actions may be ignored since $r^{\mathcal{D}'_i} \subseteq r^{\mathcal{D}_{s(i)}}$, for $i \in [0, \ell)$. Note that the domain of the function s may be finite or infinite. If its domain is infinite, i.e. when $\ell = \infty$, we require that each action in the slice is an action of the original stream of actions, i.e. $r^{\mathcal{D}'_i} \subseteq r^{\mathcal{D}_{s(i)}}$, for each $i \in \mathbb{N}$. If s's domain is finite, i.e. when $\ell \in \mathbb{N}$, we relax this requirement by not imposing any restrictions on the structures $\mathcal{D}'_i$ and the timestamps τ'_i with $i \geq \ell$. In this case, the suffix of the slice starting at time point ℓ is ignored when monitoring the slice.

To meaningfully monitor slices independently, we require that slices are *sound* and *complete*. Intuitively, this means that at least one of the monitored slices violates the given policy if and only if the original temporal structure violates the policy. We define these requirements in Definition 2 below, relative to a set $\mathcal{R} \subseteq ((V \to \mathbb{D}) \times \mathbb{N})$, called a *restriction*. We use $\mathbf{R}$ to denote the set of all such restrictions and say that a violation (v, t) is *permitted* by $\mathcal{R} \in \mathbf{R}$ if $(v, t) \in \mathcal{R}$.

Definition 2. *Let φ be a formula and $\mathcal{R} \in \mathbf{R}$.*

  (i) *$(\bar{\mathcal{D}}', \bar{\tau}') \in \mathbf{T}$ is $\mathcal{R}$-sound for $(\bar{\mathcal{D}}, \bar{\tau}) \in \mathbf{T}$ and φ if for all pairs (v, t) permitted by $\mathcal{R}$, it holds that $(\bar{\mathcal{D}}, \bar{\tau}, v, i) \models \varphi$, for all $i \in \mathbb{N}$ with $\tau_i = t$, implies $(\bar{\mathcal{D}}', \bar{\tau}', v, j) \models \varphi$, for all $j \in \mathbb{N}$ with $\tau'_j = t$.*

  (ii) *$(\bar{\mathcal{D}}', \bar{\tau}') \in \mathbf{T}$ is $\mathcal{R}$-complete for $(\bar{\mathcal{D}}, \bar{\tau}) \in \mathbf{T}$ and φ if for all pairs (v, t) permitted by $\mathcal{R}$, it holds that $(\bar{\mathcal{D}}, \bar{\tau}, v, i) \not\models \varphi$, for some $i \in \mathbb{N}$ with $\tau_i = t$, implies $(\bar{\mathcal{D}}', \bar{\tau}', v, j) \not\models \varphi$, for some $j \in \mathbb{N}$ with $\tau'_j = t$.*

We equip each slice with a restriction. The original temporal structure is equipped with the *non-restrictive* restriction $\mathcal{R}_0 := ((V \to \mathbb{D}) \times \mathbb{N})$, which permits any pair (v, t).

Slicers. We call a mechanism that splits a temporal structure into slices a *slicer*. Additionally, a slicer equips the resulting slices with restrictions. In Definition 3, we give requirements that the slices and their restrictions must fulfill. In Theorem 4, we show that these requirements suffice to ensure that monitoring the slices is equivalent to monitoring the original temporal structure.

Definition 3. *A slicer $\mathfrak{s}_\varphi$ for the formula φ is a function that maps $(\bar{\mathcal{D}}, \bar{\tau}) \in \mathbf{T}$ and $\mathcal{R} \in \mathbf{R}$ to a family of temporal structures $(\bar{\mathcal{D}}^k, \bar{\tau}^k)_{k \in K}$ and a family of restrictions $(\mathcal{R}^k)_{k \in K}$ that satisfy the following conditions.*
(S1) $(\mathcal{R}^k)_{k \in K}$ refines $\mathcal{R}$, i.e., $\bigcup_{k \in K} \mathcal{R}^k = \mathcal{R}$.
(S2) $(\bar{\mathcal{D}}^k, \bar{\tau}^k)$ is $\mathcal{R}^k$-sound for $(\bar{\mathcal{D}}, \bar{\tau})$ and φ, for all $k \in K$.
(S3) $(\bar{\mathcal{D}}^k, \bar{\tau}^k)$ is $\mathcal{R}^k$-complete for $(\bar{\mathcal{D}}, \bar{\tau})$ and φ, for all $k \in K$.

Theorem 4. *Let $\mathfrak{s}_\varphi$ be a slicer for the formula φ. Assume that $\mathfrak{s}_\varphi$ maps $(\bar{\mathcal{D}}, \bar{\tau}) \in \mathbf{T}$ and $\mathcal{R} \in \mathbf{R}$ to the family of temporal structures $(\bar{\mathcal{D}}^k, \bar{\tau}^k)_{k \in K}$ and the family of restrictions $(\mathcal{R}^k)_{k \in K}$. The following conditions are equivalent.*
(1) $(\bar{\mathcal{D}}, \bar{\tau}, v, i) \models \varphi$, for all valuations v and $i \in \mathbb{N}$ with $(v, \tau_i) \in \mathcal{R}$.
(2) $(\bar{\mathcal{D}}^k, \bar{\tau}^k, v, i) \models \varphi$, for all $k \in K$, valuations v, and $i \in \mathbb{N}$ with $(v, \tau_i) \in \mathcal{R}^k$.

Composition. We define next an operation for composing slicers. Theorem 6 shows that the composition of slicers is again a slicer. Hence we can restrict ourselves to a few basic slicers, which we provide in Section 3.2 and their algorithmic realization in Section 3.3. By composition, we obtain more powerful slicers, which may be needed to obtain slices of manageable size from very large logs.

Definition 5. *Let* $\mathfrak{s}_\varphi$ *and* $\mathfrak{s}'_\varphi$ *be slicers for the formula* φ. *The combination* $\mathfrak{s}'_\varphi \circ_{\hat{k}} \mathfrak{s}_\varphi$ *for the index* $\hat{k}$ *is the function that maps* $(\bar{\mathcal{D}}, \bar{\tau}) \in \mathbf{T}$ *and* $\mathcal{R} \in \mathbf{R}$ *to the following families of temporal structures and restrictions, assuming that* $\mathfrak{s}_\varphi$ *maps* $(\bar{\mathcal{D}}, \bar{\tau})$ *and* $\mathcal{R}$ *to* $(\bar{\mathcal{D}}^k, \bar{\tau}^k)_{k \in K}$ *and* $(\mathcal{R}^k)_{k \in K}$

– *If* $\hat{k} \notin K$ *then* $\mathfrak{s}'_\varphi \circ_{\hat{k}} \mathfrak{s}_\varphi$ *returns* $(\bar{\mathcal{D}}^k, \bar{\tau}^k)_{k \in K}$ *and* $(\mathcal{R}^k)_{k \in K}$.
– *If* $\hat{k} \in K$ *then* $\mathfrak{s}'_\varphi \circ_{\hat{k}} \mathfrak{s}_\varphi$ *returns* $(\bar{\mathcal{D}}^k, \bar{\tau}^k)_{k \in K''}$ *and* $(\mathcal{R}^k)_{k \in K''}$, *where* $K'' := (K \setminus \{\hat{k}\}) \cup K'$ *and* $(\bar{\mathcal{D}}^k, \bar{\tau}^k)_{k \in K'}$ *and* $(\mathcal{R}^k)_{k \in K'}$ *are the families returned by* $\mathfrak{s}'_\varphi$ *for the input* $(\bar{\mathcal{D}}^{\hat{k}}, \bar{\tau}^{\hat{k}})$ *and* $\mathcal{R}^{\hat{k}}$, *assuming* $K \cap K' = \emptyset$.

Intuitively, we first apply the slicer $\mathfrak{s}_\varphi$. The index $\hat{k}$ specifies which of the obtained slices should be sliced further. If there is no $\hat{k}$th slice, the second slicer $\mathfrak{s}'_\varphi$ does nothing. Otherwise, we use $\mathfrak{s}'_\varphi$ to make the $\hat{k}$th slice smaller. Note that by combing the slicer $\mathfrak{s}_\varphi$ with different indices, we can slice all of $\mathfrak{s}_\varphi$'s outputs further. Note too that an algorithmic realization of the function $\mathfrak{s}'_\varphi \circ_{\hat{k}} \mathfrak{s}_\varphi$ need not necessarily compute the output of $\mathfrak{s}_\varphi$ before applying $\mathfrak{s}'_\varphi$.

Theorem 6. *The combination* $\mathfrak{s}'_\varphi \circ_{\hat{k}} \mathfrak{s}_\varphi$ *of the slicers* $\mathfrak{s}_\varphi$ *and* $\mathfrak{s}'_\varphi$ *for the formula* φ *is a slicer for the formula* φ.

3.2 Basic Slicers

We now introduce three basic slicers. Due to space limitations, we focus on just one of them. The full version of the paper provides details on the other two.

Slicing Data. Data slicers split the relations of a temporal structure. We call the resulting slices data slices. Formally, $(\bar{\mathcal{D}}', \bar{\tau}') \in \mathbf{T}$ is a *data slice* of $(\bar{\mathcal{D}}, \bar{\tau}) \in \mathbf{T}$ if $(\bar{\mathcal{D}}', \bar{\tau}')$ is a slice of $(\bar{\mathcal{D}}, \bar{\tau})$, where the function $s : [0, \ell) \to \mathbb{N}$ in Definition 1 is the identity function and $\ell = \infty$. In the following, we introduce data slicers that return sound and complete slices relative to a restriction.

In a nutshell, a data slicer takes as input a formula φ, a *slicing variable* x, which is a free variable in φ, and *slicing sets*, which are sets of possible values for x. It constructs one slice for each slicing set. The slicing sets can be chosen freely, and can overlap, as long as their union covers all possible values for x. Intuitively, each slice excludes those elements of the relations interpreting the predicate symbols that are irrelevant to determining φ's truth value when x takes values from the slicing set. For values outside of the slicing set, the formula may evaluate to a different truth value on the slice than on the original temporal structure.

We begin by defining the slices output by our data slicer.

Definition 7. *Let* φ *be a formula,* $x \in V$, $(\bar{\mathcal{D}}, \bar{\tau}) \in \mathbf{T}$, *and* $S \subseteq \mathbb{D}$ *a slicing set. The* (φ, x, S)-*slice of* $(\bar{\mathcal{D}}, \bar{\tau})$ *is the data slice* $(\bar{\mathcal{D}}', \bar{\tau}')$, *where the relations are as follows. For all* $r \in R$, $i \in \mathbb{N}$, *and* $\bar{a} \in \mathbb{D}^{\iota(r)}$, *it holds that* $\bar{a} \in r^{\mathcal{D}'_i}$ *iff* $\bar{a} \in r^{\mathcal{D}_i}$ *and there is an atomic subformula of* φ *of the form* $r(\bar{t})$ *such that for every* j *with* $1 \leq j \leq \iota(r)$, *at least one of the following conditions is satisfied.*
(D1) t_j *is the variable* x *and* $a_j \in S$.

(D2) t_j is a variable y different from x.

(D3) t_j is a constant symbol c with $c^{\mathcal{D}} = a_j$.

Intuitively, the conditions (D1) to (D3) ensure that a slice contains the tuples from the relations interpreting the predicate symbols that are sufficient to evaluate φ when x takes values from the slicing set. For this, it suffices to consider only atomic subformulas of φ with a predicate symbol. Every item of a tuple from the symbol's interpretation must satisfy at least one of the conditions. If the subformula includes the slicing variable, then only values from the slicing set are relevant (D1). If it includes another variable, then all possible values are relevant (D2). Finally, if it includes a constant symbol, then the interpretation of the constant symbol is relevant (D3).

The following example illustrates Definition 7. It also demonstrates that the choice of the slicing variable can influence how lean the slices are and how much overhead the slicing causes in terms of duplicated log data. Ideally, each logged action appears in at most one slice. However, this is not generally the case and a logged action can appear in multiple slices. In the worst case, each slice ends up being the original temporal structure.

Example 8. Let φ be the formula $ssh\_login(c, s) \rightarrow \Diamond_{[0,6)} notify(\mathsf{reg\_server}, s)$, where c and s are variables and $\mathsf{reg\_server}$ is a constant symbol, which is interpreted by the domain element $0 \in \mathbb{D}$, with $\mathbb{D} = \mathbb{N}$. The formula φ expresses that a notification of the session identifier of an SSH login must be sent to the registration server within 5 time units. Assume that at time point 0 the relations of $\mathcal{D}_0$ of the original temporal structure $(\bar{\mathcal{D}}, \bar{\tau})$ for the predicate symbols ssh_login and $notify$ are $ssh\_login^{\mathcal{D}_0} = \{(1,1),(1,2),(3,3),(4,4)\}$ and $notify^{\mathcal{D}_0} = \{(0,1),(0,2),(0,3),(0,4)\}$.

We slice on the variable c. For the slicing set $S = \{1,2\}$, the (φ, c, S)-slice contains the structure $\mathcal{D}'_0$ with $ssh\_login^{\mathcal{D}'_0} = \{(1,1),(1,2)\}$ and $notify^{\mathcal{D}'_0} = \{(0,1),(0,2),(0,3),(0,4)\}$. For the predicate symbol ssh_login, only those tuples are included where the first parameter takes values from the slicing set. This is because the first parameter occurs as the slicing variable c in the formula. For the predicate symbol $notify$, those tuples are included where the first parameter is 0 because the constant symbol 0 occurs in the formula.

For the slicing set $S' = \{3,4\}$, the (φ, c, S')-slice contains the structure $\mathcal{D}''_0$ with $ssh\_login^{\mathcal{D}''_0} = \{(3,3),(4,4)\}$ and $notify^{\mathcal{D}''_0} = \{(0,1),(0,2),(0,3),(0,4)\}$. The tuples in the relation for the predicate symbol $notify$ are duplicated in all slices because the first element of the tuples, 0, occurs as a constant symbol in the formula. The condition (D3) in Definition 7 is therefore always satisfied and the tuple is included.

Next, we slice on the variable s instead of c. For the slicing set S, the (φ, s, S)-slice contains the structure $\mathcal{D}'_0$ with $ssh\_login^{\mathcal{D}'_0} = \{(1,1),(1,2)\}$ and $notify^{\mathcal{D}'_0} = \{(0,1),(0,2)\}$. For both of the predicate symbols ssh_login and $notify$, only those tuples are included where the second parameter takes values from the slicing set S. This is because the second parameter occurs as the slicing variable s in the formula. For the slicing set S, the (φ, s, S')-slice contains the structure $\mathcal{D}_0''$ with $ssh\_login^{\mathcal{D}_0''} = \{(3,3),(4,4)\}$ and $notify^{\mathcal{D}_0''} = \{(0,3),(0,4)\}$.

According to Definition 9 and Theorem 10 below, a data slicer is a slicer that splits a temporal structure into a family of (φ, x, S)-slices. Furthermore, it refines the given restriction with respect to the given slicing sets.

Definition 9. *Let φ be a formula, $x \in V$ a variable, and $(S^k)_{k \in K}$ a family of slicing sets. The* data slicer $\mathfrak{d}_{\varphi, x, (S^k)_{k \in K}}$ *is the function that maps a temporal structure $(\bar{D}, \bar{\tau}) \in \mathbf{T}$ and a restriction $\mathcal{R} \in \mathbf{R}$ to the family of temporal structures $(\bar{D}^k, \bar{\tau}^k)_{k \in K}$ and the family of restrictions $(\mathcal{R}^k)_{k \in K}$, where $(\bar{D}^k, \bar{\tau}^k)$ is the (φ, x, S'^k)-slice of $(\bar{D}, \bar{\tau})$, with $S'^k := S^k \cap \{v(x) \mid (v,t) \in \mathcal{R}, \text{ for some } t \in \mathbb{N}\}$, and $\mathcal{R}^k = \{(v,t) \in \mathcal{R} \mid v(x) \in S^k\}$, for each $k \in K$.*

Theorem 10. *A data slicer $\mathfrak{d}_{\varphi, x, (S^k)_{k \in K}}$ is a slicer for the formula φ if the slicing variable x is not bound in φ and $\bigcup_{k \in K} S^k = \mathbb{D}$.*

Slicing Time. Another possibility is to slice a temporal structure along its temporal dimension. A time slice contains all the logged actions over a sufficiently large time interval to determine the policy violations over a given time period. We obtain this time interval from the formula's temporal operators and their intervals. Due to space limitations, we refer to the full version of the paper for the details of how we produce the time slices, and the soundness and completeness guarantees when monitoring these slices independently. Instead, we illustrate time slicing by the following example.

Example 11. Recall the formula *(P0)* from Section 2. We can split a log into time slices that are equivalent to the original log over 1-day periods. However, to evaluate the formula over a 1-day period, each time slice must also include the log entries of the next 24 hours. This is because the formula's temporal operator $\Diamond_{[0,25)}$ refers to SSH logout events up to 24 hours into the future from a time point. Hence each time point would be monitored twice: once when checking compliance for a specific day and also in the slice for checking compliance of the previous day. If we split the log into time slices that are equivalent to the original log over 1-week periods then 6/7 of the time points are monitored once and 1/7 are monitored twice. This longer period produces less monitoring overhead. However, less parallelization is possible.

Filtering. Removing time points in which all the structures' relations are empty from a temporal structure can significantly speed up monitoring. Empty relations can, for example, originate from the application of a data slicer. Filtering empty time points is sound and complete for the formula *(P0)* from Section 2. However, in general, this is not the case. For instance, for the formula $\Box \forall x.\, p(x) \rightarrow \blacklozenge_{[0,1)} \neg q(x)$ the filtering of empty time points prior to monitoring is not sound. We refer again to the paper's full version for details, including the identification of a fragment for which it is safe to filter empty time points.

3.3   Parallel Implementation

Our slicing framework establishes the theoretical foundations for splitting logs into parts that can be monitored independently in a sound and complete fashion. We now explain how we exploit this in a concrete technical framework for parallelizing computations, the MapReduce framework [12]. Using MapReduce, we monitor a log corresponding to a temporal structure in three phases: map, shuffle, and reduce.

In the *map phase*, the log is fragmented by MapReduce. For each log fragment, we create a stream of log entries in a pointwise fashion. To this end, we implement a collection of slicing functions realizing the slicers and the composition of slicers within MapReduce. Each slicing function takes a single log entry $(\mathcal{D}, \tau)$ as an argument and returns (a) the structure $\mathcal{D}$ unmodified, (b) a structure $\mathcal{D}'$ that results from $\mathcal{D}$ by deleting actions (i.e., $r^{\mathcal{D}'} \subseteq r^{\mathcal{D}}$ must hold for each $r \in R$), or (c) the special symbol $\perp$ indicating that the log entry shall be deleted. We also associate a key with each log entry.

The *shuffle phase* reorganizes log entries into chunks, i.e., streams of key-value pairs with matching keys and each value is a single log entry from the map phase. Chunks can be viewed as slices in the sense of Definition 1. However, it is important that the associated keys are chosen in the map phase in such a way that the shuffle puts all log entries of one slice into the same chunk and that log entries of different slices are put into different chunks.

In the *reduce phase*, we individually monitor each chunk produced during the shuffle phase against the given policy and afterwards we combine the monitoring results thereby yielding the set of all violations. Due to the one-to-one correspondence between chunks and slices, Theorem 4 is applicable; hence no violations are lost by monitoring the constructed chunks in this phase.

In each of the three phases, computations are parallelized by MapReduce. In particular, the map and reduce phases comprise the parallel execution of multiple instances of a map function and a reduce function, respectively. The full version of the paper provides the details as well as pseudo code for the map, reduce, and slicing functions. Note that the shuffle phase is built into MapReduce.

4   The Google Case Study

Scenario. We consider a setting with over 35,000 computers accessing sensitive resources. These computers are used both within Google, connected directly to the corporate network, and outside of Google, accessing Google's network from remote unsecured networks.

Google uses access-control mechanisms to minimize the risk of unauthorized access to sensitive resources. In particular, computers must obtain time-limited authentication tokens using a tool, which we call AUTH. Furthermore, the Secure Shell protocol (SSH) is used to remotely login to servers. Additionally, to minimize the risk of security exploits, computers must regularly update their configuration and apply security patches according to a centrally managed configuration. To do this, every computer regularly starts an update tool, which

Table 1. Policy formalization

policy	MFOTL formula
(P1)	$\square\,\forall c.\,\forall t.\,auth(c,t) \to 1000 \prec t$
(P2)	$\square\,\forall c.\,\forall t.\,auth(c,t) \to \blacklozenge_{[0,3d]}\,\lozenge_{[0,0]}\,upd\_success(c)$
(P3)	$\square\,\forall c.\,\forall s.\,ssh\_login(c,s) \wedge$ $\quad(\lozenge_{[1min,20min]}\,net(c) \wedge \square_{[0,1d]}\,\blacksquare_{[0,0]}\,net(c) \to \lozenge_{[1min,20min]}\,net(c)) \to$ $\quad\lozenge_{[0,1d)}\,\blacklozenge_{[0,0]}\,ssh\_logout(c,s)$
(P4)	$\square\,\forall c.\,net(c) \wedge (\lozenge_{[10min,20min]}\,net(c)) \wedge (\blacklozenge_{[1d,2d]}\,alive(c)) \wedge$ $\quad\neg(\blacklozenge_{[0,3d]}\,\lozenge_{[0,0]}\,upd\_success(c)) \to \lozenge_{[0,20min)}\,\blacklozenge_{[0,0]}\,upd\_connect(c)$
(P5)	$\square\,\forall c.\,upd\_connect(c) \wedge (\lozenge_{[5min,20min]}\,alive(c)) \to$ $\quad\lozenge_{[0,30min)}\,\blacklozenge_{[0,0]}\,upd\_success(c) \vee upd\_skip(c)$
(P6)	$\square\,\forall c.\,upd\_skip(c) \to \blacklozenge_{[0,1d]}\,\lozenge_{[0,0]}\,upd\_success(c)$

we call UPD, connects to a central server to download the latest centrally managed configuration, and attempts to reconfigure and update itself. To prevent over-loading the configuration server, if the computer has recently updated its configuration then the update tool does not attempt to connect to the server.

Policies. The policies we consider specify restrictions on the authorization process, SSH sessions, and the update process. All computers are intended to comply with these policies. However, due to misconfiguration, server outages, hardware failures, and the like, this is not always the case. The policies are as follows.

(P1) Entering credentials with the tool AUTH must take at least 1 second. The motivation is that authentication with the tool AUTH should not be automated. That is, the authentication credentials must be entered manually and not by a script when executing the tool.

(P2) The tool AUTH may only be used if the computer has been updated to the latest centrally-managed configuration within the last 3 days.

(P3) Long-running SSH sessions present a security risk. Therefore, they must not last longer than 24 hours.

(P4) Each computer must be updated at least once every 3 days unless it is turned off or not connected to the corporate network.

(P5) If a computer connects to the central configuration server and downloads the new configuration, then it should successfully reconfigure itself within the next 30 minutes.

(P6) If the tool UPD aborts the update process, claiming that the computer was recently successfully updated, then this update must have occurred within the last 24 hours.

Table 1 presents our formalization of these policies, where we use the predicate symbols given in Table 2. We explain here the less obvious aspects of our formalization. The variable c represents a computer, s represents an SSH session, and t represents the time taken by a user to enter authentication credentials. In (P3), we assume that if a computer is disconnected from the corporate network, then the SSH session is closed. In (P4), because of the subformula $\blacklozenge_{[1d,2d]}\,alive(c)$, we only consider computers that have recently been used. In particular, the subformula suppresses false positives stemming from newly installed computers, which do not generate *alive* events prior to their installation. Similarly, we only require an update of a computer if it is connected to the network for a given amount of

Table 2. Predicate symbols and their interpretation

predicate symbol	description
$alive(c)$	The computer c is running. This event is generated at least once every 20 minutes when c is running but at most twice every 5 minutes.
$net(c)$	The computer c is connected to the corporate network. This event is generated at least once every 20 minutes when c is connected to the corporate network but at most once every 5 minutes.
$auth(c, t)$	The tool AUTH is invoked to obtain an authentication token on the computer c. The second argument t indicates the time in milliseconds it took the user to enter the authentication credentials.
$upd\_start(c)$	The tool UPD started on the computer c.
$upd\_connect(c)$	The tool UPD on the computer c connected to the central server and downloaded the latest configuration.
$upd\_success(c)$	The tool UPD updated the configuration and applied patches on the computer c.
$upd\_skip(c)$	The tool UPD on the computer c terminated because it believes that the computer was recently updated.
$ssh\_login(c, s)$	An SSH session with identifier s to the computer c was opened. We use the session identifier s to match the login event with the corresponding logout event.
$ssh\_logout(c, s)$	An SSH session with identifier s to the computer c was closed.

Table 3. Log statistics

event	count	
$alive$	16 B	(15,912,852,267)
net	8 B	(7,807,707,082)
$auth$	8 M	(7,926,789)
upd_start	65 M	(65,458,956)
$upd\_connect$	46 M	(45,869,101)
$upd\_success$	32 M	(31,618,594)
upd_skip	6 M	(5,960,195)
ssh_login	1 B	(1,114,022,780)
ssh_logout	1 B	(1,047,892,209)

Table 4. Monitor performance

policy	runtime (overall)	runtime (per slice)			memory (per slice)	
	[hh:mm]	median [sec]	max [hh:mm]	cumulative [days]	median [MB]	max [MB]
$(P1)$	2:04	169	0:46	21.4	6.1	6.1
$(P2)$	2:10	170	0:51	21.4	6.1	10.3
$(P3)$	11:56	170	10:40	22.7	7.1	510.2
$(P4)$	2:32	169	1:06	21.3	9.2	13.1
$(P5)$	2:28	168	1:01	21.3	6.1	6.1
$(P6)$	2:13	168	0:48	21.1	6.1	7.1

time. In $(P5)$, since a computer can be turned off after downloading the latest configuration but before modifying its local configuration, we only require a successful update if the computer is still running 5 to 20 minutes after downloading the new configuration.

Logs. The computers log entries describing their local system actions and upload their logs to a log cluster. Approximately 1 TB of log data is uploaded each day. We restricted ourselves to log data that spans approximately two years. We then processed the uploaded data to obtain a temporal structure consisting of the events relevant for the policies considered. Since events occur concurrently, we collapsed the temporal structure [8], that is, the structures at time points with equal timestamps are merged into a single structure. By doing this, we make the assumption that equally timestamped events happen simultaneously. The size of the collapsed temporal structure is approximately 600 MB per day on average and 0.4 TB for the two years, in a protocol buffers [16] format. It contains approximately 77.2 million time points and 26 billion events, i.e., tuples in the relations interpreting the predicate symbols. Table 3 presents a breakdown of the numbers of the events in the temporal structure by predicate symbols.

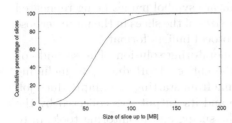

Fig. 1. Distribution of the size of the log slices

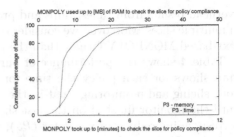

Fig. 2. Distribution of memory (upper x-axis) and time (lower x-axis) used to monitor individual slices for (*P3*)

Slicing and Monitoring. For each policy, we used 1,000 computers for slicing and monitoring. Here we used Google's MapReduce framework [12] and the MONPOLY tool [7]. We split the collapsed temporal structure into 10,000 slices so that each computer processed 10 slices on average. The decision to use 10 times more slices than computers makes the individual map and reduce computations small. This has the advantage that if the monitoring of a slice fails and must be restarted, then less computation is wasted. Furthermore, for slicing and monitoring, we used the formulas in Table 1 without universally quantifying over the variables c, t, and s. The resulting formulas fall into the fragment that the MONPOLY tool handles and our slicing techniques from Section 3 are applicable, i.e., they are sound and complete.

We employed data slicing with respect to the variable c, which occurs in all the atomic subformulas with a predicate symbol, and filtering of empty time points. We did not slice by time. Our implementation generates the primary keys of the key-value pairs emitted by a mapper from c's interpretation in an event. Concretely, we apply the MurmurHash [25] function to this value and take the remainder after dividing it by 10,000 (the number of slices). The values of the key-value pairs emitted by the implemented mappers are log entries consisting of a single event and a timestamp. Slices are generated with respect to the conjunction of all policies. Figure 1 depicts the distribution of the size of the slices. Note that generating the slices for each policy individually would result in smaller slices and thus simplify the monitoring process. Note too that although we use the same set of slices for all policies, each policy was checked separately and the slices were generated during this check.

Evaluation. Figure 1 shows the distribution of the sizes of the slices in the format used as input for MONPOLY. On the y-axis is the percentage of slices whose size is less than or equal to the value on the x-axis. The median size of a slice is 61 MB and 99% of the slices have a size of at most 135 MB. There are three slices with sizes over 1 GB and the largest slice is 1.8 GB. Recall that we used the same slicing method for all policies. The sum of the sizes of all slices (0.6 TB) is larger than the size of the collapsed temporal structure (0.4 TB). Since we slice by the computer (variable c), the slices do not overlap. However, some overhead results from timestamps and predicate symbol names being replicated in multiple slices. Moreover, we consider the sizes of the slices in the more verbose text-based MONPOLY format than the protocol buffers format.

Table 4 shows the performance of our monitoring solution. The second column shows for each policy the time for the entire MapReduce job, including both slicing and monitoring, that is, the time from starting the MapReduce job until the monitor finished on the last slice and its output was collected by the corresponding reducer. Except for $(P3)$, the slicing and monitoring took up to $2\frac{1}{2}$ hours. Slicing and monitoring $(P3)$ took almost 12 hours. Table 4 also gives details about the monitoring of the individual slices. The overhead of the MapReduce framework and time necessary for slicing is small; most resources are spent on monitoring the slices. The cumulative running times roughly amount to the time necessary to monitor all slices sequentially on a single computer.

We first discuss the time taken to monitor the individual slices and then the memory used. For $(P3)$, Figure 2 shows on the y-axis the percentage of slices for which the monitoring time is within the limit on the lower x-axis. We do not give the curves for the other policies as they are similar to $(P3)$. The similarities indicate that for most slices the monitoring time does not vary much across the considered policies. 99% of the slices are monitored within 8.2 minutes each and do not need more than 35 MB of memory.

$(P3)$ required substantially more time to monitor than the other formulas due to the nesting of temporal operators. This additional overhead is particularly pronounced on large slices and results in waiting for a few large slices that take substantially longer to monitor than the rest. There are several options to deal with such slices. We can stop the monitor after a timeout and ignore the slices and any policy violations involving them. Note that the monitoring of the other slices and the validity of violations found on them would be unaffected. Alternatively, we can split large slices into smaller ones, either prior to monitoring or after a timeout when monitoring a large slice. For $(P3)$, we can slice further by the variable c and also by s. We can also slice by time.

Due to the sensitive nature of the logged data, we do not report here on the policy violations. However, we remark that monitoring a large population of computers and aggregating the violations found can be used to identify systematic policy violations and policy violations due to system misconfiguration. An example of the former is not letting a computer update after the weekend before using it to access sensitive resources on a Monday; cf. $(P2)$. An example of the latter is that the monitoring helped determine when the update process was not operating as expected for certain types of computers during a specific time period. This information can be useful for identifying seemingly unrelated changes in the configuration of other components in the IT infrastructure.

Given the amount of logged data and the modest computational power (1,000 computers in a MapReduce cluster), the monitoring times are in general low, and reasonable even for $(P3)$. The presented monitoring solution allows us to cope with even larger logs and to speed-up the monitoring process by deploying additional slicing mechanisms provided by our general framework and by using additional computers in a MapReduce cluster.

5   Related Work

This work builds upon and extends the work by Basin et al. [7–9], where a single monitor is used to check system compliance with respect to policies expressed in metric first-order temporal logic. By parallelizing and distributing the monitoring process, we overcome a central limitation of this prior work and enable it to scale to logging scenarios that are substantially larger than those previously considered [8], namely, approximately 100 times larger in terms of the number of events and 50 times larger in the data volume.

For different logic-based specification languages, various monitoring algorithms exist, e.g., [5, 6, 10, 11, 13, 15, 17–19, 23, 24]. These algorithms have been developed with different applications in mind, such as intrusion detection [23], program verification [5], and checking temporal integrity constraints for databases [11]. In principle, these algorithms can also be used to check compliance of IT systems, where a single centralized monitor observes the system online or checks the system logs offline. However, none of these algorithms, including the one of Basin et al. [9], would scale to IT system of realistic size due to the lack of parallelization.

Similar to our work, Barre et al. [4] monitor parts of a log in parallel and independently of other log parts with a MapReduce framework. While we split the log into multiple slices and evaluate the entire formula on these slices in parallel, they evaluate the given formula in multiple iterations of MapReduce. All subformulas of the same depth are evaluated in the same MapReduce job and the results are used to evaluate subformulas of a lower depth during another MapReduce job. The evaluation of a subformula is performed in both the map and the reduce phase. While the evaluation in the map phase is parallelized for different time points of the log, the results of the map phase for a subformula for the whole log are collected and processed by a single reducer. The reducer therefore becomes a bottleneck and their approach's scalability remains unclear. Furthermore, in their experiments they used a log with fewer than five million entries and performed monitoring on a single computer with respect to formulas of a propositional temporal logic, which is limited in its ability to express realistic policies.

Roşu and Chen [22] present a generic monitoring algorithm for parametric specifications. They group logged events into slices by their parameter instances, one slice for each parameter value in case of a single parameter and one slice for each combination of values when the specification has multiple parameters. The slices are then processed by a monitoring algorithm unaware of parameters. In contrast to our work, they do not provide a solution for parallelizing the monitoring process; they provide an algorithmic solution to generate the slices online. We note that the extension of the temporal logic LTL with parameterized propositions, as considered by Roşu and Chen, is less expressive than a first-order extension like MFOTL, used in our work. Roşu and Chen also report on experiments with logs containing up to 155 million entries, all monitored on a single computer. This is orders of magnitude smaller than the log in our case study.

6 Conclusion

We presented a scalable solution for checking compliance of IT systems, where behavior is monitored offline and checked against policies. To achieve scalability, we parallelize monitoring, supported by a framework for slicing logs and an algorithmic realization within the MapReduce framework.

MapReduce is particularly well suited for implementing parallel monitoring. It allows us to efficiently reorganize huge logs into slices. It also allocates and distributes the computations for monitoring the slices, accounting for the available computational resources, the location of the logged data, failures, etc. Finally, additional computers can easily be added to speedup the monitoring process when splitting the log into more slices, thereby increasing the degree of parallelization.

Our slicing framework allows logs to be sliced in multiple dimensions by composing different slicing methods. As future work, we will evaluate different possibilities of obtaining a larger number of smaller slices that are equally expensive to monitor. We also plan to adapt our approach to check system compliance *online*. In this regard, there are extensions and alternatives to the MapReduce framework for online data processing, such as S4 [21] and STORM [20], which can potentially be used to obtain a scalable online monitoring solution.

References

1. Abiteboul, S., Hull, R., Vianu, V.: Foundations of Databases: The Logical Level. Addison Wesley (1994)
2. Alur, R., Henzinger, T.A.: Logics and models of real time: A survey. In: Huizing, C., de Bakker, J.W., Rozenberg, G., de Roever, W.-P. (eds.) REX 1991. LNCS, vol. 600, pp. 74–106. Springer, Heidelberg (1992)
3. Baier, C., Katoen, J.-P.: Principles of Model Checking. The MIT Press (2008)
4. Barre, B., Klein, M., Soucy-Boivin, M., Ollivier, P.-A., Hallé, S.: MapReduce for parallel trace validation of LTL properties. In: Qadeer, S., Tasiran, S. (eds.) RV 2012. LNCS, vol. 7687, pp. 184–198. Springer, Heidelberg (2013)
5. Barringer, H., Goldberg, A., Havelund, K., Sen, K.: Rule-based runtime verification. In: Steffen, B., Levi, G. (eds.) VMCAI 2004. LNCS, vol. 2937, pp. 44–57. Springer, Heidelberg (2004)
6. Barringer, H., Groce, A., Havelund, K., Smith, M.: Formal analysis of log files. J. Aero. Comput. Inform. Comm. 7, 365–390 (2010)
7. Basin, D., Harvan, M., Klaedtke, F., Zălinescu, E.: MONPOLY: Monitoring usage-control policies. In: Khurshid, S., Sen, K. (eds.) RV 2011. LNCS, vol. 7186, pp. 360–364. Springer, Heidelberg (2012)
8. Basin, D., Harvan, M., Klaedtke, F., Zălinescu, E.: Monitoring data usage in distributed systems. IEEE Trans. Software Eng. 39(10), 1403–1426 (2013)

9. Basin, D., Klaedtke, F., Müller, S., Pfitzmann, B.: Runtime monitoring of metric first-order temporal properties. In: Proceedings of the 28th IARCS Annual Conference on Foundations of Software Technology and Theoretical Computer Science (FSTTCS). Leibniz International Proceedings in Informatics (LIPIcs), vol. 2, pp. 49–60. Schloss Dagstuhl - Leibniz Center for Informatics (2008)
10. Bauer, A., Goré, R., Tiu, A.: A first-order policy language for history-based transaction monitoring. In: Leucker, M., Morgan, C. (eds.) ICTAC 2009. LNCS, vol. 5684, pp. 96–111. Springer, Heidelberg (2009)
11. Chomicki, J.: Efficient checking of temporal integrity constraints using bounded history encoding. ACM Trans. Database Syst. 20(2), 149–186 (1995)
12. Dean, J., Ghemawat, S.: MapReduce: Simplified data processing on large clusters. In: Proceedings of the 6th Symposium on Operating System Design and Implementation (OSDI), pp. 137–150. USENIX Association (2004)
13. Dinesh, N., Joshi, A., Lee, I., Sokolsky, O.: Checking traces for regulatory conformance. In: Leucker, M. (ed.) RV 2008. LNCS, vol. 5289, pp. 86–103. Springer, Heidelberg (2008)
14. Enderton, H.: A Mathematical Introduction to Logic, 2nd edn. Academic Press (2001)
15. Garg, D., Jia, L., Datta, A.: Policy auditing over incomplete logs: theory, implementation and applications. In: Proceedings of the 18th ACM Conference on Computer and Communications Security (CCS), pp. 151–162. ACM Press (2011)
16. Google. Protocol Buffers: Googles Data Interchange Format (2013), http://code.google.com/p/protobuf/
17. Groce, A., Havelund, K., Smith, M.: From scripts to specification: The evaluation of a flight testing effort. In: Proceedings of the 32nd ACM/IEEE International Conference on Software Engineering (ICSE), vol. 2, pp. 129–138. ACM Press (2010)
18. Hallé, S., Villemaire, R.: Runtime enforcement of web service message contracts with data. IEEE Trans. Serv. Comput. 5(2), 192–206 (2012)
19. Maggi, F.M., Montali, M., Westergaard, M., van der Aalst, W.M.P.: Monitoring business constraints with linear temporal logic: An approach based on colored automata. In: Rinderle-Ma, S., Toumani, F., Wolf, K. (eds.) BPM 2011. LNCS, vol. 6896, pp. 132–147. Springer, Heidelberg (2011)
20. Marz, N.: STORM: Distributed and fault-tolerant realtime computation, http://storm-project.net
21. Neumeyer, L., Robbins, B., Nair, A., Kesari, A.: S4: Distributed stream computing. In: Proceedings of the 11th International Conference on Data Mining Workshops (ICDMW), pp. 170–177. IEEE Computer Society (2010)
22. Roşu, G., Chen, F.: Semantics and algorithms for parametric monitoring. Log. Method. Comput. Sci. 8(1), 1–47 (2012)
23. Roger, M., Goubault-Larrecq, J.: Log auditing through model-checking. In: Proceedings of the 14th IEEE Computer Security Foundations Workshop (CSFW), pp. 220–234. IEEE Computer Society (2001)
24. Sistla, A.P., Wolfson, O.: Temporal triggers in active databases. IEEE Trans. Knowl. Data Eng. 7(3), 471–486 (1995)
25. Wikipedia. MurmurHash — Wikipedia, the free encyclopedia (2013), https://en.wikipedia.org/wiki/MurmurHash

Monitoring Systems with Extended Live Sequence Charts

Ming Chai[1] and Bernd-Holger Schlingloff[2]

[1,2] Humboldt Universität zu Berlin
[2] Fraunhofer FOKUS
{ming.chai,hs}@informatik.hu-berlin.de

Abstract. A problem with most runtime verification techniques is that the monitoring specification formalisms are often complex. In this paper, we propose an extension of live sequence charts (LSCs) which avoids this problem. We extend the standard LSCs as proposed by Damm and Harel by introducing the notion of "sufficient prechart", and by adding concatenation and iteration of charts. With these extended LSCs, necessary and sufficient conditions of certain statements can be intuitively specified. Moreover, similar as for message sequence charts, sequencing and iteration allow to express multiple scenarios. We give a translation of extended LSCs into linear temporal logic formulae, and develop online monitoring algorithms for traces with respect to extended LSCs. We use our algorithm to test a concrete example from the European Train Control System (ETCS) standard, and evaluate it on several benchmarks. The results show the feasibility of our approach.

1 Introduction

Runtime verification [17,20] is a lightweight formal verification technique, where a system's behaviour is checked while the system is running. This technique involves the use of a *monitor*, which is a device or a piece of software that observes a behaviour of the system and checks the observations against a monitoring specification. Such a monitoring specification consists of a set of correctness properties formulated in some suitable formal language.

Although runtime verification techniques continue to grow more powerful, their practical application in industry is hindered by the fact that most monitoring specification languages are quite complex. A runtime verification method typically uses some form of temporal logic linear temporal logic (LTL) [22], metric temporal logic [24], time propositional temporal logic (TPTL) [7] and first-order temporal logic [2] to specify correctness properties. Although these specification languages are expressive and technically sound for monitoring, most software engineers are not familiar with them and need extensive training to use them efficiently. Therefore, many runtime verification systems support also other specification languages that are more understood by software engineers, such as regular expressions [8] and context-free grammars [21]. Unfortunately, it is difficult to specify complex properties with multiple instances in these languages, and they are not (yet) used in practice by system designers.

B. Bonakdarpour and S.A. Smolka (Eds.): RV 2014, LNCS 8734, pp. 48–63, 2014.

Graphical languages such as message sequence charts (MSCs) and UML sequence diagrams (UML-SDs) are widely used in industry for system specifications. However, as semi-formal languages, the semantics of MSCs and UML-SDs is not defined formally. One of the central questions in this context is: "does an MSC (or a UML-SD) describe all possible executions, or does it describe a set of sample executions of the system?" [3]. Since there does not seem to be an agreement on this question, these languages are not suitable for specifying monitoring correctness properties.

In this paper, we investigate the use of live sequence charts (LSCs) as proposed by Damm and Harel [12] for monitoring specifications. The LSC language is an extension of MSC. Using the notions of universal and existential chart, it can express that a behaviour of a system is necessary or possible. A universal chart specifies a necessary (i.e., required) behaviour of the system, whereas an existential chart specifies a possible (i.e., allowed) behaviour. The LSC language also introduces the notion of "temperature" of an element (i.e., hot and cold elements) for distinguishing between mandatory (hot) elements and provisional (cold) elements.

For monitoring, we focus on universal LSCs. A universal chart typically consists of two components: a *prechart* and a *main chart*. The intended meaning is that if the prechart is executed (i.e., the underlying system exhibits an execution which is specified by the prechart), then the main chart must be executed afterwards. The standard definition thus interprets the prechart as a necessary condition for the main chart.

However, for monitoring it is also important to be able to express sufficient conditions of statements. For example, consider the statement IF a THEN b in some programming language. It indicates that b is executed if a is true; otherwise, b is not executed. This is not the same as the universal chart $(prechart(a), mainchart(b))$, because here the main chart b can still be executed if a is not satisfied.

As a possible specification for this statement, it has been suggested in UML 2.0 to use the *negation* operator to denote the case of not-executing b. As we show in this paper, sufficiency conditions of statements cannot be expressed by a finite set of negation-free universal LSCs. Since the semantics of negative LSCs is hard to define, we suggest an alternative way to specify this case. We extend LSCs to eLSCs by introducing the notion of a "sufficient" prechart. In contrast, we call the prechart of a standard universal chart a "necessary" prechart. With this extension, one can easily and intuitively express situations as above.

Alur and Yannakakis have introduced MSC-graphs to express multiple scenarios [1]. For the same reason, we introduce concatenation and iteration into the eLSC language. Since a universal chart consists of a prechart and a main chart, we define four modes of concatenation. Consequently, iteration also has four modes. In this paper, we study one mode: iteration defined on precharts.

We give a translation of eLSCs without iteration, that is, universal LSCs with necessary and sufficient precharts and concatenations, into LTL formulae. Checking whether a system run satisfies such an eLSC specification then becomes the problem of checking an execution trace against some LTL formula.

The language of an eLSC with iteration is not necessarily regular. Therefore, an eLSC with iteration cannot be translated into an equivalent LTL formula. Thus, we develop an explicit algorithm for checking arbitrary eLSC properties.

In order to demonstrate the feasibility of these algorithms, we give a concrete example from the railway domain: We formulate properties of the RBC-RBC-handover process in the European Train Control System (ETCS) standard with our eLSC language. Then, we evaluate them with several benchmark traces and give some remarks on the complexity.

Related Work

The MSC language and UML sequence diagrams are visual specification languages. They are widely used in industry. Alur et. al. study the model checking problems of MSCs, MSC-graphs and Hierarchical MSC-graphs [1]. They show that the complexity of model checking problems for MSCs and synchronous MSC-graphs are coNP-complete, and for asynchronous MSC-graphs are undecidable. Simmonds et. al. use UML-SD as the property specification language to monitor Web Service Conversations [23]. Ciraci et. al. propose a technique to check the correspondence between UML-SD models and implementations [9].

Damm et. al. defined the LSC language, which distinguishes between necessary and possible behaviours of a system [12]. Harel et. al. propose a play-in/play-out approach [14]. Behaviours of the system are captured by play-in; and the system is tested by play-out through executing the LSC specification directly. Bontemps et. al. prove that any LSC specification can be translated into LTL formulae [6]. Kugler et. al. [18] develop a translation of LSCs into LTL formulae, where the size of the resulting LTL formula is polynomial in the number of events appearing in the LSCs. The expressive power and complexity of LSCs are discussed in the survey [16]. Kumar et. al. extend the LSC language with Kleene star, subcharts, and hierarchical charts [19]. They translate an extended LSC based communication protocol specification into an automaton, and verify the specification with the resulting automaton. Since all existing works are based on the standard LSC language, they suffer from the same expressiveness problem as addressed in this paper.

LSCs have been used to model a variety of systems, such as railway systems [4], telecommunication systems [11], biological systems [13], and so on. The existing papers essentially build models of systems with the LSC language, and focus on model checking problems. To our knowledge, LSC based runtime verification approaches have not been studied yet.

2   Extended Universal Live Sequence Charts

2.1   Universal Live Sequence Charts

A basic chart of an LSC is visually similar to an MSC. It specifies the exchange of messages among a set of instances. Each instance is represented by a lifeline.

When an LSC is executed, for each message in the chart two events occur: the event of sending the message and the event of receiving it. The partial order of events induced by a basic chart is as follows.

- an event at a higher position in a lifeline precedes an event at a lower position in the same lifeline; and
- for each message m, the send-event of m precedes the receive-event of m.

Formally, basic charts can be defined as follows.

Let Σ be a finite alphabet of messages m, i.e., $m \in \Sigma$. An *event* e is a pair $e \triangleq (m, \beta)$ with $\beta \in \{s, r\}$, where (m, s) denotes the event of sending m, and (m, r) denotes the event of receiving m. We denote the set $(\Sigma \times \{s, r\})$ with $\mathcal{B}\Sigma$. A trace τ over $\mathcal{B}\Sigma$ is an element of $\mathcal{B}\Sigma^*$. The length of τ is $|\tau|$.

A lifeline l is a sequence of events $l \triangleq (e_1, e_2, ..., e_n)$. A basic chart $\mathfrak{c}$ is a set of lifelines $\mathfrak{c} \triangleq \{l_1, l_2, ..., l_n\}$, where each event (m, β) occurs at most once. Lifelines in a basic chart are usually drawn as vertical dashed lines, and messages as solid arrows between lifelines.

Now we present the trace semantics for basic charts. For a basic chart $\mathfrak{c}$, let $\mathcal{E}(\mathfrak{c})$ be the set of events appearing in $\mathfrak{c}$. The chart $\mathfrak{c}$ induces a partial order relation $\prec$ on $\mathcal{E}(\mathfrak{c})$ as follows:

1. for any $l \triangleq (e_1, e_2, ..., e_m) \in \mathfrak{c}$ and $1 \leq j < m$, it holds that $e_j \prec e_{j+1}$; and
2. for any $m \in \Sigma$, if (m, s) and $(m, r) \in \mathcal{E}(\mathfrak{c})$, then $(m, s) \prec (m, r)$.
3. $\prec$ is the smallest relation satisfying 1. and 2.

Let $\mathscr{P}(\mathfrak{c}) \triangleq \{(e, e') \mid e \prec e' \text{ with } e, e' \in \mathcal{E}(\mathfrak{c})\}$. A set of traces is defined by $\mathfrak{c}$ as follows:

$$Traces(\mathfrak{c}) \triangleq \{(e_{x1}, e_{x2}, ..., e_{xn}) \mid \{e_{x1}, e_{x2}, ..., e_{xn}\} = \mathcal{E}(\mathfrak{c}); n = |\mathcal{E}(\mathfrak{c})|; \text{ and for}$$
$$\text{all } e_{xi}, e_{xj} \in \mathcal{E}(\mathfrak{c}), \text{ if } e_{xi} \prec e_{xj}, \text{ then } xi < xj\}.$$

We call each $\sigma_{\mathfrak{c}} \in (\mathcal{B}\Sigma \backslash \mathcal{E}(\mathfrak{c}))$ a *stutter event* of $\mathfrak{c}$. For each basic chart $\mathfrak{c}$, the language $\mathcal{L}(\mathfrak{c})$ is defined by $\mathcal{L}(\mathfrak{c}) \triangleq \{(\sigma_{\mathfrak{c}}^*, e_1, \sigma_{\mathfrak{c}}^*, e_2, ..., \sigma_{\mathfrak{c}}^*, e_n, \sigma_{\mathfrak{c}}^*)\}$, where $(e_1, e_2, ..., e_n) \in Traces(\mathfrak{c})$ and each $\sigma_{\mathfrak{c}}^*$ is a finite (or empty) sequence of stutter events. A trace τ is *admitted* by a basic chart $\mathfrak{c}$ (denoted by $\tau \Vdash \mathfrak{c}$) if $\tau \in \mathcal{L}(\mathfrak{c})$.

A *universal chart* consists of two basic charts: a *prechart* (drawn with a surrounding hashed hexagon) and a *main chart* (drawn within a solid rectangle). It is formalized as a pair $\mathfrak{u} \triangleq (\mathfrak{p}, \mathfrak{m})$, where $\mathfrak{p}$ is the prechart and $\mathfrak{m}$ is the main chart. Intuitively, a universal chart specifies all traces τ such that, if τ contains a segment which is admitted by the prechart, then it must also contain a continuation segment (directly following the first segment) which is admitted by the main chart.

Given a universal chart $\mathfrak{u} \triangleq (\mathfrak{p}, \mathfrak{m})$, the stutter events of $\mathfrak{u}$ are $\sigma_{\mathfrak{u}} \in (\mathcal{B}\Sigma \backslash (\mathcal{E}(\mathfrak{p}) \cup \mathcal{E}(\mathfrak{m}))$. The languages $\mathcal{L}(\mathfrak{p})$ of the prechart and $\mathcal{L}(\mathfrak{m})$ of the main chart are defined with these stutter events as above.

For languages $\mathcal{L}$ and $\mathcal{L}'$, let $(\mathcal{L} \circ \mathcal{L}')$ be the concatenation of $\mathcal{L}$ and $\mathcal{L}'$ (i.e., $(\mathcal{L} \circ \mathcal{L}') \triangleq \{(\tau\tau') \mid \tau \in \mathcal{L} \text{ and } \tau' \in \mathcal{L}'\}$); and $\overline{\mathcal{L}}$ be the complement of $\mathcal{L}$ (i.e., for any $\tau \in \mathcal{B}\Sigma^*$, it holds that $\tau \in \overline{\mathcal{L}}$ iff $\tau \notin \mathcal{L}$). The semantics of universal charts is defined as follows (see, e.g., [5]).

Definition 1. *Given a finite alphabet Σ, the language of a universal chart $\mathsf{u} \triangleq (\mathfrak{p}, \mathfrak{m})$ is*

$$\mathcal{L}(\mathsf{u}) \triangleq \overline{\mathcal{B}\Sigma^* \circ \mathcal{L}(\mathfrak{p}) \circ \overline{\mathcal{L}(\mathfrak{m})} \circ \mathcal{B}\Sigma^*}.$$

This formalizes the intuitive interpretation given above. An LSC specification $\mathfrak{U}$ is a finite set of universal charts. The language of $\mathfrak{U}$ is $\mathcal{L}(\mathfrak{U}) \triangleq \bigcap_{\mathsf{u} \in \mathfrak{U}} \mathcal{L}(\mathsf{u})$.

2.2 Expressiveness of LSC Specifications

The standard definition of a universal chart interprets the prechart as a necessary condition of the main chart, i.e., a system is allowed to adhere to any execution, as long as it does not execute the prechart. This is not sufficient for specifying some correctness properties. For instance, for two basic charts $\mathfrak{c}$ and $\mathfrak{c}'$ we can define the statement

$$\mathsf{CS} = (\ (\mathfrak{c} \ \textit{is executed}) \ \text{IF AND ONLY IF LATER} \ (\mathfrak{c}' \ \textit{is executed})),$$

to have the semantics

$$\mathcal{L}(\mathsf{CS}) \triangleq \left(\overline{\mathcal{B}\Sigma^* \circ \mathcal{L}(\mathfrak{c}) \circ \overline{\mathcal{L}(\mathfrak{c}')} \circ \mathcal{B}\Sigma^*}\right) \cap \left(\overline{\mathcal{B}\Sigma^* \circ \overline{\mathcal{L}(\mathfrak{c})} \circ \mathcal{L}(\mathfrak{c}') \circ \mathcal{B}\Sigma^*}\right).$$

However, this can not be expressed with LSC specifications:

Lemma 1. *The language* $\left(\overline{\mathcal{B}\Sigma^* \circ \overline{\mathcal{L}(\mathfrak{c})} \circ \mathcal{L}(\mathfrak{c}') \circ \mathcal{B}\Sigma^*}\right)$ *cannot be defined by an LSC specification.*

Proof. See appendix.

2.3 Extended LSCs

One way to overcome the above expressiveness limitation is to introduce a negation operator into the LSC language. Unfortunately, the semantics of such a negation operator can be tricky, see [15]. As an alternative, we extend universal charts by introducing the notion of a *"sufficient prechart"* (drawn with a surrounding solid hexagon). This is a prechart which is interpreted as a sufficient condition for a main chart. In contrast, we label the original prechart of a universal chart as a *"necessary prechart"*. Formally, the syntax of extended LSCs is as follows.

Definition 2. *An eLSC is a tuple $\mathsf{u} \triangleq (\mathfrak{p}, \mathfrak{m}, \mathrm{Cond})$, where $\mathfrak{p}$ and $\mathfrak{m}$ are a prechart and a main chart, and $\mathrm{Cond} \in \{\mathit{Nec}, \mathit{Suff}\}$ denotes if $\mathfrak{p}$ is a necessary or sufficient prechart.*

For a chart $\mathsf{u} \triangleq (\mathfrak{p}, \mathfrak{m}, \mathit{Nec})$, the language is as defined in Definition 1. The language defined by a chart $\mathsf{u} \triangleq (\mathfrak{p}, \mathfrak{m}, \mathit{Suff})$ is

$$\mathcal{L}(\mathfrak{u}) \triangleq \left(\overline{\mathcal{B}\Sigma^* \circ \mathcal{L}(\mathfrak{p})} \circ \mathcal{L}(\mathfrak{m}) \circ \mathcal{B}\Sigma^*\right).$$

The above condition statement CS can then be specified by an LSC specification $\{(\mathfrak{c}, \mathfrak{c}', Nec), (\mathfrak{c}, \mathfrak{c}', Suff)\}$. As an abbreviation, we introduce an "iff" prechart (notated with a double dashed lines). An eLSC with an "iff" prechart is defined as $\mathfrak{u}^{iff} \triangleq \{(\mathfrak{p}, \mathfrak{m}, Nec), (\mathfrak{p}, \mathfrak{m}, Suff)\}$.

2.4   Concatenations of Universal LSCs

Concatenation of two eLSCs essentially introduces partial orders of executions of the charts. This feature can be inherited by eLSC specifications.

First, we define the concatenation of basic charts $\mathfrak{c}$ and $\mathfrak{c}'$, denoted with $(\mathfrak{c} \rightarrow \mathfrak{c}')$. Intuitively, a trace τ is in the language of $(\mathfrak{c} \rightarrow \mathfrak{c}')$ iff it contains two segments v and v' such that v precedes v' in τ, and v (resp. v') is admitted by $\mathfrak{c}$ (resp. $\mathfrak{c}'$). Formally, the language of $(\mathfrak{c} \rightarrow \mathfrak{c}')$ is given by the following clause.

$$\mathcal{L}(\mathfrak{c} \rightarrow \mathfrak{c}') \triangleq \left(\mathcal{L}(\mathfrak{c}) \cap \mathcal{L}(\mathfrak{c}') \cap \overline{\mathcal{L}(\mathfrak{c}) \circ \mathcal{L}(\mathfrak{c}')}\right).$$

Since a universal chart $\mathfrak{u}$ consists of two basic charts $\mathfrak{p}$ and $\mathfrak{m}$, there are four possibilities to define the concatenation of universal charts $\mathfrak{u}$ and $\mathfrak{u}'$: $\mathfrak{p} \rightarrow \mathfrak{p}'$, $\mathfrak{p} \rightarrow \mathfrak{m}'$, $\mathfrak{m} \rightarrow \mathfrak{p}'$ and $\mathfrak{m} \rightarrow \mathfrak{m}'$.

For monitoring, we consider only two modes of concatenation in this paper: *prechart concatenation* and *main chart concatenation*. The concatenation of two universal charts $\mathfrak{u}$ and $\mathfrak{u}'$ is defined to be a tuple $\delta \triangleq (\mathfrak{u}, \mathfrak{u}', Mode)$, where $Mode \in \{preC, mainC\}$. Formally, the semantics of the two concatenation modes is given as follows.

Definition 3. *Given two eLSCs $\mathfrak{u}$ and $\mathfrak{u}'$, The language of the concatenation of $\mathfrak{u}$ and $\mathfrak{u}'$ is*

$$\mathcal{L}(\delta) \triangleq \left(\mathcal{L}(\mathfrak{u}) \cap \mathcal{L}(\mathfrak{u}') \cap \overline{\mathcal{B}\Sigma^* \circ \mathcal{L}(\mathfrak{c})} \circ \mathcal{L}(\mathfrak{c}') \circ \mathcal{B}\Sigma^*\right),$$

where $\mathfrak{c} = \mathfrak{p}$ and $\mathfrak{c}' = \mathfrak{p}'$, if $Mode = preC$; and $\mathfrak{c} = \mathfrak{m}$ and $\mathfrak{c}' = \mathfrak{m}'$, if $Mode = mainC$.

It can be shown that the language of a concatenation $(\mathfrak{u}, \mathfrak{u}', preC)$ (resp. $(\mathfrak{u}, \mathfrak{u}', mainC)$) is the same as the language of the eLSC specification $\{\mathfrak{u}, \mathfrak{u}', (\mathfrak{p}, \mathfrak{p}', Suff)\}$ (resp. $\{\mathfrak{u}, \mathfrak{u}', (\mathfrak{m}, \mathfrak{m}', Suff)\}$). Figure 1 illustrates the two concatenation modes of eLSCs $\mathfrak{u}1$ and $\mathfrak{u}2$, where Fig. 1(a) presents a main chart concatenation and Fig. 1(b) presents a prechart concatenation. Fig. 1(c) and Fig. 1(d) present the partial orders of events of these concatenations, respectively.

To specify a repeating execution (e.g., repeating responses to requests), an iteration operator can be introduced. Such iteration operator can be directly defined from the above concatenations; $\mathfrak{u}^+ \triangleq \mathfrak{u} \cup (\mathfrak{u} \rightarrow \mathfrak{u}) \cup (\mathfrak{u} \rightarrow \mathfrak{u} \rightarrow \mathfrak{u}) \cup \dots$ Since concatenations have different modes, iteration has different modes as well.

In this paper, we consider only *iteration of necessary precharts*. Intuitively, an eLSC $\mathfrak{u}^+$ specifies that if the prechart is executed n times, then the main chart must be executed at least n times, where the executions of the main chart can be interleaved. For instance, given the eLSC u_1 in Fig. 1, a trace (... s1, r1, s2, s1, r2, r1, s2, r2,...) is admitted by u_1^+; whereas traces (... s1, s1, r1, s2, r2, r1, s2, r2,...) and (... s1, r1, s2, r2, s1, r1) are not admitted by u_1^+.

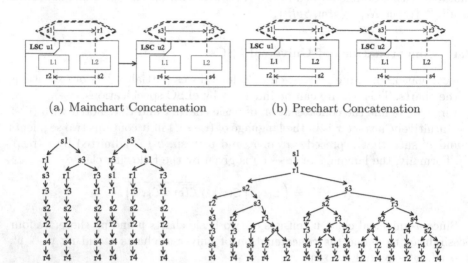

(a) Mainchart Concatenation   (b) Prechart Concatenation

(c) Partial orders induced by (d) Partial orders induced by the prechart con-
the mainchart concatenation.   catenaiton.

Fig. 1. Example: a prechart concatenation and a mainchart concatenation

3   A Translation of eLSCs into LTL Formulae

3.1   Preliminaries

We now show how to translate extended LSCs into linear temporal logic formulae for online monitoring.

Definition 4. *Given the finite alphabet Σ of messages, the formulae φ of LTL are inductively formed according to the following grammar, where, $m \in \Sigma$ and $\beta \in \{s, r\}$:*

$$\varphi ::= \perp \mid (m, \beta) \mid (\varphi_1 \Rightarrow \varphi_2) \mid (\varphi_1 \ \mathbf{U} \ \varphi_2) \mid \mathbf{X} \ \varphi.$$

In addition, we use the following shorthand: $\neg\varphi$ stands for $(\varphi \Rightarrow \perp)$, $\top$ stands for $\neg\perp$, $\mathbf{F} \ \varphi$ stands for $(\top \ \mathbf{U} \ \varphi)$, $\mathbf{G} \ \varphi$ stands for $\neg\mathbf{F} \ \neg\varphi$ and $\varphi_1 \ \mathbf{W} \ \varphi_2$ stands for $\neg (\neg\varphi_2 \ \mathbf{U} \ \neg (\varphi_1 \vee \varphi_2))$. Given an event $e \triangleq (m, \beta)$, we define $Mess(e) \triangleq m$ and $Beh(e) \triangleq \beta$. We define LTL on finite traces as follows.

Definition 5. *Let $\tau \triangleq (e_1, e_2, ..., e_n) \in \mathcal{B}\Sigma^*$ with $1 \leq i \leq n$ being a position of τ. The semantics for LTL is defined inductively as follows:*

$(\tau, i) \not\models \bot$;

$(\tau, i) \models (m, \beta)$ *iff* $m = Mess(e_i)$ *and* $\beta = Beh(e_i)$;

$(\tau, i) \models (\varphi_1 \Rightarrow \varphi_2)$ *iff* $(\tau, i) \models \varphi_1$ *implies* $(\tau, i) \models \varphi_2$;

$(\tau, i) \models (\varphi_1 \; \mathbf{U} \; \varphi_2)$ *iff there exists* $i \leq j \leq |\tau|$ *with* $(\tau, j) \models \varphi_2$,

and for all $i \leq j' < j$ *it holds that* $(\tau, j') \models \varphi_1$;

$(\tau, i) \models \mathbf{X} \; \varphi$ *iff* $i = |\tau|$ *or* $(\tau, i+1) \models \varphi$.

As usual, $\tau \models \varphi$ iff $(\tau, 1) \models \varphi$. Note that the logic is defined on events, and will be used for monitoring sequences of events.

3.2 Translation of Universal Charts

In this section, we show how to translate a universal chart into an LTL formula to check whether a trace is admitted. We follow the approach of Kugler et al. [18]. From a basic chart $\mathfrak{c}$, we define the LTL formula $\xi_\mathfrak{c} \triangleq \psi_\mathfrak{c} \wedge \gamma_\mathfrak{c} \wedge \mathfrak{y}_\mathfrak{c}$, where

$$\psi_\mathfrak{c} \triangleq \bigwedge_{(e, e') \in \mathscr{P}(\mathfrak{c})} (\neg e' \; \mathbf{W} \; e)$$

$$\gamma_\mathfrak{c} \triangleq \bigwedge_{e \in \mathscr{E}(\mathfrak{c})} (\neg e \; \mathbf{W} \; (e \wedge \mathbf{X} \; \mathbf{G} \; \neg e))$$

$$\mathfrak{y}_\mathfrak{c} \triangleq \bigwedge_{e \in \mathscr{E}(\mathfrak{c})} \mathbf{F} \; e$$

The formula $\psi_\mathfrak{c}$ specifies that e' cannot occur before e in a trace with $e \prec e'$. It does not specify e must occur at some point. The formula $\gamma_\mathfrak{c}$ specifies that each e can only occur at most one time in a trace. The formula $\mathfrak{y}_\mathfrak{c}$ specifies that every event appearing in the chart will eventually occur in a trace.

With these formulae, we can then obtain LTL formulae from eLSCs with necessary and sufficient precharts. From an eLSC $\mathfrak{u} \triangleq (\mathfrak{p}, \mathfrak{m}, Cond)$, we define the following formulae.

$$\xi_\mathfrak{p} \triangleq \psi_\mathfrak{p} \wedge \gamma_\mathfrak{p} \wedge \mathfrak{y}_\mathfrak{p}, \quad \text{and} \quad \xi_\mathfrak{m} \triangleq \psi_\mathfrak{m} \wedge \gamma_\mathfrak{m} \wedge \mathfrak{y}_\mathfrak{m},$$

$$\chi \triangleq \bigwedge_{e' \in \mathscr{E}(\mathfrak{p})} ((\bigwedge_{e \in \mathscr{E}(\mathfrak{m})} (\neg e)) \; \mathbf{W} \; e')$$

$\varphi(\mathfrak{u}) \triangleq ((\xi_\mathfrak{p} \wedge \chi) \Rightarrow \xi_\mathfrak{m})$ if $Cond = Nec$; and

$\varphi(\mathfrak{u}) \triangleq (\neg(\xi_\mathfrak{p} \wedge \chi) \Rightarrow \neg\xi_\mathfrak{m})$ if $Cond = Suff$.

The formula χ specifies that events appearing in the main chart cannot occur until all events appearing in the prechart have occurred in a trace. In can be shown that the formula $\varphi(\mathfrak{u})$ defines the language of $\mathfrak{u}$.

Lemma 2. *A trace is admitted by a universal chart* $\mathfrak{u}$ *if and only if it satisfies* $\varphi(\mathfrak{u})$: $\tau \Vdash \mathfrak{u}$ *iff* $\tau \models \varphi(\mathfrak{u})$.

Proof. Follows from the definitions. Omitted in this version of the paper.

With this translation of LSCs into LTL formulae, a system can be monitored by standard methods, e.g., formula rewriting. The size of the formula $\varphi(\mathfrak{u})$ is polynomial in the number of events appearing in $\mathfrak{u}$. Therefore, the resulting LTL formula will not explode when dealing with large eLSC specifications.

As remarked above, a concatenation $\delta = (\mathfrak{u}, \mathfrak{u}', Mode)$ of eLSCs can be expressed by a set of single eLSCs. This can be translated into an equivalent conjunction of LTL formulae as above. Thus, concatenation does not pose any additional difficulties for monitoring.

4   An Algorithm for Checking eLSCs with Iteration

The language defined by an eLSC with iteration is incomparable with LTL. Even eLSCs cannot express the temporal "next" operator. Similar with asynchronous concatenations of MSCs, the language of an eLSC with iterated precharts is not necessary regular. Therefore, for an eLSC $\mathfrak{u}^+$, in general there is no equivalent LTL formula, and the above approach to monitoring cannot be applied. For this reason, we develop an explicit algorithm for checking traces against eLSCs with prechart iterations. In the algorithm, a trace is checked against an eLSC specification $\mathfrak{u}^+$ in two steps.

1. The trace is decomposed into a set of sub-traces and a remainder sequence according to the events appearing in $\mathfrak{p}$ and $\mathfrak{m}$. Every event is unique in each sub-trace.
2. It is checked whether all sub-traces are admitted by the corresponding basic charts $\mathfrak{p}$ and $\mathfrak{m}$, and whether the begin point and the end point of each sub-trace respect the partial order implied by $\mathfrak{u}^+$.

4.1   Decomposing Traces

A trace is decomposed by two operations $\triangleright$ and $\bar{\triangleright}$. The operation $\triangleright$ generates a sub-trace τ_s from a trace τ according to a set of events E. In the resulting τ_s, each event in E occurs at most once. The order of events in τ_s is the same as in the original trace. The operation $\bar{\triangleright}$ generates the "complement" sub-trace of τ_s. These operations are formally defined as follows.

Given a trace $\tau \triangleq (e_1, ..., e_n)$ and a formula φ, we define $\kappa(\tau, \varphi)$ to be the smallest i such that $(e_1, ...e_i) \models \varphi$ (and $\kappa(\tau, \varphi) = 0$ if there is no such i). For a set of events $E = \{x_1, ..., x_m\}$, we define a sequence of points $K(\tau, E) \triangleq (k_1, ..., k_m)$ with $1 \le k_1 \le ... \le k_m \le |\tau|$ by $\{k_1, ..., k_m\} = \{\kappa(\tau, \mathbf{F}x_1), ..., \kappa(\tau, \mathbf{F}x_m)\}$. Let $\mathscr{E}(\tau)$ be the set of events appearing in τ and let ε be the empty trace. The operations $\triangleright$ and $\bar{\triangleright}$ are defined as follows.

$\triangleright$: $\mathcal{B}\Sigma^* \times 2^{\mathcal{B}\Sigma} \mapsto \mathcal{B}\Sigma^*$ such that
   $\tau \triangleright E \triangleq (e[k_1], ..., e[k_{|E|}])$ with $(k_1, ..., k_{|E|}) = K(\tau, E)$ if $E \subseteq \mathscr{E}(\tau)$;
   $\tau \triangleright E \triangleq \varepsilon$ if $E \nsubseteq \mathscr{E}(\tau)$.
$\bar{\triangleright}$: $\mathcal{B}\Sigma^* \times 2^{\mathcal{B}\Sigma} \mapsto \mathcal{B}\Sigma^*$ such that
   $\tau \bar{\triangleright} E \triangleq (e[1], ..., e[k_1 - 1], e[k_1 + 1], ..., e[k_{|E|} - 1], e[k_{|E|} + 1], ..., e[n])$ if $\tau \triangleright E \ne \varepsilon$;
   $\tau \bar{\triangleright} E \triangleq \tau$ if $\tau \triangleright E = \varepsilon$.

Given a trace τ and a basic chart $\mathfrak{c}$, we define a tuple $\mathsf{Div}(\tau, \mathfrak{c}) \triangleq (\tau_s, Pos^I, Pos^F)$, where Pos^I is the index of the initial point of τ_s, and Pos^F is the index of the final point of τ_s. Formally, $\mathsf{Div}(\tau, \mathfrak{c})$ is defined as follows.

$- \tau_s \triangleq (\tau \triangleright \mathcal{E}(c))$, $Pos^I \triangleq \bigvee_{e \in \mathcal{E}(c)} Fe$, $Pos^F \triangleq \bigwedge_{e \in \mathcal{E}(c)} Fe$,   if $\mathcal{E}(c) \subseteq \mathcal{E}(\tau)$;

$- \tau_s \triangleq \tau$ and $Pos^I = Pos^F = 0$, otherwise.

Algorithm 1. divide a trace according to a basic chart

Try typing ¡return¿ to proceed.If that doesn't work, type X ¡return¿ to quit.
procedure TraceDiv(trace τ, basic chart c) =
while $(\tau \,\overline{\triangleright}\, \mathcal{E}(c)) \neq \tau$ **do**
$\quad$ $\tau s \leftarrow (\tau \triangleright \mathcal{E}(c))$;
$\quad$ $Pos^I \leftarrow \kappa(\tau, \bigvee_{e \in \mathcal{E}(c)} Fe)$;
$\quad$ $Pos^F \leftarrow \kappa(\tau, \bigwedge_{e \in \mathcal{E}(c)} Fe)$;
$\quad$ DivSet $\leftarrow$ DivSet.add $(\tau s, Pos^I, Pos^F)$; //add the resulting tuple into the set DivSet
$\quad$ $\tau \leftarrow (\tau \,\overline{\triangleright}\, \mathcal{E}(c))$;
end
return DivSet

Next, we define a set $\mathsf{DivSet}(\tau, c) \triangleq \{(\tau_{s1}, Pos_1^I, Pos_1^F), ..., (\tau_{sn}, Pos_n^I, Pos_n^F)\}$, where

$(\tau_{s1}, Pos_1^I, Pos_1^F) \triangleq \mathsf{Div}(\tau, c)$;
$(\tau_{si}, Pos_i^I, Pos_i^F) \triangleq \mathsf{Div}((\tau_{i-1} \,\overline{\triangleright}\, c), c)$ for $1 < i \leq n$; and
$(\tau_{s(n+1)} \triangleright \mathcal{E}(c)) = \varepsilon$.

For a universal chart, we define two such sets $\mathsf{DivSet}(\tau, \mathfrak{p})$ and $\mathsf{DivSet}(\tau, \mathfrak{m})$. The calculation of these set can be done with Algorithm 1 above.

4.2 Checking Sub-traces

With the above decomposition, we can then check whether τ is admitted by u^+. An eLSC with iteration specifies repeated execution of a chart. A trace τ is admitted by u^+ if and only if

- τ is able to be decomposed into a number of sub-traces, each of which is admitted by u; and
- the order of execution of the prechart is respected.

According to the above rules, we develop algorithms for checking whether $\tau \Vdash u^+$, where Alg. 2 (resp. Alg. 3) checks the prechart (resp. the main chart) of u. The two sub-algorithms return PRes and MRes as the checking result. The satisfaction of τ against u^+ is (PRes $\wedge$ MRes) Let $\mathcal{F}$ be a formula, we define an interpretation operation $[\![\mathcal{F}]\!]$ that maps $\mathcal{F}$ to a boolean value. For a trace τ and an LTL formula φ, we say $[\![\tau \models \varphi]\!] \triangleq true$ if τ is satisfied by φ; and $[\![\tau \models \varphi]\!] \triangleq false$ if τ is violated by φ. The algorithm for checking traces against LTL formulae is developed according to an effective rewriting algorithm proposed by Havelund [17].

Algorithm 2. Checking the prechart of u^+

Try typing ¡return¿ to proceed.If that doesn't work, type X ¡return¿ to quit.
input : A trace τ and an eLSC $u \triangleq (m, \mathfrak{p}, Cond)$
output: whether τ is admitted by u^+

PRes $\leftarrow$ true; // initialize the checking result
$p \leftarrow |\mathsf{DivSet}(\tau, \mathfrak{p})|$; // the number of executions of the prechart
for $i \leftarrow 1$ **to** p **do**
    // check whether each execution of the prechart is correct
    PRes $\leftarrow$ (PRes $\wedge \llbracket \tau s_i \models \psi_\mathfrak{p} \rrbracket$);
    // check the partial order of the prechart's executions
    PRes $\leftarrow$ (PRes $\wedge \llbracket Pos_i^F < Pos_{i+1}^I \rrbracket$);
    /* if the prechart is a necessary prechart, then there is an execution of the main
    chart after each execution of the prechart */
    if $Cond == Nec$ **then**
        PRes $\leftarrow$ (PRes $\wedge \llbracket m \geq p \rrbracket$);
        if $\exists(\tau s, Pos^I, Pos^F) \in \mathsf{DivSet}(\tau, m)$ $s.t.$ $Pos^I > Pos_i^F$ **then**
          | PRes $\leftarrow$ PRes $\wedge$ true;
        else
          | PRes $\leftarrow$ false;
        end
    end
end
return PRes

5   Case Study: The RBC/RBC Handover Process

In this section, we present a concrete example from the European Train Control System (ETCS). In the ETCS level 2, the radio block center (RBC) is responsible for providing movement authorities to allow the safe movement of trains. A route is divided into several RBC supervision areas. When a train approaches the border of an RBC supervision area, an RBC/RBC handover process takes place. The current RBC is called the handing over RBC (HOVRBC), whereas the adjacent RBC is called the accepting RBC (ACCRBC)[1].

The RBC/RBC handover process is performed via exchanging a sequence of messages between the two RBCs. These messages are called NRBC messages, including "Pre-Announcement" (preAnn), "Route Related Information Request" (RRIReq), "Route Related Information" (RRI) and "Acknowledgement" (Ackn). The NRBC messages are exchanged via an open communication system GSM-R.

The safety standard EN50159 identifies the following threats to an open transmission system: corruption, masquerading, repetition, deletion, insertion, resequencing and delay. A safety protocol is added between the application layer and the transport layer for providing safe communication between RBCs. The

---

[1] Further details of this case study are provided in
http://www2.informatik.hu-berlin.de/ hs/Publikationen/2014_RV_
Ming-Schlingloff_ETCS-Case-study(description-of-RBCRBC-handover)

safety protocol provides protection against threats related to corruption and masquerading, other threats are covered elsewhere.

We use eLSC based monitors to protect against threats related to temporal relations of messages, i.e., repetition, deletion, insertion and resequencing. In this paper, we specify the following two properties with the eLSC language.

1. For a successful RBC/RBC handover process, if the train reaches the border of two RBC areas, the NRBC messages should be correctly exchanged between the two RBCs (see Fig. 2(a)).
2. The NRBC messages can only be exchanged after the two RBCs establish a safe connection (see Fig. 2(b)).

For property 1, the message preAnn is exchanged in sequence if and only if after the HOVRBC detects the handover condition. We specify the handover condition by an "HOV cond" message. Therefore, the eLSC preHOV is with an "iff" prechart, which consists of the receiving event of the message HOV cond. If HOVRBC sends an RRIReq message to ACCRBC, ACCRBC sends an RRI message to HOVRBC. HOVRBC sends an Ackn message to ACCRBC after receiving the RRI message. In fact, the accepting RBC is allowed to send an RRI without an RRI request when there is new route information. Hence, the second eLSC in Fig. 2(a) (eLSC ExdEoA) is with a necessary prechart. Since the HOVRBC can ask for new route information iteratively, the eLSC is with an iteration.

Algorithm 3. Checking the main chart of u^+

---

input : A trace τ and an eLSC $u \triangleq (m, p, Cond)$
output: whether τ is admitted by u^+

MRes $\leftarrow$ true; // initialize the checking result
$m \leftarrow |\text{DivSet}(\tau, m)|$; // the number of executions of the main chart
for $j \leftarrow 1$ **to** m **do**
  MRes $\leftarrow$ (MRes $\wedge \llbracket \tau s_j \models \psi_m \rrbracket$; // check each execution of the main chart
  /* If u is with a sufficient prechart, then there is an execution of the prechart before each execution of the main chart. */
  if $Cond == Suff$ **then**
    MRes $\leftarrow$ (MRes $\wedge \llbracket m \leq p \rrbracket$);
    if $\exists (\tau s, \text{Pos}^I, \text{Pos}^F) \in \text{DivSet}(\tau, p)$ s.t. $\text{Pos}^F < \text{Pos}_i^I$ **then**
      | MRes $\leftarrow$ MRes $\wedge$ true;
    else
      | MRes $\leftarrow$ false;
    end
  end
end
return MRes

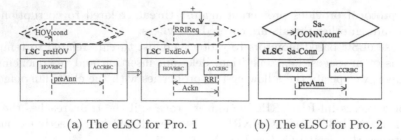

(a) The eLSC for Pro. 1   (b) The eLSC for Pro. 2

Fig. 2. Example: the RBC/RBC handover process

According to the requirements of ETCS, the messages RRIReq and RRI are allowed to be exchanged after HOVRBC receives the "preAnn" message. Thus, the eLSC ExdEoA in Fig. 2(a) cannot be executed before preHOV. The double arrow between eLSCs preHOV and ExdEoA in Fig. 2(a) denotes $\{(\mathfrak{m}, \mathfrak{m}', Suff)$, $(\mathfrak{m}, \mathfrak{p}', Suff)\}$ for $\mathfrak{u} = preHOV$ and $\mathfrak{u}' = ExdEoA$.

For property 2, the safe connection is established after HOVRBC receives a "safe connection confirm" (Sa-CONN.conf) message. As an example, we consider the message preANN: it cannot be transmitted before HOVRBC receives Sa-CONN.conf. This property is specified by an eLSC with a sufficient prechart, which consists of a receiving event of SaCONN.conf (see Fig. 2(b)).

As an example observation from the log file of RBCs (according to the specification SUBSET-039), we used the trace shown in Fig. 3(a).

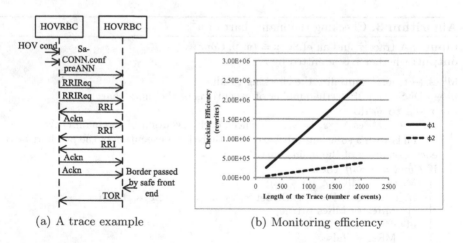

(a) A trace example   (b) Monitoring efficiency

Fig. 3. Evaulation results in Maude

To prove that the concept of eLSC based monitoring is feasible, we built a prototypical implementation of our algorithms. We translate eLSCs without iteration into LTL formulae, and implement the LTL model checking algorithm in Maude, see [17] and [7]. This is a high performance rewriting environment, which is able to execute millions of rewrites per second [10].

We checked the example trace with our prototypical implementation. The results show that it satisfies the two properties. In addition, we built some more traces by injecting errors, such as adding/removing events, and exchanging the occurrence order of events. The results show that the monitor can detect repetition, deletion, insertion and resequencing errors.

For our LTL translation, since the size of the formula is polynomial in the size of the eLSC, the monitoring complexity is the same as the complexity of LTL model checking. Thus, given an eLSC specification and a trace, the complexity of monitoring is linear in the length of the trace, and (worst-case) exponential in the number of events appearing in the eLSC. We repeated similar experiments several times with different traces. The checking efficiency is shown in Fig. 3(b). In this diagram, φ_1 and φ_2 are the resulting LTL formulae of property 1 and property 2, respectively. The difference in checking efficiency is caused by the sizes of the two formulae: φ_1 consists of approx. 630 sub-formulae, whereas φ_2 has only approx. 130 sub-formulae. The experimental results show that our approach is capable to detect failures in the executions of a system.

6   Conclusion and Discussion

In this paper, we have proposed a monitoring approach on basis of eLSC specifications. We introduced the notion of a sufficient prechart for specifying sufficiency conditions in correctness properties. Then we defined concatenation and iteration of LSCs. We have shown how to translate eLSCs without iteration into LTL formulae. A system can then be monitored by formula rewriting. For the full language, we developed an explicit monitoring algorithm. Finally, we presented a case study with a concrete example from the railway domain. The results show the feasibility of our implementation.

There are several interesting topics for future work. Firstly, the implementation reported in this paper was done as a proof-of-concept, showing that the approach of eLSC based monitoring is feasible. Since the sizes of resulting formulae are often large, translating eLSC into LTL formulae is not an efficient way for monitoring. In addition, to maintain monitors in deployed systems, one would not want to employ full Maude. Therefore, we are currently developing a more efficient implementation, which can check eLSC specifications directly.

Secondly, in this paper we only considered a subset of the original LSC language, excluding conditions and "cold" elements, where additionally all messages had to be unique. Even though we do not think that the full LSC language poses additional fundamental problems, this needs to be worked out. Moreover, the LSC language has been extended with timing constructs for specifying real-time properties. We want to investigate the translation of eLSCs with such timing constructs into TPTL formulae for monitoring purposes.

Last but not least, it remains open to define an automaton concept which has exactly the same expressiveness as our eLSCs.

References

1. Alur, R., Yannakakis, M.: Model Checking of Message Sequence Charts. In: Baeten, J.C.M., Mauw, S. (eds.) CONCUR 1999. LNCS, vol. 1664, pp. 114–129. Springer, Heidelberg (1999)
2. Bauer, A., Küster, J.-C., Vegliach, G.: From Propositional to First-order Monitoring. In: Legay, A., Bensalem, S. (eds.) RV 2013. LNCS, vol. 8174, pp. 59–75. Springer, Heidelberg (2013)
3. Ben-abdallah, H., Leue, S.: Timing Constraints in Message Sequence Chart Specifications. In: IFIP. Chapman. Hall (1997)
4. Bohn, J., Damm, W., Klose, J., Moik, A., Wittke, H., Ehrig, H., Kramer, B., Ertas, A.: Modeling and Validating Train System Applications Using Statemate and Live Sequence Charts. In: Proc. IDPT. Citeseer (2002)
5. Bontemps, Y.: Relating Inter-Agent and Intra-Agent Specifications. PhD thesis, PhD thesis, University of Namur, Belgium (2005)
6. Bontemps, Y., Schobbens, P.-Y.: The Computational Complexity of Scenario-based Agent Verification and Design. Journal of Applied Logic 5(2), 252–276 (2007)
7. Chai, M., Schlingloff, H.: A Rewriting Based Monitoring Algorithm for TPTL. In: CS&P 2013, pp. 61–72. Citeseer (2013)
8. Chen, F., Roşu, G.: Java-MOP: A Monitoring Oriented Programming Environment for Java. In: Halbwachs, N., Zuck, L.D. (eds.) TACAS 2005. LNCS, vol. 3440, pp. 546–550. Springer, Heidelberg (2005)
9. Ciraci, S., Malakuti, S., Katz, S., Aksit, M.: Checking the Correspondence between UML Models and Implementation. In: Barringer, H., et al. (eds.) RV 2010. LNCS, vol. 6418, pp. 198–213. Springer, Heidelberg (2010)
10. Clavel, M., Durán, F., Eker, S., Lincoln, P., Martí-Oliet, N., Meseguer, J., Talcott, C.: Maude Manual (version 2.6). University of Illinois, Urbana-Champaign 1(3), 4–6 (2011)
11. Combes, P., Harel, D., Kugler, H.: Modeling and Verification of a Telecommunication Application Using Live Sequence Charts and the Play-engine Tool. Software & Systems Modeling 7(2), 157–175 (2008)
12. Damm, W., Harel, D.: LSCs: Breathing Life into Message Sequence Charts. Formal Methods in System Design 19(1), 45–80 (2001)
13. Fisher, J., Harel, D., Hubbard, E.J.A., Piterman, N., Stern, M.J., Swerdlin, N.: Combining State-based and Scenario-based Approaches in Modeling Biological Systems. In: Danos, V., Schachter, V. (eds.) CMSB 2004. LNCS (LNBI), vol. 3082, pp. 236–241. Springer, Heidelberg (2005)
14. Harel, D., Kugler, H., Marelly, R., Pnueli, A.: Smart Play-out of Behavioral Requirements. In: Aagaard, M.D., O'Leary, J.W. (eds.) FMCAD 2002. LNCS, vol. 2517, pp. 378–398. Springer, Heidelberg (2002)
15. Harel, D., Maoz, S.: Assert and Negate Revisited: Modal Semantics for UML Sequence Diagrams. Software & Systems Modeling 7(2), 237–252 (2008)
16. Harel, D., Maoz, S., Segall, I.: Some Results on the Expressive Power and Complexity of LSCs. In: Avron, A., Dershowitz, N., Rabinovich, A. (eds.) Trakhtenbrot/Festschrift. LNCS, vol. 4800, pp. 351–366. Springer, Heidelberg (2008)
17. Havelund, K., Roşu, G.: Monitoring Java Programs with Java PathExplorer. Electronic Notes in Theoretical Computer Science 55(2), 200–217 (2001)
18. Kugler, H.-J., Harel, D., Pnueli, A., Lu, Y., Bontemps, Y.: Temporal Logic for Scenario-based Specifications. In: Halbwachs, N., Zuck, L.D. (eds.) TACAS 2005. LNCS, vol. 3440, pp. 445–460. Springer, Heidelberg (2005)

19. Kumar, R., Mercer, E.G.: Verifying Communication Protocols Using Live Sequence Chart Specifications. Electronic Notes in Theoretical Computer Science 250(2), 33–48 (2009)
20. Leucker, M., Schallhart, C.: A Brief Account of Runtime Verification. The Journal of Logic and Algebraic Programming 78(5), 293–303 (2009)
21. Meredith, P.O., Jin, D., Chen, F., Roşu, G.: Efficient Monitoring of Parametric Context-free Patterns. Automated Software Engineering 17(2), 149–180 (2010)
22. Roşu, G., Havelund, K.: Rewriting-based Techniques for Runtime Verification. Automated Software Engineering 12(2), 151–197 (2005)
23. Simmonds, J., Chechik, M., Nejati, S., Litani, E., O'Farrell, B.: Property Patterns for Runtime Monitoring of Web Service Conversations. In: Leucker, M. (ed.) RV 2008. LNCS, vol. 5289, pp. 137–157. Springer, Heidelberg (2008)
24. Thati, P., Roşu, G.: Monitoring Algorithms for Metric Temporal Logic Specifications. Electronic Notes in Theoretical Computer Science 113, 145–162 (2005)

A   Proof of Lemma 1

Lemma 1. *The language* $\left(\overline{\mathcal{B}\Sigma^* \circ \mathcal{L}(\mathfrak{c})} \circ \mathcal{L}(\mathfrak{c}') \circ \mathcal{B}\Sigma^*\right)$ *cannot be defined by an LSC specification.*

Proof. A universal chart $\mathfrak{u} \triangleq (\mathfrak{p}, \mathfrak{m})$ defines the language $\mathcal{L}(\mathfrak{u}) \triangleq \left(\overline{\mathcal{B}\Sigma^* \circ \mathcal{L}(\mathfrak{p})} \circ \overline{\mathcal{L}(\mathfrak{m})} \circ \mathcal{B}\Sigma^*\right)$ [5]. The language defined by an LSC specification $\mathfrak{U} \triangleq \{\mathfrak{u}_1, \mathfrak{u}_2, ..., \mathfrak{u}_n\}$ with $\mathfrak{u}_i \triangleq (\mathfrak{p}_i, \mathfrak{m}_i)$ is $X \triangleq \bigcap_{1 \leq i \leq n} \left(\overline{\mathcal{B}\Sigma^* \circ \mathcal{L}(\mathfrak{p}_i)} \circ \overline{\mathcal{L}(\mathfrak{m}_i)} \circ \mathcal{B}\Sigma^*\right)$.

We only consider the segments $S \triangleq \bigcap_{1 \leq i \leq n} \left(\mathcal{L}(\mathfrak{p}_i) \circ \overline{\mathcal{L}(\mathfrak{m}_i)}\right)$, where every word in X contains a segment in S. The complement of S is $\overline{S} \triangleq \bigcup_{1 \leq i \leq n} \left(\mathcal{L}(\mathfrak{p}_i) \circ \overline{\mathcal{L}(\mathfrak{m}_i)}\right)$. Every word in $\overline{S}$ contains a prefix $v \in \bigcup_{1 \leq i \leq n} \mathcal{L}(\mathfrak{p}_i)$. For the segment $S' \triangleq \left(\overline{\mathcal{L}(\mathfrak{c})} \circ \mathcal{L}(\mathfrak{c}')\right)$ of $Y \triangleq \left(\overline{\mathcal{B}\Sigma^* \circ \mathcal{L}(\mathfrak{c})} \circ \mathcal{L}(\mathfrak{c}') \circ \mathcal{B}\Sigma^*\right)$, a word in $\overline{S'}$ contains a segment $v' \in \overline{\mathcal{L}(\mathfrak{p}_i)}$. The language of a basic chart $\mathfrak{c}$ is defined by stutter events and a finite set $Traces(\mathfrak{c})$. Therefore, the language of $\overline{\mathfrak{c}}$ is defined by stutter events and a set $(\mathcal{B}\Sigma^* \backslash Traces(\mathfrak{c}))$, which is an infinite set. Whereas, the set $\bigcup_{1 \leq i \leq n} \mathcal{L}(\mathfrak{p}_i)$ is finite with $n < \infty$. Therefore, there exists some v' that is not expressed by $\overline{S}$. In other words, there are some segments of words in S' that are not expressed by S. Since i) X consists of S and $\mathcal{B}\Sigma^*$; ii) Y consists of S' and $\mathcal{B}\Sigma^*$; and iii) S' cannote be expressed by S, the language Y cannot be epxressed by X. ∎

Foundations of Boolean Stream Runtime Verification*

Laura Bozzelli[1] and César Sánchez[2,3]

[1] Technical University of Madrid (UPM), Madrid, Spain
[2] IMDEA Software Institute, Madrid, Spain
[3] Institute for Information Security, CSIC, Spain

Abstract. Stream runtime verification (SRV), pioneered by the tool LOLA, is a declarative approach to specify synchronous monitors. In SRV, monitors are described by specifying dependencies between output streams of values and input streams of values. The declarative nature of SRV enables a separation between (1) the evaluation algorithms, and (2) the monitor storage and its individual updates. This separation allows SRV to be lifted from conventional failure monitors into richer domains to collect statistics of traces. Moreover, SRV allows to easily identify specifications that can be efficiently monitored online, and to generate efficient schedules for offline monitors.

In spite of these attractive features, many important theoretical problems about SRV are still open. In this paper, we address complexity, expressiveness, succinctness, and closure issues for the subclass of Boolean SRV (BSRV) specifications. Additionally, we show that for this subclass, offline monitoring can be performed with only two passes (one forward and one backward) over the input trace in spite of the alternation of past and future references in the BSRV specification.

1 Introduction

Runtime verification (RV) has emerged in the last decades as an applied formal technique for software reliability. In RV, a specification, expressing correctness requirements, is automatically translated into a *monitor*. Such a monitor is then used to check either the *current* execution of a running system, or a finite set of *recorded* executions with respect to the given specification. The former scenario is called *online* monitoring, while the latter one is called *offline* monitoring. Online monitoring is used to detect and possibly handle (e.g., by the execution of additional repair code) violations of the specification when the system is in operation. On the other hand, offline monitoring is used in post-mortem analysis and it is convenient for testing large systems before deployment. Unlike static verification (such as model-checking) which formally checks that all the (infinite) executions or traces of a system satisfy the specification, RV only considers a single finite trace. Thus, this methodology sacrifices completeness guarantees to obtain an immediately applicable and formal extension of testing. See [17,14] for modern surveys on runtime verification.

---

* This work was funded in part by Spanish MINECO Project "TIN2012-39391-C04-01 STRONGSOFT" and by Spanish MINECO Project "TIN2012-38137-C02 VIVAC".

B. Bonakdarpour and S.A. Smolka (Eds.): RV 2014, LNCS 8734, pp. 64–79, 2014.
© Springer International Publishing Switzerland 2014

Stream Runtime Verification. The first specification formalisms proposed for runtime verification were based on specification languages for static verification, typically LTL [18] or past LTL adapted for finite paths [15,9,5]. Other formalisms for expressing monitors include regular expressions [23], rule based specifications as proposed in the logic Eagle [1], or rewriting [22]. Stream runtime verification (SRV), first proposed in the tool LOLA [8], is an alternative to define monitors for synchronous systems. In SRV, specifications declare explicitly the dependencies between *input* streams of values (representing the observable behavior of the system) and *output* streams of values (describing error reports and diagnosis information). These dependencies can relate the current value of an output stream with the values of the same or other streams in the present moment, in past instants (like in past temporal formulas) or in future instants. A similar approach to describe temporal relations as streams was later introduced as temporal testers [21].

Stream runtime verification offers two advantages to the description of monitors. First, SRV separates the algorithmic aspects of the runtime evaluation (by explicitly declaring the data dependencies) from the specific individual operations performed at each step (which depend on the type of data being observed, manipulated and stored). In this manner, well-known evaluation algorithms for monitoring Boolean observations – for example those from temporal logics – can be generalized to richer data domains, producing monitors that collect statistics about traces. Similarly to the Boolean case, the first approaches for collecting statistics from running traces were based on extensions of LTL [10]. SRV can be viewed as a generalization of these approaches to streams. Other modern approaches to the runtime verification for statistic collection extend first-order LTL [4,2,3]. Moreover, the declarative nature of SRV allows to identify specifications that are amenable for efficient online monitoring, essentially those specifications whose values can be resolved by past and present observations. Additionally, the analysis of dependencies also allows to generate efficient offline monitors by scheduling passes over the dumped traces, where the number of passes (back and forth) depends on the number of alternations between past and future references in the specification.

SRV can be seen as a variation of synchronous languages [7] – like Esterel [6], Lustre [13] or Signal [11] – specifically designed for observing traces of systems, removing the causality assumption. In synchronous languages, stream values can only depend on past or present values, while in SRV a dependency on future values is additionally allowed to describe future temporal observations. In recent years, SRV has also been extended to real-time systems [20,12].

When used for synthesizing monitors, SRV specifications need to be *well-defined*: for every input there is a unique corresponding output stream. However, as with many synchronous languages, the declarative style of SRV allows specifications that are not well-defined: for some observations, either there is no possible output (*over-definedness*) or there is more than one output (*under-definedness*). This anomaly is caused by circular dependencies, and in [8], a syntactical constraint called *well-formedness* is introduced in order to ensure the absence of circular dependencies, and guarantee well-definedness.

Our Contribution. In spite of its applicability, several foundational theoretical problems of SRV have not been studied so far. In this paper, we address complexity, expressiveness, succinctness, and closure properties for Boolean SRV (BSRV). Our results can be summarized as follows:

- we establish the complexity of checking whether a specification is under-defined, over-defined or well-defined. Apart from the theoretical significance of these results, many important practical properties of specifications (like semantic equivalence, implication and redundancy) can be reduced to the decision problems above.
- BSRV specifications can be naturally interpreted as language recognizers, where one selects the inputs for which the specification admits some output. We prove that in this setting, BSRV captures precisely the class of regular languages. We also show efficient closure constructions for many language operations. Additionally, BSRV specifications can be exponentially more succinct than nondeterministic finite-state automata (NFA).
- Finally, based on the construction of the NFA associated with a *well-defined* BSRV specification, we show how to schedule an offline algorithm with only two passes, one forward and one backward. This gives a partial answer (for the Boolean case) to the open problem of reducing the number of passes in offline monitoring for *well-formed* SRV specifications [8].

The rest of the paper is structured as follows. Section 2 revisits SRV. In Section 3 we establish expressiveness, succinctness, and closure results for BSRV specifications when interpreted as language recognizers. In Section 4, we describe the two-pass offline monitoring algorithm. Section 5 is devoted to the decision problems for BSRV specifications. Finally, Section 6 concludes. Due to lack of space, some proofs are omitted and are included in the longer version of this document[1].

2   Stream Runtime Verification (SRV)

In this Section, we recall the SRV framework [8]. We focus on SRV specifications over stream variables of the same type (with emphasis on the Boolean type).

A type T is a tuple $T = \langle D, F \rangle$ consisting of a countable value domain D and a finite collection F of interpreted function symbols f, where f denotes a computable function from D^k to D and $k \geq 0$ is the specific arity of f. Note that 0-ary function symbols (constants) are associated with individual values. In particular, we consider the *Boolean type*, where $D = \{0, 1\}$ and F consists of the Boolean operators $\wedge$ and $\vee$ and $\neg$. A *stream of type* T is a non-empty *finite* word w over the domain D of T. Given such a stream w, $|w|$ is the length of w and for all $1 \leq i \leq |w|$, $w(i)$ is the ith letter of w (the value of the stream at time step i). The stream w is *uniform* if there is $d \in D$ such that w is in d^*.

For a finite set Z of (stream) variables, a *stream valuation of type* T over Z is a mapping σ assigning to each variable $z \in Z$, a stream $\sigma(z)$ of type T such that

---

[1] The longer version can be obtained at `http://software.imdea.org/~cesar/`

the streams associated with the different variables in Z have the same length N for some $N \geq 1$. We also say that N is the length of σ, which is denoted by $|\sigma|$.

Remark 1. Note that for the Boolean type, a stream valuation σ over Z can be identified with the non-empty word over 2^Z of length $|\sigma|$ whose ith symbol, written $\sigma(i)$, is the set of variables $z \in Z$ such that $\sigma(z)(i) = 1$.

Stream Expressions. Given a finite set Z of variables, the set of *stream expressions* E *of type T over Z* is inductively defined by the following syntax:

$$\mathsf{E} := \tau \mid \tau[\ell|c] \mid f(\mathsf{E}_1, \ldots, \mathsf{E}_k)$$

where τ is either a constant of type T or a variable in Z, ℓ is a non-null integer, c is a constant of type T, and $f \in F$ is a function of type T and arity $k > 0$. Informally, $\tau[\ell|c]$ refers to the value of τ offset ℓ positions from the current position, and the constant c is the *default* value of type T assigned to positions from which the offset is after the end or before the beginning of the stream. Stream expressions E of type T over Z are interpreted over stream valuations σ of type T over Z. The *valuation* of E with respect to σ, written $[\![\mathsf{E}, \sigma]\!]$, is the stream of type T and length $|\sigma|$ inductively defined as follows for all $1 \leq i \leq |\sigma|$:

- $[\![c, \sigma]\!](i) = c$ and $[\![z, \sigma]\!](i) = \sigma(z)(i)$ for all $z \in Z$
- $[\![\tau[\ell|c], \sigma]\!](i) = \begin{cases} [\![\tau, \sigma]\!](i + \ell) & \text{if } 1 \leq i + \ell \leq |\sigma| \\ c & \text{otherwise} \end{cases}$
- $[\![f(\mathsf{E}_1, \ldots, \mathsf{E}_k), \sigma]\!](i) = f([\![\mathsf{E}_1, \sigma]\!](i), \ldots, [\![\mathsf{E}_k, \sigma]\!](i))$

For the *Boolean type*, we use some shortcuts: $\mathsf{E}_1 \to \mathsf{E}_2$ stands for $\neg \mathsf{E}_1 \vee \mathsf{E}_2$, $\mathsf{E}_1 \leftrightarrow \mathsf{E}_2$ stands for $(\mathsf{E}_1 \to \mathsf{E}_2) \wedge (\mathsf{E}_2 \to \mathsf{E}_1)$, and *if* E *then* E_1 *else* E_2 stands for $(\mathsf{E} \wedge \mathsf{E}_1) \vee (\neg \mathsf{E} \wedge \mathsf{E}_2)$. Additionally, we use first and last for the Boolean stream expressions $0[-1|1]$ and $0[+1|1]$, respectively. Note that for a Boolean stream, first is 1 precisely at the first position, and last is 1 precisely at the last position.

Example 1. Consider the following *Boolean* stream expression E over $Z = \{x\}$:

$$\mathsf{E} := \textit{if } x \textit{ then } x \textit{ else } x[1|0]$$

For every *Boolean* stream valuation σ over Z such that $\sigma(Z) \in (01)^+$, the valuation of E with respect to σ is the uniform Boolean stream $1^{|\sigma|}$.

Stream Runtime Verification Specification Language (SRV). Given a finite set X of *input* variables and a set $Y = \{y_1, \ldots, y_n\}$ of *output* variables with $X \cap Y = \emptyset$, an SRV φ of type T over X and Y is a set of equations

$$\varphi := \{y_1 = \mathsf{E}_1, \ldots, y_n = \mathsf{E}_n\}$$

where $\mathsf{E}_1, \ldots, \mathsf{E}_n$ are stream expressions of type T over $X \cup Y$. Note that there is exactly one equation for each output variable. A stream valuation of φ is a stream valuation of type T over $X \cup Y$, while an *input* (resp., *output*) of φ is a stream valuation of type T over X (resp., Y). Given an input σ_X of φ and an output σ_Y of φ such that σ_X and σ_Y have the same length, $\sigma_X \cup \sigma_Y$ denotes the stream valuation of φ defined in the obvious way. The SRV φ describes a relation, written $[\![\varphi]\!]$, between inputs σ_X of φ and outputs σ_Y of φ, defined as follows: $(\sigma_X, \sigma_Y) \in [\![\varphi]\!]$ iff $|\sigma_X| = |\sigma_Y|$ and for each equation $y_j = \mathsf{E}_j$ of φ,

$$[\![y_j, \sigma]\!] = [\![\mathsf{E}_j, \sigma]\!] \qquad \text{where } \sigma = \sigma_X \cup \sigma_Y$$

If $(\sigma_X, \sigma_Y) \in [\![\varphi]\!]$, we say that the stream valuation $\sigma_X \cup \sigma_Y$ is a *valuation model of* φ (associated with the input σ_X). Note that in general, for a given input σ_X, there may be zero, one, or multiple valuation models associated with σ_X. This leads to the following notions for an SRV φ:

- *Under-definedness:* for some input σ_X, there are at least two distinct valuation models of φ associated with σ_X.
- *Over-definedness:* for some input σ_X, there is no valuation model of φ associated with σ_X.
- *Well-definedness:* for each input σ_X, there is exactly one valuation model of φ associated with σ_X.

Note that an SRV φ may be both under-defined and over-defined, and φ is well-defined iff it is neither under-defined nor over-defined. For runtime verification, SRV serves as a query language on program behaviors (input streams) from which one computes a unique answer (the output streams). In this context, a specification is useful only if it is well-defined. However, in practice, it is convenient to distinguish *intermediate* output variables from *observable* output variables separating output streams that are of interest to the user from those that are used only to facilitate the computation of other streams. This leads to a more general notion of well-definedness. Given a subset $Z \subseteq Y$ of output variables, an SRV φ is *well-defined with respect to Z* if for each input σ_X, there is exactly one stream valuation σ_Z over Z having the same length as σ_X such that $\sigma_X \cup \sigma_Z$ can be extended to some valuation model of φ (*uniqueness of the output streams over Z*).

Analogously, we consider a notion of semantic equivalence between SRV of the same type and having the same input variables, which is parameterized by a set of output variables. Formally, given an SRV φ of type T over X and Y, an SRV φ' of type T over X and Y', and $Z \subseteq Y \cap Y'$, we say that φ and φ' are equivalent with respect to Z if for each valuation model σ of φ, there is a valuation model σ' of φ' such that σ and σ' coincide on $X \cup Z$, and vice versa. Moreover, if $Y' \supseteq Y$, then we say that φ' is φ-*equivalent* if φ and φ' are equivalent with respect to Y.

Remark 2. In the rest of the paper, we focus on Boolean SRV (BSRV for short). Thus, in the following, we omit the reference to the type T in the various definitions. We assume that the offsets ℓ in the subexpressions $\tau[\ell|c]$ of a BSRV are encoded in unary. For a Boolean stream expression E, we denote by $\|\mathsf{E}\|$ the offset ℓ if E is a stream expression of the form $\tau[\ell|c]$; otherwise, $\|\mathsf{E}\|$ is 1. The size $|\varphi|$ of a BSRV φ is defined as $|\varphi| := \sum_{\mathsf{E} \in SE(\varphi)} \|\mathsf{E}\|$, where $SE(\varphi)$ is the set of stream subexpressions of φ.

Example 2. Consider the following BSRV over $X = \{x\}$ and $Y = \{y\}$:

$$\varphi_1 := \{y = x \wedge y\} \quad \varphi_2 := \{y = x \wedge \neg y\} \quad \varphi_3 := \{y = \text{if } x \text{ then } x[2|0] \text{ else } x[-2|0]\}$$

The specification φ_1 is under-defined since $(1^N, 0^N)$ and $(1^N, 1^N)$ are two valuation models for each $N \geq 1$. On the other hand, the specification φ_2 is over-defined since for each $N \geq 1$, there is no valuation model associated with the input 1^N. Finally, the specification φ_3 is well-defined.

3   BSRV as Language Recognizers

BSRV can be interpreted as a simple declarative formalism to specify languages of non-empty finite words. Formally, we associate to a BSRV φ over X and Y, the language $\mathcal{L}(\varphi)$ of non-empty finite words over 2^X (or, equivalently, input stream valuations) for which the specification φ admits a valuation model, i.e.,

$$\mathcal{L}(\varphi) := \{\sigma_X \mid (\sigma_X, \sigma_Y) \in [\![\varphi]\!] \text{ for some } \sigma_Y\}$$

Example 3. Let $X = \{x\}$, $Y = \{y\}$, and $\varphi = \{y = \text{if } \mathsf{E} \text{ then } y \text{ else } \neg y\}$, where

$$\mathsf{E} := \big(\mathsf{first} \to (x \wedge y)\big) \wedge \big(y \to \neg y[+1|0]\big) \wedge \big(\neg y \to (x[+1|1] \wedge y[+1|1])\big)$$

A pair (σ_X, σ_Y) is a valuation model of φ iff the valuation of the stream expression E w.r.t. $\sigma_X \cup \sigma_Y$ is in 1^+ iff $\sigma_X(x)(i) = 1$ for all odd positions i. Hence, $\mathcal{L}(\varphi)$ is the set of Boolean streams which assume the value 1 at the odd positions.

In the following, we show that BSRV, as language recognizers, are effectively equivalent to nondeterministic finite automata (NFA) on finite words. While the translation from NFA to BSRV can be done in polynomial time, the converse translation involves an *unavoidable* singly exponential blowup. Moreover, BSRV turn out to be effectively and *efficiently* closed under many language operations.

In order to present our results, we shortly recall the class of NFA on finite words. An NFA $\mathcal{A}$ over a finite input alphabet I is a tuple $\mathcal{A} = \langle Q, q_0, \delta, F \rangle$, where Q is a finite set of states, $q_0 \in Q$ is the initial state, $\delta : Q \times I \to 2^Q$ is the transition function, and $F \subseteq Q$ is a set of accepting states. Given an input word $w \in I^*$, a run π of $\mathcal{A}$ over w is a sequence of states $\pi = q_1, \ldots, q_{|w|+1}$ such that q_1 is the initial state and for all $1 \leq i \leq |w|$, $q_{i+1} \in \delta(q_i, w(i))$. The run π is accepting if it leads to an accepting state (i.e, $q_{|w|+1} \in F$). The language $\mathcal{L}(\mathcal{A})$ accepted by $\mathcal{A}$ is the set of non-empty finite words w over I such that there is an accepting run of $\mathcal{A}$ over w. $\mathcal{A}$ is *universal* if $\mathcal{L}(\mathcal{A}) = I^+$. A language over non-empty finite words is *regular* if it is accepted by some NFA. An NFA is *unambiguous* if for each input word w, there is at most one accepting run on w.

Fix a BSRV φ on X and Y. In order to build an NFA accepting $\mathcal{L}(\varphi)$, we define an encoding of the valuation models of φ. For this, we associate to φ two parameters, the *back reference distance* $b(\varphi)$ and the *forward reference distance* $f(\varphi)$:

$$b(\varphi) := max(0, \{\ell \mid \ell > 0 \text{ and } \varphi \text{ contains a subexpression of the form } z[-\ell, c]\})$$
$$f(\varphi) := max(0, \{\ell \mid \ell > 0 \text{ and } \varphi \text{ contains a subexpression of the form } z[\ell, c]\})$$

For a stream valuation σ of φ and an expression E of φ, the value of E w.r.t. σ at a time step i is completely specified by the values of σ at time steps j such that $i - b(\varphi) \leq j \leq i + f(\varphi)$. We define the following alphabets:

$$A := 2^{X \cup Y} \qquad A_\perp := A \cup \{\perp\} \qquad P_\varphi := (A_\perp)^{b(\varphi)} \times A \times (A_\perp)^{f(\varphi)}$$

where $\perp$ is a special symbol. Note that a stream valuation of φ corresponds to a non-empty finite word over the alphabet A, and the cardinality of P_φ is singly exponential in the size of φ. For an element $p = (a_{-b(\varphi)}, \ldots, a_{-1}, a_0, a_1, \ldots, a_{f(\varphi)})$ of P_φ, the component a_0, called the *main value of p*, intuitively represents the value of some stream valuation σ at some time step i, while $a_{-b(\varphi)}, \ldots, a_{-1}$ (resp., $a_1, \ldots, a_{f(\varphi)}$) represent the values of σ at the previous $b(\varphi)$ (resp., next $f(\varphi)$) time steps, if any (the symbol $\perp$ is used to denote the absence of a previous or next time step). Let τ be either a Boolean constant or a variable in $X \cup Y$, and $a \in A$. Then, the Boolean *value* of τ in a is τ if τ is a constant, otherwise the value is 1 iff $\tau \in a$. For a Boolean stream expression E over $X \cup Y$ and an element $p = (a_{-b(\varphi)}, \ldots, a_{-1}, a_0, a_1, \ldots, a_{f(\varphi)})$ of P_φ, the *value* $[\![\mathsf{E}, p]\!]$ *of E with respect to p* is the computable Boolean value inductively defined as follows:

- $[\![c, p]\!] = c$ and $[\![z, p]\!] = $ the value of z in a_0
- $[\![\tau[\ell|c], p]\!] = \begin{cases} \text{the value of } \tau \text{ in } a_\ell \text{ if } -b(\varphi) \leq \ell \leq f(\varphi) \text{ and } a_\ell \neq \perp \\ c \hspace{4.5cm} \text{otherwise} \end{cases}$
- $[\![f(\mathsf{E}_1, \ldots, \mathsf{E}_k), p]\!] = f([\![\mathsf{E}_1, p]\!], \ldots, [\![\mathsf{E}_k, p]\!])$

We denote by Q_φ the subset of P_φ consisting of the elements p of P_φ such that for each equation $y = \mathsf{E}$ of φ, the value of y with respect to p coincides with the value of E with respect to p. Let $\#$ be an additional special symbol (which will be used as initial state of the NFA associated with φ). An *expanded valuation model* of φ is a word of the form $\# \cdot w$ such that w is a non-empty finite word w over the alphabet Q_φ satisfying the following:

- $w(1)$ is of the form $(\perp, \ldots, \perp, a_0, a_1, \ldots, a_{f(\varphi)})$;
- $w(|w|)$ is of the form $(a_{-b(\varphi)}, \ldots, a_{-1}, a_0, \perp, \ldots, \perp)$;
- if $1 \leq i < |w|$ and $w(i) = (a_{-b(\varphi)}, \ldots, a_{-1}, a_0, a_1, \ldots, a_{f(\varphi)})$, then there is $d \in A_\perp$ such that $w(i+1)$ is of the form $(a_{-b(\varphi)+1}, \ldots, a_{-1}, a_0, a_1, \ldots, a_{f(\varphi)}, d)$.

For an expanded valuation model $\# \cdot w$ of φ, the *associated stream valuation* $\sigma(w)$ is the stream valuation of φ of length $|w|$ whose ith element is the main value of the ith element of w. By construction, we easily obtain that $\sigma(w)$ is a valuation model of φ and, more precisely, the following lemma holds.

Lemma 1. *The mapping assigning to each expanded valuation model $\# \cdot w$ of φ the associated stream valuation $\sigma(w)$ is a bijection between the set of expanded valuation models of φ and the set of valuation models of φ.*

By the above characterization of the set of valuations models of a BSRV φ, we easily obtain the following result.

Theorem 1 (From BSRV to NFA). *Given a BSRV φ over X and Y, one can construct in singly exponential time an NFA $\mathcal{A}_\varphi$ over the alphabet 2^X accepting $\mathcal{L}(\varphi)$ whose set of states is $Q_\varphi \cup \{\#\}$. Moreover, for each input σ_X, the set of accepting runs of $\mathcal{A}_\varphi$ over σ_X is the set of expanded valuation models of φ encoding the valuation models of φ associated with the input σ_X.*

Proof. The NFA $\mathcal{A}_\varphi$ is defined as $\mathcal{A}_\varphi = \langle Q_\varphi \cup \{\#\}, \#, \delta_\varphi, F_\varphi \rangle$, where F_φ is the set of elements of Q_φ of the form $(a_{-b(\varphi)}, \ldots, a_{-1}, a_0, \bot, \ldots, \bot)$, and $\delta(p, \iota)$ is defined as follows for all states p and input symbol $\iota \in 2^X$:

- if $p = \#$, then $\delta_\varphi(p, \iota)$ is the set of states of the form $(\bot, \ldots, \bot, a_0, a_1, \ldots, a_{f(\varphi)})$ such that $a_0 \cap X = \iota$;
- if $p = (a_{-b(\varphi)}, \ldots, a_{-1}, a_0, a_1, \ldots, a_{f(\varphi)}) \in Q_\varphi$, then $\delta_\varphi(p, \iota)$ is the set of states of the form $(a_{-b(\varphi)+1}, \ldots, a_{-1}, a_0, a_1, \ldots, a_{f(\varphi)}, d)$ for some $d \in A_\bot$ whose main value a satisfies $a \cap X = \iota$.

By construction, for each input σ_X, the set of accepting runs of $\mathcal{A}_\varphi$ over σ_X coincides with the set of expanded valuation models $\# \cdot w$ of φ such that the stream valuation $\sigma(w)$ is associated with the input σ_X. Thus, by Lemma 1, the result follows. □

For the converse translation from NFA to BSRV, we show the following.

Theorem 2 (From NFA to BSRV). *Given an NFA $\mathcal{A}$ over the input alphabet 2^X, one can construct in polynomial time a BSRV $\varphi_{\mathcal{A}}$ with set of input variables X such that $\mathcal{L}(\varphi_{\mathcal{A}}) = \mathcal{L}(\mathcal{A})$.*

Proof. Let $\mathcal{A} = \langle Q, q_0, \delta, F \rangle$. We construct a BSRV $\varphi_{\mathcal{A}}$ over the set of input variables X as follows. First, for each input symbol ι, we use a Boolean expression E_ι over X, encoding the input symbol ι, defined as $\mathsf{E}_\iota := (\bigwedge_{x \in \iota} x) \wedge (\bigwedge_{x \in X \setminus \iota} \neg x)$. The set Y of output variables of $\varphi_{\mathcal{A}}$ is defined as follows:

$$Y = \bigcup_{q \in Q} \{\mathsf{q}\} \cup \{\mathsf{control}\}$$

Thus, we associate to each state $q \in Q$, an output variable q, whose associated equation is the trivial one given by $\mathsf{q} = \mathsf{q}$. The equation for the output variable $\mathsf{control}$ is given by

$$\mathsf{control} = if\ \mathsf{E}_{\mathsf{ev}}\ then\ \mathsf{control}\ else\ \neg\mathsf{control}$$

where the boolean stream expression E_{ev} describes accepting runs of the NFA $\mathcal{A}$ and is defined as follows:

$$\mathsf{E}_{\mathsf{ev}} = \underbrace{\bigvee_{q \in Q} (\mathsf{q} \wedge \bigwedge_{p \in Q \setminus \{q\}} \neg \mathsf{p})}_{\text{at each step, } \mathcal{A} \text{ is exactly in one state}} \wedge \underbrace{(\mathsf{first} \longrightarrow \mathsf{q_0})}_{\text{a run of } \mathcal{A} \text{ starts at the initial state}} \wedge$$

$$\underbrace{\bigwedge_{q \in Q} \bigwedge_{\iota \in I} ((\mathsf{q} \wedge \mathsf{E}_\iota) \longrightarrow \bigvee_{p \in \delta(q, \iota)} \mathsf{p}[+1|1])}_{\text{the evolution of } \mathcal{A} \text{ is } \delta\text{-consistent}} \wedge \underbrace{(\mathsf{last} \longrightarrow \bigvee_{(q, \iota) \in \{(q, \iota)\, |\, \delta(q, \iota) \cap F \neq \emptyset\}} (\mathsf{q} \wedge \mathsf{E}_\iota))}_{\text{the run of } \mathcal{A} \text{ is accepting}}$$

By construction, it easily follows that given an input stream valuation σ_X, there is a valuation model of $\varphi_\mathcal{A}$ associated with the input σ_X *if and only if* there is a stream valuation σ associated with the input σ_X such that the valuation of $\mathsf{E_{ev}}$ with respect to σ is a uniform stream in 1^+ *if and only if* there is an accepting run of $\mathcal{A}$ over the input σ_X. Hence, the result follows. $\square$

Corollary 1. *BSRV, when interpreted as language recognizers, capture the class of regular languages over non-empty finite words.*

Succinctness Issues. It turns out that the singly exponential blow-up in Theorem 1 cannot be avoided. To prove this we first show a linear time translation from standard linear temporal logic LTL with past over finite words (which captures a subclass of regular languages) into BSRV. Recall that formulas ψ of LTL with past over a finite set AP of atomic propositions are defined as follows:

$$\psi := p \mid \neg\psi \mid \psi \vee \psi \mid \bigcirc\psi \mid \ominus\psi \mid \psi\,\mathcal{U}\,\psi \mid \psi\,\mathcal{S}\,\psi$$

where $p \in AP$ and $\bigcirc, \ominus, \mathcal{U},$ and $\mathcal{S}$ are the 'next', 'previous', 'until', and 'since' temporal modalities. For a finite word w over 2^{AP} and a position $1 \leq i \leq |w|$, the satisfaction relation $(w, i) \models \psi$ is defined as follows (we omit the rules for the boolean connectives and the atomic propositions, which are standard):

$(w, i) \models \bigcirc\psi \quad\Leftrightarrow\quad i+1 \leq |w|$ and $(w, i+1) \models \psi$
$(w, i) \models \ominus\psi \quad\Leftrightarrow\quad i > 1$ and $(w, i-1) \models \psi$
$(w, i) \models \psi_1\,\mathcal{U}\,\psi_2 \Leftrightarrow \exists i \leq j \leq |w|, (w, j) \models \psi_2$ and $\forall i \leq h < j, (w, h) \models \psi_1$
$(w, i) \models \psi_1\,\mathcal{S}\,\psi_2 \Leftrightarrow \exists 1 \leq j \leq i, (w, j) \models \psi_2$ and $\forall j < h \leq i, (w, h) \models \psi_1$

The language $\mathcal{L}(\psi)$ of a LTL formula ψ is the set of non-empty finite words w over 2^{AP} such that $(w, 1) \models \psi$.

Proposition 1. *LTL with past can be translated in linear time into BSRV.*

Proof. Let ψ be a formula of LTL with past over a finite set AP of atomic propositions. We construct in linear time a BSRV specification φ over the set of input variables $X = AP$ such that $\mathcal{L}(\varphi) = \mathcal{L}(\psi)$. Let $SF(\psi)$ be the set of subformulas of ψ. Then, the set of output variables Y of φ is defined as follows.

$$Y = \bigcup_{\theta \in SF(\psi)} \{y_\theta\} \cup \{\mathsf{init}\}$$

Thus, we associate to each subformula θ of ψ, an output variable y_θ. The intended meaning is that for an input valuation σ_X (corresponding to a non-empty finite word over 2^{AP}) and a valuation model σ associated with σ_X, at each time step i, the value of variable y_θ is 1 iff θ holds at position i along σ_X. The equations for the output variables are defined as follows, where $p \in AP = X$.

$\mathsf{init} = \mathsf{first} \rightarrow (y_\psi \vee \neg\mathsf{init})$ $\qquad\qquad y_p = p$
$y_{\neg\theta} = \neg y_\theta$ $\qquad\qquad\qquad\qquad\qquad y_{\theta_1 \vee \theta_2} = y_{\theta_1} \vee y_{\theta_2}$
$y_{\bigcirc\theta} = y_\theta[+1|0]$ $\qquad\qquad\qquad\qquad y_{\ominus\theta} = y_\theta[-1|0]$
$y_{\theta_1\,\mathcal{U}\,\theta_2} = y_{\theta_2} \vee (\neg\mathsf{last} \wedge y_{\theta_1} \wedge y_{\theta_1\,\mathcal{U}\,\theta_2}[+1|1])$
$y_{\theta_1\,\mathcal{S}\,\theta_2} = y_{\theta_2} \vee (\neg\mathsf{first} \wedge y_{\theta_1} \wedge y_{\theta_1\,\mathcal{S}\,\theta_2}[-1|1])$

One can easily show that the construction is correct, i.e., $\mathcal{L}(\varphi) = \mathcal{L}(\psi)$.   □

It is well-known that there is a singly exponential succinctness gap between LTL with past and NFA [16]. Consequently, we obtain the following result.

Theorem 3. *BSRV are singly exponentially more succinct than NFA, that is, there is a finite set X of input variables and a family $(\varphi_n)_{n \geq 1}$ of BSRV such that for all $n \geq 1$, φ_n has input variables in X and size polynomial in n, and every NFA accepting $\mathcal{L}(\varphi_n)$ has at least $2^{\Omega(n)}$ states.*

Effective Closure under Language Operations. An interesting feature of the class of BSRV is that, when interpreted as language recognizers, BSRV are effectively and *efficiently* closed under many language operations. For two languages $\mathcal{L}$ and $\mathcal{L}'$ of finite words, $\mathcal{L}^R$ denotes the reversal of $\mathcal{L}$, $\mathcal{L} \cdot \mathcal{L}'$ denotes the concatenation of $\mathcal{L}$ and $\mathcal{L}'$, and $\mathcal{L}^+$ denotes the positive Kleene closure of $\mathcal{L}$.

For a BSRV φ, we say that an output variable y of φ is *uniform* if for each valuation model of φ, the stream for y is uniform.

Theorem 4. *BSRV are effectively closed under the following language operations: intersection, union, reversal, positive Kleene closure, and concatenation. Additionally, the constructions for these operations can be done in linear time.*

Proof. We illustrate the constructions for the considered language operations.
Intersection, Union, and Reversal. The constructions are illustrated in Fig. 1. For the intersection, assuming w.l.o.g. that the BSRV φ and φ' have no output variable in common, the BSRV recognizing $\mathcal{L}(\varphi) \cap \mathcal{L}(\varphi')$ is simply the joint set of the equations of φ and φ'. For the union, we use two new output variables check and main. Intuitively, check is a uniform output variable used to guess whether the input has to be considered an input for φ or for φ'. The equation for check ensures that the streams for check range over all the uniform Boolean streams. Depending on the uniform value of check (if it is in 0^+ or 1^+), the equation for the output variable main ensures that the input is recognized iff either the equations of φ are fulfilled or the equations of φ' are fulfilled. For the reversal, the BSRV recognizing $\mathcal{L}(\varphi)^R$ is obtained from φ by replacing each subexpression $\tau[k|d]$ (resp., $\tau[-k|d]$) with $k > 0$ with the subexpression $\tau[-k|d]$ (resp., $\tau[k|d]$).
Positive Kleene closure. The construction is given in Fig. 2.

The BSRV recognizing $[\mathcal{L}(\varphi)]^+$ uses two new output variables: wbegin and wend. Intuitively, wbegin and wend are used for guessing a decomposition in the given input σ_X of the form $\sigma_X = \sigma_{X,1} \cdot \ldots \cdot \sigma_{X,N}$ for some $N \geq 1$ in such a way that each component $\sigma_{X,i}$ is in $\mathcal{L}(\varphi)$. In particular, the output variable wbegin (resp., wend) is used to mark the first (resp., the last) positions of the components $\sigma_{X,i}$. Moreover, the equations for the output variables of φ are modified to allow checking for an offset k of φ and a position j inside a component $\sigma_{X,i}$ in the guessed decomposition of the input σ_X, whether $k + j$ is still a position inside $\sigma_{X,i}$.

Concatenation. The construction is given in Fig. 3. We assume w.l.o.g. that the BSRV φ and φ' have no output variables in common. The BSRV recognizing $\mathcal{L}(\varphi) \cdot \mathcal{L}(\varphi')$ uses a new output variable: wmark. This variable is used for guessing

$$\varphi = \{y_1 = \mathsf{E}_1, \dots, y_k = \mathsf{E}_k\} \quad \varphi' = \{y_1' = \mathsf{E}_1', \dots, y_h' = \mathsf{E}_h'\}$$

Intersection: $\varphi \cap \varphi' = \{y_1 = \mathsf{E}_1, \dots, y_k = \mathsf{E}_k, y_1' = \mathsf{E}_1', \dots, y_h' = \mathsf{E}_h'\}$
where $\{y_1, \dots, y_k\} \cap \{y_1', \dots, y_h'\} = \emptyset$.

Union: $\varphi \cup \varphi' = \{y_1 = y_1, \dots, y_h' = y_h', \mathsf{check} = \mathsf{E}_{\mathsf{check}}, \mathsf{main} = \mathsf{E}_{\mathsf{main}}\}$

$\mathsf{E}_{\mathsf{check}} = \mathit{if} \ \neg\mathsf{last} \to (\mathsf{check} \leftrightarrow \mathsf{check}[+1|1]) \ \mathit{then} \ \mathsf{check} \ \mathit{else} \ \neg\mathsf{check}$

$\mathsf{E}_{\mathsf{main}} = \mathit{if} \ \Big((\mathsf{check} \to \bigwedge_{i=1}^{i=k} y_i \leftrightarrow \mathsf{E}_i) \wedge (\neg\mathsf{check} \to \bigwedge_{i=1}^{i=h} y_i' \leftrightarrow \mathsf{E}'_i)\Big) \ \mathit{then} \ \mathsf{main} \ \mathit{else} \ \neg\mathsf{main}$

Reversal: $\varphi^R = \{y_1 = \mathsf{E}_1^R, \dots, y_k = \mathsf{E}_k^R\}$
E_i^R is obtained from E_i by converting each offset k in its opposite $-k$.

Fig. 1. Constructions for intersection, union, and reversal

Positive Kleene closure for $\varphi = \{y_1 = \mathsf{E}_1, \dots, y_k = \mathsf{E}_k\}$

$$\varphi^+ = \{y_1 = \mathsf{E}_1^+, \dots, y_k = \mathsf{E}_k^+, \mathsf{wbegin} = \mathsf{E}_{\mathsf{wbegin}}, \mathsf{wend} = \mathsf{E}_{\mathsf{wend}}\}$$

$\mathsf{E}_{\mathsf{wbegin}} = \mathit{if} \ (\mathsf{first} \to \mathsf{wbegin}) \wedge (\mathsf{wbegin} \to \mathsf{wend}[-1|1]) \ \mathit{then} \ \mathsf{wbegin} \ \mathit{else} \ \neg\mathsf{wbegin}$
$\mathsf{E}_{\mathsf{wend}} = \mathit{if} \ (\mathsf{last} \to \mathsf{wend}) \wedge (\mathsf{wend} \to \mathsf{wbegin}[+1|1]) \ \mathit{then} \ \mathsf{wend} \ \mathit{else} \ \neg\mathsf{wend}$

and E_i^+ is obtained from E_i by replacing each stream subexpression $\tau[k|d]$ with $\mathsf{E}_{\tau,k,d}$:

$$\mathsf{E}_{\tau,k,d} = \begin{cases} \mathit{if} \ \bigvee_{j=1}^{j=k} \mathsf{wbegin}[j|1] \ \mathit{then} \ d \ \mathit{else} \ \tau[k|d] & \text{if } k > 0 \\[2mm] \mathit{if} \ \bigvee_{j=1}^{j=-k} \mathsf{wend}[-j|1] \ \mathit{then} \ d \ \mathit{else} \ \tau[k|d] & \text{if } k < 0 \end{cases}$$

Fig. 2. Construction for positive Kleene closure

a decomposition in the given input of the form $\sigma_X \cdot \sigma_X'$ in such a way that $\sigma_X \in \mathcal{L}(\varphi)$ and $\sigma_X' \in \mathcal{L}(\varphi')$. In particular, the output variable wmark assumes the value 1 along all and only the positions of σ_X (the equation for wmark ensures that a Boolean stream for wmark is always in 1^+0^+). Moreover, the equations for the output variables of φ are modified in order to allow to check for a positive offset $k > 0$ of φ and a position j inside σ_X in the guessed decomposition $\sigma_X \cdot \sigma_X'$ of the input, whether $k+j$ is still a position inside σ_X. Analogously, the equations for the output variables of φ' are modified to allow checking for a negative offset $k < 0$ of φ' and a position j inside σ_X' in the guessed decomposition $\sigma_X \cdot \sigma_X'$ of the input, whether $k + j$ is still a position inside σ_X'. □

4 Offline Monitoring for Well-Defined BSRV

In this section, we propose an offline monitoring algorithm for well-defined BSRV based on Theorem 1. The algorithm runs in time linear in the length of the input

$$\varphi = \{y_1 = \mathsf{E}_1, \ldots, y_k = \mathsf{E}_k\} \quad \varphi' = \{y_1' = \mathsf{E}_1', \ldots, y_h' = \mathsf{E}_h'\}$$

Concatenation: $\{y_1, \ldots, y_k\} \cap \{y_1', \ldots, y_h'\} = \emptyset$

$\varphi \cdot \varphi' = \{y_1 = if \text{ wmark } then \ \widetilde{\mathsf{E}}_1 \ else \ y_1, \ldots, y_k = if \text{ wmark } then \ \widetilde{\mathsf{E}}_k \ else \ y_k,$
$y_1' = if \ \neg\text{wmark } then \ \widetilde{\mathsf{E}}_1' \ else \ y_1', \ldots, y_h' = if \ \neg\text{wmark } then \ \widetilde{\mathsf{E}}_h' \ else \ y_h', \text{wmark} = \mathsf{E}_{\text{wmark}}\}$

$\mathsf{E}_{\text{wmark}} = if \ (\text{first} \rightarrow \text{wmark}) \land (\text{last} \rightarrow \neg\text{wmark}) \land (\text{wmark} \rightarrow \text{wmark}[-1|1]) \land$
$(\neg\text{wmark} \rightarrow \neg\text{wmark}[+1|0]) \ then \text{ wmark } else \ \neg\text{wmark}$

$\widetilde{\mathsf{E}}_i$ is obtained from E_i by replacing each stream subexpression $\tau[k|d]$ s.t. $k > 0$ with:

$$if \bigvee_{j=1}^{j=k} \neg\text{wmark}[j|0] \ then \ d \ else \ \tau[k|d]$$

$\widetilde{\mathsf{E}}_i'$ is obtained from E_i' by replacing each stream subexpression $\tau[k|d]$ s.t. $k < 0$ with:

$$if \bigvee_{j=1}^{j=-k} \text{wmark}[-j|1] \ then \ d \ else \ \tau[k|d]$$

Fig. 3. Construction for concatenation

$Monitoring(\varphi, \sigma_X)$ $/^{**}$ φ is a well-defined BSRV and $\mathcal{A}_\varphi = \langle Q, q_0, \delta, F \rangle$ $^{**}/$

$\Lambda \leftarrow \{q_0\}$
for $i = 1$ upto $|\sigma_X|$ **do**
    update $\Lambda \leftarrow \{q \in Q \mid q \in \delta(p, \sigma_X(i)) \text{ for some } p \in \Lambda\}$
    store Λ at position i on the tape
for $i = |\sigma_X|$ downto 1 **do**
    let Λ be the set of states stored at position i on the tape
    if $i = |\sigma_X|$ **then** $p \leftarrow$ the *unique* accepting state in Λ
    else let q be the *unique* state in Λ such that $p \in \delta(q, \sigma_X(i+1))$; update $p \leftarrow q$
    output at position i the main value of p

Fig. 4. Offline monitoring algorithm for well-defined BSRV

---

trace (input streams) and singly exponential in the size of the specification. Additionally, we partially solve a question left open in [8] for the case of BSRV.

Let φ be a BSRV over X and Y, and $\mathcal{A}_\varphi = \langle Q, q_0, \delta, F \rangle$ be the NFA over 2^X accepting $\mathcal{L}(\varphi)$ of Theorem 1. Recall that $Q \setminus \{q_0\}$ is contained in $(A_\perp)^{b(\varphi)} \times A \times (A_\perp)^{f(\varphi)}$, where $A = 2^{X \cup Y}$ and $A_\perp := A \cup \{\perp\}$, and an expanded valuation model of φ is of the form $\pi = q_0, q_1, \ldots, q_k$, where $q_i \in Q \setminus \{q_0\}$ for all $1 \leq i \leq k$. Moreover, the valuation model of φ encoded by π is the sequence of the main values of the states q_i visited by π. By Theorem 1, the set of accepting runs of $\mathcal{A}_\varphi$ over an input σ_X is the set of expanded valuation models of φ encoding the valuation models of φ associated with the input σ_X. Hence, the following holds.

Proposition 2. *A BSRV φ is well-defined if and only if the NFA $\mathcal{A}_\varphi$ is universal and unambiguous.*

The offline monitoring algorithm for well-defined BSRV is given in Fig. 4, where we assume that the input trace σ_X is available on a tape. The algorithm operates in two phases. In the first phase, a forward traversing of the input trace is performed, and the algorithm simulates the unique run over the input σ_X of the deterministic finite state automaton (DFA) that would result from $\mathcal{A}_\varphi$ by the classical powerset construction. Let $\{q_0\}, \Lambda(1), \ldots, \Lambda(|\sigma_X|)$ be the run of this DFA over σ_X. Then, at each step i, the state $\Lambda(i)$ of the run resulting from reading the input symbol $\sigma_X(i)$ is stored in the ith position of the tape. In the second phase, a backward traversing of the input trace is performed, and the algorithm outputs a stream valuation of φ. Since φ is well-defined, by using Proposition 2, we easily deduce that the uniqueness conditions in the second phase of the algorithm are satisfied. Moreover, the sequence of states computed by the algorithm in the second phase is the unique accepting run π of $\mathcal{A}_\varphi$ over σ_X. Therefore, the algorithm outputs the valuation model of φ encoded by π, which is the unique valuation model of φ associated with the input σ_X. Thus, since the size of the NFA $\mathcal{A}_\varphi$ is singly exponential in the size of φ, we obtain the following result.

Theorem 5. *One can construct an offline monitoring algorithm for well-defined BSRV running in time linear in the length of the input trace and singly exponential in the size of the specification. Additionally, the algorithm processes a position of the input trace exactly twice.*

In [8], a syntactical condition for general SRV, called *well-formedness*, is introduced, which can be checked in polynomial time and implies well-definedness. Well-formedness ensures the absence of circular definitions by requiring that a dependency graph of the output variables have not zero-weight cycles. As illustrated in [8], for the restricted class of well-formed SRV, it is possible to construct an offline monitoring algorithm which runs in time linear in the length of the input trace and the size of the specification. Moreover, one can associate to a well-formed SRV φ a parameter $ad(\varphi)$, called *alternation depth* [8], such that the monitoring algorithm processes each position of the input trace exactly $ad(\varphi)+1$ times. An important question left open in [8] is whether for a well-formed SRV φ, it is possible to construct a φ-equivalent SRV whose alternation depth is minimal. Here, we settle partially this question for the class of BSRV. By using the same ideas for constructing the algorithm of Fig. 4, we show that for the class of BSRV, the semantic notion of well-definedness coincides with the syntactical notion of well-formedness (modulo BSRV-equivalence), and the hierarchy of well-formed BSRV induced by the alternation depth collapses to the level 1. In particular, we establish the following result.

Theorem 6. *Given a well-defined BSRV φ, one can build in doubly exponential time a φ-equivalent BSRV which is well-formed and has alternation depth 1.*

5   Decision Problems

We investigate complexity issues for some relevant decision problems on BSRV. In particular, we establish that while checking well-definedness is in EXPTIME, checking for a given BSRV φ and a given subset Z of output variables, whether φ

is well-defined with respect to Z (*generalized well-definedness problem*) is instead EXPSPACE-complete. Our results can be summarized as follows.

Theorem 7. *For BSRV:*

1. *The under-definedness problem is PSPACE-complete, the well-definedness problem is in EXPTIME and at least PSPACE-hard, while the over-definedness problem and the generalized well-definedness problem are both EXPSPACE-complete.*
2. *Checking semantic equivalence is EXPSPACE-complete.*
3. *When interpreted as language recognizers, language emptiness is PSPACE-complete, while language universality, language inclusion, and language equivalence are EXPSPACE-complete.*

Here, we illustrate the upper bounds of Theorem 7(1). We need a preliminary result (Proposition 3). For an NFA $\mathcal{A} = \langle Q, q_0, \delta, F \rangle$, a *state projection of $\mathcal{A}$* is a mapping $\Upsilon : Q \to P$ for some finite set P such that for all $q \in Q$, $\Upsilon(q)$ is computable in logarithmic space (in the size of Q). The mapping Υ can be extended to sequences of states in the obvious way. We say that the NFA $\mathcal{A}$ is *unambiguous with respect to Υ* if for all $w \in \mathcal{L}(\mathcal{A})$ and accepting runs π and π' of $\mathcal{A}$ over w, their projections $\Upsilon(\pi)$ and $\Upsilon(\pi')$ coincide.

Proposition 3. *Given an NFA $\mathcal{A}$ and a state projection Υ of $\mathcal{A}$, checking whether $\mathcal{A}$ is not unambiguous with respect to Υ can be done in NLOGSPACE.*

Upper Bounds of Theorem 7(1). Let φ be a BSRV over X and Y, and $\mathcal{A}_\varphi$ be the NFA of Theorem 1 accepting $\mathcal{L}(\varphi)$ and whose size is *singly exponential* in the size of φ.

Under-definedness: by Theorem 1 and Lemma 1, φ is under-defined iff $\mathcal{A}_\varphi$ is *not* unambiguous. Thus, since $\mathcal{A}_\varphi$ can be constructed on the fly and PSPACE = NPSPACE, by Proposition 3 (with Υ being the identity map), it follows that the under-definedness problem is in PSPACE.

Over-definedness: since $\mathcal{A}_\varphi$ accepts $\mathcal{L}(\varphi)$, φ is over-defined iff $\mathcal{A}_\varphi$ is not universal. Thus, since checking universality for NFA is a well-known PSPACE-complete problem [19], membership in EXPSPACE for checking over-definedness follows.

Well-definedness: it is well-known that checking universality of unambiguous NFA can be done in polynomial time [24]. By Proposition 2, φ is well-defined iff $\mathcal{A}_\varphi$ is universal and unambiguous. Thus, since checking that $\mathcal{A}_\varphi$ is unambiguous can be done in PSPACE (in the size of φ), membership in EXPTIME for checking well-definedness follows.

Generalized Well-definedness: let $Z \subseteq Y$. Recall that the set of non-initial states of $\mathcal{A}_\varphi$ is contained in $(A_\perp)^{b(\varphi)} \times A \times (A_\perp)^{f(\varphi)}$, where $A = 2^{X \cup Y}$ and $A_\perp := A \cup \{\perp\}$. Let Υ_Z be the state projection of $\mathcal{A}_\varphi$ assigning to the initial state q_0 of $\mathcal{A}_\varphi$ q_0 itself, and assigning to each non-initial state $(a_{-b(\varphi)}, \ldots, a_{-1}, a_0, a_1, \ldots, a_{f(\varphi)})$ of $\mathcal{A}_\varphi$ the tuple $(d_{-b(\varphi)}, \ldots, d_{-1}, d_0, d_1, \ldots, d_{f(\varphi)})$, where for all $b(\varphi) \leq i \leq f(\varphi)$, $d_i = a_i$ if $a_i = \perp$, and $d_i = a_i \cap Z$ otherwise. Now, let σ and σ' be two valuation models of φ associated with an input σ_X, and π and π' be the *expanded* valuation models encoding σ and σ', respectively. By construction, it follows that $\Upsilon_Z(\pi) = \Upsilon_Z(\pi')$ iff the restrictions of σ and σ' to Z coincide. By Theorem 1, we obtain that φ is well-defined with respect to Z iff $\mathcal{A}_\varphi$ is unambiguous with respect to Υ_Z and $\mathcal{A}_\varphi$ is universal. Thus, since checking universality for NFA is PSPACE-complete, by Proposition 3, membership in EXPSPACE for checking generalized well-definedness follows.

6   Conclusion

In this paper, we have studied some theoretical problems for the class of Boolean SRV. We have also presented an offline monitoring algorithm for well-defined BSRV that only requires two passes over the dumped trace. An open question is the exact complexity of checking well-definedness for BSRV: it lies somewhere between PSPACE and EXPTIME. Future work includes the theoretical investigation and the development of monitoring algorithms for SRV over richer data types, such as counters and stacks. In particular, the emerging field of symbolic automata and transducers [25]—that extend the classical notions from discrete alphabets to theories handled by solvers—seems very promising to study in the context of SRV, which in turn can extend automata from states and transitions to stream dependencies. The combination of these two extensions has the potential to provide a rich but *tractable* foundation for the runtime verification of values from rich types. Additionally, we are studying the extension to the monitoring of visibly pushdown systems, where SRV is extended to deal with traces containing calls and returns.

Finally, we plan to study the monitorability of well-definedness of specifications. If one cannot determine well-definedness statically, a plausible alternative would be to use a monitor that *assumes* well-definednees in tandem with a monitor that *detects* non-well-definedness (and hence, the incorrectness of the first monitor).

References

1. Barringer, H., Goldberg, A., Havelund, K., Sen, K.: Rule-based runtime verification. In: Steffen, B., Levi, G. (eds.) VMCAI 2004. LNCS, vol. 2937, pp. 44–57. Springer, Heidelberg (2004)
2. Basin, D., Harvan, M., Klaedtke, F., Zălinescu, E.: MONPOLY: Monitoring usage-control policies. In: Khurshid, S., Sen, K. (eds.) RV 2011. LNCS, vol. 7186, pp. 360–364. Springer, Heidelberg (2012)
3. Basin, D., Klaedtke, F., Müller, S.: Policy monitoring in first-order temporal logic. In: Touili, T., Cook, B., Jackson, P. (eds.) CAV 2010. LNCS, vol. 6174, pp. 1–18. Springer, Heidelberg (2010)
4. Bauer, A., Goré, R., Tiu, A.: A first-order policy language for history-based transaction monitoring. In: Leucker, M., Morgan, C. (eds.) ICTAC 2009. LNCS, vol. 5684, pp. 96–111. Springer, Heidelberg (2009)
5. Bauer, A., Leucker, M., Schallhart, C.: Runtime verification for LTL and TLTL. ACM Transactions on Software Engineering and Methodology 20(4), 14 (2011)

6. Berry, G.: The foundations of Esterel. In: Proof, Language, and Interaction: Essays in Honour of Robin Milner, pp. 425–454. MIT Press (2000)
7. Caspi, P., Pouzet, M.: Synchronous Kahn Networks. In: Proc. of ICFP 1996, pp. 226–238. ACM Press (1996)
8. D'Angelo, B., Sankaranarayanan, S., Sánchez, C., Robinson, W., Finkbeiner, B., Sipma, H.B., Mehrotra, S., Manna, Z.: LOLA: Runtime monitoring of synchronous systems. In: Proc. of TIME 2005, pp. 166–174. IEEE CS Press (2005)
9. Eisner, C., Fisman, D., Havlicek, J., Lustig, Y., McIsaac, A., Van Campenhout, D.: Reasoning with temporal logic on truncated paths. In: Hunt Jr., W.A., Somenzi, F. (eds.) CAV 2003. LNCS, vol. 2725, pp. 27–39. Springer, Heidelberg (2003)
10. Finkbeiner, B., Sankaranarayanan, S., Sipma, H.B.: Collecting statistics over runtime executions. ENTCS 70(4), 36–54 (2002)
11. Gautier, T., Le Guernic, P., Besnard, L.: SIGNAL: A declarative language for synchronous programming of real-time systems. In: Kahn, G. (ed.) FPCA 1987. LNCS, vol. 274, pp. 257–277. Springer, Heidelberg (1987)
12. Goodloe, A.E., Pike, L.: Monitoring distributed real-time systems: A survey and future directions. Technical report, NASA Langley Research Center (2010)
13. Halbwachs, N., Caspi, P., Pilaud, D., Plaice, J.: Lustre: a declarative language for programming synchronous systems. In: Proc. of POPL 1987, pp. 178–188. ACM Press (1987)
14. Havelund, K., Goldberg, A.: Verify your runs. In: Meyer, B., Woodcock, J. (eds.) Verified Software. LNCS, vol. 4171, pp. 374–383. Springer, Heidelberg (2008)
15. Havelund, K., Roşu, G.: Synthesizing monitors for safety properties. In: Katoen, J.-P., Stevens, P. (eds.) TACAS 2002. LNCS, vol. 2280, pp. 342–356. Springer, Heidelberg (2002)
16. Laroussinie, F., Markey, N., Schnoebelen, P.: Temporal logic with forgettable past. In: Proc. of LICS 2002, pp. 383–392. IEEE CS Press (2002)
17. Leucker, M., Schallhart, C.: A brief account of runtime verification. The Journal of Logic and Algebraic Programming 78(5), 293–303 (2009)
18. Manna, Z., Pnueli, A.: Temporal Verification of Reactive Systems: Safety. Springer, New York (1995)
19. Meyer, A.R., Stockmeyer, L.J.: The equivalence problem for regular expressions with squaring requires exponential space. In: Proc. of FOCS 1972, pp. 125–129. IEEE CS Press (1972)
20. Pike, L., Goodloe, A., Morisset, R., Niller, S.: Copilot: A hard real-time runtime monitor. In: Barringer, H., et al. (eds.) RV 2010. LNCS, vol. 6418, pp. 345–359. Springer, Heidelberg (2010)
21. Pnueli, A., Zaks, A.: PSL model checking and run-time verification via testers. In: Misra, J., Nipkow, T., Sekerinski, E. (eds.) FM 2006. LNCS, vol. 4085, pp. 573–586. Springer, Heidelberg (2006)
22. Roşu, G., Havelund, K.: Rewriting-based techniques for runtime verification. Autom. Softw. Eng. 12(2), 151–197 (2005)
23. Sen, K., Roşu, G.: Generating optimal monitors for extended regular expressions. ENTCS 89(2), 226–245 (2003)
24. Stearns, R.E., Hunt, H.B.: On the equivalence and containment problems for unambiguous regular expressions, regular grammars and finite automata. SIAM J. Comput. 14(3), 598–611 (1985)
25. Veanes, M., Hooimeijer, P., Livshits, B., Molnar, D., Bjrner, N.: Symbolic finite state transducers: algorithms and applications. In: Proc. of POPL 2012, pp. 137–150. ACM (2012)

Portable Runtime Verification with Smartphones and Optical Codes*

Kim Lavoie, Corentin Leplongeon, Simon Varvaressos,
Sébastien Gaboury, and Sylvain Hallé

Laboratoire d'informatique formelle
Département d'informatique et de mathématique
Université du Québec à Chicoutimi, Canada
shalle@acm.org

Abstract. We describe a prototype architecture for the runtime monitoring of Java programs using a smartphone. An online tool can produce an AspectJ file which, when woven with the program to be monitored and executed, instantiates a GUI window where XML events from the program's execution are output in the form of QR codes. We illustrate the feasibility of this approach by monitoring runtime properties on the execution of a video game by pointing a handheld Android phone at the game's screen and obtaining realtime feedback.

1 Introduction

Instrumentation forms one of the two major parts of a runtime verification architecture. While the general goal of instrumentation is generally well-understood (producing events out of the execution of a system to be processed by a monitor), the techniques advocated in past works vary widely, ranging from the manual insertion of code snippets to aspect-oriented solutions where event-generating code, and even the monitor itself, is automatically inserted in a program through a process called *weaving*. However, our past experience with industrial partners revealed a general reluctance for such an intrusive technique, where complex and untrusted monitoring code interferes with the normal execution of the program in possibly unforseen ways. This observation led us to seek instrumentation techniques that would take events out of the program as fast as possible, and to perform the bulk of the processing in a completely independent process.

Our initial solution involved a template-based instrumentation on the program side, where events were carried to the monitor as XML strings through a pipe or a TCP socket [5]. While at first sight this approach provides a reasonable separation between the monitor and the program, we discovered that it still presents a risk of "crosstalk" unacceptable in many application domains. Using a pipe forces the monitor to reside on the same computer as the program to monitor; moreover, if no monitor is present to consume events from the pipe (or fails to retrieve them fast enough), the pipe eventually reaches its maximal size, after which any write operation on the program side becomes *blocking* (i.e. halts the execution of the program) until enough space becomes available.

---

* With financial support from the Natural Sciences and Engineering Research Council of Canada (NSERC).

B. Bonakdarpour and S.A. Smolka (Eds.): RV 2014, LNCS 8734, pp. 80–84, 2014.

Using a TCP connection presents the same problems; moreover, the bidirectional nature of such a connection presents too high a risk of attacks on the program to monitor. Finally, in both cases some software setup is required to hook up the monitor to the program: defining IP addresses, pipe names, ports, etc., which again represents too much coupling in many scenarios.

In this paper, we explore an alternate instrumentation solution aimed at providing absolute isolation of the program from the monitor, while at the same time minimizing the need for establishing a link between both. We achieve this through the use of so-called "QR" codes, which are two-dimensional barcodes whose content can be read through purely optical means. This way, the communication channel between the program and the monitor is strictly unidirectional and non-blocking. In addition, monitoring boils down to pointing the device at the program's display and starting to capture the stream of events, without requiring the setup of any specific link.

The use of smartphones for runtime monitoring has already been suggested in a few works [1–3]; in this context, a monitor witnesses the execution *of* some process running inside the phone, in particular for enforcing security and usage policies. We rather propose a method for runtime monitoring *with* an Android phone —that is, the source of events is not the execution of the phone itself, which is rather used as an event-harvesting and processing device.

2 Architecture

In the proposed setup, the instrumentation on the program side instantiates a GUI window where XML events from the program's execution are output in the form of QR codes. A smartphone application, using the device's embedded camera, captures these codes and converts them back into events that are then fed to an onboard runtime monitor, or are simply relayed through a TCP connection to a monitor instance residing on some other computer.

2.1 Instrumentation

The first part of the architecture requires producing XML events from the execution of the program and outputting them as optical QR codes. The generation and display of these codes is handled by a custom-made Java library called Gyro Gearloose,[1] which provides a GUI window to which arbitrary character strings can be sent. The library uses in the background the ZXing framework[2] to convert these strings into QR codes and display them in the window in real time.

To streamline the instrumentation of an application, an online tool[3] takes as input a declaration of the method calls to trap, along with the XML template to create from each method call, and transforms it automatically into an executable AspectJ file responsible for instantiating a window where QR codes will be displayed, and declaring

---

[1] https://github.com/sylvainhalle/GyroGearloose

[2] https://github.com/zxing/zxing/

[3] http://beepbeep.sourceforge.net/qr-monitor/formatter.php

appropriate pointcuts to intercept the relevant method calls —each provoking the update of the displayed code in the window depending on the XML contents generated from the event. Figure 1 shows an example of an input specification. The PROTOTYPES section of the specification indicates what method calls should be trapped by the instrumentation, by declaring their prototypes (including argument names and types, if any). Immediately following the prototype declaration is an XML event template, which defines the contents and structure of the XML events that will be generated from every call to the method.

This event is free form; one can use arbitrary element names and whatever structure is deemed appropriate, including nested elements if necessary. Everything that does not appear between braces is copied verbatim. The portion between braces, however, is Java code. When creating the XML structure upon a method call, the formatter replaces it by the result of evaluating the enclosed expression. This expression can involve any of the arguments from the method call; in addition, the instance of the object that has been called can also be referred to using the keyword this.

Weaving the resulting AspectJ file with the application to monitor results in a program that outputs its event through QR codes. Figure 1 shows an example of an application instrumented in such a way.

```
PROTOTYPES
void Mario.jump(int height,
  Authorization auth);

<call>
  <method>withdraw</method>
  <id>
   {auth.getId()}
  </id>
  <amount>
   {auth.getAmount()}
  </amount>
<call>
```

Fig. 1. An example of an instrumentation specification (left), and an instrumented version of *Infinite Mario Bros.* outputting its XML events as QR codes in a satellite window.

2.2 Monitoring

The second part of our architecture consists of an apparatus to receive events as QR codes, decode them and feed them to a runtime monitor. We realized this part as an application running in an Android smartphone, using the device's camera to capture QR codes displayed onscreen, and convert them back into XML strings. Figure 2b shows the basic interface for this application.

This process is again separate from the monitoring itself; events can be relayed in their string form to any runtime monitor through a simple TCP socket, and in particular the monitor need not to reside directly on the phone. Nevertheless, we retrieved the code for the BeepBeep runtime monitor [4], given its ability to read XML events from a socket, and adapted it to run inside the Android operating system. In particular, we created a simple interface allowing a user to pick temporal logic properties to monitor (selected from text files copied onto the device); moreover, once the monitor's state switches from the "inconclusive" state to either "true" or "false", a message is sent in the phone's notification area, as is shown in Figure 2a and 2c.

Fig. 2. Screenshots from the prototype smartphone application. (a) The main monitor window displaying basic stats about the monitor's execution, and allowing a user to select the LTL-FO$^+$ properties to monitor. (b) The video capture window, where a user points at QR codes displayed on an external device to capture events. (c) The phone's notification area, where status updates about the monitor are displayed (at the bottom).

3 Experimental Results

We assessed the feasibility of this approach by testing it on various randomly-genrated traces of events for sample LTL properties. Our reference phone is a Sony Xperia Z running Android version 4.3 Jelly Bean. The phone's camera was set at a relatively low resolution of 800×600 pixels. The telephone was held directly in the user's hand (i.e. was not resting on any kind of stable surface), who pointed it at a code occupying a square space of 300 pixels on the computer's screen. Although the code reader and the monitor are separate processes which can run on two different devices linked through a standard TCP connection, in the experiment both were run inside the same phone and communicated through a local socket.

Table 1 shows the time required to process one frame of video containing a QR code, for varying data densities. Unsurprisingly, running times both for decoding and processing of events by the monitor are noticeably slower on a telephone than on a desktop computer. However, it is interesting to note that the bottleneck of the architecture is not the monitor, but rather the processing of video frames back into QR codes. On our reference telephone, the ZXing library takes on average 106 ms to process a video frame, while the monitor, in the worst case, was clocked at 12 ms to process the event extracted from the QR code.

Table 1. Experimental results for the decoding of video frames and the processing of XML events inside a smartphone

Code size (b)	Decoding time (ms)	Success rate		Events	Cumulative time (ms)
110	100	99%		1	3
160	106	95%		10	42
210	104	99%		100	188
260	105	91%		1000	2156
310	105	58%		5000	24848
360	105	80%		10000	63302
410	111	76%		20000	240657

Another element worthy of mention is the decoding rate, which varied from near-perfect to about 60%. It shall be noted that this figure indicates the number of *video frames* where a code could successfully be read; however, as our instrumented system produces events at a slow rate (a few events per second), each distinct code had multiple frames to be decoded. As a matter of fact, in our experiments not a single event has ever been missed.

4 Conclusion and Future Work

Early experiments on the use of analog means to transmit data from the execution of a program can be put to good use for runtime monitoring. This opens the way to various applications, such as the realtime monitoring of video games or other entertainment software by simply filming a portion of the television screen using a separate device. Future work includes the development of an efficient binary format to transmit event data in a compact form, with signalling and redundancy to compensate for poor capture conditions.

References

1. Bauer, A., Küster, J.-C., Vegliach, G.: Runtime verification meets Android security. In: Goodloe, A.E., Person, S. (eds.) NFM 2012. LNCS, vol. 7226, pp. 174–180. Springer, Heidelberg (2012)
2. Falcone, Y., Currea, S., Jaber, M.: Runtime verification and enforcement for Android applications with RV-Droid. In: Qadeer, S., Tasiran, S. (eds.) RV 2012. LNCS, vol. 7687, pp. 88–95. Springer, Heidelberg (2013)
3. Fritz, C., Arzt, S., Rasthofer, S., Bodden, E., Bartel, A., Klein, J., le Traon, Y., Octeau, D., McDaniel, P.: Flowdroid: Precise context, flow, field, object-sensitive and lifecycle-aware taint analysis for android apps. In: Proceedings of the 35th ACM SIGPLAN Conference on Programming Language Design and Implementation (PLDI) (to appear, June 2014)
4. Hallé, S., Villemaire, R.: Runtime enforcement of web service message contracts with data. IEEE T. Services Computing 5(2), 192–206 (2012)
5. Varvaressos, S., Lavoie, K., Blondin Massé, A., Gaboury, S., Hallé, S.: Automated bug finding in video games: A case study for runtime monitoring. In: Robinson, B., Williams, L., Wohlin, C. (eds.) ICST. IEEE (accepted for publication 2014)

Robust Consistency Checking for Modern Filesystems

Kuei Sun, Daniel Fryer, Dai Qin, Angela Demke Brown, and Ashvin Goel

University of Toronto

Abstract. We describe our approach to building a runtime file system checker for the emerging Linux Btrfs file system. Such checkers verify the consistency of file system metadata update operations before they are committed to disk, thus preventing corrupted updates from becoming durable. The consistency checks in Btrfs are complex and need to be expressed clearly so that they can be reasoned about and implemented reliably, thus we propose writing the checks declaratively. This approach reduces the complexity of the checks, ensures their independence, and helps identify the correct abstractions in the checker. It also shows how the checker can be made robust against arbitrary file system corruption.

Keywords: Runtime file system checker, Btrfs, Datalog, Consistency invariants.

1 Introduction

A *runtime* file-system consistency checker verifies the consistency of file-system update operations before they are committed to disk. File system metadata corruption can thus be detected *before* it propagates to disk, which minimizes data loss. In contrast, traditional offline checkers [1,4] require the file system to be taken offline to be checked for possible corruption, which can incur significant downtime [5]. Recon [3] enforces the consistency of the Linux Ext3 file system at runtime by checking that metadata updates conform to a set of rules called *consistency invariants*. These invariants are expressed in terms of the file system data structures, which are inferred outside the file system at the block layer using *metadata interpretation*, similar to semantically smart disks [6].

We describe the challenges with designing and building a robust, accurate and complete runtime checker for the Linux Btrfs file system. Since Btrfs is still under active development, a runtime checker that limits the damage caused by bugs in the file system software can both serve as a powerful debugging tool and help encourage adoption of the new file system. Compared to Ext3, Btrfs uses many more file system data structures with vastly complex relationships, which complicate both the metadata interpretation and the consistency invariants considerably. Thus, it is of paramount importance that consistency invariants for Btrfs are *expressed* clearly and concisely so that they can be reasoned about and implemented reliably.

We use a declarative language to express the Btrfs consistency invariants, which is similar in spirit to Gunawi et al.'s [4] offline consistency checker written in SQL. This approach makes it easier to reason about the runtime checker's correctness in three ways. First, each consistency invariant can be written as a set of declarative statements and run independently of the other invariants. Second, the declarative style helps to identify the appropriate abstractions for representing file system metadata updates; the

B. Bonakdarpour and S.A. Smolka (Eds.): RV 2014, LNCS 8734, pp. 85–91, 2014.

conceptual invariants are written as clearly as possible, and the metadata is interpreted accordingly. Last, the declarative approach clarified two distinct categories of invariants: the first expresses constraints on structural properties of the metadata (e.g., bounds checking) and the second expresses semantic properties (e.g., the agreement between directory entries and inode link counts).

2   Robust Consistency Checking

Our Btrfs runtime consistency checker has two goals: 1) it should detect all consistency violations, and 2) it should work correctly and predictably in the presence of arbitrary file system corruption failures. We meet these goals with two design principles. First, the semantic invariants must be written declaratively and concisely, making it easier to reason about their correctness. Second, the file system's structural invariants should be checked before performing any semantic checks so that the latter can depend on the structural integrity of the file system.

2.1   Abstractions for Runtime Checking

Here we provide an overview of how invariants are checked in a runtime file system checker. Invariant checks are expressed in terms of changes to file system objects such as directories, inodes and extents, but they may also involve querying the state of objects that have not changed. The checking operation verifies that when the logical file system changes are applied to consistent, pre-transaction file system state, they will result in consistent, post-transaction file system state.

Invariant checks are performed using two abstractions. The first is the *change record*, which captures any modifications to file system objects, such as the addition of a new object, an update to an existing object, or the removal of an object in a transaction. For example, a change record for Btrfs can be expressed as: change(TREE, ID, FIELD, OLD, NEW). Here, TREE is the Btrfs B-tree within which the object resides, while ID is the unique identifier of the object that is being changed (e.g., a Btrfs key for an inode). The TREE and ID uniquely identify Btrfs objects. The FIELD is a specific part of the object (e.g., inode size). Finally, OLD and NEW are the old and new values of the corresponding field.

The second abstraction is the query primitive, which is used to access objects or object fields that may or may not have changed in a transaction, and thus may not appear as change records. The primitives return the most recent version of the object, from either the checking framework's internal caches or the disk. There are two types of primitives, query() for retrieving an object by key, and prev()/next() for finding the previous or next Btrfs key in a tree, as shown in Figure 1.

2.2   Expressing Invariants

Btrfs is a highly complex file system with correspondingly complex consistency properties. These properties are hard to extract from the C source code of btrfsck, the file

```
% the btrfs key for an extent is [start, extent_item, size]
violation(6, TREE_ID, k(EXTENT, extent_item, SIZE)) :-
    add(TREE_ID, k(EXTENT, extent_item, SIZE)),
    prev(TREE_ID, k(EXTENT, extent_item, SIZE),
        k(EXTENT_PREV, extent_item, SIZE_PREV)),
    EXTENT < EXTENT_PREV + SIZE_PREV.

% the underscore '_' is a "don't care" or wildcard variable
violation(6, TREE_ID, k(EXTENT, extent_item, SIZE)) :-
    add(TREE_ID, k(EXTENT, extent_item, SIZE)),
    next(TREE_ID, k(EXTENT, extent_item, SIZE),
        k(EXTENT_NEXT, extent_item, _)),
    EXTENT_NEXT < EXTENT + SIZE.
```

Fig. 1. Btrfs invariant "If a new extent item is added, it must not overlap previous or next extents"

system checker for Btrfs, because they are implemented piecemeal and intermingled with the checker's metadata interpretation code. When we converted the consistency properties to their corresponding runtime invariants and implemented them in C, we found that it was hard to reason about the correctness of these invariants because their implementation was complex, with many corner cases.

Instead, we chose to express consistency invariants in Datalog, a declarative logic programming language [2]. Datalog programs consist of statements that are expressed in terms of relations, represented as a database of facts and rules. Rules take the form of *conclusion* ⊢ *premise*, where *premise* consists of one or more predicates joined by conjunction (comma) or disjunction (semicolon). We express the change records generated from a file system transaction as Datalog facts. Semantic invariants are statements that must hold true for a consistent file system. In Datalog, we negate these invariants to reach the conclusion that an invariant has been violated. For example, for an invariant $A \Rightarrow B$, the corresponding Datalog statement is *violation* ⊢ A, ¬B where A is a condition which will trigger the check B. The predicate A looks for a change in the file system by matching on the attributes of a change record. The predicate B can match change records or invoke primitives to access unmodified objects.

Figure 1 shows the Datalog invariant that checks for extent overlap. The add(TREE, ID) clause looks for an extent_item object with the Btrfs key ID that has been added to the file system and binds the TREE_ID, EXTENT and SIZE variables to its values. The prev() and next() clauses are primitives that query the file system state and bind the previous and next items in the tree to their second argument, respectively. We need a query in this case because the adjacent extents may not have changed, and thus may not be available as change records. The final clause checks for overlap between the new extent and the previous or next extents returned by the primitives. When an extent does not have a previous or next extent, the relevant query will fail, indicating that the invariant has not been violated. Note that this invariant is independent of the metadata interpretation code and other consistency invariants, making it easier to reason about.

2.3   Checking Structure before Semantics

Our second goal is to ensure that the checker works predictably in the presence of arbitrary file system failures. To do so, we need to ensure that the three components of the checker (metadata interpretation, query primitives, and invariant checking) are robust to metadata corruption. Invariant checking operates on change records generated by metadata interpretation and uses query primitives. Hence, its robustness depends on the first two components. Both metadata interpretation and query primitives access the current file system state, including the possibly corrupt metadata blocks that need to be checked. Thus, these components must perform careful validation.

Metadata interpretation requires checks to ensure that file system data structures are correctly typed, so that they can be interpreted correctly (e.g., these checks will prevent following a stray or corrupt pointer). In addition to correct typing, the primitives, which take an identifier as input, need to operate on the data structure associated with this identifier. These requirements lead to three invariants that need to be checked in order:

Type Safety: Type safety ensures that interpretation of updated metadata is robust to data corruption. Consider a query primitive query(TREE, ID, VALUE) that binds VALUE to a given object with identifier ID within tree TREE. Here ID incorporates the type of the object (e.g., the type in the Btrfs key). Type safety ensures that the object bound to VALUE will be of the same type as that specified in ID. The metadata interpretation code will therefore operate on correctly typed objects. Type safety is hard to enforce dynamically because file system data structures do not usually provide type information (e.g., a tag associated with each type). Even if they did, it could have been corrupted, possibly to another known type. Instead, we ensure type safety by validating or range checking all primitive data types that are accessed during metadata interpretation. For example, absolute disk pointers need to lie within the file system partition, while extent-relative pointers must lie within the extent. Similarly, enumerated values (enum in C) need to be valid instances, and any length fields in structures must lie within expected bounds. If these checks fail, we raise a type-safety violation.

Reachability Invariants: The query primitives require more than type safety. For example, query(TREE, ID, VALUE) would not return an existing object that has been misplaced in a B-tree, because it assumes that keys are ordered (otherwise it would need to perform an expensive full tree search). In Btrfs, we enforce reachability by checking that a parent points to the correct child node, and keys are sorted correctly. Reachability invariants also ensure that primitives will not encounter an infinite loop in the B-tree.

Uniqueness Invariants: The primitives expect that all objects are uniquely identified by an identifier. If multiple objects have the same identity several problems can arise. First, the primitives may not provide such duplicate objects deterministically, which could lead to invariant violations that are hard to analyze, or worse, allow corruption to propagate to disk. Second, duplicate change records may be generated (e.g., two objects with the same identity are modified), but since Datalog ignores duplicate facts, only one of the changes would be checked. We check reachability before uniqueness, because if an object is reachable, it is easy to test for uniqueness by first searching for the object.

```
1. nr_items != 0 && nr_items < PTRS_PER_BLOCK
2. p.ptr[i].key == c.ptr[0].key
3. p.ptr[i].blockptr == c.header.bytenr
4. p.ptr[i].generation == c.header.generation
5. ptr[i].key < ptr[i+1].key
```

Fig. 2. The structural invariants on an internal B-tree node in Btrfs (p and c are parent and child)

```
violation(16, TREE, k(INODE_NR, dir_item, CRC)) :-
    new(TREE, k(INODE_NR, dir_item, CRC), type, DIR_ITEM_TYPE),
    query(TREE, k(INODE_NR, dir_item, CRC), location, LOCATION),
    not(query(TREE, LOCATION, f(mode, s_ifmt), INODE_FILE_TYPE),
    DIR_ITEM_TYPE =:= INODE_FILE_TYPE).
```

Fig. 3. Btrfs invariant "Directory entry type is the same as the type of the inode"

After the three types of structural invariants have been checked, we are assured that query(TREE, ID, VALUE) will bind VALUE to the object associated with ID. At this point, the semantic invariants can depend on well-formed change records being generated (even though their contents may be corrupt) and the primitives working correctly.

Figure 2 shows the five structural invariants that we check for B-tree internal nodes. An internal node consists of a header and an array of key pointers. The header contains the number of key pointers in the node (nr_items), the location of the node on disk (bytenr), and the generation number of the node. A key pointer (ptr[]) contains a Btrfs key, the location of the node pointed to by the key (blockptr) and the generation of the pointed-to node. Invariant 1 is a type-safety check on the key pointer array. Invariants 2 to 4 are reachability invariants that verify that the parent points to the correct child node. Invariant 5 checks that all keys in a valid B-tree node must be monotonically increasing, a requirement that provides both reachability and uniqueness. Together, Invariants 2-5 ensure that B-tree items are ordered correctly. Similar structural invariants exist for B-tree leaf nodes. The file system metadata in the leaf nodes also has additional structural invariants such as type safety requirements for all data types.

A simple example shows the need to check structural invariants before semantic ones. Figure 3 shows the Btrfs invariant that checks that a directory entry's file type is the same as the type of the inode to which it points (e.g., both are directories or both are files). The new predicate returns the file type in a changed directory item. Suppose while creating a directory, the file system creates a directory entry and mistakenly creates two inodes with the same inode number, one of which has the file type. The second query primitive in Figure 3 (within the not clause), which returns the type of the inode, would match the two inode change records. However, the INODE_TYPE value that is bound depends on the Datalog engine, so the corruption may not be detected.

Semantic invariants can be made simpler when structural invariants are checked first, because they can depend on structural correctness. The semantic invariants can also be checked independently of each other, because the correctness of the primitives has been established by the structural invariants, rather than by the order in which semantic invariants are checked. Finally, this approach raises structural violations as early as possible, thus providing more accurate debugging information.

```
violation(12, TREE_ID, k(INODE_NUMBER, TYPE, OFFSET)) :-
    delete(TREE_ID, k(INODE_NUMBER, inode_item, _)),
    file_tree(TREE_ID),
    query(TREE_ID, k(INODE_NUMBER, TYPE, OFFSET)).
violation(12 , TREE_ID , k( INODE_NUMBER , TYPE , OFFSET)) :-
    add(TREE_ID, k( INODE_NUMBER , TYPE , OFFSET)),
    file_tree(TREE_ID), TYPE \= inode_item,
    not(query(TREE_ID, k(INODE_NUMBER, inode_item, 0))).
```

Fig. 4. Invariant 12: An inode item must exist for every distinct objectid in a file system tree

3   Experiences with Invariants

The declarative approach allows the invariants in our runtime checker to match the programmer's intent, enhancing our confidence in the correctness of the implementation. The programmer can focus on pattern matching, without worrying about the correctness of other code such as memory management. We share three examples illustrating the benefits of a declarative approach over an imperative one.

Invariant 12, shown in Figure 4, can be simply stated as "If an inode is removed, ensure that no objects with that inode number remain in the tree. If an item is added, and it's not an inode, verify that a corresponding inode exists." The Datalog invariant reflects this statement in two rules, each written in 4 lines. The corresponding implementation in C consists of 45 lines, spread across several locations.

Declarative invariants also support rapid prototyping. The Btrfs directory metadata includes Btrfs items that map the file name to an object id (i.e., inode number) and two indexes for fast lookup and iterating over all entries; each inode stores back references to all the directory entries pointing to it. The invariant that checks the consistency of the directory entries, the indexes and the back references is complicated. Its C implementation is spread in 13 locations, 1 for initializing hash tables, 4 for initializing data structures based on the different change records, and 8 for invariant checking based on different hash tables. As our understanding of the invariant evolved, significant amounts of the C code needed to be re-written. We found it simpler to reason about the invariant in Datalog, and then reimplement the equivalent version in C. The final Datalog invariant consists of 45 lines, while just the rewrite of the C invariant added 250 lines.

Fixing bugs in invariants is also easier in Datalog. Our original understanding was that all the data extents in a file must be contiguous, however, we learned that Btrfs files can have discontiguous extents beyond their logical file size. The fix for this invariant required adding a single line of Datalog to check if the offset was less than the size. The corresponding fix took roughly 20 lines (and several hours) to implement in C.

4   Conclusions

We have designed and implemented a declarative online file system checker for Btrfs, a modern file system that supports a rich set of features. The most significant challenge lies in reasoning about the correctness of the checker in the face of arbitrary file system corruption failures. A key takeaway is that the invariants should be expressed as concisely and intuitively as possible, using a declarative language such as Datalog. The rest of the checker, such as the metadata interpretation, should then be designed to support the invariants. This approach makes prototyping invariants and fixing bugs easier, significantly enhancing our confidence in their correctness. We also identified the need to check structural invariants before semantic invariants, so that arbitrary file system structural violations are caught early, and the semantic invariants can depend on the structural integrity of the file system.

References

1. Carreira, J.C.M., Rodrigues, R., Candea, G., Majumdar, R.: Scalable testing of file system checkers. In: Proc. of the 7th EuroSys, pp. 239–252 (2012)
2. Ceri, S., Gottlob, G., Tanca, L.: What you always wanted to know about datalog (and never dared to ask). IEEE Transactions on Knowledge and Data Engineering 1(1), 146–166 (1989)
3. Fryer, D., Sun, K., Mahmood, R., Cheng, T., Benjamin, S., Goel, A., Brown, A.D.: Recon: Verifying file system consistency at runtime. ACM Trans. on Storage 8(4), 15:1–15:29 (2012)
4. Gunawi, H.S., Rajimwale, A., Arpaci-Dusseau, A.C., Arpaci-Dusseau, R.H.: SQCK: A declarative file system checker. In: Proc. of the 8th USENIX OSDI (December 2008)
5. Henson, V., van de Ven, A., Gud, A., Brown, Z.: Chunkfs: Using divide-and-conquer to improve file system reliability and repair. In: Proc. of the 2nd HotDep (2006)
6. Sivathanu, M., Prabhakaran, V., Popovici, F.I., Denehy, T.E., Arpaci-Dusseau, A.C., Arpaci-Dusseau, R.H.: Semantically-smart disk systems. In: Proc. the 2nd FAST, pp. 73–88 (2003)

On the Number of Opinions Needed
for Fault-Tolerant Run-Time Monitoring
in Distributed Systems[*]

Pierre Fraigniaud[1,**], Sergio Rajsbaum[2,***], and Corentin Travers[3,†]

[1] CNRS and U. Paris Diderot, France
Pierre.Fraigniaud@liafa.univ-paris-diderot.fr
[2] Instituto de Matemáticas, UNAM, D.F. 04510, Mexico
rajsbaum@im.unam.mx
[3] CNRS and U. of Bordeaux, France
travers@labri.fr

Abstract. Decentralized runtime monitoring involves a set of monitors observing the behavior of system executions with respect to some correctness property. It is generally assumed that, as soon as a violation of the property is revealed by any of the monitors at runtime, some recovery code can be executed for bringing the system back to a legal state. This implicitly assumes that each monitor produces a binary opinion, true or false, and that the recovery code is launched as soon as one of these opinions is equal to false. In this paper, we formally prove that, in a failure-prone asynchronous computing model, there are correctness properties for which there is no such decentralized monitoring. We show that there exist some properties which, in order to be monitored in a wait-free decentralized manner, inherently require that the monitors produce a number of opinions larger than two. More specifically, our main result is that, for every k, $1 \le k \le n$, there exists a property that requires at least k opinions to be monitored by n monitors. We also present a corresponding distributed monitor using at most $k + 1$ opinions, showing that our lower bound is nearly tight.

1   Introduction

Runtime verification is concerned with monitoring software and hardware system executions. It is used after deployment of the system for ensuring reliability, safety, and security, and for providing fault containment and recovery. Its essential objective is to determine, at any point in time, whether the system is

---

[*] All authors are supported in part by the CONACYT-CNRS ECOS Nord M12M01 research grant.
[**] Additional support from the ANR project DISPLEXITY, and from the INRIA project GANG.
[***] Additional support from UNAM-PAPIIT and LAISLA.
[†] Additional support from ANR project DISPLEXITY.

B. Bonakdarpour and S.A. Smolka (Eds.): RV 2014, LNCS 8734, pp. 92–107, 2014.

in a legal or illegal state, with respect to some specification. Consider a distributed system whose execution is observed by one or several monitors. Passing messages to a *central* monitor at every event leads to severe communication and computation overhead. Therefore, recent contributions [6,9,27] on runtime verification of distributed systems focused on *decentralized* monitoring, where a set of n monitors observe the behavior of the system. As soon as a violation of the legality of the execution is revealed by any of these monitors at runtime, recovery code can be executed for bringing the system back to a legal state. For example, the recovery code can reboot the system, or release its resources. This framework implicitly assumes that each monitor i produces a binary *opinion* $o_i \in \{true, false\}$, and that the recovery code is launched as soon as one of these opinions is equal to false. In this paper, we formally prove that, in a crash-failure prone asynchronous wait-free computing model [4], there are correctness properties for which such decentralized monitoring does not exist, even if we let the number of opinions grow to an arbitrary constant $k \geq 2$.

Let us consider the following motivating example arising often in practice [8], of a system in which *requests* are sent by clients, and *acknowledged* by servers. The system is in a legal state if and only if (1) all requests have been acknowledged, and (2) every received acknowledgement corresponds to a previously sent request. Each monitor i is aware of a subset R_i of requests that has been received by the servers, and a subset A_i of acknowledgements that has been sent by the servers. To verify legality of the system, each monitor i may communicate with other monitors in order to produce some opinion o_i. In the traditional setting of decentralized monitoring mentioned in the previous paragraph, it is required that the monitors produce opinions $o_i \in \{true, false\}$ such that, whenever the system is not in a legal state, at least one monitor produces the opinion false.

In runtime monitoring, a correctness property is described by a formula in some temporal logic. In this paper, we abstract away the logic, and directly specify the property by the set of *legal* configurations of the system, that we call a *distributed language*, denoted by $\mathcal{L}$. For instance, in the request-acknowledgement example above, $\mathcal{L}$ is the set of all configurations $\{(r_i, a_i), i \in I\}$ such that $\cup_{i \in I} r_i = \cup_{i \in I} a_i$, where $I \subseteq [1, n]$. Indeed, this language is specifying that all observed requests have been acknowledged, and every observed acknowledgement corresponds to a previously sent request. The monitors must produce opinions enabling to distinguish the legal configurations, i.e., those in $\mathcal{L}$, from the illegal ones. In order to make up their opinions, the monitors are able to communicate among themselves, so that each monitor can potentially collect system observations of other monitors. Since we are mostly interested in lower bounds, we ask very little from the monitors, and simply require that, for any pair (C, C') of configurations with $C \in \mathcal{L}$ and $C' \notin \mathcal{L}$, the *multiset* of opinions produced by the monitors given the legal configuration C must be different from the multiset of opinions given the illegal configuration C'.

In the centralized setting, more than two logical values may be required to avoid evaluating prematurely the correctness of a property that cannot be decided solely based on a prefix of the execution, like request-acknowledgement.

Hence [2,7] extended linear temporal logic (LTL) to logics with three values (e.g., {true, false, inconclusive}). More recently, it was recognised [8] that even three values are not sufficient to monitor some properties, and thus extensions of LTL with four logical values (e.g., {true, false, probably true, probably false}) were introduced. In this paper we argue that, in an asynchronous failure-prone decentralized setting, even four values may not be sufficient.

Our results. We consider decentralized monitoring in the *wait-free* setting [4]. (See Section 2 for details about this model, and for the reasons why we chose it). Our main result is a lower bound on the number of opinions to be produced by a runtime decentralized monitor in an asynchronous system where monitors may crash. This lower bound depends solely on the language, i.e., on the correctness property being monitored. More specifically, we prove that, for any positive integer n, and for any k, $1 \leq k \leq n$, there exists a distributed language requiring monitors to produce at least k distinct opinions in a system with n monitors. This result holds whatever the system does with the opinions produced by the monitors. That is, our lower bound on the number of opinions is inherent to the language itself — and not to the way the opinions are handled in order to launch the recovery code to be executed in case the system misbehaves.

The number of opinions required to runtime monitor languages in a decentralized manner is actually tightly connected to an intrinsic property of each language: its *alternation number*. This parameter essentially captures the number of times a sequence of configurations of the system alternates between legal and illegal. Our main result states that, for any k, $1 \leq k \leq n$, there exists a language with alternation number k which requires at least k opinions to be monitored by n monitors. This bound is essentially tight, as we also design a distributed monitor which, for any k, $1 \leq k \leq n$, and any distributed language $\mathcal{L}$ with alternation number k, monitors $\mathcal{L}$ using at most $k + 1$ opinions in systems with n monitors.

Technically, in this paper, we establish a bridge between, on the one hand, runtime verification, and, on the other hand, distributed computability. Thanks to this bridge, we could prove our lower bound using arguments from (elementary) algebraic topology. More specifically, our impossibility result for 2 opinions is obtained using graph-connectivity techniques sharing similarities with the FLP impossibility result for consensus [15], while our general impossibility result uses higher-dimensional techniques similar to those used in set agreement impossibility results e.g. [22,23].

As far as we know, this paper is the first one studying necessary conditions for monitoring distributed systems with failures.

Related work. The main focus in the literature is on sequential runtime verification. The monitors are event-triggered [24], where every change in the state of the system triggers the monitor for analysis. There is work also in time-triggered monitoring [10], where the monitor samples the state of the program at regular time intervals. Parallel monitoring has been addressed in [20] to some extent by focusing on low-level memory architecture to facilitate communication between application and analysis threads. The concept of separating the monitor from the monitored program is considered in, e.g., [28]. Later, [9] uses a specialized parallel architecture (GPU), to implement runtime formal verification in a parallel fashion. Efficient automatic signaling monitoring in multi-core processors is considered in [13].

Closer to our setting is decentralized monitoring. In sequential runtime verification one has to monitor the requirement based on a single behavioral trace, assumed to be collected by some global observer. A central observer basically resembles classical LTL monitoring. In contrast, in decentralized monitoring, there are several partial behavioural traces, each one collected at a component of the system. Intuitively, each trace corresponds to the view that the component has of the execution. In decentralized LTL monitoring [6] a formula ϕ is decomposed into local formulas, so monitor i evaluates locally ϕ_i, and emits a boolean-valued opinion. In our terminology, an "and interpretation" is used. That is, it is assumed a global violation can always be detected locally by a process. In addition, it is assumed the set of local monitors communicate over a synchronous bus with a global clock. The goal is to keep the communication among monitors minimal. In [26] the focus is in monitoring safety properties of a distributed program's execution, also using an "and interpretation". The decentralized monitoring algorithm is based on formulae written in a variant of past time LTL. For the specific case of relaxed memory models, [11] presents a technique for monitoring that a program has no executions violating sequential consistency. There is also work [19] that targets physically distributed systems, but does not focus on distributed monitoring.

To the best of our knowledge, the effects of asynchrony and failures in a decentralized monitoring setting were considered for the first time in [17]. We extend this previous work in two ways. First, we remove the restriction that the monitors can produce only two opinions. Second, [17] investigated applications to locality, while here we extend the framework and adapt it to be able to apply it to a more general decentralized monitoring setting.

Related work in the distributed computing literature includes seminal papers such as [12] for stable property detection in a failure-free message-passing environment, and [5] for distributed program checking in the context of self-stabilization.

Organization of this paper. The distributed system model is in Section 2. Distributed languages and wait-free monitoring are presented in Section 3. In Section 4 we present the example of monitoring leader election. Our main result is in Section 5. Its proof is presented in Section 6. We conclude the paper and mention some open problems in Section 7. A full version [18] provides additional details and all the proofs.

2   Distributed System Model

There are many possible computation and communication models for distributed computation. Here we assume wait-free asynchronous processes that may fail by crashing, communicating by reading and writing a shared memory. This model serves as a good basis to study distributed computability: results in this model can often be extended to other popular models, such as when up to a fixed number of processes can crash (in a dependent or independent way). Also, message-passing, or various networking models that limit direct process-to-process connectivity, are essentially computationally equivalent or less powerful than shared memory. We recall here the main features of the wait-free model, and refer to textbooks such as [4] for a more detailed description, as well as for the relation to other distributed computing models.

The asynchronous read/write shared memory model assumes a system consisting of n asynchronous processes. Let $[n] = \{1, \ldots, n\}$. We associate each process to an integer in $[n]$. Each process runs at its own speed, that may vary along with time, and the processes may fail by *crashing* (i.e., halt and never recover). We consider *wait-free* distributed algorithms, in which a process never "waits" for another process to produce some intermediate result. This is because any number of processes may crash (and thus the expected result may never be produced).

The processes communicate through a shared memory composed of atomic registers, organised as an array of n single-writer/multiple-reader (SWMR) registers, one per process. Register $i \in [n]$ supports the operation $read()$ that returns the value stored in the register, and can be executed by any process. It also support de operation $write(v)$ that writes the value v in the register, and can be executed only by process i.

In our algorithms we use a *snapshot* operation by which a process can read all n SWMR registers, in such a way that a snapshot returns a copy of all the values that were simultaneously present in the shared memory at some point during the execution of the snapshot operation (snapshots are linearizable). Snapshots can be implemented by a wait-free algorithm (any number of processes may crash) using only the array of n SWMR registers [1] (see also textbooks such as [25]). Thus, we may assume snapshots are available to the processes, without loss of generality. The algorithms are simplified, as well as the proofs of our theorems, without modifying the outcomes of our results.

In a *distributed algorithm* each process starts with an *input value*, repeats a loop N times, consisting of writing to its register, taking a snapshot and making local computations[1]. At the end each process produces an *output value*. In a *step*, a process performs an operation on the registers (i.e., writes or snapshots). A *configuration* completely describes the state of the system. That is, a configuration specifies the state of each register as well as the local state of each process. An *execution* is a (finite) sequence of alternating configurations and steps, starting and ending in a configuration. A process *participates* in an execution if it takes at least one step in the execution. We assume that the first step of a process is a write, and it writes its input.

---

[1] If the set of possible input values is finite, all processes may execute the loop the same number of times, N (e.g. see [3]).

3   Distributed Languages and Wait-Free Monitoring

3.1   Distributed Languages

Let A be an alphabet of symbols, representing the set of possible values produced by some distributed algorithm to be monitored. Each process $i \in [n]$ has a read-only variable, $input_i$, initially equal to a symbol $\perp$ (not in A), and where the value to be monitored is deposited. We consider only the simplest scenario, where these variables change only once, from the value $\perp$, to a value in A. The goal is for the processes to monitor that, collectively, the values deposited in these variables are correct.

Formally, consider an execution $C_0, s_1, C_1, \ldots$, where each C_i is a configuration and each s_i is a step (write or snapshot) by some process, and C_0 is the initial configuration where all SWMR registers are empty. We assume the first step by a process i is to write its input, and is taken only once its variable $input_i$ is initialized to a value in A. Thus, s_1 is a write step by some process.

The correctness specification to be monitored is usually stated as a global predicate in some logic (e.g. [13,14]). We rephrase the predicate in terms of what we call a *distributed language*. An *instance* over alphabet A (we may omit A when clear from the context) is a set of pairs $s = \{(\mathrm{id}_1, a_1), \ldots, (\mathrm{id}_k, a_k)\}$, where $\{\mathrm{id}_1, \ldots, \mathrm{id}_k\} \subseteq [n]$ are distinct process identities, and $a_1, \ldots, a_k$ are (not necessarily distinct) elements of A. A distributed language $\mathcal{L}$ over the alphabet A is a collection of instances over A. Given a language $\mathcal{L}$, we say that an instance s is *legal* if $s \in \mathcal{L}$ and *illegal* otherwise.

Let $s = \{(\mathrm{id}_1, a_1), \ldots, (\mathrm{id}_k, a_k)\}$ be an instance over A. We denote by $\mathrm{ID}(s)$ the set of identities in s, $\mathrm{ID}(s) = \{\mathrm{id}_1, \ldots, \mathrm{id}_k\}$. The multiset of values in s is denoted by $val(s)$ (formally, a function that assigns to each $a \in A$ a non-negative integer specifying the number of times a is equal to one of the a_i in s).

Note that an instance s can describe an assignment of values from A to the input variables of a subset of processes. More precisely, consider an execution $C_0, s_1, C_1, \ldots, s_k, C_k$, $k \geq 1$. Suppose the processes that have taken steps in this execution are those in P, $P \subseteq [n]$. This execution defines the instance $s = \{(\mathrm{id}_1, a_1), \ldots, (\mathrm{id}_k, a_k)\}$ over A, where $\mathrm{ID}(s) = P$ and a_i is the first value written by process id_i. A configuration C_k also defines an instance, given by the input variables of processes that have written at least once (from the local state of a process, one can deduce if it has already executed a write operation).

An execution is *correct* if and only if its instance s is in $\mathcal{L}$. If the execution is correct, then processes in $\mathrm{ID}(s)$ have values as specified by the language (and the other processes have not yet been assigned a value or may be slow in announcing their values).

Consider for example the language `req-ack`, which captures a simplified version of the request-acknowledgment problem mentioned in the introduction, in which no more than q requests are sent by the clients. Requests and acknowledgments are identified with integers in $[q]$. A process id_i may know of some subset of requests $r_i \subseteq [q]$, and some subset of acknowledgments $a_i \subseteq [q]$. The language `req-ack` over alphabet $A = 2^{[q]} \times 2^{[q]}$ is defined by instances s as follows

$$s = \Big\{ (\mathrm{id}_1, (r_1, a_1)), \ldots, (\mathrm{id}_k, (r_k, a_k)) \Big\} \in \mathtt{req\text{-}ack} \iff \bigcup_{1 \le i \le k} r_i = \bigcup_{1 \le i \le k} a_i.$$

For each process i, the sets r_i and a_i denote the (possibly empty) sets of requests and acknowledgments, respectively, that process i is aware of. An instance is legal if and only if every request has been acknowledged.

As another example, consider *leader election*, for which it is required that one unique process be identified as the leader by all the other processes. This requirement is captured by the language `leader` defined over $A = [n]$ as follows:

$$s = \Big\{ (\mathrm{id}_1, \ell_1), \ldots, (\mathrm{id}_k, \ell_k) \Big\} \in \mathtt{leader} \iff \exists i \in [k] : \mathrm{id}_i = \ell_1 = \cdots = \ell_k. \quad (1)$$

An instance is legal if and only if all the processes agree on the identity ℓ of one of them.

3.2 Decentralized Monitoring

Monitoring the correctness specified by a language $\mathcal{L}$ involves two components: an *opinion-maker* M, and an *interpretation* μ. The opinion-maker is a distributed algorithm executed by the processes enabling each of them to produce an individual *opinion* about the validity of the outputs of the system. We call the processes running this algorithm *monitors*, and the (finite) set of possible individual opinions U, the *opinion set*.

The interpretation μ specifies the way one should interpret the collection of individual opinions produced by the monitors about the validity of the monitored system. We use the minimal requirement that the opinions of the monitors should be able to distinguish legal instances from illegal ones according to $\mathcal{L}$. Consider the set of all multi-sets over U, each one with at most n elements. Then $\mu = (\mathbf{Y}, \mathbf{N})$ is a partition of this set. $\mathbf{Y}$ is called the "yes" set, and $\mathbf{N}$ is called the "no" set.

For instance, when $U = \{0, 1\}$, process may produce as an opinion either 0 or 1. Together, the processes produce a multi-set of at most n boolean values. We do not consider which process produce which opinion, but we do consider how many processes produce a given opinion. The partition produced by the AND-operator [17,16] is as follows. For every multi-set of opinions S, we set $S \in \mathbf{Y}$ if every opinion in S is 1, otherwise, $S \in \mathbf{N}$.

Given a language $\mathcal{L}$ over an alphabet A, a *monitor for* $\mathcal{L}$ is a pair (μ, M), as follows.

- The opinion-maker M is a distributed wait-free algorithm that outputs an opinion u_i at every process i. The input of process i is any element a_i of A (assigned to its read-only variable $input_i$). Each process i is required to produce an opinion u_i such that: (1) every non-faulty process eventually produces an output (termination), and (2) if process i outputs u_i, then we must have: $u_i \in U$ (validity).
- Consider any execution of M where all participating processes have decided an opinion. If the instance s corresponding to the execution is legal, i.e.,

$s \in \mathcal{L}$, the monitors must produce a multiset of opinions $S \in \mathbf{Y}$, and if the instance s is illegal, i.e., $s \notin \mathcal{L}$, then they must produce a multiset of opinions in $\mathbf{N}$.

The paper focusses on the following question: given a distributed language $\mathcal{L}$, how many opinions are needed to monitor $\mathcal{L}$?

3.3 Opinion and Alternation Numbers

As stated above, we are interested in the smallest size $|U|$ of the opinion set enabling the monitors, after the execution of some distributed algorithm, to output opinions that distinguish legal instances from illegal ones. Hence, we focus on the following parameter associated with every distributed language.

Definition 1 (Opinion number). *Let $\mathcal{L}$ be a distributed language on n processes. The* opinion number *of $\mathcal{L}$ is the smallest integer k for which there exists a monitor (μ, M) for $\mathcal{L}$ using a set of at most k opinions. It is denoted by $\#\mathrm{opinion}(\mathcal{L})$.*

As we shall see, there are monitors using a small number of opinions, independent of the size of the alphabet used to define $\mathcal{L}$, and depending only on the number n of processes. The opinion number is shown to be related to a combinatorial property of languages, captured by the notion of *alternation number*. Given a language $\mathcal{L}$ over the alphabet A, the alternation number of $\mathcal{L}$ is the length of a longest increasing sequence of instances $s_1, \ldots, s_k$ with alternating legality. More formally:

Definition 2 (Alternation number). *Let $\mathcal{L}$ be a distributed language. The* alternation number *of $\mathcal{L}$ is the largest integer k for which there exists instances $s_1, \ldots, s_k$ such that, for every i, $1 \leq i < k$, $s_i \subset s_{i+1}$, and either $(s_i \in \mathcal{L}) \wedge (s_{i+1} \notin \mathcal{L})$ or $(s_i \notin \mathcal{L}) \wedge (s_{i+1} \in \mathcal{L})$. It is denoted by $\#\mathrm{altern}(\mathcal{L})$.*

Clearly, the alternation number is at most n since an instance has at most n elements.

4 Monitoring Leader Election

As a warm up example, let us show that the language `leader` of Equation 1 can be monitored using three opinions, namely, that $\#\mathrm{opinion}(\mathtt{leader}) \leq 3$. To establish this result, we describe a monitor for leader, called *traffic-light*. The set of opinions consists of three values, namely {red, orange, green}. Recall that the input of each process $i \in [n]$ is a value ℓ_i where $\ell_i \in [n]$ is supposed to be the identity of the leader. The opinion maker works as follows. Each monitor i writes its identity and it own input ℓ_i in shared memory, and then reads the whole memory with a snapshot operation. The snapshot returns a set of pairs, $s_i = \{(\mathrm{id}_j, \ell_j), j \in I\}$ for some I, that includes the values written so far in the memory. Recall that processes run asynchronously, hence a process may collect values from only a subset of all processes. Process i decides "green" if every process in s_i agrees on the same leader, and the ID of the common leader is the ID of one of the processes in s_i. Instead, if two or more processes in s_i have distinct leaders, then process i decides "red". In the somewhat "middle" case in which every process in s_i agrees on the same leader (i.e., same ID), but the ID of the common leader is not an ID of a process in s_i, then process i decides "orange".

More formally, the traffic-light opinion maker uses two procedures: "agree" and "valid". Given a set $s = \{(\mathrm{id}_1, \ell_1), \ldots, (\mathrm{id}_k, \ell_k)\}$ of pairs $(\mathrm{id}_i, \ell_i) \in [n] \times [n]$, agree($s$) is true if and only if $\ell_i = \ell_j$ for every i, j, $1 \leq i, j \leq k$. For a same s, valid(s) is true if and only if, for every ℓ_i, $1 \leq i \leq k$, there exists $j, 1 \leq j \leq k$ such that $\mathrm{id}_j = \ell_i$. Each process performs the pseudo-code below:

Opinion-maker at process p with input ℓ:
write $(\mathrm{ID}(p), \ell)$ to p's register ;
snapshot memory, to get $s = \{(\mathrm{id}_1, \ell_1), \ldots, (\mathrm{id}_k, \ell_k)\}$;
if agree(s) **and** valid(s) **then** decide "green"
else if agree(s) **but** not valid(s) **then** decide "orange" **else** decide "red".

The interpretation of the opinions produced by the monitors is the following. An opinion u_i produced by process i is an element of the set $U = \{\text{green, orange, red}\}$. The opinion-maker produces a multi-set u of opinions. We define the yes-set **Y** as the set of all multi-sets u with no red elements, and at least one green element. Hence, **N** is composed of all multi-sets u with at least one red element, or with no green elements.

Now, one can easily check that the traffic-light monitor satisfies the desired property. That is, for every set $s = \{(\mathrm{id}_1, \ell_1), \ldots, (\mathrm{id}_k, \ell_k)\}$ of pairs $(\mathrm{id}_i, \ell_i) \in [n] \times [n]$, if u denotes the multi-set of opinions produced by the monitors, then we have

$$s \in \texttt{leader} \iff u \in \mathbf{Y}.$$

Interestingly enough, one can prove that the language **leader** *cannot be monitored using fewer than three opinions*. Namely,

Proposition 1. #opinion(**leader**) $= 3$.

Crucially, the fact that three opinions are required, and that, in particular, the opinions true and false are not sufficient, is an inherent property of the language **leader**, independently of the opinion-maker algorithm, and independently of the interpretation of the opinions produced by the monitors. The lower bound argument enabling to establish this result is not hard but uses a fundamental theorem about two-process read/write wait-free computation: the graph of executions is connected (e.g. see [3]).

As we mentioned before, the number of opinions required to monitor a distributed language is strongly related to its alternation number. The sequence of instances

$$s_1 = \{(1,2)\}, \; s_2 = \{(1,2),(2,2)\}, \; \text{and} \; s_3 = \{(1,2),(2,2),(3,3)\}$$

satisfies $s_1 \subset s_2 \subset s_3$. Moreover s_1 and s_3 are illegal, while s_2 is legal (as far as `leader` is concerned). We thus infer that the alternation number of `leader` is at least 3. In fact, it can be shown that its alternation number is exactly 3. Namely,

Proposition 2. #altern(`leader`) = 3.

Intuitively, the alternation between legal and illegal instances forces the processes to use three opinions. Given s_1, process 1 may say that the instance is "probably illegal" (orange), while, given s_2, process 2 may say that the instance is "potentially legal" (green). Only process 3, given s_3, can declare that the instance is "definitively illegal" (red), no matter the number of further processes that may show up.

5 Main Result

In this section, we state our main result, that is, a lower bound on the number of opinions needed to monitor languages with n monitors.

Theorem 1. *For any $n \geq 1$, and every k, $1 \leq k < n$, there exists a language $\mathcal{L}$ on n processes, with alternation number k, that requires at least k opinions to be monitored. For $k = n$, there exists a language $\mathcal{L}$ on n processes, with alternation number n, that requires at least $n + 1$ opinions to be monitored.*

In other words, there are system properties which require a large number of opinions to be monitored. Before dwelling into the details of the proof of Theorem 1, we want to stress the fact that our lower bound is essentially the best that can be achieved in term of alternation number. Indeed, Theorem 1 says that, for every k, there exists a language $\mathcal{L}$ with alternation number k such that #opinion($\mathcal{L}$) $\geq$ #altern($\mathcal{L}$). We show that this lower bound is essentially tight. Indeed, we establish the existence of a *universal* monitor that can monitor all distributed languages using a number of opinions equal roughly to the alternation number. More specifically, we show that, for every k, and for every language $\mathcal{L}$ with opinion number k, we have #opinion($\mathcal{L}$) $\leq$ #altern($\mathcal{L}$) + 1.

Theorem 2. *There exists a monitor which, for every $k \geq 1$, monitors every language with alternation number k using at most $k + 1$ opinions.*

Since the alternation number of a language on n processes is at most n, Theorem 2 yields the following.

Corollary 1. *There exists a monitor which, for every $n \geq 1$, monitors every language on n processes, using at most $n + 1$ opinions. Moreover, this monitor uses at most $k + 1$ opinions for every execution in which at most k processes participate.*

It is worth noticing that the monitor of Corollary 1 has an interpretation μ which does not depend at all on the language to be monitored, not even on the number of processes involved in the language. (The same holds for Theorem 2). The opinion-maker (as well as the one for Theorem 2), does however depend on the language, but only up to a limited extent. Indeed, the general structure of the opinion-maker is independent of the language. It simply uses a black box that returns whether $s \in \mathcal{L}$ for any instance s. Apart from this, the opinion-maker is essentially independent of the language. In this sense it is *universal*.

The full proof of Theorem 2 is omitted for lack of space. The rest of the paper is dedicated to describing the main ideas of the proof of our main result.

6   Orientation-Detection Tasks, and Proof of Theorem 1

To establish our lower bound, we show that the design of distributed runtime monitors using few opinions is essentially equivalent to solving a specific type of tasks, that we call *orientation-detection* tasks. This equivalence is made explicit thanks to an *equivalence lemma* (Lemma 1). Introducing orientation-detection tasks requires elementary notions of combinatorial topology.

6.1   Tasks and Combinatorial Topology Terminology

When solving a distributed task[2], each process starts with a private input value and has to eventually decide irrevocably on an output value. (In our setting, the input value of a process is a symbol in a given alphabet A, and the output value is an opinion). A process $i \in [n]$ is initially not aware of the inputs of other processes. Consider an execution where only a subset of k processes participate, $1 \leq k \leq n$. These processes have distinct identities $\{\mathrm{id}_1, \ldots, \mathrm{id}_k\}$, where for every $i \in [k]$, $\mathrm{id}_i \in [n]$. A set $s = \{(\mathrm{id}_1, x_1), \ldots, (\mathrm{id}_k, x_k)\}$ is used to denote the input values, or output values, in the execution, where x_i denotes the value of the process with identity id_i — either an input value (e.g., a symbol in a given alphabet A), or a output value (e.g., an opinion).

The monitor task. An opinion-maker M for a language $\mathcal{L}$ on n processes with opinion set U, and interpretation $\mu = (\mathbf{Y}, \mathbf{N})$ is a distributed wait-free algorithm that solves the following *monitor task*. Any instance over alphabet A is a possible assignment of inputs in A to the processes. If process i has input $a_i \in A$, then i is required to produce as output an opinion $u_i \in U$ such that, in addition to satisfying termination and validity, it also satisfy *consistency*, defined as follows. Consider any execution, where I is the set of processes that do not crash, and all others crash without taking any steps. Let $s = \{(\mathrm{id}_i, a_i), i \in I\}$, and let $u = \{u_i, i \in I\}$ denote the multiset of opinions that are eventually output by the processes in I. We must have: $s \in \mathcal{L} \iff u \in \mathbf{Y}$.

---

[2] A task is the basic distributed computing problem, defined by a set of inputs to the processes and for each input to the processes, a set of legal outputs of the processes – see, e.g., [22].

Simplices and complexes. Let s' be a subset of a "full" set $s = \{(1, x_1), \ldots, (n, x_n)\}$, i.e., a set s such that $ID(s) = [n]$. Since any number of processes can crash, all such subsets s' are of interest for taking into account executions where only processes in $ID(s')$ participate. Therefore, the set of possible input sets forms a *complex* because its sets are closed under containment. Similarly, the set of possible output sets also form a complex. Following the standard terminology of combinatorial topology, the sets of a complex are called *simplexes*. Hence every set s' as above is a simplex.

More formally, a *complex* $\mathcal{K}$ is a set of vertices $V(\mathcal{K})$, and a family of finite, nonempty subsets of $V(\mathcal{K})$, called *simplexes*, satisfying: (1) if $v \in V(\mathcal{K})$ then $\{v\}$ is a simplex, and (2) if s is a simplex, so is every nonempty subset of s. The *dimension* of a simplex s is $|s| - 1$, the dimension of $\mathcal{K}$ is the largest dimension of its simplexes, and $\mathcal{K}$ is *pure* of dimension k if every simplex belongs to a k-dimensional simplex. In distributed computing, the simplexes (and complexes) are often *chromatic*, since each vertex v of a simplex is labeled with a distinct process identity $i \in [n]$.

A *distributed task* T is formally described by a triple $(\mathcal{I}, \mathcal{O}, \Delta)$ where $\mathcal{I}$ and $\mathcal{O}$ are pure $(n-1)$-dimensional complexes, and Δ is a map from $\mathcal{I}$ to the set of non-empty sub-complexes of $\mathcal{O}$, satisfying $ID(t) \subseteq ID(s)$ for every $t \in \Delta(s)$. We call $\mathcal{I}$ the input complex, and $\mathcal{O}$ the output complex. Intuitively, Δ specifies, for every simplex $s \in \mathcal{I}$, the valid outputs $\Delta(s)$ for the processes in $ID(s)$ that may participate in the computation. We assume that Δ is (sequentially) computable.

Given any finite set U and any integer $n \geq 1$, we denote by $complex(U, n)$ the $(n-1)$-dimensional *pseudosphere* [22] complex induced by U: for each $i \in [n]$ and each $x \in U$, there is a vertex labeled (i, x) in the vertex set of $complex(U, n)$. Moreover, $u = \{(id_1, u_1), \ldots, (id_k, u_k)\}$ is a simplex of $complex(U, n)$ if and only if u is properly colored with identities, that is $id_i \neq id_j$ for every $1 \leq i < j \leq k$. In particular, $complex(\{0, 1\}, n)$ is (topologically equivalent) to the $(n-1)$-dimensional sphere. For $u \in complex(U, n)$, we denote by $val(u)$ the multiset formed of all the values in U corresponding to the processes in u.

6.2 Orientation-Detection Tasks

An *oriented complex*[3] is a complex whose every simplex s is assigned a sign, $sign(s) \in \{-1, +1\}$. Given an oriented input complex, $\mathcal{J}$, a natural task consists in computing distributively the sign of the actual input simplex. That is, each process is assigned as input a vertex of $V(\mathcal{J})$, and the set of all the vertices assigned to the processes forms a simplex $s \in \mathcal{J}$. Ideally, one would like that processes individually decide "yes" if the simplex is oriented $+1$ and "no" otherwise. However, this is impossible in general because processes do not have the same view of the execution, and any form of non-trivial agreement cannot be solved in a wait-free manner [15]. Thus, we allow processes to express their knowledge through values in some larger set U.

---

[3] In the case of chromatic manifolds, our definition is equivalent to usual definition of orientation in topology textbooks.

Definition 3 (Orientation detection task). *Let $\mathcal{J}$ be a $(n-1)$-dimensional oriented complex. A task $T = (\mathcal{J}, \mathcal{U}, \Delta)$, with $\mathcal{U} = complex(U, n)$ for some set U, is an orientation detection task for $\mathcal{J}$ if and only if for every two $s, s' \in \mathcal{J}$, and every $t \in \Delta(s)$ and $t' \in \Delta(s')$: $sign(s) \neq sign(s') \Rightarrow val(t) \neq val(t')$.*

Hence, to detect the orientation of a simplex s, the processes i, $i \in I \subseteq [n]$, occurring in a simplex s have to collectively decide a multiset $val(t) = \{val(i), i \in I\}$ of values in U, where $val(i)$ denotes the value decided by process i. If $\mathcal{J}$ is non-trivially oriented, i.e., if there exist $s, s' \in \mathcal{J}$ of the same dimension, with $sign(s) \neq sign(s')$, then no orientation-detection tasks for $\mathcal{J}$ exists with $|U| = 1$, because one must be able to discriminate the different orientations of s and s'. Instead, for every oriented complex $\mathcal{J}$, there exists an orientation-detection task for $\mathcal{J}$ with $|U| = 2$. To see why, consider the task $T = (\mathcal{J}, \mathcal{U}, \Delta)$, where $\mathcal{U}$ is the $(n-1)$-dimensional sphere, and Δ maps every k-dimensional simplex $s \in \mathcal{J}$ with $sign(s) = -1$ (resp., $+1$) to the k-dimensional simplex $t \in \mathcal{U}$ with $val(t) = \{0, 0, \ldots, 0\}$ (resp., $val(t) = \{1, 1, \ldots, 1\}$). However, this latter task is not necessarily wait-free solvable (i.e., solvable in our context of asynchronous distributed computing where any number of processes can crash). The complexity of detecting the orientation of an oriented complex $\mathcal{J}$ is measured by the smallest k for which there exists an orientation-detection task $T = (\mathcal{J}, \mathcal{U}, \Delta)$ that is wait-free solvable, with $\mathcal{U} = complex(U, n)$, and $|U| = k$.

In the next subsection, we show that the problem of finding the minimum-size set U for detecting the orientation of an arbitrary given oriented complex $\mathcal{J}$ is essentially equivalent to finding the minimum-size set of opinions U for monitoring a language $\mathcal{L}_{\mathcal{J}}$ induced by $\mathcal{J}$ (and its orientation).

6.3   Equivalence Lemma

This section shows that the notion of monitoring and the notion of orientation-detection are essentially two sides of the same coin.

Let $\mathcal{L}$ be a n-process distributed language defined over an alphabet A. We define $\mathcal{J}_{\mathcal{L}} = complex(n, A)$. That is, for every collection $\{a_1, \ldots, a_k\}$ of at most k elements of A, $1 \leq k \leq n$, and every k-subset $\{id_1, \ldots, id_k\} \subseteq [n]$ of distinct identities, $\{(id_1, a_1), \ldots, (id_k, a_k)\}$ is a simplex in $\mathcal{J}_{\mathcal{L}}$. Let us orient $\mathcal{J}_{\mathcal{L}}$ as follows. For every simplex $s \in \mathcal{J}_{\mathcal{L}}$, we define:

$$sign(s) = \begin{cases} +1 \text{ if } s \in \mathcal{L}; \\ -1 \text{ otherwise.} \end{cases}$$

Conversely, let $\mathcal{J}$ be a well-formed oriented complex. We say that an oriented complex $\mathcal{J}$ on n processes is *well-formed* if for every $I \subseteq [n]$, there exists $s, s' \in \mathcal{J}$ with $\mathrm{ID}(s) = \mathrm{ID}(s') = I$ and $sign(s) = -sign(s')$. We set $\mathcal{L}_{\mathcal{J}}$ as the n-process language defined over the alphabet $A = \{+1, -1\} \times V(\mathcal{J})$. That is, each element of A is a pair (σ, v) where σ is a sign in $\{+1, -1\}$ and v a vertex of $\mathcal{J}$. The language $\mathcal{L}_{\mathcal{J}}$ is the set of instances $s = \{(id_1, (\sigma_1, v_1)), \ldots, (id_k, (\sigma_k, v_k))\}$ specified as follows:

$$s \in \mathcal{L}_{\mathcal{J}} \iff \begin{cases} t = \{(id_1, v_1), \ldots, (id_k, v_k)\} \text{ is a simplex of } \mathcal{J}, \\ \text{and } sign(t) = \sigma_i \text{ for every } i, 1 \leq i \leq k. \end{cases}$$

That is, in a legal instance, each process is assigned a vertex of some simplex $t \in \mathcal{J}$ together with the orientation of t.

We have now all ingredients to state formally the first main ingredient toward establishing Theorem 1: the equivalence between language-monitoring and orientation-detection.

Lemma 1 (Equivalence lemma)

• Let $\mathcal{L}$ be a n-process language. If there exists $k \geq 1$ and a wait-free solvable orientation-detection task for $\mathcal{J}_\mathcal{L}$ using values in some set of size k, then there exists a monitor for $\mathcal{L}$ using at most k opinions.

• Let $\mathcal{J}$ be a well-formed oriented complex, and let $k \geq 1$. If no orientation-detection task for $\mathcal{J}$ is wait-free solvable using k values, then the language $\mathcal{L}_\mathcal{J}$ requires at least $k + 1$ opinions to be monitored.

The proof of Lemma 1 is omitted from this extended abstract. This lemma establishes an equivalence between wait-free solving orientation-detection tasks and monitoring a language with few opinions. It can be shown that, in addition, this lemma preserves alternation numbers in the following sense. The concept of alternation number (for languages) can be similarly defined for oriented complexes: for an oriented complex $\mathcal{J}$, the alternation number of $\mathcal{J}$ is the length of a longest increasing sequence of simplexes of $\mathcal{J}$ with alternating orientations. Formally:

Definition 4 (Alternation number of oriented complexes). Let $\mathcal{J}$ be an oriented complex. The alternation number, $\#\mathrm{altern}(\mathcal{J})$, of $\mathcal{J}$ is the largest integer k for which there exists $s_1, \ldots, s_k \in \mathcal{J}$ such that, for every i, $1 \leq i < k$, $s_i \subset s_{i+1}$ and $\mathrm{sign}(s_i) \neq \mathrm{sign}(s_{i+1})$.

The equivalence established in Lemma 1 preserves alternation number as stated by the following result.

Lemma 2. For every language $\mathcal{L}$, and every well-formed oriented complex $\mathcal{J}$, we have $\#\mathrm{altern}(\mathcal{J}_\mathcal{L}) = \#\mathrm{altern}(\mathcal{L})$ and $\#\mathrm{altern}(\mathcal{L}_\mathcal{J}) \leq \#\mathrm{altern}(\mathcal{J}) + 1$.

6.4   Sketch of the Proof of Theorem 1

Due to lack of space, we only sketch the proof of Theorem 1. We use the correspondence between monitors and orientation-detection tasks as stated in Lemma 1, and focus on orientation-detection tasks. Given $k, 1 \leq k < n$, we carefully build an oriented complex $\mathcal{J}$ with alternation number $k - 1$ and shows that any orientation-detection task with input complex $\mathcal{J}$ cannot be solved wait-free with $k - 1$ values or less. Therefore, by the equivalence Lemma (Lemma 1), the language $\mathcal{L}_\mathcal{J}$ induced by $\mathcal{J}$ requires at least k values to be monitored. To complete the proof, we establish that the alternation number of $\mathcal{L}_\mathcal{J}$ satisfies $\#\mathrm{altern}(\mathcal{L}_\mathcal{J}) = \#\mathrm{altern}(\mathcal{J}) + 1 = k$. (The case $k = n$ is similar, except that we construct $\mathcal{J}$ with alternation number n, and $\#\mathrm{altern}(\mathcal{L}_\mathcal{J}) = \#\mathrm{altern}(\mathcal{J})$.).

The main challenge lies in constructing, and orienting the complex $\mathcal{J}$ in such a way that no orientation-detection task with input $\mathcal{J}$ is wait-free solvable with less than k values. One important ingredient in the proof is an adaptation of

Sperner's Lemma to our setting. To get an idea of how the proof proceeds, consider a ℓ-dimensional simplex $s \in \mathcal{J}$ whose all $(\ell - 1)$-dimensional simplexes have sign -1, but one which has sign $+1$. Assume moreover that ℓ values only are used to encode the signs of these faces. Recall that any wait-free distributed algorithm induces a mapping from a subdivision of the input complex to the output complex [23]. By Sperner's Lemma, we prove that, whatever the opinion-maker does, at least one ℓ-dimensional simplex s' resulting from the subdivision of s satisfies $|val(s')| = \ell + 1$. That is, $\ell + 1$ values are used to determine the orientation of s, for every monitor (μ, M). In the full paper we describe the many details omitted here, that are behind this intuition.   □

7   Conclusions and Future Work

We investigated the minimum number of opinions needed for runtime monitoring in an asynchronous distributed system where any number of processes may crash. We considered the simplest case, where each process outputs a single value just once, and the monitors verify that the values collectively satisfy a given correctness condition. A correctness condition is specified by a collection of legal sets of these values, that may occur in an execution. Each monitor expresses its opinion about the correctness of the set of outputs, based on its local perspective of the execution. We proved lower bounds on the number of opinions, and presented distributed monitors with nearly the same number of opinions.

Many avenues remain open for future research. It would be interesting to derive a temporal logic framework that corresponds to ours, and that associates to opinions a formal meaning in the logic. In our setting the processes produce just one output and the monitors must verify that, collectively, the set of outputs produced is correct. It would of course be interesting to extend our results to the case where each process produces a sequence of output values. Also, opinions are anonymous. The interpretation specifies which multisets of opinions indicate a violation, independently of the identities of the monitors that output them. We do not know whether or not taking into account the identities would help reducing the total number of opinions needed. Finally, it would be interesting to extend our results to other models, such as t-resilient models in which not more than t processes may fail.

References

1. Afek, Y., Attiya, H., Dolev, D., Gafni, E., Merritt, M., Shavit, N.: Atomic snapshots of shared memory. J. ACM 40(4), 873–890 (1993)
2. Arafat, O., Bauer, A., Leucker, M., Schallhart, C.: Runtime verification revisited. Technical Report TUM-I0518, Technischen Universität München (2005)
3. Attiya, H., Rajsbaum, S.: The Combinatorial Structure of Wait-Free Solvable Tasks. SIAM J. Comput. 31(4), 1286–1313 (2002)
4. Attiya, H., Welch, J.L.: Distributed computing: fundamentals, simulations and advanced topics. Wiley, USA (2004)
5. Awerbuch, B., Varghese, G.: Distributed Program Checking: A Paradigm for Building Self-stabilizing Distributed Protocols (Extended Abstract). In: SFCS, pp. 258–267. IEEE (1991)

6. Bauer, A., Falcone, Y.: Decentralised LTL monitoring. In: Giannakopoulou, D., Méry, D. (eds.) FM 2012. LNCS, vol. 7436, pp. 85–100. Springer, Heidelberg (2012)
7. Bauer, A., Leucker, M., Schallhart, C.: Monitoring of real-time properties. In: Arun-Kumar, S., Garg, N. (eds.) FSTTCS 2006. LNCS, vol. 4337, pp. 260–272. Springer, Heidelberg (2006)
8. Bauer, A., Leucker, M., Schallhart, C.: Comparing LTL semantics for runtime verification. J. Log. and Comput. 20(3), 651–674 (2010)
9. Berkovich, S., Bonakdarpour, B., Fischmeister, S.: Gpu-based runtime verification. In: IPDPS, pp. 1025–1036. IEEE (2013)
10. Bonakdarpour, B., Navabpour, S., Fischmeister, S.: Sampling-based runtime verification. In: Butler, M., Schulte, W. (eds.) FM 2011. LNCS, vol. 6664, pp. 88–102. Springer, Heidelberg (2011)
11. Burnim, J., Sen, K., Stergiou, C.: Sound and complete monitoring of sequential consistency for relaxed memory models. In: Abdulla, P.A., Leino, K.R.M. (eds.) TACAS 2011. LNCS, vol. 6605, pp. 11–25. Springer, Heidelberg (2011)
12. Chandy, K.M., Lamport, L.: Distributed Snapshots: Determining Global States of Distributed Systems. ACM Trans. Comput. Syst. 3(1), 63–75 (1985)
13. Chauhan, H., Garg, V.K., Natarajan, A., Mittal, N.: A distributed abstraction algorithm for online predicate detection. In: SRDS, pp. 101–110. IEEE (2013)
14. Cooper, R., Marzullo, K.: Consistent detection of global predicates. In: Workshop on Parallel and Distributed Debugging, pp. 167–174. ACM Press (1991)
15. Fischer, M.J., Lynch, N.A., Paterson, M.S.: Impossibility of distributed consensus with one faulty process. J. ACM 32(2), 374–382 (1985)
16. Fraigniaud, P., Korman, A., Peleg, D.: Local distributed decision. In: FOCS, pp. 708–717. IEEE (2011)
17. Fraigniaud, P., Rajsbaum, S., Travers, C.: Locality and checkability in wait-free computing. Distributed Computing 26(4), 223–242 (2013)
18. Fraigniaud, P., Rajsbaum, S., Travers, C.: On the Number of Opinions Needed for Fault-Tolerant Run-Time Monitoring in Distributed Systems Technical report #hal-01011079 (2014), http://hal.inria.fr/hal-01011079
19. Genon, A., Massart, T., Meuter, C.: Monitoring distributed controllers: When an efficient LTL algorithm on sequences is needed to model-check traces. In: Misra, J., Nipkow, T., Sekerinski, E. (eds.) FM 2006. LNCS, vol. 4085, pp. 557–572. Springer, Heidelberg (2006)
20. Ha, J., Arnold, M., Blackburn, S.M., McKinley, K.S.: A concurrent dynamic analysis framework for multicore hardware. In: OOPSLA, pp. 155–174. ACM (2009)
21. Henle, M.: A Combinatorial Introduction to Topology. Dover (1983)
22. Herlihy, M., Kozlov, D., Rajsbaum, S.: Distributed Computing Through Combinatorial Topology. Morgan Kaufmann-Elsevier (2013)
23. Herlihy, M., Shavit, N.: The topological structure of asynchronous computability. J. ACM 46(6), 858–923 (1999)
24. Kupferman, O., Vardi, M.Y.: Model checking of safety properties. Form. Methods Syst. Des. 19(3), 291–314 (2001)
25. Raynal, M.: Concurrent Programming - Algorithms, Principles, and Foundations. Springer (2013)
26. Sen, K., Vardhan, A., Agha, G., Rosu, G.: Efficient decentralized monitoring of safety in distributed systems. In: ICSE, pp. 418–427. IEEE (2004)
27. Sen, K., Vardhan, A., Agha, G., Rosu, G.: Decentralized runtime analysis of multithreaded applications. In: IPDPS. IEEE (2006)
28. Zhu, H., Dwyer, M.B., Goddard, S.: Predictable runtime monitoring. In: ECRTS, pp. 173–183. IEEE (2009)

Supporting the Specification and Runtime Validation of Asynchronous Calling Patterns in Reactive Systems

Jiannan Zhai[1], Nigamanth Sridhar[2], and Jason O. Hallstrom[1]

[1] School of Computing, Clemson University, Clemson, SC USA 29634
[2] Electrical and Computer Engineering, Cleveland State University,
Cleveland, OH USA 44115

Abstract. Wireless sensor networks (*"sensornets"*) are highly distributed and concurrent, with program actions bound to external stimuli. They exemplify a system class known as *reactive systems*, which comprise execution units that have "hidden" layers of control flow. A key obstacle in enabling reactive system developers to rigorously validate their implementations has been the absence of precise software component specifications and tools to assist in leveraging those specifications at runtime. We address this obstacle in three ways: (*i*) We describe a specification approach tailored for reactive environments and demonstrate its application in the context of sensornets. (*ii*) We describe the design and implementation of extensions to the popular *nesC* tool-chain that enable the expression of these specifications and automate the generation of runtime monitors that signal violations, if any. (*iii*) Finally, we apply the specification approach to a significant collection of the most commonly used software components in the *TinyOS* distribution and analyze the overhead involved in monitoring their correctness.

1 Introduction

In software development, there is a behavioral spectrum that runs from purely *synchronous* to purely *asynchronous*. A purely synchronous system contains a single thread of control, typically originating from main(). Traditional component-based specification and validation strategies were designed with these systems in mind and have proven to be effective in ensuring application correctness. Toward the middle of this spectrum are the more common applications, comprising multiple threads that communicate through narrow interfaces, or through a small set of shared variables, essentially forming a collection of synchronous, semi-independent activities. In this context, component-based specification and validation mechanisms begin to break down; they were not designed to handle frame property violations originating from outside the main control thread. At the far end of the spectrum, in the presence of pure asynchrony, component-based specification and validation mechanisms break down entirely.

B. Bonakdarpour and S.A. Smolka (Eds.): RV 2014, LNCS 8734, pp. 108–123, 2014.

A *reactive system* is one in which an invocation sequence may originate from outside the main thread of control (e.g., `main()`). Such systems are increasingly important, particularly in the context of embedded applications, which tend to spend much of their time in a reduced power state to conserve energy, waking in response to internal and external interrupts. We focus on the rigorous characterization and validation of such systems. The discussion is presented in the context of *nesC* [12], a component-based dialect of the C programming language, using examples from the *TinyOS* [14] distribution, the most popular operating system (library) of its kind for building wireless sensor network systems. However, the basic principles of the runtime verification approach are applicable to a range of languages and systems, including standard event-based systems developed in Java, and interrupt-based systems developed in other embedded C dialects.

Reactive systems often depend on external stimuli, e.g., from an attached sensor or control system. These systems are commonly implemented using an *event-driven* programming style, encoding the application's behavior in the form of a state machine, with actions tied to each state. The transitions among these states are initiated internally by the application, as well as through external signals. In this style of expression, all concurrent behaviors are explicit. So while well-suited to accommodating interrupt behavior, it poses a significant burden in terms of program understanding. Program logic is partitioned into disjoint units that are often textually distant; the state shared among these units must be managed manually, including control flow state [2]. Not only are these programs more difficult to understand, the transition from synchrony to asynchrony precludes the application of contract-based specification and validation mechanisms — arguably the most powerful tools for ensuring program correctness.

Contract specifications [23] have proven valuable for developing and validating component-based software. Unfortunately, pre- and post-conditions do not support the encoding of event semantics, which dictate properties on the *call sequence* of an execution. Without encoding call sequence properties, the contracts are not as useful; the pre- and post-conditions need to be contextualized by *when* a particular method invocation must occur. The latest attempt at defining interface contracts for TinyOS components suffers this same limitation [3]. The contracts do not preserve the timing context of method calls, offer little abstraction, and leave virtually no implementation freedom.

We use the concept of a *trace* to specify reactive behavior in a precise manner. Given the high degree of expressivity of trace variables, this may not be surprising (though our approach is novel). Here is the surprising part: The trace —traditionally viewed as a brute-force, heavy-weight mechanism— can be used to specify reactive behavior in a manner that is both *concise* and *accessible*. Using the trace construct, we define the notion of a *promise* that an operation makes about its future behavior. This promise, captured in a specialized `promises` clause, accompanies traditional pre- and post-conditions in the contract.

There has been extensive work in runtime validation using various temporal logics and associated tools. Despite their expressive power, there is little evidence of programmer adoption. The contributions of this paper are of an applied nature, serving as a bridge from the theoretical programming languages community to a popular programming domain. The goal is to provide a practical toolset, both in terms of language extensions and supporting software tools, to enable practitioners to make use of temporal concepts. Our specification approach is to recast traditional temporal specifications as time-indexed state vectors, and to introduce suitable language notations to integrate the resulting conditions as part of state-based pre- and post-conditions. The supporting tools check these conditions to the extent possible.

To support the use of promises in sensornet development, we extend the *nesC* tool-chain to accommodate an optional `promises` clause as part of a method's signature. At compile-time, the `promises` are used to generate runtime monitors that are woven throughout the resulting application image. If a `promise` is violated, the monitors signal the violation, notifying the developer, and potentially triggering corrective measures. We describe the design and implementation of the tool-chain extensions and demonstrate their use across a significant set of commonly used components within the TinyOS distribution. Finally, we present a detailed analysis of the runtime overhead these extensions introduce and show that the overhead is modest in most cases.

2   TinyOS and nesC

TinyOS [14] is a software component library designed for constructing sensornets. The components and the programs which use them are written in *nesC* [12], a dialect of C that supports component-oriented, event-driven programming.

A nesC program consists of *interfaces* and *modules*. A nesC interface is analogous to a Java interface and defines the *command* signatures that must be provided by implementations of that interface. An interface may additionally define one or more *events* that will be signaled by an implementation. An event declaration defines the signature of its callback handler.

A nesC module defines a set of interfaces *provided* by the component, and a set of interfaces *used* by the component. The module is then responsible for implementing the commands that it *provides* and relies on the commands that it *uses* to satisfy those implementations. The module is also responsible for implementing the events (i.e., handlers) defined by the interfaces that it uses.

Long-running operations in TinyOS are implemented as *split-phase* operations. In the first phase, the component that initiates the operation (e.g., sending a message) calls a command to initiate the operation (`send()`). The component that receives the command immediately returns control to the caller after registering the request. This prevents the processor from blocking, allowing the caller to continue execution. At a later point, when the operation has completed, an event is signaled (e.g., `sendDone()`, originating from interrupt context) to the calling component notifying it of the completion of the split-phase operation.

3   The Specification Approach

```
1  interface Timer {
2    modeled by: (active: boolean, period: nat number)
3    initial state: (false, 0)
4    command void start(uint32_t delay);
5    command void stop();
6    event void fired();
7  }
```

Consider the `Timer` interface shown above. The interface provides commands to start and stop a timer, and an event that serves as the timer's periodic signal. A component using this interface can start a timer, with the expectation that when `delay` time units have elapsed, the `fired()` event will be signaled. Using simple state predicates, a first spec attempt might look as follows (based on [3]):

```
1  command void start(uint32_t delay);
2    requires: !self.active
3    ensures: self.active ∧ self.period = delay
```

While the spec captures the state change induced by the call to `start()`, it does not capture the most important impact of the call — at a future time (i.e., `delay` time units later), the `fired()` event will be signaled. Using a temporal specification to capture this liveness property, a second attempt might look like:

```
1     start() ⤳ fired()
```

But such temporal specifications do not coexist well with state contracts, compromising compositional reasoning [18]. The desired goal is to express the direct relationship between the call to `start()` and the signaling of `fired()`. To do so, we introduce our main specification mechanism — namely, $f\tau$, pronounced "future trace" of execution. The future trace of a component is the sequence of method footprints (both incoming and outgoing) that the component will ultimately participate in. Using $f\tau$, we can make an assertion that as a result of the call to `start()`, the `fired()` event will be signaled in the future. To simplify the expression of assertions defined over $f\tau$, we introduce two predicates, $CallAt()$ and $CallBet()$:

$$CallAt(source, target, method, time) \equiv$$
$$(f\tau[time].s = source) \wedge (f\tau[time].t = target) \wedge (f\tau[time].m = method)$$

$CallAt()$ is *true* if the *source* object places a call to the *method* body provided by the *target* object at the specified *time*, where *time* is defined as an index into $f\tau$.

$$CallBet(source, target, method, lb, ub) \equiv$$
$$(\ \exists ft : lb < time < ub :$$
$$(f\tau[time].s = source) \wedge (f\tau[time].t = target) \wedge (f\tau[time].m = method)\ )$$

$CallBet()$ evaluates to *true* iff the call occurs within a specified window, given by lower-bound *lb*, and upper-bound *ub*, again defined as indices into $f\tau$. When applying these predicates, we often wish to disregard the *source* and/or *target* clauses. Rather than introducing additional predicates, we introduce the special object value −, indicating "don't care"; *object* = − evaluates to *true* for all *object* values. With these definitions in place, consider a third attempt at specifying `Timer.start()`:

```
1  command void start(uint32_t delay);
2    requires: !self.active
3    ensures: self.active ∧ self.period = delay ∧ CallBet(self, −, fired, now, ∞)
```

The last conjunct states that at some time in the future (*i.e.*, after the current time, *now*), a `fired` event will be signaled. Now let us consider the rest of the interface. The `stop()` command stops an active timer. In terms of $f\tau$, the command guarantees that there is no `fired()` signal in the future, between current time and the "end" of time.

```
1  command void stop();
2    requires: self.active
3    ensures: !self.active ∧ self.period = 0 ∧ ¬CallBet(self, −, fired, now, ∞)
```

While individually meaningful, the specifications miss a key relationship *between* the two commands. In the case of `start()`, the method can guarantee a `fired()` event in $f\tau$ only if there is no call to `stop()` in the intervening duration. Similarly, a call to `start()`, after a call to `stop()` will, in fact, introduce a `fired()` event in $f\tau$. Accounting for this in the specifications of `start()` and `stop()` results in this next attempt:

```
1  command void start(uint32_t delay);
2    requires: !self.active
3    ensures: self.active ∧ self.period = delay ∧
4        ∃i : now < i : [CallAt(−, self, stop, i) ∧ ¬CallBet(self, −, fired, i, ∞)] ∨
5        [¬CallBet(−, self, stop, now, i) ∧ CallAt(self, −, fired, i)]
6  command void stop();
7    requires: self.active
8    ensures: !self.active ∧ self.period = 0 ∧
9        ∀i : now < i : CallAt(self, −, fired, i) ⟹ CallBet(−, self, start, now, i)
```

While improved, the specifications are no longer independent. A post-condition is intended to capture only what is true about the component upon successful termination. The last conjunct in each post-condition is a predicate on the *future* behavior of the component. One way of addressing this is to elevate predicates on $f\tau$ to an invariant on the component, succinctly capturing all correct interleavings of command invocations. Each command specification then refers only to the corresponding command, independent of other commands. The invariant for the `Timer` interface is as follows:

```
1  ∀i : [[CallAt(−, self, start, i)
2        ⟹ ∃j : i < j : CallAt(self, −, fired, j) ∨ CallBet(−, self, stop, i, j)] ∧
3    [CallAt(self, −, fired, i)
4        ⟹ ∃h : h < i : CallAt(−, self, start, h) ∧ ¬CallBet(−, self, stop, h, i)]]
```

The first conjunct states that each call to `start()` results in a future call to `fired()`, or there is an interleaving call to `stop()`. The second conjunct states that every call to `fired()` must have been preceded by a call to `start()`, and there must have been no interleaving call to `stop()`. Given this invariant, the command contracts can again be expressed as simple state assertions on the abstract model. However, the split-phase correspondence between `start()` and `stop()` is left implicit. This is a useful relationship for developers, one that can be captured with a new `promises` clause.

The `promises` clause defines an obligation that a component must meet at some point after termination of the current command. It is the dual of the

expects clause [18], which describes the obligations that a component expects *clients* to meet after successful termination of an operation. The key difference between **expects** and **promises** is in the "direction" of the deferred method call.

```
1  command void start(uint32_t delay);
2    requires: !self.active
3    ensures: self.active ∧ self.period = delay
4    promises: signal caller.fired()
```

Operationally, in addition to the control-flow context and variable values in each state of the program, each component maintains a *promise set* – a set of actions that it has promised to other components. For example, upon successful termination of the **start()** method, the **Timer** component promises to signal **fired()** on the caller. The complete specification of **Timer** is as follows:

```
1  interface Timer {
2    modeled by: (active: boolean, period: nat number)
3    initial state: (false, 0)
4    maintains:
5    ...invariant clause presented above...
6    command void start(uint32_t delay);
7      requires: !self.active
8      ensures: self.active ∧ self.period = delay
9      promises: signal caller.fired()
10   command void stop();
11     requires: self.active
12     ensures: !self.active ∧ self.period = 0
13   event void fired();
14     requires: self.active
15     ensures: !self.active ∧ self.period = delay
16 }
```

The **promises** clause on **start()** specifies both halves of the split-phase operation, adding significant reasoning value for client programmers. Consider a program that invokes **foo()**, followed, after a delay of 1000 time units, by **bar()**:

```
1  void op1() {  foo(); call Timer.start(1000);  }
2  ...
3  event void Timer.fired() { bar();  }
```

After calling **foo()**, **op1()** starts a timer and terminates. The call to **bar()** appears within the event handler of **fired()**. Without the **promises** clause, there is no indication of where program control will continue once the timer expires.

3.1   The Invariant as an Idiom

The invariant on the future trace has broad applicability in reactive programming. In nesC, the invariant serves as an idiom for specifying interfaces that contain a split-phase operation started by **SPOpStart()** and completed by **SPOpDone()**; and contain an operation **cancelSPOp()**, used to cancel an operation after it has been initiated. The invariant idiom for such a component is:

```
1  ∀i : [[CallAt(−,self,SPOpStart, i)
2      ⟹ ∃j : i < j : CallAt(self, −,SPOpDone, j) ∨ CallBet(−,self,SPOpCancel, i, j)] ∧
3    [CallAt(self, −,SPOpDone, i)
4      ⟹ ∃h : h < i : CallAt(−,self,SPOpStart, h) ∧ ¬CallBet(−,self,SPOpCancel, h, i)]]
```

The structure mirrors the "instantiated" invariant for the `Timer` interface. As another example, consider applying the idiom to the `Send` interface in TinyOS, used to send wireless messages in a network. The idiom correspondence is as follows: `send()` corresponds to `SPOpStart()`, `sendDone()` corresponds to `SPOpDone()`, and `cancel()` corresponds to `cancelSPOp()`. Combining the instantiated specification idiom with the usual state predicates yields the following specification:

```
1  interface Send {
2    modeled by: (active: boolean, message: string)
3    initialization ensures: (false, <>)
4    maintains:
5      ...instantiated invariant...
6    command error_t send(message_t* msg, uint8_t len);
7      requires: !self.active
8      ensures: self.active ∧ self.message = #msg
9      promises: signal caller.sendDone()
10   command error_t cancel(message_t* msg);
11     ...standard state conditions...
12   event void sendDone(message_t* msg);
13     ...standard state conditions...
14 }
```

3.2 Refining Promises

Conditional Promise. Consider the `Send` interface. When `send()` is invoked, the message to be sent is placed in an outgoing buffer. If this step completes, `send()` returns `SUCCESS`; otherwise, it returns `FAIL`. The return value communicates to the client that `sendDone()` will be signaled only if the message is successfully scheduled for transmission. Accordingly, we modify the specification of `send()`:

```
1  command error_t send(message_t* msg, uint8_t len);
2    requires: !self.active
3    ensures: self.active ∧ self.message = #msg
4    promises: (retval == SUCCESS) ⟹ signal caller.sendDone()
```

Conditional promises, which allow for a promise to be made contingent on a state assertion, are a specialization of the basic idiom. The basic idiom assumes that commands always complete in a state that guarantees the promise. Conditional promises can be used in cases where such an assumption is unrealistic.

Timed Promise. It is often useful to specify *when* invocations must occur. Consider again the `Timer` interface. When a timer is started, it is not enough to promise that `fired()` will eventually be signaled. It is also necessary to state that the event will be signaled after `delay` time. We can strengthen the specification of `start()` as follows:

```
1  command void start(uint32_t delay);
2    requires: !self.active
3    ensures: self.active ∧ self.period = delay
4    promises: signal caller.fired() within delay
```

Repeat Promise. In some cases, a single split-phase `SPOpStart()` can lead to multiple event signals. Consider, for example, a periodic timer. In such cases, the promises clause includes the `repeat` keyword, signifying that the event will be signaled continuously until the `cancel` operation is called by the client. We can specify the start of a periodic timer using a repeat promise as follows:

```
1  command void startPeriodic(uint32_t delay);
2     requires: !self.active
3     ensures: self.active ∧ self.period = delay
4     promises: signal caller.fired() within delay repeat
```

Notice here that the promise includes both a time limit and a repeat condition. In practice, most promises have multiple refinement annotations.

4   nesC / TinyOS Tool-Chain Extensions

To assist developers use our approach, we have developed extensions to the nesC compiler . Specifically, we have extended the nesC parser to accommodate a variation on the specification syntax introduced in the previous sections. Further, we have modified the compiler to enable the generation of runtime monitoring logic used to detect promise violations. This logic is automatically woven throughout the source base, if requested. For our case studies, we target a significant subset of the components and applications included in the TinyOS 2.1.1 distribution.

4.1   Annotations

To support promises, we introduce command-level annotations within the nesC interface grammar. When specifying that a given command issues a promise, the developer introduces the following annotation on the event signature, where the <event> parameter specifies the signature of the event to be invoked in the future: @promises <event>

To support refined promises, three subordinate annotations (applied beneath the root @promises annotation) are introduced. The first is used to support a conditional promise; it imposes a condition on the return value of the initiating command. A <condition> clause specifies a value to compare against the initiating command's return value. Only if these values match is a promise made: @condition <condition>

The second subordinate annotation supports timed promises. The annotation specifies that the promised event will be invoked within <p> time units, where the unit of measure is (at present) specified at compile time: @within <p>

The final subordinate annotation supports repeat promises. This annotation accepts no parameters and specifies that the promised event will be invoked repeatedly: @repeat

Consider the application of these annotations in specifying the behavior of the SplitControl power management interface in TinyOS. The interface has two commands, start() and stop(), with two corresponding events, startDone() and stopDone(). The start()/ startDone() operation is used to initialize a peripheral, while the stop()/stopDone() operation is used to put a peripheral into a low-power state. The commands, return codes, and events have the usual meanings. The annotated signature of start() is:

```
1  // @promises startDone
2  // @condition SUCCESS
3  command error_t start();
```

Table 1. Annotated TinyOS 2.1.1 Interfaces

Interface	Command	Promised Event	Periodicity	Timed	Condition
Send	send	sendDone	singleton	NO	SUCCESS
AMSend	send	sendDone	singleton	NO	SUCCESS
CC2420Config	sync	syncDone	singleton	NO	SUCCESS
Tcp	connect	connectDone	singleton	NO	SUCCESS
Mount	mount	mountDone	singleton	NO	SUCCESS
Read	read	readDone	singleton	NO	SUCCESS
ReadStream	postBuffer	bufferDone	singleton	NO	SUCCESS
	read	readDone	singleton	NO	SUCCESS
SplitControl	start	startDone	singleton	NO	SUCCESS
	stop	stopDone	singleton	NO	SUCCESS
Timer	startOneShot	fired	singleton	YES	(none)
	startPeriodic	fired	repeat	YES	(none)
ConfigStorage	read	readDone	singleton	NO	SUCCESS
	write	writeDone	singleton	NO	SUCCESS
	commit	commitDone	singleton	NO	SUCCESS
LogWrite	append	appendDone	singleton	NO	SUCCESS
	erase	eraseDone	singleton	NO	SUCCESS
	sync	syncDone	singleton	NO	SUCCESS
LogRead	read	readDone	singleton	NO	SUCCESS
	seek	seekDone	singleton	NO	SUCCESS

Next recall the `Timer` interface. This interface includes a command `startPeriodic()`, which makes a promise that the event `fired()` will be invoked repeatedly, with a period specified as argument. The command does not return a value, so the promise is unconditional. Here is the annotated signature of `startPeriodic()`:

```
1  // @promises fired
2  // @within dt
3  // @repeat
4  command void startPeriodic(uint32_t dt);
```

These are demonstrative examples. We have annotated *all* of the core interfaces in TinyOS 2.1.1 to specify the appropriate promises (Table 1).

4.2 Overhead Evaluation

To use the PromiseTracker tool with TinyOS applications, we recompiled all of the constituent applications to use the annotated interfaces and corresponding runtime monitors. The number and types of promises introduced in each application are summarized in Table 2a. Each application is intended to illustrate only one or two TinyOS concepts. As such, each application uses a small number of split-phase operations. Table 2b shows the overhead introduced by Promise-Tracker. In absolute terms, the overhead is nearly the same in each application.

To evaluate PromiseTracker in a realistic scenario, we instrumented a common spanning tree data collection protocol. Upon deployment, the nodes in the network organize themselves into a spanning tree, with the base-station at the root of the tree. All nodes collect data from their sensors and transmit the data up the tree toward the root. When instrumented with PromiseTracker, the spanning tree protocol uses a total of 30 promises and nearly all of the core interfaces in TinyOS. In terms of overhead, RAM usage increased by 33% (from 1,612b to 2,138b), and ROM usage increased by 13% (from 35,404b to 40,130b).

Table 2. TinyOS Evaluation Results

(a) Number of Clauses Introduced

Application	Number of Promises		
	single basic	single timed	repeat timed
Blink	0	0	3
BaseStation	4	0	0
MultihopOscilloscope	5	0	1
MultihopOscilloscopeLqi	5	0	1
MViz	5	0	2
Oscilloscope	3	0	1
PowerUp	0	0	0
RadioSenseToLeds	3	0	1
RadioCountToLeds	3	0	1
Sense	1	0	1

(b) Application Sizes After Injection

Application	Memory Overhead	
	RAM (bytes)/ overhead (%)	ROM (bytes)/ overhead (%)
Blink	672 / 92%	10260 / 74%
BaseStation	2111 / 16%	18696 / 16%
MultihopOscilloscope	3947 / 9%	34716 / 10%
MultihopOscilloscopeLqi	3030 / 12%	30604 / 12%
MViz	2176 / 18%	38814 / 10%
Oscilloscope	1020 / 56%	24948 / 30%
PowerUp	560 / 99%	7032 / 79%
RadioSenseToLeds	990 / 58%	24890 / 30%
RadioCountToLeds	902 / 64%	19736 / 39%
Sense	696 / 83%	15480 / 48%

Fig. 1. Monitor Generation Process

4.3 Monitoring Promises at Runtime

The runtime monitoring logic generated by PromiseTracker is automatically woven into a target system image to detect and report violations at runtime. This is useful either as a debugging aid or as the foundation for fault recovery.

A summary of the monitor generation process is shown in Figure 1. The first step is the *file search*, which mirrors the behavior of the nesC *make* system. The project makefile is parsed to identify the top-level component, which is then parsed using the *nesC Analysis and Instrumentation Toolkit* [10] to identify all implementation modules linked (transitively) from the top-level component.

The next step, the *operation search*, is the most compute-intensive. All of the implementation modules identified in the previous step are parsed and analyzed. This yields three hash-tables containing information about all of the interfaces used in the target application, all of the commands invoked, and all of the events signaled, respectively.

At this point, the *promise search*, a second-level parse is performed on each of the interfaces identified in the previous step. For each command invoked in the application, the corresponding declaration in the interface is examined to determine whether there are associated promise annotations. If so, the annotations associated with the command are added to the information contained within the command hash-table.

Next, the *code injection* step is performed, which introduces the runtime monitoring logic. The most basic component of this step is the introduction of support components and data structures to record pending and failed promises. In addition, for each annotated command invoked in the application, instrumentation is introduced at the call site to capture the (perhaps conditional) promise being made. Similarly, the corresponding <event> specified in the promises annotation is instrumented to capture the attempt to satisfy the promise.

Finally, the *code regeneration* step is performed to generate augmented nesC source materials ready for compilation and installation on the target device(s).

Implementation Details. The PromiseTracker interface lies at the core of the system. The interface provides commands to register new promises, flag that particular promises have been satisfied, and check for pending promises. An implementation of this interface is linked into every monitored application. This single instance is shared across all module implementations that invoke methods involving a promise.

During code analysis, each call site involving a command that establishes a promise is identified. To differentiate these promises and monitor their correctness over time, the analysis stage assigns a unique identifier to each promise, a promiseID. The identifier serves as an index into an array that stores information about each promise. The data structure used to store information about an unbounded promise is as follows:

```
1 struct UnboundedPromise { uint8_t state; }
```

UnboundedPromise defines a single field, state, used to record the current state of the promise. There are only two possibilities, PENDING and SUCCESS. The first indicates that a promise of future behavior has been made. The latter indicates that there is no pending promise. It is interesting to note that these are the only two states required since an unbounded promise can never be violated in a finite prefix of a computation. However, recording unbounded promises at the time they are made and keeping a tally of unfulfilled promises is a valuable tool for system developers. This class of problems (unfulfilled promises) represents a large class of errors in embedded networked systems; the identification of where these errors originate is useful. The data structure used to store information about a timed promise is as follows:

```
1 struct TimeBoundedPromise {
2     bool repeat;    uint8_t state;
3     uint32_t timeConstraint, startTime;  }
```

TimeBoundedPromise defines four fields. The first, repeat, is a boolean that records whether the promise is a repeat promise. The second, timeConstraint, stores the time constraint, <p>, specified as part of the @within annotation. The third, startTime, stores the time at which the promise obligation was registered. (Comparing the current system time to startTime and timeConstraint is performed to detect timing failures.) Finally, the state field records the current state of the promise. As before, a promise may be in the PENDING or SUCCESS state. In addition, a timed promise may be in the MARKED or FAIL states. When a promise is MARKED, it indicates that the specified future event has been signaled, but the timing has not yet been checked. The FAIL state indicates that a promise of future behavior was not satisfied within the specified time limit.

The essential elements of the PromiseTracker interface are: makePromise(), markPromise(), and checkPromise(). Calls to these methods are inserted

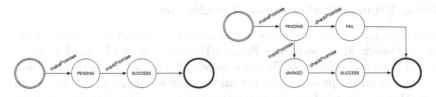

Fig. 2. Singleton, Unbnd. Tracking   **Fig. 3.** Singleton, Timed Tracking

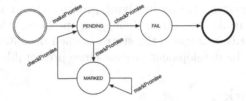

Fig. 4. Repeat, Timed Tracking

automatically during the instrumentation process. When a command that includes a `promises` clause is invoked, `makePromise()` is called to register the promise of future behavior. Note that if the promise is a conditional promise, the return value of the command is compared to the `<condition>` specified in the `@condition` annotation; `makePromise()` is not called if there is a mismatch. The call results in the corresponding promise being marked as `PENDING`. Similarly, a call to `markPromise()` is introduced in the corresponding event. In the case of an unbounded promise, the call results in the promise state being set to `SUCCESS`. In the case of a timed promise, the state is set to `MARKED`. The complete lifecycle of an unbounded promise is illustrated in Figure 2.

The lifecycle of a singleton, timed promise is more complicated, as shown in Figure 3. The call to `markPromise()` is not the end of the lifecycle; an additional step remains. Specifically, the monitoring logic must check whether the promise was satisfied within its deadline. This is done using the `checkPromise()` method. At the time the promise was made, `makePromise()` initiates a timer with a period equal to the specified promise deadline. When the timer fires, `checkPromise()` is invoked. If `checkPromise()` finds the promise in the `PENDING` state, it means the promise has not been kept, and therefore, the deadline has not been met. If the state is `MARKED`, it means the promised event has already been signaled within the deadline. For singleton, timed promises, if the deadline is met properly, the promise is marked `SUCCESS`, otherwise it is marked `FAIL`.

The lifecycle of a repeat, timed promise is similar, as shown in Figure 4. This type of promise is also examined by `checkPromise()` when the deadline timer expires. If the promised event has been signaled by the deadline (`MARKED`), the promise is returned to the `PENDING` state to wait for the next promised event. If the promised event has not yet been signaled (`PENDING`), the promise has been violated and is marked `FAIL`.

4.4 Using PromiseTracker during Development

Once interfaces have been annotated using `promises` clauses to establish links between commands and events, the PromiseTracker tool can be used as a debugging aid during development. When a developer chooses to use a particular interface, the `promises` provide a better understanding of command and event behaviors. During the development cycle, the developer can use PromiseTracker to identify the promises that have been made, and to inject code to monitor these promises. At any point during execution, the developer can query the state of all promises in the system. Errors involving promise violations are notoriously difficult to identify using traditional debugging methods. The capability that PromiseTracker affords in tracking the status of each promise provides value to developers, making the development process more predictable.

5 Related Work

Specification techniques for reactive systems usually include explicit statements of safety and progress properties. Popular specification languages such as UNITY [6] and TLA [19] model concurrency using nondeterministic interleaving of actions. Other major approaches to capturing concurrent behavior include rely-guarantee [1,15,29], hypothesis-conclusion [6], and assumption-commitment [8]. All these techniques suffer from a similar problem; they do not map well to procedural languages.

Contract specifications [23] map well to procedural code, and [18] presents techniques to capture concurrent behavior in contracts. The `promises` clause we have presented is a dual to the `expects` clause presented in [18]. Contract specifications have been written for TinyOS before [3]; however, these contracts do not capture the reactive nature of the components. In particular, these contracts do not capture the relationship between the halves of a split-phase operation.

Others have worked on capturing the behavior of TinyOS applications. [17] presents a technique to automatically derive state machines from TinyOS programs. They use symbolic execution to infer the execution trace of an application, and based on this trace, to construct a finite state machine that represents the behavior of the program. There has also been work in runtime monitoring of TinyOS applications [13]. TOSTracer is a lightweight monitor that runs concurrently with the application program and generates a sequence diagram representation of the application's execution. [4] describes work on verifying TinyOS programs using the CBMC bounded model checker [7].

Li and Regehr [22] present T-Check, a model checking approach for finding interaction bugs in sensor networks. T-Check is implemented on top of Safe TinyOS [9] and allows developers to specify both safety and liveness properties. T-Check incorporates multiple models of non-determinism in order to explore the complete state space of a sensornet. Some of the liveness bugs that T-Check can capture (node-level bugs) can be expressed as promises. Kleenet [26] is a tool based on symbolic execution for discovering interaction bugs in sensor networks. Kleenet has been integrated into Contiki [11].

Several authors have considered monitoring runtime errors using pre-defined specifications. The Monitoring and Checking framework (MaC) [20] is an approach to conducting runtime analysis of a system's execution. MaC uses a formal language to specify execution requirements, which assert events and conditions in a high-level manner. A monitoring script is used to link the high-level events and conditions with low-level information at runtime. Monitored information is converted to events, which are verified based on the requirements. Based on MaC, [28] presents an approach that uses verification results and user specifications to detect errors and adjust the system back to normal execution. [21] presents an approach that not only monitors execution and logs errors, but also takes programmers' system recovery specification as input to perform a desired repair. These efforts focus on monitoring program execution using user-defined specs, whereas our work is focused on tracking split-phase operations at runtime by extending the nesC tool-chain to support command-level annotations.

Dustminer [16] is a diagnostic tool that automatically detects root causes of interaction bugs and performance anomalies in sensor networks. For example, after analyzing collected logs from good nodes and crashed nodes in a sensor network running LiteOS [5], the *packet received* event was identified as highly correlated with the *get current radio handle* event in the good nodes, whereas it was highly correlated with the *get serial send function* event in the crashed nodes. By capturing unexpected event sequences that cause errors, Dustminer focuses on non-localized errors when nodes run distributed protocols. As such, Dustminer helps with diagnosing errors that occur in distributed scenarios, which are usually hard to reproduce. However, Dustminer is not designed to help localize the events in the code that cause these errors.

[30] presents a technique for TinyOS applications that reconstructs control-flow paths between procedures based on captured concurrent events and control-flow paths inside each event. The target program is statically analyzed, and tracing statements are inserted in each event function body. At runtime, the recorded trace is stored in RAM, and then compressed and transferred to flash. When an error is detected, the stored trace is sent to the base-station. By replaying the trace and reproducing the execution sequence in a simulator or debugger, the programmer is better able to locate the fault and the call sequence that led to the fault. This tool requires manual operations and depends highly on the capability of the programmer to identify the error and problematic trace.

There is a vast literature base exploring runtime monitoring for error detection. [27] presents an approach to monitoring the execution of reactive systems and recovering from runtime failures. This approach uses a module that learns the behavior of a reactive system, and when an error is detected, applies a repair action. The choice of which repair action to use is based on an analysis of the execution history. [24] presents a discussion of how to design runtime monitors for real-time systems. The focus is on how to enforce real-time guarantees. Copilot [25] focuses on hard real-time guarantees. The monitoring system samples observable state variables; the monitor and the system share a global clock.

6 Conclusion

Asynchronous behavior in reactive systems is difficult to capture using traditional contract-based specification mechanisms. Such behavior is usually captured using temporal specifications, but the mapping between such specifications and corresponding implementations in procedural languages is cumbersome. In this paper, we have presented a specification idiom that can be used to capture asynchronous behavior in reactive systems using the concept of a *future trace*. When a split-phase operation is initiated, the start command makes a *promise* that an event will be signaled in the future. The promise is encoded as part of the method's contract along with its pre- and post-condition.

The promises clause offers a way to capture asynchronous behavior in contract specifications that can be easily integrated with software written in procedural languages such as C. Split-phase operations are particularly common in embedded systems, where blocking operations are not viable. At this point, the promises we are able to specify and capture are only local to a single sensor node. While these represent a large class of potential interaction bugs, interactions between commands and events across nodes represent an even larger class of such bugs. These are even harder to find. We are currently working on extending the semantics of the promises clause to be able to express such cross-node promises. Once the semantics are extended, tool support can be readily added. In fact, we already have tools that can capture execution snapshots across nodes in a sensor network and check predicates; promises can be added to such a set of predicates.

As a case study, we have written specifications for TinyOS, which is designed for sensornets. As a way of enforcing promises at runtime, we have implemented a runtime monitoring infrastructure that runs in parallel with the application running on an embedded microcontroller. The runtime monitor, PromiseTracker, injects bookkeeping calls to track each promise made, and to check if the promise is satisfied. This runtime monitor, implemented for TinyOS 2.1.1, serves as a powerful debugging aid in the presence of asynchronous behavior.

Acknowledgments. This work was supported in part by NSF grants CNS-0746632, CNS-0745846, and CNS-1126344.

References

1. Abadi, M., Lamport, L.: Composing specifications. TOPLAS 15(1), 73–132 (1993)
2. Adya, A., et al.: Cooperative task management without manual stack management. In: USENIX 2002, pp. 289–302 (2002)
3. Archer, W., et al.: Interface contracts for tinyos. In: IPSN 2007, pp. 158–165. ACM Press, New York (2007)
4. Bucur, D., Kwiatkowska, M.: On software verification for sensor nodes. J. Syst. Softw. 84, 1693–1707 (2011)
5. Cao, Q., et al.: The liteos operating system: Towards unix-like abstractions for wireless sensor networks. In: IPSN 2008, Washington, DC, USA, pp. 233–244 (2008)
6. Chandy, K.M., Misra, J.: Parallel Program Design: A Foundation. Addison-Wesley, Reading (1988)

7. Clarke, E., Kroning, D., Lerda, F.: A tool for checking ansi-c programs. In: Jensen, K., Podelski, A. (eds.) TACAS 2004. LNCS, vol. 2988, pp. 168–176. Springer, Heidelberg (2004)
8. Collette, P.: Composition of assumption-commitment specifications in a UNITY style. SCP 23, 107–125 (1994)
9. Cooprider, N., et al.: Efficient memory safety for tinyos. In: SenSys 2007, pp. 205–218. ACM, New York (2007)
10. Dalton, A.R., Hallstrom, J.O.: nait: A source analysis and instrumentation framework for nesc. J. Syst. Softw. 82, 1057–1072 (2009)
11. Dunkels, A., et al.: Contiki - a lightweight and flexible operating system for tiny networked sensors. In: LCN 2004, Washington, DC, USA, pp. 455–462 (2004)
12. Gay, D., et al.: The nesC language: A holistic approach to networked embedded systems. In: PLDI 2003, pp. 1–11. ACM Press (June 2003)
13. Hammad, M., Cook, J.: Lightweight monitoring of sensor software. In: SAC 2009, pp. 2180–2185. ACM, New York (2009)
14. Hill, J., et al.: System architecture directions for networked sensors. In: ASPLOS, pp. 93–104. ACM Press (November 2000)
15. Jones, C.B.: Tentative steps toward a development method for interfering programs. TOPLAS 5(4), 596–619 (1983)
16. Khan, M.M.H., et al.: Dustminer: troubleshooting interactive complexity bugs in sensor networks. In: SenSys 2008, pp. 99–112. ACM, New York (2008)
17. Kothari, N., et al.: Deriving state machines from tinyos programs using symbolic execution. In: IPSN 2008, pp. 271–282. IEEE, Washington, DC (2008)
18. Kumar, S., et al.: Encapsulating concurrency as an approach to unification. In: SAVCBS 2004, Newport Beach, CA (October 2004)
19. Lamport, L.: The temporal logic of actions. TOPLAS 16(3), 872–923 (1994)
20. Lee, I., et al.: A monitoring and checking framework for run-time correctness assurance. In: Proc. Korea-U.S. Tech Conf. Strat. Tech., Vienna, VA (October 1998)
21. Lewis, C., Whitehead, J.: Runtime repair of software faults using event-driven monitoring. In: ICSE 2010, pp. 275–280. ACM, New York (2010)
22. Li, P., Regehr, J.: T-check: bug finding for sensor networks. In: IPSN 2010, pp. 174–185. ACM Press, New York (2010)
23. Meyer, B.: Applying "design by contract". Computer 25(10), 40–51 (1992)
24. Peters, D.K., Parnas, D.L.: Requirements-based monitors for real-time systems. SIGSOFT Softw. Eng. Notes 25, 77–85 (2000)
25. Pike, L., Goodloe, A., Morisset, R., Niller, S.: Copilot: a hard real-time runtime monitor. In: Barringer, H., et al. (eds.) RV 2010. LNCS, vol. 6418, pp. 345–359. Springer, Heidelberg (2010)
26. Sasnauskas, R., et al.: Kleenet: discovering insidious interaction bugs in wireless sensor networks before deployment. In: IPSN, New York, NY, pp. 186–196 (2010)
27. Seshia, S.A.: Autonomic reactive systems via online learning. In: Proc. IEEE ICAC. IEEE Press (June 2007)
28. Sokolsky, O., et al.: Steering of real-time systems based on monitoring and checking. In: WORDS 1999, p. 11. IEEE Computer Society, Washington, DC (1999)
29. Stark, E.W.: A proof technique for rely guarantee properties. In: Maheshwari, S.N. (ed.) FSTTCS 1985. LNCS, vol. 206, pp. 369–391. Springer, Heidelberg (1985)
30. Sundaram, V., et al.: Efficient diagnostic tracing for wireless sensor networks. In: SenSys 2010, pp. 169–182. ACM, New York (2010)
31. Yang, J.: Clairvoyant: a comprehensive source-level debugger for wireless sensor networks. In: SenSys 2007, pp. 189–203. ACM, New York (2007)

Speculative Program Parallelization with Scalable and Decentralized Runtime Verification

Aravind Sukumaran-Rajam[1], Juan Manuel Martinez Caamaño[1],
Willy Wolff[1], Alexandra Jimborean[2], and Philippe Clauss[1]

[1] INRIA, Team CAMUS, ICube Lab, CNRS, University of Strasbourg, France
{aravind.sukumaran-rajam,juan-manuel.martinez-caamano,
willy.wolff,philippe.clauss}@inria.fr
[2] Department of Information Technology, Uppsala University, Sweden
alexandra.jimborean@it.uu.se

Abstract. Thread Level Speculation (TLS) is a dynamic code parallelization technique proposed to keep the software in pace with the advances in hardware, in particular, to automatically parallelize programs to take advantage of the multi-core processors. Being speculative, frameworks of this type unavoidably rely on verification systems that are similar to software transactional memory, and that require voluminous inter-thread communications or centralized registering of the performed memory accesses. The high degree of communication is against the basic principles of high performance parallel computing, does not scale with an increasing number of processor cores, and yields weak performance. Moreover, TLS systems often apply one unique parallelization strategy consisting in slicing a loop into several parallel speculative threads. Such a strategy is also against the basic principles since loops in the original serial code are not necessarily parallel and also, it is well-known that the parallel schedule must promote data locality which is crucial in obtaining good performance. This situation appeals to scalable and decentralized verification systems and new strategies to dynamically generate efficient parallel code resulting from advanced optimizing parallelizing transformations. Such transformations require a more complex verification system that allows intra-thread iterations to be reordered. In this paper, we propose a verification system of this kind, based on a model built at runtime and predicting a linear memory behavior. This strategy is part of the Apollo speculative code parallelizer which is based on an adaptation for dynamic usage of the polyhedral model.

1 Introduction

Automatically parallelizing sequential code became increasingly important with the advent of multicore processors. However, static approaches applied at compile-time fail in handling codes which contain intractable control and memory instructions. For instance, while-loops, indirect array references or pointer accesses cannot generally be disambiguated at compile-time, thus preventing any automatic parallelization based exclusively on static dependence analysis. Such a situation appeals for the development of runtime parallelization systems, which are granted more power by the information discovered dynamically.

B. Bonakdarpour and S.A. Smolka (Eds.): RV 2014, LNCS 8734, pp. 124–139, 2014.

Runtime parallelization techniques of loop nests are usually based on thread-level speculation (TLS) [1–3] frameworks, which optimistically allow the parallel execution of code regions before all dependences are known. Hardware or software mechanisms track register and memory accesses to determine if any dependence violation occur. In such cases, the register and memory state is rolled back to a previous valid state and sequential re-execution is initiated. Traditional TLS systems perform a simple, straightforward parallelization of loop nests by simply slicing the outermost loop into consecutive parallel threads [1, 2, 4]. Verifying the speculations consists in ensuring that the schedule of the accesses to shared memory locations in the parallel code matches the one of the original code. This general verification principle is made simple in the case of straightforward parallelization, since each parallel thread consists of a slice of successive iterations of the original serial loop nest, thus following internally the original sequential schedule. Modest performance improvements have been reported, due to an expensive verification system and poor parallelizing transformations. The verification system requires communication among the parallel threads to share which memory addresses are accessed, in order to detect conflicts and preserve memory coherency by rollbacking the delinquent threads. This strategy yields a *high communication traffic* that is significantly penalizing performance, and which is against the general optimization principles in parallel computing. Another important consequence is that a *centralized verification system* does not scale with the number of processor cores. This situation calls for a different strategy where each thread takes part independently in the verification of the global correctness of the speculative parallelization. Additionally, as soon as a dependence is carried by the outermost loop, it leads to numerous rollbacks, consequently, performance drops. Moreover, even if infrequent dependences occur, there is no guarantee that the resulting instruction schedule improves performance. Indeed, *poor data locality* and a high amount of data shared between the threads can yield a parallel execution slower than the original sequential one. To gain efficiency, TLS systems must handle more complex code optimizing transformations that can be selected at runtime, depending on the current execution context.

In this paper, we propose a verification strategy as an answer to these drawbacks. Our solution relies on a *prediction model* which is built by first observing a small sample of the target loop nest execution, and then it is used to verify the speculatively optimized and parallelized code, during execution. The parallel code is generated by applying advanced code transformations, thus, the iteration schedule in the parallel threads is no longer in accordance with the original serial schedule of the iterations. This is equivalent to saying that iterations are reordered not only across threads, but also within a thread. Yet, the parallel schedule is semantically correct as long as the prediction model holds. Each thread verifies independently that its execution is compliant with the prediction model, hence the verification is entirely de-centralized. The model adopted in this work to reason about the loop transformations is an adaptation of the *polyhedral model* to dynamic and speculative parallelization.

The polyhedral model [5], originally designed for compile-time loop optimization and parallelization, is known to show immense benefits for loops with linear iteration counts and array accesses. Such loops are characteristic to scientific codes or kernels designed for embedded systems. However, frequently, applying the polyhedral model statically is prohibited by factors such as: (i) bounds that cannot be statically predicted, (ii) complex control flows, or (iii) pointers accessing dynamically allocated structures, which leads to issues such as memory aliasing. Yet, such codes, although not statically analyzable, may exhibit a linear behaviour at runtime. Thus, they are amenable to precise polyhedral dependence analysis (based on information acquired by online profiling), in the view of performing complex parallelizing code transformations at runtime. This has important consequences: (a) runtime verification is required to validate the speculative code transformations; (b) an online recovery system, which will be triggered upon a misspeculation, must be designed; (c) the system should be lightweight enough to shadow the runtime overhead[1].

In this paper, we focus on the *verification system* of a polyhedral TLS framework called Apollo, for Automatic POLydedral Loop Optimizer. Apollo takes the best of the two worlds: as a TLS system, it targets non-statically analyzable loop nests and memory accesses (including while-loops with memory accesses to dynamic data structures via pointers which exhibit a linear runtime behavior); as a polyhedral optimizer, it applies polyhedral optimizations prior to parallelization, which makes Apollo novel and conceptually different than its TLS predecessors.

The paper is organized as follows: next section describes a classic program exhibiting parallel phases, depending on the input data. This kind of programs is a typical target for Apollo. In Section 3, the global functioning of our polyhedral TLS system is depicted, while its part dedicated to runtime verification of the speculative parallelizing and optimizing transformations is thoroughly detailed in Section 4. Related work addressing runtime verification of speculations in TLS systems is summarized in Section 5. Results of experiments showing the effectiveness of our approach are given in Section 6. Finally, Section 7 presents conclusions and perspectives.

2   Motivating Example

This section underlines an example code exhibiting polyhedral behavior in some execution contexts, which cannot be detected statically, thus preventing automatic parallelization at compilation time. Apollo is tailored to detect and dynamically optimize such codes. The example is the kernel loop nest of the *breadthFirstSearch* (BFS) algorithm from the Problem Based Benchmark Suite [6] shown in Listing 1.1.

The BFS method performs a breadth first search scan of a graph in the following way. The vertices of the input graph GA are identified as integer values ranging from 0 to GA.n. Thus, array Visited is used to mark each vertex which has already been visited, by storing respectively 0 or 1 at the vertex index value. Array Frontier is used to store the list of vertices whose neighbors have to be visited in some next iterations of the outer while-loop. As long as top > bot, there are still remaining vertices that have to be visited. Before entering the loop nest, the input starting vertex is identified by the variable start: it is stored in array Frontier as the first and still unique vertex whose neighbors must be visited, and the vertex itself is marked in array Visited as having been already visited. When entering the while-loop, the current vertex whose

---

[1] Stemming from online profiling, dynamic code transformations, support for a speculative execution and recovery from invalid speculations.

Listing 1.1. Main loop nest of the breadthFirstSearch benchmark code

```
1   pair<int ,int> BFS(int start , graph<int> GA) {
2     int numVertices = GA.n;
3     int numEdges = GA.m;
4     vertex<int> *G = GA.V;
5     int* Frontier = newA(intT ,numEdges);
6     int* Visited = newA(intT ,numVertices);
7     for (intT i = 0; i < numVertices; i++) Visited[i] = 0;
8     int bot = 0;
9     int top = 1;
10    Frontier[0] = start;
11    Visited[start] = 1;
12    #pragma apollo_dcop { /* Dynamic Control OPtimization */
13    while (top > bot) {
14      int v = Frontier[bot++];
15      int k = 0;
16      for (int j=0; j < G[v].degree; j++) {
17        int ngh = G[v].Neighbors[j];
18        if (Visited[ngh] == 0) {
19          Frontier[top++] = G[v].Neighbors[k++] = ngh;
20          Visited[ngh] = 1; }
21      }
22      G[v].degree = k;
23    } // end while
24    } // end pragma
25    free(Frontier); free(Visited);
26    return pair<int ,int >(0,0);
27  }
```

neighbors are going to be visited is `Frontier[bot]`, assigned to variable v. The inner for-loop is used to scan all the neighbors of this current vertex v, their count being given by `G[v].degree`. For each neighbor, it is determined if it has already been visited by testing its corresponding element of array `Visited`. Otherwise, *i.e.* when `Visited[ngh]==0`, it is stored in array `Frontier` as a vertex whose neighbors have to be visited in the next iterations of the while-loop. The order in which vertices are stored and processed in array `Frontier` ensures the breadth first search order of the algorithm.

Compile-time automatic parallelization, as well as manual OpenMP parallelization, are prohibited by the presence of the while-loop. Additionally, the upper bound of the inner for-loop is sensitive to the input data. Dependences cannot be analyzed statically since some elements of array `Visited` may be updated several times depending on the value of `ngh = G[v].Neighbors[j]`, itself depending on the value of v = `Frontier[bot++]`. Even if experts in parallel programming would be able to handle its parallelization with considerable efforts, this loop nest is amenable to *automatic* parallelization only speculatively, at runtime. Some TLS systems would attempt to parallelize the outermost while-loop by slicing it into several speculative threads, with the assumption that values of `top` and `bot` can be predicted by the speculative system. Nevertheless, this would fail since reads of uninitialized array elements Frontier[bot++] at line 14 would be detected as faulty and not in compliance with the original serial order. In contrast, for particular input graphs, Apollo detects a Read-After-Write dependence between the update of Frontier[top++] in the inner loop and the read of Frontier[bot++] in the outer loop, from the initial run of a small instrumented slice of the outermost loop. Thus, Apollo would not attempt parallelization of the outer loop.

The unique possible loop parallelization is on the inner for-loop (for TLS systems also handling inner loops). Special care must be taken regarding accesses to array G[v].Neighbors which are carrying Write-After-Read dependences, as well as regarding read-write accesses to the variables top and k which are carrying Read-After-Write dependences. Without embedding a mechanism for privatizing in each parallel thread both latter variables and predict their values, a TLS system would fail. In contrast, thanks to instrumentation by sampling and linear interpolation, Apollo embeds their thread-privatization and the prediction of their values in the resulting parallel code. In consequence, their associated Read-After-Write dependences are eliminated.

Apollo is successful in parallelizing the inner loop for certain classes of input graphs. This example highlights a typical case where parallelization opportunities depend on the input data: for instance, if the input graph defines a regular grid, or a complete N-tree, then G[v].degree is constant, since by definition, each vertex has the same fixed number of neighbors. Also in this case, the conditional Visited[ngh]==0 is evaluated as true for a large number of successive vertices which do not share the same neighbors. Thus, variable k is equal to variable j for large execution phases, which enables an accurate prediction of the memory accesses and the parallelization of large execution phases.

Let us consider a regular grid of n vertices and of degree d defined as follows: each vertex $i < n - d$ has d neighbors ranging from $(i + 1) \bmod n$ to $(i + d) \bmod n$, and each vertex $i \geq n - d$ has one neighbor which is vertex 1. Considering this grid as input to the breadthFirstSearch algorithm (List. 1.1), Apollo was successful in automatically parallelizing the inner loop on-the-fly. A first significant phase of n/d outer loop iterations was detected as amenable for parallelization. This phase corresponds to the continuous evaluation as true of the conditional Visited[ngh]==0. A rollback was initiated at the end of this phase, followed by the run of a small slice of instrumented iterations allowing Apollo to build a new prediction model and to parallelize a larger phase of $n - d - n/d$ outer loop iterations. This latter phase corresponds to the continuous evaluation as false of the conditional Visited[ngh]==0. While this phase was ended by rollbacking, a next instrumented slice of iterations was not able to build a linear prediction model. Thus, the execution was completed using the original serial code for the remaining outer loop iterations. A 9× speed-up was obtained with $n = 10,000$ and $d = 1000$ on two AMD Opteron 6172 processors, of 12 cores each, running 32 parallel threads. Details on how Apollo handled this code, and particularly on how it ensured correctness of the speculative parallelization, are given in the next Section.

3 Dynamic and Speculative Polyhedral Parallelization with Apollo

The polytope model [7] has been proven to be a powerful mathematical and geometrical framework for analyzing and optimizing for-loop nests. The requirements are that (i) each loop iterates according to a unique index variable whose bounds are affine expressions of the enclosing loop indices, and (ii) the memory instructions are limited to accesses to simple scalar variables or to multi-dimensional array elements using affine expressions on the enclosing loop indices. Such loop nests are analyzed accurately with respect to data dependences that occur among the statements and across iterations. Thus, advanced optimizing transformations are proven to be semantically correct by preserving the dependences of the original program. The loop nest optimizations (e.g., skewing, interchange) are linear transformations of the iteration domains that are represented geometrically as polyhedra. Each tuple of loop indices values is associated with an integer point contained in the polyhedra. The order in which the iterations are executed translates to the lexicographic order of the tuples. Thus, transformations represent a reordering of the execution of iterations and are defined as scheduling matrices, which is equivalent to geometrically transforming a polyhedra into another equivalent form [7]. Representing loops nests as polyhedra enables one to reason about the valid transformations that can be performed.

Although very powerful, the polytope model is restrained to a small class of compute-intensive codes that can be analyzed accurately and transformed at compile-time. However, most legacy codes are not amenable to this model, due to dynamic data structures accessed through indirect references or pointers, which prevent a precise dependence analysis to be performed statically. On the other hand, applied entirely dynamically, the complex analyses and the polyhedral code transformations would entail significant overhead. As shown in Section 2, codes that do not exhibit characteristics suiting the polytope model may still be in compliance with the model, although this compliance can only be detected at runtime. Targeting such codes for automatic optimization and parallelization imposes to immerse the polytope model in the context of speculative and dynamic parallelization. In this context, runtime code analysis and transformation impose strategies which induce very low time-overheads that must be largely compensated by the gains provided by the polyhedral optimization and parallelization.

For loop nests that cannot be analyzed statically, our strategy for making the polyhedral model applicable at runtime relies on speculations, and thus, requires runtime verification. It consists of observing initially the original code during a very short sample of the whole run. If a polyhedral behavior has been observed on this sample, we speculate that the behavior will remain the same on the rest of the loop nest execution. Thus, we can abstract the loop to a polyhedral representation, reason about the inter-iteration dependences, and validate and apply a polyhedral optimizing and parallelizing transformation. As long as this prediction remains true, the generated parallel code is semantically correct by definition of the polyhedral model. In order to verify continuously the prediction, and thus verify the correctness of the parallel program, we implemented a decentralized runtime verification system embedded in the parallel code, as detailed in the next Section.

First, we recall the main steps of static polyhedral automatic parallelization and describe how these steps are handled in Apollo to turn this approach into its dynamic and speculative equivalent form. The framework description focuses on the two main goals: building the polyhedral prediction model and applying speculative parallelization including runtime verification of the prediction. Further details regarding dynamic code generation and other important parts of Apollo can be found in [8], where a former prototype version called VMAD is presented. Apollo consists of two main parts: a static part implemented as passes of the LLVM compiler [9], and a dynamic part implemented as a runtime system written in C++.

At compile-time, Apollo's static phase: (1) analyzes precisely memory instructions that can be disambiguated at compile-time; (2) generates an instrumented version to track memory accesses that *cannot* be disambiguated at compile-time. The instrumented version will run on a sample of the outermost loop iterations and the information acquired dynamically is used to build a prediction model of these statically non-analyzable memory accesses; (3) generates parallel code skeletons [8]. They are incomplete versions of the original loop nest and require runtime instantiation to generate the final code. Each instantiation represents a new optimization, therefore the code skeletons can be seen as highly generic templates that support a large set of optimizing and parallelizing transformations. Additionally, the skeletons embed support for speculations (e.g. verification and recovery code).

At runtime, Apollo's dynamic phase: (1) runs the instrumented version on a sample of consecutive outermost loop iterations; (2) builds a linear prediction model for the loop bounds and memory accesses; (3) computes dependences between the memory accesses; (4) instantiates a code skeleton and generates an optimized, parallel version of the original sequential code, semantically correct with respect to the prediction model; (5) during the execution of the multi-threaded code, each thread verifies independently if the prediction still holds. If not, a rollback is initiated and the system attempts to build a new prediction model. An optimization has been designed to limit the number of iterations required to rollback upon a misspeculation (see subsection 3.2).

3.1 Compliance with the Polyhedral Model

The programmer inserts a dedicated *pragma* defining regions of code in which all loop nests will be considered for a speculative execution by Apollo. At compile-time, the target loop nests are analyzed and first the instrumented versions are generated. Additional counters named *virtual loop iterators* are systematically inserted to enable the framework in handling uniformly any kind of loops, e.g. for-loops or while-loops. They are also important in the speculative parallelization phase as it will be explained later. The static analysis consists in the following steps.

Every memory instructions is classified as *static* or *dynamic*[2]. For static memory accesses, the LLVM scalar evolution pass[3] is successful in expressing the sequence of accessed locations as an affine function of the enclosing loop iterators. This approach fails on dynamic memory accesses. For each couple of static memory instructions where at least one is a store, alias analysis is performed using a dedicated LLVM pass. The collected aliasing information will be used at runtime to save some

---

[2] i.e. which can be analyzed statically or requires dynamic instrumentation.

[3] http://llvm.org/devmtg/2009-10/ScalarEvolutionAndLoopOptimization.pdf

Table 1. Prediction model characteristics for the breadthFirstSearch code

#handled scalars	predicting affine functions
4	$0i + 100; 100i + 1$
	$0i + 1j + 0; 100i + 1j + 1$
#memory instructions	**predicting affine functions**
9	$16i + 19282504; 16i + 19282496$
	$400i + 4j + 19442512$
	$400i + 4j + 27363348$
	$400i + 4j + 19442512$
	$400i + 4j + 23402932$
	$400i + 4j + 27363348$
	$16i + 0j + 19282504; 16i + 19282504$
#inner loop bounds	**predicting affine functions**
1	$0i + 100$

dependence types	dependence equations $\forall (i, j) \preceq (i', j')$
Write-After-Read	$\{\, i - i' = 0$
Write-After-Read	$\begin{cases} i - i' = 0 \\ j - j' = 0 \\ -j + j' \geq 0 \end{cases}$
Write-After-Read	$\begin{cases} i - i' = 0 \\ i - j' = 0 \end{cases}$
Write-After-Write	$\{\, i - i + 1' = 0$
Read-After-Write	$\begin{cases} i - i + 1' = 0 \\ j - j' = 0 \end{cases}$

dependence analysis time-overhead. Instrumentation instructions are inserted to collect the memory addresses touched by each dynamic memory instruction. Similarly, relying on the LLVM scalar evolution pass, Apollo attempts to build affine functions describing the loop bounds. If this attempt fails, instrumentation code is inserted to monitor the value of the loops bounds. Scalar variables required to maintain the control flow or to compute the memory addresses are also analyzed by scalar evolution or instrumented if the analysis fails. These scalar variables are detected at compile-time as being defined by phi-nodes in the LLVM Intermediate Representation (IR) which is in Static Single Assignment (SSA) form. Linearly dependent scalars are grouped to reduce instrumentation to one unique representative of the group to lower the instrumentation runtime cost. The linear functions computed by the scalar evolution pass are stored and will be transmitted to Apollo's runtime system to complete the information required for runtime dependence analysis.

The dynamic analysis consists of the following operations. When running, every instrumented instruction generates a stream of values (memory addresses or scalar values) that are interpolated as functions of the virtual loop iterators. If every stream of values, obtained from an execution sample, can be modeled as an *affine function* of the virtual loop iterators, then the target loop nest is speculatively predicted to be compliant with the polytope model. The so-built affine functions are finally used to complete the dynamic dependence analysis which is also performed using the streams of actual addresses that are collected from instrumentation.

In summary, the prediction model of each target loop nest is made of: (1) the dependence information which is used to select and validate a parallelizing code transformation; (2) the affine functions associated with the memory instructions and the scalar variables: these functions are essential for the runtime verification of the speculation and to predict the starting context of the parallel threads regarding the scalars. This part is fully detailed in the next Section. As an example, the prediction model computed by Apollo at runtime for the first phase of the breadthFirstSearch code (see Section 2) is detailed in Table 1, where $\preceq$ denotes the lexicographical order. Notice that even if some scalars and memory instructions can be intuitively related to the source code, it is generally difficult, since they are identified at compile-time on the LLVM-IR representation of the program, after some LLVM optimizations have been applied.

3.2 Speculative Parallelization and Runtime Verification

Speculative parallelization and runtime verification are performed using the prediction model as sketched in what follows. Runtime verification is specifically highlighted in the next Section.

Code skeletons: At compile-time, several variants of codes are generated from each loop nest that was marked in the source code by the user using the dedicated pragma: an instrumented version, as described in the previous subsection, but also a number of code skeletons, presented in detail in our previous work [8]. Skeletons can be seen as parametrized codes where the instantiation of their parameters results in the generation of a transformed optimized version of the target loop nest merging original computations and speculative parallelization management. They consist of three parts: the first part applies the transformation, which is populated at runtime; the second performs the original computation on the transformed iteration domain; and the third does the verification. Skeletons support classes of loop transformations as skewing, interchange, tiling, etc [10]. In the current implementation, Apollo's skeletons support skewing and interchange.

Parallelizing code transformation: As soon as the prediction model has been built, Apollo's runtime system performs a dependence analysis which determines if the target loop nest can be parallelized and optimized and what transformation has to be applied for this purpose. A polyhedral transformation merely refers to changing the order in which iterations are executed and is controlled by applying affine functions on the loop iterators. The transformation is encoded as a matrix, storing the coefficients of the affine functions which define the new schedule. Given a loop nest of depth two with iterators $\left(\begin{smallmatrix} i \\ j \end{smallmatrix} \right)$ and a transformation matrix T, polyhedral loop transformations such as skewing, interchange or any affine transformation of the iteration domains [7] are obtained as: $T \times \left(\begin{smallmatrix} i \\ j \end{smallmatrix} \right) = \left(\begin{smallmatrix} i' \\ j' \end{smallmatrix} \right)$. This is achieved by invoking the polyhedral parallelizer Pluto [7] at runtime. More precisely, only the scheduler kernel of Pluto is used. It has been slightly customized to consume our dependence analysis output and to suggest a polyhedral transformation in return. Since Pluto aims simultaneously data locality optimization and parallelization, the generated schedule is expected to lead to a well-performing parallel code. Notice also that Pluto is initially a source-to-source code transformer used at compile-time, and that Apollo is the first known dynamic framework which is using it at runtime, with very low time-overhead.

Speculative code orchestration: The different code versions (instrumented, serial original, or instantiated skeleton) are launched in chunks of fixed sizes. These chunks are running a slice of successive iterations of the outermost original loop nest. Thus, optimizing parallelizing transformations are applied on such slices. At startup, Apollo launches a small chunk running the instrumented version in order to build the prediction model and perform the dependence analysis. The transformation suggested by Pluto from the dependence information is then used to instantiate the code skeleton devoted to the corresponding class of transformations. The resulting parallel code is then launched inside a larger chunk, after having previously backed-up the memory locations that are predicted to be updated. If the verification of the speculation detects a unpredicted behavior, memory is restored to cancel the execution of the current chunk. The execution of the chunk is re-initiated using the original serial version, in order to overcome the faulty execution point. Finally, an instrumented chunk is launched again to capture the changing behavior and build a new prediction model. If no miss-prediction was detected during the run of the parallel code, a next chunk using the same parallel code and running a next slice of the loop nest is launched.

4   Runtime Verification of Speculative Polyhedral Parallelization

The model handled currently by Apollo is the polyhedral model. Thus, the speculative prediction model claims (i) that every memory instruction targets a sequence of addresses represented by an affine function of the loop iterators, (ii) that every scalar variable, that is modified across iterations, either stores values also represented by such an affine function, or carries a dependence, and finally (iii) that every loop upper bound is also such an affine function (while the lower bound is 0)[4]. Each of these three characteristics must be verified while running the speculative parallel code which is semantically correct only if the prediction model holds. This is achieved thanks to dedicated code inserted at compile-time in the parallel code skeletons, and instantiated at runtime. This code triggers a rollback as soon as the verification fails.

The skeletons are generated automatically in the LLVM IR using our dedicated compilation pass. As depicted in the previous section, they are made of three types of instructions: (1) *instructions dedicated to apply the optimizing transformation, including parallelization:* these are the for-loops iterating over the introduced virtual iterators, which are transformed into new iterators through the linear transformation suggested by Pluto; and instructions in the header of each loop of the nest which are devoted to the initialization of the predicted scalar variables; (2) *instructions of the original code:* the original loop exit conditions serve as guards of the original loop bodies which are copied in the generated skeletons at compile-time; (3) *instructions devoted to the verification:* these instructions are inserted at several relevant points of the skeleton code to verify the adherence of each linear function constituting the prediction model with the original code behavior. They are related to memory accesses, scalar initializations and loop bounds verifications, and are detailed in the following subsections.

4.1   Target Memory Address Verification

Memory instructions executed speculatively are guarded by verification instructions, ensuring that no unsafe write operations are performed. Recall that the prediction model is based on representing the sequence of the addresses accessed by an instruction as affine functions of the (virtual) loop iterators. Based on this linearity of the memory accesses, a tightly coupled dependence analysis allows to apply an optimizing transformation of the target code which is semantically correct as long as the predicted dependences are still entirely characterizing the code. Thus, verifying completeness of the predicted dependences translates to verifying that all memory accesses follow their associated affine functions. This is ensured by comparing, for each memory instruction,

---

[4] These represent the bounds of the virtual loop iterators.

the actual target address against the value resulting from the evaluation of the predicting affine function. Notice that Apollo must verify the linear functions in the transformed space, not the linear functions which were obtained during instrumentation of the original, untransformed, sequential code. An example of the code verifying the update of array G[v].Neighbors in the breadthFirstSearch code of Figure 1.1 is shown in the below pseudo source code (instead of original LLVM-IR form). Variables vi and vj denote the virtual iterators of the two nested loops.

```
if (&G[v].Neighbors[k] != linear_eq(mem_instr_ID,vi,vj))
    rollback();
G[v].Neighbors[k++] = ngh;
```

4.2 Scalars Initialization and Verification

As depicted in previous Sections, scalar variables defined as phi-nodes in the LLVM intermediate representation are taking part of the prediction model. These scalars are also carrying dependences by being used and updated among loop iterations. As it is usually done manually when parallelizing serial codes, a common approach to remove such dependences is to privatize such scalars when possible. Privatization consists of replacing their incremental updates by the direct computation of their successive values using the current values of the loop iterators. For some scalars, the scalar evolution pass of the LLVM compiler may be successful in determining statically an affine expression to compute their values. Otherwise, Apollo's instrumentation by sampling provides to compute this affine function at runtime, as soon as it can be represented in this way. However, notice that privatization of such latter scalars is therefore speculative.

Since Apollo's code transformations may not follow the original iteration order, scalar variables must be initialized at their correct starting values in the header of each iteration. This is performed in the header of each loop of the target nest, as it is shown below in pseudo source code for the breadthFirstSearch code example and its top and bot scalar variables.

```
top = linear_eq(&top,vi) ;
bot = linear_eq(&bot,vi) ;
```

However, since these scalar initializations are speculative, they must verified. Generally, scalars used in loops are initiating an iteration while being assigned the very last value that has been assigned to them among the previous iterations. The same scheme is followed by Apollo's verification strategy: at the very end of each iteration, the prediction for the next iteration initial value is compared to the actual value of the scalar, *i.e.*, its very last value before the initiation of the next iteration. If the verification fails, a rollback is triggered, as it is shown below in pseudo source code form for the breadthFirstSearch code example and its top and bot scalar variables.

```
if (top != linear_eq(&top,vi+1) rollback() ;
if (bot != linear_eq(&bot,vi+1) rollback() ;
```

Notice that this verification strategy is verifying initial values for the next iteration according to the original sequential order. Since the current schedule may follow an entirely different order resulting from a parallelizing and optimizing transformation of the original code, some iterations may be run with scalar values that have not yet been verified. But since all iterations are run inside the same chunk (slice of the outermost loop), they have all been verified regarding their scalars as soon as their preceding iteration according to the serial order has been run. Globally, all iterations inside a chunk have been inevitably verified at the chunk completion. If any of these verifications fails during the execution of the chunk, rollback for the whole chunk is initiated and memory is restored.

4.3 Loop Bounds Verification

The polyhedral model imposes loop bounds to be affine functions of the enclosing loop iterators. These bounds can be either extracted at compile-time thanks to the scalar evolution pass, or must be built at runtime through interpolation and handled speculatively. For any target loop nest, bounds of the outermost loop and of the inner loops are handled in different ways.

When undefined at compile-time, the outermost loop bound can only be known after completion of the loop nest execution. Thus it cannot be used by Apollo when analyzing and transforming speculatively the target code. However, as it is addressed in subsection 3.2, the target loop nest is launched by chunks consisting of slices of the outermost loop. Therefore, outermost loop bounds are defined by the starting and finishing borders of the current chunk. When the original loop exit condition is met during the run of a chunk and before its completion, a rollback is initiated and the last chunk is run again in the serial original order. When the outermost loop bound is discovered statically, Apollo's runtime system is able to anticipate the final loop exit by launching the very last chunk of parallel code with the exact convenient size in order to avoid any final rollback. Once they cannot be obtained at compile-time, inner loop iteration counts are being interpolated by Apollo during instrumentation. This is mostly the case with while-loops whose exit conditions are made of values that are unknown at compile-time. For this kind of bounds, predicted values are verified by comparison with the current virtual iterators values. Moreover, the original exit condition must yield the same result. Otherwise, a rollback is initiated.

5   Related Work

TLS systems are a promising solution to automatic parallelization, but suffer from a high overhead, inherent to maintaining speculative states and version management. Attempts to alleviate synchronization in verifying dependences and speculations [11] lead to increased memory management data structures and rely on hardware support.

MiniTLS [12] makes use of a compact version management structure, which however, being centralized, requires thread synchronization. Lector [12], employs the inspector-executor technique, where a lightweight inspector runs ahead and verifies if dependence violations occur. Softspec [13] is a technique whose concepts represent preliminary ideas of our approach, as it is based on a profiling step and a prediction model. However, no code transformations are performed, except slicing. The runtime verification mechanism is similar to the one presented in this paper, as it does not require inter-core communication. However, since Apollo performs advanced code transformations, it must ensure that the last iteration of the original loop may execute before other iterations are executed within the same thread, which yields a more complex verification system. ParExC [14] targets automatic speculative parallelization of code that has been optimized at compile time, but it abounds in runtime checks designed to run in parallel. ParExC speculates on a failure free execution and aborts as soon as a misspeculation is encountered, relying on a transactional memory-based solution. Steffan *et al.* [15] propose a hardware-software co-design of a runtime verification based on the coherence protocol. Recent works of Kim *et al.* [16] describe automatic parallelization on clusters, by speculating on some memory or control dependences. The system executes a master process, non-speculative, and several speculative worker processes. Verification relies on transactional logs and is supported by rollback and recovery mechanisms.

Software transactional memory (STM) [17–19] was proposed to ensure the correctness of speculative code. STM enables a group of read and write operations to execute atomically, embedded in transactions. The reader is responsible for checking the correctness of execution and must ensure that no other thread has speculatively modified the reader's target location. If validation is successful, the transaction is committed, otherwise aborted, causing all of its prior changes to rollback. Despite increasing parallelism (speculatively), STM systems are notorious for the high overhead they introduce. The work of Adl-Tabatabai *et al.* [17] develops compiler and runtime optimizations for transactional memory constructs, using JIT. Static optimizations are employed to expose safe operations, such that redundant STM operations can be removed, while the STM library interface is tailored to handle JIT-compiled and optimized code. STM-lite [18] is a tool for light-weight software transactional memory, dedicated to automatic parallelization of loops, guided by a profiling step. Raman *et al.* [19] propose software multi-threaded transactions (SMTXs), which enable combining speculative work and pipeline transformations. SMTXs use memory versioning and separate the speculative and non-speculative states in different processes. While STMX has a centralized transaction commit manager, conflict detection is decoupled from the main execution.

6   Experiments

Our benchmarks were run on a platform embedding two AMD Opteron 6172 processors, of 12 cores each, at 2.1 Ghz, running Linux 3.11.0-17-generic x86_64. The set of benchmarks has been built from a collection of benchmark suites, such that the selected codes includes a main loop nest and highlights Apollo's capabilities: backprop and needle from the Rodinia benchmark suite [20], mri-q, sgemm and stencil from the Parboil benchmark suite [21], maximalMatching and breadthFirstSearch from the Problem Based benchmark suite [6], and finally 2mm from the Polyhedral benchmark suite [22]. These codes cannot be statically analyzed and transformed for the following reasons: arrays are passed to functions using pointers, thus yielding aliasing issues, dynamic data structures, non-linear array references, conditionals inside loop bodies, while loops, and references to data structures through pointers. We compiled the original codes either using the gcc or clang compilers, with optimization flag -O3, and considered the shortest computation time among both executables, as the baseline

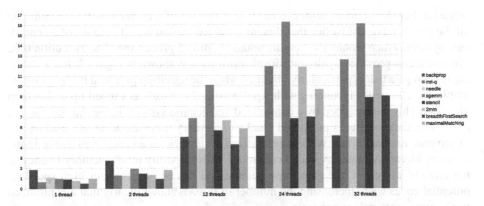

Fig. 1. Speed-ups obtained from codes speculatively parallelized with Apollo

for Apollo's speed-up (Figure 1). Apollo handled each code automatically and transparently. We measured the global resulting execution times of the target loop nests for 1, 2, 12, 24 and 32 threads and computed the resulting speed-up (Original computation time / Apollo's computation time). The execution times with Apollo from one run to another and with the same input were as stable as when running the original codes solely, since Apollo always selects the same transformation. Significant speed-ups were obtained for most of the codes, of up to $16.2\times$. Note that although some of the applications cannot be statically analyzed, they can be parallelized manually by an expert, as it is the case of the benchmarks extracted from Rodinia benchmark suite [20]. As expected, straightforward manual parallelization yields higher speed-ups, since there is no overhead incurred by instrumenting the application, generating code on-the-fly or providing support for a speculative execution. Nevertheless, the advantages of Apollo are emphasized by loops which only exhibit parallel phases (in contrast to OpenMP loops which are parallel for the entire execution), or codes which have a linear behavior and benefit from polyhedral transformations to enhance data locality or exhibit parallelism. Finally, as an automatic system, Apollo is entirely transparent and relieves the user from the parallelization effort, which is known to be an error-prone process.

An analysis of the time-overhead induced by the main processing steps of the runtime system of Apollo shows that the significant amounts of time are spent either in the memory backup (from 0.01% up to 24% of the whole execution time) or in the invocation of Pluto (up to 2%). Memory backup is costly, since it obviously involves many memory accesses. However, it has been optimized and parallelized with Apollo since each thread takes in charge the memory locations that it is supposed to touch in the next execution chunk. This approach also promotes a good data locality. Pluto is an external tool that may spend considerable times in handling some codes. Apollo could use another scheduler or define a time-out to avoid any excessive time spent by Pluto.

To exhibit the gain provided by the decentralized verification system of Apollo, we simulated the behavior of a centralized verification system regarding its additional required memory accesses. For this purpose, we annihilated our verification instructions that are associated to each memory instruction that is speculatively handled, and replaced them by memory writes to random addresses of a buffer which is common to all the parallel threads. Notice that this minimal simulation is still in favor of a centralized system, which would also require some additional processing. The execution time improvements provided by decentralized verification is shown in Figure 2. It shows the significant gain that is particularly obtained when the speed-up potential is high. For example sgemm, which is running with Apollo using 24 threads at a speed-up higher than 16×, is highly handicapped by a centralized verification system: in the Apollo parallel execution, data locality is promoted thanks to memory accesses occurring exclusively in separate memory areas, while a centralized system yields an important traffic in the memory hierarchy to ensure cache coherency, thus imposing much memory latency to the threads. Moreover, the gain improvement that can be observed for high speed-up potential codes when increasing the number of threads shows clearly that a centralized verification system does not scale.

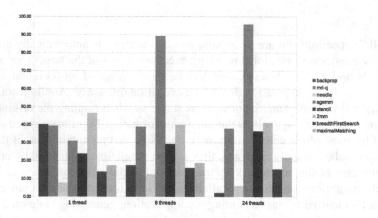

Fig. 2. Percentage of speedup attributable to decentralized verification

7   Conclusion

The software architecture of the Apollo framework is typical of TLS systems which do not require a centralized verification system and are able to apply advanced dynamic code optimizations. It encompasses two main collaborative phases combining static and dynamic analysis and transformation of the target loop nests, and is based on the lightweight construction of a prediction model at runtime. Although Apollo implements a speculative and dynamic adaptation of the polyhedral model, any model providing a sufficiently accurate characterization of the target program semantics could be used as soon as it allows to manage speculative and efficient parallel code. We currently investigate new models for handling codes that are not exhibiting a linear behavior. Alternatively, Apollo also highlights the fact that codes may exhibit interesting optimization opportunities depending on the processed input. This phenomenon opens to investigations related to new memory allocation and access strategies that may be better handled for code parallelization and optimization, either in software or hardware.

References

1. Rauchwerger, L., Padua, D.: The LRPD test: speculative run-time parallelization of loops with privatization and reduction parallelization. In: PLDI 1995. ACM (1995)
2. Liu, W., Tuck, J., Ceze, L., Ahn, W., Strauss, K., Renau, J., Torrellas, J.: POSH: a TLS compiler that exploits program structure. In: PPoPP 2006. ACM (2006)
3. Raman, E., Vachharajani, N., Rangan, R., August, D.I.: Spice: speculative parallel iteration chunk execution. In: CGO 2008. ACM (2008)
4. Johnson, T.A., Eigenmann, R., Vijaykumar, T.N.: Speculative thread decomposition through empirical optimization. In: PPoPP 2007. ACM (2007)
5. Feautrier, P., Lengauer, C.: Polyhedron model. In: Padua, D. (ed.) Encyclopedia of Parallel Computing, pp. 1581–1592. Springer, US (2011)
6. Shun, J., Blelloch, G.E., Fineman, J.T., Gibbons, P.B., Kyrola, A., Simhadri, H.V., Tangwongsan, K.: Brief announcement: the problem based benchmark suite. In: SPAA 2012. ACM (2012)
7. Bondhugula, U., Hartono, A., Ramanujam, J., Sadayappan, P.: A practical automatic polyhedral parallelizer and locality optimizer. In: PLDI 2008. ACM (2008)
8. Jimborean, A., Clauss, P., Dollinger, J.F., Loechner, V., Juan Manuel, M.: Dynamic and Speculative Polyhedral Parallelization Using Compiler-Generated Skeletons. International Journal of Parallel Programming 42(4), 529–545 (2014)
9. LLVM: LLVM compiler infrastructure, http://llvm.org
10. Banerjee, U.: Loop Transformations for Restructuring Compilers - The Foundations. Kluwer Academic Publishers (1993)
11. Oancea, C.E., Mycroft, A., Harris, T.: A lightweight in-place implementation for software thread-level speculation. In: SPAA 2009. ACM (2009)
12. Yiapanis, P., Rosas-Ham, D., Brown, G., Luján, M.: Optimizing software runtime systems for speculative parallelization. ACM TACO 9(4), 39:1–39:27 (2013)
13. Bruening, D., Devabhaktuni, S., Amarasinghe, S.: Softspec: Software-based speculative parallelism. In: Workshop on Feedback-Directed and Dynamic Optimization 2000. ACM (2000)
14. Süßkraut, M., Weigert, S., Schiffel, U., Knauth, T., Nowack, M., de Brum, D.B., Fetzer, C.: Speculation for parallelizing runtime checks. In: Guerraoui, R., Petit, F. (eds.) SSS 2009. LNCS, vol. 5873, pp. 698–710. Springer, Heidelberg (2009)
15. Steffan, J.G., Colohan, C.B., Zhai, A., Mowry, T.C.: A scalable approach to thread-level speculation. In: ISCA 2000. ACM (2000)
16. Kim, H., Johnson, N.P., Lee, J.W., Mahlke, S.A., August, D.I.: Automatic speculative doall for clusters. In: CGO 2012. ACM (2012)
17. Adl-Tabatabai, A.R., Lewis, B.T., Menon, V., Murphy, B.R., Saha, B., Shpeisman, T.: Compiler and runtime support for efficient software transactional memory. In: PLDI 2006 (2006)
18. Mehrara, M., Hao, J., Hsu, P.C., Mahlke, S.: Parallelizing sequential applications on commodity hardware using a low-cost software transactional memory. SIGPLAN Not. 44(6), 166–176 (2009)
19. Raman, A., Kim, H., Mason, T.R., Jablin, T.B., August, D.I.: Speculative parallelization using software multi-threaded transactions. In: ASPLOS 2010. ACM (2010)
20. Che, S., Boyer, M., Meng, J., Tarjan, D., Sheaffer, J.W., Lee, S.H., Skadron, K.: Rodinia: A benchmark suite for heterogeneous computing. In: IISWC 2009. IEEE (2009)
21. Stratton, J.A., Rodrigues, C., Sung, I.J., Obeid, N., Chang, L.W., Anssari, N., Liu, G.D.: mei W. Hwu, W.: The Parboil technical report. Technical report, IMPACT Technical Report, IMPACT-12-01, University of Illinois, at Urbana-Champaign (2012)
22. PolyBench, http://sourceforge.net/projects/polybench

Organising LTL Monitors
over Distributed Systems with a Global Clock

Christian Colombo[1] and Yliès Falcone[2]

[1] Department of Computer Science, University of Malta
`christian.colombo@um.edu.mt`
[2] Laboratoire d'Informatique de Grenoble, University of Grenoble-Alpes, France
`ylies.falcone@ujf-grenoble.fr`

Abstract. Users wanting to monitor distributed systems often prefer to abstract away the architecture of the system, allowing them to directly specify correctness properties on the global system behaviour. To support this abstraction, a compilation of the properties would not only involve the typical choice of monitoring algorithm, but also the organisation of submonitors across the component network. Existing approaches, considered in the context of LTL properties over distributed systems with a global clock, include the so-called orchestration and migration approaches. In the orchestration approach, a central monitor receives the events from all subsystems. In the migration approach, LTL formulae transfer themselves across subsystems to gather local information.

We propose a third way of organising submonitors: choreography — where monitors are orgnized as a tree across the distributed system, and each child feeds intermediate results to its parent. We formalise this approach, proving its correctness and worst case performance, and report on an empirical investigation comparing the three approaches on several concerns of decentralised monitoring.

1 Introduction

Due to the end of regular increase of processor speed, more systems are being designed to be decentralised to benefit from more of the multi-core feature of contemporary processors. This change in processors poses a number of challenges in the domain of runtime verification where performance is paramount.

In runtime verification one is interested in synthesizing a monitor to evaluate a stream of events (reflecting the behaviour of a system) according to some correctness properties. When the system consists of several computing units (referred to as components in the sequel), it is desirable to decentralise the monitoring process for several reasons (as seen in [1,4,5]). First, it is a solution to benefit from the plurality of computing units of the system if one can design decentralised monitors that are as independent as possible. Second, it avoids introducing a central observation point in the system that presupposes a modification of the system architecture, and it also generally reduces the communication overhead in the system. See [4,5] for more arguments along this line.

In this paper, we study these questions in the context of monitors synthesized from LTL specifications by considering three approaches, namely orchestration, migration, and choreography, to organise monitors (using terminology from [6]): (i) Orchestration

B. Bonakdarpour and S.A. Smolka (Eds.): RV 2014, LNCS 8734, pp. 140–155, 2014.

is the setting where a single node carries out all the monitoring processing whilst re-trieving information from the rest of the nodes. (ii) Migration is the setting where the monitoring entity transports itself across the network, evolving as it goes along — doing away with the need to transfer lower level (finer-grained) information. (iii) Choreography is the setting where monitors are organised into a network and a protocol is used to enable cooperation between monitors.

Note, there are two important assumptions in our study. First, we assume the existence of a global clock in the system (as in [4]). This assumption is realistic for many critical industrial systems or when the system at hand is composed of several applications executing on the same operating system. Second, we assume that local monitors are attached to the components of the system and that the monitors can directly communicate with each other through some network.

Contributions of this paper. First, we survey the work on LTL monitoring in the context of distributed systems, classifying them under orchestration, choreography, and migration. Second, we introduce choreography-based decentralised monitoring. Third, we propose an algorithm that splits the monitoring of an LTL formula into smaller monitors forming a choreography. Fourth, we empirically compare orchestration, migration (from [4]), and choreography using a benchmark implementation.

Paper Organization. The rest of the paper is organised as follows. Section 2 introduces some background. Sections 3 and 4 recall the orchestration and migration approaches for LTL monitoring, respectively. In Section 5, we introduce the setting of choreography-based decentralised monitoring. Section 6 reports on our empirical evaluation and comparison of the three approaches using a benchmark implementation. Section 7 compares this paper with related work. Finally, Section 8 concludes and proposes future work.

2 Background

In this section, we formally define a distributed system and alphabet, followed by an introduction to the syntax and semantics of LTL.

Distributed systems and alphabet. $\mathbb{N}$ is the set of natural numbers. Let a distributed system be represented by a list of components: $\mathcal{C} = [C_1, C_2, \ldots, C_n]$ for some $n \in \mathbb{N} \setminus \{0\}$, and the alphabet Σ be the set of all events of the components: $\Sigma = \Sigma_1 \cup \Sigma_2 \cup \ldots \cup \Sigma_n$, where Σ_i is the alphabet of C_i built over a set of local atomic propositions AP_i. We assume that the alphabets and sets of local atomic propositions are pair-wise disjoint[1] and define function $\#$ returning the index of the component related to an event, if it exists: $\# : \Sigma \to \mathbb{N}$ such that $\#a \stackrel{\text{def}}{=} i$ if $\exists i \in [1; n] : a \in \Sigma_i$ and undefined otherwise. The behavior of each component C_i is represented by a *trace* of events, which for t time steps is encoded as $u_i = u_i(0) \cdot u_i(1) \cdots u_i(t-1)$ with $\forall t' < t : u_i(t') \in \Sigma_i$. Finite (resp. infinite) traces over Σ are elements of Σ^* (resp. Σ^ω) and are denoted by $u, u', \ldots$ (resp. $w, w', \ldots$). The set of all traces is $\Sigma^\infty \stackrel{\text{def}}{=} \Sigma^* \cup \Sigma^\omega$. The finite or infinite sequence w^t is the *suffix* of the trace $w \in \Sigma^\infty$, starting at time t, i.e., $w^t = w(t) \cdot w(t+1) \cdots$.

---

[1] This assumption simplifies the presentation but does not affect the generality of the results.

Linear Temporal Logic. The system's global behaviour, $(u_1, u_2, \ldots, u_n)$ can now be described as a sequence of pair-wise union of the local events in component's traces, each of which at time t is of length $t + 1$ i.e., $u = u(0) \cdots u(t)$.

We monitor a system wrt. a global specification, expressed as an LTL [9] formula, that does not state anything about its distribution or the system's architecture. LTL formulae can be described using the following grammar:

$$\varphi ::= p \mid (\varphi) \mid \neg\varphi \mid \varphi \vee \varphi \mid \mathbf{X}\,\varphi \mid \varphi\,\mathbf{U}\,\varphi,$$

where $p \in AP$. Additionally, we allow the following operators, each of which is defined in terms of the above ones: $\top \overset{\text{def}}{=} p \vee \neg p$, $\bot \overset{\text{def}}{=} \neg\top$, $\varphi_1 \wedge \varphi_2 \overset{\text{def}}{=} \neg(\neg\varphi_1 \vee \neg\varphi_2)$, $\mathbf{F}\varphi \overset{\text{def}}{=} \top\,\mathbf{U}\,\varphi$, and $\mathbf{G}\varphi \overset{\text{def}}{=} \neg\,\mathbf{F}\,(\neg\varphi)$.

Definition 1 (LTL semantics [9]). *LTL semantics is defined wrt. infinite traces. Let* $w \in \Sigma^\omega$ *and* $i \in \mathbb{N}$. *Satisfaction of an LTL formula by* w *at time* i *is defined inductively:*

$$w^i \models p \Leftrightarrow p \in w(i),\ \text{for any } p \in AP$$
$$w^i \models \neg\varphi \Leftrightarrow w^i \not\models \varphi$$
$$w^i \models \varphi_1 \vee \varphi_2 \Leftrightarrow w^i \models \varphi_1 \vee w^i \models \varphi_2$$
$$w^i \models \mathbf{X}\,\varphi \Leftrightarrow w^{i+1} \models \varphi$$
$$w^i \models \varphi_1\,\mathbf{U}\,\varphi_2 \Leftrightarrow \exists k \in [i, \infty[\,\cdot\ w^k \models \varphi_2 \wedge \forall l \in [i, k[\,:\, w^l \models \varphi_1$$

When $w^0 \models \varphi$ holds, we also write $w \models \varphi$.

Several approaches have been proposed for adapting LTL semantics for monitoring purposes (cf. [2]). Here, we follow previous work [4] and consider LTL$_3$ (introduced in [3]).

Definition 2 (LTL$_3$ semantics [3]). *Let* $u \in \Sigma^*$, *the satisfaction relation of LTL$_3$,* $\models_3: \Sigma^* \times LTL \to \mathbb{B}_3$, *with* $\mathbb{B}_3 \overset{\text{def}}{=} \{\top, \bot, ?\}$, *is defined as*

$$u \models_3 \varphi = \begin{cases} \top & \text{if } \forall w \in \Sigma^\omega : u \cdot w \models \varphi, \\ \bot & \text{if } \forall w \in \Sigma^\omega : u \cdot w \not\models \varphi, \\ ? & \text{otherwise.} \end{cases}$$

3 Orchestration

The idea of orchestration-based monitoring is to use a *central observation point* in the network (see Fig. 1). The central observation point can be introduced as an additional component or it can be a monitor attached to an existing component. In orchestration-based monitoring, at any time t, the central observation point is aware of every event $u_i(t)$ occurring on each component C_i, and has thus the information about the global

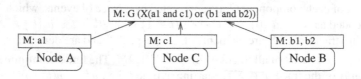

Fig. 1. An example of orchestration architecture

event $u_1(t) \cup \ldots \cup u_n(t)$ occurring in the system. Several protocols can be used by local monitors to communicate events. For instance, local monitors can send their local event at every time instance. Alternatively, the protocol may exploit the presence of a global clock in the system and just signal which propositions are true at any time instance or those whose value has changed. From a theoretical perspective, putting aside the instrumentation and communication, orchestration-based monitoring is not different from typical centralised monitoring.

4 Migration

Migration-based monitoring was introduced in [4]. The idea of migration is to represent (the state of) a monitor as an LTL formula that travels across a network. Upon the reception of a new LTL formula, a component progresses it, i.e., it rewrites the formula given the local observation, so that the resulting formula is the formula that has to hold in the next computation step. Such formula may contain references to past time instants if it has been progressed by components that could not evaluate some parts of it. More precisely, rewriting a formula is done using the so-called *progression*, adapted to the decentralised case, i.e., taking into account the fact that a component has only information about the local propositions it has access to. For example, in Fig. 2 only the valuations of $b1$ and $b2$ would be available for the monitor at component B. For the other propositions whose valuation is not available, an *obligation* is recorded which will have to be satisfied in a future time instant (by looking at the past). In the example, note that $Pa1$ and $Pc1$ refer to the previous values of $a1$ and $c1$ respectively. The rewritten formula is then sent to the most appropriate component — intuitively, the component that has the information about the proposition whose obligation reaches furthest into the past. The recipient component progresses the received formula using its local observation but also using its local history of observations to evaluate the past propositions. After sending a formula, a component is left with nothing to evaluate, unless it receives a formula from another component.

Any verdict found by a component is an actual global verdict. However, since the values of some propositions are known only one or more time instants later, the verdict is typically reached with a delay depending on the size of the network. To keep this delay to a minimum one can initially start monitoring the formula on all components, enabling different sequences of proposition processing. The downside, however, is that this increases the number of messages as well as the number of progressions.

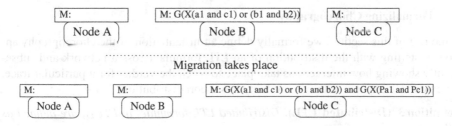

Fig. 2. An example of migrating architecture

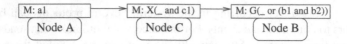

Fig. 3. An example of choreography architecture

5   Choreography

Rather than having the whole formula at a single location (whether this is fixed as in orchestration or variable as in migration), choreography breaks down the formula across the network, forming a tree structure where results from subformulae flow up to the parent formula.

5.1   Choreography at an Abstract Level

Figure 3 shows how formula $\mathbf{G}(\mathbf{X}(a1 \wedge c1) \vee b1 \wedge b2)$ is spread across a network of three nodes $A, B,$ and C with sets of local propositions $\{a1\}, \{b1, b2\},$ and $\{c1\},$ respectively. Note that each proposition is monitored in what we refer in the following as its native node, i.e., each node is monitoring a subformula that contains reference to either its local atomic propositions or *place holders*. Intuitively, place holders can be understood as three-state propositions that represent the verdict (true, false, or no verdict yet) of a remote subformula being evaluated on another component. Note also that no node is aware of all the propositional values. The progression of a choreographed monitoring network includes the following steps:

1. Progress the subformulae that do not have place holders, and forward the verdicts to their parents.
2. Upon receiving all verdicts for place holders, parent subformulae perform their progression potentially spawning new place holders (e.g., due to the progression of the *Until* operator (defined later)).
3. Verdicts continue to propagate from the leaves to the root of the tree until the root reaches a true or false verdict.

In what follows, we formalise the progression of a choreographed monitoring network, and prove two properties of the proposed choreography: the maximum number of nested place holders and the correctness of the verdict reached.

5.2   Formalizing Choreography

In the rest of this section, we formally define an instantiation of the choreography approach, starting with the distribution of an LTL formula across a network and subsequently showing how interactions take place to reach the verdict for a particular trace. We extend LTL syntax with one modality to support distribution.

Definition 3 (Distributed LTL). *Distributed LTL formulae, in LTL_D, are defined as follows:*

$$\varphi^D ::= \varphi \mid \langle\!\langle x, y \rangle\!\rangle_\varphi, \text{ where } x, y \in \mathbb{N} \text{ and } \varphi \in LTL$$

A distributed LTL formula is either an LTL formula or a place holder of the form $\langle\!\langle x, y \rangle\!\rangle_\varphi$ where natural numbers x, y act as a pointer to a subformula in the LTL network, while the LTL formula is kept as a copy.

Remark 1. The modality related to distribution is only used in our definitions and functions. The end user, i.e., the one writing properties, does not need to be aware of it.

Given a distributed LTL formula, we define a scoring function that returns a natural number representing the desirability of placing the monitor for that LTL formula on some particular component i. To choose where to place a given LTL formula, we choose the one with the highest score.

Definition 4 (Choosing component). *The scoring and choice functions are defined as follows:*

- *The scoring function* $\mathrm{scor}_i : LTL_D \to \mathbb{N}$ *is defined as follows (using $\sim$ and $\odot$ to range over unary and binary LTL operators, resp.):*

$$\mathrm{scor}_i(\varphi) = match\ \varphi\ with$$
$$\quad \mid\ \sim\!\psi \to \mathrm{scor}_i(\psi) \qquad\qquad \mid\ \psi \odot \psi' \to \mathrm{scor}_i(\psi) + \mathrm{scor}_i(\psi')$$
$$\quad \mid\ p \quad \to \begin{cases} 1\ if\ \#p = i \\ 0\ otherwise \end{cases} \qquad \mid\ \_ \quad \to 0$$

- *The choice function* $\mathrm{chc} : LTL_D \to \mathbb{N}$ *is defined as follows:*
$$\mathrm{chc}(\varphi) \stackrel{\mathrm{def}}{=} i\ such\ that\ \mathrm{scor}_i(\varphi) - \max(\mathrm{scor}_1(\varphi), \ldots, \mathrm{scor}_n(\varphi))$$

Note that this definition of chc might have several solutions but we leave it up to the implementer to choose any component with a high score, either randomly or through some other strategy.

An important condition for choreography to function correctly is to ensure that for any proposition p, $\mathrm{chc}(p) = \#p$ holds since the value of p can only be resolved at component $\#p$. In what follows we assume this is always the case.

Remark 2. There are several ways of varying the scoring function. The following two are just examples: (i) Vary the weighting of binary operators' operands, e.g., in the case of the *Until* the right subformula is given more weighting than the left; (ii) Giving more weight to a particular component, e.g., to create an orchestration where the whole formula except the remote propositions are on a single component.

Given a list of components making up a system, a monitor network is a corresponding list of monitors (with one monitor per component) where each monitor has certain LTL formulae.

Definition 5 (LTL network). *An LTL network is a function* $M : \mathbb{N} \to \mathbb{N} \to LTL$ *which given a component identifier, returns the component's monitor, which in turn is a function which given the formula identifier, returns the formula.*

We use M, N, O, P to range over the set of networks $\mathcal{M}$. As abbreviations we use M_i to refer to $M(i)$, i.e., the i-th component in network M, and M_i^j to refer to $M_i(j)$, i.e., the j-th formula of the i-th component in M. Moreover, $|M_i| = |\mathrm{dom}(M_i)|$ refers to the size of the domain of M_i, while $M_i^j \mapsto \varphi$ is used as abbreviation for $M \dagger [i \mapsto M_i \cup [(j \mapsto \varphi)]]$ and M_i^* as abbreviation for $M_i^{|M_i|}$, where $\dagger$ is the classical map override operator.[2]

Intuitively, distributing a formula across a network requires two operations: modifying the formula to point to its subparts which are in another part of the network, and inserting the formula with pointers inside the network. The function net defined below handles the latter aspect while the former is handled by distr. In turn distr (through recurs) recursively calls itself on subformulae until it encounters a subpart which belongs to a different component (due to the scoring function). In this case, function net is called once more so that the remote subformula is inserted in the network accordingly. Using function chc, the sub parts of a formula that "choose" a different component from their parent's can be marked as distributed using LTL_D modalities and placed at a different point in the network.

Definition 6 (Generating an LTL network). *Thus, we define function* net $: \mathcal{M} \times \text{LTL} \to \mathcal{M}$, *which given an (initially empty) network, distributes the LTL formula according to the scoring function as follows:*

$$
\begin{aligned}
\text{net}(M, \varphi) = \ &let\ c = \text{chc}(\varphi)\ in \\
&let\ M', \varphi' = \text{distr}_c(M, \varphi)\ in\ {M'}_c^* \mapsto \varphi'
\end{aligned}
$$

$$
\begin{aligned}
where\ \text{distr}_i(M, \varphi) = \ &match\ (M, \varphi)\ with \\
&\mid \sim \psi \quad \to let\ N, \psi' = \text{recurs}_i(M, \psi)\ in\ N, \sim \psi' \\
&\mid \psi \odot \psi' \to let\ N, \psi'' = \text{recurs}_i(M, \psi)\ in \\
&\qquad\qquad let\ O, \psi''' = \text{recurs}_i(N, \psi')\ in\ O, \psi'' \odot \psi''' \\
&\mid \psi \qquad \to M, \psi
\end{aligned}
$$

$$
and \quad \text{recurs}_i(M, \varphi) = let\ j = \text{chc}(\varphi)\ in \begin{cases} \text{distr}_i(M, \varphi) & if\ j = i \\ \text{net}(M, \varphi), \langle\!\langle j, |M_j| \rangle\!\rangle_\varphi & otherwise. \end{cases}
$$

Note that, starting with an empty network ($M_E = \{1 \mapsto \{\}, \ldots, n \mapsto \{\}\}$) where n is the number of components, this function returns a tree structure with LTL subformulae linked to their parent. We abbreviate $\text{net}(M_E, \varphi)$ to $\text{net}(\varphi)$. To denote the root of the tree for the network of an LTL formula φ, i.e., the main monitor, we use $\hat{M}$, which is defined as $M_c^{|M_c|-1}$ where $c = \text{chc}(\varphi)$.

Example 1. Consider the scenario of constructing a network for formula $\varphi = a \,\mathbf{U}\, b$ for a decentralised system with two components, A and B (numbered 1 and 2 resp.), with the former having proposition a at its disposal while the latter having proposition b.

Starting with a call to net, we note that $\text{chc}(\varphi)$ may return either 1 or 2 depending on the definition of maximum. In this case, we assume the former and call the distribution function on an empty network: $\text{distr}_1(M_E, \varphi)$. Starting with the basic definitions, the example works out as follows:

---

[2] For two functions f and g, for any element e, $(f \dagger g)(e)$ is $g(e)$ if $e \in \text{dom}(g)$, $f(e)$ if $e \in \text{dom}(f)$, and *undef* otherwise.

$$N, \varphi' = \mathrm{recurs}_1(M_E, a) = \mathrm{distr}_1(M_E, a)$$
$$= \{1 \mapsto \{\}, 2 \mapsto \{\}\}, a$$
$$O, \psi' = \mathrm{recurs}_1(N, b) = \mathrm{net}(N, b), \langle\!\langle 2, 0 \rangle\!\rangle_b$$
$$= \{1 \mapsto \{0 \mapsto b\}, 2 \mapsto \{\}\}, \langle\!\langle 2, 0 \rangle\!\rangle_b$$
$$\mathrm{distr}_1(M_E, \varphi) = \{1 \mapsto \{\}, 2 \mapsto \{0 \mapsto b\}\}, a \, \mathbf{U} \, \langle\!\langle 2, 0 \rangle\!\rangle_b$$
$$\mathrm{net}(M_E, \varphi) = \{1 \mapsto \{0 \mapsto a \, \mathbf{U} \, \langle\!\langle 2, 0 \rangle\!\rangle_b\}, 2 \mapsto \{0 \mapsto b\}\}$$

At each time step, starting from the main monitor, the network performs one choreographed progression step.

Definition 7 (Choreographed Progression). *Given an LTL network M, the index j of a formula in monitor i, and the current observation σ, the choreographed progression function $\mathrm{prog}_i : \mathcal{M} \times \mathbb{N} \times \Sigma \to \mathcal{M}$, returns the resulting LTL network:*

$$
\begin{aligned}
\mathrm{prog}_i(M, j, \sigma) = \ &match\ M_i^j\ with \\
&|\ \top\ |\ \bot\ \ \to M \\
&|\ p\ \ \ \ \ \ \ \ \to \begin{cases} M_i^j \mapsto \top\ if\ p \in \sigma \\ M_i^j \mapsto \bot\ otherwise \end{cases} \\
&|\ \neg\varphi\ \ \ \ \ \to \neg\big(\mathrm{prog}_i(M, j, \sigma)_i^j\big) \\
&|\ \mathbf{X}\varphi\ \ \ \ \to M_i^j \mapsto \varphi \\
&|\ \varphi \odot \psi\ \to let\ N = \mathrm{prog}_i(M_i^j \mapsto \varphi, j, \sigma)\ in \\
&\qquad\qquad let\ O = \mathrm{prog}_i(N_i^j \mapsto \psi, j, \sigma)\ in \\
&\qquad\qquad let\ P, \varphi' = \mathrm{distr}_i(O, \varphi \, \mathbf{U} \, \psi)\ in \\
&\qquad\qquad \begin{cases} O_i^j \mapsto N_i^j \vee O_i^j & when\ M_i^j = \varphi \vee \psi \\ P_i^j \mapsto O_i^j \vee (N_i^j \wedge \varphi') & when\ M_i^j = \varphi \, \mathbf{U} \, \psi \end{cases} \\
&|\ \langle\!\langle x, y \rangle\!\rangle_\varphi \to let\ N = \mathrm{prog}_x(M, y, \sigma)\ in \\
&\qquad\qquad \begin{cases} N_i^j \mapsto N_x^y\ if\ N_x^y \in \{\top, \bot\} \\ N\ \qquad\qquad otherwise \end{cases}
\end{aligned}
$$

Finally, due to the call to distr_i from the progression function, we overload the function to handle distributed LTL formulae by adding the following line enabling the respawning of distributed formulae:

$$\mathrm{distr}_i(M, \langle\!\langle x, y \rangle\!\rangle_\varphi) \stackrel{\mathrm{def}}{=} \mathrm{net}(M, \varphi), \langle\!\langle \, \mathrm{chc}(\varphi), |M_{\mathrm{chc}(\varphi)}| \, \rangle\!\rangle_\varphi$$

The progression mechanism in the choreography context is similar to normal LTL. However, due to remote subparts of a formula, the network may change in several parts when progressing a single formula. Thus, when handling LTL operators, subformulae should first be applied one by one on the network, each time operating on the updated network (hence N and O). Slightly more complex is the *Until* case where a fresh copy of any distributed subparts have to be respawned across the network. P handles this by calling the distribution function on the progressed network O.

Example 2. Building upon the previous example, $a \, \mathbf{U} \, b$, assuming a trace $\{a\} \cdot \{b\}$, starting with network $\{1 \mapsto \{0 \mapsto a \, \mathbf{U} \, \langle\!\langle 2, 0 \rangle\!\rangle\}, 2 \mapsto \{0 \mapsto b\}\}$, and noting that the main monitor resides at $(1, 0)$, progression would evolve as follows (again starting with the basic definitions):

1. First element of the trace: $\{a\}$

$$
\begin{aligned}
N &= \mathrm{prog}_1(\{1 \mapsto \{0 \mapsto a\}, 2 \mapsto \{0 \mapsto b\}\}, 0, \{a\}) \\
&= \{1 \mapsto \{0 \mapsto \top\}, 2 \mapsto \{0 \mapsto b\}\} \\
O &= \mathrm{prog}_1(\{1 \mapsto \{0 \mapsto \langle 2, 0 \rangle\!\rangle_b\}, 2 \mapsto \{0 \mapsto b\}\}, 0, \{a\}) \\
&= \{1 \mapsto \{0 \mapsto \bot\}, 2 \mapsto \{0 \mapsto \bot\}\} \\
P, \varphi' &= \mathrm{distr}_1(\{1 \mapsto \{0 \mapsto \bot\}, 2 \mapsto \{0 \mapsto \bot\}\}, a \, \mathbf{U} \, \langle 2, 0 \rangle\!\rangle_b) \\
&= \{1 \mapsto \{0 \mapsto \bot\}, 2 \mapsto \{0 \mapsto \bot, 1 \mapsto b\}\}, a \, \mathbf{U} \, \langle 2, 1 \rangle\!\rangle_b \\
\mathrm{prog}_1(&\{1 \mapsto \{0 \mapsto a \, \mathbf{U} \, \langle 2, 0 \rangle\!\rangle_b\}, 2 \mapsto \{0 \mapsto b\}\}, 0, \{a\}) \\
&= \{1 \mapsto \{0 \mapsto \bot \vee (\top \wedge a \, \mathbf{U} \, \langle 2, 1 \rangle\!\rangle_b)\}, 2 \mapsto \{0 \mapsto \bot, 1 \mapsto b\}\}
\end{aligned}
$$

2. Second element of the trace: $\{b\}$. (Note that the main formula has been simplified using normal LTL simplification rules and unused subformulae garbage collected.)

$$
\begin{aligned}
N &= \mathrm{prog}_1(\{1 \mapsto \{0 \mapsto a\}, 2 \mapsto \{1 \mapsto b\}\}, 0, \{b\}) \\
&= \{1 \mapsto \{0 \mapsto \bot\}, 2 \mapsto \{1 \mapsto b\}\} \\
O &= \mathrm{prog}_1(\{1 \mapsto \{0 \mapsto \langle 2, 1 \rangle\!\rangle_b\}, 2 \mapsto \{1 \mapsto b\}\}, 0, \{b\}) \\
&= \{1 \mapsto \{0 \mapsto \top\}, 2 \mapsto \{1 \mapsto \top\}\} \\
P, \varphi' &= \mathrm{distr}_1(\{1 \mapsto \{0 \mapsto \top\}, 2 \mapsto \{1 \mapsto \top\}\}, a \, \mathbf{U} \, \langle 2, 1 \rangle\!\rangle_b) \\
&= \{1 \mapsto \{0 \mapsto \top\}, 2 \mapsto \{1 \mapsto \top, 2 \mapsto b\}\}, a \, \mathbf{U} \, \langle 2, 2 \rangle\!\rangle_b \\
\mathrm{prog}_1(&\{1 \mapsto \{0 \mapsto a \, \mathbf{U} \, \langle 2, 1 \rangle\!\rangle_b\}, 2 \mapsto \{1 \mapsto b\}\}, 0, \{b\}) \\
&= \{1 \mapsto \{0 \mapsto \top \vee (\bot \wedge a \, \mathbf{U} \, \langle 2, 2 \rangle\!\rangle_b)\}, 2 \mapsto \{1 \mapsto \top, 2 \mapsto b\}\}
\end{aligned}
$$

Through simplification and garbage collection, the network resolves to $\{1 \mapsto \{0 \mapsto \top\}, 2 \mapsto \{\}\}$, i.e., the main formula is now $\top$, meaning that a verdict has been reached as defined below.

Definition 8 (Decentralised semantics). *The satisfaction relation for choreographed monitors is given according to the verdict reached by the topmost monitor as follows:*

$$
u \vDash_C \varphi \stackrel{\text{def}}{=}
\begin{cases}
\top & \textit{if } \hat{M} = \top \\
\bot & \textit{if } \hat{M} = \bot \\
? & \textit{otherwise}
\end{cases}
$$

For the purpose of guaranteeing the maximum number of indirections in a choreographed LTL network, we define two depth-measuring functions: one which measures the maximum number of nesting levels in a formula, and another which measures the number of indirections in the network (typically starting from the main formula).

Definition 9 (Depth). *The depth-measuring function* $\mathrm{dpth} : LTL_D \to \mathbb{N}$ *is defined as:*

$$
\begin{aligned}
\mathrm{dpth}(\varphi) = \textit{match } \varphi \textit{ with} & \\
\mid \sim \psi \quad &\to 1 + \mathrm{dpth}(\psi) \\
\mid \psi \odot \psi' &\to 1 + \max(\mathrm{dpth}(\psi), \mathrm{dpth}(\psi')) \\
\mid \_ \qquad &\to 1
\end{aligned}
$$

The function measuring the depth of nested distribution modalities, taking a network and an x *and* y *pointer to a formula:* $\mathrm{dpth}_D : \mathcal{M} \times \mathbb{N} \times \mathbb{N} \to \mathbb{N}$ *is defined as:*

$\text{dpth}_D(M, i, j) = \text{match } M_i^j \text{ with}$
$\quad | \; \langle\!| x, y |\!\rangle_\psi \quad \to 1 + \text{dpth}_D(M, x, y)$
$\quad | \sim \psi \quad\quad \to \text{dpth}_D(M_i^j \mapsto \psi, i, j)$
$\quad | \; \psi \odot \psi' \quad \to \max(\text{dpth}_D(M_i^j \mapsto \psi, i, j), \text{dpth}_D(M_i^j \mapsto \psi', i, j))$
$\quad | \; \_ \quad\quad\quad \to 0$

Theorem 1 (Maximum nested distributions). *The number of nested distributions in a choreographed LTL formula cannot exceed the number of levels of nesting within a formula:* $\forall \varphi \in LTL : \text{dpth}_D(\text{net}(\varphi)) < \text{dpth}(\varphi)$.

Proof. This follows from the definition of net and by extension distr which at most introduces one place holder ($\langle\!| x, y |\!\rangle_\varphi$) for any particular level and from the definitions of the functions dpth and dpth_D where for any case considered $\text{dpth}_D \le \text{dpth}$. Furthermore, we note that since a formula must have propositions, true or false at the leafs, then the distribution depth is strictly less than the formula depth.

To aid in the proof of correctness, we define the function $\overline{\text{net}}$ which given a choreography network and a pointer to the main formula, returns the LTL formula being monitored in the network, $\overline{\text{net}} : \mathcal{M} \times \mathbb{N} \times \mathbb{N} \to LTL$:

$\overline{\text{net}}(M, i, j) = \text{match } M_i^j \text{ with}$
$\quad | \sim \psi \quad\quad \to \; \sim \left(\overline{\text{net}}(M_i^j \mapsto \psi, i, j) \right)$
$\quad | \; \psi \odot \psi' \quad \to \left(\overline{\text{net}}(M_i^j \mapsto \psi, i, j) \right) \odot \left(\overline{\text{net}}(M_i^j \mapsto \psi', i, j) \right)$
$\quad | \; \langle\!| x, y |\!\rangle_\varphi \to \overline{\text{net}}(M, x, y)$
$\quad | \; \psi \quad\quad\quad \to \psi$

Theorem 2 (Correctness). *The verdict reached by choreographed monitoring is the same as the one reached under normal monitoring* $\vDash_C = \vDash_3$.

Proof. In the context of a choreography, the state of the monitor is distributed across the network. By induction on the size of the trace, we show that at every progression step, the state of the monitoring network is equivalent to the formula if monitored centrally.

BC: Initially, if we had to compare the original formula to the distributed formula but "undistributing" it, then they should be equivalent: $\varphi = \overline{\text{net}}(\text{net}(\varphi))$. This follows from the definitions of net and $\overline{\text{net}}$.

IH: After k progressions, the resulting LTL formula is equivalent to the resulting network: $_k\varphi = \overline{\text{net}}(_kM)$ (assuming no simplifications).

IC: Assuming IH, after $k + 1$ progressions the resulting formula and network should be semantically equivalent: $_{k+1}\varphi = \overline{\text{net}}(_{k+1}M)$. This follows through a case-by-case analysis of the progression function prog which correspond to the cases of the normal progression function.

6 Evaluation and Discussion

Numerous criteria can be considered for comparing different organisations of LTL monitoring over a network. Below are a number of them which are treated in this study[3]:

---

[3] We ignore implementation-dependent measurements such as actual overhead of monitors.

Delay: Because of the network organization, it takes some communication steps to propagate intermediate results.

Number and size of messages: Since no component in the network can observe the full behaviour of the system, components have to communicate. Thus, we measure how many messages are required and their size.

Progressions: Different configurations of the monitoring network affect the number of LTL progressions that need to be carried out.

Privacy and security concerns[4]: In certain cases, one might wish to avoid communicating a component's local data across the network. This might be either because of lack of trust between the components themselves or due to an unsecured network.

To compare the three approaches with respect to these criteria, we have carried out two main experiments (whose results are shown in Tables 1 and 2 resp.):

- The first one varies the size of the network, i.e., the number of components, and the number of redirections in the resulting LTL network. This experiment is crucial since the migration approach is sensitive to the size of the network [4] while intuitively we expect the choreography approach to be affected by the depth of the LTL network.
- The second experiment varies the size of the formulae being considered and the pattern of the resulting tree once the formula is distributed. This enabled us to assess the scalability of the approaches and how they react to a different network structures. In particular we considered two kinds of networks: one whose formula is generated purely randomly, and another where we biased the formula generator such that the bottom-most LTL operators always have operands from the same component; essentially emulating networks where the basic subformulae of an LTL formula can be evaluated without communicating.

Some choices needed to be made with respect to the architectural setup of the experiments:

Experiment setup: The setup is based on the tool DecentMon[5] used in a previous study comparing orchestration with migration [4]. For this study we simply extended the tool with a choreography approach[6].

Benchmark generation: For the first experiment, we generated 100 LTL formulae and distributed traces randomly, subsequently tweaking the alphabet to manipulate the number of referenced components and the depth of the resulting LTL network. For the second experiment we could not use the same formulae since one of the variables considered was the size of the formulae. The numbers shown in the tables are thus the average results obtained across the 100 formulae considered in each case.

Communication protocol: Choosing a communication protocol such as communicating only the propositions which are true while assuming that unsent ones are false, makes a significant difference to our results. The chosen protocols were as follows: In the case of orchestration, only the propositions referenced in the formula that hold true are sent. Each sent proposition is considered to be of size one. In the case of migration,

---

[4] We refrain from going into fault-tolerance issues in this study, leaving it for future work.

[5] http://decentmonitor.forge.imag.fr

[6] The new implementation is available at: http://decentmon3.forge.imag.fr

since the whole formula is sent, it is less straightforward to gain quick savings as in the case of propositions. Thus, in this case we measure the size of the formula (one for each proposition and each operator) and use it as the size of the message. In the case of choreography we have two kinds of messages: updates from subformulae to their parent's place holders and redistribution messages. The former kind are similar to those of orchestration but there is also the possibility that the subformula has neither reached true nor false. Thus, if no verdict has been reached, the subformula transmits nothing, otherwise it sends the verdict which counts as one. As for the redistribution messages, recall that each redistribution would have been already communicated during the initial setup of the network. Therefore, we assume that upon redistribution there is no need to resend the formula and we consider its size to be one.

Execution cycles: A major difference between choreography and migration is that the latter could send all the messages in one cycle while in the case of the choreography, since the distribution messages succeed the ones enabling progression, there are two messaging cycles for every time instant. However, the picture is even more complex because the progression within a component may depend on the verdict of others. Thus, while migration (as in [4]) strictly allowed one progression and messaging cycle per system cycle, in our choreography evaluation, we allowed any number of cycles that were necessary for the network to completely process the values in the current system cycle. This makes the choreography approach delay-free (and hence avoids references to the history) but relatively more expensive in terms of the number of cycles and the messages required for each system cycle.

In the following subsections, we discuss the outcome by first comparing choreography with migration, and subsequently comparing choreography to orchestration. We refrain from comparing orchestration to migration as this has already been carried out extensively in [4] and the results in the tables confirm the conclusions.

6.1 Choreography and Migration

We start by comparing the choreography approach to the migration approach by considering each criterion in turn:

Delay: As discussed earlier, since we have opted to allow the monitors to stabilise between each system cycle, we observe no delay for the choreography case. However, had this not been the case, we conjecture that the worst case delay would depend on the depth of the formula network which, as proven in Theorem 1, is less than the depth of the actual LTL formula.

Number and size of messages: A significant difference between choreography and migration is that in migration the whole formula is transmitted over the network while in choreography only when a subformula reaches true or false is the verdict transmitted. This distinction contributes to the significant difference in the size of the messages sent observed in Table 1.

However, the situation is reversed in the case of the frequency of messages. This is mainly because in choreography, not only does the network have to propagate the verdicts, but some progressions require a respawning of some submonitors. For example, consider the case of formula $\varphi\ \mathbf{U}\ \psi$ which is progressed to $\psi' \vee (\varphi' \wedge \varphi\ \mathbf{U}\ \psi)$. First, we note that φ' and ψ' are progressions of their counterparts in the context of the time instance being considered, while copies of the formulae are respawned to be progressed in the following time instance. This means that upon respawning, all remote submonitors have to be respawned accordingly. Naturally, this has to be done using messages, which as shown in Table 1, constitute more than half the total number of messages required.

Although choreography generally obtained better results with respect to the size of messages, the scale starts tipping in favour of migration the bigger the formula is. This is clearly visible in Tables 2 where for bigger formulae the results get closer, with migration surpassing choreography in the third (unbiased) case. The reason behind this is probably that simplification in the choreography context does not work optimally since the simplification function does not have the visibility of the whole network.

As part of the evaluation, we changed the number of components involved in a formula whilst keeping everything constant. Unsurprisingly, changing the number of components did not affect the performance of the choreography approach as much as it affected the performance of the migration approach. Table 1 shows this clearly: the compound size of messages transmitted over nine components is 16 times bigger than that of the three-component experiment. The results for choreography still fluctuated[7] but not clearly in any direction and less than a factor of two in the worst case.

Similarly, keeping everything constant, we altered the alphabet once more, this time keeping the number of components constant but changing the number of indirections required in the choreography, i.e., a deeper tree of monitors. Again, the results in Table 1 confirm the intuition that this change affects the choreography much more than the migration approach. In this case the distinction is somewhat less pronounced. However, if we compare the change from 96.16 to 81.3 in the migration case as opposed to the change from 2.47 to 4.16 in the case of choreography, we note that the percentage change is over four times bigger in the second case (68% as opposed to 15%).

Progressions: The variations in the number of progressions is similar to the number of messages sent/received. The two are linked indirectly in the sense that both the number of messages and progressions increase if the monitoring activity in the network increases. However, we note that this need not be the case, particularly when the number of components is small and monitoring can take place with little communication.

Privacy and security concerns: In general, in both the migration and the choreography approaches no component can view all the proposition values in the network. However, the migration approach is significantly safer in this regard as no proposition values are communicated: only LTL formulae, being less informative to an eavesdropper.

6.2 Choreography and Orchestration

In this subsection, we compare the choreography and the orchestration approaches.

Delay: Since orchestration is a special case of choreography with depth one, the delay of an orchestration is always better or as good as that of a choreography. However, in this study, since any number of monitoring cycles are allowed in between system cycles, neither approach has any delay.

---

[7] The reasons for the fluctuations are probably due to the random adaptations of the alphabet to change the number of components a formula is based upon.

Table 1. Same formulae and traces with modified components and distribution depth

Variables		Orchestration		Migration			Choreography		
comps	depth	# msgs	progs	# msgs	|msgs|	progs	# msgs	# distr[8]	progs
3	4			0.12	22.10	14.07	4.22	2.90	8.07
5	4			0.21	98.59	55.02	2.18	1.54	5.74
9	4	1.3	1.8	0.24	353.86	188.06	2.79	1.96	6.25
5	3.15			0.21	96.16	53.98	2.47	1.74	5.98
5	5.83			0.21	81.3	46.43	4.16	2.88	8.05

Table 2. Same formulae and traces with modified components and distribution depth

Variables		Orchestration		Migration			Choreography		
|frml|	bias	# msgs	progs	# msgs	|msgs|	progs	# msgs	# distr	progs
~2	×	1.97	6.15	1.37	12.05	22.08	3.39	1.19	6.83
~2	✓	1.93	5.83	0.52	4.80	16.05	0.59	0.18	5.95
~4	×	21.79	98.08	6.91	108.00	159.93	22.98	14.60	130.36
~4	✓	28.51	111.09	1.18	23.08	137.77	2.73	1.43	113.72
~8	×	193.11	833.46	26.67	944.77	1166.72	1041.97	655.42	1635.64
~8	✓	103.10	334.18	6.58	204.56	433.47	96.71	60.73	592.25
~16	×	653.20	2259.83	90.15	5828.51	4078.24	4136.77	2680.70	7271.81
~16	✓	361.54	1372.84	20.69	1802.93	1935.08	589.37	391.60	33981.28

Number and size of messages: Similar to the case of delay, in general (as shown in the empirical results) the number of messages required by an orchestration is less than that required by a choreography. However, this greatly depends on the topology of the tree. For example, having a distributed subformula $b_1 \wedge b_2$, sending updates for the conjunction is generally cheaper than sending updates for b_1 and b_2 separately. This phenomenon is hinted at in Table 1 where the results of the 3.15 depth are worse than those of depth 4 (where in general this should be the opposite). In other words, the performance of choreography is greatly dependent on how much the leaves can propagate their results towards the root of the tree without having to communicate. The hint is then confirmed in Table 2 where we intentionally biased the formula generation algorithm such that propositions from the same component are more likely to appear on the same branch. The results show a significant gain for the choreography approach, performing even better than orchestration for small formulae.

Progressions: Once more, the number of progressions behaves similarly to the number of messages.

Privacy and security concerns: In the case of orchestration, since a single component has visibility of all propositions, a security breach in that component would expose all the system information. On the contrary, generally speaking, no component has the full visibility of the system events in the case of choreography.

Clearly, none of the approaches ticks all the boxes. Rather, these experiments have shed some light as to when it makes more sense to use one approach over another

---

[8] The number of distribution messages is included in the previous column. We also note that all choreography messages are of size one and thus these two columns represent the size of the messages too.

depending on the size of the network, the structure of the LTL formula, the importance of issues such as privacy, frequency/size of messages, etc.

7 Related Work

The idea of splitting the progression of an LTL formula into subparts and propagating the results across a network is somewhat similar to the ideas used in parallel prefix networks [8]. In such networks intermediate results are evaluated in parallel and then combined to achieve the final result more efficiently. Furthermore, this work has two other main sources of inspiration: the work by Bauer and Falcone [4] about monitoring LTL properties in the context of distributed systems having a global clock, and the work by Francalanza et al. [6] which classifies modes of monitoring in the context of distributed systems. We have thus adapted the classification of distributed monitoring showing how orchestration, choreography, and migration can be applied to LTL monitors. We note, however, that we have introduced the global clock assumption which is not present in [6]. Without this assumption, our correctness theorem does not hold due to the loss of the total order between system events. From another point of view, we have classified the approach presented in [4] as a migration approach (using the terminology of [6]) and extended the work by presenting a choreography approach. Furthermore, we have also empirically compared the advantages and disadvantages of the approaches.

As pointed out in [4], decentralised monitoring is related to several techniques. We recall some of them and refer to [4] for a detailed comparison. One of the closest approaches is [10] which proposes to monitor MTTL formulae specifying the safety properties over parallel asynchronous systems. Contrary to [10], our approach considers the full set of ("off-the-shelf") LTL properties, does not assume the existence of a global observation point, and focuses on how to automatically split an LTL formula according to the architecture of the system.

Also, closely related to this paper is a monitoring approach of invariants using knowledge [7]. This approach leverages an apriori model-checking of the system to pre-calculate the states where a violation can be reported by a process acting alone. Both [7] and our approach try to minimize the communication induced by the distributed nature of the system but [7] (i) requires the property to be stable (and considers only invariants) and (ii) uses a Petri net model to compute synchronization points.

8 Conclusions and Future Work

In the context of distributed systems becoming increasingly ubiquitous, further studies are required to understand the variables involved and how these affect the numerous criteria which constitute good monitoring strategies. This would help architects to choose the correct approach depending on the circumstance.

This study shows that while choreography can be advantageous in specific scenarios such as in the case of systems with lots of components and formulae which can be shallowly distributed, generally it requires a significant number of messages and cannot fully exploit the potential of LTL simplification routines. We have noted that a substantial part of the messages required for choreography are in fact messages related to the maintenance of the network, i.e., respawning subparts of a formula. This means that LTL might not be the best candidate when going for a choreography. Contrastingly, non-progression-based monitoring algorithms where the monitors are not constantly modified, might lend themselves better to choreography.

We consider future work in three main directions: First, we would like to investigate how LTL equivalence rules can be used to make the choreography tree shallower. For example distributing $(a_1 \wedge a_2) \wedge ((a_3 \wedge b_1) \wedge b_2)$ might require two hops to reach a verdict while using associativity rules (obtaining $((a_1 \wedge a_2) \wedge a_3) \wedge (b_1 \wedge b_2))$, it can be easily reduced to one. Secondly, it would be interesting to consider the case where for each system cycle, the monitor only performs one cycle too. This introduces a delay for the choreography to reach the verdict and requires a more complex network to manage the dependencies across different time instants. Third, using other notations instead of LTL and/or different monitoring algorithms, particularly ones which are not progression-based, can potentially tip the balance more in favour of choreography approaches.

References

1. Bartocci, E.: Sampling-based decentralized monitoring for networked embedded systems. In: 3rd Int. Work. on Hybrid Autonomous Systems. EPTCS, vol. 124, pp. 85–99 (2013)
2. Bauer, A., Leucker, M., Schallhart, C.: Comparing LTL semantics for runtime verification. Logic and Computation 20(3), 651–674 (2010)
3. Bauer, A., Leucker, M., Schallhart, C.: Runtime verification for LTL and TLTL. ACM Trans. Softw. Eng. Methodol. 20(4), 14 (2011)
4. Bauer, A., Falcone, Y.: Decentralised LTL monitoring. In: Giannakopoulou, D., Méry, D. (eds.) FM 2012. LNCS, vol. 7436, pp. 85–100. Springer, Heidelberg (2012)
5. Falcone, Y., Cornebize, T., Fernandez, J.C.: Efficient and generalized decentralized monitoring of regular languages. In: Ábrahám, E., Palamidessi, C. (eds.) FORTE 2014. LNCS, vol. 8461, pp. 66–83. Springer, Heidelberg (2014)
6. Francalanza, A., Gauci, A., Pace, G.J.: Distributed system contract monitoring. J. Log. Algebr. Program. 82(5-7), 186–215 (2013)
7. Graf, S., Peled, D., Quinton, S.: Monitoring distributed systems using knowledge. In: Bruni, R., Dingel, J. (eds.) FMOODS/FORTE 2011. LNCS, vol. 6722, pp. 183–197. Springer, Heidelberg (2011)
8. Harris, D.: A taxonomy of parallel prefix networks. In: Signals, Systems and Computers, vol. 2, pp. 2213–2217 (2003)
9. Pnueli, A.: The temporal logic of programs. In: SFCS 1977: Proc. of the 18th Annual Symposium on Foundations of Computer Science, pp. 46–57. IEEE Computer Society (1977)
10. Sen, K., Vardhan, A., Agha, G., Rosu, G.: Decentralized runtime analysis of multithreaded applications. In: 20th Parallel and Distributed Processing Symposium (IPDPS). IEEE (2006)

Dynamic Verification for Hybrid Concurrent Programming Models

Erdal Mutlu[1], Vladimir Gajinov[2], Adrián Cristal[2,3],
Serdar Tasiran[1], and Osman S. Unsal[2]

[1] Koc University
{ermutlu,stasiran}@ku.edu.tr
[2] Barcelona Supercomputing Center
{vladimir.gajinov,adrian.cristal,osman.unsal}@bsc.es
[3] IIIA - CSIC - Spanish National Research Council

Abstract. We present a dynamic verification technique for a class of concurrent programming models that combine dataflow and shared memory programming. In this class of hybrid concurrency models, programs are built from tasks whose data dependencies are explicitly defined by a programmer and used by the runtime system to coordinate task execution. Differently from pure dataflow, tasks are allowed to have shared state which must be properly protected using synchronization mechanisms, such as locks or transactional memory (TM). While these hybrid models enable programmers to reason about programs, especially with irregular data sharing and communication patterns, at a higher level, they may also give rise to new kinds of bugs as they are unfamiliar to the programmers. We identify and illustrate a novel category of bugs in these hybrid concurrency programming models and provide a technique for randomized exploration of program behaviors in this setting.

Keywords: Dynamic verification, dataflow, transactional memory.

1 Introduction

Most modern computation platforms feature multiple CPU and GPU cores. For many large applications, it is more convenient for programmers to make use of multiple programming models to coordinate different kinds of concurrency and communication in the program. In this paper, we explore hybrid concurrent programming models that combine shared memory with dataflow abstractions.

Shared memory multi-threading is ubiquitous in concurrent programs. By contrast, in the dataflow programming model, the execution of an operation is constrained only by the availability of its input data – a feature that makes dataflow programming convenient and safe when it fits the problem at hand.

Using the dataflow programming model in conjunction with shared memory mechanisms can make it convenient and natural for programmers to express the parallelism inherent in a problem as evidenced by recent proposals [4,9] and adoptions [5,7,8]. The proposed hybrid programming models [4,9] provide

B. Bonakdarpour and S.A. Smolka (Eds.): RV 2014, LNCS 8734, pp. 156–161, 2014.

programmers with dataflow abstractions for defining tasks as the main execution unit with corresponding data dependencies. Contrary to the pure dataflow model which assumes side-effect free execution of the tasks, these models allow tasks to share the data using some form of thread synchronization, such as locks or transactional memory (TM). In this way, they facilitate implementation of complex algorithms for which shared state is the fundamental part of how the computational problem at hand is naturally expressed.

Enabling a combination of different programming models provides a user with a wide choice of parallel programming abstractions that can support a straightforward implementation of a wider range of problems. However, it also increases the likelihood of introducing concurrency bugs, not only those specific to a given well-studied programming model, but also those that are the result of unexpected program behavior caused by an incorrect use of different programming abstractions within the same program. Since the hybrid dataflow models we consider in this paper are quite novel, many of the bugs that belong to the latter category may not have been studied. The goal of this work is to identify these bugs and design a verification tool that can facilitate automated behavior exploration targeting their detection.

We present a dynamic verification tool for characterizing and exploring behaviors of programs written using hybrid dataflow programming models. We focus in particular on the Atomic DataFlow (ADF) programming model [4] as a representative of this class of programming models. In the ADF model, a program is based on tasks for which data dependencies are explicitly defined by a programmer and used by the runtime system to coordinate the task execution, while the memory shared between potentially concurrent tasks is managed using transactional memory (TM). While ideally these two domains should be well separated within a program, concurrency bugs can lead to an unexpected interleaving between these domains, leading to incorrect program behavior.

We devised a randomized scheduling method for exploring programs written using ADF. The key challenge in our work was precisely characterizing and exploring the concurrency visible and meaningful to the programmer, as opposed to the concurrency present in the dataflow runtime or TM implementations. For exploration of different interleavings, we adapted the dynamic exploration technique "Probabilistic Concurrency Testing (PCT)" [3] to ADF programs in order to amplify the randomness of observed schedules [2]. For shared memory concurrent programs, PCT provides probabilistic guarantees for bug detection. By properly selecting the scheduling points that PCT randomly chooses from, we aim to provide a similar guarantee for ADF programs.

In this paper, we motivate the use of and the need for a verification tool for ADF, explain our randomized behavior exploration tool and describe the experimental evaluation we are undertaking.

2   Motivation

In this section, we describe an unexpected execution scenario for motivating our dynamic verification method. Due to the asynchronous concurrent execution of

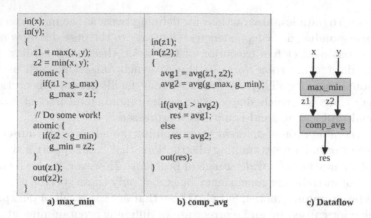

Fig. 1. Motivating example

tasks in the ADF model, users can face unexpected execution orders causing atomicity violations between dataflow tasks. To illustrate such a behavior, consider two ADF tasks in Figure 1, *max_min* that compute the maximum and minimum values from two input streams while updating a global minimum and maximum, and *comp_avg* that uses the output streams provided by *max_min* for comparing the average values of *g_max* and *g_min* with the input values and returning the bigger one. As seen in Figure 1-c, the dependencies between these tasks can be using the expressed with ADF programming model naturally as shown in Figure 1-a and b. However, while these particular implementations appear correct separately, when combined, they may result in unexpected behavior in an ADF execution. As the updates on the global variables, *g_max* and *g_min*, are performed in separate atomic blocks, concurrently running tasks can read incorrect values of global variables. Consider an execution where the first pair of integers from the input streams x and y are processed by *max_min* and then passed to *comp_avg*. During the execution of *comp_avg*, *max_min* can start to process the second pair and update *g_max* value, causing *comp_avg* to read the new *g_max* value from the second iteration while reading *g_min* value from the first one. Such concurrency scenarios that arise due to an interaction between dataflow and shared memory may be difficult to foresee for a programmer and are not addressed properly by verification methods for pure dataflow or pure shared memory model.

3 System Overview

3.1 Probabilistic Concurrency Testing

The "Probabilistic Concurrency Testing (PCT)" method relies on the observation that concurrency bugs typically involve unexpected interactions among few instructions that are executed by a small number of threads [6]. For capturing these unexpected thread interactions, PCT defines a *bug depth* parameter as the minimum number of ordering constraints that are sufficient to find a bug and uses a randomized scheduling method, with provably good probabilistic guarantees, to find all bugs of low depth.

PCT makes use of a priority based scheduler that maintains randomly assigned priorities for each thread. During execution, the scheduler schedules only the thread with the highest priority until it becomes blocked by another thread or finishes its execution. For simulating the ordering constraints, the PCT scheduler also maintains a list of *priority change points*. Whenever the execution reaches a priority change point, the scheduler changes the priority of the running thread to a predetermined priority associated with the change point. With this mechanism, the PCT method can potentially exercise all bugs of depth d by simply using $d - 1$ points.

Consider a program with n threads that together execute at most k instructions. Assuming that we want to find bugs with depth d, PCT provides a guarantee of finding a bug of depth d with the probability at least $1/nk^{d-1}$.

3.2   Our Method and Implementation

The ADF programming model has an inherently asynchronous concurrent execution model, where tasks can be enabled and executed multiple times. In addition, programmers are allowed to provide their custom synchronization using transactional memory to protect certain code blocks (not necessarily entire tasks) in ADF tasks. This can potentially influence the dataflow execution. In order to fully investigate behaviors of programs written using a hybrid model such as ADF, the dynamic exploration technique has to be aware of both the dataflow structure and the specifics of the shared memory synchronization mechanism. Furthermore, the dynamic verification tool should not simply instrument the platform implementations for transactional memory, atomic blocks and dataflow. This would not only be very inefficient, but it would also not provide value to the programmer. The user of a hybrid concurrent programming model is not interested in the concurrency internal to the platform implementing the model, which should be transparent to the programmer, but only in the non-determinism made visible at the programming model level.

We build upon the PCT algorithm but redefine priority assignment points, making use of TM transaction boundaries for priority change point assignment. Rather than using the original ADF work-stealing scheduler based on a pool of worker threads, we have devised a new scheduler that creates a thread with a randomly assigned priority for each enabled task and sequentially schedules the threads by honoring their priorities. Likewise, instead of using the original priority change point assignment from the PCT method, we narrowed possible priority change point locations to the beginning and the end of atomic regions only.

Given an ADF program with at most n enabled tasks that together execute at most k regions (atomic and non-atomic), our exploration method tries to find bugs of depth d as follows.

1. Whenever a task becomes enabled, randomly assign one of n priority values between d and $d + n$ to a thread associated with the task.
2. Pick $d - 1$ random priority change points $k_1,...,k_{d-1}$ in the range of $[1, k]$ and associate priority value of i to k_i.

3. Schedule a thread with the highest priority and execute it sequentially. When a thread reaches the i-th change point, change its priority to i.

With this randomized scheduler, our exploration technique provides the following guarantee.

Given an ADF program with at most n enabled tasks that together execute at most k regions (atomic and non-atomic), our exploration method finds a bug of depth d with probability at least $1/nk^{d-1}$.

We implemented our exploration technique as a separate testing mechanism into the ADF framework. With this mechanism, users can choose the testing scheduler for exploring the behaviors of their applications with different task ordering for a given bug depth. Differently from conventional testing, our technique provides probabilistic guarantees for finding bugs and the overall detection probability can be increased by running our technique multiple times.

Our tool also provides a monitoring mechanism for checking globally-defined invariants during an execution. We provide the users with the capability to write global invariants on shared variables. These can be checked at every step by our tool, or at randomly assigned points in the execution.

Consider the motivating example in Figure 1 with input streams of length 2, our exploration technique can catch the the described buggy behavior with bug depth 2 as follow:

Initialization. Random priorities between d-$(n + d)$ (2-6 as the length of the input streams is 2, there can be at most 4 enabled tasks) will be assigned to the enabled tasks. As the only enabled task is max_min, let's assume it is given a priority of 4.

Later, $d - 1$ (1) priority change points will be assigned randomly among the start and end points of all atomic sections, assume this change point (as we are exploring bug depth 2) is chosen to be at the end of first atomic block in max_min task.

First iteration. The scheduler starts the execution by choosing the task with the highest priority. When the execution comes to a priority change point, the priority is lowered causing scheduler to check for a task with higher priority. In this case, max_min will continue to execute as there is no other enabled task.

After finishing the execution max_min task will enable the $comp\_avg$ task resulting in a priority assignment to it. Assume that the scheduler assigned 2 as the priority for the $comp\_avg$.

The next set of inputs from the streams will enable max_min task again with new assigned priority to be 3.

Second iteration. Now scheduler will choose the enabled task with the highest priority for execution, which is max_min in this case.

While executing the max_min task, the priority will be changed at the priority change point and set to 1.

As a result scheduler will now choose $comp\_avg$ to execute causing the buggy behavior explained in Section 2.

4   Conclusion and Ongoing Work

This paper identifies and illustrates a novel category of bugs in the hybrid concurrency programming models that make use of dataflow and shared memory programming models, and provides a technique for randomized exploration of program behaviors in this setting.

We have started investigating ADF implementations of DWARF [1] benchmark applications. These applications are mostly numerical computations that have a structured dataflow with little shared memory accesses. We believe these to be a good initial set of benchmarks for discovering possibly missed cases in dataflow-heavy implementations.

In later experimental work, we plan to investigate the dynamic verification of the ADF implementation of a parallel game engine. In this complex application, the game map is divided between different tasks that process the objects moving between map regions. Dataflow is used to coordinate the execution of tasks that correspond to different game regions, whereas the TM synchronization is used to protect lists of objects, associated with each game region, that hold all the objects physically located within a region. By using the game engine application, we wish to evaluate how well our exploration method behaves with performance-critical applications characterized with highly-irregular behavior.

References

1. Asanovic, K., Bodik, R., Demmel, J., Keaveny, T., Keutzer, K., Kubiatowicz, J., Morgan, N., Patterson, D., Sen, K., Wawrzynek, J., Wessel, D., Yelick, K.: A view of the parallel computing landscape. Commun. ACM 52(10), 56–67 (2009)
2. Ben-Asher, Y., Eytani, Y., Farchi, E., Ur, S.: Producing scheduling that causes concurrent programs to fail. In: PADTAD 2006, pp. 37–40. ACM (2006)
3. Burckhardt, S., Kothari, P., Musuvathi, M., Nagarakatte, S.: A randomized scheduler with probabilistic guarantees of finding bugs. In: ASPLOS XV, pp. 167–178. ACM (2010)
4. Gajinov, V., Stipic, S., Unsal, O., Harris, T., Ayguade, E., Cristal, A.: Integrating dataflow abstractions into the shared memory model. In: SBAC-PAD, pp. 243–251 (2012)
5. Intel: Intel threading building blocks - flow graph,
   http://www.threadingbuildingblocks.org/docs/help/
   reference/flow_graph.htm
6. Lu, S., Park, S., Seo, E., Zhou, Y.: Learning from mistakes: A comprehensive study on real world concurrency bug characteristics. In: ASPLOS XIII, pp. 329–339. ACM (2008)
7. Microsoft: Task parallel library - dataflow,
   http://msdn.microsoft.com/en-us/library/hh228603.aspx
8. OpenMP: Openmp 4.0 specification,
   http://www.openmp.org/mp-documents/OpenMP4.0.0.pdf
9. Seaton, C., Goodman, D., Luján, M., Watson, I.: Applying dataflow and transactions to Lee routing. In: Workshop on Programmability Issues for Heterogeneous Multicores (2012)

Abstraction and Mining of Traces
to Explain Concurrency Bugs

Mitra Tabaei Befrouei[1,*], Chao Wang[2,**], and Georg Weissenbacher[1,*]

[1] Vienna University of Technology, Vienna, Austria
[2] Virginia Tech, Blacksburg, VA, USA

Abstract. We propose an automated mining-based method for explaining concurrency bugs. We use a data mining technique called *sequential pattern mining* to identify problematic sequences of concurrent read and write accesses to the shared memory of a multi-threaded program. Our technique does not rely on any characteristics specific to one type of concurrency bug, thus providing a general framework for concurrency bug explanation. In our method, given a set of concurrent execution traces, we first mine sequences that frequently occur in failing traces and then rank them based on the number of their occurrences in passing traces. We consider the highly ranked sequences of events that occur frequently only in failing traces an explanation of the system failure, as they can reveal its causes in the execution traces. Since the scalability of sequential pattern mining is limited by the length of the traces, we present an abstraction technique which shortens the traces at the cost of introducing spurious explanations. Spurious as well as misleading explanations are then eliminated by a subsequent filtering step, helping the programmer to focus on likely causes of the failure. We validate our approach using a number of case studies, including synthetic as well as real-world bugs.

1 Introduction

While Moore's law is still upheld by increasing the number of cores of processors, the construction of parallel programs that exploit the added computational capacity has become significantly more complicated. This holds particularly true for *debugging* multi-threaded shared-memory software: unexpected interactions between threads may result in erroneous and seemingly non-deterministic program behavior whose root cause is difficult to analyze.

To detect concurrency bugs, researchers have focused on a number of problematic program behaviors such as data races (concurrent conflicting accesses to the same memory location) and atomicity/serializability violations (an interference between supposedly indivisible critical regions). The detection of data races requires no knowledge of the program semantics and has therefore received

---

* Supported by the Austrian National Research Network S11403-N23 (RiSE) and the LogiCS doctoral program W1255-N23 of the Austrian Science Fund (FWF) and by the Vienna Science and Technology Fund (WWTF) through grant VRG11-005.
** Supported in part by the NSF CAREER award CCF-1149454.

B. Bonakdarpour and S.A. Smolka (Eds.): RV 2014, LNCS 8734, pp. 162–177, 2014.
© Springer International Publishing Switzerland 2014

ample attention (see Section 5). Freedom from data races, however, is neither a necessary nor a sufficient property to establish the correctness of a concurrent program. In particular, it does not guarantee the absence of atomicity violations, which constitute the predominant class of non-deadlock concurrency bugs [12]. Atomicity violations are inherently tied to the intended granularity of code segments (or operations) of a program. Automated atomicity checking therefore depends on heuristics [25] or atomicity annotations [6] to obtain the boundaries of operations and data objects.

The past two decades have seen numerous tools for the exposure and detection of race conditions [22,16,4,5,3], atomicity or serializability violations [6,11,25,20], or more general order violations [13,18]. These techniques have in common that they are geared towards common bug characteristics [12].

We propose a technique to explain concurrency bugs that is oblivious to the nature of the specific bug. We assume that we are given a set of concurrent execution traces, each of which is classified as successful or failed. This is a reasonable assumption, as this is a prerequisite for systematic software testing.

Although the traces of concurrent programs are lengthy sequences of events, only a small subset of these events is typically sufficient to explain an erroneous behavior. In general, these events do not occur consecutively in the execution trace, but rather at an arbitrary distance from each other. Therefore, we use data mining algorithms to isolate ordered sequences of non-contiguous events which occur frequently in the traces. Subsequently, we examine the *differences* between the common behavioral patterns of failing and passing traces (motivated by Lewis' theory of causality and counterfactual reasoning [10]).

Our approach combines ideas from the fields of runtime monitoring [2], abstraction and refinement [1], and sequential pattern mining [14]. It comprises the following three phases:

- We systematically generate execution traces with different interleavings, and record all global operations but not thread-local operations [27], thus requiring only limited observability. We justify our decision to consider only shared accesses in Section 2. The resulting data is partitioned into successful and failed executions.
- Since the resulting traces may contain thousands of operations and events, we present a novel abstraction technique which reduces the length of the traces as well as the number of events by mapping sequences of concrete events to single abstract events. We show in Section 3 that this abstraction step preserves all original behaviors while reducing the number of patterns to consider.
- We use a sequential pattern mining algorithm [26,23] to identify sequences of events that frequently occur in failing execution traces. In a subsequent filtering step, we eliminate from the resulting sequences spurious patterns that are an artifact of the abstraction and misleading patterns that do not reflect problematic behaviors. The remaining patterns are then ranked according to their frequency in the passing traces, where patterns occurring in failing traces exclusively are ranked highest.

In Section 4, we use a number of case studies to demonstrate that our approach yields a small number of relevant patterns which can serve as an explanation of the erroneous program behavior.

2   Executions, Failures, and Bug Explanation Patterns

In this section, we define basic notions such as program semantics, execution traces, and faults. We introduce the notion of bug explanation patterns and provide a theoretical rationale as well as an example of their usage. We recap the terminology of sequential pattern mining and explain how we apply this technique to extract bug explanation patterns from sets of execution traces.

2.1   Programs and Failing Executions

A multi-threaded program comprises a set V of memory locations or variables and k threads with thread indices $\{1, \ldots, k\}$. Each thread is represented by a control flow graph whose edges are annotated with atomic instructions. We use guarded statements $\varphi \triangleright \tau$ to represent atomic instructions, where φ is a predicate over the program variables and τ is an (optional) assignment $v := \phi$ (where $v \in V$ and ϕ is an expression over V). An atomic instruction $\varphi \triangleright \tau$ is executable in a given state (which is a mapping from V to the values of a domain) if φ evaluates to true in that state. The execution of the assignment $v := \phi$ results in a new state in which v is assigned the value of ϕ in the original state. Since an atomic instruction is indivisible, acquiring and releasing a lock l in a thread with index i is modeled as $(l = 0) \triangleright l := i$ and $(l = i) \triangleright l := 0$, respectively. Fork and join can be modeled in a similar manner using auxiliary synchronization variables.

Each thread executes a sequence of atomic instructions in *program order* (determined by the control flow graph). During the execution, the scheduler picks a thread and executes the next atomic instruction in the program order of the thread. The execution halts if there are no more executable atomic instructions.

The sequence of states visited during an execution constitutes a program behavior. A *fault* or *bug* is a defect in a program, which if triggered leads to an *error*, which in turn is a discrepancy between the intended and the actual behavior. If an error propagates, it may eventually lead to a *failure*, a behavior contradicting the specification. We call executions leading to a failure *failing* or *bad*, and all other executions *passing* or *good* executions.

Errors and failures are manifestations of bugs. Our goal is to explain why a bug results in a failure.

2.2   Events, Transactions, and Traces

Each execution of an atomic instruction $\varphi \triangleright v := \phi$ generates read events for the memory locations referenced in φ and ϕ, followed by a write event for v.

Definition 1 (Events). *An* event *is a tuple* $\langle \mathsf{id}\#n, \mathsf{tid}, \ell, \mathsf{type}, \mathsf{addr} \rangle$, *where* id *is an identifier and* n *is an instance number,* $\mathsf{tid} \in \{1, \ldots, k\}$ *and* ℓ *are the* *thread identifier and the program location of the corresponding instruction,* type $\in$ $\{R, W\}$ *is the type (or direction) of the memory access, and* addr $\in \mathbb{V}$ *is the memory location or variable accessed.*

Two events have the same identifier id if they are issued by the same thread and agree on the program location, the type, and the address. The instance number enables us to distinguish these events. We use $R_{tid}(addr) - \ell$ and $W_{tid}(addr) - \ell$ to refer to read and write events to the object with address addr issued by thread tid at location ℓ, respectively. The program order of a thread induces a partial order po on the set of events $\mathbb{E}$ with equivalent tids issued by a program execution. For each $i \in \{1, \ldots, k\}$ the set of events in $\mathbb{E}$ with tid $= i$ (denoted by $\mathbb{E}|_{(tid=i)}$) is totally ordered by po.

Two events conflict if they are issued by different threads, access the same memory address, and at least one of them is a write. Given two conflicting events e_1 and e_2 such that e_1 is issued before e_2, we distinguish three cases of data dependency: (a) flow-dependence: e_2 reads a value written by e_1, (b) anti-dependence: e_1 reads a value before it is overwritten by e_2, and (c) output-dependence: e_1 and e_2 both write the same memory location.

We use dep to denote the partial order over $\mathbb{E}$ representing the data dependencies that arise from the order in which the instructions of a program are executed. Thus, $\langle \mathbb{E}, \text{po} \cup \text{dep} \rangle$ is a partially ordered set. This poset induces a *schedule*. In the terminology of databases [17], a schedule is a sequence of interleaving transactions, where each *transaction* comprises a set of atomic read events followed by a set of corresponding atomic write events of the same thread which record the result of a local computation on the read values. A transaction in a schedule is *live* if it is either the final transaction writing to a certain location, or if it writes a value read by a subsequent live transaction. Two schedules are *view-equivalent* if their sets of live transactions coincide, and if a live transaction i reads the value of variable v written by transaction j in one schedule then so does transaction i in the other [17, Proposition 1].

Two equivalent schedules, if executed from the same initial state, yield the same final state. Failing executions necessarily deviate from passing executions in at least one state. Consequently, the schedules of good and bad program executions started in the same initial state either (a) differ in their flow-dependencies dep over the shared variables, and/or (b) contain different live transactions. The latter case may arise if the local computations differ or if two variables are output dependent in one schedule but not in the other.

Our method aims at identifying sequences of events that explain this discrepancy. We focus on concurrency bugs that manifest themselves in a deviation of the accesses to and the data dependencies between *shared* variables, thus ignoring failures caused purely by a difference of the local computations. As per the argument above, this criterion covers a large class of concurrency bugs, including data races, atomicity and order violations.

To this end, we log the order of read and write events (for shared variables) in a number of passing and failing executions. We assume that the addresses of variables are consistent across executions, which is enforced by our logging tool.

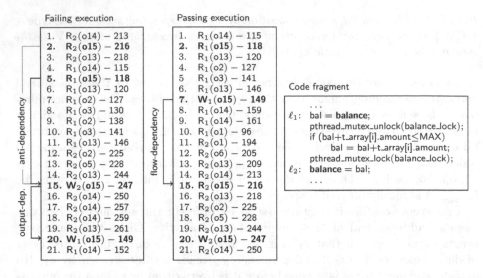

Fig. 1. Conflicting update of bank account balance

Let tot be a linear extension of po ∪ dep reflecting the total ordering introduced during event logging. An execution trace is then defined as follows:

Definition 2. *An execution trace* $\sigma = \langle e_1, e_2, ..., e_n \rangle$ *is a finite sequence of events* $e_i \in \mathbb{E}$, $i \in \{1, ..., n\}$ *ordered by* tot.

2.3   Bug Explanation Patterns

We illustrate the notion of bug explanation patterns or sequences using a well-understood example of an atomicity violation. Figure 1 shows a code fragment that non-atomically updates the balance of a bank account (stored in the shared variable balance) at locations ℓ_1 and ℓ_2. The example does not contain a data race, since balance is protected by the lock balance_lock. The array t_array contains the sequence of amounts to be transferred. At the left of Figure 1, we see a failing and a passing execution of our example. The identifiers on (where n is a number) represent the addresses of the accessed shared objects, and o15 corresponds to the variable balance. The events $R_1(o15) - 118$ and $W_1(o15) - 149$ correspond to the read and write instructions at ℓ_1 and ℓ_2, respectively.

The execution at the very left of Figure 1 fails because its final state is inconsistent with the expected value of balance. The reason is that o15 is overwritten with a stale value at position 20 in the trace, "killing" the transaction of thread 2 that writes o15 at position 15. This is reflected by the output dependency of the events $W_1(o15) - 149$ and $W_2(o15) - 247$ and the anti-dependencies between the highlighted *write-after-read* couples in the failing trace.

This combination of events and the corresponding dependencies do not arise in any passing trace, since no context switch occurs between the events $R_1(o15) - 118$ and $W_1(o15) - 149$. Accordingly, the sequence of events highlighted in the left trace in Figure 1 in combination with the dependencies reveals the problematic memory accesses to balance. We refer to this sequence as a *bug explanation pattern*. We emphasize that the events belonging to this pattern do not occur consecutively inside the trace, but are interspersed with other unrelated events. In general, events belonging to a bug explanation pattern can occur at an arbitrary distance from each other due to scheduling. Our explanations are therefore, in general, *subsequences* of execution traces. Formally, $\pi = \langle e_0, e_1, e_2, ..., e_m \rangle$ is a *subsequence* of $\sigma = \langle E_0, E_1, E_2, ..., E_n \rangle$, denoted as $\pi \sqsubseteq \sigma$, if and only if there exist integers $0 \leq i_0 < i_1 < i_2 < i_3 ... < i_m \leq n$ such that $e_0 = E_{i_0}, e_1 = E_{i_1}, ..., e_m = E_{i_m}$. We also call σ a *super-sequence* of π.

2.4 Mining Bug Explanation Patterns

In this section, we recap the terminology of sequential pattern mining and adapt it to our setting. For a more detailed treatment, we refer the interested reader to [14]. Sequential pattern mining is a technique to extract frequent subsequences from a dataset. In our setting, we are interested in subsequences occurring frequently in the sets Σ_G and Σ_B of passing (good) and failing (bad) execution traces, respectively. Intuitively, bug explanation patterns occur more frequently in the bad dataset Σ_B. While the bug pattern in question may occur in passing executions (since a fault does not necessarily result in a failure), our approach is based on the assumption that it is less frequent in Σ_G.

In a sequence dataset $\Sigma = \{\sigma_1, \sigma_2, ..., \sigma_n\}$, the *support* of a sequence π is defined as $\mathsf{support}_\Sigma(\pi) = |\{\sigma \mid \sigma \in \Sigma \land \pi \sqsubseteq \sigma\}|$. Given a minimum support threshold min_supp, the sequence π is considered a sequential pattern or a frequent subsequence if $\mathsf{support}_\Sigma(\pi) \geq$ min_supp. $\mathrm{FS}_{\Sigma,\mathsf{min\_supp}}$ denotes the set of all sequential patterns mined from Σ with the given support threshold min_supp and is defined as $\mathrm{FS}_{\Sigma,\mathsf{min\_supp}} = \{\pi \mid \mathsf{support}_\Sigma(\pi) \geq \mathsf{min\_supp}\}$. As an example, for $\Sigma = \{\langle a, b, c, e, d \rangle, \langle a, b, e, a, c, f \rangle, \langle a, g, b, c, h \rangle, \langle a, b, i, j, c \rangle, \langle a, k, l, c \rangle\}$ we obtain $\mathrm{FS}_{\Sigma,4} = \{\langle a \rangle : 5, \langle b \rangle : 4, \langle c \rangle : 5, \langle a, b \rangle : 4, \langle a, c \rangle : 5, \langle b, c \rangle : 4, \langle a, b, c \rangle : 4\}$, where the numbers following the patterns denote the respective supports of the patterns. In $\mathrm{FS}_{\Sigma,4}$, patterns $\langle a, b, c \rangle : 4$ and $\langle a, c \rangle : 5$ which do not have any super-sequences with the same support value are called *closed* patterns. A closed pattern encompasses all the frequent patterns with the same support value which are all subsequences of it. For example, in $\mathrm{FS}_{\Sigma,4}$ $\langle a, b, c \rangle : 4$ encompasses $\langle b \rangle : 4$, $\langle a, b \rangle : 4$, $\langle b, c \rangle : 4$ and similarly $\langle a, c \rangle : 5$ encompasses $\langle a \rangle : 5$ and $\langle c \rangle : 5$. Closed patterns are the lossless compression of all the sequential patterns. Therefore, we apply algorithms [26,23] that mine *closed* patterns only in order to avoid a combinatorial explosion. $\mathrm{CS}_{\Sigma,\mathsf{min\_supp}}$ denotes the set of all closed sequential patterns mined from Σ with the support threshold min_supp and is defined as

$$\{\pi \mid \pi \in \mathrm{FS}_{\Sigma,\mathsf{min\_supp}} \land \nexists \pi' \in \mathrm{FS}_{\Sigma,\mathsf{min\_supp}} . \pi \sqsubset \pi' \land \mathsf{support}(\pi) = \mathsf{support}(\pi')\}.$$

To extract bug explanation patterns from Σ_G and Σ_B, we first mine closed sequential patterns with a given minimum support threshold min_supp from Σ_B. At this point, we ignore the instance number which corresponds to the index of events in a totally ordered trace and identify events using their id. This is because in mining we do not distinguish between the events according to where they occurred inside an execution trace. The event $R_1(o15) - 118$ in Figure 1, for instance, has the same id in the failing and passing traces, even though the instances numbers (5 and 2) differ. After mining the closed patterns from Σ_B, we determine which patterns are only frequent in Σ_B but not in Σ_G by computing their value of *relative support*:

$$\mathsf{rel\_supp}(\pi) = \frac{\mathsf{support}_{\Sigma_B}(\pi)}{\mathsf{support}_{\Sigma_B}(\pi) + \mathsf{support}_{\Sigma_G}(\pi)}.$$

Patterns occur more frequently in the bad dataset are thus ranked higher, and those that occur in Σ_B exclusively have the maximum relative support of 1.

We argue that the patterns with the highest relative support are indicative of one or several faults inside the program of interest. These patterns can hence be used as clues for the exact location of the faults inside the program code.

Support Thresholds and Datasets. Which threshold is adequate depends on the number and the nature of the bugs. Given a single fault involving only one variable, every trace in Σ_B presumably contains only few patterns reflecting that fault. Since the bugs are not known up-front, and lower thresholds result in a larger number of patterns, we gradually decrease the threshold until useful explanations emerge. Moreover, the quality of the explanations is better if the traces in Σ_G and Σ_B are similar. Our experiments in Section 4 show that the sets of execution traces need not necessarily be exhaustive to enable good explanations.

3   Mining Abstract Execution Traces

With increasing length of the execution traces and number of events, sequential pattern mining quickly becomes intractable [8]. To alleviate this problem, we introduce *macro-events* that represent events of the same thread occurring consecutively inside an execution trace, and obtain *abstract* events by grouping these macros into equivalence classes according to the events they replace. Our abstraction reduces the length of the traces as well as the number of the events at the cost of introducing spurious traces. Accordingly, patterns mined from the abstract traces may not reflect actual faults. Therefore, we eliminate spurious patterns using a subsequent feasibility check.

3.1   Abstracting Execution Traces

In order to obtain a more compact representation of a set Σ of execution traces, we introduce *macros* representing substrings of the traces in Σ. A substring of a trace σ is a sequence of events that occur consecutively in σ.

Definition 3 (Macros). *Let Σ be a set of execution traces. A macro-event (or macro, for short) is a sequence of events $m \stackrel{\text{def}}{=} \langle e_1, e_2, ..., e_k \rangle$ in which all the events e_i ($1 \leq i \leq k$) have the same thread identifier, and there exists $\sigma \in \Sigma$ such that m is a substring of σ.*

We use events(m) to denote the set of events in a macro m. The concatenation of two macros $m_1 = \langle e_i, e_{i+1}, \ldots e_{i+k} \rangle$ and $m_2 = \langle e_j, e_{j+1}, \ldots e_{j+l} \rangle$ is defined as $m_1 \cdot m_2 = \langle e_i, e_{i+1}, \ldots e_{i+k}, e_j, e_{j+1}, \ldots e_{j+l} \rangle$.

Definition 4 (Macro trace). *Let Σ be a set of execution traces and $\mathbb{M}$ be a set of macros. Given a $\sigma \in \Sigma$, a corresponding macro trace $\langle m_1, m_2, \ldots, m_n \rangle$ is a sequence of macros $m_i \in \mathbb{M}$ $(1 \leq i \leq n)$ such that $m_1 \cdot m_2 \cdots m_n = \sigma$. We say that $\mathbb{M}$ covers Σ if there exists a corresponding macro trace (denoted by* macro(σ)*) for each $\sigma \in \Sigma$.*

Note that the mapping macro : $\mathbb{E}^+ \to \mathbb{M}^+$ is not necessarily unique. Given a mapping macro, every macro trace can be mapped to an execution trace and vice versa. For example, for $\mathbb{M} = \{m_0 \overset{\text{def}}{=} \langle e_0, e_2 \rangle, m_1 \overset{\text{def}}{=} \langle e_1, e_2 \rangle, m_2 \overset{\text{def}}{=} \langle e_3 \rangle, m_3 \overset{\text{def}}{=} \langle e_4, e_5, e_6 \rangle, m_4 \overset{\text{def}}{=} \langle e_8, e_9 \rangle, m_5 \overset{\text{def}}{=} \langle e_5, e_6, e_7 \rangle \}$ and the traces σ_1 and σ_2 as defined below, we obtain

$$
\begin{array}{ll}
\sigma_1 = \langle \overbrace{e_0, e_2, e_3}^{\text{tid}=1}, \overbrace{e_4, e_5, e_6}^{\text{tid}=2}, \overbrace{e_8, e_9}^{\text{tid}=1} \rangle & \text{macro}(\sigma_1) = \langle \overbrace{m_0, m_2}^{\text{tid}=1}, \overbrace{m_3}^{\text{tid}=2}, \overbrace{m_4}^{\text{tid}=1} \rangle \\
\sigma_2 = \langle \underbrace{e_1, e_2}_{\text{tid}=1}, \underbrace{e_5, e_6, e_7}_{\text{tid}=2}, \underbrace{e_3, e_8, e_9}_{\text{tid}=1} \rangle & \text{macro}(\sigma_2) = \langle \underbrace{m_1}_{\text{tid}=1}, \underbrace{m_5}_{\text{tid}=2}, \underbrace{m_2, m_4}_{\text{tid}=1} \rangle
\end{array} \tag{1}
$$

This transformation reduces the number of events as well as the length of the traces while preserving the context switches, but hides information about the frequency of the original events. A mining algorithm applied to the macro traces will determine a support of one for m_3 and m_5, even though the events $\{e_5, e_6\} = $ events$(m_3) \cap $ events(m_5) have a support of 2 in the original traces. While this problem can be amended by *refining* $\mathbb{M}$ by adding $m_6 = \langle e_5, e_6 \rangle$, $m_7 = \langle e_4 \rangle$, and $m_8 = \langle e_6 \rangle$, for instance, this increases the length of the trace and the number of events, countering our original intention.

Instead, we introduce an abstraction function $\alpha : \mathbb{M} \to \mathbb{A}$ which maps macros to a set of abstract events $\mathbb{A}$ according to the events they share. The abstraction guarantees that if m_1 and m_2 share events, then $\alpha(m_1) = \alpha(m_2)$.

Definition 5 (Abstract events and traces). *Let R be the relation defined as $R(m_1, m_2) \overset{\text{def}}{=} ($events$(m_1) \cap $events$(m_2) \neq \emptyset)$ and R^+ its transitive closure. We define $\alpha(m_i)$ to be $\{m_j \mid m_j \in \mathbb{M} \wedge R^+(m_i, m_j)\}$, and the set of abstract events $\mathbb{A}$ to be $\{\alpha(m) \mid m \in \mathbb{M}\}$. The abstraction of a macro trace* macro$(\sigma) = \langle m_1, m_2, \ldots, m_n \rangle$ *is $\alpha($macro$(\sigma)) = \langle \alpha(m_1), \alpha(m_2), \ldots, \alpha(m_n) \rangle$.*

The concretization of an abstract trace $\langle u_1, u_2, \ldots, u_n \rangle$ is the set of macro traces $\gamma(\langle a_1, a_2, \ldots, a_n \rangle) \overset{\text{def}}{=} \{\langle m_1, \ldots, m_n \rangle \mid m_i \in a_i, 1 \leq i \leq n\}$. Therefore, we have macro$(\sigma) \in \gamma(\alpha($macro$(\sigma)))$. Further, since for any $m_1, m_2 \in \mathbb{M}$ with $e \in $events$(m_1)$ and $e \in $events$(m_2)$ it holds that $\alpha(m_1) = \alpha(m_2) = a$ with $a \in \mathbb{A}$, it is guaranteed that support$_\Sigma(e) \leq $support$_{\alpha(\Sigma)}(a)$, where $\alpha(\Sigma) = \{\alpha($macro$(\sigma)) \mid \sigma \in \Sigma\}$. For the example above (1), we obtain $\alpha(m_i) = \{m_i\}$ for $i \in \{2, 4\}$, $\alpha(m_0) = \alpha(m_1) = \{m_0, m_1\}$, and $\alpha(m_3) = \alpha(m_5) = \{m_3, m_5\}$ (with support$_{\alpha(\Sigma)}(\{m_3, m_5\}) = $support$_\Sigma(e_5) = 2$).

3.2 Mining Patterns from Abstract Traces

As we will demonstrate in Section 4, abstraction significantly reduces the length of traces, thus facilitating sequential pattern mining. We argue that the patterns mined from abstract traces over-approximate the patterns of the corresponding original execution traces:

Lemma 1. *Let Σ be a set of execution traces, and let $\pi = \langle e_0, e_1 \ldots e_k \rangle$ be a frequent pattern with $\mathsf{support}_\Sigma(\pi) = n$. Then there exists a frequent pattern $\langle a_0, \ldots, a_l \rangle$ (where $l \leq k$) with support at least n in $\alpha(\Sigma)$ such that for each $j \in \{0..k\}$, we have $\exists m . e_j \in m \wedge \alpha(m) = a_{i_j}$ for $0 = i_0 \leq i_1 \leq \ldots \leq i_k = l$.*

Lemma 1 follows from the fact that each e_j must be contained in some macro m and that $\mathsf{support}_\Sigma(e_j) \leq \mathsf{support}_{\alpha(\Sigma)}(\alpha(m))$. The pattern $\langle e_2, e_5, e_6, e_8, e_9 \rangle$ in the example above (1), for instance, corresponds to the abstract pattern $\langle \{m_0, m_1\}, \{m_3, m_5\}, \{m_4\} \rangle$ with support 2. Note that even though the abstract pattern is significantly shorter, the number of context switches is the same.

While our abstraction preserves the original patterns in the sense of Lemma 1, it may introduce spurious patterns. If we apply γ to concretize the abstract pattern from our example, we obtain four patterns $\langle m_0, m_3, m_4 \rangle$, $\langle m_0, m_5, m_4 \rangle$, $\langle m_1, m_3, m_4 \rangle$, and $\langle m_1, m_5, m_4 \rangle$. The patterns $\langle m_0, m_5, m_4 \rangle$ and $\langle m_1, m_3, m_4 \rangle$ are *spurious*, as the concatenations of their macros do not translate into valid subsequences of the traces σ_1 and σ_2. We filter spurious patterns and determine the support of the macro patterns by mapping them to the original traces in Σ (aided by the information about which traces the macros derive from).

3.3 Filtering Misleading Patterns

Sequential pattern mining ignores the underlying semantics of the events and macros. This has the undesirable consequences that we obtain numerous patterns that are not explanations in the sense of Section 2.3, since they do not contain context switches or data-dependencies.

Accordingly, we define a set of constraints to eliminate *misleading* patterns:

1. Patterns must contain events of at least two different threads. The rationale for this constraint is that we are exclusively interested in concurrency bugs.
2. We lift the data-dependencies introduced in Section 2.2 to macros as follows: Two macros m_1 and m_2 are data-dependent iff there exist $e_1 \in \mathsf{events}(m_1)$ and $e_2 \in \mathsf{events}(m_2)$ such that e_1 and e_2 are related by dep. We require that for each macro in a pattern there is a data-dependency with at least one other macro in the pattern.
3. We restrict our search to patterns with a limited number (at most 4) of context switches, since there is empirical evidence that real world concurrency bugs involve only a small number of threads, context switches, and variables [12,15]. This heuristic limits the length of patterns and increases the scalability of our analysis significantly.

These criteria are applied during sequential pattern mining as well as in a post-processing step.

3.4   Deriving Macros from Traces

The precision of the approximation as well as the length of the trace is inherently tied to the choice of macros $\mathbb{M}$ for Σ. There is a tradeoff between precision and length: choosing longer subsequences as macros leads to shorter traces but also more intersections between macros.

In our algorithm, we start with macros of maximal length, splitting the traces in Σ into subsequences at the context switches. Subsequently, we iteratively refine the resulting set of macros by selecting the shortest macro m and splitting all macros that contain m as a substring. In the example in Section 3.1, we start with $\mathbb{M}_0 = \{m_0 \stackrel{\text{def}}{=} \langle e_0, e_2, e_3 \rangle, m_1 \stackrel{\text{def}}{=} \langle e_4, e_5, e_6 \rangle, m_2 \stackrel{\text{def}}{=} \langle e_8, e_9 \rangle, m_3 \stackrel{\text{def}}{=} \langle e_1, e_2 \rangle, m_4 \stackrel{\text{def}}{=} \langle e_5, e_6, e_7 \rangle, m_5 \stackrel{\text{def}}{=} \langle e_3, e_8, e_9 \rangle\}$. As m_2 is contained in m_5, we split m_5 into m_2 and $m_6 \stackrel{\text{def}}{=} \langle e_3 \rangle$ and replace it with m_6. The new macro is in turn contained in m_0, which gives rise to the macro $m_7 = \langle e_0, e_2 \rangle$. At this point, we have reached a fixed point, and the resulting set of macros corresponds to the choice of macros in our example.

For a fixed initial state, the execution traces frequently share a prefix (representing the initialization) and a suffix (the finalization). These are mapped to the same macro events by our heuristic. Since these macros occur at the beginning and the end of all good as well as bad traces, we prune the traces accordingly and focus on the deviating substrings of the traces.

4   Experimental Evaluation

To evaluate our approach, we present 7 case studies which are listed in Table 1 (6 of them are taken from [13]). The programs are bug kernels capturing the essence of bugs reported in Mozilla and Apache, or synthetic examples created to cover a specific bug category.

We generate execution traces using the concurrency testing tool INSPECT [27], which systematically explores all possible interleavings for a fixed program input. The generated traces are then classified as bad and good traces with respect to the violation of a property of interest. We implemented our mining algorithm in C#. All experiments were performed on a 2.93 GHz PC with 3.5 GB RAM running 32-bit Windows XP 32-bit.

In Table 1, the last column shows the length reduction (up to 95%) achieved by means of abstraction. This amount is computed by comparing the minimum length of the original traces with the maximum length of abstracted traces given in the preceding columns. The number of traces inside the bad and good datasets are given in columns 2 and 3, respectively. State-of-the-art sequential pattern mining algorithms are typically applicable to sequences of length less than 100 [26,14]. Therefore, the reduction of the original traces is crucial. For all benchmarks except two of them, we used an exhaustive set of interleavings. For the remaining benchmarks, we took the first 100 bad and 100 good traces from the sets of 32930 and 1427 traces we were able to generate. Moreover, for these two benchmarks, evaluation has also been done on the datasets generated by randomly choosing 100 bad and 100 good traces from the set of available traces.

Table 1. Length reduction results by abstracting the traces

Prog. Category	Name	$|\Sigma_B|$	$|\Sigma_G|$	Min. Trace Len.	Max. Abst. Trace Len	Len Red.
Synthetic	BankAccount	40	5	178	13	93%
	CircularListRace	64	6	184	9	95%
	WrongAccessOrder	100	100	48	20	58%
Bug Kernel	Apache-25520(Log)	100	100	114	16	86%
	Moz-jsStr	70	66	404	18	95%
	Moz-jsInterp	610	251	430	101	76%
	Moz-txtFrame	99	91	410	57	86%

Table 2. Mining results

Program	min_supp	#α	#γ	#feas	#filt	#rs = 1	#grp
BankAccount	100%	65	13054	19	10	10	3
CircularListRace	95%	12	336	234	18	14	12
WrongAccessOrder	100%	5	8	11	1	1	1
WrongAccessOrder$_{rand}$	100%	41	62	88	1	1	1
Apache-25520(Log)	100%	160	1650	667	16	12	12
Apache-25520(Log)$_{rand}$	100%	76	968	51	15	13	6
Apache-25520(Log)$_{rand}$	95%	105	1318	598	61	39	28
Moz-jsStr	100%	83	615056	486	90	76	4
Moz-jsInterp	100%	83	279882	49	23	23	4
Moz-txtFrame	90%	1192	5137	2314	200	32	11

The results of mining for the given programs and traces are provided in Table 2. For the randomly generated datasets, namely WrongAccessOrder$_{rand}$ and Apache-25520(Log)$_{rand}$, the average results of 5 experiments are given. The column labeled min_supp shows the support threshold required to obtain at least one bug explanation pattern (lower thresholds yield more patterns). For the given value of min_supp, the table shows the number of resulting abstract patterns (#α), the number of patterns after concretization (#γ), the number of patterns remaining after removing spurious patterns (#feas), and the patterns remaining after filtering misleading sequences (#filt). Mining, concretization, and the elimination of spurious patterns takes only 263ms on average. With an average runtime of 100s, filtering misleading patterns is the computationally most expensive step, but is very effective in eliminating irrelevant patterns.

The number of patterns with a relative support 1 (which only occur in the bad dataset) is given in column 7. Finally, we group the resulting patterns according to the set of data-dependencies they contain; column #grp shows the resulting number of groups. Since we may get multiple groups with the same relative support as the column #grp shows, we sort descendingly groups with the same relative support according to the number of data-dependencies they contain. Therefore, in the final result set a group of patterns with the highest value of relative support and maximum number of data-dependencies appears at the top. The patterns at the top of the list in the final result are inspected first by the user for understanding a bug. We verified manually that all groups with the relative support of 1 are an adequate explanation of at least one concurrency bug in the corresponding program. In the following, we explain for each case study how the inspection of only a single pattern from these groups can expose the bug. These patterns are given in Figure 2. For each case study, the given pattern belongs to group of patterns which appeared at the top of the list in the final result set, hence inspected first by the user. To save space, we only show the ids of the events and the data-dependencies relevant for understanding the bugs. Macros are separated by extra spaces between the corresponding events.

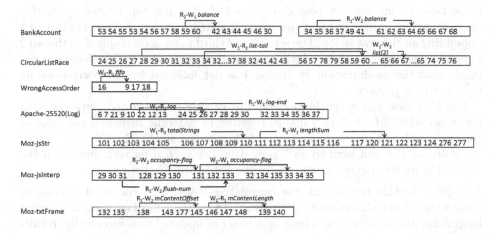

Fig. 2. Bug explanation patterns-case studies

Bank Account. The update of the shared variable balance in Figure 1 in Section 2.3 involves a *read* as well as a *write* access that are not located in the same critical region. Accordingly, a context switch may result in writing a stale value of balance. In Figure 2, we provide two patterns for *BankAccount*, each of which contains two macro events. From the anti-dependency ($R_2 - W_1$ balance) in the left pattern, we infer an atomicity violation in the code executed by thread 2, since a context switch occurs after R_2(balance), consequently it is not followed by the corresponding W_2(balance). Similarly, from the anti-dependency $R_1 - W_2$ balance in the right pattern we infer the same problem in the code executed by the thread 1. In order to obtain the bug explanation pattern given in Figure 1 for this case study, we reduced the min_supp to 60%.

Circular List Race. This program removes elements from the end of a list and adds them to the beginning using the methods getFromTail and addAtHead, respectively. The update is expected to be atomic, but since the calls are not located in the same critical region, two simultaneous updates can result in an incorrectly ordered list if a context switch occurs. The first and the second macros of the pattern in Figure 2 correspond to the events issued by the execution of addAtHead by the threads 1 and 2, respectively. From the given data-dependencies it can be inferred that these two calls occur consecutively during the program execution, thus revealing the atomicity violation.

Wrong Access Order. In this program, the main thread spawns two threads, consumer and output, but it only joins output. After joining output, the main thread frees the shared data-structure which may be accessed by consumer which has not exited yet. The flow-dependency between the two macros of the pattern in Figure 2 implies the wrong order in accessing the shared data-structure.

Apache-25520(Log). In this bug kernel, Apache modifies a data-structure log by appending an element and subsequently updating a pointer to the log. Since these two actions are not protected by a lock, the log can be corrupted if a context switch occurs. The first macro of the pattern in Figure 2 reflects thread 1 appending an element to log. The second and third macros correspond to thread 2 appending an element and updating the pointer, respectively. The dependencies imply that the modification by thread 1 is not followed by the corresponding update of the pointer.

For this case study, evaluation on the randomly generated datasets with min_supp $=100\%$ (row 7 in Table 2) resulted in patterns revealing only one of the two problematic data dependencies in Figure 2, namely $(R_1 - W_2 \log - \text{end})$. By reducing the min_supp to 95% (row 8 in Table 2), a pattern similar to the one in Figure 2 appeared at the top of the list in the final result set.

Moz-jsStr. In this bug kernel, the cumulative length and the total number of strings stored in a shared cache data-structure are stored in two variables named lengthSum and totalStrings. These variables are updated non-atomically, resulting in an inconsistency. The pattern and the data-dependencies in Figure 2 reveal this atomicity violation: the values of totalStrings and lengthSum read by thread 2 are inconsistent due to a context switch that occurs between the updates of these two variables by thread 1.

Moz-jsInterp. This bug kernel contains a non-atomic update to a shared data-structure Cache and a corresponding occupancy flag, resulting in an inconsistency between these objects. The first and last macro-events in Figure 2 of the pattern correspond to populating Cache and updating the occupancy flag by thread 1, respectively. The given data-dependencies suggest these two actions are interrupted by thread 2 which reads an inconsistent flag.

Moz-txtFrame. The patterns and data-dependencies at the bottom of Figure 2 reflect a non-atomic update to the two fields mContentOffset and mContentLength, which causes the values of these fields to be inconsistent: the values of these variables read by thread 1 in the second and forth macros are inconsistent due to the updates done by thread 2 in the third macro.

5   Related Work

Given the ubiquity of multithreaded software, there is a vast amount of work on finding concurrency bugs. A comprehensive study of concurrency bugs [12] identifies data races, atomicity violations, and ordering violations as the prevalent categories of non-deadlock concurrency bugs. Accordingly, most bug detection tools are tailored to identify concurrency bugs in one of these categories. AVIO [11] only detects single-variable atomicity violations by learning acceptable memory access patterns from a sequence of passing training executions, and then monitoring whether these patterns are violated. SVD [25] is a tool that relies on heuristics to approximate atomic regions and uses deterministic replay to detect serializability violations. Lockset analysis [22] and happens-before analysis [16] are popular approaches focusing only on data race detection. In contrast to these approaches, which rely on specific characteristics of concurrency bugs and lack generality, our bug patterns can indicate any type of concurrency bugs. The algorithms in [24] for atomicity violations detection rely on input from the user in order to determine atomic fragments of executions. Detection of atomic-set serializability violations by the dynamic analysis method in [7] depends on a set of given problematic data access templates. Unlike these approaches, our algorithm does not rely on any given templates or annotations. BUGABOO [13] constructs bounded-size context-aware communication graphs during an execution, which encode access ordering information including the context in which the accesses occurred. BUGABOO then ranks the recorded access patterns according to their frequency. Unlike our approach, which analyzes entire execution traces (at the cost of having to store and process them in full), context-aware communication graphs may miss bug patterns if the relevant ordering information is not encoded. FALCON [19] and the follow-up work UNICORN [18] can detect single- and multi-variable atomicity violations as well as order violations by monitoring pairs of memory accesses, which are then combined into problematic patterns. The suspiciousness of a pattern is computed by comparing the number of times the pattern appears in a set of failing traces and in a set of passing traces. UNICORN produces patterns based on pattern templates, while our approach does not rely on such templates. In addition, UNICORN restricts these patterns to windows of some specific length, which results in a local view of the traces. In contrast to UNICORN, we abstract the execution traces without losing information.

Leue et al. [8,9] have used pattern mining to explain concurrent counterexamples obtained by explicit-state model checking. In contrast to our approach, [8] mines frequent substrings instead of subsequences and [9] suggests a heuristic to partition the traces into shorter sub-traces. Unlike our abstraction-based technique, both of these approaches may result in the loss of bug explanation sequences. Moreover, both methods are based on *contrasting* the frequent patterns of the bad and the good datasets rather than ranking them according to their relative frequency. Therefore, their accuracy is contingent on the values for the *two* support thresholds of the bad as well as the good datasets.

Statistical debugging techniques which are based on comparison of the characteristics of a number of failing and passing traces are broadly used for localizing faults in sequential program code. For example, a recent work [21] statically ranks the differences between a few number of similar failing and passing traces, producing a ranked list of facts which are strongly correlated with the failure. It

then systematically generates more runs that can either further confirm or re-
fute the relevance of a fact. As opposed to this approach, our goal is to identify
problematic sequences of interleaving actions in concurrent systems.

6   Conclusion

We introduced the notion of bug explanation patterns based on well-known
ideas from concurrency theory, and argued their adequacy for understanding
concurrency bugs. We explained how sequential pattern mining algorithms can
be adapted to extract such patterns from logged execution traces. By applying a
novel abstraction technique, we reduce the length of these traces to an extent that
pattern mining becomes feasible. Our case studies demonstrate the effectiveness
of our method for a number of synthetic as well as real world bugs.

As future work we plan to apply our method for explaining other types of
concurrency bugs such as *deadlocks* and *livelocks*.

References

1. Clarke, E.M., Grumberg, O., Jha, S., Lu, Y., Veith, H.: Counterexample-guided
   abstraction refinement. In: Emerson, E.A., Sistla, A.P. (eds.) CAV 2000. LNCS,
   vol. 1855, pp. 154–169. Springer, Heidelberg (2000)
2. Delgado, N., Gates, A.Q., Roach, S.: A taxonomy and catalog of runtime software-
   fault monitoring tools. IEEE Transactions on Software Engineering (TSE) 30(12),
   859–872 (2004)
3. Elmas, T., Qadeer, S., Tasiran, S.: Goldilocks: a race-aware Java runtime. Communications of the ACM 53(11), 85–92 (2010)
4. Engler, D.R., Ashcraft, K.: RacerX: effective, static detection of race conditions and
   deadlocks. In: Symposium on Operating Systems Principles (SOSP), pp. 237–252.
   ACM (2003)
5. Flanagan, C., Freund, S.N.: FastTrack: efficient and precise dynamic race detection.
   Communications of the ACM 53(11), 93–101 (2010)
6. Flanagan, C., Qadeer, S.: A type and effect system for atomicity. In: PLDI,
   pp. 338–349. ACM (2003)
7. Hammer, C., Dolby, J., Vaziri, M., Tip, F.: Dynamic detection of atomic-set-
   serializability violations. In: International Conference on Software Engineering
   (ICSE), pp. 231–240. ACM (2008)
8. Leue, S., Tabaei Befrouei, M.: Counterexample explanation by anomaly detection. In: Donaldson, A., Parker, D. (eds.) SPIN 2012. LNCS, vol. 7385, pp. 24–42.
   Springer, Heidelberg (2012)
9. Leue, S., Tabaei Befrouei, M.: Mining sequential patterns to explain concurrent
   counterexamples. In: Bartocci, E., Ramakrishnan, C.R. (eds.) SPIN 2013. LNCS,
   vol. 7976, pp. 264–281. Springer, Heidelberg (2013)
10. Lewis, D.: Counterfactuals. Wiley-Blackwell (2001)
11. Lu, S., Tucek, J., Qin, F., Zhou, Y.: AVIO: detecting atomicity violations via access
    interleaving invariants. In: Architectural Support for Programming Languages and
    Operating Systems, ASPLOS (2006)

12. Lu, S., Park, S., Seo, E., Zhou, Y.: Learning from mistakes: a comprehensive study on real world concurrency bug characteristics. ACM Sigplan Notices 43, 329–339 (2008)
13. Lucia, B., Ceze, L.: Finding concurrency bugs with context-aware communication graphs. In: Symposium on Microarchitecture (MICRO), pp. 553–563. ACM (2009)
14. Mabroukeh, N.R., Ezeife, C.I.: A taxonomy of sequential pattern mining algorithms. ACM Computing Surveys 43(1), 3:1–3:41 (2010)
15. Musuvathi, M., Qadeer, S.: Iterative context bounding for systematic testing of multithreaded programs. In: PLDI, pp. 446–455. ACM (2007)
16. Netzer, R.H.B., Miller, B.P.: Improving the accuracy of data race detection. SIGPLAN Notices 26(7), 133–144 (1991)
17. Papadimitriou, C.H.: The serializability of concurrent database updates. Journal of the ACM 26(4), 631–653 (1979)
18. Park, S., Vuduc, R., Harrold, M.J.: A unified approach for localizing non-deadlock concurrency bugs. In: Software Testing, Verification and Validation (ICST), pp. 51–60. IEEE (2012)
19. Park, S., Vuduc, R.W., Harrold, M.J.: Falcon: fault localization in concurrent programs. In: International Conference on Software Engineering (ICSE), pp. 245–254. ACM (2010)
20. Park, S., Lu, S., Zhou, Y.: CTrigger: exposing atomicity violation bugs from their hiding places. In: Architectural Support for Programming Languages and Operating Systems (ASPLOS), pp. 25–36. ACM (2009)
21. Rößler, J., Fraser, G., Zeller, A., Orso, A.: Isolating failure causes through test case generation. In: International Symposium on Software Testing and Analysis, pp. 309–319. ACM (2012)
22. Savage, S., Burrows, M., Nelson, G., Sobalvarro, P., Anderson, T.: Eraser: A dynamic data race detector for multithreaded programs. Transactions on Computer Systems (TOCS) 15(4), 391–411 (1997)
23. Wang, J., Han, J.: Bide: Efficient mining of frequent closed sequences. In: ICDE (2004)
24. Wang, L., Stoller, S.D.: Runtime analysis of atomicity for multithreaded programs. TSE 32(2), 93–110 (2006)
25. Xu, M., Bodík, R., Hill, M.D.: A serializability violation detector for shared-memory server programs. In: PLDI, pp. 1–14. ACM (2005)
26. Yan, X., Han, J., Afshar, R.: CloSpan: Mining closed sequential patterns in large datasets. In: Proceedings of 2003 SIAM International Conference on Data Mining, SDM 2003 (2003)
27. Yang, Y., Chen, X., Gopalakrishnan, G.C., Kirby, R.M.: Distributed dynamic partial order reduction based verification of threaded software. In: Bošnački, D., Edelkamp, S. (eds.) SPIN 2007. LNCS, vol. 4595, pp. 58–75. Springer, Heidelberg (2007)

Online Monitoring of Metric Temporal Logic*

Hsi-Ming Ho, Joël Ouaknine, and James Worrell

Department of Computer Science, University of Oxford,
Wolfson Building, Parks Road, Oxford, OX1 3QD, UK

Abstract. Current approaches to monitoring real-time properties suffer either from unbounded space requirements or lack of expressiveness. In this paper, we adapt a separation technique enabling us to rewrite arbitrary MTL formulas into LTL formulas over a set of atoms comprising bounded MTL formulas. As a result, we obtain the first trace-length independent online monitoring procedure for full MTL in a dense-time setting.

1 Introduction

In recent years, there has been increasing interest in *runtime verification* as a complement to traditional model checking techniques (see [21, 29] for surveys). Runtime monitoring, for example, may be used in situations in which we wish to evaluate a system that is either too complex to model or whose internal details are not accessible. Moreover, logics whose model-checking problems are undecidable may become tractable in this more restricted setting. The latter is the case in the present paper, which is concerned with runtime monitoring of *Metric Temporal Logic* with both forwards and backwards temporal modalities (MTL[U, S]).

MTL[U, S] was introduced almost 25 years ago by Koymans [19] and has since become the most widely studied real-time temporal logic. Over the reals, it has been shown that MTL[U, S] has the same expressiveness as *Monadic First-Order Logic of Order and Metric* (FO[<, +ℚ]) [17]. In this paper, we study the **monitoring** problem for MTL[U, S] over *timed words*. This so-called *pointwise semantics* is more natural and appropriate when we consider systems modelled as timed automata. Also, monitoring timed words is often conceptually simpler and more efficient [6].

Given an MTL[U, S] formula φ and a finite timed word ρ, the *prefix* problem asks whether all infinite timed words extending ρ satisfy φ. The monitoring problem can be seen as an *online* version of the prefix problem where ρ is given incrementally, one event at a time. The monitoring procedure is required to output an answer when either (i) all infinite extensions of the current trace satisfy the specification, or (ii) no infinite extension of the current trace can possibly meet the specification. In this paper, we consider a variant of the monitoring problem, based on the notion of *informative prefixes* [20].

---

* More extensive technical details as well as all proofs can be found in the full version of this paper [16].

B. Bonakdarpour and S.A. Smolka (Eds.): RV 2014, LNCS 8734, pp. 178–192, 2014.
© Springer International Publishing Switzerland 2014

Ideally, for a monitoring procedure to be practical, we require that it be *trace-length independent* [7] in the sense that the total space requirement should not depend on the length of the input trace. With this objective in mind, the principal difficulty in monitoring MTL[U, S] is that it allows unbounded intervals and nesting of future and past operators, and hence the truth value of a formula at some point may depend on the truth values of its subformulas arbitrarily far in the future or past. For this reason, most real-time monitoring procedures in the literature impose certain syntactic or semantic restrictions, e.g., only allowing bounded future modalities[1] or assuming integer-time traces. A notable exception is [4] which handles the full logic MTL[U, S] over dense-time signals, but which unfortunately fails to be trace-length independent.

The main contribution of this paper is a new online monitoring procedure for MTL[U, S] over dense-time traces. The procedure we give handles the full logic MTL[U, S] and is trace-length independent,[2] making it suitable for traces with potentially unbounded lengths, e.g., network activity logs. For a given formula, we first adapt a separation theorem of [17] to rewrite an MTL[U, S] formula into an LTL[U, S] formula over a set of atoms comprising bounded MTL[U, S] formulas, whose truth values are computed and stored efficiently. The remaining untimed component is then handled via translation to deterministic finite automata. The resulting algorithm is free of dynamic memory allocations, linked lists, etc., and hence can be implemented efficiently.

2 Related Work

The most closely related work to the present paper is that of Finkbeiner and Kuhtz [13], which concerns monitoring MTL over a discrete-time semantics. They handle bounded formulas in a similar fashion to us and highlight the problematic role of unbounded temporal operators. However they do not exploit a syntactic rewriting of unbounded operators from the scope of bounded operators, and are forced to apply specialised constructions in this case.

Another highly relevant work is that of Nickovic and Piterman [26], in which a translation from MTL to deterministic timed automata is proposed. The essence of the method is the observation that, while the truth values of unbounded subformulas must necessarily be guessed, the truth values of bounded subformulas can be obtained via bounded look-ahead. In spirit, this is very similar to our approach. The main differences are that they consider only the future fragment, and we handle bounded subformulas explicitly rather than encoding them into clock constraints.

---

[1] Note in passing that, unlike for LTL, past modalities strictly increase the expressiveness of MTL [9].

[2] As shown in [22], trace-length independence necessarily requires a global bound on the *variability* of time sequences, i.e., the maximum number of events which can occur in any given unit-duration time interval. This is a standard assumption which is in practice always met by physical systems. The proof in [22] is carried out in the continuous semantics, but it goes through in the pointwise setting as well.

Regarding real-time logics with past, it is known that the non-punctual fragment of MTL[U, S], called MITL[U, S], can be translated into timed automata [1, 2, 11, 18, 23]. The difficulty in using such approaches for monitoring lies in the fact that timed automata cannot be determinised in general. In principle one can carry out determinisation on-the-fly for timed words of bounded variability; however, it is not clear that this approach can yield an efficient procedure.

Automata-free monitoring procedures also appear in the literature. For example, in a pioneering paper, Thati and Roşu [30] propose a rewriting-based monitoring procedure for MTL[U, S]. Their procedure is trace-length independent and amenable to efficient implementations. However, the procedure only works for integer-time traces and hence does not appear applicable to our setting.

Online monitoring of real-time properties is still a very active topic of research. Recently, there have been some attempts to extend temporal logics with (restricted) first-order quantifiers for monitoring (see, e.g., [5, 7, 10, 15, 28]). The work in the present paper can be seen as orthogonal to these advances.

3   Background

3.1   Metric Temporal Logic

A *time sequence* $\tau = \tau_1 \tau_2 \ldots$ is a non-empty strictly increasing sequence of rational numbers such that $\tau_1 = 0$. We consider both finite and infinite time sequences, denoting by $|\tau|$ the length of such a sequence. If τ is infinite we require it to be unbounded, i.e., we disallow the so-called Zeno sequences.

A *timed word* over a finite alphabet Σ is a pair $\rho = (\sigma, \tau)$, where $\sigma = \sigma_1 \sigma_2 \ldots$ is a non-empty finite or infinite word over Σ and τ is a time sequence of the same length. We equivalently consider a timed word as a sequence of events $(\sigma_1, \tau_1)(\sigma_2, \tau_2) \ldots$. The finite timed words considered in this paper arise as prefixes of infinite timed words, and so we sometimes use the term *prefix* to denote an arbitrary finite timed word. We write $T\Sigma^*$ and $T\Sigma^\omega$ for the respective sets of finite and infinite timed words over Σ. For a set of propositions P we write $\Sigma_P = 2^P$.

For a space-bounded online monitoring procedure to be possible, we must impose a global bound on the variability of time sequences, cf. [22]. Henceforth we assume that all timed words have variability at most k_{var} for some (*a priori* known) absolute constant k_{var}, i.e., there are at most k_{var} events in any unit time interval.

We specify properties of timed words using *Metric Temporal Logic* with both the 'Until' and 'Since' modalities, denoted MTL[U, S]. Given a set of propositions P, the formulas of MTL[U, S] are given by the following grammar

$$\varphi ::= p \mid \mathbf{true} \mid \varphi_1 \wedge \varphi_2 \mid \neg\varphi \mid \varphi_1 \, \mathbf{U}_I \, \varphi_2 \mid \varphi_1 \, \mathbf{S}_I \, \varphi_2$$

where $p \in P$ and $I \subseteq (0, \infty)$ is an interval with endpoints in $\mathbb{Q}_{\geq 0} \cup \{\infty\}$. We sometime omit the subscript I if $I = (0, \infty)$. Given $x \in \mathbb{Q}$, we write $x < I$ to mean $x < \sup(I)$. Additional temporal operators and dual operators are defined in the standard way, e.g., $\mathbf{P}_I\varphi \equiv \mathbf{true}\mathbf{S}_I\varphi$ and $\mathbf{H}_I\varphi \equiv \neg\mathbf{P}_I\neg\varphi$. For an MTL[U, S] formula φ, we denote by $|\varphi|$ the number of subformulas of φ.

The satisfaction relation $\rho, i \models \varphi$ for an MTL[U, S] formula φ, an infinite timed word $\rho = (\sigma, \tau)$ and a position $i \geq 1$ is defined as follows:

- $\rho, i \models p$ iff $p \in \sigma_i$
- $\rho, i \models \varphi_1 \mathbf{U}_I \varphi_2$ iff there exists $j > i$ such that $\rho, j \models \varphi_2$, $\tau_j - \tau_i \in I$, and $\rho, k \models \varphi_1$ for all k with $i < k < j$
- $\rho, i \models \varphi_1 \mathbf{S}_I \varphi_2$ iff there exists j, $1 \leq j < i$ such that $\rho, j \models \varphi_2$, $\tau_i - \tau_j \in I$ and $\rho, k \models \varphi_1$ for all k with $j < k < i$.[3]

The semantics of the Boolean connectives is defined in the expected way.

We say that ρ satisfies φ, denoted $\rho \models \varphi$, if $\rho, 1 \models \varphi$. We write $\mathcal{L}(\varphi)$ for the set of infinite timed words that satisfy φ. Abusing notation, we also write $\mathcal{L}(\psi)$ for the set of infinite (untimed) words that satisfy the LTL[U, S] formula ψ, and $\mathcal{L}(\mathcal{A})$ for the set of infinite words accepted by automaton $\mathcal{A}$.

3.2   Truncated Semantics and Informative Prefixes

Since in online monitoring one naturally deals with truncated paths, it is useful to define a satisfaction relation of formulas over finite timed words. To this end we adopt a timed version of the *truncated semantics* [12] which incorporates *strong* and *weak* views on satisfaction over truncated paths. These views indicate whether the evaluation of the formula 'has completed' on the finite path, i.e., whether the truth value of the formula on the whole path is already determined. For example, the formula $\mathbf{F}_{(0,5)}p$ is weakly satisfied by any finite timed word whose time points are all strictly less than 5 since there is an extension that satisfies the formula. We also consider the *neutral* view, which extends to MTL[U, S] the traditional LTL semantics over finite words [24].

The respective strong, neutral and weak satisfaction relations will be denoted by $\models_f^+$, $\models_f$ and $\models_f^-$ respectively. The definitions below closely follow [12].

Definition 1. *The satisfaction relation* $\rho, i \models_f^+ \varphi$ *for an* MTL[U, S] *formula* φ, *a finite timed word* $\rho = (\sigma, \tau)$ *and a position* i, $1 \leq i \leq |\rho|$ *is defined as follows:*

- $\rho, i \models_f^+ p$ *iff* $p \in \sigma_i$
- $\rho, i \models_f^+ \mathbf{true}$
- $\rho, i \models_f^+ \varphi_1 \wedge \varphi_2$ *iff* $\rho, i \models_f^+ \varphi_1$ *and* $\rho, i \models_f^+ \varphi_1$
- $\rho, i \models_f^+ \neg\psi$ *iff* $(\rho, i) \not\models_f^- \psi$
- $\rho, i \models_f^+ \varphi_1 \mathbf{U}_I \varphi_2$ *iff there exists* j, $i < j \leq |\rho|$, *such that* $\rho, j \models_f^+ \varphi_2$, $\tau_j - \tau_i \in I$, *and* $\rho, j' \models_f^+ \varphi_1$ *for all* j' *with* $i < j' < j$
- $\rho, i \models_f^+ \varphi_1 \mathbf{S}_I \varphi_2$ *iff there exists* j, $1 \leq j < i$, *such that* $\rho, j \models_f^+ \varphi_2$, $\tau_i - \tau_j \in I$ *and* $\rho, j' \models_f^+ \varphi_1$ *for all* j' *with* $j < j' < i$.

---

[3] Note that we adopt *strict* interpretations to $\mathbf{U}_I$ and $\mathbf{S}_I$. It is easy to see that, e.g., weak-future until operators can be defined in strict-future ones.

Definition 2. *The satisfaction relation* $\rho, i \models_f^- \varphi$ *for an* MTL[U, S] *formula* φ, *a finite timed word* $\rho = (\sigma, \tau)$ *and a position* i, $1 \le i \le |\rho|$ *is defined as follows:*

- $\rho, i \models_f^- p$ *iff* $p \in \sigma_i$
- $\rho, i \models_f^-$ **true**
- $\rho, i \models_f^- \varphi_1 \wedge \varphi_2$ *iff* $\rho, i \models_f^- \varphi_1$ *and* $\rho, i \models_f^- \varphi_1$
- $\rho, i \models_f^- \neg \varphi$ *iff* $(\rho, i) \not\models_f^+ \varphi$
- $\rho, i \models_f^- \varphi_1 \mathbf{U}_I \varphi_2$ *iff either of the following holds:*
  - *there exists* j, $i < j \le |\rho|$, *such that* $\rho, j \models_f^- \varphi_2$, $\tau_j - \tau_i \in I$, *and* $\rho, j' \models_f^- \varphi_1$ *for all* j' *with* $i < j' < j$
  - $\tau_{|\rho|} - \tau_i < I$ *and* $\rho, j' \models_f^- \varphi_1$ *for all* j' *with* $i < j' \le |\rho|$
- $\rho, i \models_f^- \varphi_1 \mathbf{S}_I \varphi_2$ *iff there exists* j, $1 \le j < i$, *such that* $\rho, j \models_f^- \varphi_2$, $\tau_i - \tau_j \in I$ *and* $\rho, j' \models_f^- \varphi_1$ *for all* j' *with* $j < j' < i$.

The following proposition which helps explain the terms strong, neutral and weak, can be proved by a simple induction on the structure of φ.

Proposition 1. *For a finite timed word* ρ, *a position* i *in* ρ *and an* MTL[U, S] *formula* φ,

$$\rho, i \models_f^+ \varphi \to \rho, i \models_f \varphi \text{ and } \rho, i \models_f \varphi \to \rho, i \models_f^- \varphi.$$

A closely related notion, *informative prefixes* [20], has been adopted in several works on online monitoring of untimed properties, e.g., [3, 14]. Intuitively, an informative prefix for a formula φ is a prefix that 'tells the whole story' about the fulfilment or violation of φ.[4] We give two examples before the formal definition.

Example 1. Consider the following formula over $\{p_1\}$:

$$\varphi = \mathbf{FG}(\neg p_1) \wedge \mathbf{G}(p_1 \to \mathbf{F}_{(0,3)} p_1).$$

The finite timed word $\rho = (\{p_1\}, 0)(\{p_1\}, 2)(\emptyset, 5.5)$ is an informative bad prefix for φ, since no extension satisfies the second conjunct. On the other hand, while $\rho' = (\{p_1\}, 0)(\{p_1\}, 2)(\{p_1\}, 4)$ is a bad prefix for φ, it has (different) extensions that satisfy, respectively, the left and right conjuncts. Thus we do not consider it an informative bad prefix.

Example 2. Consider the following formula over $\{p_1\}$:

$$\varphi' = \mathbf{G}(\neg p_1) \wedge \mathbf{G}(p_1 \to \mathbf{F}_{(0,3)} p_1).$$

This formula is equivalent to the formula φ in the previous example. However, all bad prefixes for φ' are informative.

---

[4] Our usage of the term *informative* slightly deviates from [20] as in that paper the term refers exclusively to bad prefixes.

If a prefix ρ strongly satisfies φ then we say that it is an *informative good prefix* for φ. Similarly we say ρ is an *informative bad prefix* for φ when it fails to weakly satisfy φ. Finally ρ is an *informative prefix* if it is either an informative good prefix or an informative bad prefix. Here we have adopted the semantic characterisation of informative prefixes in terms of the truncated semantics from [12], rather than the original syntactic definition [20].

The following proposition follows immediately from the definition of informative prefixes.

Proposition 2. *ρ is informative for φ iff ρ is informative for $\neg\varphi$.*

Since $\rho \models_f \varphi \leftrightarrow \rho \not\models_f \neg\varphi$, negating a formula essentially exchanges its set of informative good prefixes and informative bad prefixes. The following proposition says 'something good remains good' and 'something bad remains bad'.

Proposition 3. *For a finite timed word ρ, a position i in ρ and an $\mathsf{MTL}[\mathbf{U}, \mathbf{S}]$ formula φ, if ρ is a prefix of the finite timed word ρ', then*

$$\rho, i \models_f^+ \varphi \rightarrow \rho', i \models_f^+ \varphi \ and \ \rho, i \not\models_f^+ \varphi \rightarrow \rho', i \not\models_f^+ \varphi.$$

4   LTL[U, S] over Bounded Atoms

In this section we present a series of logical equivalences that can be used to rewrite a given $\mathsf{MTL}[\mathbf{U}, \mathbf{S}]$ formula into an equivalent formula in which no unbounded temporal operator occurs within the scope of a bounded operator. Only the rules for future modalities and open intervals are given, as the rules for past modalities are symmetric and the rules for other types of intervals are straightforward variants. Since we work in the pointwise semantics, the techniques in [17] (developed for the continuous semantics) must be carefully adapted.

4.1   Normal Form

We say an $\mathsf{MTL}[\mathbf{U}, \mathbf{S}]$ formula is in *normal form* if it satisfies the following.

(i) All occurrences of unbounded temporal operators are of the form $\mathbf{U}_{(0,\infty)}$, $\mathbf{S}_{(0,\infty)}$, $\mathbf{G}_{(0,\infty)}$, $\mathbf{H}_{(0,\infty)}$.
(ii) All other occurrences of temporal operators are of the form $\mathbf{U}_I$, $\mathbf{S}_I$ with bounded I.
(iii) Negation is only applied to propositions or bounded temporal operators (except that we allow $\mathbf{G}_{(0,\infty)}$, $\mathbf{H}_{(0,\infty)}$).
(iv) In any subformula of the form $\varphi_1 \mathbf{U}_I \varphi_2$, $\varphi_1 \mathbf{S}_I \varphi_2$, $\mathbf{F}_I\varphi_2$, $\mathbf{P}_I\varphi_2$ where I is bounded, φ_1 is a disjunction of temporal subformulas and propositions and φ_2 is a conjunction thereof.

We describe how to rewrite a given formula into normal form. To satisfy (i) and (ii), apply the usual rules (e.g., $\mathbf{G}_I\varphi \leftrightarrow \neg\mathbf{F}_I\neg\varphi$) and the rule:

$$\varphi_1 \mathbf{U}_{(a,\infty)} \varphi_2 \leftrightarrow \varphi_1 \mathbf{U} \varphi_2 \wedge \left(\mathbf{F}_{(0,a]}\mathbf{true} \rightarrow \mathbf{G}_{(0,a]}(\varphi_1 \wedge \varphi_1 \mathbf{U} \varphi_2)\right).$$

To satisfy (iii), use the usual rules and the rule:

$$\neg(\varphi_1 \mathbf{U} \varphi_2) \leftrightarrow \mathbf{G}\neg\varphi_2 \vee \left(\neg\varphi_2 \mathbf{U} \left(\neg\varphi_2 \wedge \neg\varphi_1\right)\right).$$

For (iv), use the usual rules of Boolean algebra and the rules below:

$$\phi \mathbf{U}_I (\varphi_1 \vee \varphi_2) \leftrightarrow (\phi \mathbf{U}_I \varphi_1) \vee (\phi \mathbf{U}_I \varphi_2)$$
$$(\varphi_1 \wedge \varphi_2) \mathbf{U}_I \phi \leftrightarrow (\varphi_1 \mathbf{U}_I \phi) \wedge (\varphi_2 \mathbf{U}_I \phi).$$

4.2   Extracting Unbounded Operators from Bounded Operators

We now provide a set of rewriting rules that extract unbounded operators from the scopes of bounded operators. In what follows, let $\varphi_{xlb} = \mathbf{false}\,\mathbf{U}_{(0,b)}\,\mathbf{true}$, $\varphi_{ylb} = \mathbf{false}\,\mathbf{S}_{(0,b)}\,\mathbf{true}$ and

$$\varphi_{ugb} = \left(\left((\varphi_{xlb} \to \mathbf{G}_{(b,2b)}\varphi_1) \wedge (\neg\varphi_{ylb} \to (\varphi_1 \wedge \mathbf{G}_{(0,b]}\varphi_1))\right)\right.$$
$$\left.\mathbf{U}\left((\varphi_1 \wedge (\varphi_1 \mathbf{U}_{(b,2b)} \varphi_2)) \vee \left(\neg\varphi_{ylb} \wedge \left(\varphi_2 \vee (\varphi_1 \wedge (\varphi_1 \mathbf{U}_{(0,b]} \varphi_2))\right)\right)\right)\right),$$
$$\varphi_{ggb} = \mathbf{G}\left(\left((\varphi_{xlb} \to \mathbf{G}_{(b,2b)}\varphi_1) \wedge (\neg\varphi_{ylb} \to (\varphi_1 \wedge \mathbf{G}_{(0,b]}\varphi_1))\right)\right).$$

Proposition 4. *The following equivalences hold over infinite timed words.*

$$\theta \mathbf{U}_{(a,b)} \left((\varphi_1 \mathbf{U} \varphi_2) \wedge \chi\right) \leftrightarrow \theta \mathbf{U}_{(a,b)} \left((\varphi_1 \mathbf{U}_{(0,2b)} \varphi_2) \wedge \chi\right)$$
$$\vee\left(\left(\theta \mathbf{U}_{(a,b)} (\mathbf{G}_{(0,2b)}\varphi_1 \wedge \chi)\right) \wedge \varphi_{ugb}\right)$$
$$\theta \mathbf{U}_{(a,b)} (\mathbf{G}\varphi \wedge \chi) \leftrightarrow \left(\theta \mathbf{U}_{(a,b)} (\mathbf{G}_{(0,2b)}\varphi \wedge \chi)\right) \wedge \varphi_{ggb}$$
$$\theta \mathbf{U}_{(a,b)} \left((\varphi_1 \mathbf{S} \varphi_2) \wedge \chi\right) \leftrightarrow \theta \mathbf{U}_{(a,b)} \left((\varphi_1 \mathbf{S}_{(0,b)} \varphi_2) \wedge \chi\right)$$
$$\vee\left(\left(\theta \mathbf{U}_{(a,b)} (\mathbf{H}_{(0,b)}\varphi_1 \wedge \chi)\right) \wedge \varphi_1 \mathbf{S} \varphi_2\right)$$
$$\theta \mathbf{U}_{(a,b)} (\mathbf{H}\varphi \wedge \chi) \leftrightarrow \left(\theta \mathbf{U}_{(a,b)} (\mathbf{H}_{(0,b)}\varphi \wedge \chi)\right) \wedge \mathbf{H}\varphi$$
$$\left((\varphi_1 \mathbf{U} \varphi_2) \vee \chi\right) \mathbf{U}_{(a,b)} \theta \leftrightarrow \left((\varphi_1 \mathbf{U}_{(0,2b)} \varphi_2) \vee \chi\right) \mathbf{U}_{(a,b)} \theta$$
$$\vee\left(\left(((\varphi_1 \mathbf{U}_{(0,2b)} \varphi_2) \vee \chi) \mathbf{U}_{(0,b)} (\mathbf{G}_{(0,2b)}\varphi_1)\right)\right.$$
$$\wedge$$
$$\left.\mathbf{F}_{(a,b)}\theta \wedge \varphi_{ugb}\right)$$
$$\left((\mathbf{G}\varphi) \vee \chi\right) \mathbf{U}_{(a,b)} \theta \leftrightarrow \chi \mathbf{U}_{(a,b)} \theta$$
$$\vee\left(\chi \mathbf{U}_{(0,b)} (\mathbf{G}_{(0,2b)}\varphi_1) \wedge \mathbf{F}_{(a,b)}\theta \wedge \varphi_{ggb}\right)$$

$$((\varphi_1 \mathbf{S} \varphi_2) \vee \chi) \mathbf{U}_{(a,b)} \theta \leftrightarrow ((\varphi_1 \mathbf{S}_{(0,b)} \varphi_2) \vee \chi) \mathbf{U}_{(a,b)} \theta$$
$$\vee \Bigl(\bigl((\mathbf{H}_{(0,b)} \varphi_1 \vee (\varphi_1 \mathbf{S}_{(0,b)} \varphi_2) \vee \chi) \mathbf{U}_{(a,b)} \theta \bigr)$$
$$\wedge$$
$$\varphi_1 \mathbf{S} \varphi_2 \Bigr)$$
$$((\mathbf{H}\varphi) \vee \chi) \mathbf{U}_{(a,b)} \theta \leftrightarrow \chi \mathbf{U}_{(a,b)} \theta \vee \Bigl(((\mathbf{H}_{(0,b)}\varphi \vee \chi) \mathbf{U}_{(a,b)} \theta) \wedge \mathbf{H}\varphi \Bigr).$$

Proof. We sketch the proof for the first rule as the proofs for the other rules are similar. In the following, let the current position be i and the position of an (arbitrary) event in $(\tau_i + a, \tau_i + b)$ be j.

For the forward direction, let the witness position where φ_2 holds be w. If $\tau_w < \tau_j + 2b$, the subformula $\varphi_1 \mathbf{U}_{(0,2b)} \varphi_2$ clearly holds at j and we are done. Otherwise, $\mathbf{G}_{(0,2b)} \varphi_1$ holds at j and it follows that $(\varphi_{xlb} \to \mathbf{G}_{(b,2b)} \varphi_1)$ and φ_{ylb} (and vacuously $\neg \varphi_{ylb} \to (\varphi_1 \wedge \mathbf{G}_{(0,b]} \varphi_1)$) hold at all positions j', $i < j' < j$. Let $l > j$ be the first position such that $\tau_w \in (\tau_l + b, \tau_l + 2b)$. Consider the following cases:

- There is such l: It is clear that $(\varphi_1 \wedge (\varphi_1 \mathbf{U}_{(b,2b)} \varphi_2))$ holds at l. Since $\mathbf{G}_{(b,2b)} \varphi_1$ holds at all positions j'', $j \leq j'' < l$ by the minimality of l, $(\varphi_{xlb} \to \mathbf{G}_{(b,2b)} \varphi_1)$ also holds at these positions. For the other conjunct, note that φ_{ylb} holds at j and $\varphi_1 \wedge \mathbf{G}_{(0,b]} \varphi_1$ holds at all positions j''', $j < j''' < l$.
- There is no such l: Consider the following cases:
  - $\neg \varphi_{ylb}$ and $\neg \mathbf{P}_{[b,b]} \mathbf{true}$ hold at w: There is no event in $(\tau_w - 2b, \tau_w)$. The proof is similar to the case where l exists.
  - $\neg \varphi_{ylb}$ and $\mathbf{P}_{[b,b]} \mathbf{true}$ hold at w: Let l' be the position such that $\tau_{l'} = \tau_w - b$. There must be no event in $(\tau_{l'} - b, \tau_{l'})$. It follows that $\neg \varphi_{ylb}$ and $(\varphi_1 \wedge (\varphi_1 \mathbf{U}_{(0,b]} \varphi_2))$ hold at l'. The proof is similar.
  - φ_{ylb} holds at w: By assumption, there is no event in $(\tau_w - 2b, \tau_w - b)$. It is easy to see that there is a position such that $\neg \varphi_{ylb} \wedge (\varphi_1 \wedge (\varphi_1 \mathbf{U}_{(0,b]} \varphi_2))$ holds. The proof is again similar.

We prove the other direction by contraposition. Consider the interesting case where $\mathbf{G}_{(0,2b)} \varphi_1$ holds at j yet $\varphi_1 \mathbf{U} \varphi_2$ does not hold at j. If φ_2 never holds in $[\tau_j + 2b, \infty)$ then we are done. Otherwise, let $l > j$ be the first position such that both φ_1 and φ_2 do not hold at l (note that $\tau_l \geq \tau_j + 2b$). It is clear that

$$\Bigl((\varphi_1 \wedge (\varphi_1 \mathbf{U}_{(b,2b)} \varphi_2)) \vee \bigl(\neg \varphi_{ylb} \wedge (\varphi_2 \vee (\varphi_1 \wedge (\varphi_1 \mathbf{U}_{(0,b]} \varphi_2))) \bigr) \Bigr)$$ does not hold

at all positions j', $i < j' \leq l$. Consider the following cases:

- φ_{ylb} does not hold at l: $\varphi_1 \wedge \mathbf{G}_{(0,b]} \varphi_1$ does not hold at l, and hence φ_{ugb} fails to hold at i.
- φ_{ylb} holds at l: Consider the following cases:
  - There is an event in $(\tau_l - 2b, \tau_l - b)$: Let this event be at position j''. We have $j'' + 1 < l$, $\tau_{j''+1} - \tau_{j''} \geq b$ and $\tau_l - \tau_{j''+1} < b$. However, it follows that φ_{ylb} does not hold at $j'' + 1$ and $\varphi_1 \wedge \mathbf{G}_{(0,b]} \varphi_1$ holds at $j'' + 1$, which is a contradiction.

- There is no event in $(\tau_l - 2b, \tau_l - b)$: Let the first event in $[\tau_l - b, \tau_l)$ be at position j''. It is clear that φ_{ylb} does not hold at j'' and $\varphi_1 \wedge \mathbf{G}_{(0,b]}\varphi_1$ must hold at j'', which is a contradiction.

$\square$

Proposition 5. *For an* MTL[**U, S**] *formula* φ, *we can use the rules above to obtain an equivalent formula* $\hat{\varphi}$ *in which no unbounded temporal operator appears in the scope of a bounded temporal operator.*

Proof. Define the *unbounding depth* $ud(\varphi)$ of a formula φ to be the modal depth of φ counting only unbounded operators. We demonstrate a rewriting process on φ which terminates in an equivalent formula $\hat{\varphi}$ such that any subformula $\hat{\psi}$ of $\hat{\varphi}$ with outermost operator bounded has $ud(\hat{\psi}) = 0$.

Assume that the input formula φ is in normal form. Let k be the largest unbounding depth among all subformulas of φ with bounded outermost operators. We pick all minimal (wrt. subformula order) such subformulas ψ with $ud(\psi) = k$. By applying the rules in Section 4.2, we can rewrite ψ into ψ' where all subformulas of ψ' with bounded outermost operators have unbounded depths strictly less than k. We then substitute these ψ' back into φ to obtain φ'. We repeat this step until there remain no bounded operators with unbounding depth k. Rules that rewrite a formula into normal form are used whenever necessary on relevant subformulas—this will never affect their unbounding depths. It is easy to see that we will eventually obtain such a formula φ^*. Now rewrite φ^* into normal form and start over again. This is to be repeated until we reach $\hat{\varphi}$. $\square$

Given the input formula φ over propositions $P = \{p_1, \ldots, p_n\}$, we can apply the rewriting process above to obtain a formula $\hat{\varphi}$. Since each rewriting rule is a logical equivalence, we have the following theorem.

Theorem 1. $\mathcal{L}(\varphi) = \mathcal{L}(\hat{\varphi})$.

The syntactic separation of the original formula could potentially induce a non-elementary blow-up. However, such behaviour does not seem to be realised in practice. In our experience, the syntactically separated formula is often of comparable size to the original formula, which itself is typically small. For example, consider the following formula:

$$\mathbf{G}\big(\texttt{ChangeGear} \rightarrow \mathbf{F}_{(0,30)}(\texttt{InjectFuel} \wedge \mathbf{P}\texttt{InjectLubricant})\big).$$

The syntactically separated version of the formula is

$$\mathbf{G}\big[\texttt{ChangeGear} \rightarrow \mathbf{F}_{(0,30)}(\texttt{InjectFuel} \wedge \mathbf{P}_{(0,30)}\texttt{InjectLubricant})$$
$$\vee \big(\mathbf{F}_{(0,30)}(\texttt{InjectFuel}) \wedge \mathbf{P}\texttt{InjectLubricant}\big)\big].$$

In any case, Proposition 5 and Theorem 1 imply that we may even require the input formula to be in 'separated form' without sacrificing any expressiveness.

5 Online Monitoring Procedure

Having obtained $\hat{\varphi} = \Phi(\psi_1, \ldots, \psi_m)$ where $\psi_1, \ldots, \psi_m$ are bounded formulas over P and Φ is an LTL[U, S] formula, we now introduce new propositions $Q = \{q_1, \ldots, q_m\}$ that correspond to bounded subformulas. In this way, we can monitor Φ as an untimed property over Q, only that now we obtain the truth values of $q_1, \ldots, q_m$ by simple dynamic programming procedures. As these propositions correspond to bounded formulas, we only need to store a 'sliding window' on the input timed word.

5.1 Untimed LTL[U, S] Part

We describe briefly the standard way to construct automata that detect informative prefixes [20]. For a given LTL formula Θ, first use a standard construction [31] to obtain a language-equivalent alternating Büchi automaton $\mathcal{A}_\Theta$. Then redefine its set of accepting states to be the empty set and treat it as an automaton over finite words. The resulting automaton $\mathcal{A}_\Theta^{true}$ accepts exactly all informative good prefixes for Θ. For online monitoring, one can then determinise $\mathcal{A}_\Theta^{true}$ with the usual subset construction. The same can be done for $\neg \Theta$ to obtain a deterministic automaton detecting informative bad prefixes for Θ.

In our case, we first translate the LTL[U, S] formulas Φ and $\neg \Phi$ into a pair of *two-way* alternating Büchi automata. It is easy to see that, with the same 'tweaks', we can obtain two automata that accept informative good prefixes and informative bad prefixes for Φ (by Proposition 2). We then apply existing procedures that translate two-way alternating automata over finite words into deterministic automata, e.g., [8]. We call the resulting automata $\mathcal{D}_{good}$ and $\mathcal{D}_{bad}$ and execute them in parallel.

5.2 Bounded Metric Part

We define $fr(\varphi)$ and $pr(\varphi)$ (*future-reach* and *past-reach*) for an MTL[U, S] formula φ as follows (the cases for boolean connectives are defined as expected):

- $fr(\mathbf{true}) = pr(\mathbf{true}) = fr(p) = pr(p) = 0$ for all $p \in P$
- $fr(\varphi_1 \, \mathbf{U}_I \, \varphi_2) = \sup(I) + \max(fr(\varphi_1), fr(\varphi_2))$
- $pr(\varphi_1 \, \mathbf{S}_I \, \varphi_2) = \sup(I) + \max(pr(\varphi_1), pr(\varphi_2))$
- $fr(\varphi_1 \, \mathbf{S}_I \, \varphi_2) = \max(fr(\varphi_1), fr(\varphi_2) - \inf(I))$
- $pr(\varphi_1 \, \mathbf{U}_I \, \varphi_2) = \max(pr(\varphi_1), pr(\varphi_2) - \inf(I))$.

Intuitively, these indicate the lengths of the time horizons needed to determine the truth value of φ. We also define $l_f(\psi) = k_{var} \cdot \lceil fr(\psi) \rceil$ and $l_p(\psi) = k_{var} \cdot \lceil pr(\psi) \rceil$ (recall that we assume that timed words are of bounded variability k_{var}).

Naïve Method. Suppose that we would like to obtain the truth value of q_i at position j in the input (infinite) timed word $\rho = (\sigma, \tau)$. Observe that only events occurring between $\tau_j - pr(\psi_i)$ and $\tau_j + fr(\psi_i)$ can affect the truth value of ψ_i at j. This implies that $\rho, j \models \psi_i \leftrightarrow \rho', j \models_f \psi_i$, given that ρ' is a prefix of ρ that contains all events between $\tau_j - pr(\psi_i)$ and $\tau_j + fr(\psi_i)$. Since ρ is of bounded variability k_{var}, there will be at most $l_p(\psi_i) + 1 + l_f(\psi_i)$ events between $\tau_j - pr(\psi_i)$ and $\tau_j + fr(\psi_i)$. It follows that we can simply record all events in this interval. Events outside of this interval are irrelevant as they do not affect whether $\rho', j \models_f \psi_i$. In particular, we maintain a two-dimensional array of $l_p(\psi_i) + 1 + l_f(\psi_i) + 1$ rows and $1 + |\psi|$ columns. The first column is used to store timestamps of the corresponding events.[5] The last $|\psi|$ columns are used to store the truth values of subformulas. We then use dynamic programming procedures (cf. [25]) to evaluate whether $\rho', j \models_f \psi_i$. These procedures fill up the array in a bottom-up manner, starting from minimal subformulas. The columns for boolean combinations can be filled in the natural way.

Now consider all propositions in Q. We can obtain the truth values of them at all positions in the 'sliding window' by using an array of $l_p^Q + 1 + l_f^Q + 1$ rows and $1 + |\psi_1| + \cdots + |\psi_m|$ columns, where $l_p^Q = \max_{i \in [1,m]} l_p(\psi_i)$ and $l_f^Q = \max_{i \in [1,m]} l_f(\psi_i)$. Each column can be filled in time linear in its length. Overall, we need an array of size $O(k_{var} \cdot c_{sum} \cdot |\hat{\varphi}|)$ where c_{sum} is the sum of the constants in $\hat{\varphi}$, and for each position j we need time $O(k_{var} \cdot c_{sum} \cdot |\hat{\varphi}|)$ to obtain the truth values of all propositions in Q. This method is not very efficient as for each j we need to fill all columns for temporal subformulas from scratch. Previously computed entries cannot always be reused as certain entries are 'wrong'—they were computed without the knowledge of events outside of the interval.

Incremental Evaluation. We describe an optimisation which allows effective reuse of computed entries stored in the table. The idea is to treat entries that depend on future events as 'unknown' and not to fill them. By construction, these unknown entries will not be needed for the result of the evaluation.

For a past subformula, e.g., $\varphi_1 \mathbf{S}_{(a,b)} \varphi_2$, we can simply suspend the column-filling procedure when we filled all entries using the truth values of φ_1 and φ_2 (at various positions) that are currently known. We may continue when the truth values of φ_1 and φ_2 (at some other positions) that are previously unknown become available. The case for future subformulas is more involved. Suppose that we are filling a column for $p_1 \mathbf{U}_{(a,b)} p_2$ with the naïve method. Denote the corresponding timestamp of an index i in the column by $t(i)$ and the timestamp of the last acquired event by t_{max}. Observe that not all of the truth values at indices j, $t(j) + b > t_{max}$ can be reused later, as they might depend on future events. However, if we know that φ_1 does not hold at some j', $t(j') + b > t_{max}$, then all the truth values at indices $< j'$ can be reused in the following iterations as they cannot depend on future events. Now consider the general case of filling the column for $\psi = \varphi_1 \mathbf{U}_{(a,b)} \varphi_2$. We keep an index j_ψ that points to the first unknown entry in the column, and we now let $t_{max} = \min(t(j_{\varphi_1} - 1), t(j_{\varphi_2} - 1))$. In each iteration, if j_{φ_1} and j_{φ_2} are updated to some new values, t_{max} also changes accordingly. If this happens, we first check if $t(j_\psi) + b > t_{max}$. If this

---

[5] We assume the timestamps can be finitely represented, e.g., with a built-in data type, and additions and subtractions on them can be done in constant time.

is the case, we do nothing (observe the fact that φ_1 must hold at all indices l, $t(j_\psi) < t(l) \leq t_{\max}$, thus the truth value at j_ψ must remain unknown). Otherwise we find the least index $l' > j_\psi$ such that $t(l') + b > t_{\max}$. Additionally, we check if all truth values of φ_1 between $t_{\max}$ and $t_{\max}^{old}$ are **true**, starting from $t_{\max}$. If φ_1 is not satisfied at some (maximal) position j' then start filling at $\max(l', j') - 1$. Otherwise we start filling from $l' - 1$.

Observe that we can use a variable to keep track of the least index $l' > j_\psi$ such that $t(l') + b > t_{\max}$ instead of finding it each time since it increases monotonically. Also we can keep track of the greatest index where φ_2 holds. With these variables, we can easily make the extra 'sweeping' happen only twice (once for φ_1 and once for φ_2) over newly acquired truth values. Also observe that the truth value of a subformula at a certain position will be filled only once. These observations imply that each entry in the array can be filled in amortised constant time. Assuming that each step of an deterministic automaton takes constant time, we can state the following theorem.

Theorem 2. *For an* MTL[U, S] *formula* φ, *the automata* $\mathcal{D}_{good}$ *and* $\mathcal{D}_{bad}$ *have size* $2^{2^{O(|\Phi|)}}$ *where* Φ *is the* LTL[U, S] *formula described above. Moreover, for an infinite timed word of bounded variability* k_{var}, *our procedure uses space* $O(k_{var} \cdot c_{sum} \cdot |\hat{\varphi}|)$ *and amortised time* $O(|\hat{\varphi}|)$ *per event, where* $\hat{\varphi}$ *is the syntactically separated equivalent formula of* φ *and* c_{sum} *is the sum of the constants in* $\hat{\varphi}$.

5.3 Correctness

One may think of the monitoring process on an infinite timed word $\rho \in T\Sigma_P^\omega$ as continuously extending a corresponding finite timed word $\rho' \in T\Sigma_Q^*$. Suppose that, instead of $\mathcal{D}_{good}$ and $\mathcal{D}_{bad}$, we now execute a deterministic ω-automaton $\mathcal{D}_\Phi$ such that $\mathcal{L}(\mathcal{D}_\Phi) = \mathcal{L}(\Phi)$. Since we are implicitly ensuring that the truth values of propositions in Q are valid along the way, it is easy to see that the corresponding run on $\mathcal{D}_\Phi$ will be accepting iff $\rho \models \varphi$. However, for the purpose of online monitoring, we will be more interested in deciding whether $\rho \models \varphi$ given only a finite prefix of ρ. In this subsection we show that our approach is both sound and complete for detecting informative prefixes.

The following proposition is immediate since three views of the truncated semantics coincide in this case.

Proposition 6. *For a bounded* MTL[U, S] *formula* ψ, *a finite timed word* $\rho = (\sigma, \tau)$ *and a position* $1 \leq i \leq |\rho|$ *such that* $\tau_i + fr(\psi) \leq \tau_{|\rho|}$ *and* $\tau_i - pr(\psi) \geq 0$, *we have*

$$\rho, i \models_f^+ \psi \leftrightarrow \rho, i \models_f \psi \leftrightarrow \rho, i \models_f^- \psi.$$

The following lemma implies that the rewriting process outlined in Section 4 preserves the 'informativeness' of prefixes.

Lemma 1. *For an* MTL[U, S] *formula* φ, *let* φ' *be the formula obtained after applying one of the rewriting rules in Section 4 on some of its subformula. We have*

$$\rho \models_f^+ \varphi \leftrightarrow \rho \models_f^+ \varphi' \text{ and } \rho \models_f^- \varphi \leftrightarrow \rho \models_f^- \varphi'.$$

Given the lemma above, we can state the following theorem.

Theorem 3. *The set of informative good prefixes of φ coincides with the set of informative good prefixes of $\hat{\varphi}$. The same holds for informative bad prefixes.*

Now we state the main result of the paper in the following two theorems.

Theorem 4 (Soundness). *In our procedure, if we ever reach an accepting state of $\mathcal{D}_{good}$ ($\mathcal{D}_{bad}$) via a finite word $u \in \Sigma_Q^*$, then the finite timed word $\rho \in T\Sigma_P^*$ that we have read must be an informative good (bad) prefix for φ.*

Proof. For such u and the corresponding ρ (note that $|u| \le |\rho|$),

$$\forall i \in [1, |u|] \left((u, i \not\models_f^- \Theta \to \rho, i \not\models_f^- \vartheta) \wedge (u, i \models_f^- \Theta \to \rho, i \models_f^- \vartheta) \right)$$

where Θ is a subformula of Φ and $\vartheta = \Theta(\psi_1, \ldots, \psi_m)$. This can easily be proved by structural induction. If u is accepted by $\mathcal{D}_{good}$, we have $u \models_f^- \Phi$ by construction. By the above we have $\rho \models_f^- \Phi(\psi_1, \ldots, \psi_m)$, as desired. The case for $\mathcal{D}_{bad}$ is symmetric. □

Theorem 5 (Completeness). *Whenever we read an informative good (bad) prefix $\rho = (\sigma, \tau)$ for φ, $\mathcal{D}_{good}$ ($\mathcal{D}_{bad}$) must eventually reach an accepting state.*

Proof. For the finite word u' obtained a bit later with $|u'| = |\rho|$,

$$\forall i \in [1, |u'|] \left((\rho, i \models_f^- \vartheta \to u', i \models_f^- \Theta) \wedge (\rho, i \not\models_f^- \vartheta \to u', i \not\models_f^- \Theta) \right)$$

where Θ is a subformula of Φ and $\vartheta = \Theta(\psi_1, \ldots, \psi_m)$. Again, this can be proved by structural induction (the base step holds by Proposition 3). The theorem follows. □

Remark 1. As pointed out in Example 1, is possible that some of the bad prefixes for the input formula φ are not informative. Certain syntactic restrictions can be imposed on φ to avoid such a situation. For example, it can be shown that all bad prefixes of Safety-MTL [27] formulas will inevitably be extended to informative bad prefixes.[6]

6   Conclusion

We have proposed a new trace-length independent dense-time online monitoring procedure for MTL[U, S], based on rewriting the input MTL[U, S] formula into an LTL[U, S] formula over a set of bounded MTL[U, S] atoms. The former is converted into a deterministic (untimed) automaton, while the truth values of the latter are maintained through dynamic programming. We circumvent the

---

[6] As noted by Kupferman and Vardi [20], all Safety-MTL properties are either *intentionally safe* or *accidentally safe*.

potentially delicate issue of translating MTL[U, S] to a class of deterministic timed automata.

We are currently investigating whether the procedure can be extended to support more expressive modalities. Another possible direction for future work is to improve the monitoring procedure. For example, the dynamic programming procedures in Section 5.2 can support subformulas with unbounded past. This can be exploited to use a smaller equivalent formula in place of $\hat{\varphi}$.

References

1. Alur, R., Feder, T., Henzinger, T.: The benefits of relaxing punctuality. Journal of the ACM 43(1), 116–146 (1996)
2. Alur, R., Henzinger, T.: Back to the future: towards a theory of timed regular languages. In: Proceedings of FOCS 1992, pp. 177–186. IEEE Computer Society Press (1992)
3. Armoni, R., Korchemny, D., Tiemeyer, A., Vardi, M.Y., Zbar, Y.: Deterministic dynamic monitors for linear-time assertions. In: Havelund, K., Núñez, M., Roşu, G., Wolff, B. (eds.) FATES/RV 2006. LNCS, vol. 4262, pp. 163–177. Springer, Heidelberg (2006)
4. Baldor, K., Niu, J.: Monitoring dense-time, continuous-semantics, metric temporal logic. In: Qadeer, S., Tasiran, S. (eds.) RV 2012. LNCS, vol. 7687, pp. 245–259. Springer, Heidelberg (2013)
5. Basin, D., Klaedtke, F., Müller, S., Pfitzmann, B.: Runtime monitoring of metric first-order temporal properties. In: Proceedings of FSTTCS 2008. LIPIcs, vol. 2, pp. 49–60. Schloss Dagstuhl–Leibniz-Zentrum fuer Informatik (2008)
6. Basin, D., Klaedtke, F., Zălinescu, E.: Algorithms for monitoring real-time properties. In: Khurshid, S., Sen, K. (eds.) RV 2011. LNCS, vol. 7186, pp. 260–275. Springer, Heidelberg (2012)
7. Bauer, A., Küster, J., Vegliach, G.: From propositional to first-order monitoring. In: Legay, A., Bensalem, S. (eds.) RV 2013. LNCS, vol. 8174, pp. 59–75. Springer, Heidelberg (2013)
8. Birget, J.C.: State-complexity of finite-state devices, state compressibility and incompressibility. Mathematical Systems Theory 26(3), 237–269 (1993)
9. Bouyer, P., Chevalier, F., Markey, N.: On the expressiveness of TPTL and MTL. In: Sarukkai, S., Sen, S. (eds.) FSTTCS 2005. LNCS, vol. 3821, pp. 432–443. Springer, Heidelberg (2005)
10. Chai, M., Schlingloff, H.: A rewriting based monitoring algorithm for TPTL. In: Proceedings of CS&P 2013. CEUR Workshop Proceedings, vol. 1032, pp. 61–72. CEUR-WS.org (2013)
11. D'Souza, D., Matteplackel, R.: A clock-optimal hierarchical monitoring automaton construction for MITL. Tech. Rep. 2013-1, Department of Computer Science and Automation, Indian Institute of Science (2013), http://www.csa.iisc.ernet.in/TR/2013/1/lics2013-tr.pdf
12. Eisner, C., Fisman, D., Havlicek, J., Lustig, Y., McIsaac, A., Van Campenhout, D.: Reasoning with temporal logic on truncated paths. In: Hunt Jr., W.A., Somenzi, F. (eds.) CAV 2003. LNCS, vol. 2725, pp. 27–39. Springer, Heidelberg (2003)
13. Finkbeiner, B., Kuhtz, L.: Monitor circuits for LTL with bounded and unbounded future. In: Bensalem, S., Peled, D.A. (eds.) RV 2009. LNCS, vol. 5779, pp. 60–75. Springer, Heidelberg (2009)

14. Geilen, M.: On the construction of monitors for temporal logic properties. Electronic Notes in Theoretical Computer Science 55(2), 181–199 (2001)
15. Gunadi, H., Tiu, A.: Efficient runtime monitoring with metric temporal logic: A case study in the android operating system. In: Jones, C., Pihlajasaari, P., Sun, J. (eds.) FM 2014. LNCS, vol. 8442, pp. 296–311. Springer, Heidelberg (2014)
16. Ho, H.M., Ouaknine, J., Worrell, J.: Online monitoring of metric temporal logic (2014), full version:
    http://www.cs.ox.ac.uk/people/hsi-ming.ho/monitoring-full.pdf
17. Hunter, P., Ouaknine, J., Worrell, J.: Expressive completeness of metric temporal logic. In: Proceedings of LICS 2013, pp. 349–357. IEEE Computer Society Press (2013)
18. Kini, D.R., Krishna, S.N., Pandya, P.K.: On construction of safety signal automata for MITL[U,S] using temporal projections. In: Fahrenberg, U., Tripakis, S. (eds.) FORMATS 2011. LNCS, vol. 6919, pp. 225–239. Springer, Heidelberg (2011)
19. Koymans, R.: Specifying real-time properties with metric temporal logic. Real-Time Systems 2(4), 255–299 (1990)
20. Kupferman, O., Vardi, M.Y.: Model checking of safety properties. Formal Methods in System Design 19(3), 291–314 (2001)
21. Leucker, M., Schallhart, C.: A brief account of runtime verification. Journal of Logic and Algebraic Programming 78(5), 293–303 (2009)
22. Maler, O., Nickovic, D., Pnueli, A.: Real time temporal logic: Past, present, future. In: Pettersson, P., Yi, W. (eds.) FORMATS 2005. LNCS, vol. 3829, pp. 2–16. Springer, Heidelberg (2005)
23. Maler, O., Nickovic, D., Pnueli, A.: From MITL to timed automata. In: Asarin, E., Bouyer, P. (eds.) FORMATS 2006. LNCS, vol. 4202, pp. 274–289. Springer, Heidelberg (2006)
24. Manna, Z., Pnueli, A.: Temporal verification of reactive systems: safety, vol. 2. Springer (1995)
25. Markey, N., Raskin, J.: Model checking restricted sets of timed paths. Theoretical Computer Science 358(2-3), 273–292 (2006)
26. Ničković, D., Piterman, N.: From MTL to deterministic timed automata. In: Chatterjee, K., Henzinger, T.A. (eds.) FORMATS 2010. LNCS, vol. 6246, pp. 152–167. Springer, Heidelberg (2010)
27. Ouaknine, J., Worrell, J.: Safety metric temporal logic is fully decidable. In: Hermanns, H., Palsberg, J. (eds.) TACAS 2006. LNCS, vol. 3920, pp. 411–425. Springer, Heidelberg (2006)
28. de Matos Pedro, A., Pereira, D., Pinho, L.M., Pinto, J.S.: A compositional monitoring framework for hard real-time systems. In: Badger, J.M., Rozier, K.Y. (eds.) NFM 2014. LNCS, vol. 8430, pp. 16–30. Springer, Heidelberg (2014)
29. Sokolsky, O., Havelund, K., Lee, I.: Introduction to the special section on runtime verification. International Journal on Software Tools for Technology Transfer 14(3), 243–247 (2011)
30. Thati, P., Roşu, G.: Monitoring algorithms for metric temporal logic specifications. Electronic Notes in Theoretical Computer Science 113, 145–162 (2005)
31. Vardi, M.Y.: An automata-theoretic approach to linear temporal logic. In: Moller, F., Birtwistle, G. (eds.) Logics for Concurrency. LNCS, vol. 1043, pp. 238–266. Springer, Heidelberg (1996)

On Real-Time Monitoring
with Imprecise Timestamps[*]

David Basin[1], Felix Klaedtke[2], Srdjan Marinovic[1], and Eugen Zălinescu[1]

[1] Institute of Information Security, ETH Zurich, Switzerland
[2] NEC Europe Ltd., Heidelberg, Germany

Abstract. Existing real-time monitoring approaches assume traces with precise timestamps. Their correctness is thus indefinite when monitoring the behavior of systems with imprecise clocks. We address this problem for a metric temporal logic: We identify classes of formulas for which we can leverage existing monitors to correctly reason about observed system traces.

1 Introduction

Existing runtime-verification approaches for real-time logics, e.g., [1, 2, 5, 6], assume that the monitored system emits events with precise (i.e. exact) timestamps. This assumption however does not hold for real-world systems, and thus monitors may produce incorrect outputs. To account for the clocks' imprecision, an error may be associated with events' timestamps. For instance, Google's distributed database Spanner [3] associates a time interval with each event, and Spanner guarantees that each event happened at some point in its associated interval.

This paper poses and explores the problem of whether existing monitoring approaches for real-time logics can account for timestamp imprecision, and thereby provide correctness guarantees for the monitors' outputs. In our study, we focus on the real-time temporal logic MTL [4] over a continuous dense time domain, for which we propose a monitoring approach that accounts for imprecise timestamps. For monitoring, we (a) first modify the specification by syntactically rewriting the MTL formula and (b) use an existing monitor for precise timestamps on the modified specification over one precisely timestamped trace that is obtained from the given imprecisely timestamped one. We identify MTL formulas for which conformance with the modified specification implies conformance with the given specification of all possible precise traces corresponding to the given imprecise trace. We also identify formulas for which the approach provides a weaker—but still a useful—guarantee that there is some precise trace satisfying the specification.

In summary, our contributions are the following. (1) We raise the problem of imprecise timestamps in runtime verification with respect to specifications in

---

[*] This work was partially supported by the Zurich Information Security and Privacy Center (www.zisc.ethz.ch).

B. Bonakdarpour and S.A. Smolka (Eds.): RV 2014, LNCS 8734, pp. 193–198, 2014.

real-time logics. (2) We provide correctness guarantees for the use of existing monitors over imprecise traces for certain MTL fragments.

Related to this work are the results of Zhang et al. [8] and Wang et al. [7]. Zhang et al. [8] explore the issue of imprecise timestamps in data-stream processing. In contrast to our approach, their solution is for a more restrictive specification language, relies on a discrete time domain, and outputs probabilistic verdicts. In runtime verification, Wang et al. [7] explore trace imprecision due to an unknown ordering between events. Events do not have explicit timestamps and thus only linear time properties (in LTL) are considered. In contrast, we monitor real-time properties (expressed in MTL). Furthermore, they propose a specialized monitoring algorithm, while we leverage existing monitoring algorithms.

2   Preliminaries

Let $\mathbb{T} := \mathbb{R}_{\geq 0}$ be the time domain and let P be a nonempty finite set of atomic propositions. A *timeline* is a function $\pi : \mathbb{T} \to 2^P$ in which values do not change infinitely often over bounded intervals. That is, for any bounded nonempty interval $I \subseteq \mathbb{T}$, there is a partition of I into nonempty intervals $I_1, \ldots, I_n$ for some $n \geq 1$ such that π is constant on each I_i.

MTL formulas are given by the grammar

$$\varphi ::= p \mid \neg\varphi \mid \varphi \wedge \varphi \mid \varphi \, \mathsf{S}_I \, \varphi \mid \varphi \, \mathsf{U}_I \, \varphi,$$

where p ranges over P and I over the intervals of $\mathbb{T}$ with rational endpoints or ∞ as a right endpoint. Given a timeline π, a time $t \in \mathbb{T}$, and a formula φ, the satisfaction relation $\models$ is defined as follows.

$$
\begin{array}{lll}
\pi, t \models p & \text{iff} & p \in \pi(t) \\
\pi, t \models \neg\varphi & \text{iff} & \pi, t \not\models \varphi \\
\pi, t \models \varphi \wedge \psi & \text{iff} & \pi, t \models \varphi \text{ and } \pi, t \models \psi \\
\pi, t \models \varphi \, \mathsf{S}_I \, \psi & \text{iff} & \text{there is some } t' \in \mathbb{T} \text{ with } t - t' \in I \text{ such that} \\
& & \pi, t' \models \psi \text{ and } \pi, t'' \models \varphi, \text{ for all } t'' \in \mathbb{T} \text{ with } t' < t'' \leq t \\
\pi, t \models \varphi \, \mathsf{U}_I \, \psi & \text{iff} & \text{there is some } t' \in \mathbb{T} \text{ with } t' - t \in I \text{ such that} \\
& & \pi, t' \models \psi \text{ and } \pi, t'' \models \varphi, \text{ for all } t'' \in \mathbb{T} \text{ with } t \leq t'' < t'
\end{array}
$$

Note that MTL's time domain is dense and its semantics is continuous. We use standard syntactic sugar. For instance, we define $\varphi \, \mathsf{T}_I \, \psi := \neg(\neg\varphi \, \mathsf{S}_I \, \neg\psi)$, $\varphi \, \mathsf{R}_I \, \psi := \neg(\neg\varphi \, \mathsf{U}_I \, \neg\psi)$, $\blacklozenge_I \, \varphi := \mathsf{true} \, \mathsf{S}_I \, \varphi$, $\blacksquare_I \, \varphi := \mathsf{false} \, \mathsf{T}_I \, \varphi$, $\lozenge_I \, \varphi := \mathsf{true} \, \mathsf{U}_I \, \varphi$, and $\square_I \, \varphi := \mathsf{false} \, \mathsf{R}_I \, \varphi$, with $\mathsf{true} := p \vee \neg p$ and $\mathsf{false} := p \wedge \neg p$, for some $p \in P$.

A *timed word* is a sequence $(a_i, \tau_i)_{i \in \mathbb{N}}$ of tuples with $a_i \in 2^P$ and $\tau_i \in \mathbb{T}$, for any $i \in \mathbb{N}$, such that the sequence $(\tau_i)_{i \in \mathbb{N}}$ is non-strictly ascending and progressing. Intuitively, a timed word represents the observed, imprecisely timestamped trace, while a timeline represents the real system behavior. In the following, we assume a timestamp imprecision of $\delta \geq 0$, which we fix for the rest of the paper. For an "observed" timed word $(a_i, \tau_i)_{i \in \mathbb{N}}$, it would be natural to additionally assume that the τ_is are from a discrete infinite subset of $\mathbb{T}$, in which all elements have a finite representation. However, our results are valid without this additional assumption.

Given a timed word $\bar{\sigma} = (\bar{a}, \bar{\tau})$, the set of *possible timelines* of $\bar{\sigma}$, denoted $TL(\bar{\sigma})$, is the set of functions $\pi : \mathbb{T} \to 2^P$ with

$$\pi(t) := \begin{cases} a_i & \text{if } ts^{-1}(t) = \{i\} \text{ for some } i \in \mathbb{N}, \\ \emptyset & \text{otherwise,} \end{cases}$$

for any $t \in \mathbb{T}$, where $ts : \mathbb{N} \to \mathbb{T}$ is an injective function such that $ts(i) \in [\tau_i - \delta, \tau_i + \delta]$, for any $i \in \mathbb{N}$. We remark that the progress condition on $(\tau_i)_{i \in \mathbb{N}}$ ensures that the elements of $TL(\bar{\sigma})$ are indeed timelines. Furthermore, note that the requirement that ts is injective corresponds to the assumption that, in reality, no two events happen at the same point in time.

Example 1. Given $\delta := 1$ and the time word $\bar{\sigma} := (\{p\}, 1)(\{q\}, 1)(\{r\}, 2)(\{s\}, 5)\ldots$, one of the timelines in $TL(\bar{\sigma})$ is π where $\pi(0.6) = \{q\}$, $\pi(1.2) = \{r\}$, $\pi(1.3) = \{p\}$, and $\pi(t) = \emptyset$ for $t \in [0, 4) \setminus \{0.6, 1.2, 1.3\}$. Note that the ordering of events in $\bar{\sigma}$ differs from that in π.

3 MTL Monitoring of Imprecisely Timestamped Traces

Informally, we are interested in what can be said about the conformance of the possible timelines of an observed timed word $\bar{\sigma}$ with respect to a given formula φ, where $\bar{\sigma}$ is observed incrementally. Formally, we focus on the following problems, where a problem instance consists of a formula φ, a timed word $\bar{\sigma}$, and a time $t \in \mathbb{T}$. For $\ell \in \{\exists, \forall\}$, the question is whether $\bar{\sigma}, t \models_\ell \varphi$ holds, where we write (i) $\bar{\sigma}, t \models_\exists \varphi$ if $\pi, t \models \varphi$, for *some* $\pi \in TL(\bar{\sigma})$, and (ii) $\bar{\sigma}, t \models_\forall \varphi$ if $\pi, t \models \varphi$, for *all* $\pi \in TL(\bar{\sigma})$. We focus on answering these questions online, using monitoring.

Given a formula φ and an iteratively presented timed word $\bar{\sigma}$, our monitoring approach is the following, where formal definitions are given below:

1. Transform the formula φ into the formula $\mathsf{tf}(\varphi)$.
2. Transform at runtime the timed word $\bar{\sigma}$ into the timeline $\rho_{\bar{\sigma}}$.
3. Monitor the timeline $\rho_{\bar{\sigma}}$ with respect to the formula $\mathsf{tf}(\varphi)$.

The transformed formula $\mathsf{tf}(\varphi)$ accounts for timestamp imprecision by relaxing the implicit temporal constraints on atoms, that is, relaxing "atom p holds now" to "atom p holds within a $\pm\delta$ interval". Formally, for $p \in P$, we define $\mathsf{tf}(p) := (\blacklozenge_{[0,\delta]} p) \vee (\lozenge_{[0,\delta]} p)$ and extend tf homomorphically to non-atomic formulas.

The timeline $\rho_{\bar{\sigma}}$ is obtained by simply ignoring timestamp imprecision. For the timed word $\bar{\sigma} = (\bar{a}, \bar{\tau})$, we define the *monitored timeline* $\rho_{\bar{\sigma}}$ as $\rho_{\bar{\sigma}}(t) := \bigcup_{i \in \mathbb{N}} \{a_i \mid \tau_i = t\}$, for any $t \in \mathbb{T}$. Note that the timeline $\rho_{\bar{\sigma}}$ is easily built at runtime from the timed word $\bar{\sigma}$. In fact, if $t \in \mathbb{T}$ is the current time, then the value of $\rho_{\bar{\sigma}}$ at t can be obtained as soon as a tuple (a_i, τ_i) of elements of the timed word $\bar{\sigma}$ with $\tau_i > t$ arrives.

The following theorem states the guarantees provided by our monitoring approach. Concretely, for each of the two posed questions, we identify two classes of formulas for which the approach provides correct answers. We define these formula classes syntactically using the rules in Figure 1. We say that a formula φ in negation normal form is *labeled by* (ℓ) with $\ell \in \{\exists, \forall\}$ if $\varphi : (\ell)$ is derivable

$$\frac{}{\mathsf{true}:(\forall)} \quad \frac{}{\mathsf{false}:(\forall)} \quad \frac{}{p:(\exists)} \quad \frac{}{\neg p:(\forall)} \quad \frac{\varphi:(\forall) \quad \psi:(\forall)}{\varphi \,\mathsf{op}\, \psi:(\forall)} \;\; \mathsf{op} \in \{\wedge, \vee, \mathsf{S}_I, \mathsf{T}_I, \mathsf{U}_I, \mathsf{R}_I\}$$

$$\frac{\varphi:(\exists) \quad \psi:(\forall)}{\varphi \wedge \psi:(\exists)} \quad \frac{\varphi:(\exists) \quad \psi:(\exists)}{\varphi \vee \psi:(\exists)} \quad \frac{\varphi:(\forall) \quad \psi:(\exists)}{\varphi \,\mathsf{op}_I\, \psi:(\exists)} \;\; \mathsf{op} \in \{\mathsf{S}, \mathsf{T}, \mathsf{U}, \mathsf{R}\} \quad \frac{\varphi:(\forall)}{\varphi:(\exists)}$$

Fig. 1. Labeling Rules

using the rules in Figure 1. For the negation normal form, we assume that the formulas true and false, and the connectives $\vee$, T, and R are language primitives, while the connectives $\blacklozenge$, $\blacksquare$, $\Diamond$, and $\square$ are still syntactic sugar. We denote by $nnf(\varphi)$ the negation normal form of φ.

Theorem 2. *Let $\bar{\sigma}$ be a timed word, $\ell \in \{\exists, \forall\}$, and φ a formula with $nnf(\varphi)$ labeled by (ℓ). For any $t \in \mathbb{T}$, if $\rho_{\bar{\sigma}}, t \models \mathsf{tf}(\varphi)$, then $\bar{\sigma}, t \models_\ell \varphi$.*

Due to space limitations, we omit the theorem's proof, which is by induction over the formula structure, and give instead the intuition behind the theorem and some of the rules in Figure 1. The true and false formulas can be labeled by $(\forall)$ as their satisfaction does not depend on the trace. Positive literals p can only be labeled by $(\exists)$. If $\mathsf{tf}(p)$ is satisfied at t, then p is satisfied at some t' within the interval $[t - \delta, t + \delta]$, and thus there is a possible timeline for which p is satisfied at t. However, in general the other possible timelines do not satisfy p at t. In contrast, negative literals $\neg p$ can be labeled by $(\forall)$. If p is not satisfied on the interval $[t - \delta, t + \delta]$ on the monitored timeline, then there is no possible timeline satisfying p at t. Any formula of the form $\varphi \,\mathsf{op}\, \psi$ can be labeled by $(\forall)$, as long as φ and ψ can both be labeled by $(\forall)$. That is, the $(\forall)$ fragment consists of those formulas in which atomic propositions occur only negatively. The last rule expresses that if all possible timelines satisfy φ at t then there is a possible timeline satisfying φ at t. Thus the $(\forall)$ fragment is included in the $(\exists)$ fragment.

By monitoring $\rho_{\bar{\sigma}}$ with respect to $\mathsf{tf}(\varphi)$ and using Theorem 2, we may obtain correctness guarantees about whether some or all timelines in $TL(\bar{\sigma})$ satisfy φ. This depends on whether the negation normal form of φ or $\neg\varphi$ can be labeled, and on the monitoring result for $\mathsf{tf}(\varphi)$ on $\rho_{\bar{\sigma}}$ at t. To clarify when guarantees are obtained, we consider the following cases.

- *Neither $nnf(\varphi)$ nor $nnf(\neg\varphi)$ can be labeled.* Then we cannot apply Theorem 2 to obtain the guarantees.
- *Only $nnf(\varphi)$ is labeled.* If the monitoring result is positive, i.e. $\rho_{\bar{\sigma}}, t \models \mathsf{tf}(\varphi)$, then we simply apply Theorem 2 to obtain the guarantees. If however $\rho_{\bar{\sigma}}, t \not\models \mathsf{tf}(\varphi)$, then nothing can be concluded about the system's conformance with respect to φ.
- *Only $nnf(\neg\varphi)$ is labeled.* This case is similar to the previous one, and we only obtain the guarantees if the monitoring result is negative. That is, when $\rho_{\bar{\sigma}}, t \not\models \mathsf{tf}(\varphi)$, we can apply Theorem 2 to $\neg\varphi$. This is because $\mathsf{tf}(\neg\varphi) \equiv \neg\mathsf{tf}(\varphi)$, and thus $\rho_{\bar{\sigma}}, t \not\models \mathsf{tf}(\varphi)$ iff $\rho_{\bar{\sigma}}, t \models \mathsf{tf}(\neg\varphi)$.
- *Both $nnf(\varphi)$ and $nnf(\neg\varphi)$ are labeled.* We obtain the guarantees regardless of the monitoring result. If $\rho_{\bar{\sigma}}, t \models \mathsf{tf}(\varphi)$ then we apply Theorem 2 to φ; otherwise, we apply it to $\neg\varphi$.

The last case is illustrated through the following example.

Example 3. Let $\varphi := \neg p \to \Diamond_I q$. We have that $nnf(\varphi) = p \vee (\text{true}\, \mathsf{S}_I\, q) : (\exists)$ and $nnf(\neg\varphi) = \neg p \wedge (\text{false}\, \mathsf{T}_I \, \neg q) : (\forall)$. According to Theorem 2, the guarantees that we obtain by monitoring $\rho_{\bar{\sigma}}$ with respect to $\text{tf}(\varphi)$ are as follows. For any $t \in \mathbb{T}$, (1) if $\rho_{\bar{\sigma}}, t \models \text{tf}(\varphi)$, then there is a $\pi \in TL(\bar{\sigma})$ with $\pi, t \models \varphi$, and (2) if $\rho_{\bar{\sigma}}, t \not\models \text{tf}(\varphi)$, then $\pi, t \not\models \varphi$, for all $\pi \in TL(\bar{\sigma})$.

We remark that one can build the monitored timeline $\rho_{\bar{\sigma}}$ in different manners. Instead of taking the middle of the "uncertainty" intervals $[\tau_i - \delta, \tau_i + \delta]$ as the representative point in the monitored timeline, one could take another point as representative, provided that subsequent points have the same offset to the middle of the corresponding interval. The formula transformation must then be adjusted accordingly. However, monitoring such other timelines does not result in new conformance (with respect to the given property) guarantees as the following proposition demonstrates. In other words, it is sufficient to monitor the timeline considered in Theorem 2.

We first generalize the formula transformation. Given $\epsilon \in [0, \delta]$ and $* \in \{+, -\}$, let $\text{tf}_{*\epsilon}(p) := (\blacklozenge_{[0,\delta * \epsilon]}\, p) \vee (\Diamond_{[0, \delta \,\bar{*}\, \epsilon]}\, p)$, for any $p \in P$, where $\bar{*}$ switches $*$ to its dual value. For instance, $\text{tf}_0(p) = \text{tf}(p)$ and $\text{tf}_{-\delta}(p) = (\blacklozenge_{[0,0]}\, p) \vee (\Diamond_{[0,2\delta]}\, p)$. As before, $\text{tf}_{*\epsilon}(\cdot)$ is extended homomorphically to non-atomic formulas.

Proposition 4. *Let* $\delta \in \mathbb{T}$, $\epsilon_1, \epsilon_2 \in [0, \delta]$, $*_1, *_2 \in \{+, -\}$, *a timed word* $\bar{\sigma} = (a_i, \tau_i)_{i \in \mathbb{N}}$, *and the timelines* ρ_1 *and* ρ_2 *be given with* $\rho_j(t) := \bigcup_{i \in \mathbb{N}} \{a_i \mid \tau_i = t *_j \epsilon_j\}$, *for any* $l \in \mathbb{T}$ *and* $j \in \{1, 2\}$. *For any formula* φ *and any* $t \in \mathbb{T}$, *we have that* $\rho_1, t \models \text{tf}_{*_1 \epsilon_1}(\varphi)$ *iff* $\rho_2, t \models \text{tf}_{*_2 \epsilon_2}(\varphi)$.

4 Discussion

Fragments. The $(\exists)$ fragment is practically relevant because the negation normal form of various common specifications patterns are included in it. For instance, consider the common specification pattern $\Box\varphi$ with $\varphi = (p \wedge \alpha) \to \blacklozenge_I(q \wedge \beta)$, for some $p, q \in P$ and some formulas α and β. When $nnf(\neg\alpha)$ is labeled by $(\exists)$ and $nnf(\beta)$ is labeled by $(\forall)$, then $nnf(\varphi)$ is labeled by $(\exists)$. Similarly, when $nnf(\alpha)$ is labeled by $(\forall)$ and $nnf(\neg\beta)$ is labeled by $(\forall)$, then $nnf(\neg\varphi)$ is labeled by $(\exists)$. Observe that $nnf(\varphi)$ and $nnf(\neg\varphi)$ can both be labeled only in some special cases, for instance, when both $nnf(\alpha)$ and $nnf(\neg\alpha)$ can be labeled and when $\beta = \text{true}$. Furthermore, the $(\exists)$ fragment is limited in that conformance guarantees are given for only one possible timeline. In contrast, the $(\forall)$ fragment offers strong conformance guarantees; however, it is practically less relevant. Note that a formula in the $(\forall)$ fragment requires that all propositions occur negatively in φ. This is a strong restriction on the form of φ.

We do not, however, see how to extend the fragments in any significant way. For instance, the given rules cannot be strengthened by using stronger labels. This is illustrated by the following example, which shows that a rule that labels $\varphi \wedge \psi$ by $(\exists)$ whenever φ and ψ are labeled by $(\exists)$ is not sound. Let $\varphi := p \wedge \blacklozenge_{[1,1]} q$ and $\psi := p \wedge$

$\Diamond_{[1,1]}\, q$. Let $\delta := 2$ and consider the timed word $\bar{\sigma} := (\{p\}, 2)(\{q\}, 3)(\{r\}, 10)\dots$. We have $\rho_{\bar{\sigma}}(2) = \{p\}$, $\rho_{\bar{\sigma}}(3) = \{q\}$, and $\rho_{\bar{\sigma}}(t) = \emptyset$, for any $t \in [0,5] \setminus \{2,3\}$, and $\mathsf{tf}(\varphi \wedge \psi) \equiv (\blacklozenge_{[0,2]} \Diamond_{[0,2]}\, p) \wedge (\blacklozenge_{[0,3]} \Diamond_{[0,1]}\, q) \wedge (\blacklozenge_{[0,1]} \Diamond_{[0,3]}\, q)$. Clearly $\rho_{\bar{\sigma}}, 2 \models \mathsf{tf}(\varphi \wedge \psi)$ but $\pi, 2 \not\models \varphi \wedge \psi$, for any $\pi \in TL(\bar{\sigma})$.

Point-based Monitoring. It is appealing to monitor directly the observed timed word $\bar{\sigma}$ using a monitor for the more prevalent point-wise semantics of MTL. See [1] for a comparison of the two semantics with respect to monitoring. However, it is harder to obtain correctness guarantees for such a setting because one must use two different MTL semantics, the point-wise one for the monitored traces and the continuous one for the possible timelines. Note that monitoring precise traces with respect to a point-wise semantics is inappropriate as there is no reference evaluation point for comparing the evaluation of the observed trace with the evaluation of the precise traces. Recall that, under a point-wise semantics, evaluation points are event indices and these depend on the events' occurrence times.

Conclusions. The previous discussion motivates the need for alternative approaches. We are investigating a quantitative MTL monitoring approach along the lines explored in [8]. However, the raised problem may require not only new algorithmic solutions, but also specification languages that allow for the explicit reasoning about timestamp imprecision.

References

1. Basin, D., Klaedtke, F., Zălinescu, E.: Algorithms for monitoring real-time properties. In: Khurshid, S., Sen, K. (eds.) RV 2011. LNCS, vol. 7186, pp. 260–275. Springer, Heidelberg (2012)
2. Bauer, A., Leucker, M., Schallhart, C.: Runtime verification for LTL and TLTL. ACM Transactions on Software Engineering and Methodology 20(4) (2011)
3. Corbett, J.C., Dean, J., Epstein, M., Fikes, A., Frost, C., Furman, J.J., Ghemawat, S., Gubarev, A., Heiser, C., Hochschild, P., Hsieh, W.C., Kanthak, S., Kogan, E., Li, H., Lloyd, A., Melnik, S., Mwaura, D., Nagle, D., Quinlan, S., Rao, R., Rolig, L., Saito, Y., Szymaniak, M., Taylor, C., Wang, R., Woodford, D.: Spanner: Google's globally distributed database. ACM Transactions on Computer Systems 31(3), 8 (2013)
4. Koymans, R.: Specifying real-time properties with metric temporal logic. Real-Time Systems 2(4), 255–299 (1990)
5. Maler, O., Nickovic, D.: Monitoring temporal properties of continuous signals. In: Lakhnech, Y., Yovine, S. (eds.) FORMATS/FTRTFT 2004. LNCS, vol. 3253, pp. 152–166. Springer, Heidelberg (2004)
6. Thati, P., Roşu, G.: Monitoring algorithms for metric temporal logic specifications. In: Proceedings of the 4th Workshop on Runtime Verification. ENTCS, vol. 113, pp. 145–162. Elsevier (2005)
7. Wang, S., Ayoub, A., Sokolsky, O., Lee, I.: Runtime verification of traces under recording uncertainty. In: Khurshid, S., Sen, K. (eds.) RV 2011. LNCS, vol. 7186, pp. 442–456. Springer, Heidelberg (2012)
8. Zhang, H., Diao, Y., Immerman, N.: Recognizing patterns in streams with imprecise timestamps. Proceedings of the VLDB Endowment 3(1-2), 244–255 (2010)

ModelPlex: Verified Runtime Validation
of Verified Cyber-Physical System Models*

Stefan Mitsch and André Platzer

Computer Science Department
Carnegie Mellon University, Pittsburgh PA 15213, USA
{smitsch,aplatzer}@cs.cmu.edu

Abstract. Formal verification and validation play a crucial role in making cyber-physical systems (CPS) safe. Formal methods make strong guarantees about the system behavior *if* accurate models of the system can be obtained, including models of the controller and of the physical dynamics. In CPS, models are essential; but any model we could possibly build necessarily deviates from the real world. If the real system fits to the model, its behavior is guaranteed to satisfy the correctness properties verified w.r.t. the model. Otherwise, all bets are off. This paper introduces ModelPlex, a method ensuring that verification results about models apply to CPS implementations. ModelPlex provides correctness guarantees for CPS executions at runtime: it combines offline verification of CPS models with runtime validation of system executions for compliance with the model. Model-Plex ensures that the verification results obtained for the model apply to the actual system runs by monitoring the behavior of the world for compliance with the model, assuming the system dynamics deviation is bounded. If, at some point, the observed behavior no longer complies with the model so that offline verification results no longer apply, ModelPlex initiates provably safe fallback actions. This paper, furthermore, develops a systematic technique to synthesize provably correct monitors automatically from CPS proofs in differential dynamic logic.

1 Introduction

Cyber-physical systems (CPS) span controllers and the relevant dynamics of the environment. Since safety is crucial for CPS, their models (e. g., hybrid system models [29]) need to be verified formally. Formal *verification* guarantees that a model is safe w.r.t. a safety property. The remaining task is to *validate* whether those models are adequate, so that the verification results transfer to the system implementation [16,38]. This paper introduces ModelPlex, a method to *synthesize monitors by theorem proving*: it uses sound proof rules to formally verify that a model is safe and to synthesize provably correct monitors that validate compliance of system executions with that model.

System execution, however, provides many opportunities for surprising deviations from the model: faults may cause the system to function improperly [39], sensors may deliver uncertain values, actuators suffer from disturbance, or the formal verification

* This material is based on research sponsored by DARPA under agreement number DARPA FA8750-12-2-0291. The U.S. Government is authorized to reproduce and distribute reprints for Governmental purposes notwithstanding any copyright notation thereon.

B. Bonakdarpour and S.A. Smolka (Eds.): RV 2014, LNCS 8734, pp. 199–214, 2014.
© Springer International Publishing Switzerland 2014

may have assumed simpler ideal-world dynamics for tractability reasons or made unrealistically strong assumptions about the behavior of other agents in the environment. Simpler models are often better for real-time decisions and optimizations, because they make predictions feasible to compute at the required rate. The same phenomenon of simplicity for predictability is often exploited for the models in formal verification and validation. As a consequence, the *verification results obtained about models of a CPS only apply to the actual CPS at runtime to the extent that the system fits to the model.*

Validation, i. e., checking whether a CPS implementation fits to a model, is an interesting but difficult problem. Even more so, since CPS models are more difficult to analyze than ordinary (discrete) programs because of the physical plant, the environment, sensor inaccuracies, and actuator disturbance. In CPS, models are essential; but any model we could possibly build necessarily deviates from the real world. Still, good models are approximately right, i. e., within certain error margins.

In this paper, we settle for the question of *runtime model validation*, i. e. validating whether the model assumed for verification purposes is adequate for a *particular system execution* to ensure that the verification results apply *to the current execution*.[1] But we focus on *verifiably correct runtime validation* to ensure that verified properties of models provably apply, which is important for safety and certification [5].

If the observed system execution fits to the verified model, then this execution is safe according to the offline verification result about the model. If it does not fit, then the system is potentially unsafe because it no longer has an applicable safety proof, so we initiate a verified fail-safe action to avoid safety risks. Checking whether a system execution fits to a verified model includes checking that the actions chosen by the (unverified) controller implementation fit to *one of* the choices and requirements of the verified controller model. It also includes checking that the observed states can be explained by the plant model. The crucial questions are: How can a compliance monitor be synthesized that provably represents the verified model? How much safety margin does a system need to ensure that fail-safe actions are initiated early enough for the system to remain safe even if its behavior ceases to comply with the model?

The second question is related to feedback control and can only be answered when assuming constraints on the deviation of the real system dynamics from the plant model [33]. Otherwise, i. e., if the real system can be infinitely far off from the model, safety guarantees are impossible. By the sampling theorem in signal processing [37], such constraints further enable compliance monitoring solely on the basis of sample points instead of the unobservable intermediate states about which no sensor data exists.[2] This paper presents ModelPlex, a method to synthesize verifiably correct runtime validation monitors automatically. ModelPlex uses theorem proving with sound proof rules [29] to

---

[1] ModelPlex checks system execution w.r.t. a monitor specification, and thus, belongs to the field of runtime verification [16]. In this paper we use the term *runtime validation* in order to clearly convey the purpose of monitoring (i. e., runtime verification: monitor properties without offline verification; ModelPlex: monitor model adequacy to transfer offline verification results).

[2] When such constraints are not available, our method still generates verifiably correct *runtime tests*, which detect deviation from the model at the sampling points, just not between them. A fail-safe action will then lead to best-effort mitigation of safety risks (rather than guaranteed safety).

Table 1. Hybrid program representations of hybrid systems

Statement	Effect
$\alpha; \beta$	sequential composition, first run hybrid program α, then hybrid program β
$\alpha \cup \beta$	nondeterministic choice, following either hybrid program α or β
α^*	nondeterministic repetition, repeats hybrid program α $n \geq 0$ times
$x := \theta$	assign value of term θ to variable x (discrete jump)
$x := *$	assign arbitrary real number to variable x
$?F$	check that a particular condition F holds, and abort if it does not
$(x_1' = \theta_1, \ldots,$	evolve x_i along differential equation system $x_i' = \theta_i$
$x_n' = \theta_n \ \& \ F)$	restricted to maximum evolution domain F

turn hybrid system models into monitors in a verifiably correct way. Upon noncompliance, ModelPlex initiates provably safe fail-safe actions. System-level challenges w.r.t. monitor implementation and violation cause diagnosis are discussed elsewhere [8,19,41].

2 Preliminaries: Differential Dynamic Logic

For hybrid systems verification we use *differential dynamic logic* dℒ [27,29,31], which has a notation for hybrid systems as *hybrid programs*. dℒ allows us to make statements that we want to be true for all runs of a hybrid program ($[\alpha]\phi$) or for at least one run ($\langle\alpha\rangle\phi$). Both constructs are necessary to derive safe monitors: we need $[\alpha]\phi$ proofs so that we can be sure all behavior of a model (including controllers) are safe; we need $\langle\alpha\rangle\phi$ proofs to find monitor specifications that detect whether or not system execution fits to the verified model. Table 1 summarizes the relevant syntax fragment of hybrid programs together with an informal semantics. The semantics $\rho(\alpha)$ of hybrid program α is a relation on initial and final states of running α (defined in [27,32]). The set of dℒ formulas is generated by the following grammar ($\sim \in \{<, \leq, =, \geq, >\}$ and θ_1, θ_2 are arithmetic expressions in $+, -, \cdot, /$ over the reals):

$$\phi ::= \theta_1 \sim \theta_2 \mid \neg\phi \mid \phi \wedge \psi \mid \phi \vee \psi \mid \phi \rightarrow \psi \mid \forall x\phi \mid \exists x\phi \mid [\alpha]\phi \mid \langle\alpha\rangle\phi$$

Differential dynamic logic comes with a verification technique to prove correctness properties of hybrid programs (cf. [31] for an overview of dℒ and KeYmaera).

3 ModelPlex Approach for Verified Runtime Validation

CPS are almost impossible to get right without sufficient attention to prior analysis, for instance by formal verification and formal validation techniques. We assume to be given a verified model of a CPS, i.e. formula (1) is proved valid,[3] for example using [27,31].

$$\psi \rightarrow [\alpha^*]\psi \quad \text{with invariant } \varphi \rightarrow [\alpha]\varphi \text{ s.t. } \phi \rightarrow \varphi \text{ and } \varphi \rightarrow \psi \qquad (1)$$

---

[3] We use differential dynamic logic (dℒ) and KeYmaera as a theorem prover to illustrate our concepts throughout this paper. The concept of ModelPlex is not predicated on the use of KeYmaera to prove (1). Other verification techniques could be used to establish validity of this formula. The flexibility of the underlying logic dℒ, its support for both $[\alpha]\phi$ and $\langle\alpha\rangle\phi$, and its proof calculus, however, are exploited for systematically constructing monitors from proofs in the sequel.

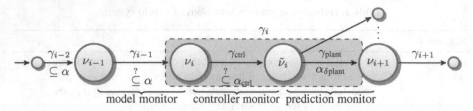

Fig. 1. Use of ModelPlex monitors along a system execution

Formula (1) expresses that all runs of the hybrid system α^*, which start in states that satisfy the precondition ϕ and repeat the model α arbitrarily many times, must end in states that satisfy the postcondition ψ. Formula (1) is proved using some form of induction, which shows that a loop invariant φ holds after every run of α if it was true before. The model α is a *hybrid system model* of a CPS, which means that it describes both the discrete control actions of the controllers in the system and the continuous physics of the plant and the system's environment.

The safety guarantees that we obtain by proving formula (1) about the model α^* transfer to the real system, *if* the actual CPS execution fits to α^*. Since we want to preserve safety properties, a CPS γ fits to a model α^*, *if* the CPS reaches at most those states that are reachable by the model, i.e., $\rho(\gamma) \subseteq \rho(\alpha^*)$. However, we do not know γ and therefore need to find a condition based on α^* that we can check at runtime to see if concrete runs of γ behave like α^*. Checking the postcondition ψ is not sufficient because, if ψ does not hold, the system is already unsafe. Checking the invariant φ is insufficient as well, because if φ does not hold the controller can no longer guarantee safety, even though the system may not yet be unsafe. But if we detect when a CPS is about to deviate from α^* *before* leaving φ, we can still switch to a fail-safe controller to avoid $\neg\psi$ from happening.

ModelPlex derives three kinds of monitors (model monitor, controller monitor, and prediction monitor, cf. Fig. 1). We check reachability between consecutive states in α, α_{ctrl}, and $\alpha_{\delta\text{plant}}$ by verifying states during execution against the corresponding monitor.

Model monitor. In each state ν_i we test the sample point ν_{i-1} from the previous execution γ_{i-1} for deviation from the single α, not α^* i.e., test $(\nu_{i-1}, \nu_i) \in \rho(\alpha)$. If violated, other verified properties may no longer hold for the system; the system, however, is still safe if a prediction monitor was satisfied on ν_{i-1}. Frequent violations indicate an inadequate model that should be revised to better reflect reality.

Controller monitor. In intermediate state $\tilde{\nu}_i$ we test the current controller decisions of the implementation γ_{ctrl} for compliance with the model, i.e., test $(\nu_i, \tilde{\nu}_i) \in \rho(\alpha_{\text{ctrl}})$. Controller monitors are designed for switching between controllers similar to Simplex [36]. If violated, the commands from a fail-safe controller replace the current controller's decisions to ensure that no unsafe commands are ever actuated.

Prediction monitor. In intermediate state $\tilde{\nu}_i$ we test the worst-case safety impact of the current controller decisions w.r.t. the predictions of a bounded deviation plant model $\alpha_{\delta\text{plant}}$, which has a tolerance around the model plant α_{plant}, i.e., check $\nu_{i+1} \models \varphi$ for all ν_{i+1} such that $(\tilde{\nu}_i, \nu_{i+1}) \in \rho(\alpha_{\delta\text{plant}})$. Note, that we simultaneously check all ν_{i+1} by checking $\tilde{\nu}_i$ for a characterizing condition of $\alpha_{\delta\text{plant}}$. If violated, the current control choice is not guaranteed to keep the system safe until the next control cycle and, thus, a fail-safe controller takes over.

The assumption for the prediction monitor is that the real execution is not arbitrarily far off the plant models used for safety verification, because otherwise guarantees can be neither made on unobservable intermediate states nor on safety of the future system evolution [33]. We propose separation of disturbance causes in the models: ideal plant models α_{plant} for correctness verification purposes, implementation deviation plant models $\alpha_{\delta plant}$ for monitoring purposes. We support any deviation model (e. g., piecewise constant disturbance, differential inclusion models of disturbance), as long as the deviation is bounded and differential invariants can be found. We further assume that monitor evaluations are at most some ε time units apart (e. g., along with a recurring controller execution). Note that disturbance in $\alpha_{\delta plant}$ is more manageable compared to α^*, because we can focus on single runs α instead of repetitions for monitoring.

3.1 Relation between States

We systematically derive a check that inspects states of the actual CPS to detect deviation from the model α^*. We first establish a notion of state recall and show that, when all previous state pairs complied with the model, compliance of the entire execution can be checked by checking the latest two states (ν_{i-1}, ν_i) (see [25, App. A] for proofs).

Definition 1 (State recall). *We use V to denote the set of variables whose state we want to recall. We use $\Upsilon_V^- \equiv \bigwedge_{x \in V} x = x^-$ to express a characterization of the values of variables in a state prior to a run of α, where we always assume the fresh variables x^- to occur solely in Υ_V^-. The variables in x^- can be used to recall this state. Likewise, we use $\Upsilon_V^+ \equiv \bigwedge_{x \in V} x = x^+$ to characterize the posterior states and expect fresh x^+.*

With this notation the following lemma states that an interconnected sequence of α transitions forms a transition of α^*.

Lemma 1 (Loop prior and posterior state). *Let α be a hybrid program and α^* be the program that repeats α arbitrarily many times. Assume that all consecutive pairs of states $(\nu_{i-1}, \nu_i) \in \rho(\alpha)$ of $n \in \mathbb{N}^+$ executions, whose valuations are recalled with $\Upsilon_V^i \equiv \bigwedge_{x \in V} x = x^i$ and Υ_V^{i-1} are plausible w.r.t. the model α, i. e., $\models \bigwedge_{1 \leq i \leq n} (\Upsilon_V^{i-1} \rightarrow \langle \alpha \rangle \Upsilon_V^i)$ with $\Upsilon_V^- = \Upsilon_V^0$ and $\Upsilon_V^+ = \Upsilon_V^n$. Then, the sequence of states originates from an α^* execution from Υ_V^0 to Υ_V^n, i. e., $\models \Upsilon_V^- \rightarrow \langle \alpha^* \rangle \Upsilon_V^+$.*

Lemma 1 enables us to check compliance with the model α^* up to the current state by checking reachability of a posterior state from a prior state on each execution of α (i. e., online monitoring [16], which is easier because the loop was eliminated). To find compliance checks systematically, we construct formula (2), which relates a prior state of a CPS to its posterior state through at least one path through the model α. [4]

$$\Upsilon_V^- \rightarrow \langle \alpha \rangle \Upsilon_V^+ \tag{2}$$

---

[4] Consecutive states for α^* mean before and after executions of α (i. e., $\alpha\overset{\downarrow}{;}\alpha\overset{\downarrow}{;}\alpha$, not within α).

This formula is satisfied in a state ν, if there is at least one run of the model α starting in the state ν recalled by Υ_V^- and results in a state ω recalled using Υ_V^+. In other words, at least one path through α explains how the prior state ν got transformed into the posterior state ω. The d$\mathcal{L}$ formula (2) characterizes the state transition relation of the model α directly. Its violation witnesses compliance violation. Compliance at all intermediate states cannot be observed by real-world sensors, see Section 3.5.

In principle, formula (2) would be a monitor, because it relates a prior state to a posterior state through the model of a CPS; but the formula is hard if not impossible to evaluate at runtime, because it refers to a hybrid system α, which includes nondeterminism and differential equations. The basic observation is that any formula that is equivalent to (2) but conceptually easier to evaluate in a state would be a correct monitor. We use theorem proving for simplifying formula (2) into quantifier-free first-order real arithmetic form so that it can be evaluated efficiently at runtime. The resulting first-order real arithmetic formula can be easily implemented in a runtime monitor and executed along with the actual controller. A monitor is executable code that only returns true if the transition from the prior system state to the posterior state is compliant with the model. Thus, deviations from the model can be detected at runtime, so that appropriate fallback and mitigation strategies can be initiated.

Remark 1. The complexity for evaluating an arithmetic formula over the reals for concrete numbers is linear in the formula size, as opposed to deciding the validity of such formulas, which is doubly exponential. Evaluating the same formula on floating point numbers is inexpensive, but may yield wrong results due to rounding errors; on exact rationals the bit-complexity can be non-negligible. We use interval arithmetic to obtain reliable results efficiently (cf. [25, App. C]).

Example 1. We will use a simple water tank as a running example to illustrate the concepts throughout this section. The water tank has a current level x and a maximum level m. The water tank controller, which runs at least every ε time units, nondeterministically chooses any flow f between a maximum outflow -1 and a maximum inflow $\frac{m-x}{\varepsilon}$. This water tank never overflows, as witnessed by a proof for the following d$\mathcal{L}$ formula.

$$\underbrace{0 \leq x \leq m \wedge \varepsilon > 0}_{\phi} \rightarrow \Big[\big(f := *; \, ?\big(-1 \leq f \leq \tfrac{m-x}{\varepsilon}\big); \\ t := 0; \, (x' = f, \, t' = 1 \,\&\, x \geq 0 \wedge t \leq \varepsilon)\big)^* \Big] \overbrace{(0 \leq x \leq m)}^{\psi}$$

3.2 ModelPlex Monitor Synthesis

This section introduces the nature of ModelPlex monitor specifications, our approach to generate such specifications from hybrid system models, and how to turn those specifications into monitor code that can be executed at runtime along with the controller.

A ModelPlex specification corresponds to the d$\mathcal{L}$ formula (2). If the current state of a system does not satisfy a ModelPlex specification, some behavior that is not reflected in the model occurred (e. g., the wrong control action was taken, unanticipated dynamics in the environment occurred, sensor uncertainty led to unexpected values, or the system was applied outside the specified operating environment).

A *model monitor* χ_m checks that two consecutive states ν and ω can be explained by an execution of the model α, i. e., $(\nu, \omega) \in \rho(\alpha)$. In the sequel, $BV(\alpha)$ are bound variables in α, $FV(\psi)$ are free variables in ψ, Σ is the set of all variables, and $A\backslash B$ denotes the set of variables being in some set A but not in some other set B. Furthermore, we use $\nu|_A$ to denote ν projected onto the variables in A.

Theorem 1 (Model monitor correctness). *Let α^* be provably safe, so $\models \phi \rightarrow [\alpha^*]\psi$. Let $V_m = BV(\alpha) \cup FV(\psi)$. Let $\nu_0, \nu_1, \nu_2, \nu_3 \ldots \in \mathbb{R}^n$ be a sequence of states, with $\nu_0 \models \phi$ and that agree on $\Sigma\backslash V_m$, i.e., $\nu_0|_{\Sigma\backslash V_m} = \nu_k|_{\Sigma\backslash V_m}$ for all k. We define $(\nu, \nu_{i+1}) \models \chi_m$ as χ_m evaluated in the state resulting from ν by interpreting x^+ as $\nu_{i+1}(x)$ for all $x \in V_m$, i.e., $\nu_{x^+}^{\nu_{i+1}(x)} \models \chi_m$. If $(\nu_i, \nu_{i+1}) \models \chi_m$ for all $i < n$ then we have $\nu_n \models \psi$ where*

$$\chi_m \equiv \left(\phi|_{const} \rightarrow \langle\alpha\rangle\Upsilon_{V_m}^+\right) \tag{3}$$

and $\phi|_{const}$ denotes the conditions of ϕ that involve only constants that do not change in α, i.e., $FV(\phi|_{const}) \cap BV(\alpha) = \emptyset$.

Our approach to generate monitor specifications from hybrid system models takes a verified d$\mathcal{L}$ formula (1) as input and produces a monitor χ_m in quantifier-free first-order form as output. The algorithm, listed in [25, App. D], involves the following steps:

1. A d$\mathcal{L}$ formula (1) about a model α of the form $\phi \rightarrow [\alpha^*]\psi$ is turned into a specification conjecture (3) of the form $\phi|_{const} \rightarrow \langle\alpha\rangle\Upsilon_{V_m}^+$.
2. Theorem proving on the specification conjecture (3) is applied until no further proof rules are applicable and only first-order real arithmetic formulas remain open.
3. The monitor specification χ_m is the conjunction of the unprovable first-order real arithmetic formulas from open sub-goals.

Generate the monitor conjecture. We map d$\mathcal{L}$ formula (1) syntactically to a specification conjecture of the form (3). By design, this conjecture will not be provable. But the unprovable branches of a proof attempt will reveal information that, had it been in the premises, would make (3) provable. Through $\Upsilon_{V_m}^+$, those unprovable conditions collect the relations of the posterior state of model α characterized by x^+ to the prior state x, i.e., the conditions are a representation of (2) in quantifier-free first-order real arithmetic.

Example 2. The specification conjecture for the water tank model is given below. It is constructed from the model by removing the loop, flipping the modality, and formulating the specification requirement as a property, since we are interested in a relation between two consecutive states ν and ω (recalled by x^+, f^+ and t^+). Using theorem proving [34], we analyze the conjecture to reveal the actual monitor specification.

$$\underbrace{\varepsilon > 0}_{\phi|_{const}} \rightarrow \Big\langle f := *; ?\left(-1 \leq f \leq \tfrac{m-x}{\varepsilon}\right); \quad t := 0;\ (x' = f,\ t' = 1\ \&\ x \geq 0 \wedge t \leq \varepsilon) \Big\rangle \overbrace{(x = x^+ \wedge f = f^+ \wedge t = t^+)}^{\Upsilon_{V_m}^+}$$

Use theorem proving to analyze the specification conjecture. We use the proof rules of d$\mathcal{L}$ [27,31] to analyze the specification conjecture χ_m. These proof rules syntactically decompose a hybrid model into easier-to-handle parts, which leads to sequents with first-order real arithmetic formulas towards the leaves of a proof. Using real arithmetic quantifier elimination we close sequents with logical tautologies, which do not need to be checked at runtime since they always evaluate to *true* for any input. The conjunction of the remaining open sequents is the monitor specification; it implies (2).

A complete sequence of proof rules applied to the monitor conjecture of the water tank is described in [25, App. B]. Most steps are simple when analyzing specification conjectures: sequential composition ($\langle ; \rangle$), nondeterministic choice ($\langle \cup \rangle$), deterministic assignment ($\langle := \rangle$) and logical connectives ($\wedge$r etc.) replace current facts with simpler ones or branch the proof (cf. rules in [27,32]). Challenge arise from handling nondeterministic assignment and differential equations in hybrid programs.

Let us first consider nondeterministic assignment $x := *$. The proof rule for nondeterministic assignment ($\langle * \rangle$) results in a new existentially quantified variable. By sequent proof rule $\exists$r, this existentially quantified variable is instantiated with an arbitrary term θ, which is often a new logical variable that is implicitly existentially quantified [27]. Weakening (Wr) removes facts that are no longer necessary.

$$(\langle * \rangle) \ \frac{\exists X \langle x := X \rangle \phi}{\langle x := * \rangle \phi} {}_1 \qquad (\exists r) \ \frac{\Gamma \vdash \phi(\theta), \exists x\, \phi(x), \Delta}{\Gamma \vdash \exists x\, \phi(x), \Delta} {}_2 \qquad (\text{Wr}) \ \frac{\Gamma \vdash \Delta}{\Gamma \vdash \phi, \Delta}$$

---

[1] X is a new logical variable
[2] θ is an arbitrary term, often a new (existential) logical variable X.

Optimization 1 (Instantiation Trigger). *If the variable is not changed in the remaining* α, $x_i = x_i^+$ *is in* $\Upsilon_{V_m}^+$ *and* X *is not bound in* $\Upsilon_{V_m}^+$, *then instantiate the existential quantifier by rule* $\exists$r *with the corresponding* x_i^+ *that is part of the specification conjecture (i. e.,* $\theta = x_i^+$), *since subsequent proof steps are going to reveal* $\theta = x_i^+$ *anyway.*

Otherwise, we introduce a new logical variable, which may result in an existential quantifier in the monitor specification if no further constraints can be found later in the proof.

Example 3. The corresponding steps in the water tank proof use $\langle * \rangle$ for the nondeterministic flow assignment ($f := *$) and $\exists$r to instantiate the resulting existential quantifier $\exists F$ with a new logical variable F (*plant* is an abbreviation for $x' = f, t' = 1 \ \& \ 0 \le x \wedge t \le \varepsilon$). We show the proof without and with application of Opt. 1.

$$\langle * \rangle \frac{ \exists r, \text{Wr} \frac{\phi \vdash \langle f := F \rangle \langle ?-1 \le f \le \frac{m-x}{\varepsilon} \rangle \langle plant \rangle \Upsilon^+}{\phi \vdash \exists F \langle f := F \rangle \langle ?-1 \le f \le \frac{m-x}{\varepsilon} \rangle \langle plant \rangle \Upsilon^+}}{\phi \vdash \langle f := *; ?-1 \le f \le \frac{m-x}{\varepsilon} \rangle \langle plant \rangle \Upsilon^+}$$

w/o Opt. 1

with Opt. 1 (anticipate $f = f^+$ from Υ^+)

$$\exists r, \text{Wr} \frac{\phi \vdash \langle f := f^+ \rangle}{\langle ?-1 \le f \le \frac{m-x}{\varepsilon} \rangle \langle plant \rangle \Upsilon^+} \cdots$$

Next, we handle differential equations. Even when we can solve the differential equation, existentially and universally quantified variables remain. Let us inspect the corresponding proof rule from the d$\mathcal{L}$ calculus [31]. For differential equations we have to prove that there exists a duration t, such that the differential equation stays within the evolution domain H throughout all intermediate times $\tilde{t}$ and the result satisfies ϕ at the end. At this point we have three options:

- we can instantiate the existential quantifier, if we know that the duration will be t^+;
- we can introduce a new logical variable, which is the generic case that always yields correct results, but may discover monitor specifications that are harder to evaluate;

$$(\langle'\rangle) \quad \frac{\exists T \geq 0 \left((\forall 0 \leq \tilde{t} \leq T \, \langle x := y(\tilde{t}) \rangle H) \wedge \langle x := y(T) \rangle \phi \right)}{\langle x' = \theta \, \& \, H \rangle \phi} \, {}^{1} \qquad (\text{QE}) \quad \frac{\text{QE}(\phi)}{\phi} \, {}^{2}$$

---

[1] T and $\tilde{t}$ are fresh logical variables and $\langle x := y(T) \rangle$ is the discrete assignment belonging to the solution y of the differential equation with constant symbol x as symbolic initial value

[2] iff $\phi \equiv \text{QE}(\phi)$, ϕ is a first-order real arithmetic formula, $\text{QE}(\phi)$ is an equivalent quantifier-free formula computable by [7]

- we can use quantifier elimination (QE) to obtain an equivalent quantifier-free result (a possible optimization could inspect the size of the resulting formula).

Example 4. In the analysis of the water tank example, we solve the differential equation (see $\langle'\rangle$) and apply the substitutions $f := F$ and $t := 0$. In the next step (see $\exists$r,Wr), we instantiate the existential quantifier $\exists T$ with t^+ (i. e., we choose $T = t^+$ using Opt. 1 with the last conjunct) and use weakening right (Wr) to systematically get rid of the existential quantifier that would otherwise still be left around by rule $\exists$r. Finally, we use quantifier elimination (QE) to reveal an equivalent quantifier-free formula.

$$\text{QE} \, \frac{\phi \vdash F = f^+ \wedge x^+ = x + Ft^+ \wedge t^+ \geq 0 \wedge x \geq 0 \wedge \varepsilon \geq t^+ \geq 0 \wedge Ft^+ + x \geq 0}{\phi \vdash \forall 0 \leq \tilde{t} \leq T \, (x + f^+ \tilde{t} \geq 0 \wedge \tilde{t} \leq \varepsilon) \wedge F = f^+ \wedge x^+ = x + Ft^+ \wedge t^+ = t^+}$$

$$\exists \text{r,Wr} \, \frac{}{\phi \vdash \exists T \geq 0 ((\forall 0 \leq \tilde{t} \leq T \, (x + f^+ \tilde{t} \geq 0 \wedge \tilde{t} \leq \varepsilon)) \wedge F = f^+ \wedge (x^+ = x + FT \wedge t^+ = T))}$$

$$\langle'\rangle \, \frac{}{\phi \vdash \langle f := F; t := 0 \rangle \langle \{x' = f, t' = 1 \, \& \, x \geq 0 \wedge t \leq \varepsilon \} \rangle \Upsilon^+}$$

The analysis of the specification conjecture finishes with collecting the open sequents from the proof to create the monitor specification $\chi_m \overset{\text{def}}{\equiv} \bigwedge (\textit{open sequent})$. The collected open sequents may include new logical variables and new (Skolem) function symbols that were introduced for nondeterministic assignments and differential equations when handling existential or universal quantifiers. We use the invertible quantifier rule i∃ to re-introduce existential quantifiers for the new logical variables (universal quantifiers for function symbols, see [27] for calculus details). Often, the now quantified logical variables are discovered to be equal to one of the post-state variables later in the proof, because those variables did not change in the model after the assignment. If this is the case, we can use proof rule $\exists \sigma$ to further simplify the monitor specification by substituting the corresponding logical variable x with its equal term θ.

$$(\text{i}\exists) \quad \frac{\Gamma \vdash \exists X \left(\bigwedge_i (\Phi_i \vdash \Psi_i) \right), \Delta}{\Gamma, \Phi_1 \vdash \Psi_1, \Delta \quad \cdots \quad \Gamma, \Phi_n \vdash \Psi_n, \Delta} \, {}^{1} \qquad (\exists \sigma) \quad \frac{\phi(\theta)}{\exists x \, (x = \theta \wedge \phi(x))} \, {}^{2}$$

---

[1] Among all open branches, free logical variable X only occurs in the branches $\Gamma, \Phi_i \vdash \Psi_i, \Delta$

[2] Logical variable x does not appear in term θ

Example 5. The two open sequents of Examples 3 and 4 use a new logical variable F for the nondeterministic flow assignment $f := *$. After further steps in the proof, the assumptions reveal additional information $F = f^+$. Thus, we re-introduce the existential quantifier over all the open branches (i∃) and substitute f^+ for F ($\exists\sigma$). The sole open sequent of this proof attempt is the monitor specification χ_m of the water tank model.

$$\begin{array}{c}
\cfrac{\phi \vdash -1 \leq f^+ \leq \frac{m-x}{\varepsilon} \wedge x^+ = x + f^+ t^+ \wedge t^+ \geq 0 \wedge x \geq 0 \ldots}{\cfrac{\phi \vdash \exists F(-1 \leq F \leq \frac{m-x}{\varepsilon} \wedge F = f^+ \wedge x^+ = x + Ft^+ \wedge t^+ \geq 0 \wedge x \geq 0 \ldots)}{\phi \vdash -1 \leq F \leq \frac{m-x}{\varepsilon} \quad \phi \vdash F = f^+ \wedge x^+ = x + Ft^+ \wedge t^+ \geq 0 \wedge x \geq 0 \ldots}} \, {}^{\text{i}\exists}}\, {}^{\exists\sigma}
\end{array}$$

3.3 Controller Monitor Synthesis

A *controller monitor* χ_c checks that two consecutive states ν and ω are reachable with one controller execution α_{ctrl}, i.e., $(\nu, \omega) \in \rho(\alpha_{\text{ctrl}})$ with $V_c = BV(\alpha_{\text{ctrl}}) \cup FV(\psi)$. We systematically derive controller monitors from formulas $\phi|_{\text{const}} \to \langle \alpha_{\text{ctrl}} \rangle \Upsilon_{V_c}^+$. A controller monitor can be used to initiate controller switching similar to Simplex [36].

Theorem 2 (Controller monitor correctness). *Let α of the canonical form $\alpha_{\text{ctrl}}; \alpha_{\text{plant}}$. Assume $\models \phi \to [\alpha^*]\psi$ has been proven with invariant φ as in* (1). *Let $\nu \models \phi|_{\text{const}} \wedge \varphi$, as checked by χ_m (Theorem 1). Furthermore, let $\tilde{\nu}$ be a post-controller state. If $(\nu, \tilde{\nu}) \models \chi_c$ with $\chi_c \equiv \phi|_{\text{const}} \to \langle \alpha_{\text{ctrl}} \rangle \Upsilon_{V_c}^+$ then we have that $(\nu, \tilde{\nu}) \in \rho(\alpha_{\text{ctrl}})$ and $\tilde{\nu} \models \varphi$.*

3.4 Monitoring in the Presence of Expected Uncertainty and Disturbance

Up to now we considered exact ideal-world models. But real-world clocks drift, sensors measure with some uncertainty, and actuators are subject to disturbance. This makes the exact models safe but too conservative, which means that monitors for exact models are likely to fall back to a fail-safe controller rather often. In this section we discuss how we find ModelPlex specifications so that the safety property (1) and the monitor specification become more robust to expected uncertainty and disturbance. That way, only unexpected deviations beyond those captured in the normal operational uncertainty and disturbance of α^* cause the monitor to initiate fail-safe actions.

In d$\mathcal{L}$, we can, for example, use nondeterministic assignment from an interval to model sensor uncertainty and piecewise constant actuator disturbance (e. g., as in [22]), or differential inequalities for actuator disturbance (e. g., as in [35]). Such models include nondeterminism about sensed values in the controller model and often need more complex physics models than differential equations with polynomial solutions.

Example 6. We incorporate clock drift, sensor uncertainty and actuator disturbance into the water tank model to express expected deviation. The measured level x_s is within a known sensor uncertainty u of the real level x (i.e. $x_s \in [x - u, x + u]$). We use differential inequalities to model clock drift and actuator disturbance. The clock, which wakes the controller, is slower than the real time by at most a time drift of c; it can be arbitrarily fast. The water flow disturbance is at most d, but the water tank is allowed to drain arbitrarily fast (even leaks when the pump is on). To illustrate different modeling possibilities, we use additive clock drift and multiplicative actuator disturbance.

$$0 \leq x \leq m \wedge \varepsilon > 0 \wedge c < 1 \wedge 0 \leq u \wedge 0 < d$$
$$\to \Big[\big(x_s := *; ? (x - u \leq x_s \leq x + u); \ f := *; ? \big(-1 \leq f \leq \tfrac{m - x_s - u}{d\varepsilon}(1 - c)\big);$$
$$t := 0; \ \{x' \leq fd, \ 1 - c \leq t' \ \& \ x \geq 0 \wedge t \leq \varepsilon\}\big)^* \Big] (0 \leq x \leq m)$$

We analyze Example 6 in the same way as the previous examples, with the crucial exception of the differential inequalities. We cannot use the proof rule $\langle' \rangle$ to analyze this model, because differential inequalities do not have polynomial solutions. Instead, we use the DR and DE proof rules of d$\mathcal{L}$ [28,29] to turn differential inequalities into a differential-algebraic constraint form that lets us proceed with the proof. Rule DE turns a differential inequality $x' \leq \theta$ into a quantified differential equation $\exists \tilde{d}(x' = \tilde{d} \ \& \ \tilde{d} \leq \theta)$ with an equivalent differential-algebraic constraint. Rule DR turns a differential-algebraic constraint $\mathcal{E}$ into another differential-algebraic constraint $\mathcal{D}$, which implies $\mathcal{E}$, written $\mathcal{D} \to \mathcal{E}$, as defined in [28] (cf. [25, App. B] for an example).

$$
\text{(DR)} \ \frac{\mathcal{D} \to \mathcal{E} \quad \langle \mathcal{D} \rangle \phi}{\langle \mathcal{E} \rangle \phi} \ _1 \qquad \text{(DE)} \ \frac{\forall X (\exists \tilde{d}(X = \tilde{d} \wedge \tilde{d} \leq \theta \wedge H) \to X \leq \theta \wedge H)}{\langle x' \leq \theta \ \& \ H \rangle \phi} \langle \exists \tilde{d}(x' = \tilde{d} \ \& \ \tilde{d} \leq \theta \wedge H) \rangle \phi \ _2
$$

---

[1] differential refinement: differential-algebraic constraints $\mathcal{D}$, $\mathcal{E}$ have the same changed variables
[2] differential inequality elimination: special case of DR, which rephrases the differential inequalities $\leq$ as differential-algebraic constraints (accordingly for other or mixed inequalities systems).

Currently, for finding model monitors our prototype tool solves differential equations by the proof rule $\langle' \rangle$. Thus, it finds model monitor specifications for differential algebraic equations with polynomial solutions and for differential algebraic inequalities, which can be refined into solvable differential algebraic equations as in Example 6. For prediction monitors (discussed in Section 3.5) we use d$\mathcal{L}$ techniques for finding differential variants and invariants, differential cuts [28], and differential auxiliaries [30] to handle differential equations and inequalities *without polynomial solutions*.

3.5 Monitoring Compliance Guarantees for Unobservable Intermediate States

With controller monitors, non-compliance of a controller implementation w.r.t. the modeled controller can be detected right away. With model monitors, non-compliance of the actual system dynamics w.r.t. the modeled dynamics can be detected when they first occur. We switch to a fail-safe action, which is verified using standard techniques, in both non-compliance cases. The crucial question is: can such a method always guarantee safety? The answer is linked to the image computation problem in model checking (i. e., approximation of states reachable from a current state), which is known to be not semi-decidable by numerical evaluation at points; approximation with uniform error is only possible if a bound is known for the continuous derivatives [33]. This implies that we need additional assumptions about the deviation between the actual and the modeled continuous dynamics to guarantee compliance for unobservable intermediate states. Unbounded deviation from the model between sample points just is unsafe, no matter how hard a controller tries. Hence, worst-case bounds capture how well reality is reflected in the model.

We derive a prediction monitor to check whether a current control decision will be able to keep the system safe for time ε even if the actual continuous dynamics deviate from the model. A prediction monitor checks the current state, because all previous states are ensured by a model monitor and subsequent states are then safe by (1).

Definition 2 (ε-**bounded plant with disturbance** δ). *Let α_{plant} be a model of the form $x' = \theta \,\&\, H$. An ε-bounded plant with disturbance δ, written $\alpha_{\delta plant}$, is a plant model of the form $x_0 := 0;\ (f(\theta, \delta) \le x' \le g(\theta, \delta) \,\&\, H \wedge x_0 \le \varepsilon)$ for some f, g with fresh variable $\varepsilon > 0$ and assuming $x_0' = 1$. We say that disturbance δ is constant if $x \notin \delta$; it is additive if $f(\theta, \delta) = \theta - \delta$ and $g(\theta, \delta) = \theta + \delta$.*

Theorem 3 (Prediction monitor correctness). *Let α^* be provably safe, i. e., $\models \phi \to [\alpha^*]\psi$ has been proved using invariant φ as in (1). Let $V_p = BV(\alpha) \cup FV([\alpha]\varphi)$. Let $\nu \models \phi|_{const} \wedge \varphi$, as checked by χ_m from Theorem 1. Further assume $\tilde{\nu}$ such that $(\nu, \tilde{\nu}) \in \rho(\alpha_{ctrl})$, as checked by χ_c from Theorem 2. If $(\nu, \tilde{\nu}) \models \chi_p$ with $\chi_p \equiv (\phi|_{const} \wedge \varphi) \to \langle \alpha_{ctrl}\rangle(\Upsilon_{V_p}^+ \wedge [\alpha_{\delta plant}]\varphi)$, then we have for all $(\tilde{\nu}, \omega) \in \rho(\alpha_{\delta plant})$ that $\omega \models \varphi$.*

Remark 2. By adding a controller execution $\langle \alpha_{ctrl}\rangle$ prior to the disturbed plant model, we synthesize prediction monitors that take the actual controller decisions into account. For safety purposes, we could just as well use a monitor definition without controller $\chi_p \equiv (\phi|_{const} \wedge \varphi) \to [\alpha_{\delta plant}]\varphi$. But doing so results in a conservative monitor, which has to keep the CPS safe without knowledge of the actual controller decision.

3.6 Decidability and Computability

One useful characteristic of ModelPlex beyond soundness is that monitor synthesis is computable, which yields a synthesis algorithm, and that the correctness of those synthesized monitors w.r.t. their specification is decidable, cf. Theorem 4.

Theorem 4 (Monitor correctness is decidable and monitor synthesis computable).
We assume canonical models of the form $\alpha \equiv \alpha_{ctrl};\alpha_{plant}$ without nested loops, with solvable differential equations in α_{plant} and disturbed plants $\alpha_{\delta plant}$ with constant additive disturbance δ (see Def. 2). Then, monitor correctness is decidable, i. e., the formulas $\chi_m \to \langle \alpha\rangle\Upsilon_V^+$, $\chi_c \to \langle \alpha_{ctrl}\rangle\Upsilon_V^+$, and $\chi_p \to \langle \alpha\rangle(\Upsilon_V^+ \wedge [\alpha_{\delta plant}]\phi)$ are decidable. Also, monitor synthesis is computable, i. e., the functions $synth_m : \langle \alpha\rangle\Upsilon_V^+ \mapsto \chi_m$, $synth_c : \langle \alpha_{ctrl}\rangle\Upsilon_V^+ \mapsto \chi_c$, and $synth_p : \langle \alpha\rangle(\Upsilon_V^+ \wedge [\alpha_{\delta plant}]\phi) \mapsto \chi_p$ are computable.

4 Evaluation

We developed a software prototype, integrated into our modeling tool Sphinx [24], to automate many of the described steps. The prototype generates χ_m, χ_c, and χ_p conjectures from hybrid programs, collects open sequents, and interacts with KeYmaera [34].

To evaluate our method, we created monitors for prior case studies of non-deterministic hybrid models of autonomous cars, train control systems, and robots (adaptive cruise control [18], intelligent speed adaptation [23], the European train control system [35], and ground robot collision avoidance [22]). Table 2 summarizes the evaluation. For the model, we list the dimension in terms of the number of function symbols and state variables, and the size of the safety proof (i. e., number of proof steps and branches). For the monitor, we list the dimension of the monitor conjecture in terms of the number of variables, compare the number of steps and open sequents when deriving the monitor using manual proof steps to apply Opt. 1 and fully automated w/o Opt. 1,

Table 2. Monitor complexity case studies

Case Study	Model		Monitor				
	dim.	proof size (branches)	dim.	steps (open seq.) w/ Opt. 1	steps (open seq.) auto	proof steps (branches)	size
χ_m Water tank	5	38 (4)	3	16 (2)	20 (2)	64 (5)	32
Cruise control [18]	11	969 (124)	7	127 (13)	597 (21)	19514 (1058)	1111
Speed limit [23]	9	410 (30)	6	487 (32)	5016 (126)	64311 (2294)	19850
χ_c Water tank	5	38 (4)	1	12 (2)	14 (2)	40 (3)	20
Cruise control [18]	11	969 (124)	7	83 (13)	518 (106)	5840 (676)	84
Robot [22]	14	3350 (225)	11	94 (10)	1210 (196)	26166 (2854)	121
ETCS safety [35]	16	193 (10)	13	162 (13)	359 (37)	16770 (869)	153
χ_p Water tank	8	80 (6)	1	135 (4)	N/A	307 (12)	43

http://www.cs.cmu.edu/~smitsch/resource/modelplex_study.zip

and the number of steps in the monitor correctness proof. Finally, we list the monitor size in terms of arithmetic, comparison, and logical operators in the monitor formula. Although the number of steps and open sequents differ significantly between manual interaction for Opt. 1 and fully automated synthesis, the synthesized monitors are logically equivalent. But applying Opt. 1 usually results in structurally simpler monitors, because the conjunction over a smaller number of open sequents (cf. Table 2) can still be simplified automatically. The model monitors for cruise control and speed limit control are significantly larger than the other monitors, because their size already prevents automated simplification by Mathematica. As future work, KeYmaera will be adapted to allow user-defined tactics in order to apply Opt. 1 automatically.

5 Related Work

Runtime verification and monitoring for finite state discrete systems has received significant attention (e. g., [9,14,20]). Other approaches monitor continuous-time signals (e. g., [10,26]). We focus on hybrid systems models of CPS to combine both.

Several tools for formal verification of hybrid systems are actively developed (e. g., SpaceEx [12], dReal [13], extended NuSMV/MathSat [6]). For monitor synthesis, however, ModelPlex crucially needs the rewriting capabilities and flexibility of (nested) $[\alpha]$ and $\langle\alpha\rangle$ modalities in d$\mathcal{L}$ [29] and KeYmaera [34]; it is thus an interesting question for future work if other tools could be adapted to ModelPlex.

Runtime verification is the problem of checking whether or not a trace produced by a program satisfies a particular formula (cf. [16]). In [40], a method for runtime verification of LTL formulas on abstractions of concrete traces of a flight data recorder is presented. The RV system for Java programs [21] predicts execution traces from actual traces to find concurrency errors offline (e. g., race conditions) even if the actual trace did not exhibit the error. We, instead, use prediction on the basis of disturbed plant models for *hybrid systems* at runtime to ensure safety for future behavior of the system and switch to a fail-safe fallback controller if necessary. Adaptive runtime verification [4] uses state estimation to reduce monitoring overhead by sampling while still maintaining accuracy with Hidden Markov Models, or more recently, particle filtering [15] to fill the sampling gaps. The authors present interesting ideas for managing the overhead of runtime monitoring, which could be beneficial to transfer into the hybrid systems world. The approach, however, focuses purely on the discrete part of CPS.

The Simplex architecture [36] (and related approaches, e. g., [1,3,17]) is a control system principle to switch between a highly reliable and an experimental controller at runtime. Highly reliable control modules are assumed to be verified with some other approach. Simplex focuses on switching when timing faults or violation of controller specification occur. Our method complements Simplex in that *(i)* it checks whether or not the current system execution fits the entire model, not just the controller; *(ii)* it systematically derives provably correct monitors for hybrid systems; *(iii)* it uses prediction to guarantee safety for future behavior of the system.

Further approaches with interesting insights on combined verification and monitor/controller synthesis for discrete systems include, for instance, [2,11].

Although the related approaches based on offline verification derive monitors and switching conditions from models, none of them validates whether or not the model is adequate for the current execution. Thus, they are vulnerable to deviation between the real world and the model. In summary, this paper addresses safety at runtime as follows:

- Unlike [36], who focus on timing faults and specification violations, we propose a systematic principle to derive monitors that react to any deviation from the model.
- Unlike [4,15,17,21], who focus on the discrete aspects of CPS, we use hybrid system models with differential equations to address controller and plant.
- Unlike [17,36], who assume that fail-safe controllers have been verified with some other approach and do not synthesize code, we can use the same technical approach (d$\mathcal{L}$) for verifying controllers and synthesizing provably correct monitors.
- ModelPlex combines the leight-weight monitors and runtime compliance of online runtime verification with the design time analysis of offline verification.
- ModelPlex synthesizes provably correct monitors, certified by a theorem prover
- To the best of our knowledge, our approach is the first to guarantee that verification results about a hybrid systems model transfer to a particular execution of the system by verified runtime validation. We detect deviation from the verified model when it first occurs and, given bounds, can guarantee safety with fail-safe fallback. Other approaches (e. g., [3,17,36]) assume the system perfectly complies with the model.

6 Conclusion

ModelPlex is a principle to build and verify high-assurance controllers for safety-critical computerized systems that interact physically with their environment. It guarantees that verification results about CPS models transfer to the real system by safeguarding against deviations from the verified model. Monitors created by ModelPlex are provably correct and check at runtime whether or not the actual behavior of a CPS complies with the verified model and its assumptions. Upon noncompliance, ModelPlex initiates fail-safe fallback strategies. In order to initiate those strategies early enough, ModelPlex uses prediction on the basis of disturbed plant models to check safety for the next control cycle. This way, ModelPlex ensures that verification results about a model of a CPS transfer to the actual system behavior at runtime.

Future research directions include extending ModelPlex with advanced $d\mathcal{L}$ proof rules for differential equations [31], so that differential equations without polynomial solutions, as we currently handle for prediction monitor synthesis, can be handled for model monitor synthesis as well. An interesting question for certification purposes is end-to-end verification from the model to the final machine code.

References

1. Aiello, A.M., Berryman, J.F., Grohs, J.R., Schierman, J.D.: Run-time assurance for advanced flight-critical control systems. In: AIAA Guidance, Nav. and Control Conf. AIAA (2010)
2. Alur, R., Bodík, R., Juniwal, G., Martin, M.M.K., Raghothaman, M., Seshia, S.A., Singh, R., Solar-Lezama, A., Torlak, E., Udupa, A.: Syntax-guided synthesis. In: FMCAD, pp. 1–17. IEEE (2013)
3. Bak, S., Greer, A., Mitra, S.: Hybrid cyberphysical system verification with Simplex using discrete abstractions. In: Caccamo, M. (ed.) IEEE Real-Time and Embedded Technology and Applications Symposium, pp. 143–152. IEEE Computer Society (2010)
4. Bartocci, E., Grosu, R., Karmarkar, A., Smolka, S.A., Stoller, S.D., Zadok, E., Seyster, J.: Adaptive runtime verification. In: Qadeer, S., Tasiran, S. (eds.) RV 2012. LNCS, vol. 7687, pp. 168–182. Springer, Heidelberg (2013)
5. Blech, J.O., Falcone, Y., Becker, K.: Towards certified runtime verification. In: Aoki, T., Taguchi, K. (eds.) ICFEM 2012. LNCS, vol. 7635, pp. 494–509. Springer, Heidelberg (2012)
6. Cimatti, A., Mover, S., Tonetta, S.: SMT-based scenario verification for hybrid systems. Formal Methods in System Design 42(1), 46–66 (2013)
7. Collins, G.E., Hong, H.: Partial cylindrical algebraic decomposition for quantifier elimination. J. Symb. Comput. 12(3), 299–328 (1991)
8. Daigle, M.J., Roychoudhury, I., Biswas, G., Koutsoukos, X.D., Patterson-Hine, A., Poll, S.: A comprehensive diagnosis methodology for complex hybrid systems: A case study on spacecraft power distribution systems. IEEE Transactions on Systems, Man, and Cybernetics, Part A 40(5), 917–931 (2010)
9. D'Angelo, B., Sankaranarayanan, S., Sánchez, C., Robinson, W., Finkbeiner, B., Sipma, H.B., Mehrotra, S., Manna, Z.: LOLA: Runtime monitoring of synchronous systems. In: TIME, pp. 166–174. IEEE Computer Society (2005)
10. Donzé, A., Ferrère, T., Maler, O.: Efficient robust monitoring for STL. In: Sharygina, N., Veith, H. (eds.) CAV 2013. LNCS, vol. 8044, pp. 264–279. Springer, Heidelberg (2013)
11. Ehlers, R., Finkbeiner, B.: Monitoring realizability. In: Khurshid, S., Sen, K. (eds.) RV 2011. LNCS, vol. 7186, pp. 427–441. Springer, Heidelberg (2012)
12. Frehse, G., et al.: SpaceEx: Scalable verification of hybrid systems. In: Gopalakrishnan, G., Qadeer, S. (eds.) CAV 2011. LNCS, vol. 6806, pp. 379–395. Springer, Heidelberg (2011)
13. Gao, S., Kong, S., Clarke, E.M.: dReal: An SMT solver for nonlinear theories over the reals. In: Bonacina, M.P. (ed.) CADE 2013. LNCS (LNAI), vol. 7898, pp. 208–214. Springer, Heidelberg (2013)
14. Havelund, K., Roşu, G.: Efficient monitoring of safety properties. STTT 6(2), 158–173 (2004)
15. Kalajdzic, K., Bartocci, E., Smolka, S.A., Stoller, S.D., Grosu, R.: Runtime verification with particle filtering. In: Legay, A., Bensalem, S. (eds.) RV 2013. LNCS, vol. 8174, pp. 149–166. Springer, Heidelberg (2013)
16. Leucker, M., Schallhart, C.: A brief account of runtime verification. J. Log. Algebr. Program. 78(5), 293–303 (2009)
17. Liu, X., Wang, Q., Gopalakrishnan, S., He, W., Sha, L., Ding, H., Lee, K.: ORTEGA: An efficient and flexible online fault tolerance architecture for real-time control systems. IEEE Trans. Industrial Informatics 4(4), 213–224 (2008)

18. Loos, S.M., Platzer, A., Nistor, L.: Adaptive cruise control: Hybrid, distributed, and now formally verified. In: Butler, M., Schulte, W. (eds.) FM 2011. LNCS, vol. 6664, pp. 42–56. Springer, Heidelberg (2011)

19. McIlraith, S.A., Biswas, G., Clancy, D., Gupta, V.: Hybrid systems diagnosis. In: Lynch, N.A., Krogh, B.H. (eds.) HSCC 2000. LNCS, vol. 1790, pp. 282–295. Springer, Heidelberg (2000)

20. Meredith, P.O., Jin, D., Griffith, D., Chen, F., Roşu, G.: An overview of the MOP runtime verification framework. STTT 14(3), 249–289 (2012)

21. Meredith, P., Roşu, G.: Runtime verification with the RV system. In: Barringer, H., et al. (eds.) RV 2010. LNCS, vol. 6418, pp. 136–152. Springer, Heidelberg (2010)

22. Mitsch, S., Ghorbal, K., Platzer, A.: On provably safe obstacle avoidance for autonomous robotic ground vehicles. In: Robotics: Science and Systems (2013)

23. Mitsch, S., Loos, S.M., Platzer, A.: Towards formal verification of freeway traffic control. In: Lu, C. (ed.) ICCPS, pp. 171–180. IEEE (2012)

24. Mitsch, S., Passmore, G.O., Platzer, A.: Collaborative verification-driven engineering of hybrid systems. J. Math. in Computer Science (2014)

25. Mitsch, S., Platzer, A.: ModelPlex: Verified runtime validation of verified cyber-physical system models. Tech. Rep. CMU-CS-14-121, Carnegie Mellon (2014)

26. Nickovic, D., Maler, O.: AMT: A property-based monitoring tool for analog systems. In: Raskin, J.-F., Thiagarajan, P.S. (eds.) FORMATS 2007. LNCS, vol. 4763, pp. 304–319. Springer, Heidelberg (2007)

27. Platzer, A.: Differential dynamic logic for hybrid systems. J. Autom. Reas. 41(2), 143–189 (2008)

28. Platzer, A.: Differential-algebraic dynamic logic for differential-algebraic programs. J. Log. Comput. 20(1), 309–352 (2010); advance access published on November 18, 2008

29. Platzer, A.: Logical Analysis of Hybrid Systems. Springer (2010)

30. Platzer, A.: The structure of differential invariants and differential cut elimination. Logical Methods in Computer Science 8(4) (2011)

31. Platzer, A.: The complete proof theory of hybrid systems. In: LICS. IEEE (2012)

32. Platzer, A.: Logics of dynamical systems. In: LICS, pp. 13–24. IEEE (2012)

33. Platzer, A., Clarke, E.M.: The image computation problem in hybrid systems model checking. In: Bemporad, A., Bicchi, A., Buttazzo, G. (eds.) HSCC 2007. LNCS, vol. 4416, pp. 473–486. Springer, Heidelberg (2007)

34. Platzer, A., Quesel, J.-D.: KeYmaera: A hybrid theorem prover for hybrid systems. In: Armando, A., Baumgartner, P., Dowek, G. (eds.) IJCAR 2008. LNCS (LNAI), vol. 5195, pp. 171–178. Springer, Heidelberg (2008)

35. Platzer, A., Quesel, J.-D.: European Train Control System: A case study in formal verification. In: Breitman, K., Cavalcanti, A. (eds.) ICFEM 2009. LNCS, vol. 5885, pp. 246–265. Springer, Heidelberg (2009)

36. Seto, D., Krogh, B., Sha, L., Chutinan, A.: The Simplex architecture for safe online control system upgrades. In: American Control Conference, pp. 3504–3508 (1998)

37. Shannon, C.: Communication in the presence of noise. Proc. of the IRE 37(1), 10–21 (1949)

38. Srivastava, A.N., Schumann, J.: Software health management: a necessity for safety critical systems. ISSE 9(4), 219–233 (2013)

39. Wang, D., Yu, M., Low, C.B., Arogeti, S.: Model-based Health Monitoring of Hybrid Systems. Springer (2013)

40. Wang, S., Ayoub, A., Sokolsky, O., Lee, I.: Runtime verification of traces under recording uncertainty. In: Khurshid, S., Sen, K. (eds.) RV 2011. LNCS, vol. 7186, pp. 442–456. Springer, Heidelberg (2012)

41. Zhao, F., Koutsoukos, X.D., Haussecker, H.W., Reich, J., Cheung, P.: Monitoring and fault diagnosis of hybrid systems. IEEE Transactions on Systems, Man, and Cybernetics, Part B 35(6), 1225–1240 (2005)

Runtime Observer Pairs and Bayesian Network Reasoners On-board FPGAs: Flight-Certifiable System Health Management for Embedded Systems*

Johannes Geist[1], Kristin Y. Rozier[2], and Johann Schumann[3]

[1] USRA/RIACS, Mountain View, CA, USA
jgeist@usra.edu
[2] NASA ARC, Moffett Field, CA, USA
Kristin.Y.Rozier@nasa.gov
[3] SGT, Inc., NASA Ames, Moffett Field, CA, USA
Johann.M.Schumann@nasa.gov

Abstract. Safety-critical systems, like Unmanned Aerial Systems (UAS) that must operate totally autonomously, e.g., to support ground-based emergency services, must also provide assurance they will not endanger human life or property in the air or on the ground. Previously, a theoretical construction for paired synchronous and asynchronous runtime observers with Bayesian reasoning was introduced that demonstrated the ability to handle runtime assurance within the strict operational constraints to which the system must adhere. In this paper, we show how to instantiate and implement temporal logic runtime observers and Bayesian network diagnostic reasoners that use the observers' outputs, on-board a field-standard Field Programmable Gate Array (FPGA) in a way that satisfies the strict flight operational standards of REALIZABILITY, RESPONSIVENESS, and UNOBTRUSIVENESS. With this type of compositionally constructed diagnostics framework we can develop compact, hierarchical, and highly expressive health management models for efficient, on-board fault detection and system monitoring. We describe an instantiation of our System Health Management (SHM) framework, rt-R2U2, on standard FPGA hardware, which is suitable to be deployed on-board a UAS. We run our system with a full set of real flight data from NASA's Swift UAS, and highlight a case where our runtime SHM framework would have been able to detect and diagnose a fault from subtle evidence that initially eluded traditional real-time diagnosis procedures.

1 Introduction

Totally autonomous systems operating in hazardous environments save human lives. In order to operate, they must both be able to intelligently react to unknown environments to carry out their missions and adhere to safety regulations to prevent causing harm.

---

* Additional artifacts to enable reproducibility are available at http://research.kristinrozier.com/RV14.html. This work was supported in part by ARMD 2014 Seedling Phase I and Universities Space Research Association under NASA Cooperative Agreement, International Research Initiative for Innovation in Aerospace Methods and Technologies (I3AMT), NNX12AK33A.

B. Bonakdarpour and S.A. Smolka (Eds.): RV 2014, LNCS 8734, pp. 215–230, 2014.

NASA's Swift Unmanned Aerial System (UAS) [6] is tasked with intelligently mapping California wildfires for maximally effective deployment of fire-fighting resources yet faces obstacles to deployment, i.e., from the FAA because it must also provably avoid harming any people or property in the air or on the ground in case of off-nominal conditions. Similar challenges are faced by NASA's Viking Sierra-class UAS, tasked with low-ceiling earthquake surveillance, as well as many other autonomous vehicles, UAS, rovers, and satellites. To provide assurance that these vehicles will not cause any harm during their missions, we propose a framework designed to deliver runtime System Health Management (SHM) [7] while adhering to strict operational constraints, all aboard a low-cost, dedicated, and separate FPGA; FPGAs are standard components used in such vehicles. We name our framework **rt-R2U2** after these constraints:

real-time: SHM must detect and diagnose faults in real time during any mission.

REALIZABLE: We must utilize existing on-board hardware (here an FPGA) providing a generic interface to connect a wide variety of systems to our plug-and-play framework that can efficiently monitor different requirements during different mission stages, e.g., deployment, measurement, and return. New specifications do not require lengthy recompilation and we use an intuitive, expressive specification language; we require real-time projections of Linear Temporal Logic (LTL) since operational concepts for UASs and other autonomous vehicles are most frequently mapped over timelines.

RESPONSIVE: We must continuously monitor the system, detecting any deviations from the specifications within a tight and a priori known time bound and enabling mitigation or rescue measures. This includes reporting intermediate status and satisfaction of timed requirements as early as possible and utilizing them for efficient decision making.

UNOBTRUSIVE: We must not alter any crucial properties of the system, use commercial-off-the-shelf (COTS) components to avoid altering cost, and above all not alter any hardware or software components in such a way as to lose flight-certifiability, which limits us to read-only access to the data from COTS components. In particular, we must not alter functionality, behavior, timing, time or budget constraints, or tolerances, e.g., for size, weight, power, or telemetry bandwidth.

Unit: The rt-R2U2 is a self-contained unit.

Previously, we defined a compositional design for combining building blocks consisting of paired temporal logic observers; Boolean functions; data filters, such as smoothing, Kalman, or FFT; and Bayesian reasoners for achieving these goals [17]. We require the temporal logic observer pairs for efficient temporal reasoning but since temporal monitors don't make decisions, Bayesian reasoning is required in conjunction with our temporal logic observer pairs in order to enable the decisions required by this safety-critical system. We designed and proved correct a method of synthesizing paired temporal logic observers to monitor, both synchronously and asynchronously, the system safety requirements and feed this output into Bayesian network (BN) reasoner back ends to enable intelligent handling and mitigation of any off-nominal operational conditions [15]. In this paper, we show how to create those BN back ends and how to efficiently encode the entire rt-R2U2 runtime monitoring framework on-board a standard FPGA to enable intelligent runtime SHM within our strict operational constraints. We demonstrate that our implementation can significantly outperform expert human operators by running it in a hardware-supported simulation with real flight data from a test flight of the Swift UAS during which a fluxgate magnetometer malfunction caused a hard-to-diagnose failure that grounded the flight test for 48 hours, a costly disturbance in terms of both time and money. Had rt-R2U2 been running on-board during the flight test it would have diagnosed this malfunction in real time and kept the UAS flying.

1.1   Related Work

While there has been promising work in Bayesian reasoning for probabilistic diagnosis via efficient data structures in software [16,18], this does not meet our UNOBTRU-SIVENESS requirement to avoid altering software or our REALIZABILITY requirement because it does not allow efficient reasoning over temporal traces. For that, we need dynamic Bayes Nets, which are much more complex and necessarily cannot be RE-SPONSIVE in real time.

There is a wealth of promising temporal-logic runtime monitoring techniques in software, including automata-based, low-overhead techniques, i.e., [5,19]. The success of these techniques inspires our research question: how do we achieve the same efficient, low-overhead runtime monitoring results, but in hardware since we cannot modify system software without losing flight certifiability? Perhaps the most pertinent is Copilot [14], which generates constant-time and constant-space C programs implementing hard real-time monitors, satisfying our RESPONSIVENESS requirement. Copilot is unobtrusive in that it does not alter functionality, schedulability, certifiability, size, weight, or power, but the software implementation still violates our strict UNOBTRUSIVENESS requirement by executing software. Copilot provides only sampling-based runtime monitoring whereas rt-R2U2 provides complete SHM including BN reasoning.

BusMOP [13,10] is perhaps most similar to our rt-R2U2 framework. Exactly like rt-R2U2, BusMOP achieves zero runtime overhead via a bus-interface and an implementation on a reconfigurable FPGA and monitors COTS peripherals. However, Bus-MOP only reports property failure and (at least at present) does not handle future-time logic, whereas we require early-as-possible reporting of future-time temporal properties passing and intermediate status updates. The time elapsed from any event that triggers a property resolution to executing the corresponding handler is up to 4 clock cycles for BusMOP whereas rt-R2U2 always reports in 1 clock cycle. Most importantly, although BusMOP can monitor multiple properties at once, it handles diagnosis on a single-property-monitoring basis, executing arbitrary user-supplied code on the occurrence of any property violation whereas rt-R2U2 performs SHM on a system level, synthesizing BN reasoners that utilize the passage, failure, and intermediate status of multiple properties to assess overall system health and reason about conditions that require many properties to diagnose. Also rt-R2U2 never allows execution of arbitrary code as that would violate UNOBTRUSIVENESS, particularly flight certifiability requirements.

The gNOSIS [8] framework also utilizes FPGAs, but assesses FPGA implementations, mines assertions either from simulation or hardware traces, and synthesizes LTL into, sometimes very large, Finite State Machines that take time to be re-synthesized between missions, violating our REALIZABILITY requirement. Its high bandwidth, automated probe insertion, ability to change timing properties of the system, and low sample-rate violate our UNOBTRUSIVENESS and RESPONSIVENESS requirements, though gNOSIS may be valuable for design-time checking of rt-R2U2 in the future.

1.2 Contributions

We define hardware, FPGA encodings for both the temporal logic runtime observer pairs proposed in [15] and the special BN reasoning units required to process their three-valued output for diagnostics and decision-making. We detail novel FPGA implementations within a specific architecture to exhibit the strengths of an FPGA implementation in hardware in order to fulfill our strict operational requirements; this construction incurs zero runtime overhead. We provide a specialized construction rather than the standard "algorithm-rewrite-in-VHDL" that may be acceptable for less-constrained systems. We provide timing and performance data showing reproducible evidence that our new rt-R2U2 implementation performs within our required parameters of REALIZABILITY, RESPONSIVENESS, and UNOBTRUSIVENESS in real time. Finally, we highlight implementation challenges to provide instructive value for others looking to reproduce our work, i.e., implementing theoretically proven temporal logic observer constructions on a real-world UAS. Using full-scale, real flight test data streams from NASA's Swift UAS, we demonstrate this real-time execution and prove that rt-R2U2 would have pinpointed in real time a subtle buffer overflow issue that grounded the flight test and stumped human experts for two days in real life.

This paper is organized as follows: Section 2 provides the reader with theoretical principles of our approach. Section 3 provides an overview of the various parts and Sections 4 and 5 give more details about the hardware implementation. A real-world test case of NASA's Swift UAS is evaluated in Section 6. Section 7 concludes this paper with a summary of our findings.

2 Preliminaries

Our system health models are comprised of paired temporal observers, sensor filters, and Bayesian network probabilistic reasoners, all encoded on-board an FPGA; see [17] for a detailed system-level overview.

2.1 Temporal-Logic Based Runtime Observer Pairs [15]

We encode system specifications in real-time projections of LTL. Specifically, we use Metric Temporal Logic (MTL), which replaces the temporal operators of LTL with operators that respect time bounds [1] and mission-time LTL [15], which reduces to MTL with all operator bounds being between now (i.e., time 0) and the mission termination time.

Definition 1 (Discrete-Time MTL [15]). *For atomic proposition* $\sigma \in \Sigma$, σ *is a formula. Let time bound* $J = [t, t']$ *with* $t, t' \in \mathbb{N}_0$. *If* φ *and* ψ *are formulas, then so are:*

$$\neg\varphi \mid \varphi \wedge \psi \mid \varphi \vee \psi \mid \varphi \rightarrow \psi \mid \mathcal{X}\varphi \mid \varphi \mathcal{U}_J \psi \mid \Box_J\varphi \mid \Diamond_J\varphi.$$

Time bounds are specified as intervals: for $t, t' \in \mathbb{N}_0$, we write $[t, t']$ for the set $\{i \in \mathbb{N}_0 \mid t \le i \le t'\}$. We interpret MTL formulas over executions of the form

$e : \omega \rightarrow 2^{Prop}$; we define φ *holds at time* n *of execution* e, denoted $e^n \models \varphi$, inductively as follows:

$$e^n \models true \qquad \text{is } \textbf{true}, \qquad\qquad e^n \models \sigma \qquad \text{iff } \sigma \text{ holds in } s_n,$$

$$e^n \models \neg\varphi \quad \text{iff } e^n \nvDash \varphi, \qquad\qquad e^n \models \varphi \wedge \psi \text{ iff } e^n \models \varphi \text{ and } e^n \models \psi,$$

$$e^n \models \mathcal{X}\varphi \quad \text{iff } e^{n+1} \models \varphi, \qquad\qquad e^n \models \varphi \vee \psi \text{ iff } e^n \models \varphi \text{ or } e^n \models \psi,$$

$$e^n \models \varphi \, \mathcal{U}_J \, \psi \text{ iff } \exists i (i \geq n) : (i - n \in J \wedge e^i \models \psi \wedge \forall j (n \leq j < i) : \; e^j \models \varphi).$$

Since systems in our application domain are usually bounded to a certain mission time $\tau \in \mathbb{N}_0$, we also encode *mission-time LTL* [15]. For a formula φ in LTL, we create mission-bounded formula φ_m by replacing every $\square$, $\Diamond$, and $\mathcal{U}$ operator in φ with its bounded MTL equivalent using the bounds $J = [0, \tau]$. An execution sequence for an MTL formula φ, denoted by $\langle T_\varphi \rangle$, is a sequence of tuples $T_\varphi = (v, \tau_e)$ where $\tau_e \in \mathbb{N}_0$ is a time stamp and $v \in \{\textbf{true}, \textbf{false}, \textbf{maybe}\}$ is a verdict.

For every temporal logic system specification, we synthesize a pair of runtime observers, one asynchronous and one synchronous, using the construction defined and proved correct in [15]. *Asynchronous observers* are *evaluated with every new input*, in this case with every tick of the system clock. For every generated output tuple T we have that $T.v \in \{\textbf{true}, \textbf{false}\}$ and $T.\tau_e \in [0, n]$. Since verdicts are exact evaluations of a future-time specification φ, for each clock tick they may resolve φ for clock ticks prior to the current time n if the information required for this resolution was not available until n. *Synchronous observers* are *evaluated at every tick of the system clock* and their output tuples T are guaranteed to be synchronous to the current time stamp n. Thus, for each time n, a synchronous observer outputs a tuple T with $T.\tau_e = n$. This eliminates the need for synchronization queues. Outputs of these observers are three-valued verdicts: $T.v \in \{\textbf{true}, \textbf{false}, \textbf{maybe}\}$ depending on whether we can concretely valuate that the observed formula holds at this time point (**true**), does not hold (**false**), or cannot be evaluated due to insufficient information (**maybe**). Verdicts of **maybe** are later resolved concretely by the matching asynchronous observers in the first clock tick when sufficient information is available.

2.2 Bayesian Networks for Health Models

In order to maximize the reasoning power of our health management system, we use Bayesian networks (BN). BNs have been well established in the area of diagnostic and health management (e.g., [12,9]) as they can cope with conflicting sensor signals and priors. BNs are directed acyclic graphs, where each node represents a statistical variable. Directed edges between nodes correspond to (local) conditional dependencies. For our health models, we are using BNs of a general structure as shown in Figure 1A. We do not use dynamic BNs, because all temporal aspects are being dealt with by the temporal observers described above. Discrete sensor signals or outputs of the synchronous temporal observers (**true, false, maybe**) are clamped to the "sensor" and "command" nodes of the BN as observable. Since sensors can fail, they have (unobservable) health nodes attached. As priors, these health nodes can contain information on how reliable the component is, e.g., by using a Mean Time To Failure (MTTF) metric.

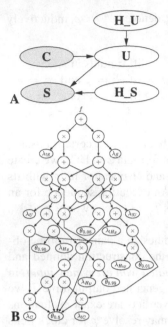

Fig. 1. A: BN for Health management. **B:** Arithmetic circuit

Unobservable nodes U may describe the behavior of the system or component as it is defined and influenced by the sensor or software information. Often, such nodes are used to define a mode or state of the system. For example, it is likely that the UAS is climbing if the altimeter sensor says "altitude increasing." Such (desired) behavior can also be affected by faults, so behavior nodes have health nodes attached. For details of modeling see [16]. The local conditional dependencies are stored in the Conditional Probability Table (CPT) of each node. For example, the CPT of the sensor node S defines its probabilities given its dependencies: $P(S|U, H\_S)$.

In our health management system, we, at each time stamp, calculate the posterior probabilities of the BN's health nodes, given the sensor and command values e as evidence. The probability $Pr(H\_S = good|\mathbf{e})$ gives an indication of the status of the sensor or component. Reasoning in real-time avionics applications requires aligning resource consumption of diagnostic computations with tight resource bounds [11]. We are therefore using a representation of BNs that is based upon arithmetic circuits (AC), which are directed acyclic graphs where leaf nodes represent indicators (λ in Fig. 1) and parameters (θ) while all other nodes represent addition and multiplication operators. AC based reasoning algorithms are powerful, as they provide predictable real-time performance [2,9].

The AC is factually a compact encoding of the joint distribution into a network polynomial [3]. The marginal probability (see Corollary 1 in [3]) for a variable x given evidence e can then be calculated as $Pr(x | \mathbf{e}) = \frac{1}{Pr(\mathbf{e})} \cdot \frac{\partial f}{\partial \lambda_x}(\mathbf{e})$ where $Pr(\mathbf{e})$ is the probability of the evidence. In a first, bottom-up pass, the λ indicators are clamped according to the evidence and the probability of this particular evidence setting is evaluated. A subsequent top-down pass over the circuit computes the partial derivatives $\frac{\partial f}{\partial \lambda_x}$. Based upon the structure of the AC, this algorithm only requires —except for the final division by $Pr(\mathbf{e})$— only additions and multiplications. Since the structure of the AC is determined at compile time, a fixed, reproducible timing behavior can be guaranteed.

2.3 Digital Design 101 and FPGAs

Integrated circuits (ICs) have come a long way from the first analog, vacuum tube-based switching circuits, over discrete semiconductors to sub-micron feature size for modern ICs. Our ability to implement rt-R2U2 in hardware is strongly based upon high-level hardware definition languages and tools to describe the functionality of the hardware design, and FPGAs, which make it possible to "instantiate" the hardware on-the-fly without having to go through costly silicon wafer production.

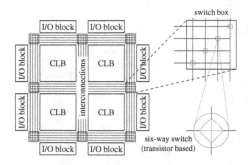

Fig. 2. Simplified representation of a modern FPGA architecture

VHDL - Very High Speed Integrated Circuit Hardware Definition Language. This type-safe programming language allows the concise description of concurrent systems, supporting the inherent nature of any IC. Therefore, programming paradigms are substantially different from software programming languages, e.g., memory usage and mapping has to be considered explicitly and algorithms with loops have to be rewritten into finite state machines. In general, a lot more time and effort has to be put into system design.

FPGA - Field Programmable Gate Array is a fast, cheap, and efficient way to produce a custom-designed digital system or prototype. Basically an FPGA consists of logic cells (Figure 2), that can be programmed according to its intended use. A modern FPGA is composed of three main parts *Configurable Logic Blocks* (CLBs), long and short *interconnections* with six-way programmable switches, and *I/O blocks*. The CLBs are elementary Look Up Tables (LUTs) where, depending on the input values, a certain output value is presented to the next cell. Hence, every possible combination of unary operations can be programmed. Complex functionality can be achieved by connecting different CLBs using short (between neighboring cells) and long interconnections. These interconnections need the most space on an FPGA, because in general every cell can be connected to every other cell. The I/O cells are also connected to this interconnection grid. To be able to route the signals in all directions there is a "switch box" on every intersection. This six-way switch is based on 6 transistors that can be programmed to route the interconnection accordingly. In order to achieve higher performance modern FPGAs have hardwired blocks for certain generic or complex operations (adder, memory, multiplier, I/O transceiver, etc.).

3 System Overview

Our system health models are constructed based upon information extracted from system requirements, sensor schematics, and specifications of expected behaviors, which are usually written in natural language. In a manual process (Figure 3) we develop the health model in our framework, which is comprised of temporal components (LTL and MTL specifications), Bayesian networks (BNs), and signal processing. Our tool chain compiles the individual parts and produces binary files, which, after linking, are downloaded to the FPGA. The actual hardware architecture, which is defined in VHDL, is compiled using a commercial tool chain[1] and used to configure the FPGA. This lengthy process, which can take more than 1 hour on a high-performance workstation needs to be carried out only once, since it is independent of the actual health model.

---

[1] http://www.xilinx.com/products/design-tools/ise-design-suite/index.htm

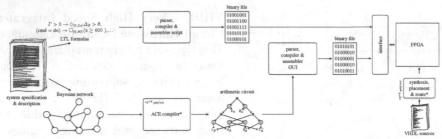

Fig. 3. rt-R2U2 software tool chain

3.1 Software

The software tool chain for creating the code for the temporal logic specifications is straightforward and only translates the given formulas to a binary representation with mapping information. Significantly more effort goes into preparing a BN for our system. First, the given network is translated into an optimized arithmetic circuit (AC) using the Ace[2] tool. Then, the resulting AC must be compiled and mapped for efficient execution on the FPGA. This process, which will be described in more detail in Section 5, is controlled with a Java GUI.

3.2 Hardware

The hardware architecture (Figure 4A) of our implementation is built out of three components: the *control subsystem*, the *runtime verification* (RV) unit, and the *runtime reasoning* (RR) unit. Whereas the control subsystem establishes the communication link to the external world (e.g., to load health models and to receive health results), the RV and RR units comprise the proper health management hardware, which we will discuss in detail in the subsequent sections. Any sensor and software data passed along the Swift UAS bus can be directly fed into the signals' filters and pre-processing modules of the *atChecker*, which are a part of the RV unit, where they are converted into streams of Boolean values.

Our architecture is designed in such a way that its requirements with respect to gates and look-up tables only depend on the number of signals we monitor, not on the temporal logic formulas or the Bayesian networks. In the configuration used for our case study (with 12 signals), the monitoring device synthesized for the Xilinx Virtex 5 XC5VFX130T FPGA needed 28849 registers, 24450 look-up tables, 63 blocks of RAM, and 25 digital signal processing units. These numbers clearly strongly depend on the architecture of the FPGA, and, in our case used 35% of the registers, 29% of the LUTs, 21% of the RAM, and 7% of the DSP blocks.

The runtime verification subsystem evaluates the compiled temporal logic formulas over the Boolean signals prepared by the atChecker. Since evaluations of the past-time variations of our logics (MTL and mission-time LTL) are naturally synchronous, we can essentially duplicate the synchronous observer construction, but with past-time evaluation, to add support for past-time formulas should they prove useful in the context of the

---

[2] http://reasoning.cs.ucla.edu/ace/

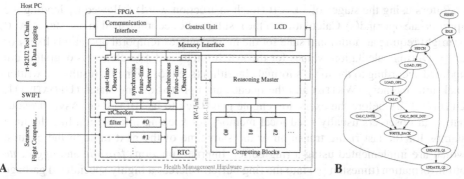

Fig. 4. A: Overview of the rt-R2U2 architecture. **B:** FSM for the ftObserver

system specifications. Depending on the type of logic encoding each individual formula (past or future time), it is either evaluated by the past-time or future-time subsystem. As the algorithms are fundamentally different for the two time domains we use two separate entities in the FPGA. A real time clock (RTC) establishes a global time domain and provides a time base for evaluating the temporal logic formulas.

After the temporal logic formulas have been evaluated, the results are transferred to the runtime reasoning (RR) subsystem, where the compiled Bayesian network is evaluated to yield the posterior marginals of the health model. For easier debugging and evaluation, a memory dump of the past and future time results as well as of the posterior marginals has been implemented. After each execution cycle, the evaluation is paused and the memory dump is transferred to the host PC for further analysis.

4   FPGA Implementation of MTL/Mission-Time LTL

As shown in Figure 4A, incoming sensor and software signals, which consist of vectors of binary fixed-point numbers, are first processed and discretized by the atChecker unit. This hardware component can contain filters to smooth the signal, Fast Fourier Transforms, or Kalman Filters, and performs scaling and comparison operations to yield a Boolean value. Each discretizer block can process one or two signals s_1, s_2 according to $(\pm 2^{p_1} \times F_1^2(F_1^1(s_1)) \pm 2^{p_2} \times F_2^2(F_2^1(s_2))) \bowtie c$ for integer constants p_1, p_2, and c, filters F_j^i, and a comparison operator $\bowtie \in \{=, <, \leq, \geq, >, \neq\}$. For example, the discrete signal "UAS is at least 400ft above ground" would be specified by: $(mvg\_avg(alt_{UAS}) - alt_{gnd}) > 400$, where the altitude measurements of the UAS would be smoothed out by a moving average filter before the altitude of the ground is subtracted. Note that several blocks can be necessary for thresholding, e.g., to determine if the UAS is above 400ft, 1000ft, or 5000ft.

Each temporal logic processing unit (ptObserver, ftObserver) is implemented as a processor, which executes the compiled formulas instruction by instruction. It contains its own program and data memory, and finite-state-machine (FSM) based execution unit (Figure 4B[3]). Individual instructions process Boolean operators and temporal logic

---

[3] The architecture and FSM for processing the past time fragment is similar to this unit and thus will not be discussed here.

operators using the stages of FETCH (fetch instruction word) followed by loading the appropriate operand(s). Calculation of the result can be accomplished in one step (CALC) or might require an additional state for the more complex temporal operations like $\mathcal{U}$ or $\Box_{[.,.]}$. During calculation, values for the synchronous and asynchronous operators are updated according to the logic's formal algorithm (see [15]). Finally, results are written back into memory (WRITE) and the queues are updated during states (UPDATE_Q1, UPDATE_Q2), before the execution engine goes back to its IDLE state. Asynchronous temporal observers usually need local memory for keeping information like the time stamps for the last rising transition or the start time of the next tuple in the queues, which are implemented using a ring buffer. Internal functions *feasible* and *aggregate* put information (timestamps) into the ring buffer, whereas a highly specialized garbage collecting function removes time stamps that can no longer contribute to the validity of the formula, thus keeping memory requirements low. These updates to the queues happen during the UPDATE states of the processor ([15]).

In contrast to asynchronous observers, which require additional memory for keeping internal history information, *synchronous* observers are realized as memoryless Boolean networks. Their three-valued logic {**false**, **true**, **maybe**} is encoded in two binary signals as $\langle 0, 0 \rangle$, $\langle 0, 1 \rangle$, and $\langle 1, 0 \rangle$, respectively.

Let us consider the following specification, which expresses that the UAS, after receiving the takeoff command must reach an altitude alt above ground of at least 600ft within 40 seconds: cmd = takeoff $\rightarrow \Diamond_{[0,40s]}(alt \geq 600)$. Obviously, synchronous and asynchronous observers report **true** before the takeoff. After takeoff, the synchronous observer immediately returns **maybe** until the 40-second time window has expired or the altitude exceeds 600ft, whichever comes first. Then the formula can be decided to yield **true** or **false**. In contrast, the asynchronous observer always yields the concrete valuation of the formula, **true** or **false**, for every time stamp; however this result (which is always tagged with a time stamp) might retroactively resolve an earlier point in time.

For rt-R2U2, both types of observers are important. Whereas asynchronous observers guarantee the concrete result but might refer to an earlier system state, synchronous observers immediately yield some information, which can be used by the Bayesian network to disambiguate failures. In our example, this information can be used to express that, with a certain (albeit unknown) probability, the UAS still can reach the desired target in time, but hasn't done so yet. Our Bayesian health models can reflect that fact by using three-valued sensor and command nodes.

5   FPGA Implementation of Bayesian Networks

The BN reasoning has been implemented on the FPGA as a Multiple Instruction, Multiple Data (MIMD) architecture. This means that every processing unit calculates a part of the AC using its individual data and program memory. That way, a high degree of parallelism can be exploited and we can obtain a high performance and low latency evaluation unit. Therefore, our architectural design process led to a simple, tightly coupled hardware architecture, which relies on optimized instructions provided by the BN compiler (Figure 3). The underlying idea of this architecture is to partition the entire arithmetic circuit into small parts of constant size, which in turn are processed by a

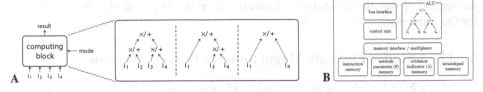

Fig. 5. A: A computing block and its three modes of operation. **B:** Internals of a computing block.

number of parallel execution units with the goal of minimizing inter-processor data exchanges and synchronization delays. We will first describe the hardware architecture and then focus on the partitioning algorithm in the BN compiler.

BN Computing Block. We designed an elementary BN processor (BN computing block) that can process three different kinds of small "elementary" arithmetic circuits. A number of identical copies (the number depends on the size of the FPGA) of these computing blocks work as slaves in a master-slave configuration. Figure 5A shows the three different patterns. Each pattern consists of up to three arithmetic operators (addition or multiplication) and can have 2, 3, or 4 inputs. Such a small pattern can be efficiently executed by a BN computing block. Figure 5B shows a BN computing block, which is built from several separate hardware units (bus interface, local memory, instruction decoder, ALU, etc.). On an abstract level the calculation is based on a generic four-stage pipeline execution (FETCH, DECODE, CALCULATE, and WRITE-BACK). To achieve this performance-focused behavior, each subsystem runs independently. Therefore, a handshake synchronizing protocol between each internal component is used. As a MIMD processor, each BN computing block keeps its own instruction memory as well as local storage for network parameters and evidence indicators. A local scratchpad memory is used to store intermediate results.

Although probabilities are best represented using floating-point numbers according to IEEE 754, we chose to use an 18-bit fixed-point representation, because floating-point ALUs are resource-intensive in terms of both number of logic gates used and power, and would drastically reduce the number of available parallel BN computing blocks. Our chosen resolution is based on the 18-bit hardware multiplier that is available on our Xilinx Virtex 5 FPGA. We achieve a resolution of $2^{-18} = 3.8 \cdot 10^{-6}$, which is sufficient for our purposes to represent probability values.

All slave processors are connected via a bus to the BN master processor. Besides programming, data handling, and controlling their execution, the master also calculates the final result $Pr(x \mid e) = \frac{1}{Pr(e)} \cdot \frac{\partial f}{\partial \lambda_x}(e)$, because the resources needed to perform the division are comparatively high and therefore not replicated over the slave processors.

Mapping of AC to BN computing units. Our software tool chain tries to achieve an optimal mapping of the AC to the different BN computation units during compile time, using a pattern-matching-based algorithm. We "tile" the entire AC with the three small patterns (Figure 5A) in such a way that the individual BN processing units operate as parallel as possible and communication and data transfer is reduced to a minimum. For this task, we use a Bellman-Ford algorithm to obtain the optimal placement. Furthermore, all scheduling information (internal reloads and communication on the hardware bus to exchange data with other computing blocks) as well as the configuration for the master and probability values for the Conditional Probability Table (CPT) are prepared for the framework.

6   Case Study: Fluxgate Magnetometer Buffer Overflow

In 2012, a NASA flight test of the Swift UAS was grounded for 48 hours as system engineers worked to diagnose an unexpected problem with the UAS that ceased vital data transmissions to the ground. All data of the scientific sensors on the UAS (e.g., laser altimeter, magnetometer, etc.) were collected by the Common Payload System (CPS). The fluxgate magnetometer (FG), which measures strength and direction of the Earth's magnetic field, had previously failed and was replaced before the flight test. System engineers eventually determined that the replacement was not configured correctly; firmware on-board the fluxgate magnetometer was sending data to its internal transmit buffer at high speed although the intended speed of communication with the CPS was 9600 baud. As the rate was set to a higher value and the software in the magnetometer did not catch this error, internal buffer overflows started to occur, resulting in an increasing number of corrupted packets sent to the CPS. This misconfiguration in the data flow was very difficult to deduce by engineers on the ground because they had to investigate the vast number of possible scenarios that could halt data transmission.

In this case study, we use the original data as recorded by the Swift Flight Computer (FC) and the CPS. At this time, no publicly available report on this test flight has been published; the tests and their resulting data are identified within NASA by the date and location, Surprise Valley, California on May 8, 2012, starting at 7:50 am. With our rt-R2U2 architecture, which continuously monitors our standard set of rates, ranges, and relationships for the on-board sensors, we have been able to diagnose this problem in real-time, and could have avoided the costly delay in the flight tests.

The available recorded data are time series of continuous and discrete sensor and status data for navigational, sensor, and system components. From the multitude of signals, we selected, for the purpose of this case study, the signals shown in Table 1. We denote the total number of packets from the FG with $N_{tot} = N_g + N_b$; $X^R = X^t - X^{t-1}$ is the rate of signal X, and X^N denotes the normalized vector X.

Table 1. Signals and sources used in this health model, sampled with a 1Hz sampling rate

Signal	description	Source
N_g	number of good FG packets since start of mission	CPS
N_b	number of bad FG packets since start of mission	CPS
E^{log}	logging event	CPS
$FG_{x,y,z}$	directional fluxgate magnetometer reading	CPS
$Hd_{x,y}$	aircraft heading	FC
p, q, r	pitch, roll, and yaw rate	FC

6.1   The Bayesian Health Model

The results of the temporal specifications $S_1, \ldots, S_6$ alone are not sufficient to disambiguate the different failure modes. We are using the Bayesian network as shown in

Table 2. Temporal formula specifications that are translated into paired runtime observers for the fluxgate magnetometer (FG) health model

Description	Formula
S_1: The FG packet transmission rate N_{tot}^R is appropriate: about 64 per second.	$63 \leq N_{tot}^R \leq 66$
S_2: The number of bad packets N_b^R is low, no more than one bad packet every 30 seconds.	$\square_{[0,30]}(N_b^R = 0 \vee (N_b^R \geq 1 \, \mathcal{U}_{[0,30]} N_b^R = 0))$
S_3: The bad packet rate N_b^R does not appear to be increasing; we do not see a pattern of three bad packets within a short period of time.	$\neg(\Diamond_{[0,30]} N_b^R \geq 2 \wedge \Diamond_{[0,100]} N_b^R \geq 3)$
S_4: The FG sensor is working, i.e., the data appears good. Here, we use a simple, albeit noisy sanity check by monitoring if the aircraft heading vector with respect to the x and y coordinates (Hd_x, Hd_y) calculated by the flight computer using the magnetic compass and inertial measurements roughly points in the same direction (same quadrant) as the normalized fluxgate magnetometer reading (FG_x^N, FG_y^N). To avoid any false positive evaluations due to a noisy sensor, we filter the input signal.	$((Hd_x \geq 0 \rightarrow FG_x^N \geq 0) \wedge$ $(Hd_x < 0 \rightarrow FG_x^N < 0)) \vee$ $((Hd_y \geq 0 \rightarrow FG_y^N \geq 0) \wedge$ $(Hd_y < 0 \rightarrow FG_y^N < 0))$
S_5: We have a subformula Eul that states if the UAS is moving (Euler rates of pitch p, roll q, and yaw r are above the tolerance thresholds $\theta = 0.05$) then the fluxgate magnetometer should also register movement above its threshold $\theta_{FG} = 0.005$. The formula states that this should not fail more than three times within 100 seconds of each other.	$Eul := (\|p\| > \theta \vee \|q\| > \theta \vee \|r\| > \theta) \rightarrow$ $(\|FG_x\| > \theta_{FG} \vee \|FG_y\| > \theta_{FG} \vee$ $\|FG_z\| > \theta_{FG})$ $\neg(\neg Eul \wedge (\Diamond_{[2,100]}(\neg Eul \wedge \Diamond_{[2,100]} \neg Eul)))$
S_6: Whenever a logging event occurs, the CPS has received a good or a bad packet. S_6 needs a sampling rate of at least 64Hz.	$E^{log} \rightarrow ((E_g^{log} \wedge \neg E_b^{log}) \vee (E_b^{log} \wedge \neg E_g^{log}))$
S_6': This case study uses a 1Hz sampling rate. We are losing precision and S_6 becomes $N_g^R +$ $N_b^R = N_{tot}^R = 64$.	$N_{tot}^R = 64$

Figure 6A, which receives, as evidence, the results of each specification S_i and produces posterior marginals of the health nodes for the various failure modes. All health nodes are shown in Figure 6A. H_FG indicates the health of the FG sensor itself. It is obviously related to evidence that the measurements are valid (S_4) and that the measurements are changing over time (S_5). The two causal links from these health nodes indicate that relationship. Failure modes H_FG_TxERROR and H_FG_TxOVR indicate an error in the transmission circuit/software and overflow of the transmission buffer of the fluxgate magnetometer, respectively. The final two failure modes H_FC_RxOVR and H_FC_RxUR concern the receiver side of the CPS and denote problems with receiver buffer overflow and receiver buffer underrun, respectively.

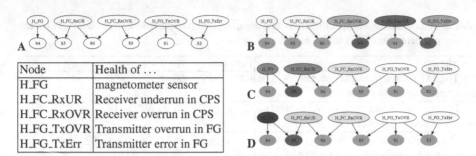

Node	Health of ...
H_FG	magnetometer sensor
H_FC_RxUR	Receiver underrun in CPS
H_FC_RxOVR	Receiver overrun in CPS
H_FG_TxOVR	Transmitter overrun in FG
H_FG_TxErr	Transmitter error in FG

Fig. 6. A: Bayesian network for our example with legend of health nodes. **B, C, D**: posterior probabilities (lighter shading corresponds to values closer to 1.0) for different input conditions.

Figure 6B shows the reasoning results of this case study, where the wrong configuration setting of the fluxgate magnetometer produces an increasing number of bad packets. The posterior of the node H_FG_TxOVR is substantially lower, compared to the other health nodes, indicating that a problem in the fluxgate magnetometer's transmitter component is most likely. So, debugging and repair attempts or on-board mitigation can be focused on this specific component, thus our SHM could have potentially avoided the extended ground time of the Swift UAS. This situation also indicates that, with a smaller likelihood, this failure might have been caused by some kind of overrun of the receiver circuit in the flight computer, or specific errors during transmission.

Figures 6C, D show the use of prior information to help disambiguate failures. Assume that we detected that the FG data are not changing, i.e., $S_5 =$ **false**, despite the fact that the aircraft is moving. This could have two causes: the sensor itself is broken, or something in the software is wrong and no packets are reaching the receiver, causing an underrun there. When this evidence is applied (red indicates **false**, green indicates **true**), the posterior of all nodes is close to 1 (white); only H_FG and H_FC_RxUR show values around 0.5 (gray), indicating that these two failures cannot be properly distinguished. This is not surprising, since we set the priors to $P(H_{sensor} = ok) = P(H\_FC\_RxUR) = 0.99$. Making the sensor less reliable, i.e., $P(H_{sensor} = ok) = 0.95$, now enables the BN to clearly disambiguate both failure modes. Further disambiguation information is provided by S_5, which indicates that we actually receive valid (i.e., UAS is moving) packets.

As the case study is based on a real event, we ran it on our hardware and extracted a trace of the sensor signals and specifications. Figure 7 shows a small snippet from this trace. The results of the atChecker evaluation of certain sensor signals can be seen on the

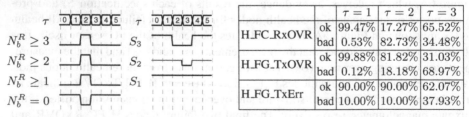

		$\tau = 1$	$\tau = 2$	$\tau = 3$
H_FC_RxOVR	ok	99.47%	17.27%	65.52%
	bad	0.53%	82.73%	34.48%
H_FG_TxOVR	ok	99.88%	81.82%	31.03%
	bad	0.12%	18.18%	68.97%
H_FG_TxErr	ok	90.00%	90.00%	62.07%
	bad	10.00%	10.00%	37.93%

Fig. 7. Recorded traces: sensor signals (left), trace of $S_1 \ldots S_3$ (middle). Data of health nodes (right) reflecting the buffer overflow situation shown in 6B.

left. On the right we show the results of S_1 to S_3. The system model delivers different health estimations during this trace. While at $\tau = 1$ the system is perfectly healthy, at $\tau = 2$ the rate of bad packets drastically increases. More than 3 bad packets have been received within 30 seconds. While the violation of S_3 would suggest a receiver overrun at this time, the indication for a buffer overflow becomes concrete at $\tau = 3$. This is indicated in the table on the right in Figure 7. The high probability of a transmitter overrun at the fluxgate magnetometer side with the reduced confidence of an error-free transition, leads to determining a root cause at the fluxgate magnetometer buffer.

7 Conclusion

We have presented an FPGA-based implementation for our health management framework called rt-R2U2 for the runtime monitoring and analysis of important safety and performance properties of a complex unmanned aircraft, or other autonomous systems. A combination of temporal logic observer pairs and Bayesian networks makes it possible to define expressive, yet compact health models. Our hardware implementation of this health management framework using efficient special-purpose processors allows us to execute our health models in real time. Furthermore, new or updated health models can be loaded onto the FPGA quickly between missions without having to re-synthesize its entire configuration in a time-consuming process.

We have demonstrated modeling and analysis capabilities on a health model, which monitors the serial communication between the payload computer and sensors (e.g., an on-board fluxgate magnetometer) on NASA's Swift UAS. Using data from an actual test flight, we demonstrated that our health management system could have quickly detected a configuration problem of the fluxgate magnetometer as the cause for a buffer overflow—the original problem grounded the aircraft for two days until the root cause could be determined.

Our rt-R2U2 system health management framework is applicable to a wide range of embedded systems, including CubeSats and rovers. Our independent hardware implementation allows us to monitor the system without interfering with the previously-certified software. This makes rt-R2U2 amenable both for black-box systems, where only the external connections/buses are available (like the Swift UAS), and monitoring white-box systems, where potentially each variable of the flight software could be monitored.

There is of course a question of trade-offs in any compositional SHM framework like the one we have detailed here: for any combination of data stream and off-nominal behavior, where is the most efficient place to check for and handle that off-nominal behavior? Should a small wobble in a data value be filtered out via a standard analog filter, accepted by a reasonably lenient temporal logic observer, or flagged by the BN diagnostic reasoner? In the future, it would be advantageous to complete a study of efficient design patterns for compositional temporal logic/BN SHM and map the types of checks we need to perform and the natural variances in sensor readings that we need to allow for their most efficient implementations.

Future work will also address the challenges of automatically generating health models from requirements and design documents, and carrying out flight tests with our FPGA-based rt-R2U2 on-board. In a next step, the output of rt-R2U2 could be connected to an on-board decision-making component, which could issue commands to loiter, curtail the mission, execute an emergency landing, etc.. Here, probabilistic information and confidence intervals calculated by the Bayesian networks of our approach can play an important role in providing solid justifications for decisions made.

References

1. Alur, R., Henzinger, T.A.: Real-time Logics: Complexity and Expressiveness. In: LICS, pp. 390–401. IEEE Computer Society Press (1990)
2. Chavira, M., Darwiche, A.: Compiling Bayesian networks with local structure. In: Proceedings of the 19th International Joint Conference on Artificial Intelligence (IJCAI), pp. 1306–1312 (2005)
3. Darwiche, A.: A differential approach to inference in Bayesian networks. Journal of the ACM 50(3), 280–305 (2003)
4. Darwiche, A.: Modeling and reasoning with Bayesian networks. In: Modeling and Reasoning with Bayesian Networks (2009)
5. Drusinsky, D.: The temporal rover and the ATG rover. In: Havelund, K., Penix, J., Visser, W. (eds.) SPIN 2000. LNCS, vol. 1885, pp. 323–330. Springer, Heidelberg (2000)
6. Ippolito, C., Espinosa, P., Weston, A.: Swift UAS: An electric UAS research platform for green aviation at NASA Ames Research Center. In: CAFE EAS IV (April 2010)
7. Johnson, S., Gormley, T., Kessler, S., Mott, C., Patterson-Hine, A., Reichard, K., Philip Scandura, J.: System Health Management: with Aerospace Applications. Wiley & Sons (2011)
8. Majzoobi, M., Pittman, R.N., Forin, A.: gNOSIS: Mining FPGAs for verification (2011)
9. Mengshoel, O.J., Chavira, M., Cascio, K., Poll, S., Darwiche, A., Uckun, S.: Probabilistic model-based diagnosis: An electrical power system case study. IEEE Trans. on Systems, Man and Cybernetics, Part A: Systems and Humans 40(5), 874–885 (2010)
10. Meredith, P.O., Jin, D., Griffith, D., Chen, F., Roşu, G.: An overview of the mop runtime verification framework. International Journal on Software Tools for Technology Transfer 14(3), 249–289 (2012)
11. Musliner, D., Hendler, J., Agrawala, A.K., Durfee, E., Strosnider, J.K., Paul, C.J.: The challenges of real-time AI. IEEE Computer 28, 58–66 (1995),
    citeseer.comp.nus.edu.sg/article/musliner95challenges.html
12. Pearl, J.: A constraint propagation approach to probabilistic reasoning. In: UAI, pp. 31–42. AUAI Press (1985)
13. Pellizzoni, R., Meredith, P., Caccamo, M., Rosu, G.: Hardware runtime monitoring for dependable COTS-based real-time embedded systems. In: RTSS, pp. 481–491 (2008)
14. Pike, L., Wegmann, N., Niller, S., Goodloe, A.: Copilot: monitoring embedded systems. Innovations in Systems and Software Engineering 9(4), 235–255 (2013)
15. Reinbacher, T., Rozier, K.Y., Schumann, J.: Temporal-logic based runtime observer pairs for system health management of real-time systems. In: Ábrahám, E., Havelund, K. (eds.) TACAS 2014. LNCS, vol. 8413, pp. 357–372. Springer, Heidelberg (2014)
16. Schumann, J., Mbaya, T., Mengshoel, O.J., Pipatsrisawat, K., Srivastava, A., Choi, A., Darwiche, A.: Software health management with Bayesian networks. Innovations in Systems and Software Engineering 9(2), 1–22 (2013)
17. Schumann, J., Rozier, K.Y., Reinbacher, T., Mengshoel, O.J., Mbaya, T., Ippolito, C.: Towards real-time, on-board, hardware-supported sensor and software health management for unmanned aerial systems. In: Proceedings of the 2013 Annual Conference of the Prognostics and Health Management Society (PHM 2013), pp. 381–401 (October 2013)
18. Srivastava, A.N., Schumann, J.: Software health management: a necessity for safety critical systems. Innovations in Systems and Software Engineering 9(4), 219–233 (2013)
19. Tabakov, D., Rozier, K.Y., Vardi, M.Y.: Optimized temporal monitors for SystemC. Formal Methods in System Design 41(3), 236–268 (2012)

On-Line Monitoring for Temporal Logic Robustness

Adel Dokhanchi, Bardh Hoxha, and Georgios Fainekos

School of Computing, Informatics and Decision Systems Engineering,
Arizona State University, USA
{adokhanc,bhoxha,fainekos}@asu.edu

Abstract. In this paper, we provide a Dynamic Programming algorithm for on-line monitoring of the state robustness of Metric Temporal Logic specifications with past time operators. We compute the robustness of MTL with unbounded past and bounded future temporal operators ($MTL_{+pt}^{<+\infty}$) over sampled traces of Cyber-Physical Systems. We implemented our tool in Matlab as a Simulink block that can be used in any Simulink model. We experimentally demonstrate that the overhead of the $MTL_{+pt}^{<+\infty}$ robustness monitoring is acceptable for certain classes of practical specifications.

1 Introduction

Modern airplanes, automobiles and medical devices are prime examples of safety critical Cyber-Physical Systems (CPS). Nowadays, the majority of safety critical functions in such systems is controlled by embedded computers. Due to the critical nature of these components, it is of paramount importance to verify the functional correctness of the embedded software. However, as the number of computer controlled components increases so does the complexity of the verification of functional correctness. Moreover, the verification problem of most classes of CPS is even an undecidable problem [1].

As an alternative to verification and off-line testing, runtime monitoring has been proposed. The underlying idea is that given a set of formal requirements, these requirements are analyzed at runtime by an independent monitor and if a violation is detected, it is reported to a supervisor. The supervisor can then decide on remedial actions to fix the problem or reduce its impact to the system. The monitoring problem has been extensively studied [2–14] for the cases where the formal requirements are expressed in Linear Temporal Logic (LTL) [15] or in Metric Temporal Logic (MTL) [16].

In this paper, we revisit the MTL runtime monitoring problem when targeted to CPS. In particular, we claim that the classical Boolean semantics (or even three valued semantics) are not sufficiently informative for CPS behaviors. For instance, consider the specification "*After a takeoff command is received, then reach altitude of 600ft within 5 minutes*" for an autonomous Unmanned Aerial Vehicle (UAV) as introduced in [8]. Clearly, knowing that the specification failed or passed at runtime is important. However, more useful information from the perspective of the supervisor would be the knowledge of how far is the aircraft from satisfying the requirement. More specifically, -10ft from the requirement of 600ft at 1 min away from the 5 min threshold should potentially be less alarming than -100ft at exactly the same time. A supervisor that has a model of the dynamics of the aircraft can determine whether the UAV can climb 100ft

B. Bonakdarpour and S.A. Smolka (Eds.): RV 2014, LNCS 8734, pp. 231–246, 2014.
© Springer International Publishing Switzerland 2014

within 1 min or not. We remark that the determination of the climb rate can only occur at runtime since this depends on the atmospheric parameters, the payload of the UAV, etc. Hence, the climb rate cannot be a precomputed parameter unless it is very conservatively set.

Our goal is to construct MTL monitors for estimating the robustness of satisfaction [17–19]. Temporal logic robustness gives a quantitative interpretation of satisfaction of an MTL formula. In detail, if an MTL formula valuates to positive robustness ε, then the specification is true and, moreover, the state sequences can tolerate perturbations up to ε and still satisfy the specification. Similarly, if the robustness is negative, then the specification is false and, moreover, the state sequences under ε perturbations still do not satisfy the specification. Thus, robust semantics can be used to give quantitative values to the satisfaction of MTL formulas when the target is CPS.

The challenge here is that automata based monitors [13, 14] cannot be synthesized for computing the robustness valuations. Therefore, formula rewriting methods [11] or dynamic programming [9] methods must be used. Here, we take the latter approach for combined unbounded past time and bounded future time MTL specifications. Since we are working with CPS, we assume that it is possible - if desired - to have a model predictive component in the system [20] which will provide a finite horizon prediction of the system behavior. That finite horizon prediction could be appended with the observed system behavior to provide a robustness estimate of a likely system behavior. Hence, it becomes possible to monitor specifications such as *"If at anytime in the past a take-off command is issued, then within 5 min the altitude of 600ft is reached"*. Thus, such requirements can now be monitored using only the actual observed system behavior or the observed system behavior with the predicted system behavior.

Our contributions in this paper are as follows: We provide a dynamic programming algorithm for on-line monitoring of the robustness metric of MTL formulas with bounded future and unbounded past. In addition, we provide a Matlab/Simulink toolbox that can be used in any Simulink model for runtime monitoring of MTL robustness. The memory usage of our method is bounded and its runtime overhead is negligible for practical applications. Additional benefits in utilizing an on-line monitor are that it can be used in temporal logic testing algorithms [21, 22], where it may be desirable that the simulation stops as soon as the property is violated, as well as in feedback control for MTL specifications. Although temporal logic robustness has been considered in previous works [17–19], the solutions were provided for off-line testing. To the best of our knowledge, this is the first attempt to solve the on-line MTL robustness monitoring problem efficiently.

2   Problem Formulation

In the following, we represent the set of natural numbers including zero by $\mathbb{N}$ and the finite interval of $\mathbb{N}$ up to m by $\mathbb{N}_m = \{0, 1, \ldots, m\}$. In this work, we consider monitoring of Cyber-Physical Systems (CPS). We assume that we have access to some discrete time execution or simulation traces of the CPS. We view *(execution or simulation) traces* as

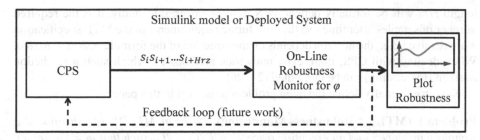

Fig. 1. Overview of the solution of the $\text{MTL}_{+pt}^{<+\infty}$ on-line monitoring problem. The monitored robustness values could be used as feedback to the CPS or it could be plotted to be observed by a human supervisor if needed.

timed state sequences $\mathcal{T} = \mathcal{T}_0\mathcal{T}_1\mathcal{T}_2 \ldots \mathcal{T}_m = (\tau_0, s_0)\,(\tau_1, s_1)\,(\tau_2, s_2)\ldots(\tau_m, s_m)$ where for each $k \in \mathbb{N}_m$, $\tau_k \in \mathbb{R}_{\geq 0}$ is a time stamp and $s_k \in S$ is a vector containing the values of the state variables of the system at each sampling instance k. For example, for $m = 2$, the trace $\mathcal{T} = (0, (2, 0.34))(0.1, (3, 0.356))(0.2, (2, 0.36))$ captures the finite time execution of a CPS with two state variables in the vector s_k: one ranging over the natural numbers $\mathbb{N}$ and the other over the reals $\mathbb{R}$. That is, for $k = 1$, the state of the system at time $\tau_1 = 0.1$ was $s_1 = (3, 0.356) \in \mathbb{N} \times \mathbb{R}$. We further assume that $\mathcal{S} = (S, d)$ is a generalized quasi-metric space [23]. The existence of metrics is necessary so that distances can be defined for quantitative valuations of the atomic propositions [18, 21].

Throughout the paper, the variable i, which ranges over $\mathbb{N}$, is used to represent the current simulation step or the current index of the sampling process. We assume a fixed sampling period for the monitored system. Thus, there exists a fixed time period between consecutive time stamps. For this fixed period $\Delta t > 0$, for all $i \geq 0$, we have $\tau_{i+1} - \tau_i = \Delta t$ (or equivalently $\tau_i = i\Delta t$). As a result, we can simply compute each time stamp τ_i knowing the trace index (or simulation step) i by multiplication ($\tau_i = i\Delta t$). Therefore, we use the trace index (simulation step i) as the reference of time.

The property of interest is stated in Metric Temporal Logic (MTL) with bounded future and unbounded past ($\text{MTL}_{+pt}^{<+\infty}$) for timed state sequences [11]. More specifically, at each time i, we would like to monitor safety requirements represented as $\text{MTL}_{+pt}^{<+\infty}$ formulas. These formulas capture safety properties of the system, such as bounded reactivity, which can be periodically analyzed for violation. In our formulation, we use the robust (quantitative) semantics [18] that quantify the distance between a given execution trace of a CPS and all the execution traces that violate the property. The robustness of a formula $[\![\varphi]\!]$ with respect to a trace $\mathcal{T}$ at time i is a value that measures how far is the trace from the satisfaction/falsification. This measure is an extension of boolean values representing satisfaction or falsification which is used in conventional monitoring. A positive robustness value means that the trace satisfies the property and a negative robustness means that the specification is not satisfied.

Our goal in this paper is to provide monitoring tools for temporal logic robustness. We assume that at each time i, the CPS outputs its current state s_i along with a finite prediction $s_{i+1}, s_{i+2}, \ldots, s_{i+Hrz}$ of horizon length $Hrz \in \mathbb{N}$ (see Fig. 1). The horizon length Hrz will be formally defined in Sec. 4; however, informally, it is the required number of samples after time i so that any future requirements in the MTL specification ϕ are resolved, i.e., the horizon depends on the structure of the formula ϕ, $Hrz = hrz(\phi)$. When dealing with CPS, there exist numerous methods by which such a prediction horizon (forecasting) can be computed [24–26].

Next, we formally define the main problem presented in this paper.

Problem 1 (MTL$_{+pt}^{<+\infty}$ Robustness Monitoring). *Given an MTL$_{+pt}^{<+\infty}$ specification φ, a sampling instance i and an execution trace $\mathcal{T} = \mathcal{T}_0 \mathcal{T}_1 \ldots \mathcal{T}_m$ such that $m = i + hrz(\varphi)$, compute the current robustness estimate $[\![\varphi]\!](\mathcal{T}, i)$ at time τ_i.*

Intuitively, φ represents a system invariant that must hold at every point in the system execution. This can also be viewed as testing for the specification robustness $[\![\Box\varphi]\!](\mathcal{T}, 0)$, where $\Box$ is the operator for "*always in the future*" and φ is an arbitrary MTL$_{+pt}^{<+\infty}$ specification. However, instead of caring about the satisfaction of the formula at the beginning of the time, we care about the potential of violating φ for which we design an on-line monitor.

Overview of solution and summary of contributions: We provide an on-line monitoring approach for computing the robustness of an MTL$_{+pt}^{<+\infty}$ formula with respect to execution traces of a CPS. An overview of the solution for the MTL$_{+pt}^{<+\infty}$ on-line monitoring problem appears in Fig. 1. Our method monitors the behavior of a CPS as it executes. Our toolbox is also useful for applications where Simulink models are actually used for process monitoring (and not simulation). In addition, it can also be used for code generation for general MTL$_{+pt}^{<+\infty}$ monitors for deployment on actual systems. Our method computes the robustness of invariants $[\![\varphi]\!](\mathcal{T}, i)$ by storing previous specification robustness values – if needed – and by only utilizing a bounded number of pairs of the execution trace $\mathcal{T}_{Hst}, \ldots, \mathcal{T}_{Hrz}$ where $Hst \in \mathbb{N}_i$ and it will be formally defined in Sec. 4. Our monitor uses bounded memory and, in the worst case, it has quadratic time complexity that depends on the magnitude of $Hrz - Hst$. In principle, our solution for robustness monitoring is inspired by the boolean temporal logic monitoring algorithm in [2].

3   Robustness of Metric Temporal Logic Specifications

In digital control and monitoring of CPS, it is inevitable that physical quantities are measured through a sampling process. As mentioned in the Problem Formulation section, when we mention time, we are actually referring to the corresponding sampling index i. With a slight abuse of notation and under the assumption of constant sampling rate, an execution trace $\mathcal{T}$ can also be represented by a function $s : \mathbb{N}_{i+Hrz} \rightarrow S$. The view of the sequence $s_0 s_1 \ldots s_{i+Hrz}$ as a function s simplifies the presentation of the robust semantics for MTL.

Using a metric d [23], we can define a distance function that captures how far away a point $x \in X$ is from a set $S \subseteq X$. Intuitively, the distance function assigns positive values when x is in the set S and negative values when x is outside the set S. The metric

d must be at least a generalized quasi-metric as described in [21] which also includes the case where d is a metric as it was introduced in [18].

Definition 1 (Signed Distance). *Let $x \in X$ be a point, $S \subseteq X$ be a set and d be a metric. Then, we define the Signed Distance from x to S to be*

$$\mathbf{Dist}_d(x, S) := \begin{cases} -\inf\{d(x, y) \mid y \in S\} & \text{if } x \notin S \\ \inf\{d(x, y) \mid y \in X \setminus S\} & \text{if } x \in S \end{cases}$$

where inf is the infimum.

Metric Temporal Logic (MTL) was introduced by Koymans [16] to reason about the quantitative timing properties of boolean signals. In this paper, we use the standard fragment of MTL with bounded future, but also we allow the use of past time operators.

Definition 2 (MTL$_{+pt}^{<+\infty}$ Syntax). *Let AP be the set of atomic propositions and I be any non-empty interval of $\mathbb{N}$, and $\overline{I}$ be any non-empty interval of $\mathbb{N} \cup \{+\infty\}$. The set MTL$_{+pt}^{<+\infty}$ formulas is inductively defined as $\varphi ::= \top \mid p \mid \neg\varphi \mid \psi \vee \varphi \mid \psi \mathcal{U}_I \varphi \mid \psi \mathcal{S}_{\overline{I}} \varphi$ where $p \in AP$ and $\top$ stands for* true.

Note that we use the number of samples to represent the time interval constraints of temporal operators. For example assume that $\Delta t = 0.1$, then the MTL formula $\Diamond_{[0,0.5]} a$ where the timing constraints are over time is instead represented by $\Diamond_{[0,5]} a$ in MTL$_{+pt}^{<+\infty}$.

The propositional operators conjunction ($\wedge$) and implication ($\rightarrow$) are defined the usual way. All other bounded future temporal operators can be syntactically defined using Until ($\mathcal{U}_I$), where $\bigcirc$ (Next), $\Diamond$ (Eventually), and $\square$ (Always) are defined as $\bigcirc\varphi \equiv \top\mathcal{U}_{[1,1]}\varphi$, $\Diamond_I\varphi \equiv \top\mathcal{U}_I\varphi$, and $\square_I\varphi \equiv \neg\Diamond_I\neg\varphi$ respectively. The intuitive meaning of the $\psi\mathcal{U}_{[a,b]}\varphi$ operator at sampling time i is a follows: ψ has to hold at least until φ becomes true within the time interval of $[i + a, i + b]$ in the future. Similarly, all other bounded/unbounded past temporal operators can be defined using Since ($\mathcal{S}_{\overline{I}}$), where $\odot$ (Previous), $\Diamondblack$ (Eventually in the past), and $\boxminus$ (Always in the past) are defined as $\odot\varphi \equiv \top\mathcal{S}_{[1,1]}\varphi$, $\Diamondblack_{\overline{I}}\varphi \equiv \top\mathcal{S}_{\overline{I}}\varphi$, and $\boxminus_{\overline{I}}\varphi \equiv \neg\Diamondblack_{\overline{I}}\neg\varphi$ respectively. The intuitive meaning of the $\psi\mathcal{S}_{[a,b]}\varphi$ operator at sampling time i is as follows: since φ becomes true within the interval $[i - b, i - a]$ in the past, ψ must hold till now (current time i).

MTL$_{+pt}^{<+\infty}$ can state requirements over the observable trajectories of a CPS. In order to capture these requirements, each predicate $p \in AP$ is mapped to a subset of the metric space X. We use an observation map O to interpret each predicate $p \in AP$. In other words, the observation map is defined as $O : AP \rightarrow P(X)$ such that for each $p \in AP$ the corresponding set is $O(p)$. Here, $P(S)$ denotes the powerset of a set S. We define the robust valuation of an MTL$_{+pt}^{<+\infty}$ formula φ over a trace s as follows [17].

Definition 3 (MTL$_{+pt}^{<+\infty}$ Robustness Semantics). *Let s be a trace $s : \mathbb{N} \rightarrow X$, and O be an observation map $O : AP \rightarrow P(X)$, then the robust semantics of any formula $\varphi \in$ MTL$_{+pt}^{<+\infty}$ with respect to s is recursively defined as:*

$$[\![\top]\!](s,i) := +\infty$$

$$[\![p]\!](s,i) := \mathbf{Dist}_d(s(i), O(p))$$

$$[\![\neg\varphi]\!](s,i) := -[\![\varphi]\!](s,i)$$

$$[\![\psi \lor \varphi]\!](s,i) := [\![\psi]\!](s,i) \sqcup [\![\varphi]\!](s,i)$$

$$[\![\psi \mathcal{U}_{[l,u]}\varphi]\!](s,i) := \bigsqcup_{j=i+l}^{i+u}\left([\![\varphi]\!](s,j) \sqcap \prod_{k=i}^{j-1}[\![\psi]\!](s,k)\right)$$

$$[\![\psi S_{[l',u'\rangle}\varphi]\!](s,i) := \bigsqcup_{j=max\{0,i-u'\}}^{i-l'}\left([\![\varphi]\!](s,j) \sqcap \prod_{k=j+1}^{i}[\![\psi]\!](s,k)\right)$$

where $\sqcup$ *stands for max,* $\sqcap$ *stands for min,* $p \in AP$, $l, u, l' \in \mathbb{N}$ *and* $u' \in \mathbb{N} \cup \{\infty\}$. *Furthermore, the symbol* $\rangle$ *in* $S_{[l',u'\rangle}$ *will be* $)$ *when* $u' = +\infty$ *and* $]$ *when* $u' \neq +\infty$.

We should point out that we use the extended definition of maximum ($\sqcup$) and minimum ($\sqcap$), with slight abuse of notation, we let $max(\emptyset) = -\infty$ and $min(\emptyset) = +\infty$. i.e., over empty sets we treat min and max as infimum and supremum, respectively. For exact definition of infimum and supremum see [27].

4   Robustness Monitoring of $MTL_{+pt}^{<+\infty}$

4.1   Finite Horizon and History of $MTL_{+pt}^{<+\infty}$

For each $MTL_{+pt}^{<+\infty}$ formula ψ we define the finite horizon $hrz(\psi)$ as the number of samples we need to consider in the future. In MTL, the satisfaction of the formula depends on what will happen in the future. In bounded MTL, the finite horizon $hrz(\psi)$ is the number of steps (samples) which we need to consider in the future in order to evaluate the formula ψ at the current time i. In other words, $hrz(\psi)$ is the number of steps into the future for which the truth value of the sub-formula ψ depends on [2]. Similarly, we define the finite history $hst(\psi)$ of ψ as the number of samples we need to look into the past. That is, the number of steps in the past for which the truth value of the sub-formula ψ depends on. Intuitively, the $hst(\psi)$ is the size of the history we need to consider in order to keep track of what happened in the past to evaluate the formula ψ at present time. The finite horizon and the history can be defined recursively. We define $hrz(\psi)$ (similar to $h(\psi)$ in [2]) and we add the recursive definition of $hst(\psi)$ in the following:

$hrz(p) = 0$ $hst(p) = 0$

$hrz(\neg\psi) = hrz(\psi)$ $hst(\neg\psi) = hst(\psi)$

$hrz(\psi\ \mathbf{OP}\ \varphi) = max\{hrz(\psi), hrz(\varphi)\}$ $hst(\psi\ \mathbf{OP}\ \varphi) = max\{hst(\psi), hst(\varphi)\}$

$hrz(\psi\mathcal{U}_{[l,u]}\varphi) = max\{hrz(\psi) + u - 1, hrz(\varphi) + u\}$ $hst(\psi\mathcal{U}_{[l,u]}\varphi) = max\{hst(\psi), hst(\varphi)\}$

$hrz(\psi S_{[l',u'\rangle}\varphi) = max\{hrz(\psi), hrz(\varphi)\}$

$$hst(\psi S_{[l',u'\rangle}\varphi) = \begin{cases} max\{hst(\psi) + u' - 1, hst(\varphi) + u'\} & \text{if } u' \neq +\infty \\ max\{hst(\psi) + l' - 1, hst(\varphi) + l'\} & \text{if } u' = +\infty \end{cases}$$

where $p \in AP$. Here, **OP** is any binary operator in propositional logic, and ψ, φ are $MTL_{+pt}^{<+\infty}$ formulas. For the unbounded $S_{[0,+\infty)}$ operator, the computation of finite history is more involved and needs more explanation. Namely, we need to restate the dynamic programming algorithm for monitoring a sub-formula $\psi S_{[0,+\infty)}\varphi$ based on the

Table 1. Pre Vector and Robustness Table

Pre[k]	$T_{k,j}$	column $j \Rightarrow$	-2	-1	0	1	2
	row $k \Downarrow$	Time(i)	$i-2$	$i-1$	i	$i+1$	$i+2$
	$\psi_1 = \varphi$	$\psi_2 \wedge \psi_3$	$[\![\varphi]\!](s, i-2)$	$[\![\varphi]\!](s, i-1)$	$[\![\varphi]\!](s, i)$	$[\![\varphi]\!](s, i+1)$	$[\![\varphi]\!](s, i+2)$
	ψ_2	$\square_{[1,2]}q$	$[\![\psi_2]\!](s, i-2)$	$[\![\psi_2]\!](s, i-1)$	$[\![\psi_2]\!](s, i)$	$[\![\psi_2]\!](s, i+1)$	$[\![\psi_2]\!](s, i+2)$
$[\![\psi_3]\!](s, i-3)$	ψ_3	$\boxdot_{[0,+\infty)}p$	$[\![\psi_3]\!](s, i-2)$	$[\![\psi_3]\!](s, i-1)$	$[\![\psi_3]\!](s, i)$	$[\![\psi_3]\!](s, i+1)$	$[\![\psi_3]\!](s, i+2)$
	ψ_4	p	$[\![\psi_4]\!](s, i-2)$	$[\![\psi_4]\!](s, i-1)$	$[\![\psi_4]\!](s, i)$	$[\![\psi_4]\!](s, i+1)$	$[\![\psi_4]\!](s, i+2)$
	ψ_5	q	$[\![\psi_5]\!](s, i-2)$	$[\![\psi_5]\!](s, i-1)$	$[\![\psi_5]\!](s, i)$	$[\![\psi_5]\!](s, i+1)$	$[\![\psi_5]\!](s, i+2)$

following works [9, 5]. According to the robustness semantics, the robustness of $\psi S_{[0,+\infty)}\varphi$ at time i is as follows:

$$[\![\psi S_{[0,+\infty)}\varphi]\!](s, i) = \bigsqcup_{j=0}^{i}\left([\![\varphi]\!](s, j) \sqcap \prod_{k=j+1}^{i}[\![\psi]\!](s, k)\right)$$

also robustness of $\psi S_{[0,+\infty)}\varphi$ at time $i - 1$ is

$$[\![\psi S_{[0,+\infty)}\varphi]\!](s, i - 1) = \bigsqcup_{j=0}^{i-1}\left([\![\varphi]\!](s, j) \sqcap \prod_{k=j+1}^{i-1}[\![\psi]\!](s, k)\right)$$

Thus, we can rewrite $[\![\psi S_{[0,+\infty)}\varphi]\!](s, i)$ as

$$[\![\psi S_{[0,+\infty)}\varphi]\!](s, i) = [\![\varphi]\!](s, i) \sqcup \left([\![\psi]\!](s, i) \sqcap \left(\bigsqcup_{j=0}^{i-1}\left([\![\varphi]\!](s, j) \sqcap \prod_{k=j+1}^{i-1}[\![\psi]\!](s, k)\right)\right)\right) =$$

$$= [\![\varphi]\!](s, i) \sqcup \left([\![\psi]\!](s, i) \sqcap \left([\![\psi S_{[0,+\infty)}\varphi]\!](s, i - 1)\right)\right)$$

Therefore, similar to [5] we recursively update the robustness of $\psi S_{[0,+\infty)}\varphi$ at the current time i and save it in a variable called "*Pre*" to reuse it for the computation of the next time step (see [5] for more details). As a result, when we have an unbounded past time operator, we do not need the full history table. However, if the formula contains a nested future time operator, we need to extend the history to be long enough to contain the actual values. In other words, although for unbounded past time operators we do not need the whole history table, we should still extend the history to be able to store the actual simulation values (not the predicted values) in "*Pre*".

4.2 Robustness Computation Algorithm

For each MTL$_{+pt}^{<+\infty}$ formula φ we construct a table called **Robustness Table** with width of $Hst + 1 + Hrz$, where $Hrz = hrz(\varphi)$ is the finite horizon of the specification formula φ, and, $Hst = Hrz + hst(\varphi)$, where $hst(\varphi)$ is the finite history of the specification φ. Hst is extended conservatively due to the fact that "*Pre*" value can only store the robustness values corresponding to the actual simulation. The height of the robustness table is the size of the formula φ ($|\varphi|$), where $|\varphi|$ is the number of sub-formulas of φ including itself. For example, assume we have a formula $\varphi = \boxdot_{[0,+\infty)}p \wedge \square_{[1,2]}q$ and we intend to compute $[\![\varphi]\!](\mathcal{T}, i)$ at each time i. In formula φ, $Hst = 2$ and $Hrz = 2$. Since φ has unbounded past-time operators, it needs the *Pre* vector as well as the Robustness Table. The *Pre*

Algorithm 1. On-Line Monitor

Input: φ, $s'_i = s_i s_{i+1} \ldots s_{i+Hrz}$, $\mathbf{d}$, O; **Global variables:** T, Pre; **Output:** $T_{1,0}(robustness\ value)$.

procedure MONITOR(φ, s'_i, $\mathbf{d}$, O)
1: **for** $k \leftarrow 1$ to $|\varphi|$ **do**
2:      $Pre(k) \leftarrow T_{k,(-Hst+hst(\varphi_k))}$
3: **end for**
4: **for** $j \leftarrow 1 - Hst$ to Hrz **do**
5:      **for** $k \leftarrow 1$ to $|\varphi|$ **do**
6:          **if** $\varphi_k = p \in AP$ **then**
7:              $T_{k,j-1} \leftarrow T_{k,j}$
8:          **end if**
9:      **end for**
10: **end for**
11: **for** $k \leftarrow |\varphi|$ down to 1 **do**
12:     **if** $\varphi_k = \varphi_m S_{[l',u']} \varphi_n$ **then**
13:         **for** $j \leftarrow -Hst$ to Hrz **do**
14:             $T_{k,j} \leftarrow CR(\phi_k, j, s'_i, \mathbf{d}, O)$
15:         **end for**
16:     **else**
17:         **for** $j \leftarrow Hrz$ down to $-Hst$ **do**
18:             $T_{k,j} \leftarrow CR(\phi_k, j, s'_i, \mathbf{d}, O)$
19:         **end for**
20:     **end if**
21: **end for**
22: **return** $T_{1,0}$
end procedure

---

vector appended to the Robustness Table is presented in Table 1. In particular, the *Pre* vector contains the value of past sub-formulas from the beginning of the time up to the current time.

In the following, we explain how the values of Table 2, the robustness table, are computed using Algorithms 1 and 2. In order to make our algorithms more readable, we used a vector to show the CPS output s_i, s_{i+1}, ..., s_{i+Hrz} to the monitoring (see Fig. 1). We define a vector $s'_i = s_i s_{i+1} \ldots s_{i+Hrz}$ which appends current state s_i with predictions s_{i+1}, s_{i+2}, ..., s_{i+Hrz}. In Table 1, i is the current simulation step which corresponds to column 0. At each simulation step i, for each unbounded past time sub-formula ϕ, we first save the values of the column $-Hst + hst(\phi)$ in the *Pre* vector (Algorithm 1 lines 1-3) since the column $-Hst + hst(\phi)$ contains the robustness value of ϕ from the beginning of the simulation. We need the *Pre* vector to compute the robustness of ϕ at the next sampling time using the dynamic programming method. In the above example, for $\square_{[0,+\infty)}p$ the value at column -2 is saved in *Pre* to be used during robustness computation. Then, we shift all the robustness table entries of the predicates by one position to the left (Algorithm 1, lines 4-10). Then the loop (Algorithm 1, lines 11-21) recursively calls Algorithm 2 to fill the robustness table for each sub-formula from bottom to top.

Each call of Algorithm 2 (CR) computes each table entry $T_{k,j}$ (see tables 1,2) where column j is the horizon/history index and row k is the sub-formula index. For past

Table 2. Robustness Computation of each table entries (Gray cells are unused)

$T_{k,j}$	$i-2$	$i-1$	i	$i+1$	$i+2$
$k \Downarrow, j \Rightarrow$	$j = -2$	$j = -1$	$j = 0$	$j = 1$	$j = 2$
$Pre[1]$	$T_{2,-2} \sqcap T_{3,-2}$	$T_{2,-1} \sqcap T_{3,-1}$	$T_{2,0} \sqcap T_{3,0}$	$T_{2,1} \sqcap T_{3,1}$	$T_{2,2} \sqcap T_{3,2}$
$Pre[2]$	$T_{5,-1} \sqcap T_{5,0}$	$T_{5,0} \sqcap T_{5,1}$	$T_{5,1} \sqcap T_{5,2}$	$T_{5,2}$	$+\infty$
$Pre[3]$	$Pre[3] \sqcap T_{4,-2}$	$T_{3,-2} \sqcap T_{4,-1}$	$T_{3,-1} \sqcap T_{4,0}$	$T_{3,0} \sqcap T_{4,1}$	$T_{3,1} \sqcap T_{4,2}$
$Pre[4]$	$\mathbf{Dist}_d(s_{i-2}, O(p))$	$\mathbf{Dist}_d(s_{i-1}, O(p))$	$\mathbf{Dist}_d(s_i, O(p))$	$\mathbf{Dist}_d(s_{i+1}, O(p))$	$\mathbf{Dist}_d(s_{i+2}, O(p))$
$Pre[5]$	$\mathbf{Dist}_d(s_{i-2}, O(q))$	$\mathbf{Dist}_d(s_{i-1}, O(q))$	$\mathbf{Dist}_d(s_i, O(q))$	$\mathbf{Dist}_d(s_{i+1}, O(q))$	$\mathbf{Dist}_d(s_{i+2}, O(q))$

Algorithm 2. Robustness Computation (CR)

Input: φ_k, j, $s'_i = s_i s_{i+1} \ldots s_{i+Hrz}$, d, O; Global variables: T, Pre; Output: $T_{k,j}$.

procedure CR(φ_k, j, s'_i, d, O)
1:   if $\varphi_k = \top$ then $T_{k,j} \leftarrow +\infty$
2:   else if $\varphi_k = p \in AP$ then
3:     if $j >= 0$ then
4:       $T_{k,j} \leftarrow Dist_d(s_{i+j}, O(p))$
5:     end if
6:   else if $\varphi_k = \neg\varphi_m$ then
7:     $T_{k,j} \leftarrow -T_{m,j}$
8:   else if $\varphi_k = \varphi_m \vee \varphi_n$ then
9:     $T_{k,j} \leftarrow T_{m,j} \sqcup T_{n,j}$
10:   else if $\varphi_m \mathcal{U}_{[l,u]} \varphi_n$ then
11:     if $j + l \leq Hrz$ then
12:       $tmp_{min} \leftarrow \sqcap_{j \leq j' < j+l} T_{m,j'}$
13:       $T_{k,j} = -\infty$
14:       for $j' \leftarrow j+l$ to $min\{Hrz, u+j\}$ do
15:         $T_{k,j} \leftarrow T_{k,j} \sqcup (tmp_{min} \sqcap T_{n,j'})$
16:         $tmp_{min} = tmp_{min} \sqcap T_{m,j'}$
17:       end for
18:     else
19:       $T_{k,j} = -\infty$
20:     end if
21:   else if $\varphi_m \mathcal{S}_{[l',u']} \varphi_n$ then
22:     if $j - l' \geq -Hst$ then

23:       $tmp_{min} \leftarrow \sqcap_{j-l' < j' \leq j} T_{m,j'}$
24:       if $u' \neq +\infty$ then
25:         $T_{k,j} = -\infty$
26:         for $j' \leftarrow j-l'$ down to $max\{-Hst, j-u'\}$ do
27:           $T_{k,j} \leftarrow T_{k,j} \sqcup (tmp_{min} \sqcap T_{n,j'})$
28:           $tmp_{min} = tmp_{min} \sqcap T_{m,j'}$
29:         end for
30:       else
31:         if $j - hst(\varphi_k) = -Hst$ then
32:           $tmp_S \leftarrow Pre[k] \sqcap T_{m,j}$
33:         else
34:           $tmp_S \leftarrow T_{k,j-1} \sqcap T_{m,j}$
35:         end if
36:         $T_{k,j} \leftarrow (T_{n,j-l'} \sqcap tmp_{min}) \sqcup tmp_S$
37:       end if
38:     else
39:       $T_{k,j} = -\infty$
40:     end if
41:   end if
42:   return $T_{k,j}$
end procedure

---

sub-formulas the table entries are computed from left to right (Algorithm 1, lines 12-15), and for future sub-formulas the table entries are computed from right to left (Algorithm 1, lines 16-19). New values for predicates (according to execution traces) will be placed in column 0 and the predicted values of the predicates will be saved in columns 1 to Hrz (Algorithm 2, lines 2-5). Table 2 shows the updates of predicate values in rows 4, and 5 which correspond to Algorithm 2, line 4.

In the following, we explain how the CR Algorithm 2 computes the MTL robustness values for three different cases of MTL:

Case 1 (Lines 10-20): The robustness of bounded future temporal sub-formulas with interval $[l, u]$ at each column j is computed given the values of its operands for columns j up-to $min\{j + u, Hrz\}$ (Line 14). For example, this case is used in table 2 to compute the robustness of sub-formula $\psi_2 = \square_{[1,2]} q$ from right to left. Case 1 in CR Algorithm is similar to the DP-TALIRO algorithm [28].

Case 2 (Lines 24-29): The robustness of bounded past temporal sub-formulas with interval $[l', u']$ at each column j is computed given the values of its operands for columns j down-to $max\{j - u', -Hst\}$ (Line 26).

Case 3 (Lines 30-37): The robustness of unbounded past temporal sub-formulas with interval $[l', +\infty)$ for column j is computed using the stored value in column $j - 1$ in dynamic programming fashion (Line 34) and using the Pre vector (Line 32). For example, Case 3 is used to compute the robustness of $\psi_3 = \Box_{[0,+\infty]}p$ using $Pre[3]$ from left to right in table 2.

Finally, we update table entries for the top row which corresponds to $\psi_1 = \varphi$. Since its corresponding operator $\wedge$ is propositional (Algorithm 2 Lines 6-9), we can update its value from any direction. The high level explanation of Algorithm 1 is described as follows:

1. Store values of column $-Hst + hst(\phi_k)$ for each unbounded past sub-formula ϕ_k in $Pre[k]$ and shift the table entries of predicates to the left (Lines 1-10).
2. For each row i from $|\varphi|$ to 1 compute the robustness values according to:
   (a) If φ_i is a future temporal operator, for each column j from Hrz down to $-Hst$, update table entry $T_{i,j}$ using Algorithm 2.
   (b) If φ_i is a past temporal operator, for each column j from $-Hst$ up to Hrz update table entry $T_{i,j}$ using Algorithm 2.
3. Return the robustness $(T_{1,0})$.

5   Experimental Analysis and Case Studies

5.1   Runtime Overhead

First, we measure the overhead of the proposed monitoring framework on a slightly modified version of the Automatic Transmission (AT) model provided by Mathworks as a Simulink demo[1]. The experiments were conducted on a Windows 7, Intel Core2 Quad (2.99 GHz) with 8 GB RAM.

The physical model of the AT system has two continuous (real-valued) state variables which are also its monitored outputs: the speed of the engine ω and the speed of the vehicle v. The model includes an automatic transmission controller that exhibits both continuous and discrete behavior. It is a typical CPS model and specifications over both boolean and continuous variables can be formalized. However, since the valuation of the robustness of predicates over continuous state variables is computationally more expensive than a boolean valuation, we consider only specifications over continuous state variables for the impact analysis.

We introduce our $MTL_{+pt}^{<+\infty}$ monitoring block in the AT model and test the performance over a set of specifications. In order to test the runtime overhead of our work, we artificially generate 30 different $MTL_{+pt}^{<+\infty}$ formulas based on typical critical safety formulas to show that the runtime overhead depends on both of the size of the formula and the horizon/history. We test our method for 100 runs of monitoring algorithm for each specification (formula), and for each run we use 100 simulation steps. Then, we compute the mean and variance of the overhead for each simulation step which is the execution time of Algorithm 1 in table 3. In this table, the overhead is measured on specifications that contain either nested Until operators (U columns) or nested Eventually operators (E columns).

We generate 30 formulas according to the following templates:

---

[1] Available at: http://www.mathworks.com/help/simulink/examples/
modeling-an-automatic-transmission-controller.html

Table 3. The overhead on each simulation step on the Automatic Transmission model with specifications of increasing length. Table entries are in milliseconds.

#	H=1,000				H=2,000				H=10,000			
	E		U		E		U		E		U	
	Mean	Var.	Mean	Var.	Mean	Var.	Mean	Var.	Mean	Var.	Mean	Var.
$\phi_1(H)$	2.39	0.00	4.83	0.00	8.03	0.00	15.8	0.001	188.8	0.001	358.5	0.036
$\phi_3(H)$	4.24	0.00	7.5	0.001	12.7	0.00	25.09	0.005	314.4	0.01	599	0.665
$\phi_5(H)$	4.66	0.00	8.36	0.001	14.01	0.00	27.8	0.005	309.2	0.077	650	0.014
$\phi_7(H)$	4.95	0.00	8.94	0.00	14.83	0.00	29.33	0.006	311	0.013	674.2	0.033
$\phi_9(H)$	5.23	0.00	9.46	0.001	15.4	0.001	30.56	0.007	317.5	0.011	683.5	0.698

- **E formulas:** $\phi_n(H) = p_j \longrightarrow \psi_n(H/n)$
  where $H \in \mathbb{N}$ is the finite horizon of the formula. In table 3, we used 1,000, 2,000 and 10,000 for the size of the horizon. Here, p_j is an arbitrary predicate and $\psi_n(H/n)$ is defined recursively as follows:
  $$\psi_1(h) = \Diamond_{[0,h]} p_k \text{ and } \psi_n(h) = \Diamond_{[0,h]}(p_l \wedge \psi_{n-1}(h)), \text{ for } 1 < n \leq 10$$
  where $h = H/n$, i.e., the finite horizon H divided by the number of nested subformulas n and p_k, p_l are arbitrary predicates.
- **U formulas:** $\phi_n(H) = p_j \longrightarrow \psi_n(H/n)$
  where $H \in \mathbb{N}$ is the finite horizon of the formula. In table 3, we used 1,000, 2,000 and 10,000 for the size of the horizon of H. Here, p_j is an arbitrary predicate and $\psi_n(H/n)$ is defined recursively as follows:
  $$\psi_1(h) = p_k \, \mathcal{U}_{[0,h]} p_l \text{ and } \psi_n(h) = p_m \, \mathcal{U}_{[0,h]}(p_n \wedge \psi_{n-1}(Y)), \text{ for } 1 < n \leq 10$$
  where $h = H/n$ and p_k, p_l, p_m, p_m are arbitrary predicates.

As illustrated in table 3, the computational complexity of the monitoring algorithm is closely related to the horizon and history size. Since the algorithm's complexity is of order $O(n^2)$ where n is the horizon/history, the added overhead (in worst case execution) is quadratic in terms of the size of the horizon for some formulas in table 3 (like $\phi_1(H)$). Moreover, in most cases, the impact of the number of nested temporal operators is not significant compared to the size of horizon/history windows. From table 3, we notice that when the horizon and history size is less than 2,000, the overhead for each simulation step is negligible with our prototype implementation. Furthermore, for most practical reactivity requirements, it is quite unlikely that even a window size of 2,000 sampling points is necessary. Therefore, the method could be utilized in real world monitoring applications.

5.2 Case Study

In the following, we utilize the monitoring method on an industrial size high-fidelity engine model. The model is part of the SimuQuest Enginuity [29] Matlab/Simulink tool package. The Enginuity tool package includes a library of modules for engine component blocks. It also includes pre-assembled models for standard engine configurations. In this work, we use the Port Fuel Injected (PFI) spark ignition, 4 cylinder inline engine configuration. It models the effects of combustion from first physics principles on a cylinder-by-cylinder basis, while also including regression models for particularly complex physical phenomena. The model includes a tire-model, brake system model, and a drive train model (including final drive, torque converter and transmission). The input to the system is the throttle schedule. The output is the normalized air-to-fuel(A/F) ratio. Simulink reports that this is a 56 state model. Note that this number represents only the visible states. It is possible that more states are present in the blackbox s-functions which are not accessible. This is a high dimensional non-linear system for which reachability analysis is very difficult. It also includes lookup tables, non-linear components, and inputs that affect the switching guards.

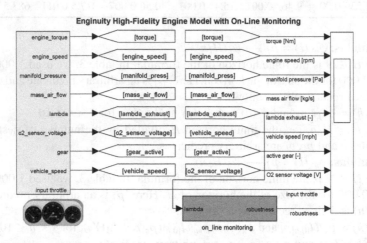

Fig. 2. SimuQuest [29] Enginuity Matlab Simulink engine model with the on-line monitoring block

A specification of practical interest for an engine is the settling time for the A/F ratio, which is the quotient between the air mass and fuel mass flow. Ideally, the normalized A/F ratio λ should always be 1, indicating that the ratio of the air and fuel flow is the same as the stoichiometric ratio. Under engine operating conditions, this output fluctuates $\pm\%10$. We add the on-line monitoring block to the Simulink model as presented in Fig. 2.

Our goal is to monitor the engine while allowing temporary fluctuations to λ. We formally define the specification as follows:

$$\phi_{pt} = (\lambda \text{ out of bounds}) \rightarrow \Diamond_{[0,1]} \boxdot_{[0,1]} \neg(\lambda \text{ out of bounds})$$

Here, the formal specification states that if the A/F ratio exceeds the allowed bounds, then the ratio should have been settled for at least one second within the last two seconds.

Notice that an alternative presentation of the formula would be to use the future eventually and always operators, i.e. the formula would be defined as follows:

$$\phi_{ft} = (\lambda \text{ out of bounds}) \rightarrow \Diamond_{[0,1]} \Box_{[0,1]} \neg(\lambda \text{ out of bounds})$$

In this case, the specification states that always, if the A/F ratio output exceeds the allowed bounds, then within one second it should settle inside the bounds and stay there for a second.

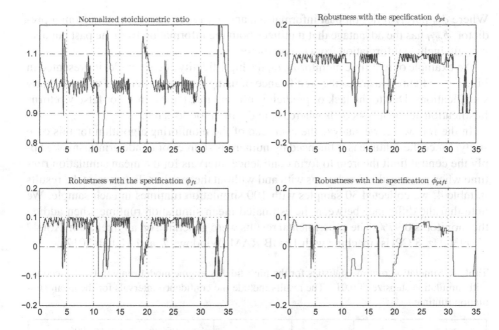

Fig. 3. Runtime monitoring of specifications ϕ_{pt}, ϕ_{ft} and ϕ_{ptft} on the high-fidelity engine model. The figure presents a normalized stoichiometric ratio, and the corresponding robustness values for specifications ϕ_{pt}, ϕ_{ft} and ϕ_{ptft}. Note that no predictor is utilized when computing the robustness values.

Clearly, both ϕ_{pt} and ϕ_{ft} are equivalent in terms of the set of traces that satisfy/falsify each specification[2]. However, in real-time robustness monitoring, there is an important distinction between the two. When the specification requires future information, either a predictor is put in place or the semantics will handle only the current information. In this case, without a predictor, the future time formula reduces to the propositional formula $\phi_{ft} = (\lambda \text{ out of bounds}) \rightarrow \neg(\lambda \text{ out of bounds}) \equiv (\lambda \text{ out of bounds})$. Therefore, past time operators should be used. Recall that when monitoring robustness, our goal is to provide early warning on when the specification may fail by approaching dangerously an undesired threshold. In other words, the past formula allows us to reason about the robustness of the actual system observations, while the future formula in collaboration with a forecast model would allow us to estimate the likely robustness. This is in contrast to many boolean monitoring algorithms which issue an *"undecided until further notice"* verdict that does not provide any actionable information.

A third alternative monitoring specification is the following formula:

$$\phi_{ptft} = \Box_{[0,2]}((\lambda \text{ out of bounds}) \rightarrow \Diamond_{[0,1]}\Box_{[0,1]}\neg(\lambda \text{ out of bounds}))$$

This specification states that at some point in the last two seconds, when λ is out of bounds then within the next second, λ will not be out of bounds and stay there for one second. This alternative seems to be the balance between the ϕ_{pt} and ϕ_{ft} formulas.

---

[2] Formally, this is the case if we ignore the first 2 seconds of the execution trace as well as the last 2 seconds – if the execution trace is finite.

Where ϕ_{pt} purely relies on past information, and ϕ_{ft} relies on information from a predictor, ϕ_{ptft} has the advantage that it utilizes both the information from the past but also it could include information from the predictor.

An example of real-time monitoring on the high-fidelity engine model is presented in Fig. 3. The figure illustrates the significance of using past time operators when defining specifications. Due to the lack of predictor information, the ϕ_{ft} monitor falsely returns falsification at about 4 seconds whereas the ϕ_{pt} monitor does not.

In the following, we analyze the overhead of the monitoring algorithm for this case study. Since the runtime is influenced by numerous sources of nondeterminism, we apply the central limit theorem to form confidence intervals for the mean simulation runtime when running the simulations with and without the monitor. To generate the results in table 4, we collected 30 samples with 100 simulation runtimes in each sample. We note that the difference between the estimated mean simulation runtime when adding the monitor is 0.97%. The experimental results were generated on an Intel Xeon X5647 (2.993GHz, 8 CPUs) machine with 12 GB RAM, Windows 7, and Matlab 2012a.

Table 4. Simulation runtime statistics for the high-fidelity engine model running for 35 seconds with simulation stepsize of 0.01s. The results include the confidence intervals for the mean simulation runtime.

Simulation runtime(sec.)	Est. Mean	Est. Std. Dev	95%		99%	
			LB	UB	LB	UB
Without monitor	10.811	0.090	10.778	10.844	10.766	10.857
With monitor	10.987	0.086	10.955	11.019	10.944	11.030

6   Conclusions and Future Work

We have presented an algorithm for monitoring the robustness of combined past and future MTL specifications. Our framework can incorporate predicted or estimated data as provided by a model predictive component. We have created a Simulink toolbox for MTL robustness monitoring which is distributed with the S-Taliro tools [30]. Our experiments indicate that the toolbox adds minimal overhead to the simulation time of Simulink models and it can be used for both runtime analysis of the models and for off-line testing. Our future work will concentrate on several aspects. First, the current version of the tool allows reasoning over timed state sequences generated under a constant sampling rate. We would like to relax this constraint so that we allow arbitrary sampling functions. Second, we would like to investigate the possibility of porting our monitor on FPGA platforms similar to [2, 8]. Finally, we envision that utilizing information about the system through the form of a model will permit us to move to an event based monitoring framework while still sufficiently approximating the robustness estimate.

Acknowledgments. This work was partially supported by NSF awards CNS 1116136 and CNS 1319560. The authors would also like to thank the anonymous reviewers for the very detailed comments.

References

1. Alur, R., Courcoubetis, C., Halbwachs, N., Henzinger, T.A., Ho, P.H., Nicollin, X., Olivero, A., Sifakis, J., Yovine, S.: The algorithmic analysis of hybrid systems. Theoretical Computer Science 138, 3–34 (1995)
2. Finkbeiner, B., Kuhtz, L.: Monitor circuits for ltl with bounded and unbounded future. In: Bensalem, S., Peled, D.A. (eds.) RV 2009. LNCS, vol. 5779, pp. 60–75. Springer, Heidelberg (2009)
3. Havelund, K., Rosu, G.: Monitoring programs using rewriting. In: Proceedings of the 16th IEEE International Conference on Automated Software Engineering (2001)
4. Havelund, K., Roşu, G.: Synthesizing monitors for safety properties. In: Katoen, J.-P., Stevens, P. (eds.) TACAS 2002. LNCS, vol. 2280, pp. 342–356. Springer, Heidelberg (2002)
5. Havelund, K., Rosu, G.: Efficient monitoring of safety properties. STTT 6, 158–173 (2004)
6. Kristoffersen, K.J., Pedersen, C., Andersen, H.R.: Runtime verification of timed LTL using disjunctive normalized equation systems. In: Proceedings of the 3rd Workshop on Run-time Verification. ENTCS, vol. 89, pp. 1–16 (2003)
7. Maler, O., Nickovic, D.: Monitoring temporal properties of continuous signals. In: Lakhnech, Y., Yovine, S. (eds.) FORMATS/2004. LNCS, vol. 3253, pp. 152–166. Springer, Heidelberg (2004)
8. Reinbacher, T., Rozier, K.Y., Schumann, J.: Temporal-logic based runtime observer pairs for system health management of real-time systems. In: Ábrahám, E., Havelund, K. (eds.) TACAS 2014. LNCS, vol. 8413, pp. 357–372. Springer, Heidelberg (2014)
9. Rosu, G., Havelund, K.: Synthesizing dynamic programming algorithms from linear temporal logic formulae. Technical report, Research Institute for Advanced Computer Science (RIACS) (2001)
10. Tan, L., Kim, J., Sokolsky, O., Lee, I.: Model-based testing and monitoring for hybrid embedded systems. In: Proceedings of the 2004 IEEE International Conference on Information Reuse and Integration, pp. 487–492 (2004)
11. Thati, P., Rosu, G.: Monitoring algorithms for metric temporal logic specifications. In: Runtime Verification. ENTCS, vol. 113, pp. 145–162. Elsevier (2005)
12. Basin, D., Klaedtke, F., Zălinescu, E.: Algorithms for monitoring real-time properties. In: Khurshid, S., Sen, K. (eds.) RV 2011. LNCS, vol. 7186, pp. 260–275. Springer, Heidelberg (2012)
13. Geilen, M.: On the construction of monitors for temporal logic properties. In: Proceedings of the 1st Workshop on Runtime Verification. ENTCS, vol. 55, pp. 181–199 (2001)
14. Maler, O., Nickovic, D., Pnueli, A.: From MITL to Timed Automata. In: Asarin, E., Bouyer, P. (eds.) FORMATS 2006. LNCS, vol. 4202, pp. 274–289. Springer, Heidelberg (2006)
15. Pnueli, A.: The temporal logic of programs. In: Proceedings of the 18th IEEE Symposium Foundations of Computer Science, pp. 46–57 (1977)
16. Koymans, R.: Specifying real-time properties with metric temporal logic. Real-Time Systems 2, 255–299 (1990)
17. Fainekos, G., Pappas, G.J.: Robustness of temporal logic specifications. In: Havelund, K., Núñez, M., Roşu, G., Wolff, B. (eds.) FATES/RV 2006. LNCS, vol. 4262, pp. 178–192. Springer, Heidelberg (2006)
18. Fainekos, G., Pappas, G.J.: Robustness of temporal logic specifications for continuous-time signals. Theor. Comput. Sci. 410, 4262–4291 (2009)
19. Donzé, A., Ferrère, T., Maler, O.: Efficient robust monitoring for stl. In: Sharygina, N., Veith, H. (eds.) CAV 2013. LNCS, vol. 8044, pp. 264–279. Springer, Heidelberg (2013)
20. Garcia, C.E., Prett, D.M., Morari, M.: Model predictive control: Theory and practice - a survey. Automatica 25, 335–348 (1989)

21. Abbas, H., Fainekos, G.E., Sankaranarayanan, S., Ivancic, F., Gupta, A.: Probabilistic tempo-
    ral logic falsification of cyber-physical systems. ACM Trans. Embedded Comput. Syst. 12,
    95 (2013)
22. Jin, X., Donze, A., Deshmukh, J., Seshia, S.: Mining requirements from closed-loop control
    models. In: Hybrid Systems: Computation and Control. ACM Press (2013)
23. Seda, A.K., Hitzler, P.: Generalized distance functions in the theory of computation. The
    Computer Journal 53, 443–464 (2008)
24. Eklund, J.M., Sprinkle, J., Sastry, S.: Implementing and testing a nonlinear model predictive
    tracking controller for aerial pursuit/evasion games on a fixed wing aircraft. In: American
    Control Conference (2005)
25. Bakirtzis, A., Petridis, V., Kiartzis, S., Alexiadis, M., Maissis, A.: A neural network short
    term load forecasting model for the greek power system. IEEE Transactions on Power Sys-
    tems 11, 858–863 (1996)
26. Monteiro, C., Bessa, R., Miranda, V., Botterud, A., Wang, J., Conzelmann, G.: Wind power
    forecasting: State-of-the-art 2009. Technical Report ANL/DIS-10-1, Argonne National Lab-
    oratory (2009)
27. Davey, B.A., Priestley, H.A.: Introduction to Lattices and Order, 2nd edn. Cambridge Uni-
    versity Press (2002)
28. Fainekos, G., Sankaranarayanan, S., Ueda, K., Yazarel, H.: Verification of automotive control
    applications using s-taliro. In: Proceedings of the American Control Conference (2012)
29. Simuquest: Enginuity (2013), http://www.simuquest.com/products/enginuity (ac-
    cessed: October 14, 2013)
30. Annpureddy, Y., Liu, C., Fainekos, G., Sankaranarayanan, S.: S-taliro: A tool for temporal
    logic falsification for hybrid systems. In: Abdulla, P.A., Leino, K.R.M. (eds.) TACAS 2011.
    LNCS, vol. 6605, pp. 254–257. Springer, Heidelberg (2011)

ROSRV: Runtime Verification for Robots

Jeff Huang[1], Cansu Erdogan[1], Yi Zhang[1], Brandon Moore[1], Qingzhou Luo[1],
Aravind Sundaresan[2], and Grigore Rosu[1]

[1] University of Illinois at Urbana-Champaign
[2] SRI International, Menlo Park, CA 94025
{smhuang,bmmoore,cerdoga2,qluo2,grosu}@illinois.edu,
aravind@ai.sri.com

Abstract. We present ROSRV, a runtime verification framework for robotic applications on top of the Robot Operating System (ROS [8]), a widely used open-source framework for robot software development. ROSRV aims to address the safety and security issues of robots by providing a transparent monitoring infrastructure that intercepts and monitors the commands and messages passing through the system. Safety and security properties can be defined in a formal specification language, and are ensured by automatically generated monitors. ROSRV integrates seamlessly with ROS—no change in ROS nor the application code is needed. ROSRV has been applied and evaluated on a commercial robot.

1 Introduction

The Robot Operating System (ROS [4]) is an open-source meta-operating system for robot software development. With the increasing popularity of programmable robots, ROS has become the de facto standard for robotic applications such as perception [3], motion planning [1], object detection [2], etc. ROS provides common robot-specific libraries as well as standard operating system services such as hardware abstraction, low-level device control, etc[1]. At the lowest level, ROS offers a message passing interface that provides inter-process communication including publish/subscribe messages and distributed parameter configuration. The message passing is based on a graph architecture where computation takes place in ROS processes (called *nodes*) that may receive, post and multiplex messages.

With the wide adoption of ROS, however, its safety and security are becoming an important concern. For instance, any node is allowed to publish/subscribe arbitrary messages on any topic[2], which can be easily abused by attackers. Moreover, ROS is designed to be highly dynamic and distributed, making it hard or impossible to verify statically. For example, nodes running on different hardware devices can join and leave dynamically, changing parameters and namespaces,

---

[1] Note that ROS is not a traditional operating system. For example, it does not deal with process scheduling.

[2] In ROS, topics are communication channels between publishers and subscribers which identify the content of the message.

B. Bonakdarpour and S.A. Smolka (Eds.): RV 2014, LNCS 8734, pp. 247–254, 2014.

and creating new message topics. A node can be killed by another node via a shutdown command or accidentally replaced by a new node with the same name.

In this paper, we present a runtime verification framework, ROSRV, for improving the safety and security of robots running ROS. ROSRV is designed to be lightweight, expressive, and transparent, with no changes to ROS or the application running on top of ROS. Its core is a runtime monitoring infrastructure that intercepts, observes and optionally modifies the commands and messages passing through the system, and performs actions upon relevant events defined over the messages. Safety properties are implemented as monitors on top of this infrastructure, such that all relevant messages are monitored and property-triggered user-specified actions are performed. For example, to prevent a robot from overturn, a safety monitor can intercept and modify the robot speed/acceleration messages. ROSRV provides a specification language for safety properties, and monitors are automatically generated from specifications. For security, ROSRV provides a specification language for access control policies and enforces them at runtime. For example, it is possible to specify which nodes are permitted to publish messages on certain topics or to send shutdown signals to kill other nodes.

ROSRV integrates seamlessly with ROS and has been applied on the Land-Shark[3], an unmanned ground vehicle (UGV) robot running ROS. We illustrate ROSRV via a case study on LandShark and demonstrate how ROSRV improves the safety and security of LandShark through monitoring safety properties and enforcing access control policies. All the ROSRV source code, materials, and demos are publicly available at http://fsl.cs.illinois.edu/rosrv.

2   Robot Operating System (ROS)

We briefly overview ROS communication concepts [7], highlighting its safety and security limitations. ROS is a peer-to-peer network of nodes that communicate with each other using XMLRPC and custom ROS messages that are based on TCP/IP. Each message has a type and is transported on a channel called a *topic*, and each node may subscribe and publish to arbitrarily many topics. A special node, the *Master*, coordinates the communication and provides global services such as naming, registration, parameter updates and lookups.

Fig. 1 depicts the ROS communication architecture. Node communication is initiated with a sequence of XMLRPC requests. First, nodes register with the Master; e.g., the publisher may register that it publishes messages on topic "chat" at address "foo:1234", and then when a subscriber registers to topic "chat" the Master passes it the publisher's address. Second, the subscriber contacts the publisher to obtain a topic connection and negotiate the transport protocol. Finally, the subscriber connects to the publisher and starts receiving messages. ROS also supports commands that query/update the system state, such as the name, address, and published/subscribed topics of a node, query published topics, kill a node, etc.

---

[3]   The LandShark UGV is a product of Black-i Robotics (www.blackirobotics.com).

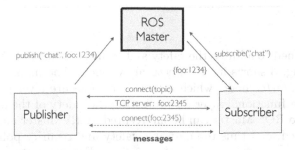

Fig. 1. ROS Communication Architecture

Fig. 2. Safety issues: LandShark shoots itself and tips over

2.1 ROS Safety and Security Issues

Safety is often application specific and challenging to address in a generic distributed communication framework such as ROS. Also, since ROS is designed to be open and dynamic, it lacks any security protection mechanism. For example, an attacker can easily create a node, query the Master about the system state, and send shutdown commands to kill any node. Moreover, nodes are uniquely identified by their name, with newly created nodes replacing existing ones with the same name. Thus, an attacker can easily fake a node to publish bogus messages on important topics. For instance, a navigation node in a robot may be killed and replaced by a fake node that misdirects the robot.

The LandShark UGV has an onboard Linux box connected to various devices: GPS, radar, cameras, motor and turret controllers, a paintball gun, etc. The paintball gun can fire on receiving a trigger message. Each device has a driver and a corresponding ROS node (wrapper) which publishes sensor data and/or accepts commands as ROS messages. An operator control unit (OCU) node listens to messages from the robot and sends it user commands.

Fig. 2 shows two scenarios where the safety of the robot is infringed. The first, "robot shoots itself", is motivated by the fact that no mechanism in the LandShark or ROS prevents this behavior, so the LandShark can shoot itself (inadvertently or maliciously, by an attacker). The second, "LandShark tips over", occurs when it accelerates too quickly or becomes unbalanced. This scenario is typical for UGVs but there is no safety mechanism in ROS to prevent it.

3   ROSRV

ROSRV is designed to address the safety and security issues in ROS-based robot applications. Fig. 3 shows its architectural overview. The main difference from ROS is the *RVMaster* node, which acts as both a secure layer protecting ROS Master and as a functional layer for protecting the safety of the application: all node requests to ROS Master can be intercepted by RVMaster and all messages can be monitored, and thus the desirable safety and security policies enforced.

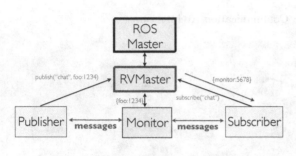

Fig. 3. ROSRV Architecture

For example, access control policies such as allowing only certain nodes to publish messages on a certain topic can be enforced by checking the node identity and topic name in the request and rejecting it if they do not match the policy. We have developed an IP address-based access control specification that allows the security policies to be enforced as system configuration.

Monitors are generated by RVMaster from safety specifications and implemented as ordinary ROS nodes that can subscribe and publish messages. However, RVMaster keeps track of all the communication requests by the other nodes in the system and manipulates the point-to-point communication addresses so that the generated monitors act as men-in-the-middle. For example, a monitor can drop the triggering message of LandShark when the position of the gun is within the range of pointing at itself, or modify the acceleration message when the LandShark is moving too fast to prevent it from tipping.

An important property of ROSRV is that it does not require any change to ROS or the application code. The only requirement is to configure the RVMaster to listen at the standard port and the ROS Master to listen at a hidden port visible only to RVMaster. This is implemented using a firewall to block access to the ROS master port. In this way, all the ordinary nodes in the system remain the same (sending requests to the default port, sending and receiving messages from normal ROS nodes), and are not even aware of being monitored.

3.1   Monitoring Safety Properties

A safety property is specified by means of events and actions based on event sequences. Fig. 4 shows a simple example to illustrate the idea. The property we want to monitor here requires that the robot can only fire in certain safe poses. There are two events, checkPosition and safeTrigger. Each event has its own parameters and the topic and type of the messages being monitored. For example, checkPosition is used to check whether the gun is at a safe position: "position > -0.45" (not pointing at itself). It listens to topic */landshark/joint* _states_ with message type _sensor_msgs/JointState_, which holds two arrays: name and position. The second elements of these arrays are bound to variables N and P, respectively. They are used as the parameters of the event and in the event handler code. Event handler code is used to trigger actions under certain conditions. For example, in checkPosition the global variable isSafeTrigger will be set to true if and only if the gun is at an angle larger than -0.45; later on it is used in safeTrigger to determine whether the trigger is allowed or not.

```
safeTrigger() {
    bool isSafeTrigger = false;
    event checkPosition(string N, double P)
        /landshark/joint_states sensor_msgs/JointState
        '{name[1]:N, position[1]:P}'  {
    if (N=="turret_tilt"){if (P > -0.45){ //check gun position
            isSafeTrigger = true;
        }else{
            isSafeTrigger = false;
    }   }   }
    event safeTrigger() /landshark_control/trigger
        landshark_msgs/PaintballTrigger '{}'  {
        if(!isSafeTrigger) return; //drop trigger message
    }
}
```

Fig. 4. Safe Trigger Specification

Our monitoring infrastructure enables us to use any _logic plugins_ of Monitoring-Oriented Programming (MOP [5]) to specify temporal properties over events, such as regular expressions, linear temporal logics, context-free grammars, etc., and to trigger actions only when certain patterns of event sequences are matched, because such specifications translate into ordinary code that implements corresponding monitors, which are executed as event actions.

ROSRV automatically generates C++ monitoring code from all the user-defined specifications, and creates nodes that act as monitors as explained above. Each event generates one call back method and all the call back methods are registered by RVMaster. Parameters of events are treated as references to fields in monitored messages, so users can modify messages in event handler code. Event handlers are inserted in call back methods that are called at runtime.

3.2 Enforcing Security Policies

ROSRV enforces access control based on a user-provided specification of access policies as input configuration. On receiving any XMLRPC request, RVMaster decides whether the request is allowed to go to the ROS Master according the specification. The policies are currently categorized into four different sections: [Nodes], [Subscribers], [Publishers], and [Commands]. Under each section, the access policy is written as a key followed by an assignment symbol and a list of values. For [Nodes], "key" is the node name, and "value" is the machine identity allowed to create nodes with the name "key". For [Subscribers] and [Publishers], "key" is the topic name and "value" is the node identity allowed to subscribe/publish to the topic. For [Commands], "key" is the command name and "value" is the node identity allowed to perform the command. We support access granularity at a host level. We use the source IP address of the request

```
[Groups]
localhost = 127.0.0.1                [Publishers]                    [Commands]
certikos = ip1 ip2 ip3 ip4           default=localhost certikos      # Commands: full access
ocu = ip5 ip6 ip7 ip8                /landshark_control/trigger= ocu getSystemState = localhost certikos ocu
                                                                     # Commands: limited access
[Nodes]                              [Subscribers]                   lookupNode = localhost certikos
default=localhost                    default = localhost certikos    # Commands: local access only
/landshark_radar=certikos            /landshark/gps = ocu            shutdown = localhost
```

Fig. 5. Sample access control policy for LandShark

to identify the host, because the node name itself is self-reported. IP address aliases and groups are also supported in our specification language.

Fig. 5 shows a snippet of the LandShark access policy. The [Group] section defines three groups of IP addresses. In the [Nodes] section, "default=localhost" means that by default "localhost" is allowed to create a node with any name, and "/landshark_radar=certikos" that the alias "certikos" is allowed to create a node with name "/landshark_radar". In [Publishers], only nodes running on machine "ocu" can publish to topic "/landshark_control/trigger". In [Commands], "getSystemState=localhost certikos ocu" means that nodes running on machines "localhost", "certikos", or "ocu" are allowed to send "getSystemState" requests to ROS Master, and "shutdown=localhost" that only nodes on "localhost" are allowed to "shutdown" other nodes.

4   Current Limitations and Future Work

Security The main limitation of the current implementation is the reliance on IP addresses in particular and on network routing in general to guarantee security. Naively trusting IP addresses does not protect against attackers who can run processes on the same (virtual) machines as trusted nodes, or spoof packets on physical network segments carrying unencrypted traffic. To defend against local attacks, the RVMaster and the mutually distrustful nodes can be run on separate (virtual) machines. To protect against spoofed IP addresses, the machines can be configured to receive packets from other machines on distinct virtual network interfaces, with the link between interface and machine using encrypted tunnels or relying on the virtual machine monitor to provide private local connections. Then routing can be configured so that only packets from specific machines can claim recognized IP addresses, and also to prevent nodes from being accessed directly. We intend to augment RVMaster with tools to automate the creation and configuration of virtual machines to more easily provide this level of security.

Scalability Currently ROSRV is centralized. All the monitor nodes live in the same multithreaded process, and all communication in the system is monitored. We tested the performance of monitoring with 10+ nodes in Landshark. The message delay caused by monitoring is on small digits of milliseconds. Although this is acceptable in our current project, the centralized monitoring may face scalability problems with a large number of nodes. We plan to investigate decentralized mechanisms such as multimaster [6] to improve scalability. The multimaster approach also enriches the fault tolerance of the system, as the current ROS master is a single point of failure.

Formal verification Currently the runtime verified system is not formally verified. This would require a formal model of ROS itself, as well as proving that the generated monitors and glue code guarantee the desired global system properties. At the implementation level, this would consist of showing that RVMaster respects the given model of ROS and invokes the monitor code at correct times to impose monitoring, and developing tools to prove that monitor code generated from higher level specifications actually correctly monitors those specifications.

5   Conclusion

With our society increasingly depending on robots, the importance of their safe and secure operation cannot be overstated. This paper makes first steps towards the runtime verification of robot applications. Users provide formal safety and security specifications, and monitors are automatically generated and incorporated in the system to ensure the safety and security of robots.

Acknowledgement. This material is based on research sponsored by DARPA under agreement number FA8750-12-C-0284. The U.S. Government is authorized to reproduce and distribute reprints for Governmental purposes notwithstanding any copyright notation thereon. The views and conclusions contained herein are those of the authors and should not be interpreted as necessarily representing the official policies or endorsements, either expressed or implied, of DARPA or the U.S. Government.

References

1. Kalakrishnan, M., Chitta, S., Theodorou, E., Pastor, P., Schaal, S.: STOMP: Stochastic trajectory optimization for motion planning. In: ICRA, pp. 4569–4574. IEEE (2011)
2. Klank, U., Carton, D., Beetz, M.: Transparent object detection and reconstruction on a mobile platform. In: ICRA, pp. 5971–5978. IEEE (2011)
3. Pitzer, B., Styer, M., Bersch, C., DuHadway, C., Becker, J.: Towards perceptual shared autonomy for robotic mobile manipulation. In: ICRA, pp. 6245–6251. IEEE (2011)
4. Quigley, M., Conley, K., Gerkey, B.P., Faust, J., Foote, T., Leibs, J., Wheeler, R., Ng, A.Y.: ROS: an open-source robot operating system. In: ICRA Workshop on Open Source Software (2009)
5. Roşu, G., Chen, F.: Semantics and algorithms for parametric monitoring. Logical Methods in Computer Science 8(1), 1–47 (2012)
6. ROS contributors. ROS Multimaster, http://wiki.ros.org/rocon_multimaster (accessed April 25, 2014)
7. ROS contributors. ROS technical overview, http://wiki.ros.org/ROS/Technical%20verview (accessed April 25, 2014)
8. ROS contributors. ROS.org, http://wiki.ros.org (accessed April 25, 2014)

A   Demo Overview

The ROSRV tool consists of the RVMaster node written in C++, a monitor generator (called *rosmop*) written in Java and JavaCC, and a set of bash scripts to compile and start ROS. The tool works on Ubuntu 12.04 with ROS Groovy distribution release. The user simply describes the property or a set of properties using the monitor specification language and specifies the access control policy in a configuration file. Taking the property specifications as input, ROSRV first automatically generates all the monitors, with each monitor corresponding to one property. The user can run *rosmop* with either a single property specification or the directory containing a set of property specifications, to generate the monitors and compile the whole system.

In the accompanying video, we demonstrate the use of ROSRV with three monitors and four access control policies on the Landshark robot.

- *Safe Trigger*: we first show that by default the Landshark can shoot itself when we move the gun to point at itself. We then enable the safe trigger monitor and show the gun is no longer allowed to shoot when pointing at Landshark, but can still shoot when pointing at the ground.
- *Safe Zone*: this monitor monitors the location of Landshark against a zone, and ensures that once Landshark enters the zone it cannot move out. Within the zone, we also show Landshark is disallowed to shoot itself, to demonstrate that the tool can support multiple monitors working simultaneously.
- *Logging*: in many cases, users want to log messages in the robot to understand the runtime behavior of the system. We show a logging monitor that, once enabled, prints out the messages that the user is interested in, which could be useful for debugging.
- *Access control policies*: we demonstrate a policy for each of the four sections in the sample access control policies in Fig. 5. We run this demo with two machines: one running ROSRV and all the legal nodes, and the other running the attacker nodes. We show the attacker nodes cannot perform any action not specified in the access control policy file, such as publishing messages on a certain topic, killing another node, or pretending to be an existing legal node.

The demonstration video is available at:
  http://fsl.cs.illinois.edu/index.php/ROSRV

Symbolic Execution Debugger (SED)

Martin Hentschel, Richard Bubel, and Reiner Hähnle

TU Darmstadt, Dept. of Computer Science, Darmstadt, Germany
{hentschel,bubel,haehnle}@cs.tu-darmstadt.de

Abstract. We present the Symbolic Execution Debugger for sequential JAVA programs. Being based on symbolic execution, its functionality goes beyond that of traditional interactive debuggers. For instance, debugging can start directly at any method or statement and all program execution paths are explored simultaneously. To support program comprehension, execution paths as well as intermediate states are visualized.

Keywords: Symbolic Execution, Debugging, Program Execution Visualization.

1 Introduction

We present the Symbolic Execution Debugger (SED),[1] a language independent extension of the Eclipse debug platform for symbolic execution. Symbolic execution [3,4,9,10] is a program analysis technique based on the interpretation of a program with symbolic values. This makes it possible to explore *all* concrete execution paths (up to a finite depth). We describe an SED implementation that uses KeY [2] as the underlying symbolic execution engine, supporting sequential JAVA without floats, garbage collection and dynamic class loading. Our main contributions are the SED platform, interactive symbolic execution of JAVA and visualization of program behavior including unbounded loops and method calls.

The SED supports traditional debugger functionality like step-wise execution or breakpoints, and enhances it as follows: Debugging can begin at any method or any other statement in a program, no fixture is required. The initial state can be specified partially or not at all. During symbolic execution all feasible execution paths are discovered, thus it is not necessary to set up a concrete initial program state leading to an execution where a targeted bug occurs. At any time each intermediate state can be inspected using the SED. Intermediate states tend to be small and simple, because symbolic execution can be started close to the suspected location of a bug and the symbolic states contain only program variables accessed during execution. This makes it easy for the bug hunter to comprehend intermediate states and the actions performed on them to find the origin of a bug. Heisenbugs [5], a class of program errors that disappear while debugging, are avoided as the behavior of a program is correctly reflected in its symbolic execution. Besides debugging the SED platform allows to visualize and explore results of static analysis based on symbolic execution.

---

[1] The website www.key-project.org/eclipse/SED provides an installation & user guide (with instructions on how to use API classes), screencast and theoretical background.

B. Bonakdarpour and S.A. Smolka (Eds.): RV 2014, LNCS 8734, pp. 255–262, 2014.
© Springer International Publishing Switzerland 2014

2   Symbolic Execution

Symbolic execution (SE) means to execute a program with symbolic values in lieu of concrete values. We explain SE and how it is used interactively in the SED by example: method eq shown in the listing in Fig. 1 compares the given Number instance with the current one.

For a JAVA method to be executed it must be called explicitly. For instance, the expression **new** Number().eq(**new** Number()); invokes eq on a fresh instance with a different instance as argument. This results in a single execution path: first the guard in line 5 is evaluated to true, as fields of integer type are initialized with 0 by default. Finally, true is returned as result. To inspect another execution path the method has to be called in a different state.

Let us execute method eq symbolically, i.e., without a concrete argument, but a reference to a symbolic value n which can represent any object or **null**. In our SE tree notation we use different icons to underscore the semantics of nodes. As Fig. 1 shows, the root is a *Start Node* representing the initial state and the program fragment (any method or any block of statements) to execute. Here a call to eq is represented by its *Method Call* child node.

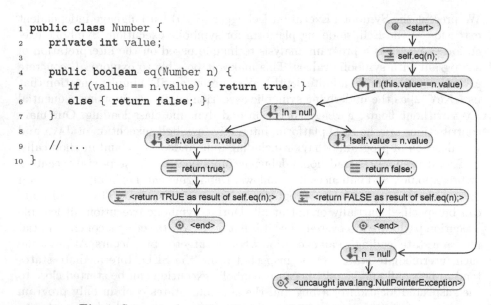

```
1  public class Number {
2      private int value;
3
4      public boolean eq(Number n) {
5          if (value == n.value) { return true; }
6          else { return false; }
7      }
8
9  // ...
10 }
```

Fig. 1. Source code of class Number and SE tree of method eq

The **if**-guard, represented as a *Branch Statement* node, splits execution when the field value is accessed on the symbolic object n. Because nothing is known about n, it could be **null**. The *Branch Condition* children nodes show the condition under which each path is taken. On the left, where n is not **null**, the comparison in the **if**-guard splits execution again. If both values are the same, the **return** statement is executed, indicated by a *Statement* node. Now the symbolic path of the method is fully executed and returns true in the *Method Return* child node. This SE path ends in the *Termination* node. The branch where the values are different looks similar, but false is returned instead. In the rightmost branch the parameter n has the value **null** and SE ends with an uncaught NullPointerException, visualized as an *Exceptional Termination* node.[2]

In contrast to concrete execution, SE does not require fixture code and discovers all feasible execution paths (up to its execution depth). Each SE path through an SE tree may represent infinitely many concrete executions and is characterized by its path condition (the conjunction of all branch conditions on it). SE may not terminate in presence of loops and recursive methods which can be avoided by applying loop invariants or method contracts, see Section 4.

3   Basic Usage of the Symbolic Execution Debugger

The SED is realized as an Eclipse plugin. SE of a selected method or selected statements in a method can be started via the Eclipse context menu item *Debug As, Symbolic Execution Debugger (SED)*. The user is then offered to switch to the *Symbolic Debug* perspective, which provides all relevant views for interactive symbolic execution (see Fig. 2).

The *Debug* view allows, as usual, to switch between debug sessions and to control program execution. In case of SE, the view shows the traversed SE tree, instead of the current stack trace. The SE tree is also visualized in the *Symbolic Execution Tree* view (it is identical to the tree in Fig. 1). An SE tree sketch is provided by the *Symbolic Execution Tree (Thumbnail)* view to help navigation. The symbolic program state of a node consists of variables and their symbolic values. It can be inspected in the *Variables* view. Breakpoints suspend execution and are managed in the *Breakpoints* view. The details of a selected node (path condition, call stack, etc.) are available in the *Properties* view. The source code line corresponding to the selected SE tree node is highlighted in the editor. The *Symbolic Execution Settings* view lets one customize SE, e.g., choose between method inlining and method contract application.

In Fig. 2 the SE tree node **return true;** is selected. In the *Variables* view we can see that the symbolic values of field value are identical for the objects referenced by self (the current instance) and parameter n. This is exactly what is enforced by the path condition. In an object-oriented setting one could think that self and n refer to different instances, but this needs not to be the case. The path condition is also satisfied if n and self reference the same object. Unintended *aliasing* is a source of bugs. The SED helps to find these by determining and visualizing all possible memory layouts w.r.t. the path condition.

Selecting context menu item *Visualize Memory Layouts* of an SE tree node creates a visualization of possible memory layouts as a *symbolic object diagram* (see Fig. 3). It resembles a UML object diagram and shows the dependencies

---

[2] The instantiation of the thrown exception is not visualized since we do not include execution of JAVA API methods for simplicity.

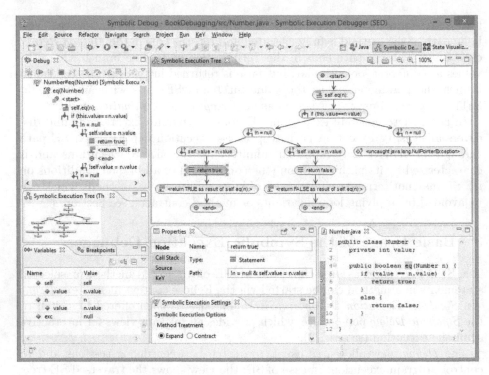

Fig. 2. Symbolic Execution Debugger: Interactive symbolic execution

between objects, the values of object fields and the local variables of the current state.

The root of the symbolic object diagram is visualized as a rounded rectangle and shows all local variables visible at the current node. In Fig. 3, the local variables n and self refer to objects visualized as rectangles. The content of the instance field value is shown in the lower compartment of each object.

The toolbar (near the origin of the callout) allows to select different possible layouts and to switch between the current and the initial state of each layout. The initial state shows how the memory layout looked before the execution started resulting in the current state. Fig. 3 shows both possible layouts of the selected node **return true**; in the current state. The second memory layout (inside the callout) represents the situation, where n and self are aliased.

4   Usage Scenarios

Like a traditional debugger, the SED helps the user to control execution and to comprehend each performed step. It is helpful to focus on a single branch where a buggy state is suspected. (To change the focus to a different branch, no new debugging session or new input values are needed). It is always possible to revisit previous steps, because each node in the SE tree provides the full state.

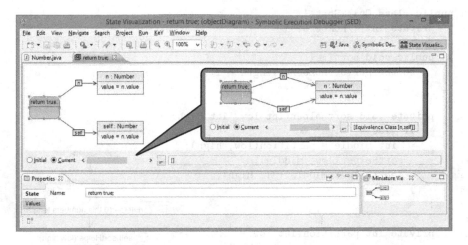

Fig. 3. Symbolic Execution Debugger: Different memory layouts

Finding the Origin of Bugs The explicit rendering of different control flow branches in the SE tree constitutes a major advantage over traditional debuggers. Unexpected or missing expected branches are good candidates for possible sources of bugs. Fig. 4a shows a buggy part of a Quicksort implementation for sorting array numbers. Within a concrete execution of a large application a StackOverflowError was thrown. It indicates that method sortHelper calls itself infinitely often. Using SED we start debugging close to the suspected location of the bug, namely, at method sort. Executing the method stepwise, exhibits execution paths taken when invoking the method in an illegal state. Exploration of such cases can be avoided by providing a precondition which limits the initial symbolic state. In this example, we exclude empty arrays by specifying the precondition numbers != **null** && numbers.length >= 1 in the debug configuration. After a few steps, the SE tree produced by SED (see Fig. 4b) shows that the **if** statement is not branching. This is suspicious and deserves closer attention. Inspecting the **if** guard shows that the comparison should have been low < high and the source of the bug is found.[3]

Program and Specification Understanding SE trees show control and data flow at the same time. Thus they can be used to help understanding programs and specifications just by inspecting them. This can be useful during code reviews or in early prototyping phases, where the full implementation is not yet available. It works best, when partial method contracts and invariants are available to achieve compact and finite SE trees. However, useful specifications can be much weaker than what would be required for verification. The listing in Fig. 5 shows a buggy implementation of method indexOf with a very simple loop invariant written in JML. We configured the symbolic execution engine to apply

---

[3] Without the precondition the bug can be observed as well, but a little later.

```
1  public class QuickSort {
2     private int[] numbers;
3
4     public void sort() {
5        sortHelper(0, numbers.length - 1);
6     }
7
8     private void sortHelper(int low, int high) {
9        if (low <= high) {
10           int middle = partition(low, high);
11          sortHelper(low, middle);
12          sortHelper(middle + 1, high);
13       }
14    }
15
16    private int partition(int low,
17                          int high) {
18       // ...
19    }
20 }
```

(a) Buggy Quicksort implementation (from [6])   (b) SE tree

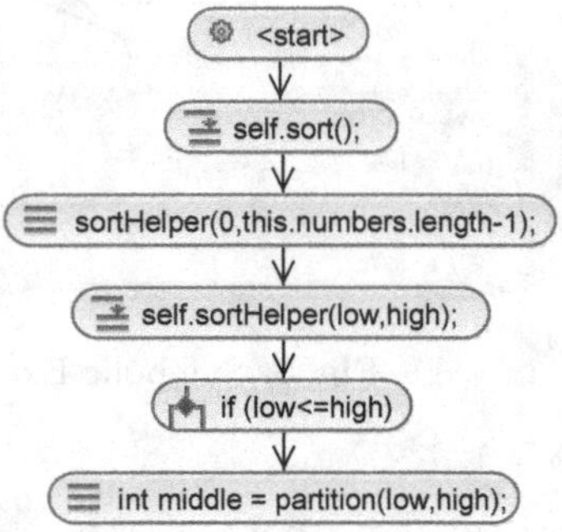

Fig. 4. Quicksort example

loop invariants instead of unrolling loops, which guarantees a finite SE tree. The resulting SE tree under precondition a != **null** is also shown in Fig. 5. Application of the loop invariant splits execution into two branches. *Body Preserves Invariant* represents all loop iterations and *Use Case* continues execution after the loop (full branch conditions are not shown for brevity).

Without checking further details, one can see that the leftmost branch terminates in a state where the loop invariant is not preserved. Now, closer inspection shows the reason to be that, when the array element is found, the variable i is not increased, hence the **decreasing** clause (a.length - i) of the invariant is violated. The two branches below the *Use Case* branch correspond to the code after the loop has terminated. In one case an element was found, in the other not. Looking at the return node, however, we find that in both cases instead of the index computed in the loop, the value of i is returned.

Our examples demonstrate that SE trees can be used to answer questions about thrown exceptions or returned values. In SED the full state of each node is available and can be visualized. Thus it is easily possible to see whether and where new objects are created and which fields are changed when (comparison between initial and current memory layout).

Using breakpoints, symbolic execution is continued until a breakpoint is hit on any branch. Breakpoints can be attached to a line of code with or without a condition or they may consist only of a condition. Thus they can be used to find execution paths that (i) throw a specified exception, (ii) access or modify a specified field, (iii) invoke or return from a specified method. Breakpoints can

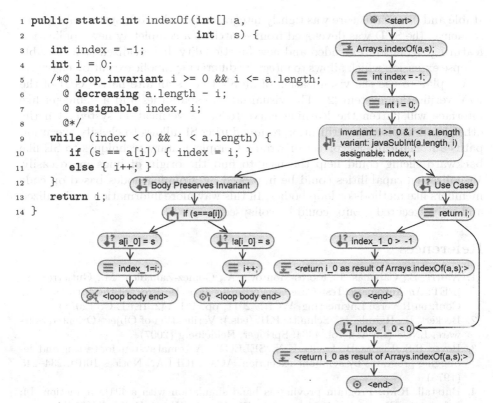

```
1  public static int indexOf(int[] a,
2                             int  s) {
3      int index = -1;
4      int i = 0;
5      /*@ loop_invariant i >= 0 && i <= a.length;
6        @ decreasing a.length - i;
7        @ assignable index, i;
8        @*/
9      while (index < 0 && i < a.length) {
10         if (s == a[i]) { index = i; }
11         else { i++; }
12     }
13     return i;
14 }
```

Fig. 5. Buggy and partially specified implementation of indexOf and its SE Tree

also be used to (iv) control loop unwinding and recursive method invocation and (v) to stop at an intermediate state that has a specified property.

5   Related and Future Work

A number of recent tools implement SE for program verification [8] or test generation [1,12], which are complementary to SED. In fact, SED could be employed to control or visualize these tools. As far as we know, EFFIGY [10] was the first system that allowed to interactively execute a program symbolically in the context of debugging. It did not support specifications or visualization.

The Eclipse plugin of Java Path Finder (JPF) [11] prints the analysis results obtained from SE as a text report, but does neither provide graphical visualization nor interactive control of SE. JPF is prototypically supported by SED as an alternative SE engine.

The SE engine and its Eclipse integration described in [7] features non-interactive graphic visualization of the SE tree. SED allows to interact with the visualization as a means to control SE and to inspect symbolic states.

A prototypic symbolic state debugger that could not make use of method contracts and loop invariants was presented in [6]. However, that tool was not very stable and its architecture was tightly integrated into the KeY system. As a consequence, the SED was developed from scratch as a completely new application featuring significant extended and new functionality. It is realized as a reusable Eclipse extension which allows to integrate different symbolic execution engines.

We plan to use the visualization of an SE tree as an alternative GUI of the KeY verification system [2]. The visualization capabilities and a debugger-like interface will flatten the learning curve to use a verification system. On the other hand, exploiting verification results during SE allows to classify execution paths automatically as correct or wrong. Complementary techniques to SE like backward slicing could help the user to find the origin of bugs more easily. Visualization capabilities could be improved by grouping nodes based on code members like methods or loop bodies. In this way more information is visualized and fully executed groups could be collapsed.

References

1. Albert, E., Cabanas, I., Flores-Montoya, A., Gomez-Zamalloa, M., Gutierrez, S.: jPET: An Automatic Test-Case Generator for Java. In: Proc. of the 18th Working Conf. on Reverse Engineering, WCRE 2011, pp. 441–442. IEEE CS (2011)
2. Beckert, B., Hähnle, R., Schmitt, P.H. (eds.): Verification of Object-Oriented Software. LNCS (LNAI), vol. 4334. Springer, Heidelberg (2007)
3. Boyer, R.S., Elspas, B., Levitt, K.N.: SELECT—A formal system for testing and debugging programs by symbolic execution. ACM SIGPLAN Notices 10(6), 234–245 (1975)
4. Burstall, R.M.: Program proving as hand simulation with a little induction. In: Information Processing 1974, pp. 308–312. Elsevier/North-Holland (1974)
5. Grottke, M., Trivedi, K.S.: A classification of software faults. Journal of Reliability Engineering Association of Japan 27(7), 425–438 (2005)
6. Hähnle, R., Baum, M., Bubel, R., Rothe, M.: A visual interactive debugger based on symbolic execution. In: ASE, pp. 143–146 (2010)
7. Ibing, A.: Parallel SMT-Constrained Symbolic Execution for Eclipse CDT/Codan. In: Yenigün, H., Yilmaz, C., Ulrich, A. (eds.) ICTSS 2013. LNCS, vol. 8254, pp. 196–206. Springer, Heidelberg (2013)
8. Jacobs, B., Smans, J., Philippaerts, P., Vogels, F., Penninckx, W., Piessens, F.: VeriFast: A Powerful, Sound, Predictable, Fast Verifier for C and Java. In: Bobaru, M., Havelund, K., Holzmann, G.J., Joshi, R. (eds.) NFM 2011. LNCS, vol. 6617, pp. 41–55. Springer, Heidelberg (2011)
9. Katz, S., Manna, Z.: Towards automatic debugging of programs. In: Proc. of the Intl. Conf. on Reliable Software, Los Angeles, pp. 143–155. ACM Press (1975)
10. King, J.C.: Symbolic Execution and Program Testing. Communications of the ACM 19(7), 385–394 (1976)
11. Păsăreanu, C.S., Mehlitz, P.C., Bushnell, D.H., Gundy-Burlet, K., Lowry, M., Person, S., Pape, M.: Combining Unit-level Symbolic Execution and System-level Concrete Execution for Testing Nasa Software. In: Proc. of the 2008 Intl. Symposium on Software Testing and Analysis, ISSTA 2008, pp. 15–26. ACM (2008)
12. Tillmann, N., de Halleux, J.: Pex: White Box Test Generation for .NET. In: Beckert, B., Hähnle, R. (eds.) TAP 2008. LNCS, vol. 4966, pp. 134–153. Springer, Heidelberg (2008)

Checking Data Structure Properties
Orders of Magnitude Faster

Emmanouil Koukoutos and Viktor Kuncak

EPFL, Lausanne, Switzerland
{emmanouil.koukoutos,viktor.kuncak}@epfl.ch

Abstract. Executable formal contracts help verify a program at run-time when static verification fails. However, these contracts may be prohibitively slow to execute, especially when they describe the transformations of data structures. In fact, often an efficient data structure operation with $O(\log(n))$ running time executes in $O(n\log(n))$ when naturally written specifications are executed at run time.

We present a set of techniques that improve the efficiency of run-time checks by orders of magnitude, often recovering the original asymptotic behavior of operations. Our implementation first removes any statically verified parts of checks. Then, it applies a program transformation that changes recursively computed properties into data structure fields, ensuring that properties are evaluated no more than once on a given data structure node. We present evaluation of our techniques on the Leon system for verification of purely functional programs.

1 Introduction

Static verifiers can demonstrate program correctness for any given input. However, their limitations prevent them from proving complex programs. Runtime verification can be of great help in such circumstances. Unfortunately, contracts that are good for static verification are often expensive to check at runtime, and may even degrade program performance asymptotically.

Related Work. There have been some attempts to mitigate the performance penalty of runtime checks. Shankar and Bodík [7] present DITTO, an automatic incrementalizer for imperative data structure invariant checking. The system memoizes results of runtime checks for data structures, and recomputes them only when the data structure is mutated, rather than every time it is accessed. Memoization itself is first proposed by Michie [5]. Hughes [4] introduces lazy memo-functions, which optimize memoization by computing the results of the memoized functions lazily. Memoization (or tabling) has also been included as a built-in feature in XSB and other variants of Prolog [9], providing both theoretical and practical benefits to performance and termination of Prolog programs.

Another popular strategy for optimizing runtime checks is partially evaluating checks ahead of time, i.e. running a static verification step before executing the program, in order to simplify or completely remove runtime checks. This idea

B. Bonakdarpour and S.A. Smolka (Eds.): RV 2014, LNCS 8734, pp. 263–268, 2014.

```
sealed abstract class Tree
case class Leaf() extends Tree
case class Node(left : Tree, value : Int, right: Tree) extends Tree
def insert(t: Tree, e : Int) : Tree = {
  require(isBST(t))
  t match {
    case Leaf() ⇒ Node(Leaf(), e, Leaf())
    case Node(l,v,r) ⇒ if (e == v) t
      else if (e < v) Node(insert(l,e), v, r)
      else Node(l, v, insert(r,e))}
} ensuring (res ⇒ isBST(res))

def isBST(t:Tree) : Boolean = t match {
  case Leaf() ⇒ true
  case Node(l,v,r) ⇒ isBST(l) && isBST(r) && treeMax(l) < v && v < treeMin(r) }
```

Fig. 1. Binary Search Tree

```
case class TreeFields(isBST: Boolean, treeMin : Int, treeMax : Int)
sealed abstract class Tree
case class Leaf(treeFields : TreeFields) extends Tree
case class Node(left : Tree, value : Int, right: Tree, treeFields : TreeFields) extends Tree
def makeNode(left : Tree, value : Int, right: Tree) = Node(left, value, right, {
  val lmin = left.treeFields.min; val lmax = left.treeFields.max
  val rmin = right.treeFields.min; val rmax = right.treeFields.max
  val thisBST = left.treeFields.isBST && right.treeFields.isBST && lmax < v && v < rmin
  TreeFields(thisBST, min3(lmin,value,rmin), max3(lmax,value,rmax)) }
def isBST(t:Tree) : Boolean = t.treeFields.isBST
```

Fig. 2. Binary Search Tree with Memoization

has been applied to partially evaluate finite-state properties [2] as well as for dynamically typed languages and languages with expressive type systems [3].

Contributions. In this paper, we show that a particular, predictable form of memoization, which introduces extra fields into data structures, can substantially improve the performance of runtime checks that remain after static verification attempts. Our system works for a purely functional subset of Scala recognized by the Leon verification tool [1], [8]. It provides executable formal contracts in the form of pre- and postconditions of functions, and supports algebraic data types (ADTs). Our implementation and the benchmarks we used to evaluate it are available at https://github.com/manoskouk/leon/tree/memoization.

Example. Consider the example in Fig. 1, which defines a tree datatype along with a decorated insert operation in PureScala. **require** denotes a precondition, whereas **ensuring** denotes a postcondition that takes an anonymous function that applies to function result. isBST is a function used as a specification, denoting that its argument is indeed a binary search tree. treeMin and treeMax are full tree traversals, so isBST would also need to traverse the whole tree when executed. If executed directly as written, each recursive call of insert calls isBST, which makes insert on unbalanced trees quadratic instead of linear. To avoid such costly computation without losing any information, we add extra fields into Tree to denote the result of isBST, treeMin and treeMax for each node. Fig. 2 sketches such transformed version of the data structure. The information that was previously computed using recursive functions is now available with a field lookup. We use constructor functions such as makeNode to compute the additional fields when creating a node, using a constant amount of additional work. The next sections present and evaluate an automated transformation that performs such rewriting.

2   Our Approach

In our system, memoization and static verification jointly reduce the cost of runtime checks.

2.1   Memoizing Fields for Formal Contracts

Intuitively, we memoize whatever the program's formal contracts need, and use the data structure itself as the storage space. A function is eligible to be memoized, if 1) it is called (directly or indirectly) from a formal contract (otherwise its value is not needed for runtime checks), 2) it has a single argument of a class type, i.e. an ADT (to ensure that a single memoized field can indeed uniquely describe the result of the function for the object it is applied to), 3) it is recursive, possibly through mutual recursion (to make memoization worthwhile), 4) its return type is not the same as its argument type (as a heuristic to exclude storing large fields). Our system memoizes each function that fits the above criteria by turning it into an extra field. Each invocation of the function in the program is substituted with a field retrieval. Every instantiation of a class that was enhanced with extra fields is modified to initialize these fields correctly.

Memoizing further fields. The above memoization technique is not specific to runtime checks, but can also memoize bookkeeping fields for data structures that require them, such as AVL sub-tree heights. This saves the programmer the effort to prove that the memoized field matches a definition. Our system therefore supports an explicit annotation in the source code to memoize additional functions. We have used this functionality to simplify some of our benchmarks.

2.2   Utilizing Static Verification

Memoization, although useful on its own, does not yield the optimal results in isolation. This is because we often end up memoizing fields to monitor properties that have already been proven statically. This may have large associated cost, especially when complex properties are involved (e.g. the contents of a data structure).

Therefore, in our system, memoization is preceded by static verification. Each statically verified postcondition is removed from the program, and each precondition verified at a call site is removed from this call site. Additionally, all formal contracts expressed as conjuncts of simpler contracts are split and the conjuncts are verified separately, to remove as many checks as possible.

3   Evaluation

To demonstrate how this transformation can improve programs, we evaluated it on benchmarks available at `https://github.com/manoskouk/leon/tree/memoization`. We consider benchmarks where we perform a series of element insertions to a data structure, and benchmarks where we sort a list.

In Table 1, we compare the asymptotic running time bounds for the original version of each benchmark with the fully optimized version, where we have removed statically verified formal contracts and then applied memoization. This analysis demonstrates that our approach indeed restores the asymptotic bounds of programs in many cases.

Table 1. Asymptotic time bounds. [1]Per element insertion. [2]Amortized.

Benchmark	SortedList[1]	AVLTree[1]	RBTree[1]	AmQueue[1,2]	HeapSort	InsertionSort
Original	$O(n^2)$	$O(n \log n)$	$O(n)$	$O(n)$	$O(n^2 \log n)$	$O(n^3)$
Optimized	$O(n)$	$O(\log n)$	$O(n)$	$O(1)$	$O(n \log n)$	$O(n^2)$

To further confirm the results, we compiled and ran these benchmarks. The tests were compiled to JVM bytecode with the internal compiler of Leon. The input used was a sequence of pseudorandom numbers produced by a simple arithmetic function (using linear and *mod* operators). For each benchmark, we present four sets of measurements, corresponding to the original program, and the version of the program after applying each of our two techniques, isolated or together ("Original", "Memoized", "Static" and "Static+Memoized").

Note that the AVLTree and HeapSort benchmarks had the subtree height automatically memoized rather than manually in the original version, which makes the "Original" and "Static" versions slower; however, this influences asymptotically only the "Static" version of HeapSort (by a logarithmic factor), since in all other cases the performance penalty is at least matched by unverified checks. Also, we use an implementation of AmortizedQueue that uses the sizes of the front and back stacks to decide when it has to reverse the former onto the latter [6]. So our system memoizes the size of both stacks.

The results are presented in Fig. 3. Missing measurement points mean that the corresponding benchmark timed out with a timeout of 100 seconds.

Our techniques improved the performance of programs by orders of magnitude. In several of these benchmarks, all checks were removed statically; this is because we originally started from benchmarks that were used to show the

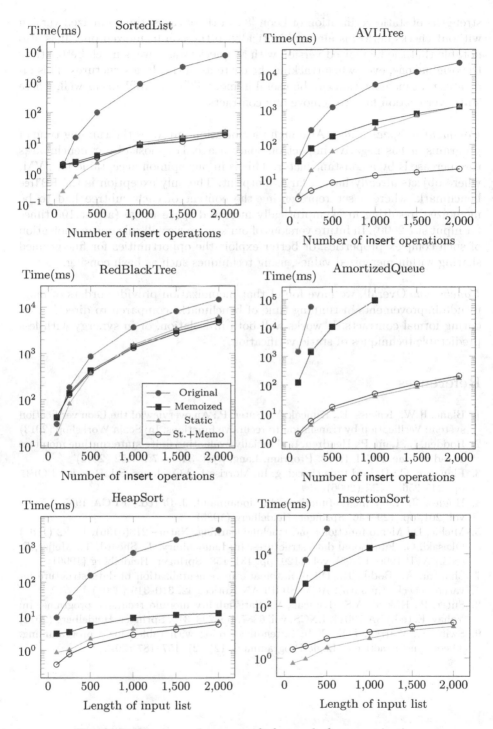

Fig. 3. Performance of programs before and after memoization

strengths of static verification of Leon [8]. In these cases, the memoized version without checks performs almost identically to the non-memoized one. It is also notable that the memoized version with all checks was always much better than the original one, even when tracking the contents of the data structures. This indicates that memoization can be useful in more difficult problems as well, where static verification fails to remove any contracts.

Comment on space usage. Although memoization improves the running time of programs, it has negative impact on space usage. For most of our benchmarks the increase is by a constant factor. This is in our opinion acceptable for JVM, where objects already have a large footprint. The only exception is the RBTree benchmark, where a set representing the content of each subtree had to be memoized, resulting in asymptotically increased space usage (about 100 times for input size 2000). In future versions of our system we will rule out memoization of such complex properties, or better exploit the opportunities for fine-grained sharing within memoized values, using techniques such as hash consing.

Conclusion. Overall, we have found that memoization provides orders of magnitude improvements in running time of benchmarks compared to directly executing formal contracts. It works well both in isolation, or in synergy with less predictable techniques of static verification.

References

1. Blanc, R.W., Kneuss, E., Kuncak, V., Suter, P.: An overview of the Leon verification system: Verification by translation to recursive functions. In: Scala Workshop (2013)
2. Bodden, E., Lam, P., Hendren, L.: Partially evaluating finite-state runtime monitors ahead of time. ACM Trans. Program. Lang. Syst. 34(2), 7:1–7:52 (2012)
3. Flanagan, C.: Hybrid type checking. In: Morrisett, J.G., Jones, S.L.P. (eds.) POPL, pp. 245–256. ACM (2006)
4. Hughes, J.: Lazy memo-functions. In: Jouannaud, J.-P. (ed.) FPCA 1985. LNCS, vol. 201, pp. 129–146. Springer, Heidelberg (1985)
5. Michie, D.: Memo functions and machine learning. Nature 218(5136), 19–22 (1968)
6. Okasaki, C.: Functional data structures. In: Launchbury, J., Sheard, T., Meijer, E. (eds.) AFP 1996. LNCS, vol. 1129, pp. 131–158. Springer, Heidelberg (1996)
7. Shankar, A., Bodik, R.: Ditto: automatic incrementalization of data structure invariant checks (in Java). ACM SIGPLAN Notices 42, 310–319 (2007)
8. Suter, P., Köksal, A.S., Kuncak, V.: Satisfiability modulo recursive programs. In: Yahav, E. (ed.) SAS 2011. LNCS, vol. 6887, pp. 298–315. Springer, Heidelberg (2011)
9. Swift, T., Warren, D.S.: Xsb: Extending Prolog with tabled logic programming. Theory and Practice of Logic Programming 12(1-2), 157–187 (2012)

Dynamic Test Generation
with Static Fields and Initializers

Maria Christakis, Patrick Emmisberger, and Peter Müller

Department of Computer Science,
ETH Zurich, Switzerland
{maria.christakis,peter.mueller}@inf.ethz.ch, empatric@student.ethz.ch

Abstract. Static state is common in object-oriented programs. However, automatic test case generators do not take into account the potential interference of static state with a unit under test and may, thus,
miss subtle errors. In particular, existing test case generators do not treat
static fields as input to the unit under test and do not control the execution of static initializers. We address these issues by presenting a novel
technique in automatic test case generation based on static analysis and
dynamic symbolic execution. We have applied this technique on a suite
of open-source applications and found errors that go undetected by existing test case generators. Our experiments show that this problem is
relevant in real code, indicate which kinds of errors existing techniques
miss, and demonstrate the effectiveness of our technique.

1 Introduction

In object-oriented programming, data stored in static fields is common and potentially shared across the entire program. In case developers choose to initialize
a static field to a value different from the default value of its declared type, they
typically write initialization code. The initialization code is executed by the runtime environment at *some* time prior to the first use of the static field. The time
at which the initialization code is executed depends on the programming language and may be chosen non-deterministically, which makes the semantics of
the initialization code non-trivial, even to experienced developers.

In C#, initialization code has the form of a static
initializer, which may be inline or explicit. The C#
code on the right shows the difference: field f0 is initialized with an inline static initializer, and field f1
with an explicit static initializer. If any static initializer exists, inline or explicit, the C# compiler always generates an explicit initializer. This compiler-
generated explicit initializer first initializes the static
fields of the class that are assigned their initial value
with inline initializers and then incorporates the code
of the original explicit initializer (if any) written by
the developer, as shown below for class C.

```
class C {
  // inline
  static int f0 = 19;
  static int f1;

  // explicit
  static C() {
    f1 = 23;
  }
}
```

B. Bonakdarpour and S.A. Smolka (Eds.): RV 2014, LNCS 8734, pp. 269–284, 2014.

However, the semantics of the compiler-generated static initializer depends on whether the developer has indeed written an explicit initializer. If this is the case, the compiler-generated initializer has *precise* semantics: the body of the initializer is executed (*triggered*) exactly on the first access to any (non-inherited) member of the class (that is, static field, static method, or instance constructor).

```
// compiler-generated
static C() {
    f0 = 19;
    f1 = 23;
}
```

Otherwise, the compiler-generated initializer has *before-field-init* semantics: the body of the initializer is executed no later than the first access to any (non-inherited) static field of the class [3]. This means that the initializer could be triggered by the runtime environment at any point prior to the first static-field access.

In Java, static (initialization) blocks are the equivalent of explicit static initializers with precise semantics in C# [8]. In C++, static initialization occurs before the program entry point in the order in which the static fields are defined in a single translation unit. However, when linking multiple translation units, the order of initialization between the translation units is undefined [2].

Even though static state is common in object-oriented programs and the semantics of static initializers is non-trivial, automatic test case generators do not take into account the potential interference of static state with a unit under test. They may, thus, miss subtle errors. In particular, existing test case generators do not solve the following issues:

1. *Static fields as input*: When a class is initialized before the execution of the unit under test, the values of its static fields are part of the state and should, thus, be treated as inputs to the unit under test. Existing tools fail to do that and may miss bugs when the unit under test depends on the values stored in static fields (for instance, to determine control flow or evaluate assertions).

2. *Initialization and uninitialization*: Existing tools do not control whether static initializers are executed before or during the execution of the unit under test. The point at which the initializer is executed may affect the test outcome since it may affect the values of static fields and any other variables assigned to by the static initializer. Ignoring this issue may cause bugs to be missed. A related issue is that existing tools do not undo the effect of a static initializer between different executions of the unit under test such that the order of executing tests may affect their outcomes.

3. *Eager initialization*: For static initializers with before-field-init semantics, a testing tool should not only control whether the initializer is run before or during test execution; in the latter case, it also needs to explore all possible program points at which initialization of a class may be triggered (non-deterministically).

4. *Initialization dependencies*: The previous issues are further complicated by the fact that the order of executing static initializers may affect the resulting state due to their side effects. Therefore, a testing tool needs to consider all relevant execution orders in order not to miss bugs.

We address these issues by designing and implementing a novel technique in automatic test case generation based on dynamic symbolic execution [7] (*concolic testing* [13]) and static analysis. Our technique treats static fields as input to the unit under test and systematically controls the execution of static initializers. The dynamic symbolic execution collects constraints describing the static-field inputs that will cause the unit under test to take a particular branch in the execution or violate an assertion. It also explores the different program points at which a static initializer might be triggered. The static analysis improves performance by pruning program points at which the execution of a static initializer does not lead to any new behaviors of the unit under test.

We have implemented our technique as an extension to the testing tool Pex [14] for .NET. We have applied it on a suite of open-source applications and found errors that go undetected by existing test case generators. Our results show that this problem is relevant in real code, indicate which kinds of errors existing techniques miss, and demonstrate the effectiveness of our technique.

Related Work. Most existing automatic test case generation tools ignore the potential interactions of a unit under test with static state. These tools range from random testing (like JCrasher [1] for Java), over feedback-directed random testing (like Randoop [10] for Java), to symbolic execution (like Symbolic Java PathFinder [11]) and dynamic symbolic execution (like Pex for .NET or jCUTE [12] for Java).

To the best of our knowledge, existing testing tools such as the above do not take into account the interference of static state with a unit under test, with the exception of JCrasher. JCrasher ensures that each test runs on a "clean slate"; it resets all static state initialized by any previous test runs either by using a different class loader to load each test, or by rewriting the program under test at load time to allow re-initialization of static state. Nevertheless, JCrasher does not address the four issues described above.

Unit testing frameworks, like NUnit for .NET and JUnit for Java, require the tester to manage static state manually in set-up methods in order to ensure the clean execution of the unit tests. Therefore, the tester must be aware of all interactions of the unit under test with static state. As a result, these frameworks become significantly less automatic for unit tests that interact with static state.

Static analysis tools for object-oriented languages, such as Clousot [5] for .NET and ESC/Java [6] for Java, do not reason about static initialization. An extension of Spec# [9] supports static verification in the presence of static initializers, but requires significant annotation overhead.

We are, therefore, not aware of any tool that automatically takes static state into account and detects the kinds of errors described in this paper.

Outline. Sect. 2 explains how we explore static input state where all relevant classes are initialized. Sects. 3 and 4 show we handle static initializers with precise and before-field-init semantics, respectively. Sect. 5 demonstrates the effectiveness of this technique by applying it on a suite of open-source applications.

2   Static Fields as Input

In this section, we address the issue of treating static fields of *initialized* classes as input to the unit under test. The case that a class is not yet initialized is discussed in the next two sections.

```
1 public class C {
2   public static int F;
3
4   static C() {
5     F = 0;
6   }
7
8   public static void M() {
9     F++;
10    if (F == 2) abort;
11  }
12 }
```

Fig. 1. A C# method accessing static state. To cover all branches, dynamic symbolic execution must treat static field F as an input to method M and collect constraints on its value.

The example in Fig. 1 illustrates the issue. Existing automatic test case generators do not treat static field F of class C as input to method M. In particular, testing tools based on dynamic symbolic execution generate only one unit test for method M since there are no branches on a method parameter of M. Since the body of method M contains a branch on static field F (line 10), they achieve low code coverage of M and potentially miss bugs.

Dynamic Symbolic Execution. To address this issue, we treat static fields as inputs to the method under test and assign to them symbolic variables. This causes the dynamic symbolic execution to collect constraints on the static fields and use them to generate inputs that force the execution to explore all branches in the code. As usual with the automatic generation of unit tests, these generated inputs might not occur in any actual execution of the program; to avoid false positives, developers may write specifications (preconditions or invariants) that further constrain the possible values of these inputs.

Treating *all* static fields of a program as inputs is not practical. It is also not modular and defeats the purpose of unit testing. Therefore, we determine at runtime which static fields are read during the execution of a unit test and treat only those as inputs to the unit under test.

We implement this approach in a procedure DSE(*UUT*, *IC*), which performs dynamic symbolic execution of the unit under test *UUT*. *IC* is the set of classes that have been initialized *before* the execution of the unit under test. For all other classes, initialization may be triggered *during* the execution of the generated unit tests. The DSE procedure treats the static fields of all classes in the IC set as symbolic inputs. It returns the set TC of classes whose initialization is triggered during the execution of the generated unit tests. The static fields of the classes in $IC \cup TC$ include all static fields that are read by the unit tests. We call the DSE procedure repeatedly to ensure that the static fields of all of these classes are treated as inputs to the unit under test. The precise algorithm for this exploration as well as more details of the DSE procedure are described in the next section.

Consider the dynamic symbolic execution DSE(M, {}) of method M from Fig. 1. This dynamic symbolic execution generates one unit test that calls method M. The execution of this unit test triggers the initialization of class C due to the access to static field F (line 9). Therefore, procedure DSE returns the singleton set {C}. As a result, our exploration algorithm will call DSE(M, {C}). This second dynamic symbolic execution treats static field F as a symbolic input to method M and collects constraints on its value. For instance, assuming that the first unit test of the second dynamic symbolic execution executes M in a state where F is zero, the conditional statement introduces the symbolic constraint $\neg(F + 1 = 2)$. The dynamic symbolic execution subsequently negates and solves the symbolic constraints on M's inputs. Consequently, a second unit test is generated that first assigns the value 1 to field F and then calls M. The second unit test now reaches the abort statement and reveals the bug. We will see in the next section that, even though the second call to DSE is the one that explores the unit under test for different values of static field F, the first call to DSE is also important; besides determining which static fields should be treated symbolically, it is also crucial to handle uninitialized classes.

3 Initialization with Precise Semantics

In the previous section, we addressed the issue of treating static fields of initialized classes as input to the unit under test. In this section, we explain how our technique (1) controls the execution of static initializers and (2) explores executions that trigger static initializers. Here, we consider only static initializers with precise semantics; initializers with before-field-init semantics are discussed in the next section.

3.1 Controlling Initialization

In order to explore the interaction between a unit under test and static initializers, we must be able to control for each execution of a unit test which classes are initialized before the execution of the unit test and which ones are not. This could be achieved by restarting the runtime environment (virtual machine) before each execution of a unit test and then triggering the initialization of certain classes. To avoid the high performance overhead of this naïve approach, we instrument the unit under test such that the execution *simulates* the effects of triggering an initializer and restarting the runtime environment.

Initialization. We insert calls to the dynamic symbolic execution engine at all points in the entire program where a static initializer could be triggered according to its semantics. For static initializers with precise semantics, we insert instrumentation calls to the dynamic symbolic execution engine on the first access to any (non-inherited) member of their class. Where to insert these instrumentation calls is determined using the inter-procedural control-flow graph of the unit under test. This means that we might insert an instrumentation call at a point in the code where, along certain execution paths, the corresponding class has already been initialized. Note that each .NET bytecode instruction triggers at most one static initializer; therefore, there is at most one instrumentation call at each program point.

For an exploration DSE(UUT, IC), the instrumentation calls in UUT have the following effect. If the instrumentation call is made for a class C that is in the IC set, then C has already been initialized before executing UUT and, thus, the instrumentation call has no effect. Otherwise, if this is the first instrumentation call for C in the execution of this unit test, then we use reflection to explicitly invoke C's static initializer. That is, we execute the static initializer no matter if the runtime environment has initialized C during the execution of a previous unit test or not. Moreover, we add class C to the TC set of classes returned by procedure DSE. If the same unit test has already initialized C during its execution, the instrumentation call has no effect.

In method M from Fig. 1, we add instrumentation calls for class C before the two accesses to static field F, that is, between lines 8 and 9 and between lines 9 and 10. (Our implementation omits the second instrumentation call in this example, but this is not always possible for methods with more interesting control flow.) Consider again the exploration DSE(M, {}). During the execution of the generated unit test, the instrumentation call at the first access to static field F calls C's static initializer such that the unit test continues with F = 0. The instrumentation call for the second access to F has no effect since this unit test already initialized class C. DSE returns the set {C} as described above.

Note that an explicit call to a static initializer is itself an access to a class member and, thus, causes the runtime environment to trigger another call to the same initializer. To prevent the initializer from executing twice (and thereby duplicating its side effects), we instrument each static initializer such

```
static C() {
  if (/* this is the first call */)
    return;
  // body of original
  // static initializer
}
```

that its body is skipped on the first call, as shown on the right.

This instrumentation decouples the execution of a unit test from the initialization behavior of the runtime environment. Static initializers triggered by the runtime environment have no effect and, thus, do not actually initialize the classes, whereas our explicit calls to static initializers initialize the classes even in cases where the runtime environment considers them to be initialized already.

Uninitialization. To avoid the overhead of restarting the runtime environment after each unit test, we simulate the effect of a restart through code instrumentation. Since our technique does not depend on the behavior of the runtime environment to control class initialization, we do not have to actually uninitialize classes. It is sufficient to reset the static fields of all classes initialized by the unit under test to the default values of their declared types after each execution of a unit test. Therefore, the next execution of the static initializer during the execution of the next unit test behaves as if it ran on an uninitialized class.

Existing automatic test case generators (with the exception of JCrasher) do not reset static fields to their initial values between test runs. For code like in Fig. 1, Pex emits a warning that the unit under test might not leave the dynamic symbolic execution engine in a clean state. Therefore, the deterministic re-execution of the generated unit tests is not guaranteed. In fact, the Pex documentation suggests that the tester should mock all interactions of the unit under test with static state. However, this requires the tester to be aware of these interactions and renders Pex significantly less automatic.

3.2 Dynamic Symbolic Execution

The core idea of our exploration is as follows. Assume that we knew the set *classes* of all classes whose initialization may be triggered by executing the unit under test *UUT*. For each subset $IC \subseteq classes$, we perform dynamic symbolic execution of *UUT* such that the classes in *IC* are initialized before executing *UUT* and their static fields are symbolic inputs. The classes in $classes \setminus IC$ are not initialized (that is, their initializers may be triggered when executing a unit test). We can then explore all possible initialization behaviors of *UUT* by testing it for each possible partition of *classes* into initialized and uninitialized classes.

Algorithm. Alg. 1 is a dynamic-symbolic-execution algorithm that implements this core idea, but also needs to handle the fact that the set of relevant classes is not known upfront, but determined during the execution. Procedure EXPLORE takes as argument a unit under test *UUT*, which has been instrumented as described above. Local variable *classes* is the set of relevant classes determined

---

Alg. 1 Dynamic symbolic execution for exploring the interactions of a unit under test with static state.

```
1  procedure EXPLORE(UUT)
2      classes ← {}
3      explored ← {}
4      while ∃IC ⊆ classes · IC ∉ explored do
5          IC ← choose({IC | IC ⊆ classes ∧ IC ∉ explored})
6          TC ← DSE(UUT, IC)
7          classes ← classes ∪ TC
8          explored ← explored ∪ {IC}
9      end while
10 end procedure
```

so far, while local variable *explored* is the set of sets of classes that have been treated as initialized in the exploration so far; that is, *explored* keeps track of the partitions that have been explored. As long as there is a partition that has not been explored (that is, a subset IC of *classes* that is not in *explored*), the algorithm picks any such subset and calls the dynamic symbolic execution procedure DSE, where classes in IC are initialized and their static fields are treated symbolically. If this procedure detects any classes that are initialized during the dynamic symbolic execution, they are added to *classes*. The EXPLORE procedure terminates when all possible subsets of the relevant classes have been explored.

Initialization Dependencies. Alg. 1 enumerates all combinations of initialized and uninitialized classes in the input state of the method under test, that is, all possible partitions of *classes* into IC and *classes* $\setminus IC$. This includes combinations that cannot occur in any actual execution. If the static initializer of a class E triggers the static initializer of a class D, then there is no input state in which E is initialized, but D is not. To avoid such situations and, thus, false positives during testing, we trigger the static initializers of all classes in IC before invoking the method under test. In the above example, this ensures that both E and D will be initialized in the input state of the method under test, and D's initializer will not be triggered during the execution of the method. Since the outcome of running several static initializers may depend on the order in which they are triggered, we explore all orders among dependent static initializers.

The triggering of the static initializers of the classes in IC happens at the beginning of the set-up code that precedes the invocation of the method under test in every generated unit test. This set-up code is also responsible for creating the inputs for the method under test, for instance, for allocating objects that will be passed as method arguments. Therefore, the set-up code may itself trigger static initializers, for instance, when a constructor reads a static field. To handle the dependencies between set-up code and initialization, we treat set-up code as a regular part of the unit test (like the method under test itself), that is, apply the same instrumentation and explore all possible execution paths during dynamic symbolic execution.

Handling dependencies between static initializers is particularly useful in C++, where static initialization happens before the program entry point. When linking multiple translation units, the order of initialization between the translation units is undefined. By exploring all orders of execution of dependent initializers, developers can determine dependencies that may crash a program before its entry point is reached.

Example. The example in Fig. 2 illustrates our approach. The assertion on line 13 fails only if N is executed in a state in which class D is initialized (such that the if-statement may be executed), the static field G is negative (such that the if-statement will be executed and E's initialization will be triggered), and class E is not initialized (such that its static initializer will affect the value of G).

We will now explain how Alg. 1 reveals such subtle bugs. In the first iteration, IC is the empty set, that is, no class is considered to be initialized. Therefore,

```
 1 public class D {                 16 public class E {
 2   public static int G;           17   public static int H;
 3                                   18
 4   static D() {                    19   static E() {
 5     G = 0;                        20     H = 0;
 6   }                               21     D.G = 1;
 7                                   22   }
 8   public static void N() {        23 }
 9     if (G < 0) {
10       E.H++;
11       G = -G;
12     }
13     assert 0 <= G;
14   }
15 }
```

Fig. 2. An example illustrating the treatment of static initializers with precise semantics. We use the special `assert` keyword to denote Code Contracts [4] assertions. The assertion on line 13 fails only if N is called in a state where class D is initialized, but E is not.

when the DSE procedure executes method N, class D is initialized right before line 9. Consequently, static field G is zero, the if-statement is skipped, and the assertion holds. DSE returns the set {D}.

In the second iteration, IC will be {D}, that is, the static initializer of class D is triggered by the set-up code, and static field G is treated symbolically. Since there are no constraints on the value of G yet, the dynamic symbolic execution executes method N with an arbitrary value for G, say, zero. This unit test passes and produces the constraint G < 0 for the next unit test. For any such value of G, the unit test will now enter the if-statement and initialize class E before the access to E's static field H. This initialization assigns 1 to G, such that the subsequent negation makes the assertion fail, and we have detected the bug. The call to the DSE procedure in the second iteration returns {D, E}.

The two remaining iterations of Alg. 1 cover the cases that IC is {E} or {D, E}. The former case illustrates how we handle initialization dependencies. The static initializer of class E accesses static field G of class D. Therefore, when E's initializer is called by the set-up code of the generated unit test, D's initializer is also triggered (recall that the set-up code and all static initializers are instrumented like the method under test). This avoids executing N in the impossible situation where E is initialized, but D is not. The rest of this iteration is analogous to the first iteration, that is, class D gets initialized (this time while executing the set-up code), the if-statement is skipped, and the assertion holds.

Finally, for $IC = \{D, E\}$, all relevant classes are initialized. The dynamic symbolic execution will choose negative and non-negative values for G. The assertion holds in either case.

Discussion. Alg. 1 can be implemented in any testing tool based on dynamic symbolic execution. We have implemented it in Pex, whose existing dynamic symbolic execution engine is invoked by our DSE procedure. Alg. 1 could also be implemented in jCUTE for testing how static fields and static blocks in Java interact with a unit under test. Moreover, this algorithm can be adjusted to perform all dynamic tasks statically for testing tools based on static symbolic execution. For instance, Symbolic Java PathFinder could then be extended to take static state into account.

By treating static fields symbolically, our technique gives meaning to specifications that refer to static fields, like assertions or preconditions. For example, an assertion about the value of a static field is now treated as a branch by the symbolic execution. One could also support preconditions that express which classes are required to be initialized before the execution of a method.

As part of the integration with unit testing frameworks, many automatic test case generators support defining set-up methods for a unit under test. Such methods allow testers to initialize and reset static fields manually. Since set-up methods might express preconditions on static fields (in the form of code), we extended our technique not to override the functionality of these methods. That is, when a set-up method assigns to a static field of a class C, we do not trigger the initialization of class C and do not treat its static fields symbolically. We do, however, reset the values of all static fields in class C after each execution of a unit test such that the next execution of the set-up method starts in a fresh state.

This technique could also be used in existing frameworks for detecting whether a set-up method allows for any static fields to retain their values between runs of the unit under test. This is achieved by detecting which static fields are modified in the unit under test, but have not been manually set up. If such fields exist, an appropriate warning could be emitted by the unit testing framework.

4   Initialization with Before-Field-Init Semantics

The technique presented in the previous section handles static initializers with precise semantics. Static initializers with before-field-init semantics, which may be triggered at any point before the first access to a static field of the class, impose two additional challenges. First, they introduce non-determinism because the static initializer of any given class may be triggered at various points in the unit under test. Second, in addition to the classes that have to be initialized in order to execute the unit under test, the runtime environment could in principle choose to trigger any other static initializer with before-field-init semantics, even initializers of classes that are completely unrelated. In this section, we describe how we solve these challenges. Our solution uses a static program analysis to determine the program points at which the execution of a static initializer with before-field-init semantics may affect the behavior of the unit under test. Then, we use a modified dynamic symbolic execution procedure to explore each of these possibilities.

As the running example of this section, consider method P in Fig. 3. The static initializer of class D has before-field-init semantics and must be executed before the access to field D.Fd on line 10. If the initializer runs on line 5 or 9, then the assertion on line 8 succeeds. If, however, the initializer runs on line 7, the assertion fails because the value of field C.Fc has been incremented (line 15) and is no longer equal to 2. This bug indicates that the unit under test is affected by the non-deterministic behavior of a static initializer with before-field-init semantics. Such errors are particularly difficult to detect with standard unit testing since they might not manifest themselves reproducibly.

```
 1 public static class C {
 2   static int Fc = 0;
 3
 4   public static void P() {
 5     // static initializer of 'D'
 6     Fc = 2;
 7     // static initializer of 'D'
 8     assert Fc == 2;
 9     // static initializer of 'D'
10     if (D.Fd == 3)
11       Fc = E.Fe;
12   }
13
14   static class D {
15     public static int Fd = C.Fc++;
16   }
17
18   static class E {
19     public static int Fe = 11;
20   }
21 }
```

Fig. 3. A C# example illustrating the non-determinism introduced by static initializers with before-field-init semantics. The assertion on line 8 fails if D's static initializer is triggered on line 7.

Critical Points. A static initializer with before-field-init semantics may be triggered at any point before the first access to a static field of its class. To reduce the non-determinism that needs to be explored during testing, we use a static analysis to determine the *critical points* in a unit under test, that is, those program points where triggering a static initializer might actually affect the execution of the unit under test. All other program points can be ignored during testing because no new behavior of the unit under test will be exercised.

A critical point is a pair consisting of a program point i and a class C. It indicates that there is an instance or static field f that is accessed both by the instruction at program point i and the static initializer of class C such that the instruction or the static initializer or both modify the field. In other words, a critical point indicates that the overall effect of executing the static initializer of C and the instruction at i depends on the order in which the execution takes place. Moreover, a pair (i, C) is a critical point only if program point i is not dominated in the control-flow graph by an access to a static field of C, that is, if it is possible to reach program point i without initializing C first.

In the example of Fig. 3, there are five critical points: (6, C), (6, D), (8, D), (10, D), and (11, E), where we denote program points by line numbers. Note that even though the static initializer of class E could be triggered anywhere before line 11, there is only one critical point for E because the behavior of method P is the same for all these possibilities.

We determine the critical points in a method under test in two steps. First, we use a simple static analysis to compute, for each program point i, the set of classes with before-field-init initializers that might get triggered at program point i. This set is denoted by $prospectiveClasses(i)$. In principle, it includes all classes with before-field-init initializers in the entire program, except those that are definitely triggered earlier. Since it is not feasible to consider all of them during testing, we focus on those classes whose static fields are accessed by the method under test. This is not a restriction in practice: even though the Common Language Infrastructure *standard* [3] allows more initializers to be triggered, the Common Language Runtime *implementation*, version 4.0, triggers the initialization of exactly the classes whose static fields are accessed by the method. Therefore, in Fig. 3, $prospectiveClasses(8)$ is the set $\{D, E\}$.

Second, we use a static analysis to determine for each program point i and class C in $prospectiveClasses(i)$ whether (i, C) is a critical point. For this purpose, the static analysis approximates the read and write effects of the instruction at program point i and of the static initializers of all classes in $prospectiveClasses(i)$. The *read effect* of a statement is the set of fields read by the statement or by any method the statement calls directly or transitively. Analogously, the *write effect* of a statement is the set of fields written by the statement or by any method the statement calls directly or transitively. The pair (i, C) is a critical point if (1) i's read effect contains a (static or instance) field f that is included in the write effect of C's static initializer, or (2) i's write effect contains a (static or instance) field f that is included in the read or write effect of C's static initializer. For instance, for line 8 of our example, (8, D) is a critical point because the statement on line 8 reads field Fc, which is written by the static initializer of class D, and D is in $prospectiveClasses(8)$. However, even though class E is in $prospectiveClasses(8)$, (8, E) is not a critical point because the effects of the statement on line 8 and of E's static initializer are disjoint.

Read and write effects are sets of fully-qualified field names, which allows us to approximate them without requiring alias information. Our static effect analysis is inter-procedural. It explores the portion of the whole program it can access (in particular, the entire assembly of the method under test) to compute a call graph that includes information about dynamically-bound calls. Therefore, our analysis may miss critical points (for instance, when it fails to consider a method override in an assembly that is not accessible to the analysis) and, thus, testing might not explore all possible behaviors. It may also yield irrelevant critical points (for instance, when the instruction and the static initializer both have an instance field f in their effects, but at runtime, access f of different objects) and, thus, produce redundant unit tests.

A critical point (i, C) indicates that the dynamic symbolic execution should trigger the initialization of class C right before program point i. However, C's static initializer might lead to more critical points, because its effects may overlap with the effects of other static initializers and because it may trigger the initialization of additional classes, which, thus, must be added to *prospectiveClasses*. To handle this interaction, we iterate over all options for critical points and, for each choice, inline the static initializer and recursively invoke our static analysis.

Dynamic Symbolic Execution. We instrument the unit under test to include a marker for each critical point (i, C). We enhance the DSE procedure called from Alg. 1 to trigger the initialization of class C when the execution hits such a marker. If there are several markers for one class, the DSE procedure explores all paths of the unit under test for each possible point. Conceptually, one can think of adding an integer argument n_C to the unit under test and interpreting the n-th marker for class C as a conditional statement if $(n_C == n)$ { init_C }, where init_C calls the static initializer of class C if it has not been called earlier during the execution of the unit test. Dynamic symbolic execution will then explore all options for the initialization of a class C by choosing different values for the input n_C.

Since $(8, \text{D})$ is a critical point in our example, DSE will trigger the initialization of class D right before line 8 during the symbolic execution of method P. As a result, the assertion violation is detected.

5   Experimental Evaluation

We have evaluated the effectiveness of our technique on 30 open-source applications written in C#. These applications were arbitrarily selected from applications on Bitbucket, CodePlex, and GitHub. Our suite of applications contains a total of 423,166 methods, 47,515 (11%) of which directly access static fields. All classes of these applications define a total of 155,632 fields (instance and static), 28,470 (18%) of which are static fields; 14,705 of the static fields (that is, 9% of all fields) are static read-only fields. There is a total of 1,992 static initializers, 1,725 (87%) of which have precise semantics, and 267 (13%) of which have before-field-init semantics.

To determine which of the 47,515 methods that directly access static fields are most likely to have bugs, we implemented a lightweight scoring mechanism. This mechanism statically computes a score for each method and ranks all methods by their score. The score for each method is based on vulnerability and accessibility scores. The *vulnerability score* of a method indicates whether the method directly accesses static fields and how likely it is to fail at runtime because of a static field, for instance, due to failing assertions, or division-by-zero and arithmetic-overflow exceptions involving static fields. This score is computed based on nesting levels

Tab. 1. Summary of our experiments. The first column shows the name of each application. The second column shows the total number of tested methods from each application. The two rightmost columns show the number of errors detected without and with treating static fields as inputs to the unit under test, respectively.

Application	Methods	Number of errors	
		init	init&input
Boggle	60	-	24
Boogie	21	-	6
Ncqrs	38	1	1
NRefactory	37	-	9
Scrabble	64	-	2
Total	220	1	42

of expressions and how close a static field is to an operation that might throw an exception. The *accessibility score* of a method indicates how accessible the method and the accessed static fields are from potential clients of the application. In particular, this score indicates the level of accessibility from the public interface of the application, and suggests whether a potential bug in the method is likely to be reproducible by clients of the application. The final score for each method is the product of its vulnerability and accessibility scores.

To compare the number of errors detected with and without our technique, we ran Pex with and without our implementation on all methods with a non-zero score. There were 454 methods with a non-zero score in the 30 applications. Tab. 1 summarizes the results of our experiments on the applications in which bugs were detected. The first column of the table shows the name of each application[1]. The second column shows the total number of methods with a non-zero score for each application. The two rightmost columns of the table show the number of errors that our technique detected in these methods. These errors do not include errors already detected by Pex without our technique; they are all caused by interactions of the methods under test with static state.

More specifically, column "init" shows the number of errors detected by simply triggering static initializers at different points in the code. These errors are, thus, caused by calling static initializers (with both semantics) during the execution of the unit tests without treating static fields as inputs. Column "init&input" shows the number of errors detected by our technique, that is, by treating static fields symbolically and systematically controlling the execution of static initializers.

As shown in the last column of the table, our technique detected 42 bugs that are not found by Pex. Related work suggests that existing test case generators would not find these bugs either. A failed unit test does not necessarily mean that the application actually contains code that exhibits the detected bug; this

---

[1] The applications can be found at:

http://boggle.codeplex.com, rev: 20226

http://boogie.codeplex.com, rev: e80b2b9ac4aa

http://github.com/ncqrs/ncqrs, rev: 0102a001c2112a74cab906a4bc924838d7a2a965

http://github.com/icsharpcode/NRefactory, rev: ae42ed27e0343391f7f30c1ab250d729fda9f431

http://wpfscrabble.codeplex.com, rev: 20226

uncertainty is inherent to unit testing since methods are tested in isolation rather than in the context of the entire application. However, all of the detected bugs may surface during maintenance or code reuse. In particular, for 25 of the 42 detected bugs, both the buggy method and the accessed static fields are public. Therefore, when the applications are used as libraries, client code can easily exhibit these bugs.

We have also manually inspected static initializers from all 30 applications and distilled their three most frequent usage patterns. Static initializers are typically used for:

1. Initializing static fields of the same class to constants or simple computations; these initializers are often inline initializers, that is, have before-field-init semantics. However, since they neither read static fields of other classes nor have side effects besides assigning to the static fields of their class, the non-determinism of the before-field-init semantics does not affect program execution.

2. Implementing the singleton pattern in a lazy way; these initializers typically have precise semantics.

3. Initializing public static fields that are mutable; these fields are often meant to satisfy invariants such as non-nullness. However, since they are public, these invariants can easily be violated by client code or during maintenance. This pattern is especially susceptible to static-field updates after the initialization, a scenario that we cover by treating static fields as inputs of the unit under test.

In none of these common usage patterns do initializers typically have side effects besides assigning to static fields of their class. This might explain why we did not find more bugs that are caused by static initialization alone (column "init" in Tab. 1); it is largely irrelevant when such initializers are triggered.

An interesting example of the third pattern was found in application Boggle, which uses the Caliburn.Micro library. This library includes a public static field LogManager.GetLog, which is initialized by LogManager's static initializer to a non-null value. GetLog is read by several other static initializers, for instance, the static initializer of class Coroutine, which assigns the value of GetLog to a static field Log. If client code of the Caliburn.Micro library assigned null to the public GetLog field before the initialization of class Coroutine is triggered, the application might crash; Coroutine will then initialize Log with the null value, which causes a null-pointer exception when Coroutine's BeginExecute method dereferences Log. Our technique reveals this issue when testing BeginExecute; it explores the possibility that LogManager is initialized before BeginExecute is called whereas Coroutine is not, and it treats GetLog as an input to BeginExecute such that the dynamic symbolic execution will choose null as a possible value. Note that this issue is indeed an initialization problem. Since Coroutine.Log is not public, a client could not cause this behavior by assigning null directly to Log.

6   Conclusion

To automatically check the potential interactions of static state with a unit under test, we have proposed a novel technique in automatic test case generation based on static analysis and dynamic symbolic execution. Our technique treats static fields as input to the unit under test and systematically controls the execution of static initializers. We have implemented this technique as an extension to Pex and used it to detect errors in open-source applications. As future work, one could prune redundant explorations more aggressively; this is promising since our evaluation suggests that many static initializers have very small read and write effects and, thus, very limited interactions with the unit under test.

Acknowledgments. We are grateful to Nikolai Tillman and Jonathan "Peli" de Halleux for sharing the Pex source code with us. We also thank Dimitar Asenov, Valentin Wüstholz, and the reviewers for their constructive feedback.

References

1. Csallner, C., Smaragdakis, Y.: JCrasher: An automatic robustness tester for Java. SPE 34, 1025–1050 (2004)
2. Du Toit, S.: Working Draft, Standard for Programming Language C++ (2013), http://www.open-std.org/jtc1/sc22/wg21/docs/papers/2013/n3691.pdf
3. ECMA. ECMA-335: Common Language Infrastructure (CLI). ECMA (2012)
4. Fähndrich, M., Barnett, M., Logozzo, F.: Embedded contract languages. In: SAC, pp. 2103–2110. ACM (2010)
5. Fähndrich, M., Logozzo, F.: Static contract checking with abstract interpretation. In: Beckert, B., Marché, C. (eds.) FoVeOOS 2010. LNCS, vol. 6528, pp. 10–30. Springer, Heidelberg (2011)
6. Flanagan, C., Leino, K.R.M., Lillibridge, M., Nelson, G., Saxe, J.B., Stata, R.: Extended static checking for Java. In: PLDI, pp. 234–245. ACM (2002)
7. Godefroid, P., Klarlund, N., Sen, K.: DART: Directed automated random testing. In: PLDI, pp. 213–223. ACM (2005)
8. Gosling, J., Joy, B., Steele, G., Bracha, G., Buckley, A.: The Java Language Specification. Oracle, java SE, 7th edn. (2012)
9. Leino, K.R.M., Müller, P.: Modular verification of static class invariants. In: Fitzgerald, J.S., Hayes, I.J., Tarlecki, A. (eds.) FM 2005. LNCS, vol. 3582, pp. 26–42. Springer, Heidelberg (2005)
10. Pacheco, C., Lahiri, S.K., Ernst, M.D., Ball, T.: Feedback-directed random test generation. In: ICSE, pp. 75–84. IEEE Computer Society (2007)
11. Păsăreanu, C.S., Mehlitz, P.C., Bushnell, D.H., Gundy-Burlet, K., Lowry, M., Person, S., Pape, M.: Combining unit-level symbolic execution and system-level concrete execution for testing NASA software. In: ISSTA, pp. 15–26. ACM (2008)
12. Sen, K., Agha, G.: CUTE and jCUTE: Concolic unit testing and explicit path model-checking tools. In: Ball, T., Jones, R.B. (eds.) CAV 2006. LNCS, vol. 4144, pp. 419–423. Springer, Heidelberg (2006)
13. Sen, K., Marinov, D., Agha, G.: CUTE: A concolic unit testing engine for C. In: ESEC, pp. 263–272. ACM (2005)
14. Tillmann, N., de Halleux, J.: Pex—White box test generation for .NET. In: Beckert, B., Hähnle, R. (eds.) TAP 2008. LNCS, vol. 4966, pp. 134–153. Springer, Heidelberg (2008)

RV-Monitor: Efficient Parametric Runtime Verification with Simultaneous Properties

Qingzhou Luo[1], Yi Zhang[1], Choonghwan Lee[1], Dongyun Jin[2],
Patrick O'Neil Meredith[1], Traian Florin Şerbănuţă[3], and Grigore Roşu[1]

[1] University of Illinois at Urbana-Champaign, Urbana IL, USA
{qluo2,yzhng173,grosu}@illinois.edu, {linjus.yi,pmeredit}@gmail.com
[2] Samsung Electronics, Suwon, Korea
dongyun.jin@samsung.com
[3] University of Bucharest, Bucharest, Romania
traian.serbanuta@fmi.unibuc.ro

Abstract. Runtime verification can effectively increase the reliability of software systems. In recent years, parametric runtime verification has gained a lot of traction, with several systems proposed. However, lack of real specifications and prohibitive runtime overhead when checking numerous properties simultaneously prevent developers or users from using runtime verification. This paper reports on more than 150 formal specifications manually derived from the Java API documentation of commonly used packages, as well as a series of novel techniques which resulted in a new runtime verification system, RV-Monitor. Experiments show that these specifications are useful for finding bugs and bad software practice, and RV-Monitor is capable of monitoring all our specifications simultaneously, and runs substantially faster than other state-of-the-art runtime verification systems.

1 Introduction

Runtime verification (RV) can increase the reliability of software systems by dynamically verifying property specifications during program execution. Runtime verification has gained significant interest from the research community and there are increasingly broad uses of Runtime Verification (RV) in software development and analysis, as reflected, for example, by abundant approaches proposed recently ([14, 10, 4, 19, 1, 6, 7, 13, 8, 20] among others).

Runtime verification systems typically take a possibly unsafe system as input together with specifications of events and desired properties, and yield as output a modified version of the input system which checks the input specification during its execution, possibly triggering recovery code if specifications are violated. Fig. 1 illustrates this by means of an example using the state-of-the-art monitoring system JavaMOP [20, 15]. An *event* is an abstraction of an action of interest (method invocation, field access, etc.) that occurs during program execution. A *trace* is a finite sequence of events, and a *property* (specification) is a formal description of a set of (desired or undesired) traces. The specification in Fig. 1 has three parameters (line 1): m, c and i. These are bound to concrete objects provided by events at runtime. For example, the event getI defined on

B. Bonakdarpour and S.A. Smolka (Eds.): RV 2014, LNCS 8734, pp. 285–300, 2014.

```
1  Map_UnsafeIterator(Map m, Collection c, Iterator i) {
2    creation event getC after(Map m) returning(Collection c) :
3      ( call(Set Map+.keySet()) || ... ) && target(m) {}
4    event getI after(Collection c) returning(Iterator i) :
5      call(Iterator Iterable+.iterator()) && target(c) {}
6    event modifyM before(Map m) :
7      ( call(* Map+.clear*(..)) || ... ) && target(m) {}
8    event modifyC before(Collection c) :
9      ( call(* Collection+.clear(..)) || ... ) && target(c) {}
10   event useI before(Iterator i) :
11     ( call(* Iterator.hasNext(..)) ||
12       call(* Iterator.next(..)) ) && target(i) {}
13
14   ere : getC (modifyM | modifyC)* getI useI*
15         (modifyM | modifyC)+ useI
16
17   @match { print("Map was modified while being iterated"); }
18 }
```

Fig. 1. A JavaMOP specification Map_UnsafeIterator

lines 4–5 is fired when the `iterator()` of an `Iterable` implementation is invoked, and carries two concrete objects that c and i are bound to. The property, given as an extended regular expression (ERE) (lines 14–15), specifies bad behaviors. The `@match` *handler* (line 17) says what to do when a trace matches the pattern, i.e., when a map is modified while being iterated. Handlers can contain any code, for example, error recovery code.

Despite the usefulness of runtime verification, we believe there are a few hurdles that make developers or users reluctant to use RV systems in practice:

1. It is not easy to write specifications for RV systems to check against;
2. Even if the specifications are available, existing RV systems usually incur large overhead when checking multiple properties simultaneously in real world software.

We next introduce background knowledge and elaborate on the points above in detail.

Lack of Specifications: specifications are key to runtime verification. However it is not easy to produce correct specifications, as it requires a deep understanding of the underlying system. There are several hand-written specifications shipped with monitoring systems, as well as a few specifications produced by automated specification mining approaches. These face a few common problems: 1) Correctness. Most specifications are written in ad-hoc ways without rigorous procedures, which make their correctness questionable; 2) Coverage. Most existing specifications only focus on limited coverage of the software system; 3) Reusability. Most existing specifications are specific to the underlying software system. They cannot be applied to different software systems.

High Monitoring Overhead: producing a highly reliable system while maintaining a low overhead was always a major concern of runtime verification. Most state-of-the-art monitoring systems employ *parametricity* to ensure correctness of the monitored behaviors. Conceptually, parametric monitoring systems maintain a separate trace for each parameter binding and separately check if each trace matches the pattern. As an example in Fig. 1, a `useI` event with an `Iterator` object $i1$ does not affect traces that correspond to the parameter binding where i is bound to $i2$ while m and c can be

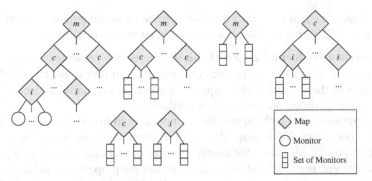

Fig. 2. Indexing trees for Map_UnsafeIterator

bound to any object, denoted as $\langle m \mapsto *, c \mapsto *, i \mapsto i2 \rangle$. Instead of maintaining traces, an efficient monitoring system, such as JavaMOP, actually uses a monitor instance for each parameter binding; when an event occurs, it is dispatched to every monitor instance whose parameter binding contains concrete objects carried by the event. If no such instances exist and the event is a *creation event*, a new monitor instance is created.

For fast lookup of monitor instances, JavaMOP employs *indexing trees*, which precisely return all the related monitor instances. An indexing tree is a multi-level map that, at each level, indexes each concrete object of the parameter binding. For example, when a parameter binding is $\langle m \mapsto m1, c \mapsto c1, i \mapsto i1 \rangle$ (m is bound to $m1$, c is bound to $c1$ and i is bound to $i1$), one can retrieve the related monitor instance by searching for $m1$, $c1$ and $i1$ at each level in the 3-level map, shown in the top-left of Fig. 2. However, not all parameters are always bound; e.g., getI in Fig. 1 does not carry m, which makes it ineffective to retrieve all the related instances using this map. To handle such case efficiently, another map, shown in the top-right of Fig. 2, is constructed as well. Unlike the 3-level map, where a leaf corresponds to one monitor instance, this 2-level map has a set of instances at each leaf, because there can be multiple parameter bindings that bind c and i to the same Collection and Iterator.

If an indexing tree holds a strong reference (i.e., an ordinary Java reference) to a concrete object, this object becomes ineligible for garbage collection, which leads to a memory leak. To avoid this, indexing trees store only weak references, which enables the garbage collector to reclaim the referents. Since a weak reference gives indication that the referent has been reclaimed by returning *null*, a monitoring system can detect broken mappings in the indexing trees and clean them up. In addition to indexing trees, an indexing cache that stores the previously accessed monitor instance(s) is used [20].

Even with the use of indexing trees and weak references, the runtime overhead is still large when monitoring multiple parametric properties simultaneously. From a thorough profiling of JavaMOP, [16] identifies the main remaining bottleneck to runtime performance is the excessive memory usage, which is caused by the large size/number of indexing trees. Indeed, when there are hundreds of properties being monitored and each property has a few parameters, the total memory and runtime overhead associated with all the indexing trees will dominate the program execution time. This urges us to design new techniques to further reduce the number and memory overhead of indexing trees.

In this paper, we aim to address the above problems in order to make runtime verification practical. This paper makes the following specific contributions:

– **Comprehensive formal Java API specifications:** We presented a comprehensive set (179 in total) of formal specifications which cover four of the most widely used packages of the Java API. These specifications were manually produced following rigorous procedures, and are publicly available [3].
– **Novel optimization techniques:** We re-implemented JavaMOP, separating its monitoring (as a new RV system, RV-Monitor) from its event firing (as an AspectJ front-end of RV-Monitor). We employ a series of techniques to make RV-Monitor more efficient, especially when monitoring multiple properties simultaneously. Our techniques can also be easily adopted by other RV systems, such as MOPBox.
– **Large scale evaluation:** We monitored all the Java API specifications we produced with RV-Monitor against the DaCapo [5] benchmark suite. Results show that RV-Monitor is capable of finding property violations (potential bugs) in DaCapo while monitoring hundreds of properties at the same time. Our comparison also shows that RV-Monitor runs substantially faster than other monitoring systems.

2 Formal Specifications from the Java API Specification

Almost all Java programs make use of the Java API. Moreover, misuses of the Java API can result in runtime errors or nondeterministic behavior. It is therefore important to obey the usage protocols of the Java API. In this section we describe our formalization of several Java API specifications. All our tools and specifications are publicly available and can be used and verified by any RV systems [3].

2.1 Java API Specification

A Java platform, such as Java Platform Standard Edition 6, implements various libraries that are commonly needed to implement applications, such as data structures (e.g., `List` and `HashMap`), and I/O functions (e.g., `FileInputStream` and `FileOutputStream`). Besides such library implementations, a Java platform provides the *API Specification*, which describes all aspects of the behavior of each method on which user's programs may rely. For example, the API specification for the `Map` interface states:

> If the map is modified while an iteration over the set is in progress ... the results of the iteration are undefined.

We believe the Java API documentation is a good source for formal specifications. First of all, the Java API is commonly used by virtually all Java programs. Thus the use protocols of those API methods should always be obeyed. Second, the Java API specification is well written, clearly stating what the correct/incorrect usage of API methods is. For example, in the above `Map` specification it can be inferred that any methods that modify the `Map` (`put()`, `remove()`, `etc.`) should *not* be called *before* the iteration of the `Map` is done. Violations of such properties usually indicate a bug or bad programming practice.

We have carefully read and analyzed the complete Java API documentation for four of the most commonly used packages: `java.io`, `java.lang`, `java.net` and `java.util`. We employed a multi-step approach to formalizing all the specifications in these four packages and produced 179 formal specifications. Next we describe our approach.

2.2 Separating Specification-Implying Text

Although the API specification includes contracts (Sec. 2.1), sentences referring to different purposes are mingled in API specifications. As a preparation step, we marked specification-implying text versus descriptive text using a specially defined javadoc tag. This facilitates the review of relevant parts when writing specifications (Sec. 2.3).

While it might seem obvious to distinguish between descriptive and specification-implying text, there are unclear cases. One case is the description of conditions involving external environments. Here is an example for the `FileOutputStream` constructor:

> If the file exists but is a directory rather than a regular file, does not exist but cannot be created, or cannot be opened for any other reason, then a `FileNot-FoundException` is thrown.

We decided to not formalize this property, because the state of the file system can externally and dynamically change without notifying the RV system and, consequently, it is impossible to reliably check whether a file can be created or opened.

It is difficult to formalize a specific set of rules that resolves all of the unclear cases, but the rule of thumb was that a chunk of text is specification-implying only if a desirable or undesirable behavior is apparent and it is defined in terms of noticeable events, such as class loadings, method invocations and field accesses.

2.3 Writing Formal Specifications

For each chunk of text that we marked as specification-implying, we wrote JavaMOP specifications. We chose the JavaMOP specification syntax because JavaMOP was the most efficient and expressive, in that it allows us to write a property in various formalisms. As shown in Fig. 1, a typical specification contains three parts: a set of event definitions, a desirable or undesirable behavioral pattern (i.e., property), and a handler for violations. An event in our specifications is mostly a method invocation, a field access, an end of an execution, or a construction of an object. Depending on the pattern, we chose the most intuitive formalism, among an ERE, a finte-state machine (FSM) or a linear temporal logic (LTL) formula, for expressing a property. Our handlers simply output a warning message in case of a violation.

There are some cases where we intentionally did not write formal specifications. Below we explain such cases with rationales.

Non-monitorable Behaviors. We considered only runtime-monitorable specifications because we intended to use a RV system; e.g., consider the following:

> The implementor must also ensure that the relation is transitive: (`x.compareTo(y)` > 0 && `y.compareTo(z)` > 0) implies `x.compareTo(z)` > 0.

Although this implies a certain behavior, checking whether it holds is infeasible at runtime. Not having a means of describing and checking it, we did not write formal specifications for such cases.

Already Enforced Behaviors. We did not write formal specifications if the desirable behavior is already enforced by compilers. For example, consider the following, which states the requirement of InputStream's subclasses:

Applications that need to define a subclass of InputStream must always provide a method that returns the next byte of input.

Java compilers enforce the requirement because read(), the method implied by the comment, is an abstract method. Such guarantee obviates the need for additional runtime specifications; thus, we did not formalize such cases.

Internal Behaviors. When all the events in the implied specification are never exposed to clients (e.g., they are private method invocations or field accesses), we did not write specifications. For example, consider the API specification for GregorianCalendar. getYearOffsetInMillis():

This Calendar object must have been normalized.

A specification on this is feasible but useless because user's programs cannot invoke it anyway, due to the access control—it is defined as private. We did not write specifications in such cases because there is no benefit from a user's perspective.

2.4   Classifying Formal Specifications

Not all violations are equally important; violations of some specifications are harmless in certain applications and users may want to suppress them. To facilitate such filtering, we classified our specifications into three groups: suggestion, warning and error. We use suggestion if a violation is merely a bad practice. If a violation is not necessarily erroneous but potentially wrong, we use warning. We use the last group, error, if a violation indicates an error.

3   Scalable Runtime Verification

Many RV systems are able to monitor *one* property efficiently. However, to make runtime verification practical, an RV system should be able to efficiently monitor *multiple* properties simultaneously. In this section we present our optimizations to reduce runtime overhead. Since JavaMOP was the most efficient RV system when this paper was written, we built upon several of its optimizations, especially upon its indexing tree idea. Most of our techniques focus on making the indexing tree accesses faster, which reduce the monitoring overhead when multiple properties and monitor instances are present.

Note that the idea of using indexing trees and caches for managing multiple monitor instances is commonly used among other RV systems. For example, MOPBox uses JavaMOP's indexing algorithm to map variable bindings to monitors. We believe our improvement of JavaMOP, such as the merging of indexing trees, can also be directly applied to other RV systems and can indirectly inspire other systems, such as the more general RuleR or Eagle [4, 9]. Besides, some other systems propose static analysis on top of the JavaMOP technique; those systems will also benefit from our techniques.

3.1 Global Weak Reference Table

Even monitoring a single specification causes multiple weak references for a single object in JavaMOP because it constructs multiple indexing trees for a specification and each indexing tree stores its own copy of the weak reference. From the specification shown in Fig. 1, for example, JavaMOP can create four weak references for a single Collection object: one at the second level of the top-left tree, another at the first level of the bottom-left tree, and so forth in Fig. 2.

When multiple specifications are monitored, redundancy is more severe because JavaMOP creates separate indexing trees for each specification. That is, indexing trees for another specification create their own (possibly multiple) weak references for the same object, in addition to those already created for the first specification. For example, both Map_UnsafeIterator and Iterator_HasNext—it states that Iterator.next() should not be called without checking for the existence of the next element—create their own weak references to the same Iterator objects.

We avoid such intra/inter-specification redundancy by employing a global weak reference table (GWRT) that stores only one weak reference for each distinct object. As in string interning, however, keeping only one copy requires extra computation for creation—it is necessary to check whether or not a weak reference for the given object has been previously created, in order to guarantee uniqueness of weak reference. To eliminate redundancy with little performance compromise, we use a separate GWRT for each parameter type; e.g., three GWRTs will be used by Map_UnsafeIterator. A GWRT functions as a dictionary where a concrete object is used as a key and a weak reference is used as a value. That is, this table allows one to retrieve the weak reference associated with the concrete object. Since this table is globally shared among all specifications and a key can appear at most once in it as in other typical dictionaries, it allows only a single copy of weak reference for each object.

While the GWRT may seem to be the same as any other hashtable with weak reference values, its internal structure is further optimized to reduce memory consumption. First, it does not hold a strong reference to a concrete object, which would cause memory leaks. More importantly, this table does not actually store pairs of objects and their weak references; only weak references are stored because one can retrieve the object from the weak reference by invoking WeakReference.get(). Fast lookup, achieved using a hash function, is still viable by locating the slot based on the hash value of the object and searching weak references in the slot.

We further reduce the memory overhead incurred from GWRTs by merging them with the first levels of indexing trees. The first level of an indexing tree holds all the weak references to the objects of a certain type, as does the GWRT for that type. Therefore, the GWRT can be embedded in the first level of the indexing tree, without losing any weak reference, introducing wasted space, or compromising fast lookup. The GWRT for Map, for example, is embedded in the first level of the top-left tree in Fig. 2, which holds entries for all the weak references, one per each Map object. Embedding eliminates all memory overhead of said GWRT. Most GWRTs can be embedded because RV-Monitor needs to create indexing trees with many different types. For example, RV-Monitor creates at least one indexing tree for each parameter type for Map_UnsafeIterator, as shown in Fig. 2, which allows the three GWRTs to be embedded. In our experiments, all GWRTs were embedded when the 137 specifications from [18] were monitored simultaneously. However, there are some theoretical cases where embedding is not possible.

Moreover, reducing the number of invocations of System.identityHashCode() is also beneficial. Therefore, a subclass of the WeakReference class, Java's weak reference implementation, was created in such a way that the hash value of the referent is computed at most once and then stored in a dedicated field by the constructor. This subclass is used in place of the WeakReference class in both GWRTs and indexing trees. With this subclass, calls to System.identityHashCode() can be replaced by a field access, which is less expensive, at the cost of adding one int field to each weak reference. Adding this field to each weak reference does not cause a significantly larger expenditure of memory because only a single weak reference is created for each distinct object thanks to GWRTs.

Another benefit of GWRTs is that it is easier to check if there exists a monitor instance referring to a given object. Because a GWRT holds all the weak references of one type, the lack of the weak reference for an object implies that none of specifications have created any monitor instance for that object. For this reason, when handling a non-creation event (see Section 1), we can safely skip the other steps of monitoring if there are no weak references for every parameter carried by the event. In contrast, JavaMOP, where indexing trees are separately created for each specification, must check indexing trees for each specification that shares a given event.

3.2 Caches for the Global Weak Reference Table

GWRTs are frequently accessed because weak references for each parameter object bound in a given event must be retrieved. As a result, optimizing this data structure has a large impact on performance. We first reduce the number of accesses to a GWRT by extending each indexing cache. Temporal locality is often exhibited in the access patterns of objects related to monitoring a given specification. For example, consider a specification that formalizes a resource management pattern on the Reader class: "a reader can perform the read operation until it is closed." While monitoring this specification, it is likely that there would be a long sequence of read() calls on a particular Reader object until close() is called. To utilize such locality, JavaMOP already has an indexing cache that stores the recently accessed monitor instance(s).

While this cache allows for quick retrieval of the monitor instance(s), weak references for all of the parameter objects associated with those instance(s) are often necessary during the process of updating said instance(s). Quick retrieval of a monitor instance followed by retrieving weak references for every single parameter object from the GWRT would be contrary to the whole purpose of the indexing cache. We therefore extended the indexing cache in such a way that, when it caches monitor instance(s), it also caches the weak references that point to the parameter objects bound by those monitor instance(s). As a result, when an event carries the recently handled objects, the indexing cache can return not only the relevant monitor instance(s) but also weak references, without the need to consult the GWRT for each bound parameter object.

Second, we add to each GWRT a cache, called the GWRTCache, which is used to store recently requested weak references. As stated previously, multiple specifications

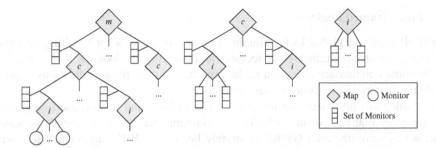

Fig. 3. Indexing trees for Map_UnsafeIterator after combining

commonly share event definitions, thus a single method invocation can trigger multiple events, one per each specification. For example, an invocation of Reader.read() triggers not only an event of the aforementioned resource management specification but also the "mark/reset" specification: "a reader's mark position, set by Reader.mark(), is invalidated after reading the specified number of bytes." Without the GWRTCache, when read() is invoked on an unprecedented Reader object, indexing caches for both specifications will miss—while handling the two events—and both caches would query the GWRT for the Reader object, in order to create or retrieve the weak reference (whichever request occurs first will create the weak reference). Using the GWRTCache, however, the first miss causes this cache to hold the created Reader object and, consequently, a hash lookup in the GWRT for each subsequent request is replaced by a lookup in this cache, which is faster.

3.3 Combining Indexing Trees

As we mentioned in Section 1, monitoring a real program causes millions of monitor instances and, consequently, the size of indexing trees becomes large because they store references to monitor instances at leaves. In the presence of hundreds of specifications, the size of indexing trees is likely to become even larger, causing excessive memory overhead. To mitigate such overhead, we combine indexing trees originating from the same specification, if they share the same prefix; e.g., indexing trees for ⟨Collection, Iterator⟩ and ⟨Collection⟩ are combined, but trees for ⟨Map, Collection, Iterator⟩ and ⟨Collection, Iterator⟩ are not.

Consider the indexing trees for ⟨Collection, Iterator⟩ and ⟨Collection⟩, shown in Fig. 2. Since both trees index all the Collection objects at the first level, their first level maps contain the exactly same keys (i.e., weak references); the only difference is that, by the same key, a second level map is mapped to in the first tree, whereas a set of monitor instances is mapped to in the second tree. We combined these two trees by allowing a second level map and set of monitor instances pair to be mapped to by a key, as shown at the bottom tree of Fig. 3. Choosing which part of the pair can be done depending on whether or not a Collection object is carried by an event. Three indexing trees, shown at the top of Fig. 2, are also combined into one tree, shown at the left top of Fig. 3, similarly. By combining compatible trees, only three trees, out of six, remain as shown in Fig. 3.

3.4   Fine-Grained Locking

JavaMOP uses one global lock throughout all the operations for handling an event, which may involve multiple GWRT accesses and indexing tree lookups. This can significantly hinder concurrent execution in the presence of multiple specifications because it is likely that more events occur simultaneously.

To reduce this hindrance, we remove the global lock, and instead use fine-grained locking given that each of the GWRTs and indexing trees is independently accessed. First, we synchronize each GWRT separately because GWRTs do not interfere with each other. This enables multiple threads to run concurrently, unless they handle the same type of parameters—recall that one GWRT is created for each parameter type. Second, we synchronize each level of an indexing tree separately. For example, consider a getC event in Fig. 1, which brings two parameters: m and c. When looking up the left tree in Fig. 3 for retrieving monitor instances corresponding to the provided parameters, we first acquire a lock corresponding to the first level. On retrieving the node at the second level according to the object bound to m, we immediately release the lock. This way, another request on the first level of this tree can be served with relatively short delay.

In order to promote concurrent execution further, we moved to thread-local storage (TLS) two caches: the cache in each indexing tree and the GWRTCache in each GWRT (Section 3.2). This is based on the observation that most objects bound to parameters are solely used in a single thread. With this change, if a request is served by the cache, no synchronization is performed, at the cost of adding a few cache entries to each GWRT and each level of indexing trees, per thread.

4   Implementation and Evaluation

In this section we describe our implementation of RV-Monitor and evaluate the correctness of all our formal specifications as well as the performance of RV-Monitor.

4.1   Implementation

We have developed RV-Monitor in such a way that it can be used as a universal platform for building various monitoring systems. To achieve this, we re-implemented JavaMOP and separated event monitoring functionality from event firing functionality. RV-Monitor implements only the common and indispensable monitoring functionality-such as listening to events and triggering handlers when a pattern matches. Using RV-Monitor, one can generate a monitoring library that exposes an interface—more specifically, a set of methods, each of which corresponds to an event definition—for listening to events. One can then monitor a program by notifying the library of events; i.e., inserting invocations of such methods either manually, or systematically using instrumentation tools. Having this separate system enables one to write a specification in terms of virtually any event, from method invocation to monitor (in the context of locking) wait, using diverse means, such as bytecode instrumentation or JVMTI. No matter how events are fired, monitoring can be efficient because it is entirely delegated to the code generated by RV-Monitor.

We also re-implemented the event firing functionality of JavaMOP as an AspectJ front end of RV-Monitor. All the original JavaMOP specifications can be translated into simple AspectJ code. Inside those AspectJ code, RV-Monitor event monitoring library methods are now called. The AspectJ front end of RV-Monitor enables us to easily compare the performance of RV-Monitor with JavaMOP.

4.2 Correctness of Formal Specifications

The correctness of specifications is vital, because incorrect specifications would miss bugs or give out false alarms. However there is no silver bullet to guarantee the correctness of specifications other than careful inspection and thorough testing. All of our specifications were reviewed by at least two authors who are knowledgeable about Java. In addition to peer review, we wrote small defective Java programs and tested if the formal specification can reveal violations. We have written more than 100 (publicly available) small programs in total, and all the tests revealed the inserted defects, which brings evidence that these specifications are capable of detecting errors. All our specifications and tests can be found at [3].

4.3 Runtime Overhead

Comparison with JavaMOP. To measure the efficiency of RV-Monitor, we compare the overhead of RV-Monitor (with the AspectJ front end) with that of the latest version of JavaMOP (v2.3). We chose JavaMOP because, at the time of writing this paper, it was the most efficient system, to the best of our knowledge. All our experiments were conducted on Sun Java SE 6 (build 1.6.0_35) under a system with a 3.5 GHz Intel Core i7 and 32GB of memory running Linux 3.2.

We collected the execution time for each benchmark, as shown in Table 1, under a steady state using DaCapo 9.12's -converge option. We took the average time of the last five runs. The "Original" column shows the unmonitored runs of benchmarks, whereas the other columns show the monitored runs with all the specifications. The "overhead" columns indicate the percentage overhead.

In average, the percentage overhead of RV-Monitor is less than half of that of Java-MOP. In particular, improvement was significant for four benchmarks that caused excessive overheads under JavaMOP; avrora, lusearch, pmd and xalan under JavaMOP respectively showed 150%, 654%, 797% and 2,968% overheads, but they caused only 22%, 420%, 261% and 97% overheads under RV-Monitor. On one benchmark, fop, RV-Monitor was noticeably worse. This is because fop is single-threaded, and RV-Monitor has been geared toward increasing concurrency, such as fine-grained locking and thread-local storage (TLS) caches (Section 3.4), which are beneficial to multi-threaded programs but may end up adding extra computation when concurrency is not needed.

Note that in xalan, RV-Monitor performs much better than JavaMOP. The reason is that the program itself is computation intensive. Many monitor instances are created and used only once, incurring a large memory overhead with JavaMOP. Therefore, RV-Monitor is able to greatly reduce the overhead by merging indexing trees and using global caches. If we exclude this program, the average overhead of RV-Monitor will be 143%, still better than JavaMOP with 163%. We believe the DaCapo benchmark has been conceived as a whole, to test various aspects of the language, and established itself

Table 1. Execution time and the number of allocations during execution

Benchmark	Original	JavaMOP†		RV-Monitor		MOPBox		
	time (s)	time (s)	overhead	time (s)	overhead	times (s)	overhead	GCs
avrora	4.55	11.36	150%	5.55	22%	>600	-	142
batik	0.80	0.96	20%	1.27	59%	>600	-	195
eclipse	10.77	10.51	-2%	10.68	-1%	>600	-	216
fop	0.23	0.92	300%	1.85	704%	>600	-	193
h2	4.59	6.44	40%	10.64	132%	>600	-	176
jython	1.33	2.98	124%	3.84	189%	>600	-	209
luindex	0.56	0.60	7%	0.57	2%	383.76	68428%	199
lusearch	0.50	3.77	654%	2.60	420%	>600	-	111
pmd	1.71	15.34	797%	6.17	261%	>600	-	198
sunflow	1.31	1.77	35%	1.57	20%	>600	-	73
tomcat	1.36	1.36	0%	2.09	54%	1.37	0%	18
tradebeans	6.52	6.33	-2%	6.91	6%	6.84	4%	44
tradesoap	3.88	3.91	1%	3.83	-1%	3.70	-4%	87
xalan	0.38	11.66	2,968%	0.75	97%	>600	-	88
Average			364%		140%		-	

as the most suitable benchmark for runtime verification. Therefore, we think the huge overhead reduction case shows a big improvement of our technique, not an isolated case.

It should be noted that the runtime overhead may look high, for some benchmarks, but those cases are extreme: here we monitored programs that intensively use the Java API against lots of specifications, and this is indeed a challenging task. For example, most benchmarks emitted millions of events; in particular, avrora, h2 and pmd emitted 32,804,400, 65,647,663 and 48,866,293 events, respectively. In usual cases, however, one can expect moderate overhead.

Comparison with MOPBox. MOPBox [21] is the most similar RV system to RV-Monitor. MOPBox [21] requires one to construct an FSM by setting alphabets, states, and transitions using its API and it does not support other formalisms. Because of that, we tested only the most heavily used specification in DaCapo, Collection_UnsafeIterator, which warns if a collection is modified while an iterator is being used.

Table 1 shows the execution time and the number of garbage collections. Even though only one specification was monitored, most benchmarks barely finished the first iteration in 10 minutes, except three benchmarks that fire relatively few events: tomcat, tradebeans and tradesoap. One of reasons for such excessive overhead was memory consumption: we noticed that an execution under MOPBox triggered garbage collections frequently as shown in Table 1, whereas that under RV-Monitor triggered merely at most 5 garbage collections, for each iteration, in the worst case.

Overall, the result shows that the overhead of MOPBox with one specification is by far more than that of RV-Monitor with 179 specifications. There could be many possible reasons for the big difference. First, RV-Monitor enables the monitored program to directly pass parameters to events (through generated AspectJ code), while MOPBox requires a VariableBinding object to be created for each parameter. This may cause

Table 2. The number of specifications, violated specifications and violations

Package	io			lang			net			util		
Severity	err.	warn.	sugg.	err.	warn.	sugg.	err.	warn.	sugg.	err.	warn.	sugg.
# of specs	19	6	5	23	11	14	31	12	1	43	11	3
# of violated specs	3	1	3	2	0	11	1	2	0	6	4	1
# of violations	19	14	12	36	0	4724	3	2	0	14	134	60

extra runtime overhead. Also, MOPBox uses the $C^+\langle X \rangle$ algorithm [8], which is less efficient than $D\langle X \rangle$ [8], used by RV-Monitor. Moreover, MOPBox does not use all the efficient data structures for handling monitor instances, such as indexing trees.

We believe that our comparison with MOPBox, as well as that with JavaMOP, shows that engineering a high-performance runtime verification system for parametric specifications is a highly challenging task.

4.4 Bug Finding

Runtime monitoring is capable of finding bugs and bad practices even from widely used benchmarks. Compared with JavaMOP, RV-Monitor is able to monitor all the properties simultaneously on large programs, makes it practical for finding bugs. Table 2 summarizes the number of specifications, the number of violated specifications, and the number of violations for each severity level from all the benchmarks of DaCapo 9.12. When we counted the number of violations, we counted all violations caused by the same call site as one. Here we focus on the violations of specifications that are marked as error and warning among thousands of violations.

Reader_ManipulateAfterClose, which warns if a read operation is performed after a Reader object has been closed, was violated by 13 out of 14 benchmarks of DaCapo. In fact, read() failed and the reader was immediately closed, but read() was invoked again on that closed reader. The latter read() call was reached because the exception raised at the first failure was discarded by a method and it returned as if there were no errors. Since the Reader implementation raises IOException anyway and it is properly handled, this violation does not result in a notable failure. Nevertheless, we believe it is a bad practice to rely on an exception even when a violation is predictable.

ShutdownHook_LateRegister, which warns if one registers or unregisters a shutdown hook [1] after the Java Virtual Machine (JVM)'s shutdown sequence has begun, was violated by h2—this program attempted to unregister a shutdown hook. One may think that such attempt would be safe as long as the resulting exception is properly handled, but it is unsafe because registered hooks are started in unspecified order and, consequently, the hook to be unregistered may have been already started.

Collections_SynchronizedCollection, which warns if a synchronized (thread-safe) collection is accessed in an unsynchronized manner, was violated by jython. This program created a synchronized collection, using Collections.synchronizedList(), but iterated over the collection without synchronizing on it, which may result in non-deterministic behavior, according to the API specification.

---

[1] According to the API specification, a *shutdown hook* is an initialized but unstarted thread.

Besides these violations that imply notable problems, we also found many minor yet informative violations that static analysis might not be able to detect. One such example is a violation of Math_ContendedRandom, which recommends one to create a separate pseudorandom-number generator per thread for better performance if multiple threads invoke `Math.random()`. Another example is StringBuffer_SingleThreadUsage, which checks if a `StringBuffer` object is solely used by a single thread. To detect such violations without false positives, it is necessary to accurately count how many threads access an object or a method, which is impossible for static checkers in full generality.

4.5   Ineffectual Approaches

In this section, we discuss some ineffectual approaches that we have tried while improving the scalability of parametric monitoring. Although they turn out to be ineffectual for parametric monitoring, some of them might be useful in different settings or they might inspire new effectual ideas.

Combining Indexing Trees between Specifications. As mentioned in Section 3.3, we combine indexing trees only within each specification. If we combine indexing trees for different specifications, as well, we can reduce the number of indexing trees even more. However, there is a lot of wasted space in the combined indexing tree. For example, an indexing tree A maps p_1 to m_1 and p_2 to m_2, and another indexing tree B maps p_2 to m_3 and p_3 to m_4. The combined indexing tree of A and B will map p_1 to $(m_1, \varnothing)$, p_2 to (m_2, m_3), and p_3 to $(\varnothing, m_4)$. All empty spaces indicated by $\varnothing$ will be wasted while the indexing trees A and B do not have empty space. More memory overhead from wasted space triggers more garbage collection, slowing down the monitoring.

Enhanced Indexing Cache. The indexing cache provides faster retrieval of monitors from the indexing tree. There are several ideas to improve its hit ratio. We can apply a multi-entry cache from Section 3.2. Also, we can cache not only monitors but also lack thereof to save searching the indexing tree for nothing. However, since the indexing cache already has a high hit ratio, these enhancements do not improve the ratio enough to justify their overhead.

Indexing Tree Cleaning by GWRT. Since we can manage all weak references for each parameter type in one place, the GWRT, we can let the GWRT clean up the indexing trees. In this way, we can remove garbage collected parameter objects from all indexing trees at once, eliminating the need for partial cleanups. Note that partial cleanups could occur even when there is no garbage collected parameter object. We can also have a bit map in the weak reference to indicate to which indexing trees the referent belongs so that we need check only the indexing trees that actually contain it. However, this approach only moves cleanup costs from indexing trees to the GWRT, showing no improvement. The cleanup by the GWRT is more effective because it knows which weak references should be removed. However, cleaning up from outside of the indexing tree costs more because we must locate the entry before we can remove it.

Statistics-Based Indexing Tree Cleaning. As mentioned previously, partial cleanups at indexing trees can occur even when there are no garbage collected parameter objects.

Since we have the GWRT, we can keep statistics about garbage collected parameter objects and use it for deciding whether to trigger a partial cleanup. However, in most cases, there are garbage collected parameter objects. Saving a relatively small number of partial cleanups does not compensate the overhead necessary.

5 Related Work

Producing Specifications. Many automated specification mining approaches [2, 12, 11, 17] has been proposed to reduce the considerable human effort in writing specifications. Unfortunately, they tend to have a few problems in general. First, many of them require or assume non-trivial inputs to yield a meaningful specification [2]. Second, many approaches support only very particular properties [12, 11]. Last but not least, most of them do not guarantee correctness of their results [17].

Monitoring Specifications. Many approaches have been proposed for runtime verification [10, 4, 19, 1, 6, 7, 13]. Most of them do not focus on reducing the overhead of monitoring multiple properties simultaneously. Recently Purandare et al. [22] presents the first study of overhead arising during the simultaneous monitoring of multiple finite-state machine (FSM) specifications. Their approach reduces runtime overhead by merging FSM monitors into bigger monitors, resulting in significant runtime overhead reduction (~50%) over JavaMOP v2.1; it is unknown how that compares with the more recent JavaMOP v2.3, which added several optimizations over v2.1 that minimize the number of created monitors. Their monitor-merging idea is orthogonal and complementary to ours techniques of merging indexing trees and using global caches, as our techniques do not take into account the internal structure of each monitor.

Except for that work, most existing monitoring systems are not capable of handling multiple specifications simultaneously, or have rudimentary support, considering each specification separately. Since each specification is individually handled, the runtime overhead for running them simultaneously is likely to be at least the summation of the overheads of running each in isolation. In fact, our preliminary experiment with JavaMOP (v2.3) showed that the overhead of monitoring several specifications simultaneously is higher than the summation of the overheads of monitoring each in isolation, probably because more memory pressure and less cache hit.

6 Conclusion

Runtime verification has not been widely adopted by developers and users, mainly because of lack of usable specifications and large runtime monitoring overhead. In this paper we have presented a set of 179 formal specifications covering most commonly used Java packages. We have also employed a series of techniques to decrease runtime overhead of monitoring multiple properties simultaneously, which resulted in a new monitoring system, RV-Monitor. Results showed that: 1) our specifications help finding bugs or bad practice coding in real world benchmarks; 2) our techniques make RV-Monitor runs significantly faster than other state-of-the-art RV systems.

Acknowledgement. The work presented in this paper was supported in part by the Boeing grant on "Formal Analysis Tools for Cyber Security" 2014-2015, the NSF grants CCF-1218605, CCF-1318191 and CCF-1421575, and the DARPA grant under agreement number FA8750-12-C-0284.

References

[1] Allan, C., Avgustinov, P., Christensen, A.S., Hendren, L.J., Kuzins, S., Lhoták, O., de Moor, O., Sereni, D., Sittampalam, G., Tibble, J.: Adding trace matching with free variables to AspectJ. In: OOPSLA (2005)

[2] Ammons, G., Bodík, R., Larus, J.R.: Mining specifications. In: POPL (2002)

[3] Annotated Java API Specifications, https://code.google.com/p/annotated-java-api/

[4] Barringer, H., Rydeheard, D., Havelund, K.: Rule systems for run-time monitoring: from EAGLE to RULER. J. Logic Computation (November 2008)

[5] Blackburn, S.M., Garner, R., Hoffman, C., Khan, A.M., McKinley, K.S., Bentzur, R., Diwan, A., Feinberg, D., Frampton, D., Guyer, S.Z., Hirzel, M., Hosking, A., Jump, M., Lee, H., Moss, J.E.B., Phansalkar, A., Stefanović, D., VanDrunen, T., von Dincklage, D., Wiedermann, B.: The DaCapo benchmarks: Java benchmarking development and analysis. In: OOPSLA (2006)

[6] Bodden, E.: J-LO, a tool for runtime-checking temporal assertions. Master's thesis, RWTH Aachen University (2005)

[7] Chaudhuri, S., Alur, R.: Instrumenting C programs with nested word monitors. In: Bošnački, D., Edelkamp, S. (eds.) SPIN 2007. LNCS, vol. 4595, pp. 279–283. Springer, Heidelberg (2007)

[8] Chen, F., Meredith, P., Jin, D., Rosu, G.: Efficient formalism-independent monitoring of parametric properties. In: ASE (2009)

[9] d'Amorim, M., Havelund, K.: Event-based runtime verification of Java programs. SIGSOFT Softw. Eng. Notes (2005)

[10] Drusinsky, D.: The Temporal Rover and the ATG Rover. In: Havelund, K., Penix, J., Visser, W. (eds.) SPIN 2000. LNCS, vol. 1885, pp. 323–330. Springer, Heidelberg (2000)

[11] Ernst, M.D., Czeisler, A., Griswold, W.G., Notkin, D.: Quickly detecting relevant program invariants. In: ICSE (2000)

[12] Gabel, M., Su, Z.: Symbolic mining of temporal specifications. In: ICSE (2008)

[13] Goldsmith, S., O'Callahan, R., Aiken, A.: Relational queries over program traces. In: OOPSLA (2005)

[14] Havelund, K., Roşu, G.: Monitoring Java programs with Java PathExplorer. In: RV (2001)

[15] Jin, D., Meredith, P.O., Griffith, D., Roşu, G.: Garbage collection for monitoring parametric properties. In: PLDI (2011)

[16] Jin, D., Meredith, P.O., Roşu, G.: Scalable parametric runtime monitoring. Technical Report, Department of Computer Science, University of Illinois at Urbana-Champaign (2012), http://hdl.handle.net/2142/30757

[17] Lee, C., Chen, F., Roşu, G.: Mining parametric specifications. In: ICSE (2011)

[18] Lee, C., Jin, D., Meredith, P.O., Roşu, G.: Towards categorizing and formalizing the JDK API. Technical Report, Department of Computer Science, University of Illinois at Urbana-Champaign (2012), http://hdl.handle.net/2142/30006

[19] Martin, M., Livshits, V.B., Lam, M.S.: Finding application errors and security flaws using PQL: a program query language. In: OOPSLA. ACM (2005)

[20] Meredith, P.O., Jin, D., Griffith, D., Chen, F., Roşu, G.: An overview of the MOP runtime verification framework. STTT (2011)

[21] MOPBox, https://code.google.com/p/mopbox/

[22] Purandare, R., Dwyer, M.B., Elbaum, S.G.: Optimizing monitoring of finite state properties through monitor compaction. In: ISSTA (2013)

Improving Dynamic Inference
with Variable Dependence Graph

Anand Yeolekar

Tata Research Development and Design Centre
anand.yeolekar@tcs.com
www.tcs-trddc.com

Abstract. Dynamic detection of program invariants infers relationship between variables at program points using trace data, but reports a large number of irrelevant invariants. We outline an approach that combines lightweight static analysis with dynamic inference that restricts irrelevant comparisons. This is achieved by constructing a variable dependence graph relating a procedure's input and output variables. Initial experiments indicate the advantage of this approach over the dynamic analysis tool Daikon.

Keywords: program invariants, dynamic inference, variable dependence graph.

1 Introduction

Dynamic inference of program invariants analyzes trace data to infer *likely* invariants at program points. Inferred invariants are generally instantiated from templates relating program variables. The Daikon tool [1,2] infers program invariants in the form of unary ($x = k, x \neq 0$), binary ($x \geq y$), etc. relationships between variables. This simple yet effective approach of inferring relations from trace data has found many applications as in [3,4]. Dynamically inferred invariants have been used to summarize procedures [5,6], improve test suites [7], etc.

While dynamic analysis scales in general, there are two issues of concern:(i) the large number of invariants reported by the analysis, and (ii) *irrelevant* comparisons between variables, leading to over-fitting or imprecision. Both issues can affect the subsequent application of inferred invariants, in particular where correctness of the inference matters. To tackle the large number of inferences, Daikon allows the user to specify filters enabling/disabling families of invariants, statistical justification, pruning redundant ones using logical implications and some other heuristics. Using statistical justification, Daikon checks if some threshold of samples have been observed for each candidate invariant. Redundant ones are identified and suppressed using various heuristics e.g. whenever both a==b and a-1==b-1 hold, the latter redundant candidate is suppressed [1]. Nevertheless, it still reports a large number of invariants [5,6,8] forcing users to figure out other means of filtering such invariants.

B. Bonakdarpour and S.A. Smolka (Eds.): RV 2014, LNCS 8734, pp. 301–306, 2014.

A more serious issue is that of reporting irrelevant comparisons e.g. `shoe_size` < `age` that may escape Daikon's heuristics. We have found such irrelevant comparisons almost always getting falsified by some valid test case. Even when such comparisons turn out to be true, they are often uninteresting. A dynamic type inference-based component within Daikon, called DynComp [9], attempts to reduce irrelevant comparisons. DynComp achieves this by *bucketing* variables based on their inferred abstract type. However, once the variables are bucketed, Daikon still *blindly* explores large number of combinations of these variables sharing the same abstract type to report potential invariants.

When subjected to a correctness check as in [6,10], many of the inferred invariants get falsified. While dynamic analysis is known to be unsound and dependent on the test suite quality, it is desirable that the analysis reports likely invariants such that *as few as possible* get falsified. Irrelevant comparisons are closely related to this set of falsified invariants, as we have observed experimentally. Note that when a decision procedure is invoked to prune the set of inferred invariants over the program code, it is desirable to minimize calls to the solver.

We propose to address these issues by using statically obtained program information in the form of a *variable dependence graph* [11]. Intuitively, a variable dependence graph (VDG) allows to discover input-output relations between variables.

1.1   Motivating Example

As an example, consider the procedure in figure 1(a), adapted from [9][1]. DynComp analysis buckets variables `price`, `tax`, `shippingFee`, `returnValue` together, while separating variables `miles` and `year` into different buckets[2], as shown in figure 2(a). With random inputs to variables `miles`, `price`, `tax`, Daikon reports invariants at the exit of procedure `totalCost`, shown in figure 1(b)[3].

Consider invariants 7, 8 and 10: they share the same abstract type yet can be falsified with suitable inputs. Purely from a correctness point of view, we consider these as *irrelevant* comparisons. We propose to reduce such comparisons by referring to the VDG of the procedure, shown in figure 2(b). We obtain a VDG for each modified (i.e. output) variable of the procedure at the exit point. We propose a set of heuristics for variable comparisons based on the VDG, one of which is: *compare a variable with those in its VDG*. With this heuristic, our technique reports only *relevant* comparisons as potential invariants, namely, invariants 9 and 11-13 from figure 1(b).

Intuitively, such invariants have a better chance of being *proven* as correct, as the comparison is more meaningful compared to trying all possible pairs when, statistically, all pairs appear justified.

---

[1] We have converted the arguments of `totalCost` to globals.
[2] `Comparability` values are 1,2,3 respectively.
[3] Without DynComp mode, Daikon reports 22 invariants.

```
int miles, price, tax;          0)  miles == orig(::miles)
int totalCost() {               1)  price == orig(::price)
int year = 2006;                2)  tax == orig(::tax)
if ((miles > 1000)              3)  year == orig(::year)
    && (year > 2000)) {         4)  shipFee==orig(::shipFee)
int shipFee = 10;               5)  year == 2006
return price + tax + shipFee;   6)  shippingFee == 10
 } else                         7)  price > ::tax
 {                              8)  price > ::shippingFee
 return price + tax;            9)  price < return
 }                              10) tax <= ::shippingFee
}                               11) tax < return
                                12) shippingFee < return
                                13) price+tax-return+10==0
      (a)                                 (b)
```

Fig. 1. Example C procedure from [9] and invariants reported by Daikon+DynComp

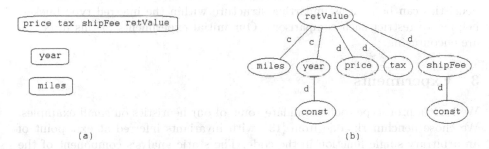

         (a)   (b)

Fig. 2. (a) DynComp-based variable bucketing (b) VDG

2   Relating VDG to Invariants

Given the program dependence graph (PDG) for a procedure and reaching definitions at the procedure exit, we can obtain the VDG for each output variable. This requires locating the nodes corresponding to the reaching definitions and traversing the PDG to identify control and data dependencies, akin to slicing. The VDG obtained for the return value of the procedure in figure 1(a) is illustrated in figure 2(b), with labels c,d on the edges representing control and data dependency.

We now present heuristics for relating variables using VDG to infer potential invariants.

– *For binary invariants, pair the variable with one in its VDG having data dependency.* Such comparisons relate the procedure's output variables with inputs. This heuristic particularly reduces comparisons between variables *within* a bucket, which we have experimentally observed to be irrelevant, as seen for the example in figure 1(a).

- *For binary invariants, compare output variables only when they share inputs.* Reporting comparisons in the absence of common inputs is another source of irrelevant invariants, as suggested by our experiments.

- *For conditional invariant $p \Rightarrow q$, use control dependency to obtain p and data dependency to obtain q.* Daikon supports a notion of conditional invariant inference of the form $p \Rightarrow q$ where p is a branch condition in the program. This heuristic allows to generalize conditional invariants by investigating the VDGs of p, q.

These heuristics seek to reduce noise in the dynamic analysis, over and above Daikon's statistical justification measures and abstract type inference. The authors note in [9] that the bucketing corresponds to variables obtained via (static) slicing (but without control dependencies). A VDG is similar to a slice. While type inference buckets *related* variables, we feel the bucket sizes can be large for programs with tens and hundreds of variables, again leading to large number of invariants with irrelevant comparisons. The VDG analysis combined with our heuristics can be seen as imparting structure within the inferred type bucket, helping to restrict such comparisons. Our initial experiments in this direction are encouraging.

3 Experiments

We built a prototype tool to validate some of our heuristics on small examples. We chose benchmark code from [13], with invariants inferred at exit point of an arbitrary single function in the code. The static analysis component of the tool utilises Prism [12] to build VDGs for procedures. The dynamic analysis component implements a subset of Daikon's invariant detection template (unary, binary, range) and reports invariants, given trace data.

Table 1 presents the results of our experiments. The table reports number of invariants inferred and falsified by Daikon with DynComp mode and our tool using the VDG approach, respectively. For a fair comparison, we restricted Daikon's invariants to match the template set implemented in our tool. Invariants were checked for correctness using the CBMC model checker. The VDG construction is a one-time activity and the time taken on this set of benchmark code was a small fraction of the time taken by the decision procedure.

From the table, our tool appears to report lesser number of invariants mainly because we suppress `var==orig(var)` family of invariants, whenever we can statically figure out that `var` is unmodified in the procedure. Our tool reports these invariants only when `var` is modified along some path and the relation holds on the trace data. When Daikon reports these invariants, they may hold, but are not useful, as seen in figure 1(b). Note that the two techniques can report slightly different sets of invariants, due to the internal heuristics of Daikon.

Our technique seeks to reduce the number of potentially irrelevant comparisons. For this small set of experiments, our technique does better than Daikon+DynComp. In this set of experiments, we observed we did not miss any

Table 1. Experimental Results

code	Daikon+DynComp		VDG	
	reported	falsified	reported	falsified
totalCost	14	3	6	1
kundu	4	0	4	0
bist_cell	9	4	5	0
pc_sfifo3	4	2	1	0

relevant (correct) invariant that Daikon inferred. As this is work-in-progress, we plan to accumulate more experimental data on larger code size to validate our hypothesis.

4   Conclusion and Future Work

Identifying (ir)relevant invariants either dynamically or from program text (statically) remains a challenge. Our technique based on VDG construction offers new heuristics to combine static and dynamic analysis seeking to reduce irrelevant program invariants. We plan to conduct more experiments to understand the tradeoffs in the technique, such as experimenting with the full invariant template of Daikon, applying the heuristics on diverse code and analyzing precision (retaining irrelevant invariants), false positive rate (eliminating relevant invariants) and performance of our technique.

Acknowledgements. The author would like to thank Abhishek Patel, Vishwa Patel and Divyesh Unadkat for their help in this work.

References

1. Ernst, M.D., Perkins, J.H., Guo, P.J., McCamant, S., Pacheco, C., Tschantz, M.S., Xiao, C.: The daikon system for dynamic detection of likely invariants. Sci. Comput. Program. 69, 35–45 (2007)
2. Ernst, M., et al.: The daikon invariant detector, http://pag.lcs.mit.edu/daikon
3. Nimmer, J.W., Ernst, M.D.: Invariant inference for static checking. In: SIGSOFT FSE, pp. 11–20 (2002)
4. Win, T., Ernst, M.: Verifying distributed algorithms via dynamic analysis and theorem proving (2002)
5. Yeolekar, A., Unadkat, D., Agarwal, V., Kumar, S., Venkatesh, R.: Scaling model checking for test generation using dynamic inference. In: International Conference on Software Testing, Verification and Validation (ICST 2013). IEEE (2013)
6. Yeolekar, A., Unadkat, D.: Assertion checking using dynamic inference. In: Bertacco, V., Legay, A. (eds.) HVC 2013. LNCS, vol. 8244, pp. 199–213. Springer, Heidelberg (2013)
7. Xie, T., Notkin, D.: Tool-assisted unit test selection based on operational violations. In: Proc. 18th IEEE International Conference on Automated Software Engineering, pp. 40–48 (2003)

8. Arthur, D.: Evaluating daikon and its applications (2003),
   http://people.duke.edu/dga2/cps208/Daikon.pdf
9. Guo, P.J., Perkins, J.H., McCamant, S., Ernst, M.D.: Dynamic inference of abstract
   types. In: Proceedings of the 2006 International Symposium on Software Testing
   and Analysis, ISSTA 2006, pp. 255–265. ACM, New York (2006)
10. Zhang, L., Yang, G., Rungta, N., Person, S., Khurshid, S.: Feedback-driven dy-
    namic invariant discovery (2014)
11. Harman, M., Fox, C., Hierons, R., Hu, L., Danicic, S., Wegener, J.: Vada: A
    transformation-based system for variable dependence analysis. In: Proceedings of
    the Second IEEE International Workshop on Source Code Analysis and Manipu-
    lation 2002, pp. 55–64. IEEE (2002)
12. TCS Embedded Code Analyzer, http://www.tcs.com/resources/
    brochures/Pages/ TCSEmbeddedCodeAnalyzer.aspx
13. Cimatti, A., Griggio, A., Micheli, A., Narasamdya, I., Roveri, M.: Kratos bench-
    marks, https://es.fbk.eu/tools/kratos/index.php?n=Main.Benchmarks

The TTT Algorithm: A Redundancy-Free Approach to Active Automata Learning

Malte Isberner[1], Falk Howar[2], and Bernhard Steffen[1]

[1] TU Dortmund University, Dept. of Computer Science,
Otto-Hahn-Str. 14, 44227 Dortmund, Germany
{malte.isberner,steffen}@cs.tu-dortmund.de
[2] Carnegie Mellon University, Silicon Valley,
Moffett Field, CA 94043, USA
howar@cmu.edu

Abstract. In this paper we present TTT, a novel active automata learning algorithm formulated in the Minimally Adequate Teacher (MAT) framework. The distinguishing characteristic of TTT is its redundancy-free organization of observations, which can be exploited to achieve optimal (linear) space complexity. This is thanks to a thorough analysis of counterexamples, extracting and storing only the essential refining information. TTT is therefore particularly well-suited for application in a runtime verification context, where counterexamples (obtained, e.g., via monitoring) may be excessively long: as the execution time of a test sequence typically grows with its length, this would otherwise cause severe performance degradation. We illustrate the impact of TTT's consequent redundancy-free approach along a number of examples.

1 Introduction

The wealth of model-based techniques developed in Software Engineering – such as model checking [10] or model-based testing [7] – is starkly contrasted with a frequent lack of formal models. Sophisticated static analysis techniques for obtaining models from a source- or byte-code representation (e.g., [11]) have matured to close this gap to a large extent, yet they might fall short on more complex systems: be it that no robust decision procedure for the underlying theory (e.g., floating-point arithmetics) is available, or that the system performs calls to external, closed source libraries or remote services.

Dynamic techniques for model generation have the advantage of providing models reflecting actual execution behavior of a system. *Passive* approaches (e.g., [21]) construct finite-state models from previously recorded traces, while *active* techniques (e.g., [2]) achieve this by directly interacting with ("querying") the system. In this paper, we focus on the latter; in particular, we consider Angluin-style active automata learning [2], or simply active automata learning.

Active automata learning allows to obtain finite-state models approximating the runtime behavior of systems. These models are *inferred* by invoking sequences of operations (so-called *membership queries*) on the system, and observing the system's response. The technique relies on the following assumptions:

B. Bonakdarpour and S.A. Smolka (Eds.): RV 2014, LNCS 8734, pp. 307–322, 2014.

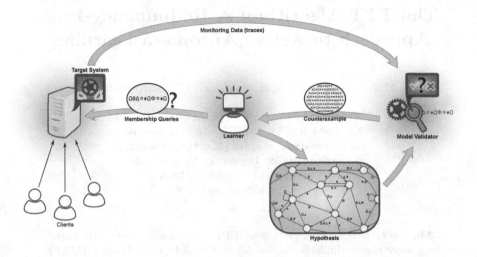

Fig. 1. Active automata learning setup with monitoring in the loop

- the set of operations that can be invoked has to be known a priori (e.g., from a public API),
- the reaction of the system to a membership query must be observable,
- the system has to behave deterministically, under the chosen output abstraction, and
- a way of *resetting* the system is required, i.e., subsequent membership queries have to be independent.

While some of these assumptions seem rather strong, the work of Cho *et al.* [8] on inferring botnet protocols has shown that active learning is a viable technique for obtaining useful models even in highly adverse scenarios.

A practical problem is that Angluin-style automata learning relies on *counterexamples* for model refinement, which are to be provided by an external source. Without such counterexamples, the inferred automata usually remain very small. Bertolino *et al.* [5] have thus suggested to combine active learning with *monitoring*, continuously validating inferred hypotheses against actual system traces. The setup is sketched in Figure 1: a learner infers an initial hypothesis through queries. The system is further instrumented to report its executions during regular operation to a *model validator* component in real-time. This component checks whether the monitored traces conform to the model. In case of a violation, a trace forming a counterexample is reported to the learner, which then refines its hypothesis.

The problem with this approach is that counterexamples obtained through monitoring can be very long. In the following section, by means of a simple example we sketch why virtually all existing active learning algorithms are not prepared to deal with such long counterexamples.

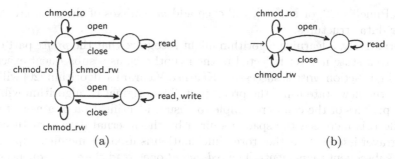

Fig. 2. (a) Example target system, (b) inferred approximation

1.1 Practical Motivation

Consider the behavioral fragment of the system depicted in Figure 2a, representing a stripped-down version of a resource access protocol. A resource can be opened, read from, and closed. Reading from and closing the resource is possible only if it has been opened before. A resource can only be opened if it is closed. Additionally, it is possible to write to a resource. This requires the access mode of this resource to be set to read/write previously (chmod_rw). It is not possible to change the access mode of an open resource.

Active automata learning aims at inferring such a behavioral model by executing test cases and observing the outcome (i.e., whether a sequence of operations is legal or not). The chmod_rw action does not have an *immediate* effect: to notice a difference, the resource needs to be opened *and then* written to. The model inferred by a learning algorithm might therefore be an incorrect *approximation*, as depicted in Figure 2b. If writing is a rare operation compared to reading, this incompleteness will go unnoticed for a long time. Only if the access mode is set to read/write *and* the resource is opened *and* written to, our hypothesis will fail to explain the observed behavior.

If we validate the inferred model by monitoring the actual system, the causal relationship between these three events might not at all be easily identifiable from a counterexample trace. Consider the following trace, not supported by the hypothesis in Fig. 2b:

$$\overbrace{\text{open read close open read close chmod\_rw}}^{prefix} \underbrace{\text{open read close open read close open write}}_{suffix}$$

When presented with such a counterexample, a learning algorithm needs to incorporate the contained information into its internal data structures. Most algorithms implement a variant of one of the following strategies: they identify that the chmod_rw transition in Figure 2b is wrongly routed, as a subsequent execution of the *suffix* part yields a different outcome than executing the suffix only (i.e., from the initial state). Rivest&Schapire's algorithm [26], for example, will add the suffix part to its internal data structures. Other algorithms, such as

Maler&Pnueli's [22] or NL* [6], will even add *all* suffixes of the counterexample to their data structures.

Alternatively, a learning algorithm might recognize that the *prefix* part corresponds to a state not yet reflected in the hypothesis, as a subsequent execution of the single action write is successful. Kearns&Vazirani's algorithm [20] will thus identify the new state using the prefix part. The original L* algorithm will even use *all* prefixes of the counterexample to ensure identification of a new state.

While this increases the space required by the internal data structures, the much graver issue is that the stored information is used for membership queries during subsequent refinements. The *redundant* open read close... sequences thus have to be executed again and again, even if no valuable information can be gained from them. Furthermore, as these redundancies appear both *before* and *after* the actual point of interest (chmod_rw), neither entirely prefix- nor entirely suffix-based approaches will avoid this problem.

In this paper, we present the TTT algorithm, which eliminates all future performance impacts caused by redundancies in counterexamples. In particular, after the refinement step is completed, the internal data structures maintained by TTT after processing the above counterexample would be completely indistinguishable from those resulting from processing the stripped-down counterexample chmod_rw open write.

Outline. After establishing notation in the next section, the main contribution is presented in Section 3: the description of the novel TTT algorithm, particularly highlighting the above-described approach. Section 4 reports on the results of a first experimental evaluation of TTT. Section 5 gives an overview on related work in the field of active automata learning, before Section 6 concludes the paper with an outlook on future work.

2   Preliminaries

2.1   Alphabets, Words, Languages

Let Σ be a finite set of *symbols* (we call such a set a (finite) *alphabet*). By Σ^* we denote the set of all finite *words* (i.e., finite sequences) over symbols in Σ, including the empty word ε. We define $\Sigma^+ = \Sigma^* \setminus \{\varepsilon\}$. The *length* of a word $w \in \Sigma^*$ is denoted by $|w|$. For words $w, w' \in \Sigma^*$, $w \cdot w'$ is the *concatenation* of w and w'. Unless we want to emphasize the concatenation operation, we will usually omit the concatenation operator $\cdot$ and just write ww'.

2.2   Deterministic Finite Automata

As DFA are one of the fundamental concepts in computer science, we will only give a very brief recount for the sake of establishing notation.

Definition 1 (DFA). *Let Σ be a finite alphabet. A deterministic finite automaton (DFA) $\mathcal{A}$ over Σ is a 5-tuple $\mathcal{A} = \langle Q^{\mathcal{A}}, \Sigma, q_0^{\mathcal{A}}, \delta^{\mathcal{A}}, F^{\mathcal{A}} \rangle$, where*

- $Q^{\mathcal{A}}$ is a finite set of states,
- $q_0^{\mathcal{A}} \in Q^{\mathcal{A}}$ is the initial state,
- $\delta^{\mathcal{A}}: Q^{\mathcal{A}} \times \Sigma \to Q^{\mathcal{A}}$ is the transition function, and
- $F^{\mathcal{A}} \subseteq Q^{\mathcal{A}}$ is the set of final (or accepting) states.

For $a \in \Sigma$ and $q \in Q^{\mathcal{A}}$, we call $q' = \delta^{\mathcal{A}}(q, a)$ the a-successor of q. Slightly abusing notation, we extend the transition function to words by defining $\delta^{\mathcal{A}}(q, \varepsilon) = q$ and $\delta^{\mathcal{A}}(q, wa) = \delta^{\mathcal{A}}(\delta^{\mathcal{A}}(q, w), a)$ for $q \in Q, a \in \Sigma, w \in \Sigma^*$.

The following shorthand notations will greatly ease presentation. For $q \in Q^{\mathcal{A}}$, we define the *output function* $\lambda_q^{\mathcal{A}}: \Sigma^* \to \{\top, \bot\}$ of q as $\lambda_q^{\mathcal{A}}(v) = \top$ iff $\delta^{\mathcal{A}}(q, v) \in F$ for all $v \in \Sigma^*$. We denote by $\lambda^{\mathcal{A}}$ the output function of $q_0^{\mathcal{A}}$. For the (extended) transition function, we use a notation borrowed from [20]: for $u \in \Sigma^*$, $\mathcal{A}[u] = \delta^{\mathcal{A}}(q_0^{\mathcal{A}}, u)$ is the state reached by u.

We conclude this section with an important property of DFA.

Definition 2 (Canonicity). *Let $\mathcal{A}$ be a DFA. $\mathcal{A}$ is canonical iff:*

1. $\forall q \in Q^{\mathcal{A}} : \exists u \in \Sigma^* : \mathcal{A}[u] = q$ *(all states are reachable)*
2. $\forall q \neq q' \in Q^{\mathcal{A}} : \exists v \in \Sigma^* : \lambda_q^{\mathcal{A}}(v) \neq \lambda_{q'}^{\mathcal{A}}(v)$ *(all states are pairwisely separable, and we call v a separator).*

It is well known that canonical (i.e., minimal) DFA are unique up to isomorphism [24].

3 The TTT Algorithm

In this section, we will present our main contribution: a new algorithm for actively inferring DFA. We start by giving a brief recount of active automata learning, defining the problem statement and sketching common assumptions and techniques. After this, we will introduce our running example that will accompany the explanation of the key steps, given in Section 3.4. We will also use this opportunity to provide the reader with a high-level idea of the interplay between TTT's data structures. Finally, we conclude the section with remarks on complexity.

3.1 Active Automata Learning in the MAT Model

In active automata learning, the goal is to infer an unknown target DFA $\mathcal{A}$ over a given alphabet Σ. For the remainder of the paper, we fix both the alphabet and the target DFA $\mathcal{A}$, which w.l.o.g. we assume to be canonical. The entity confronted with this task is called a *learner*, and to accomplish this task it may pose queries to a *teacher* (also called *Minimally Adequate Teacher*, MAT) [2]. Two kinds of queries are allowed: the *Membership Query* (MQ) of a word $w \in \Sigma^*$ corresponds to a function evaluation of $\lambda^{\mathcal{A}}(w)$. Whenever the learner has conjectured a hypothesis DFA $\mathcal{H}$, it may subject this to an *Equivalence Query* (EQ). Such a query either signals success (the hypothesis is correct) or yields a

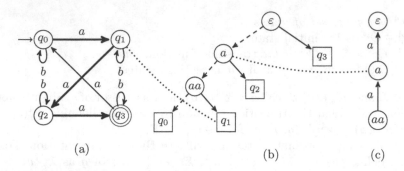

Fig. 3. Running example: (a) target DFA $\mathcal{A}$ and final hypothesis $\mathcal{H}_2$, (b) final discrimination tree $\mathcal{T}_2''$, (c) discriminator trie for final hypothesis

counterexample. A counterexample is a word $w \in \Sigma^*$ for which $\lambda^{\mathcal{A}}(w) \neq \lambda^{\mathcal{H}}(w)$. If presented with a counterexample, the learner needs to *refine* its hypothesis by asking additional membership queries, to conjecture a subsequent hypothesis $\mathcal{H}'$. These steps of hypothesis construction/refinement and equivalence checking are iterated until an equivalence query signals success. Note that in this setting, the learner is not in control over the appearance of counterexamples.

Many learning algorithms work by maintaining a finite, prefix-closed set $\mathcal{S}p \subset \Sigma^*$ identifying states in the target DFA $\mathcal{A}$. Each element of $\mathcal{S}p$ corresponds to a state of the hypothesis $\mathcal{H}$, and vice versa. For $q \in Q^{\mathcal{H}}$, we call its corresponding element $u \in \mathcal{S}p$ the *access sequence* of q, denoted by $\lfloor q \rfloor_{\mathcal{H}}$, and we have $\mathcal{H}[u] = q$. We extend this notation to arbitrary words, allowing to *transform* them into access sequences: for $w \in \Sigma^*$, we define $\lfloor w \rfloor_{\mathcal{H}} = \lfloor \mathcal{H}[w] \rfloor_{\mathcal{H}}$.

It is desirable to ensure that distinct prefixes in $\mathcal{S}p$ also correspond to distinct states in the target DFA $\mathcal{A}$. To accomplish this, the learner maintains a finite set of *distinguishing suffixes* (or *discriminators*) $\mathcal{D} \subset \Sigma^*$. It then constructs $\mathcal{S}p$ in such a way that, for any distinct pair of prefixes $u \neq u' \in \mathcal{S}p$, there exists a discriminator $v \in \mathcal{D}$ such that $\lambda^{\mathcal{A}}(u \cdot v) \neq \lambda^{\mathcal{A}}(u' \cdot v)$ has been observed through membership queries. Due to determinism in $\mathcal{A}$, this implies $\mathcal{A}[u] \neq \mathcal{A}[u']$. We denote the set of states of $\mathcal{A}$ that the learner has identified (or *discovered*) through words in $\mathcal{S}p$ by $\mathcal{A}[\mathcal{S}p] = \{\mathcal{A}[u] \mid u \in \mathcal{S}p\}$.

3.2 Running Example

We will now introduce our running example. We will also use this opportunity to briefly sketch the ideas behind the TTT algorithm's organization in terms of data structures.

Consider the DFA $\mathcal{A}$ in Figure 3a, defined over the alphabet $\Sigma = \{a, b\}$. This DFA accepts words containing $4i + 3$ a's, $i \in \mathbb{N}$. The rest of Figure 3 shows the state of TTT's eponymous data structures for inferring this DFA as its final hypothesis.

First, some of the transitions in (a) are highlighted in bold. These transitions form a *spanning Tree*, and they correspond to the prefix-closed set $\mathcal{S}p$ maintained by TTT; here, $Sp = \{\varepsilon, a, aa, aaa\}$. Conversely, since paths in a tree are uniquely defined, the spanning tree itself *defines* the access sequences of states, and can be used to compute $\lfloor \cdot \rfloor_{\mathcal{H}}$. States of the hypothesis correspond to leaves of the binary tree shown in (b), the *discrimination Tree* (DT). This discrimination tree maintains the information on which discriminators in $\mathcal{D}$ separate states: for every distinct pair of states, a separator can be obtained by looking at the label of the *lowest common ancestor* of the corresponding leaves. Thus, the labels of inner nodes act as discriminators (or separators). As they form a suffix-closed set, they can compactly be stored in a trie [12] – the *discriminator Trie*, shown in (c): each node in this trie represents a word, and this word can be constructed by following the path to the root.[1] The root itself thus corresponds to the empty word ε.

3.3 Discrimination Trees

Discrimination trees (DT) were first used in an active learning context by Kearns and Vazirani [20]. They replaced the *observation table* used in previous algorithms [2,26]: whereas an observation table requires to pose a membership query for every pair $(u, v) \in Sp \times \mathcal{D}$, a DT is redundancy-free in the sense that only MQs that contribute to the distinction of states have to be performed.

As can be seen in Figure 3b, a DT $\mathcal{T}$ is a rooted binary tree. Inner nodes are labeled by discriminators $v \in \mathcal{D}$, and leaves are labeled by hypothesis states $q \in Q^{\mathcal{H}}$. The two children of an inner node correspond to labels $\ell \in \{\top, \bot\}$: we call them the $\bot$-child (dashed line) and the $\top$-child (solid line), respectively.

The nature of a discrimination tree is best explained by considering the operation of *sifting* a word $u \in \Sigma^*$ into the tree. Starting at the root of $\mathcal{T}$, at every inner node labeled by $v \in \mathcal{D}$ we branch to the $\top$- or $\bot$-child depending on the value of $\lambda^{\mathcal{A}}(u \cdot v)$. This procedure is iterated until a leaf is reached, which forms the result of the sifting operation. Sifting thus requires a number of membership queries bounded by the height of the tree.

3.4 Key Steps

In this section, we will present the key steps of TTT. We will use the example presented in Section 3.2 to clarify the effects of the presented steps. A complete and thorough description of the algorithm is beyond the scope of this paper. For technical details, we refer to the source code, which we made publicly available under the GPL license at https://github.com/LearnLib/learnlib-ttt.

Hypothesis Construction. It has already been mentioned in Section 3.1 that states are identified by means of a *prefix-closed set* $Sp \subset \Sigma^*$. Furthermore, these states correspond to leaves in the discrimination tree. Using this information, a hypothesis can be constructed from a set Sp and a discrimination tree $\mathcal{T}$ as follows:

---

[1] This is a slight modification to the usual interpretation of a trie, which considers paths *from* the root.

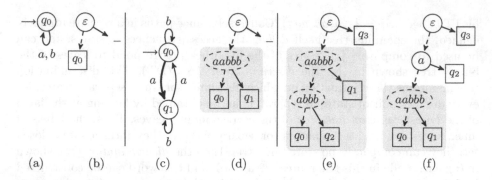

Fig. 4. Evolution of hypotheses and discrimination trees during a run of TTT: (a) initial hypothesis $\mathcal{H}_0$, (b) initial discrimination tree $\mathcal{T}_0$, (c) second hypothesis $\mathcal{H}_1$ (instable), (d) discrimination tree $\mathcal{T}_1$ for $\mathcal{H}_1$, (e) discrimination tree $\mathcal{T}_2$ for final hypothesis $\mathcal{H}_2$ showing blocks in blue, (f) discrimination tree $\mathcal{T}_2'$ after first discriminator finalization

- the *initial state* $q_0^{\mathcal{H}}$ is identified with the empty word $\varepsilon \in \mathcal{S}p$.
- transition targets are determined by means of *sifting*: given a state $q \in Q^{\mathcal{H}}$ identified by a prefix $u \in \mathcal{S}p$, its a-successor ($a \in \Sigma$) is determined by sifting ua into $\mathcal{T}$.
- a state $q \in Q^{\mathcal{H}}$ is in $F^{\mathcal{H}}$ if and only if its associated discrimination tree leaf is in the $\top$-subtree of the root of $\mathcal{T}$.

In the initial hypothesis $\mathcal{H}_0$ and discrimination tree $\mathcal{T}_0$, the setup is fairly simple: the initial state is the only state in the hypothesis, hence $\mathcal{S}p = \{\varepsilon\}$. As the corresponding DT leaf is in the $\bot$-subtree, q_0 is rejecting. Sifting $\varepsilon \cdot a$ and $\varepsilon \cdot b$ into $\mathcal{T}_0$ results in q_0. All transitions therefore form reflexive edges.

Hypothesis Refinement. Key to refining a hypothesis by means of a *counterexample*, i.e., a word $w \in \Sigma^+$ satisfying $\lambda^{\mathcal{H}}(w) \neq \lambda^{\mathcal{A}}(w)$, is Rivest&Schapire's observation [26,28] that w can be *decomposed* in the following way: there exist $u \in \Sigma^*$, $a \in \Sigma$, $v \in \Sigma^*$ such that $w = u \cdot a \cdot v$ and $\lambda^{\mathcal{A}}(\lfloor u \rfloor_{\mathcal{H}} a \cdot v) \neq \lambda^{\mathcal{A}}(\lfloor ua \rfloor_{\mathcal{H}} \cdot v)$.

Such a decomposition makes apparent that the words $\lfloor u \rfloor_{\mathcal{H}} a$ and $\lfloor ua \rfloor_{\mathcal{H}}$ lead to different states in $\mathcal{A}$ (as their output for v differs), but to the same state in $\mathcal{H}$. Therefore, the state $q_{old} = \mathcal{H}[ua]$ needs to be *split*. In the hypothesis, this is achieved by introducing a new state q_{new} with access sequence $\lfloor u \rfloor_{\mathcal{H}} a$ (note that this preserves prefix-closedness of $\mathcal{S}p$). In the discrimination tree, the leaf corresponding to q_{new} is split, introducing v as a *temporary* discriminator.

A possible counterexample for $\mathcal{H}_0$ could be $w = bbbaaabbb$, since $\lambda^{\mathcal{A}}(w) = \top \neq \lambda^{\mathcal{H}_0}(w)$. This counterexample contains a lot of redundant information: the b symbols exercise only self loops in $\mathcal{A}$, and thus do not contribute to the discovery of new states. Part – but not all – of the redundant information will be eliminated by the first counterexample analysis step, which yields the decomposition $\langle bbbb, a, aabbb \rangle$. Hence, a state with access sequence a is added to the next hypothesis $\mathcal{H}_1$ (Fig. 4c), and the corresponding discrimination tree $\mathcal{T}_1$ (Fig. 4d) contains a new inner node labeled with $aabbb$.

Hypothesis Stabilization. As a result of the previous step, it might happen that the constructed hypothesis contradicts information that is present in the discrimination tree. Consider, for example, the hypothesis $\mathcal{H}_1$ and its associated discrimination tree $\mathcal{T}_1$, shown in Figures 4c and d, respectively. State q_1 is identified by prefix $a \in \mathcal{S}p$. Since it is the $\top$-child of the inner node labeled with $aabbb$, we can deduce that $\lambda^{\mathcal{A}}(a \cdot aabbb) = \top$. However, the hypothesis $\mathcal{H}_1$ predicts output $\bot$.

An important observation is that the word $aaabbb$ again forms a counterexample. This counterexample is treated in the same way as described in the previous step: by first decomposing it and then splitting the corresponding leaf in the discrimination tree, thus introducing a new state in the hypothesis. The resulting discrimination tree $\mathcal{T}_2$ can be seen in Figure 4e, and the corresponding hypothesis $\mathcal{H}_2$ is already the final one, i.e., the automaton shown in Figure 3a. We call a hypothesis like $\mathcal{H}_1$ *instable*, as it is refined without a call to an "external" equivalence oracle.

Discriminator Finalization. When comparing the inferred discrimination tree $\mathcal{T}_2$ (Fig. 4e) to the one shown in Figure 3b, one notices immediately that the discriminators occurring in $\mathcal{T}_2$ are much longer. This is due to the fact that the counterexample $w = bbbaaabbb$ contained a lot of redundant information, which is in part still present in the data structure. If these redundancies were not eliminated, subsequent refinements (if there were any) would frequently pose membership queries involving $aabbb$ while sifting new transitions into the tree. To underline the dramatic impact this has, note that any word $aaab^i$, $i \in \mathbb{N}$, would have been a valid counterexample. Thus, the amount of redundancy that is present in these discriminators is generally unbounded.

TTT treats discriminators derived directly from counterexamples as *temporary* (represented by the dashed outlines of the inner nodes in Fig. 4). Furthermore, in Figures 4 d through f, parts of the discrimination tree are enclosed in rectangular regions. These correspond to maximal subtrees of the discrimination tree with temporary discriminators, and we refer to them as *blocks*. The TTT algorithm will *split* these blocks by subsequently replacing temporary discriminators at block roots with *final* ones. New final discriminators v' are obtained by prepending a symbol $a \in \Sigma$ to an existing final discriminator $v \in \mathcal{D}$, i.e., $v' = av$. This can be understood as adding a single node to the *discriminator trie* (cf. Fig. 3c). In Figure 4e, the effect of replacing the temporary discriminator $aabbb$ in $\mathcal{T}_2$ with the final discriminator a is shown, resulting in the discrimination tree $\mathcal{T}_2'$. Note that the replacement discriminator does not need to partition the states in the same way as the temporary discriminators, but it needs to separate at least two states in the respective block. In particular, $aabbb$ still occurs in $\mathcal{T}_2''$ (Fig. 4f), but $abbb$ has vanished.

After replacing $aabbb$ in $\mathcal{T}_2''$ with the final discriminator aa, the discrimination tree already shown in Figure 3b is obtained. As can be seen, it no longer contains any redundant information (i.e., b's) in any of the discriminators. Without discriminator finalization, this would have required the stripped-down, minimal counterexample aaa in the first place.

3.5   Complexity

We now briefly report the complexity of the TTT algorithm. In particular, we focus on three complexity measures:

- *Query complexity*, i.e., the number of overall membership queries posed by the algorithm.
- *Symbol complexity*, i.e., the total number of symbols contained in all these membership queries.
- *Space complexity*, i.e., the amount of space taken up by the internal data structures of the algorithm.

We neglect the time spent on internal computations of the algorithm (e.g., for organizing data structures). This is well-justified by existing reports on practical applications of automata learning, which usually mention the time required for either symbol executions [8], system resets [9], or the space taken up by the observation table data structure [4] as bottlenecks.

Query and Symbol Complexity. We limit ourselves to a brief sketch of query and symbol complexity. Basically, for both correctness and (query) complexity, the same arguments as for other active learning algorithms apply (cf., e.g., [20,28]). We assume that k is the size of the alphabet Σ, the target DFA $\mathcal{A}$ has n states, and the length of the longest counterexample returned by an equivalence query is m. TTT in the worst case requires $O(n)$ equivalence queries and $O(kn^2 + n \log m)$ membership queries, each of length $O(n+m)$. This pessimistic estimate is due to the fact that (degenerate) DTs can be of height $O(n)$ (cf. Fig. 3b). This worst-case query and symbol complexity coincides with Rivest and Schapire's algorithm [26], though we will see in Section 4 that in practice there is a huge gap between the two.

Space Complexity. Interesting from a theoretical perspective is the fact that the TTT algorithm exhibits *optimal* space complexity, not considering the (temporary) storage required for storing counterexamples. In general, the optimality becomes apparent when looking at Figure 3. All of the data structures are (based on) trees, which require an amount of space linear in the number of the leaves. Thus, the space required for the complete hypothesis (with all transitions, i.e., $\Theta(kn)$) dominates the overall space complexity.

Intuitively, it is obvious that every correct learning algorithm has to store the hypothesis (as it constitutes its output), and thus requires space in $\Omega(kn)$. Therefore, TTT has optimal space complexity. Furthermore, this space complexity is significantly below the space complexity of other algorithms, such as L* [2], Rivest and Schapire's [26], or Kearns and Vazirani's [20]. These require space in $\Theta(kn \cdot (n+m))$, $\Theta(kn^2 + nm)$, or $\Theta(kn + nm)$, respectively.

Let us briefly remark that to formally prove space optimality, the above intuition is not sufficient. In particular, it does not take into account the reduction of the search space due to the restriction to *canonical* automata only. However, Domaratzki *et al.* [13] proved a lower bound of $f_k(n) \geq (k - o(1))n2^{n-1}n^{(k-1)n}$ on the number of distinct canonical DFA with n states over an input alphabet of size k. This implies that encoding a canonical DFA requires, on average,

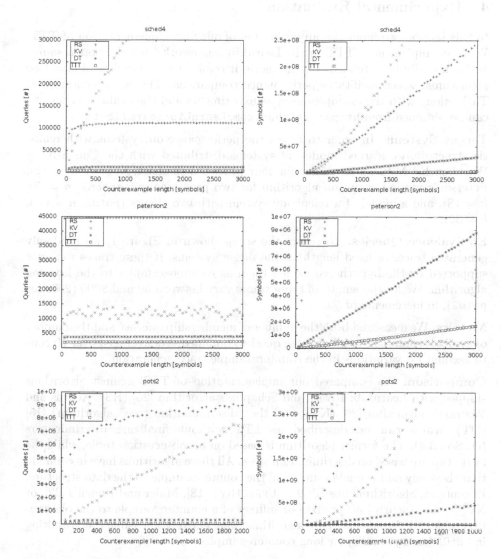

Fig. 5. Experimental results for the CWB examples sched4, peterson2, and pots2 (top to bottom). Queries (left) and symbols (right) are shown as a function of the counterexample length.

$\Omega(\log f_k(n)) = \Omega(nk \log n)$ bits, which coincides with TTT's space complexity in the logarithmic cost model.

4   Experimental Evaluation

In this section, we report on an evaluation of our first implementation of TTT. We have implemented TTT in the LearnLib framework,[2] which is open source and can easily be extended. Furthermore, it comes with a number of standard algorithms, which facilitates performance comparison. The implementation of TTT, along with the examples used as experiments and the evaluation scripts, can be obtained from https://github.com/LearnLib/learnlib-ttt.

Target Systems. In order to assess the performance on systems with realistic structure, we learned models of systems distributed with the Concurrency Workbench:[3] Milner's scheduler for four processes (sched4, $n = 97, k = 12$), Peterson's mutual exclusion algorithm for two processes (peterson2, $n = 50$, $k = 18$), and a model of a telephony system with two clients (pots2, $n = 664$, $k = 32$).

Equivalence Queries. To reflect the setup shown in Figure 1, we randomly generated traces of fixed length on the target systems. If these traces were not supported by the hypothesis, we fed them as counterexamples to the learning algorithm. We let the length of these traces vary between 50 and 3000 (2000 for pots2), in increments of 50.

Metrics. We measured both the number of membership queries, and the number of symbols contained in all of these queries combined. We averaged over 10 runs to account for variations in the counterexample trace generation.

Comparison. We compared our implementation of TTT against algorithms shipped with LearnLib: Rivest and Schapire's algorithm [26] (RS), Kearns and Vazirani's algorithm [20] (KV), and the "discrimination tree" algorithm[4] [15] (DT), which can be described as TTT without finalizing discriminators (cf. Sec. 3.4). The former algorithm is based on an observation table, while the latter two are based on discrimination trees. All these algorithms have in common that they only add a single suffix from the counterexample to the data structure. In contrast, algorithms like L* [2], SUFFIX1BY1 [18], Maler and Pnueli's [22], or NL* [6] add (nearly) *all* prefixes or suffixes of a counterexample to the observation table. We found that these algorithms were entirely infeasible (i.e., resulting in OutOfMemoryErrors) for long counterexamples.

4.1   Results

The results of our evaluation on the three systems (top to bottom: sched4, peterson2, pots2) are displayed in Figure 5. Both the number of membership

---

[2] http://www.learnlib.de/
[3] http://homepages.inf.ed.ac.uk/perdita/cwb/
[4] This algorithm is also known as the *Observation Pack* algorithm.

queries (left column) and the total number of symbols (right column) are plotted as a function of the length of counterexample traces.

In terms of membership queries, TTT outperforms all other algorithms on all examples. When compared to the DT algorithm, the difference is comparatively small, with TTT requiring 25%–50% as many membership queries. However, this is still remarkable when considering that the main difference between TTT and DT is the *extra effort* for finalizing discriminators (cf. Sec. 3.4). We conclude from this that by discriminator finalization, we obtain "more general" discriminators, which lead to better-balanced trees than the very specific, long ones directly extracted from the counterexamples. When compared to the RS and KV algorithms, the difference in membership queries spans several orders of magnitude.

When looking at the number of symbols, TTT consistently beats DT. On the sched4 and peterson2 examples, we observe a reduction in the number of symbols by approximately one order of magnitude. On the pots2 example, which is the largest of the systems we considered, there even is a 60× reduction!

The peterson2 example poses a special case. Here, the number of membership queries apparently is nearly constant for all counterexample lengths, but the variation for the KV algorithm is considerable. In terms of symbols, the KV algorithm outperforms TTT when counterexamples consists of 800 symbols or more (for a length of 3000, TTT needs roughly 4.5× as many symbols as KV). Manual inspection of the model showed that it is structured in a DAG-like fashion, with only very few loops. Hence, counterexamples on this system contain relatively little redundant information. However, this was the only example we investigated[5] where KV performed that strongly in terms of symbols. Furthermore, especially the pots2 example underlines that preferring the KV algorithm over TTT might be an extremely poor choice: for a counterexample length of 2000, KV on average requires 670× more symbol executions than TTT does. When considering Rivest&Schapire, this factor increases to up to 1100×.

5 Related Work

The MAT model for active automata learning was established by Angluin [2], along with the presentation of the famous observation table-based L* algorithm. The technique gained major interest after it was discovered as a means of enabling model-based techniques in scenarios where no such models were available. Notable works in this direction include its application to model checking [25], and to model-driven test-case generation [14]. The practical applicability was further improved by adapting the L* DFA learning algorithm to Mealy machines [14,27].

While much effort has been devoted to optimizations in practical scenarios (e.g., using various filters [23]), improvements at the "pure" algorithmic level are

---

[5] Other examples included randomly generated DFA, and instances of Figure 2a for up to 5 resources, which we do not report upon due to size constraints. All data necessary to run these experiments can be obtained via GitHub.

comparably rare. Maler and Pnueli [22] suggested adding all suffixes of the counterexample to the table. Rivest and Schapire [26] found that adding a single suffix was sufficient, and that this suffix could be determined using a binary search. It has been observed that this leads to non-canonical intermediate hypotheses [28]. Several heuristics have thus been proposed to maintain suffix-closedness of the discriminators, such as Shahbaz's algorithm and SUFFIX1BY1 [18].

Kearns and Vazirani [20] were the first to employ a *discrimination tree*. A general framework for active learning named *Observation Packs* was introduced by Balcazar *et al.* [3]. This framework provides a unifying view on the aforementioned algorithms. Its name has been adopted for an algorithm developed by Howar [15], which can be summarized as combining the discrimination tree data structure with Rivest and Schapire's counterexample analysis.

A fairly recent contribution in the classical scenario of black-box inference of regular languages is the NL* algorithm [6], inferring NFA instead of DFA. These NFA may be exponentially more succinct than the corresponding DFA, and can in such cases be learned with less membership queries. However, the number of required equivalence queries grows from linear to quadratic. Furthermore, it is unclear how (or even if) the NL* algorithm could be adapted to infer Mealy machines.

6 Conclusion

We have presented TTT, an active automata learning algorithm which stores the essential data in three tree-like data structures: a *spanning tree* defining unique access sequences, embedded into the hypothesis' transition graph, a *discrimination tree* for distinguishing states, and a *discriminator trie* for storing the suffix-closed set of discriminators. This leads to an extremely compact representation, as it strips all the information down to the *essentials* for learning. In fact, the combined space required for all data structures is asymptotically the same as the size of the hypothesis, $\Theta(kn)$. We demonstrated the effects of this *redundancy-free* data structure on a number of examples. TTT outperformed other learning algorithms when considering the total number of membership queries on all of the examples. When considering the number of symbols, Kearns&Vazirani's algorithm in fact outperformed TTT in one out of three systems (even though it required a much higher number of membership queries). However, the system in question was the smallest one, and on all other systems, Kearns&Vazirani's algorithm performed poorly. On average, TTT yields a one to two orders of magnitude reduction in terms of symbol executions, and a 50%–75% reduction in terms of membership queries when compared to the Observation Pack algorithm, which ranks second. We conclude that the "cleanup" of the internal data structures that TTT performs is well worth the extra effort.

6.1 Future Work

There are several lines of work we want to explore. The first one is to further investigate the impact of TTT in practical setups. A necessary step for this will be to adapt TTT to learn Mealy machines [14,27], an extension we expect to be straightforward. We then plan to evaluate the *life-long learning* approach [5] in larger case studies, using learning in the loop with monitoring.

The second line concerns improving the practical applicability in general settings. While most of the optimizing filter techniques [23] work with any learning algorithm, an important optimization is the parallelization of membership queries [8,16]. The challenge that presents itself here is the fact that when sifting a word into a discrimination tree, the next query to be asked depends on the outcome of the previous one.

The third – and probably the most challenging – line of future research is to adapt TTT to richer modeling formalisms, in particular register automata [17,19]. Unlike approaches that separate the inference of the control skeleton from that of the *mapper* responsible for handling data [1], adapting TTT to *natively* infer register automata will require non-trivial modifications at the algorithmic level.

Acknowledgement. We thank Maren Geske and Dennis Kühn for their help with preparing the illustrations.

References

1. Aarts, F., Heidarian, F., Kuppens, H., Olsen, P., Vaandrager, F.: Automata Learning through Counterexample Guided Abstraction Refinement. In: Giannakopoulou, D., Méry, D. (eds.) FM 2012. LNCS, vol. 7436, pp. 10–27. Springer, Heidelberg (2012), http://dx.doi.org/10.1007/978-3-642-32759-9_4
2. Angluin, D.: Learning Regular Sets from Queries and Counterexamples. Inf. Comput. 75(2), 87–106 (1987)
3. Balcázar, J.L., Díaz, J., Gavaldà, R.: Algorithms for Learning Finite Automata from Queries: A Unified View. In: Advances in Algorithms, Languages, and Complexity, pp. 53–72 (1997)
4. Berg, T., Jonsson, B., Leucker, M., Saksena, M.: Insights to Angluin's Learning. Electron. Notes Theor. Comput. Sci. 118, 3–18 (2005), http://dx.doi.org/10.1016/j.entcs.2004.12.015
5. Bertolino, A., Calabrò, A., Merten, M., Steffen, B.: Never-Stop Learning: Continuous Validation of Learned Models for Evolving Systems through Monitoring. ERCIM News 2012(88) (2012)
6. Bollig, B., Habermehl, P., Kern, C., Leucker, M.: Angluin-style Learning of NFA. In: Proc. IJCAI 2009, San Francisco, CA, USA, pp. 1004–1009 (2009)
7. Broy, M., Jonsson, B., Katoen, J.-P., Leucker, M., Pretschner, A. (eds.): Model-Based Testing of Reactive Systems. LNCS, vol. 3472. Springer, Heidelberg (2005)
8. Cho, C.Y., Babić, D., Shin, R., Song, D.: Inference and Analysis of Formal Models of Botnet Command and Control Protocols. In: CCS 2010, pp. 426–440. ACM, Chicago (2010)
9. Choi, W., Necula, G., Sen, K.: Guided GUI Testing of Android Apps with Minimal Restart and Approximate Learning. In: Proc. OOPSLA 2013, pp. 623–640. ACM, New York (2013), http://doi.acm.org/10.1145/2509136.2509552
10. Clarke, E.M., Grumberg, O., Peled, D.A.: Model Checking. MIT Press (1999)

11. Corbett, J., Dwyer, M., Hatcliff, J., Laubach, S., Pasareanu, C., Robby, Z.H.: Bandera: Extracting Finite-state Models from Java Source Code. In: Proc. Software Engineering, pp. 439–448 (2000)
12. De La Briandais, R.: File Searching Using Variable Length Keys. In: Western Joint Computer Conference, IRE-AIEE-ACM 1959, Western, pp. 295–298. ACM, New York (1959), http://doi.acm.org/10.1145/1457838.1457895
13. Domaratzki, M., Kisman, D., Shallit, J.: On the Number of Distinct Languages Accepted by Finite Automata with n States. Journal of Automata, Languages and Combinatorics 7(4), 469–486 (2002)
14. Hagerer, A., Hungar, H.: Model generation by moderated regular extrapolation. In: Kutsche, R.-D., Weber, H. (eds.) FASE 2002. LNCS, vol. 2306, pp. 80–95. Springer, Heidelberg (2002)
15. Howar, F.: Active Learning of Interface Programs. Ph.D. thesis, TU Dortmund University (2012), http://dx.doi.org/2003/29486
16. Howar, F., Bauer, O., Merten, M., Steffen, B., Margaria, T.: The Teachers Crowd: The Impact of Distributed Oracles on Active Automata Learning. In: Hähnle, R., Knoop, J., Margaria, T., Schreiner, D., Steffen, B. (eds.) ISoLA 2011 Workshops 2011. CCIS, vol. 336, pp. 232–247. Springer, Heidelberg (2012)
17. Howar, F., Steffen, B., Jonsson, B., Cassel, S.: Inferring Canonical Register Automata. In: Kuncak, V., Rybalchenko, A. (eds.) VMCAI 2012. LNCS, vol. 7148, pp. 251–266. Springer, Heidelberg (2012)
18. Irfan, M.N., Oriat, C., Groz, R.: Angluin Style Finite State Machine Inference with Non-optimal Counterexamples. In: 1st Int. Workshop on Model Inference in Testing (2010)
19. Isberner, M., Howar, F., Steffen, B.: Learning Register Automata: From Languages to Program Structures. Machine Learning 96(1-2), 65–98 (2014), http://dx.doi.org/10.1007/s10994-013-5419-7
20. Kearns, M.J., Vazirani, U.V.: An Introduction to Computational Learning Theory. MIT Press, Cambridge (1994)
21. Lorenzoli, D., Mariani, L., Pezzè, M.: Inferring State-based Behavior Models. In: Proc. WODA 2006, pp. 25–32. ACM, New York (2006)
22. Maler, O., Pnueli, A.: On the Learnability of Infinitary Regular Sets. Information and Computation 118(2), 316–326 (1995)
23. Margaria, T., Raffelt, H., Steffen, B.: Knowledge-based Relevance Filtering for Efficient System-level Test-based Model Generation. Innovations in Systems and Software Engineering 1(2), 147–156 (2005)
24. Nerode, A.: Linear Automaton Transformations. Proceedings of the American Mathematical Society 9(4), 541–544 (1958)
25. Peled, D., Vardi, M.Y., Yannakakis, M.: Black Box Checking. In: Wu, J., Chanson, S.T., Gao, Q. (eds.) Proc. FORTE 1999, pp. 225–240. Kluwer Academic (1999)
26. Rivest, R.L., Schapire, R.E.: Inference of Finite Futomata Using Homing Sequences. Inf. Comput. 103(2), 299–347 (1993)
27. Shahbaz, M., Groz, R.: Inferring Mealy Machines. In: Cavalcanti, A., Dams, D.R. (eds.) FM 2009. LNCS, vol. 5850, pp. 207–222. Springer, Heidelberg (2009)
28. Steffen, B., Howar, F., Merten, M.: Introduction to Active Automata Learning from a Practical Perspective. In: Bernardo, M., Issarny, V. (eds.) SFM 2011. LNCS, vol. 6659, pp. 256–296. Springer, Heidelberg (2011)

Lazy Symbolic Execution for Enhanced Learning

Duc-Hiep Chu, Joxan Jaffar, and Vijayaraghavan Murali

National University of Singapore
{hiepcd,joxan,m.vijay}@comp.nus.edu.sg

Abstract. The performance of symbolic execution based verifiers relies heavily on the quality of "interpolants", formulas which succinctly describe a generalization of states proven safe so far. By default, symbolic execution along a path stops the moment when infeasibility is detected in its path constraints, a property we call "eagerness". In this paper, we argue that eagerness may hinder the discovery of good quality interpolants, and propose a systematic method that ignores the infeasibility in pursuit of better interpolants. We demonstrate with a state-of-the-art system on realistic benchmarks that this "lazy" symbolic execution outperforms its eager counterpart by a factor of two or more.

1 Introduction

Symbolic execution has been largely successful in program verification, testing and analysis [16,24,28,14,13]. It is a method for program reasoning that uses symbolic values as inputs instead of actual data, and it represents the values of program variables as symbolic expressions on the input symbolic values. As symbolic execution reaches each program point along different paths, different "symbolic states" are created. For each symbolic state, a path condition is maintained, which is a formula over the symbolic inputs built by accumulating constraints that those inputs must satisfy in order for execution to reach the state. A symbolic execution tree depicts all executed paths during symbolic execution.

We say that a state is *infeasible* if its path condition is unsatisfiable, therefore one obviously cannot reach an **error** location from this state. Whenever an infeasible state is encountered, symbolic execution will backtrack along the edge(s) just executed. In that regard, symbolic execution by default is *eager*. This eagerness has been considered as a clear advantage of symbolic execution, in comparison with Abstract Interpretation (AI) [7] or Counterexample-Guided Abstraction Refinement (CEGAR) [6], since it avoids the exploration of *infeasible paths* which could block exponentially large symbolic trees in practice.

This paper considers symbolic execution in the context of software verification. One main challenge is to address the path explosion problem. The approaches of [16,24,15,14] tackle this fundamental issue by eliminating from the model those facts which are irrelevant or too-specific for proving the unreachability of the error nodes. This "learning" phase consists of computing *interpolants* in the same spirit of conflict-driven learning in SAT solvers. Informally, the interpolant at a given program point can be seen as a formula that succinctly captures the reason of infeasibility of paths which go through that program point. In

B. Bonakdarpour and S.A. Smolka (Eds.): RV 2014, LNCS 8734, pp. 323–339, 2014.

other words it succinctly captures the reason why paths through the program point are safe. As a result, if the program point is encountered again through a different path such that its path condition implies the interpolant, the new path can be *subsumed*, because it can be guaranteed to be safe. Interpolation has been empirically shown to be crucial in scaling symbolic execution because it can potentially result in exponential savings by pruning large sub-trees. It is also generally known that the quality of interpolants greatly affects the amount of savings provided.

This is where a conflict between eagerness and learning arises. Eagerly stopping and backtracking at an infeasible state can make the learned interpolants unnecessarily too *restrictive* – while the interpolant would typically capture the reason for infeasibility of the state, the infeasibility could have nothing to do with the safety of the program. In practice, safety properties often involve a small number of variables whereas conditional expressions, which act as guards by causing infeasibility in paths, could be on any unrelated variable. Ultimately, this causes the (restrictive) interpolant to disallow subsumption in future, mitigating its benefit. In other words, eagerness hinders a *property-directed* approach.

In this paper, we propose a new method to enhance the learning of powerful interpolants but without losing the intrinsic benefits of symbolic execution. Whenever an infeasible path is encountered, instead of backtracking immediately, we *selectively abstract* the infeasible state so that it becomes feasible, and proceed with the search. By performing such an abstraction, we say that we have entered *speculation mode*. More generally, as we progressively abstract away infeasibility from a symbolic path, we are exhibiting a property-directed strategy, i.e., ignoring the infeasibility along the path until the real reason why the path is safe is found. Note that the sole purpose of speculation is to find better interpolants – we already know any path with an infeasible prefix is safe.

However, since exploration of infeasible states is in general a wasteful effort, we subject the speculation to a *bound*. This mitigates the potential blowup of the speculative search, while still retaining the possibility of discovering good interpolants. Intuitively, this bound should be at least linearly related to the program size: anything less than this could make the speculation phase arbitrarily short. It is a main contribution of this paper, that in the other direction, a linear bound is *good enough*.

Finally, we remark that though this paper studies and quantifies the "enhanced learning" for symbolic execution in the setting of static analysis, its impact is relevant to runtime verification as well. In our previous work [13], we have demonstrated the benefits of interpolation in speeding up *concolic* testing for better coverage. By being lazy, we expect the enhanced interpolants to result in further speedup. As another example, Navabpour et al. [25] propose a method, which leverages symbolic execution to predict the program's execution path, in order to effectively reduce the overhead of time-triggered runtime verification (TTRV). In fact, improvements in symbolic execution, as demonstrated in this paper, can lead to improvements in their runtime verification.

2   Examples

We first exemplify the case when (eager) symbolic execution is clearly not an efficient way to conduct a proof. For the programs in Fig. 1, assume (1) the boolean expressions e_i do not involve the variables x and y, and (2) the desired postcondition is $y \leq n$ for some constant $n > 0$. A *path expression* is of the form $E_1 \wedge E_2 \wedge \cdots \wedge E_n$ where each E_i is either e_i or its negation. Note that each of the (2^n) path expressions represents a unique path through each of the programs.

```
x = y = 0                 x = y = 0                 x = y = 0
if (e₁) y++ else x++      if (e₁) y += 2            if (e₁) y++ else x++
if (e₂) y++ else x++      if (e₂) y += 2            ...
...                       ...                       if (eⱼ) y++ else y = n+1
if (eₙ) y++ else x++      if (eₙ) y += 2            ...
                                                    if (eₙ) y++ else x++

  (a) Lazy is Good          (b) Eager is Good         (c) Lazy is Still Better
```

Fig. 1. Proving $y \leq n$: Eager vs Lazy

Given the first program in Fig. 1(a), we can reason that the postcondition $y \leq n$ always holds, *without considering* the satisfiability of the path expressions. Using symbolic execution, in contrast, many of the unsatisfiable path expressions need to be detected and worse, their individual reasons for unsatisfiability (the "interpolants") need to be recorded and managed. Note that if we used a CEGAR approach [6] here, where *abstraction refinements* are performed only when a spurious counter-example is encountered, we would have a very efficient (linear) proof.

In the next program in Fig. 1(b), slightly modified from the previous, we present a dual and opposite situation. Note that the program is safe just if, amongst the path expressions that are satisfiable, less than $n/2$ of these involve a distinct and positive expression e_i (as opposed to the negation of e_i), for i ranging from 1 to n. This means that the number of times the "then" bodies of the if-statements are (symbolically) executed is less than $n/2$. Here, it is in fact necessary to record and manage the unsatisfiable path expressions as they are encountered during symbolic execution. CEGAR, in contrast, would require a large number of abstraction refinements in order to remove counter-examples arising from not recognizing the unsatisfiability of "unsafe" path expressions, i.e. those corresponding to $n/2$ or more increments of y.

In principle, a typical program would correspond to being in between the above two extreme cases in Fig. 1(a) and 1(b). Our key intuition, however, is that in fact a typical program lies closer to the first example rather than the second, because in practice safety properties are typically on a small subset of variables, whereas program guards, which are the cause of infeasibilities, can be on any (unrelated) variables. This intuition is later confirmed empirically.

For the final example program in Fig. 1(c), assume that all and only the path expressions which contain the subexpression e_j are unsatisfiable. (In other words, the only way to execute the jth if-statement is through its "then" body.)

Here we clearly need to detect the presence of the expression e_j and not any of the other expressions. More generally, we argue that while some path expressions must be recorded and managed, this number is small. The challenge is, of course, is how to *find* these important path expressions, which is precisely the objective of our speculation algorithm. We next exemplify this.

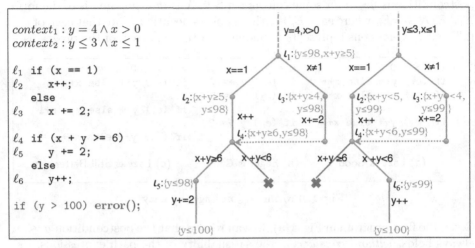

Fig. 2. A Symbolic Execution (Eager) Tree with Learning

Consider the program fragment in Fig. 2 executed under two different initial contexts: $y = 4 \wedge x > 0$ and $y \leq 3 \wedge x \leq 1$. In both contexts, the program is safe because $y \leq 100$ at the end. Throughout the example, assume weakest preconditions (WP) are used as interpolants.

Symbolic execution (eager) would start at program point ℓ_1 with the first context $y = 4 \wedge x > 0$. Assume it first takes the then branch with condition x==1, executing x++ and reaching ℓ_4. Proceeding along the then branch from ℓ_4, it executes y+=2 and reaches the end of the safe path, generating the (WP) interpolant $y \leq 98$ at ℓ_5. Now from ℓ_4, it finds that the else branch is infeasible as the path condition $y = 4 \wedge x > 0 \wedge x = 1 \wedge x' = x+1 \wedge x'+y < 6$ is unsatisfiable. Being eager, symbolic execution would immediately backtrack, and to preserve this infeasibility, it would learn the interpolant $x' + y \geq 6$. Combining the then and else body's interpolants, it would generate $x' + y \geq 6 \wedge y \leq 98$ at ℓ_4 (note that in Fig. 2 we project the formula on the original variable names). Passing this back through WP propagation would result in $x + y \geq 5 \wedge y \leq 98$ at ℓ_2.

Now, executing the else body x+=2 from ℓ_1, it would reach ℓ_4 with the path condition $y = 4 \wedge x > 0 \wedge x \neq 1 \wedge x' = x + 2$, which implies the interpolant $x' + y \geq 6 \wedge y \leq 98$. Therefore the path would be *subsumed* (dotted line). Propagating this interpolant through x+=2 would result in $x + y \geq 4 \wedge y \leq 98$ at ℓ_3. Now, combining the then and else body's interpolant at ℓ_1 would result in the disjunction: $(x = 1 \Rightarrow (x+y \geq 5 \wedge y \leq 98)) \wedge (x \neq 1 \Rightarrow (x+y \geq 4 \wedge y \leq 98))$. For the sake of clarity, we strengthen this to $y \leq 98 \wedge x + y \geq 5$, but we assure the reader that our discussion is not affected by this. Thus, the final symbolic execution tree explored for this context will be the one on the left in Fig. 2.

Now, when the program fragment is reached along the second context $y \leq 3 \wedge x \leq 1$, subsumption cannot take place at ℓ_1 as the context does not imply the interpolant $y \leq 98 \wedge x + y \geq 5$. Symbolic execution would therefore proceed to generate the symbolic tree shown on the right. It is worth noting that even if the program was explored with the order of the contexts swapped, subsumption cannot take place at the top level.

Consider now our lazy symbolic execution process invoked on this program. We would perform symbolic execution exactly the same as before, except when the unsatisfiable path condition $y = 4 \wedge x > 0 \wedge x = 1 \wedge x' = x + 1 \wedge x' + y < 6$ is encountered, instead of backtracking, we selectively abstract the formula to make it satisfiable. Since we are doing forward symbolic execution, we selectively abstract by *deleting* the constraint(s) from the latest guard that we encountered (i.e., $x' + y < 6$) to make the formula satisfiable.[1]

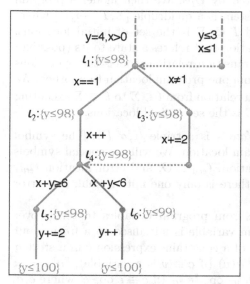

Fig. 3. Lazy Symbolic Execution Tree

After performing selective abstraction, we enter "speculation mode" with the abstracted path condition $y = 4 \wedge x > 0 \wedge x = 1 \wedge x' = x + 1$. A problem now is that in general, the sub-tree underneath the infeasible branch may be exponentially large, exploring which is wasteful as we already know that it is safe. Therefore it is necessary to impose a bound on the speculative search. We remark on our design choice of such a bound in later technical Sections.

Triggering speculation at ℓ_4, we execute the statement y++ at ℓ_6 and reach the end of the (safe) path. Speculation has now succeeded, hence we annotate ℓ_6 with $y \leq 99$. Combining the interpolants at ℓ_4, we get $y \leq 98$. Propagating it back through the tree as shown in Fig. 3 we get the interpolant $y \leq 98$ at ℓ_1. Now, when the program fragment is reached along the second context $y \leq 3 \wedge x \leq 1$, the interpolant is implied at ℓ_1, and the entire tree can be subsumed at the top level. Note that we applied strengthening of WP as before, but we assure that even without strengthening the subsumption will still take place.

This example has shown that speculation can potentially result in exponential savings. The reason speculation works in practice is that safety properties

---

[1] In principle, selective abstraction can be done in many ways, for instance, by also deleting $y = 4$, $x' = x + 1$ or any combination. We defer to Section 5 the reasoning behind our design choice of deleting the latest guard.

are only on a small subset of variables whereas program guards that cause in-feasibility can be on any of them. Temporarily ignoring the infeasibility helps in discovering interpolants closely related to the safety, such as those in Fig. 3, rather than interpolants that blindly preserve the infeasibility, such as those in Fig. 2. In Section 5, we empirically show that the exponential gains provided by speculation clearly outweigh its cost.

3   Preliminaries

Syntax. We restrict our presentation to a simple imperative programming lan-guage where all basic operations are either assignments or assume operations, and the domain of all variables are integers. The set of all program variables is denoted by *Vars*. An *assignment* x := e corresponds to assign the evaluation of the expression e to the variable x. In the *assume* operator, assume(c), if the Boolean expression c evaluates to *true*, then the program continues, otherwise it halts. The set of operations is denoted by *Ops*. We then model a program by a *transition system*. A transition system is a quadruple $[\Sigma, I, \longrightarrow, O]$ where Σ is the set of program locations and $I \subseteq \Sigma$ is the set of initial locations. $\longrightarrow \subseteq \Sigma \times \Sigma \times Ops$ is the transition relation that relates a state to its (possible) successors executing operations. This transition relation models the operations that are executed when control flows from one program location to another. We shall use $\ell \xrightarrow{\text{op}} \ell'$ to denote a transition relation from $\ell \in \Sigma$ to $\ell' \in \Sigma$ executing the operation op $\in Ops$. Finally, $O \subseteq \Sigma$ is the set of final locations.

Symbolic Execution. A *symbolic state* s is a triple $\langle \ell, \sigma, \Pi \rangle$. The symbol $\ell \in \Sigma$ corresponds to the current program location. We will use special symbols for initial location, $\ell_{\text{start}} \in I$, final location, $\ell_{\text{end}} \in O$, and error location $\ell_{\text{error}} \in O$ (if any). W.l.o.g we assume that there is only one initial, final, and error location in the transition system.

The symbolic store σ is a function from program variables to terms over input symbolic variables. Each program variable is initialised to a fresh input symbolic variable. The *evaluation* $[\![c]\!]\sigma$ of a constraint expression c in a store σ is defined recursively as usual: $[\![v]\!]\sigma = \sigma(v)$ (if $c \equiv v$ is a variable), $[\![n]\!]\sigma = n$ (if $c \equiv n$ is an integer), $[\![e \text{ op}_r e']\!]\sigma = [\![e]\!]\sigma \text{ op}_r [\![e']\!]\sigma$ (if $c \equiv e \text{ op}_r e'$ where e, e' are expressions and op$_r$ is a relational operator $<, >, ==, ! =, >=, <=$), and $[\![e \text{ op}_a e']\!]\sigma = [\![e]\!]\sigma \text{ op}_a [\![e']\!]\sigma$ (if $c \equiv e \text{ op}_a e'$ where e, e' are expressions and op$_a$ is an arithmetic operator $+, -, \times, \ldots$).

Finally, Π is called *path condition*, a first-order formula over the symbolic inputs that accumulates constraints which the inputs must satisfy in order for an execution to follow the particular corresponding path. The set of first-order formulas and symbolic states are denoted by *FOL* and *SymStates*, respectively. Given a transition system $[\Sigma, I, \longrightarrow, O]$ and a state $s \equiv \langle \ell, \sigma, \Pi \rangle \in SymStates$, a 'symbolic step' of transition $t : \ell \xrightarrow{\text{op}} \ell'$ returns another symbolic state s' defined as:

$$s' \equiv \text{SYMSTEP}(s, t) \triangleq \begin{cases} \langle \ell', \sigma, \Pi \wedge [\![c]\!]\sigma \rangle & \text{if op} \equiv \text{assume(c)} \\ \langle \ell', \sigma[x \mapsto [\![e]\!]\sigma], \Pi \rangle & \text{if op} \equiv \text{x := e} \end{cases} \quad (1)$$

Given a symbolic state $s \equiv \langle \ell, \sigma, \Pi \rangle$ we define $[\![s]\!] : SymStates \to FOL$ as the formula $(\bigwedge_{v \in Vars} [\![v]\!]\sigma) \wedge \Pi$ where $Vars$ is the set of program variables.

A *symbolic path* $\pi \equiv s_0 \cdot s_1 \cdot \ldots \cdot s_n$ is a sequence of symbolic states such that $\forall i \cdot 1 \leq i \leq n$ the state s_i is a *successor* of s_{i-1}, denoted as $\mathsf{SUCC}(s_{i-1}, s_i)$. A path $\pi \equiv s_0 \cdot s_1 \cdot \ldots \cdot s_n$ is *feasible* if $s_n \equiv \langle \ell, \sigma, \Pi \rangle$ such that $[\![\Pi]\!]\sigma$ is satisfiable. If $\ell \in O$ and s_n is feasible then s_n is called *terminal* state. If $[\![\Pi]\!]\sigma$ is unsatisfiable the path is called *infeasible* and s_n is called an *infeasible* state. If there exists a feasible path $\pi \equiv s_0 \cdot s_1 \cdot \ldots \cdot s_n$ then we say s_k $(0 \leq k \leq n)$ is *reachable* from s_0. A *symbolic execution tree* contains all the execution paths explored during the symbolic execution of a transition system by triggering Equation (1). The nodes represent symbolic states and the arcs represent transitions between states. Verification is done by exploring the symbolic execution tree and ensuring that the error location ℓ_{error} is not reachable. Finally, we define a "selective abstraction" operator $\overline{\nabla} : FOL \times FOL$ that accepts an *unsatisfiable* formula Π and returns a satisfiable formula that is an abstraction of Π.

Interpolation. The main challenge for symbolic execution is the path explosion problem. This issue has been addressed using the concept of interpolation.

Definition 1 (Craig Interpolant). *Given two formulas A and B such that $A \wedge B$ is unsatisfiable, a Craig interpolant [8], $\mathsf{INTP}(A, B)$, is another formula $\overline{\Psi}$ such that (a) $A \models \overline{\Psi}$, (b) $\Psi \wedge B$ is unsatisfiable, and (c) all variables in $\overline{\Psi}$ are common to A and B.*

An interpolant allows us to remove irrelevant information in A that is not needed to maintain the unsatisfiability of $A \wedge B$. That is, the interpolant captures the essence of the reason of unsatisfiability of the two formulas. Efficient interpolation algorithms exist for quantifier-free fragments of theories such as linear real/integer arithmetic, uninterpreted functions, pointers and arrays, and bitvectors (e.g., see [5] for details) where interpolants can be extracted from the refutation proof in linear time on the size of the proof.

Definition 2 (Subsumption check). *Given a current symbolic state $s \equiv \langle \ell, \sigma, \cdot \rangle$ and an already explored symbolic state $s' \equiv \langle \ell, \cdot, \cdot \rangle$ annotated with the interpolant $\overline{\Psi}$, we say s is subsumed by s', $\mathsf{SUBSUME}(s, \langle s', \overline{\Psi} \rangle)$, if $[\![s]\!]\sigma \models \overline{\Psi}$.*

To understand the intuition behind the subsumption check, it helps to know what an interpolant at a node actually represents. An interpolant $\overline{\Psi}$ at a node s' succinctly captures the reason of infeasibility of all infeasible paths in the symbolic tree rooted at s'. Let us call this tree T_1. Then, if another state s at ℓ implies $\overline{\Psi}$, it means the tree rooted at s, say T_2, has exactly the same or more (in a superset sense), infeasible paths compared to T_1. In other words, T_2 has exactly the same, or *less feasible paths* (in a subset sense) compared to T_1. Since T_1 did not contain any feasible path that was buggy, we can guarantee the same for T_2 as well, thus subsuming it.

Eager vs. Lazy. We say that a symbolic execution approach is *eager* if the successor relation is defined only for feasible states. In other words, when we encounter an infeasible state, we immediately backtrack and compute an interpolant, succinctly capturing the reason of the infeasibility. Though different systems might employ different search strategies for symbolic execution (our formulation above is called *forward* symbolic execution [20]), it is worth to note that all common symbolic execution engines are indeed eager. This eagerness has been considered as a clear advantage of symbolic execution, since it avoids the consideration of infeasible paths, which could be exponential in number.

However, with learning (interpolation), being eager might not give us the best performance. The intuition behind this is that we are using the learned interpolant from T_1 to subsume T_2, which has less feasible paths than T_1. Therefore, if T_1 itself has very few feasible paths due to eagerness, it is unlikely that the learned interpolant would be able to subsume many of such T_2s.

4   Algorithm

We present our algorithm as a symbolic execution engine with interpolation and speculative abstraction. In Fig. 4, the recursive procedure SymExec is of the type SymExec : $SymStates \times \mathbb{N} \to FOL \cup \{\epsilon\}$. It takes two parameters – a symbolic state s typically on which to do symbolic execution, and a number representing

---

Assume initial state $s_0 \equiv \langle \ell_{\mathsf{start}}, \cdot, true \rangle$
$\langle 1 \rangle$ *Initially* : SymExec($s_0, 0$)
function SymExec($s \equiv \langle \ell, \sigma, \Pi \rangle$, AbsLevel)
$\langle 2 \rangle$ **if** AbsLevel > 0 **then**
$\langle 3 \rangle$ **if** (bounds violated) or ($\ell \equiv \ell_{\mathsf{error}}$) **then return** ϵ **endif**
$\langle 4 \rangle$ **else if** $\ell \equiv \ell_{\mathsf{error}}$ **then** report error and halt
$\langle 5 \rangle$ **endif**

$\langle 6 \rangle$ **if** TERMINAL(s) **then** $\overline{\Psi} := true$
$\langle 7 \rangle$ **else if** $\exists\, s' \equiv \langle \ell, \cdot, \cdot \rangle$ annotated with $\overline{\Psi}$ s.t. SUBSUME($s, \langle s', \overline{\Psi}' \rangle$) **then** $\overline{\Psi} := \overline{\Psi}'$
$\langle 8 \rangle$ **else if** INFEASIBLE(s) **then**
$\langle 9 \rangle$ $s' := \langle \ell, \sigma, \overline{\nabla}(\Pi) \rangle$
$\langle 10 \rangle$ $\overline{\Psi}' :=$ SymExec(s', AbsLevel $+ 1$)
$\langle 11 \rangle$ **if** $\overline{\Psi}' \equiv \epsilon$ **then** $\overline{\Psi} := false$ **else** $\overline{\Psi} := \overline{\Psi}'$ **endif**
$\langle 12 \rangle$ **if** AbsLevel $\equiv 0$ **then** clear data on bounds **endif**
$\langle 13 \rangle$ **else**
$\langle 14 \rangle$ $\overline{\Psi} := true$
$\langle 15 \rangle$ **foreach** transition $t: \ell \longrightarrow \ell'$ **do**
$\langle 16 \rangle$ $s' :=$ SYMSTEP(s, t)
$\langle 17 \rangle$ $\overline{\Psi}' :=$ SymExec(s', AbsLevel)
$\langle 18 \rangle$ **if** $\overline{\Psi}' \equiv \epsilon$ **then return** ϵ
$\langle 19 \rangle$ **else** $\overline{\Psi} := \overline{\Psi} \wedge$ INTP($\Pi, constraints(t) \wedge \neg\, \overline{\Psi}'$)
$\langle 20 \rangle$ **endfor**
$\langle 21 \rangle$ **endif**
$\langle 22 \rangle$ annotate s with $\overline{\Psi}$ and **return** ($\overline{\Psi}$)
end function

Fig. 4. A Framework for Lazy Symbolic Execution with Speculative Abstraction

the current level of speculative abstraction, which we will define soon. Its return value is a FOL formula representing the interpolant it generated at s. A special value of ϵ is used to signify failure of speculation.

Initially, SymExec is called with the initial state s_0 with ℓ_{start} as the program point, an empty symbolic store, and the path condition *true*. For clarity, ignore lines 2-5 which we will come to later. Lines 6-12, represent the three base cases of eager symbolic execution in general – terminal, subsumed and infeasible node (of course, in our lazy method infeasible node is not a base case). In line 6, if the current symbolic state s is a terminal node (defined by ℓ being the same as ℓ_{end}), we simply set the current interpolant $\overline{\Psi}$ to *true*, as the path is safe and there is no infeasibility to preserve. In line 7, the subsumption check is performed to see if there exists another symbolic state s' at the same program point ℓ such that s' subsumes s (see Definition 2). If so, the current interpolant $\overline{\Psi}$ is set to be the same as the subsuming node's interpolant $\overline{\Psi}'$. Note that this is an important case for symbolic execution to scale as it can result in exponential savings.

In line 8, we check if the current state s is infeasible, defined by $[\![s]\!]_\sigma$ being unsatisfiable. Normally at this point, eager symbolic execution would simply generate the interpolant *false* to denote the infeasibility of s and return. For lazy symbolic execution, we begin our speculation procedure here. Line 9 creates a new symbolic state s' such that it has the same program point ℓ and symbolic store σ as s, but its (unsatisfiable) path condition Π is selectively abstracted using $\overline{\nabla}$ to make the new path condition, which is satisfiable. In our implementation of $\overline{\nabla}$, since SymExec does forward symbolic execution, the path condition would have been feasible until the preceding state whose successor is s. That is, the state s'' such that $\mathsf{SUCC}(s'', s)$ must have been a feasible state. Hence simply setting Π to the path condition of s'' would make it satisfiable. This mimics *deleting* the latest constraint(s) from Π that caused its infeasibility. In Section 5, we discuss the reasons for implementing $\overline{\nabla}$ in this way.

Once the abstraction is made, we now speculate by recursively calling SymExec with s' and incrementing the abstraction level by 1. An abstraction level greater than 0 means that we are under speculation mode. SymExec essentially performs symbolic execution on the selectively abstracted state but with a condition – focus now on lines 2-5. Running under speculation mode, if at any point the bound is violated or if the error location ℓ_{error} is encountered, it means the speculation failed. In this case, we return a special value ϵ to signify the failure (line 3). Of course, if we are not speculating and ℓ_{error} is encountered (line 4), then it is a real error to be reported and the entire verification process halts. Otherwise, SymExec proceeds to normally explore s and finally return an interpolant.

Now in line 10, the interpolant returned from speculation is stored in $\overline{\Psi}'$. If ϵ was returned, indicating that speculation failed, we simply resort to using *false* as the interpolant, just like a fully eager symbolic execution procedure. Otherwise, we use the interpolant computed by speculation (line 11). Finally, in line 12, if the current abstraction level is 0 (i.e., we are at the 'root' of the speculation tree), then regardless of whether we succeeded or not, we reset all the data that count towards the bounds. For instance, in our implementation, we restrict the speculation to not explore more than one state per program point ℓ, which would result in a bound that is linear in the program's size. In this case, we have to maintain a count of the number of states explored for each program point. At line 12 this data is cleared since the speculation has finished.

Note that there are two reasons why speculation can fail. A first reason is simply that an abstracted guard is needed to *avoid a counter-example*. If this guard corresponds to abstraction level 0, speculation resulted in nothing learnt *at this program point* (but we could have learnt something from the start of speculation until encountering the counter-example, for descendant program points). If however the guard abstraction is at a deeper level, the top-level invocation of speculation still can learn new interpolants. The second reason why speculation can fail is that the *bound was exceeded*. In this case, we put forward that, by increasing the bound, it is not likely to result in significant learning. That is, increasing the bound is a strategy of diminishing returns. We will return to this point when we discuss certain statistics in Section 5.

If none of the base cases were activated, SymExec proceeds to unwind the path, in lines 13-20. It first initialises the interpolant $\overline{\Psi}$ to *true*. Then, for every transition from the current program point ℓ, it does the following. First it performs a symbolic step (SYMSTEP) to obtain the next symbolic state s' along the transition $t : \ell \longrightarrow \ell'$. Then, it recursively calls itself with s' to obtain an interpolant $\overline{\Psi}'$ for s' (note that we are not speculating here so the abstraction level is unchanged). Now, if the returned interpolant is ϵ, it means further down some speculation resulted in failure. Hence it simply propagates back this failure by returning ϵ (line 18). Otherwise, it computes the current interpolant by invoking INTP on the path condition Π and the conjunction of the constraints of the current transition, $constraints(t)$, with the negation of $\overline{\Psi}'$ (where $\Pi \wedge constraints(t) \wedge \neg\overline{\Psi}'$ is unsatisfiable). The result is conjoined with any existing interpolant (line 19). Finally, in line 22 the current state s is annotated with the interpolant $\overline{\Psi}$, which is then returned. This annotation is persistent such that the subsumption check at line 7 can utilise this information.

On loop handling: In the presence of unbounded loops, symbolic execution might not terminate in general. Handling unbounded loops, however, is often considered as an orthogonal problem. Indeed, we were able to incorporate the loop handling technique proposed by [15] into the implementation of our algorithm without difficulty.

We conclude this section with some insights about the new interpolants discovered by speculation. At the root of speculation, the eager algorithm would have returned *false* as an interpolant. Therefore any other valid interpolant is clearly better. However, is it the case that using the new (and better) interpolant here, results in better interpolants higher up in the tree? Intuitively the answer is yes, provided that the interpolation algorithm is, in some sense, well behaved. We formalize this as follows.

Definition 3 (Monotonic Interpolation). *The interpolation method used in our algorithm is said to be* monotonic *if for all transition t, path condition Π,* and formulas $\overline{\Psi}_1, \overline{\Psi}_2 \bullet \overline{\Psi}_1 \models \overline{\Psi}_2$ implies $INTP(\Pi, constraints(t) \wedge \neg \overline{\Psi}_1) \models INTP(\Pi, constraints(t) \wedge \neg \overline{\Psi}_2)$

Monotonicity ensures that better interpolants at a program point translate into better interpolants at a predecessor point. The supreme interpolation algorithm, based on the weakest precondition, is of course monotonic. A more practical algorithm, however, may not be guaranteed to be monotonic. For example, an algorithm which is based on computing an unsatisfiable core (i.e., simply disregarding constraints which do not affect unsatisfiability), is in general not monotonic because it can arbitrarily choose between choices of cores.

Nevertheless, we noticed in our experiments, detailed in Section 5, that new interpolants from speculation do translate into better interpolants and this, in turn, produces more subsumption. This indicates that the interpolation algorithm employed in [14], is indeed relatively well behaved. Some random inspections of the interpolants obtained in the experiments showed that we often have monotonic behavior in practice, although not theoretically. We show via concrete statistics that as a result of this, we obtain fewer and yet better interpolants.

5   Implementation and Evaluation

We implemented our lazy algorithm on top of TRACER [14], an eager symbolic execution system, and made use of the same interpolation method and theory solver presented in [14]. Let us now remark on our two design choices.

Selective Abstraction: in principle, selective abstraction ($\overline{\nabla}$) can be done in many ways, formally, by deleting any "correction subset" [19] of the unsatisfiable formula. We implemented selective abstraction by deleting constraint(s) from the latest guard that we encountered during forward symbolic execution. The reason is two-fold. Firstly, deleting the latest guard *guarantees* the formula to become satisfiable without requiring to compute any of its correction subsets (the latest guard is trivially a *minimal* correction subset), which could be expensive. Secondly, given an *incremental* theory solver, deleting the latest constraints can be implemented more efficiently than deleting those encountered earlier. Although we believe that more sophisticated analysis can be employed to make a well-informed decision, the empirical results show that this approach works well in practice.

Speculation Bound: we used a *linear* bound for the speculation. In particular, during speculation if a program point is visited more than once and it cannot be subsumed, we stop the speculative search, and use the interpolant *false* at the latest speculation point. Intuitively, anything less than a linear bound could make speculation arbitrarily short, hence we need to give each program point *at least* one chance to be explored. Our experiments confirm that often, a linear bound that gives each program point *at most* one chance, is good enough.

We used as benchmarks sequential C programs from a varied pool – five device drivers from the ntdrivers-simplified category of SV-COMP 2013 [2]: cdaudio, diskperf, floppy, floppy2 and kbfiltr, two linux drivers qpmouse and tlan, an air

Table 1. Verification Statistics for Eager and Lazy SE (A T/O is 180s (3 mins))

Bench-mark	CPA Time (sec)	IMP Time (sec)	TRACER								
			Time (sec)			States			#Interpolants		
			EAG	LZY	Speedup	EAG	LZY	Red.	EAG	LZY	Red.
cdaudio	19	30	41	23	1.78	4396	2864	35%	3854	2689	30%
diskperf	28	149	53	19	2.79	4309	1617	62%	4012	1514	62%
floppy	27	36	25	12	2.08	3535	1635	54%	3208	1534	52%
floppy2	98	40	42	29	1.45	5063	3153	38%	4536	2863	37%
kbfiltr	3	8	4	3	1.33	973	756	22%	860	691	20%
qpmouse	3	8	32	15	2.13	1313	779	41%	1199	723	40%
tlan	T/O	T/O	41	26	1.58	3895	2545	35%	3542	2324	34%
nsichneu	5	41	40	5	8.00	4481	1027	77%	4379	1018	77%
statemate	2	T/O	72	5	14.40	6680	616	91%	4370	471	89%
tcas	2	11	19	1	19.00	5500	369	93%	5248	348	93%
Total	**367**	**683**	**369**	**138**	**2.67**	**40145**	**15361**	**62%**	**35208**	**14175**	**60%**

traffic collision avoidance system tcas, and two programs from the Mälardalen WCET benchmark [21] statemate and nsichneu for which the safety property was the approximate WCET. We chose only safe programs for our benchmarks as they ensure a full search of the program's state space. With unsafe programs, if the error is encountered very early in the search process (e.g., due to good heuristics), hardly any useful comparison can be drawn. All experiments are carried out on an Intel 2.3 Ghz machine with 2GB memory.

To give a perspective of where TRACER stands in the spectrum of verification tools, we compare its performance with two competitive verifiers CPA-CHECKER [30] (ABM version) and IMPACT [23]. Of these, IMPACT implements an interpolation-based model checking procedure, whereas CPA-CHECKER is a hybrid of SMT-based search and CEGAR. Since IMPACT is not publicly available, we use CPA-CHECKER's implementation of the IMPACT algorithm [23].

For each benchmark, we record in the shaded columns in Table 1 the verification time (in seconds) of CPA-CHECKER (CPA), IMPACT (IMP) and TRACER with *eager* symbolic execution (TRACER EAG.), respectively. As it can be seen TRACER is generally faster than IMPACT but sometimes slower than CPA-CHECKER so it can be roughly positioned between the two (closer to CPA-CHECKER) in terms of performance. This comparison is to show that we chose a competitive verifier to implement our algorithm and we expect the same benefits to be provided to other similar verifiers.

We now present the main results in the rest of Table 1. In the set of columns labelled Time (sec) we show the verification time of TRACER in seconds for each benchmark. In this, the (shaded) column EAG which we just saw, performed eager symbolic execution, while the LZY column performed lazy symbolic execution, and Speedup is the ratio of the two. It can be seen that in all programs, laziness makes the verification much faster, providing an average speedup of 2.67. This also makes lazy TRACER perform much better than eager TRACER. We notice enormous improvement for nsichneu, statemate and tcas, as these are programs with a large number of infeasible paths and the safety property on a small number of variables, the perfect scenario for our speculation to shine.

We move on to a more fine-grained measurement than time in the next set of columns States, which shows the number of symbolic states TRACER encountered during verification. In total, we found that 40145 states were encountered without speculation (EAG) and just 15361 states with speculation (LZY), a reduction of about 62%. This shows that speculation results in more subsumption, which thereby causes a reduction in the search space.

Next, we measure the improvement in memory provided by speculation. In the set of columns #Interpolants, we show the total number of interpolants stored by TRACER at the end of the verification process. Interpolants typically contribute to a major part of memory used by modern symbolic execution verifiers. In this regard, laziness reduced the number of interpolants in TRACER from 35208 (EAG) to 14175 (LZY), a reduction of 60% across all benchmarks.

We focus on the two metrics seen above: number of interpolants (#Interpolants), and amount of subsumption, in terms of states (States) encountered. The critical point is the inverse relationship: *laziness provided a much smaller number of interpolants while simultaneously increasing subsumption*. In other words, the *quality* of interpolants discovered through speculation is enhanced.

We conclude this section with a few more statistics which, while not directly linked to absolute performance, nevertheless shed additional insight. First, consider the number of distinct program variables that are involved in the interpolants. In the case without speculation, we noticed across all benchmarks that there were **363** such variables. In contrast, with speculation, the number is only **229**. This means that many (134) variables were not required to determine the safety of the program. They were being needlessly tracked by interpolants simply to preserve infeasible paths.

Next consider the "success rate" of speculation: how often does speculation find an alternative interpolant? For simplicity, consider only those speculations triggered at the top-level of the algorithm (from abstraction level 0 to 1). We found, across the benchmark programs, a rate of **40-90%**, more often at the higher end. This means that speculation returns something useful most of the time. However, note importantly that even when speculation was not successful at the top-level, there is likely to have been interpolants discovered at the lower levels. These are interpolants one would have not found without speculation.

To elaborate on the success rate of 40-90%, programs having large number of infeasible paths tend to produce a high success rate, because as per our key intuition, many such paths will be unrelated to the safety. Similarly, programs with few infeasible paths produce a low success rate. In our experiments, the highest success rates (90%) were from nsichneu, tcas and statemate, which have a large number of infeasible paths as mentioned before.

Finally, reconsider the bound. The above success rate also indicates that there are a significant, though minor, number of failures. We wish to mention that when we do fail, the overwhelming reason is *not the bound*, but instead, the (spurious) counter-examples. In summary, the rather high rate of success, and the rather low rate of failure caused by the bound, together suggest that increasing the bound would be a strategy of diminishing returns.

6   Related Work and Concluding Discussion

Symbolic execution [17] has been widely used for program understanding and program testing. We name a few notable systems: KLEE [3], Otter [26], and SAGE [11]. Traditionally, execution begins at the first program point and then proceeds according to the program flow. Thus symbolic execution is actually *forward* execution. Recently, [20] proposed a variation, *directed* symbolic execution, making use of heuristics to guide symbolic execution toward a particular target. This has shown some initial benefits in program testing.

For the purpose of having scalability in program verification, however, symbolic execution needs to be equipped with *learning*, particularly in the form of interpolation [16,24,15,14,1]. Due to the requirement of *exhaustive* search, as in the case of this paper, these systems naturally implement forward symbolic execution. Recently, interpolation has also been applied to the context of concolic testing [13]. All the above-mentioned approaches can be classified as *eager* symbolic execution. In other words, we do not continue a path when the accumulated constraints are enough to decide its infeasibility.

In the domain of SAT solving and hardware verification, *property directed reachability* (PDR) [10] has recently emerged as an alternative to interpolation [22]. Some notable extensions of PDR are [12,4,29]. However, the impact of PDR to the area of software verification is still unclear. While such "backward" execution has merits in terms of being goal directed, it has lost the advantage of using the (forward) computation to limit the scope of consideration.

In contrast, our lazy symbolic execution preserves the intrinsic benefits of symbolic execution while at the same time, by opening the infeasible paths selectively, it enables the learning of *property directed* interpolants. We believe this is indeed the reason for the efficiency achieved and demonstrated in Section 5.

The traditional CEGAR-based approach to verification may also be thought of a "lazy". This is because it starts from a coarsely abstracted model and subsequently refines it. Such concept of laziness is, therefore, different from what discussed in this paper. In the context of this paper, given a refined abstract domain, a CEGAR-based approach is in fact considered as eager, since it avoids traversal of infeasible paths, which are blocked by the abstract domain. Some of such paths are indeed counter-examples learned from the previous phases. The work [24] discussed this as a disadvantage of CEGAR-based approaches: they might not recover from over-specific refinements. Our contribution, therefore, is plausibly applicable in a CEGAR-based setting.

There is now an emerging trend of employing generic SMT solvers for (bounded) symbolic execution, and since modern SMT solvers, e.g. [9], do possess the similar power of interpolation – in the form of conflict clause learning or lemma generation – we now make a few final comments in this regard.

First, note that lazy symbolic execution has no relation with the concept of *lazy* SMT. In particular, the dominating architecture DPLL(T), which underlies most state-of-the-art SMT tools, is based on the integration of a SAT solver and one (or more) T-solver(s), respectively handling the Boolean and the theory-specific components of reasoning. On the one hand, the SAT solver enumerates truth assignments which satisfy the Boolean abstraction of the input formula. On the other hand, the T-solver checks the consistency in T of the set of literals corresponding to the assignments enumerated. This approach is called lazy (encoding), and in contrast to the eager approach, it encodes an SMT formula into an equivalently-satisfiable Boolean formula and feeds the result to a SAT solver. See [27] for a survey.

Second, we note that though the search strategies used in modern DPLL-based SMT solvers would be more dynamic and different from the forward symbolic execution presented in this paper, it is safe to classify these SMT solvers as *eager* symbolic execution. This is because, in general, whenever a conflict is encountered, a DPLL-based algorithm would analyze the conflict, learn and/or propagate new conflict clauses or lemmas, and then immediately backtrack (backjump) to some previous decision, dictated by its heuristics [18].

We believe that for the purpose of program verification, the benefit of being lazy by employing speculative abstraction, would also be applicable to SMT approaches. This is because, in general, we can always miss out useful (good) interpolants if we have not yet seen the complete path. In this paper, we have demonstrated that in verification, property directed learning usually outperforms learning from "random" infeasible paths. Eagerly stopping when the set of constraints is unsatisfiable might prevent a solver from learning the conflict clauses which are more relevant to the safety of the program. In SMT solvers, the search, however, is structured around the decision graph. Therefore, some technical adaptations to our linear bound need to be reconsidered. For example, a bound based on the number of decisions seems to be a good possibility. Moreover, in SMT setting, there are no error locations. One possible idea is, when compiling a verification problem into SMT input format, we specially "mark" the constraints guarding the error locations, so that unsatisfiable cores involving marked constraints can be favored over those not.

7   Conclusion

We presented a systematic approach to perform speculative abstraction in symbolic execution in pursuit of program verification. The basic idea is simple: when a symbolic path is first found to be infeasible, we abstract the cause of infeasibility and enter speculation mode. In continuing along the path, more abstractions may be performed, while remaining in speculation mode. Crucially, speculation is only permitted up to a given bound, which is a linear function of the program size. A number of reasonably sized and varied benchmark programs then showed that our speculative abstraction produced speedups of a factor of two and more.

References

1. Albarghouthi, A., Gurfinkel, A., Chechik, M.: Whale: An interpolation-based algorithm for inter-procedural verification. In: Kuncak, V., Rybalchenko, A. (eds.) VMCAI 2012. LNCS, vol. 7148, pp. 39–55. Springer, Heidelberg (2012)

2. Beyer, D.: Second competition on software verification. In: Piterman, N., Smolka, S.A. (eds.) TACAS 2013. LNCS, vol. 7795, pp. 594–609. Springer, Heidelberg (2013)
3. Cadar, C., Dunbar, D., Engler, D.: Klee: Unassisted and automatic generation of high-coverage tests for complex systems programs. In: OSDI (2008)
4. Cimatti, A., Griggio, A., Mover, S., Tonetta, S.: Ic3 modulo theories via implicit predicate abstraction. CoRR (2013)
5. Cimatti, A., Griggio, A., Sebastiani, R.: Efficient interpolant generation in satisfiability modulo theories. In: Ramakrishnan, C.R., Rehof, J. (eds.) TACAS 2008. LNCS, vol. 4963, pp. 397–412. Springer, Heidelberg (2008)
6. Clarke, E., Grumberg, O., Jha, S., Lu, Y., Veith, H.: CounterExample-Guided Abstraction Refinement. In: Emerson, E.A., Sistla, A.P. (eds.) CAV 2000. LNCS, vol. 1855, Springer, Heidelberg (2000)
7. Cousot, P., Cousot, R.: Abstract Interpretation: A Unified Lattice Model for Static Analysis. In: POPL (1977)
8. Craig, W.: Three uses of Herbrand-Gentzen theorem in relating model theory and proof theory. Journal of Symbolic Computation 22 (1955)
9. de Moura, L., Bjørner, N.S.: Z3: an efficient smt solver. In: Ramakrishnan, C.R., Rehof, J. (eds.) TACAS 2008. LNCS, vol. 4963, pp. 337–340. Springer, Heidelberg (2008)
10. Een, N., Mishchenko, A., Brayton, R.: Efficient implementation of property directed reachability. In: FMCAD (2011)
11. Godefroid, P., Levin, M.Y., Molnar, D.: Sage: Whitebox fuzzing for security testing. Queue (2012)
12. Hoder, K., Bjørner, N.: Generalized property directed reachability. In: Cimatti, A., Sebastiani, R. (eds.) SAT 2012. LNCS, vol. 7317, pp. 157–171. Springer, Heidelberg (2012)
13. Jaffar, J., Murali, V., Navas, J.: Boosting Concolic Testing via Interpolation. In: FSE (2013)
14. Jaffar, J., Murali, V., Navas, J., Santosa, A.: TRACER: A symbolic execution engine for verification. In: CAV (2012)
15. Jaffar, J., Navas, J.A., Santosa, A.E.: Unbounded Symbolic Execution for Program Verification. In: Khurshid, S., Sen, K. (eds.) RV 2011. LNCS, vol. 7186, pp. 396–411. Springer, Heidelberg (2012)
16. Jaffar, J., Santosa, A.E., Voicu, R.: An interpolation method for clp traversal. In: Gent, I.P. (ed.) CP 2009. LNCS, vol. 5732, pp. 454–469. Springer, Heidelberg (2009)
17. King, J.C.: Symbolic Execution and Program Testing. Com. ACM (1976)
18. Kroening, D., Strichman, O.: Decision procedures: An algorithmic point of view (2008)
19. Liffiton, M.H., Sakallah, K.A.: Algorithms for computing minimal unsatisfiable subsets of constraints. J. Automated Reasoning (2008)
20. Ma, K.-K., Yit Phang, K., Foster, J.S., Hicks, M.: Directed symbolic execution. In: Yahav, E. (ed.) SAS 2011. LNCS, vol. 6887, pp. 95–111. Springer, Heidelberg (2011)
21. Mälardalen WCET research group benchmarks (2006), http://www.mrtc.mdh.se/projects/wcet/benchmarks.html
22. McMillan, K.L.: Interpolation and SAT-based model checking. In: Hunt Jr., W.A., Somenzi, F. (eds.) CAV 2003. LNCS, vol. 2725, pp. 1–13. Springer, Heidelberg (2003)
23. McMillan, K.L.: Lazy abstraction with interpolants. In: Ball, T., Jones, R.B. (eds.) CAV 2006. LNCS, vol. 4144, pp. 123–136. Springer, Heidelberg (2006)
24. McMillan, K.L.: Lazy annotation for program testing and verification. In: Touili, T., Cook, B., Jackson, P. (eds.) CAV 2010. LNCS, vol. 6174, pp. 104–118. Springer, Heidelberg (2010)

25. Navabpour, S., Bonakdarpour, B., Fischmeister, S.: Path-aware time-triggered runtime verification. In: Qadeer, S., Tasiran, S. (eds.) RV 2012. LNCS, vol. 7687, pp. 199–213. Springer, Heidelberg (2013)
26. Reisner, E., Song, C., Ma, K.-K., Foster, J.S., Porter, A.: Using symbolic evaluation to understand behavior in configurable software systems. In: ICSE (2010)
27. Sebastiani, R.: Lazy satisability modulo theories. JSAT (2007)
28. Visser, S.W., Păsăreanu, C.: Test input generation with java pathfinder. In: ISSTA (2004)
29. Welp, T., Kuehlmann, A.: Qf bv model checking with property directed reachability. In: DATE (2013)
30. Wonisch, D.: Block Abstraction Memoization for CPAchecker. In: Flanagan, C., König, B. (eds.) TACAS 2012. LNCS, vol. 7214, pp. 531–533. Springer, Heidelberg (2012)

Faster Statistical Model Checking
by Means of Abstraction and Learning[*]

Ayoub Nouri[1], Balaji Raman[1], Marius Bozga[1],
Axel Legay[2], and Saddek Bensalem[1]

[1] Univ. Grenoble Alpes, VERIMAG, F-38000 Grenoble, France
CNRS, VERIMAG, F-38000 Grenoble, France
[2] INRIA/IRISA, Rennes, France

Abstract. This paper investigates the combined use of abstraction and probabilistic learning as a means to enhance statistical model checking performance. We are given a property (or a list of properties) for verification on a (large) stochastic system. We project on a set of traces generated from the original system, and learn a (small) abstract model from the projected traces, which contain only those labels that are relevant to the property to be verified. Then, we model-check the property on the reduced, abstract model instead of the large, original system. In this paper, we propose a formal definition of the projection on traces given a property to verify. We also provide conditions ensuring the correct preservation of the property on the abstract model. We validate our approach on the Herman's Self Stabilizing protocol. Our experimental results show that (a) the size of the abstract model and the verification time are drastically reduced, and that (b) the probability of satisfaction of the property being verified is correctly estimated by statistical model checking on the abstract model with respect to the concrete system.

1 Introduction

Statistical Model-Checking (SMC) [12,17,24,27] has recently emerged as an alternative to standard model-checking to avoid exhaustive exploration of the state-space and its associated explosion problem. SMC combines Monte-Carlo simulation [11] on model traces with statistical techniques in order to decide whether some stochastic model satisfies a given property or to compute its satisfaction probability. Nowadays, SMC is getting increased industrial attention [4] and several modeling and/or analysis frameworks include it amongst their (usually, most successful) analysis techniques [5,16,15,3].

SMC is however not a panacea for automated verification. As many other analysis techniques, it still encounters significant difficulties when used on real-life systems. First, the stochastic modeling of these systems might be extremely

---

[*] Research supported by the European Community's Seventh Framework Programme [FP7] under grant agreements No. 257414 (ASCENS), No. 288175 (CERTAINTY), and the French BGLE project ACOSE.

B. Bonakdarpour and S.A. Smolka (Eds.): RV 2014, LNCS 8734, pp. 340–355, 2014.

cumbersome. Actually, high expertise is generally required to produce any kind of meaningful formal models. For stochastic models, besides functional aspects, they must include stochastic information in form of probabilities. These are hardly available and usually incomprehensible by an average system designer. Second, whenever such stochastic models exist, they can be very detailed and contain too much information than actually needed for verification purposes. This is usually the case when stochastic system models are automatically generated from higher level descriptions, e.g., as part of various designs/analysis flows [2]. In this case, Monte-Carlo simulation becomes problematic as individual simulation time (time to obtain a single execution trace) could be very long. Henceforth, it could not be possible to obtain any but only a limited number of traces and consequently, prevent the use of SMC techniques. Moreover, it is worth mentioning that for verification of system-level properties, the observation of any such trace in detail is rarely needed. Most of the time, such properties are expressed in terms of few observable actions/states of the system while the remaining are completely irrelevant and can be safely ignored.

Our aim is to improve general applicability of SMC techniques. In this work, we propose the combined use of abstraction and learning techniques to automatically construct faithful abstractions of system models and therefore to overcome the issues discussed earlier. Nowadays, machine learning is an active field of research and learning algorithms are constantly developed and improved in order to address new challenges and new classes of problems (see [26] for a recent survey on grammatical inference). In our context, learning is combined with abstraction as follows. Given a property of interest and a (usually large) sample of partial traces generated from a concrete system (model), we first use abstraction to restrict the amount of visible information on traces to the minimum required to evaluate the property and then, use learning to construct an abstract, probabilistic model which conforms to the abstracted sample set. Under some additional restrictions discussed later, the resulting model is a sound abstraction of the concrete model with respect to the satisfaction of the property. Hence, it can be used to correctly predict/generate the entire abstract behavior of the model, in particular, as an input model for SMC.

The above approach has multiple benefits. First of all, the sample set of traces can be generated directly from an existing black-box implementation of the system, as opposed to a concrete detailed model. In many practical situations, such detailed system models simply do not exist and the cost for building them using reverse-engineering could be prohibitive. In such cases, learning provides an effective, automated way to obtain a model and to get some valuable insight on the system behavior. The use of projection is also mostly beneficial. In most of the cases, the complexity of the learning algorithms as well as the complexity of the resulting models are directly correlated to the the number of distinct observations (the alphabet) of traces. Moreover, under normal considerations, a large alphabet requires a large size for the sample set. Intuitively, the more complex the final model is, the more traces are needed to learn it correctly. Nevertheless, one should mention that a bit of care is needed to meaningfully combine abstraction and learning. That is, abstraction may change a deterministic model into a non-deterministic one, and henceforth has an impact on the learning algorithms needed for it.

The contributions of the paper are as follows. We propose a general approach to compute abstract stochastic models using learning and projection and discuss conditions under which the obtained model is a correct abstraction of the original system. We provide a first simple definition for a projection operator on execution traces given an LTL property and an implementation of the whole procedure. We finally validate the approach on the Herman's Self Stabilizing protocol. The obtained results show an important reduction of the model size, the SMC time, and accurate probability estimations of the verified properties.

The remainder of this paper is organized as follows. The basic formalisms for probabilistic modeling and learning techniques are briefly recalled in Section 2. In Section 3, we present our contribution, that is the joint use of abstraction and learning as a means to speed-up statistical model checking. We discuss the restrictions needed for convergence and correctness. In Section 4, we present the experimental set-up and concrete results. Related work is discussed in Section 5. Finally, conclusions and directions for future research are presented in Section 6.

2   Background

Let AP be a finite set of atomic propositions. We define the alphabet $\Sigma = 2^{AP}$ and denote the elements of Σ (subsets of AP) as symbols. The empty symbol is denoted by τ. As usual, we denote by Σ^ω (resp. Σ^*) the sets of infinite (resp. finite) words over Σ. For an infinite word $\sigma = \sigma_0\sigma_1...$ and $i \geq 0$, we define the ith suffix (resp. prefix) of σ as $\sigma[i..] = \sigma_i\sigma_{i+1}...$ (resp. as $\sigma[..i] = \sigma_0...\sigma_i$).

2.1   Probabilistic Models

Definition 1. *A labeled Markov chain (LMC) M is a tuple $\langle S, \iota, \pi, L \rangle$ where,*

- *S is a finite set of states,*
- *$\iota : S \to [0,1]$ is the initial states distribution such that $\sum_{s \in S} \iota(s) = 1$,*
- *$\pi : S \times S \to [0,1]$ is the probability transition function such that for each $s \in S$, $\sum_{s' \in S} \pi(s, s') = 1$ and*
- *$L : S \to \Sigma$ is a state labeling function.*

A *run* is a possible behavior (infinite execution) of the LMC. A *trace* is the sequence of labels associated to the states of the run. Formally:

Definition 2. *Let $M = \langle S, \iota, \pi, L \rangle$ be a LMC. A run of M is an infinite sequence of states $s_0 s_1 ... s_n s_{n+1}...$ such that $\iota(s_0) > 0$ and $\pi(s_i, s_{i+1}) > 0$, for all $i \geq 0$. A trace σ associated to a run $s_0 s_1 ... s_n s_{n+1}...$ is the infinite word*

$L(s_0)L(s_1)...L(s_n)L(s_{n+1})....$ *A finite run (resp. finite trace) is any finite prefix of a run (resp. trace).*

We denote by $Runs(M)$ the set of runs and by $Traces(M)$ the set of traces of M. Moreover, we denote by Pr_M the underlying probability measure induced by M on the set of its traces. This measure is well-defined in the context of Markov chains (see [1]). Two LMCs M_1 and M_2 are called equivalent, and denoted $M_1 \approx M_2$ if they have identical probability measures on traces, that is, $Pr_{M_1} = Pr_{M_2}$.

A labeled Markov chain is *deterministic* (DLMC) iff (i) $\exists s_0 \in S$ such that $\iota(s_0) = 1$, and (ii) $\forall s \in S$, $\forall \sigma \in \Sigma$ there exists at most one $s' \in S$ such that $\pi(s, s') > 0$ and $L(s') = \sigma$.

Probabilistic finite automata (PFA) are an alternative model for probabilistic systems. They are defined similarly to LMC with the following modification: π is now defined on $S \times S \cup \{\$\}$ and $\pi(s, \$)$ stands for the probability to terminate execution at state s. Henceforth, the associated notions of runs and traces correspond to finite runs and finite traces for a LMC. The probability of a finite run $\mathbf{s} = s_0 s_1 ... s_n$ of a PFA is $Pr(\mathbf{s}) = \iota(s_0) \cdot (\prod_{i=0}^{n-1} \pi(s_i, s_{i+1})) \cdot \pi(s_n, \$)$. Deterministic PFA are denoted as DPFA.

Example. We consider the Craps Gambling Game [1] as an illustrative example. A player starts by rolling two fair six-sided dice. The outcome of the two dice determines whether he wins or not. If the outcome is 7 or 11, the player wins. If the outcome is 2, 3, or 12, the player looses. Otherwise, the dice are rolled again taking into account the previous outcome (called point). If the new outcome is 7, the player looses. If it is equal to point, he wins. For all other outcome, the dice are rolled again and the process continue until the player wins or looses. Figure 1 illustrates the DLMC model that describes the game behavior. A possible run of the DLMC below is $r = S_0 S_5 S_5 S_7 S_7 ...$ The corresponding trace is $t = start$ $point6$ $point6$ won won ... and $Pr(t) = 1 \times \frac{5}{36} \times \frac{25}{36} \times \frac{5}{36} \times 1 \times ... = 0.0277$.

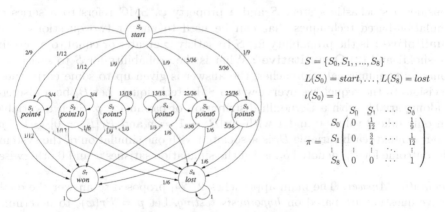

Fig. 1. A DLMC model for the Craps Gambling Game

2.2   Probabilistic Linear Time Temporal Logic (PLTL)

The linear time temporal logic (LTL) formula φ built over a set of atomic propositions AP is defined by the following syntax:

$$\varphi := true \mid p \mid \neg\varphi \mid \varphi_1 \wedge \varphi_2 \mid N\varphi \mid \varphi_1 U \varphi_2 \mid \varphi_1 U^i \varphi_2 \quad (p \in AP)$$

N, U and U^i are respectively the next, until and bounded until operators. Additional Boolean operators can be inferred from negation $\neg$ and conjunction $\wedge$. Moreover, temporal operators such as G (always) and F (eventually) are defined as $F\varphi \equiv true \ U\varphi$ and $G\varphi \equiv \neg F \neg \varphi$. The bounded fragment of LTL (denoted BLTL) restricts the use of the *until* operator U to its bounded variant U^i. LTL formula are interpreted on infinite traces $\sigma = \sigma_0 \sigma_1 \ldots \in \Sigma^\omega$ as follows:

- $\sigma \vDash true$; $\sigma \vDash p$ iff $p \in \sigma_0$; $\sigma \vDash \neg\varphi$ iff $\sigma \nvDash \varphi$;
- $\sigma \vDash \varphi_1 \wedge \varphi_2$ iff $\sigma \vDash \varphi_1$ and $\sigma \vDash \varphi_2$; $\sigma \vDash N\varphi$ iff $\sigma[1..] \vDash \varphi$;
- $\sigma \vDash \varphi_1 U \varphi_2$ iff $\exists k \geq 0$ s.t. $\sigma[k..] \vDash \varphi_2$ and $\forall j \in [0, k[$ holds $\sigma[j..] \vDash \varphi_1$;
- $\sigma \vDash \varphi_1 U^i \varphi_2$ iff $\exists k \in [0, i]$ s.t. $\sigma[k..] \vDash \varphi_2$ and $\forall j \in [0, k[$ holds $\sigma[j..] \vDash \varphi_1$.

Definition 3. *Given an LMC M and an LTL property φ, the probability for M to satisfy φ denoted by $Pr(M \vDash \varphi)$ is given by the measure $Pr_M\{\sigma \in Traces(M) \mid \sigma \models \varphi\}$. In addition, we say that M satisfies φ denoted by $M \vDash \varphi$ iff $\forall \sigma \in Traces(M), \sigma \vDash \varphi$.*

Example. Given the Craps Gambling Game model in Figure 1, one could check for instance the following probabilistic (B)LTL properties. The probability to eventually loose is $Pr(F \ lost) = 0.51$, and the probability to win in two steps is $Pr(true \ U^2 \ won) = 0.3$.

2.3   Statistical Model Checking (SMC)

Consider a stochastic system S and a property φ. SMC refers to a series of simulation-based techniques that can be used to answer two questions : (1) **Qualitative :** Is the probability for S to satisfy φ greater or equal to a certain threshold? and (2) **Quantitative :** What is the probability for S to satisfy φ? Contrary to numerical approaches, the answer is given up to some correctness precision. In the sequel, we overview two SMC techniques. Let B_i be a discrete random variable with a Bernoulli distribution of parameter p. Such a variable can only take 2 values 0 and 1 with $Pr[B_i = 1] = p$ and $Pr[B_i = 0] = 1 - p$. In our context, each variable B_i is associated with one simulation of the system. The outcome for B_i, denoted b_i, is 1 if the simulation satisfies φ and 0 otherwise.

Qualitative Answer. The main approaches [27,24] proposed to answer the qualitative question are based on *hypothesis testing*. Let $p = Pr(\varphi)$, to determine whether $p \geq \theta$, we can test $H : p \geq \theta$ against $K : p < \theta$. A test-based solution does not guarantee a correct result but it is possible to bound the probability of error. The *strength* of a test is determined by two parameters, α and β, such that the probability of accepting K (respectively, H) when H (respectively, K) holds, called a Type-I error (respectively, a Type-II error) is less or equal to α (respectively, β). A test has *ideal performance* if the probability of the Type-I error (respectively, Type-II error) is exactly α (respectively, β). However, these requirements make it impossible to ensure a low probability for both types of errors simultaneously (see [27] for details). A solution is to use an *indifference region* $[p_1, p_0]$ (given some δ, $p_1 = \theta - \delta$ and $p_0 = \theta + \delta$) and to test $H_0 : p \geq p_0$ against $H_1 : p \leq p_1$. We now sketch the Sequential Probability Ratio Test (SPRT). In this algorithm, one has to choose two values A and B $(A > B)$ that ensure that the strength of the test is respected. Let m be the number of observations that have been made so far. The test is based on the following quotient: $\frac{p_{1m}}{p_{0m}} = \prod_{i=1}^{m} \frac{Pr(B_i = b_i | p = p_1)}{Pr(B_i = b_i | p = p_0)} = \frac{p_1^{d_m}(1-p_1)^{m-d_m}}{p_0^{d_m}(1-p_0)^{m-d_m}}$, where $d_m = \sum_{i=1}^{m} b_i$. The idea is to accept H_0 if $\frac{p_{1m}}{p_{0m}} \geq A$, and H_1 if $\frac{p_{1m}}{p_{0m}} \leq B$. The algorithm computes $\frac{p_{1m}}{p_{0m}}$ for successive values of m until either H_0 or H_1 is satisfied. This has the advantage of minimizing the number of simulations.

Quantitative Answer. In [12,17] Peyronnet et al. propose an estimation procedure to compute the probability p for S to satisfy φ. Given a *precision* δ, Peyronnet's procedure, which we call PESTIM, computes a value for p' such that $|p' - p| \leq \delta$ with *confidence* $1 - \alpha$. The procedure is based on the *Chernoff-Hoeffding bound* [14]. Let m be the number of simulations of the system and $p' = (\sum_{i=1}^{m} b_i)/m$, then Chernoff-Hoeffding bound [14] gives $Pr(|p' - p| > \delta) < 2e^{-\frac{m\delta^2}{4}}$. As a consequence, if we take $m \geq \frac{4}{\delta^2} \log(\frac{2}{\alpha})$, then $Pr(|p' - p| \leq \delta) \geq 1 - \alpha$.

2.4   Probabilistic Learning

Learning probabilities distributions over traces is a hard problem [7] with potential applications in a wide range of domains, far beyond formal verification. Many methods have been proposed in the research literature and are continuously improved and challenged on learning research competitions [26]. The family of state merging techniques is one of the most successful nowadays. Intuitively, these techniques proceed by first constructing some large automata-based representation of the set of input traces and then progressively compacting them, by merging states, into a smaller automaton, while preserving as much as possible trace occurrence frequencies/probabilities. Different algorithms in this family can learn either DPFA models [6,9,8] or general PFA models [25,22,10].

In this paper, we use AAlergia [19] which is a state merging algorithm that exclusively learn deterministic models. Given a sample of traces, the algorithm proceeds in three steps. It first builds an intermediate representation, a *Frequency Prefix Tree Acceptor* (FPTA), which is a restricted form of DPFA that represents all the traces in the input sample and their corresponding frequencies. Seconds, based on a compatibility criterion parametrized by α_A (automatically computed, as explained in [19]), it iteratively merges states of the FPTA having the same labels and similar probability distributions until reaching a compact DPFA. Finally, it transforms the obtained DPFA into a DLMC model.

AAlergia is proven to converge to the correct model in the limit [19] if the input traces are generated, with random lengths, from an LMC model. A first consequence concerns verification on DLMCs and ensures that, in the limit (with sufficiently big sample set of traces), a given LTL property will hold on the original and the learned model with the same probability. This result is partially extended to LMC. That is, for arbitrary Markov chain models, the algorithm might not converge to the good model in general. In the case of input traces from a non-deterministic LMC model (which moreover, does not have an equivalent deterministic representation), as the sample size increases, AAlergia will build a sequence of DLMCs (usually, of increasing size) tending to approximate the original model. It is however proven that, in the limit, these learned DLMC models provide an increasingly better approximation for the initial (prefix) behavior, and hence preserve the satisfaction of bounded LTL properties.

3   Learning Abstract Models

The verification problem in the stochastic setting amounts to compute $Pr(M \models \varphi)$ for an LMC model M and an LTL property φ. Moreover, M might not be explicitly known, that is, it could be a black-box probabilistic system which can be executed arbitrarily many times in order to produce arbitrarily long traces.

Due to the reasons introduced earlier, we would like to avoid the verification of φ on the original model M. Instead, we would like to perform it on a smaller, abstract model $M^\sharp$ which preserves the satisfaction probability of φ, that is, $Pr(M \models \varphi) = Pr(M^\sharp \models \varphi)$. We propose hereafter a method to compute such an abstraction $M^\sharp$ by combining learning and a projection operator on traces parametrized by the property φ. The idea is based on the simple observation that, when checking a model against a property, only a subset of the atomic propositions is really relevant. In fact, only the atomic propositions mentioned explicitly in the property are useful while the others can be safely ignored.

$$M = \langle S, \tau, \pi, L \rangle \xrightarrow{\textit{(Execution)}} \textit{traces } T \xrightarrow{\textit{(Learning)}} M' \quad (M' \approx M)$$

$$\textit{(Relabeling)} \downarrow \qquad (\textit{Projection}_\varphi) \downarrow$$

$$M_a = \langle S, \tau, \pi, L_a \rangle \dashrightarrow \textit{(Execution)} \textit{traces } T_a \xrightarrow{\textit{(Learning)}} M^\sharp \quad (M^\sharp \approx M_a)$$

Fig. 2. Learning abstract models: approach overview

The proposed approach is depicted in Figure 2. It consists of initially generating a finite set of random finite traces T (with random lengths) from M (Sampling). In a second step, a projection is applied on traces T in order to restrict the atomic propositions to the ones needed for the evaluation of the property φ. The projection is detailed below. Third, the set of projected traces is used as an input to a learning algorithm. For experiments, we have used AAlergia [19], however, any other algorithm could be used. The output of the learning denoted $M^\sharp$ on Figure 2 will be used to evaluate the property of interest φ.

It is worthwhile to mention that, in our approach, the sampling step (which could be time consuming) is done only once, while the following steps could be repeated given different properties. Our approach ensures a significant time reduction with respect to applying SMC directly on the black-box system since it generally requires trace re-sampling every time. In [24], re-sampling is avoided but raises confidence level issues as discussed in Section 5. In addition, some SMC algorithms, besides their termination guarantee, might potentially need a huge number/length of traces depending on the required confidence level.

The soundness of this approach is however justified only under particular considerations. Note that a projection may potentially introduce non-deterministic behavior at the level of traces. We then need to distinguish several cases. The first one is when the traces are generated from a DLMC and the projection operation does not introduce any non-determinism. In this case any learning algorithm should work, for instance, AAlergia. Another case is when the traces are generated from an LMC and/or the projection introduces non-determinism. This case is divided into two sub-cases depending on the type of non-determinism. If the non-deterministic model has an equivalent deterministic one, then any learning algorithm can be used. Otherwise, one needs to use learning algorithms capable to learn non-deterministic models such as [25,10]. We detail the main steps of the approach and illustrate them on the running example. The correctness is formally established by Theorem 1.

3.1 Main Steps

Projection. The projection is defined on traces so as to reduce the number of labels and henceforth, later on, the number of states in the learned model. We introduce a first syntactic definition of a projection operator. It basically consists of ignoring the atomic propositions that are not relevant to the property under verification as formally defined below.

Definition 4. *Let* $V_\varphi \subseteq AP$ *called the support of* φ *be the set of atomic propositions occurring explicitly in* φ. *The projection* $\mathcal{P}_\varphi : \Sigma^* \to \Sigma^*$ *is defined as* $\mathcal{P}_\varphi(\sigma_0\sigma_1...\sigma_n) = \sigma'_0\sigma'_1...\sigma'_n$ *where* $\sigma'_i = \sigma_i \cap V_\varphi$ *for all* $i \in [0, n]$.

Example. Given a set T of traces generated from the Craps Gambling Game model in Figure 1 and the properties $\varphi_1 = F$ *won* and $\varphi_2 = F$ (*won* $\vee$ *lost*), Definition 4 is applied to compute the corresponding sets of projected traces T_{a_1} and T_{a_2}: $T = \{start\ won,\ start\ lost\ lost,\ start\ won\ won\ won\ won\ won\ won\ won\ won,\ start\ point5,\ start\ point10\ point10\ point10\ point10\ point10,\ start\ point9\ point9,\ ...\};\ T_{a_1} = \{\tau\ won,\ \tau\ \tau\ \tau,\ \tau\ won\ won\ won\ won\ won\ won\ won\ won,\ \tau\ \tau,\ \tau\ \tau\ \tau\ \tau\ \tau\ \tau,\ \tau\ \tau\ \tau,\ ...\};\ T_{a_2} = \{\tau\ won,\ \tau\ lost\ lost,\ \tau\ won\ won\ won\ won\ won\ won\ won\ won,\ \tau\ \tau,\ \tau\ \tau\ \tau\ \tau\ \tau\ \tau,\ \tau\ \tau\ \tau,\ ...\}$

Learning. We briefly illustrate the learning phase using AAlergia on the running example. Figure 3 shows three learned models of the Craps Gambling Game obtained using the set T of 5000 traces generated from the model in Figure 1. One can note, out of this figure, the important reduction of the obtained models sizes with respect to the original one. Figure 3a shows the model learned by AAlergia taking as input the set T_{a_2}, that is, with respect to property $\varphi_2 = F\ (won \lor lost)$. Figure 3b is obtained by applying AAlergia on the set T_{a_1}, that is, projected with respect to $\varphi_1 = F\ won$. Remark that this model is not equivalent but only an approximation of the original model in Figure 1. That is, in the latter there exists some non null probability to never reach the *won* state. Whereas, in the learned model the *won* state is reachable with probability 1. This approximation could however improve if a larger set of traces is used for learning as stated in the previous section. Finally, the third learned model shown in Figure 3c is equally obtained from T_{a_1} but when using an algorithm able to learn non-deterministic models such as the one proposed by Stolcke [25].

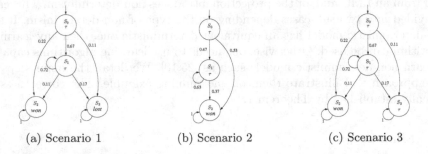

(a) Scenario 1   (b) Scenario 2   (c) Scenario 3

Fig. 3. Learned Markov Chains for Craps Gambling Game using 5000 traces

Statistical Model Checking. The last step evaluates the considered property on the learned model. Table 1 provides results of verifying the property $\varphi_1 = F\ won$ on the Craps Gambling Game models. It shows that the model in Figure 3a exhibits similar probability to the original Craps model, whereas the one in Figure 3b shows different ones. The reason is that the projection introduced a non-determinism in the input sample. In addition, it seems that in this case there is no equivalent deterministic model that could be learned by AAlergia.

Table 1. Verifying φ_1 on the original and the learned Craps Gambling Game models using SMC (PESTIM)

Models	$Pr(\varphi_1)$
Scenario 1 (Figure 3a)	0.485
Scenario 2 (Figure 3b)	1
Original Model (Figure 1)	0.493

3.2   Correctness

The correctness of our approach is formally stated as follows.

Theorem 1. *Let M be an LMC model and let φ be an LTL property. Let $M^\sharp$ be the learned model from a sample set of traces generated from M and projected according to φ as in definition 4. Then, in the limit, $M^\sharp$ is a correct abstraction for the verification of φ, that is $Pr(M \models \varphi) = Pr(M^\sharp \models \varphi)$ if either*

i) φ belongs to the bounded fragment BLTL and the learning algorithm converges for DLMC models, or

ii) the learning algorithm converges for arbitrary LMC models

Proof. First, let us remark that $M^\sharp$ is constructed as illustrated by the thick line in Figure 2. Let us moreover observe that any sample set of projected traces T_a obtained from M is equally obtained from M_a, that is, the "abstracted" version of M where only the labeling function has changed from L into L_a by taking $L_a(s) = L(s) \cap V_\varphi$, for all $s \in S$. In other words, the left-hand side of the diagram shown in Figure 2 commutes. Henceforth, M and M_a are identical with respect to the satisfaction of φ. The underlying set of runs and their associated probabilities are the same in M and M_a. As the atomic propositions occurring in φ are preserved by relabeling, it obviously holds that $Pr(M \models \varphi) = Pr(M_a \models \varphi)$.

Moreover, learning from the sample set T_a leads eventually to M_a. That is, under particular restrictions specific to the learning algorithms and limit conditions, the learned model $M^\sharp$ will be an equivalent representation of M_a, that is, $M^\sharp \approx M_a$. We distinguish two cases depending on the learning algorithm:

i) In the case of deterministic models learning (e.g., AAlergia), the learned model $M^\sharp$ is provable equivalent only for a deterministic input model M_a. But, in addition, for the general case, this models is also providing good approximations for the initial (prefix) behavior of M_a and hence preserve the probability of satisfaction for properties in the BLTL fragment (see Theorem 3 in [19]). Thereof, by using AAlergia or a similar learning algorithm, it holds that $Pr(M_a \models \varphi) = Pr(M^\sharp \models \varphi)$ whenever φ belongs to BLTL.

ii) In the general case of non-deterministic models learning, it is guaranteed in the limit that $M_a \approx M^\sharp$. Thereof, one can safely conclude that $Pr(M_a \models \varphi) = Pr(M'_a \models \varphi)$ for any φ.

Henceforth, in both cases it holds $Pr(M \models \varphi) = Pr(M^\sharp \models \varphi)$.   □

4   Case Study: Herman's Self Stabilizing Protocol

To experiment our approach, we use the Herman's Self Stabilizing Protocol [13]. The goal of such a protocol is to perform fault tolerance by enabling a distributed system starting in an arbitrary state to converge to a legitimate one in a finite time. Given a token ring network where the processes are indexed from 1 to N (N must be odd) and ordered anticlockwise, the algorithm operates synchronously.

Processes can possess tokens, which circulate in one direction around the ring. At every step, each process with a token tosses a coin. Depending on the outcome, it decides to keep it or to pass it on to the right neighbor. When a process holds two tokens, they are eliminated. Thus, the number of tokens remains odd. The network is said to be stable if exactly one process has a token. Once such a configuration is reached, the token circulate forever, fairly, around the ring.

We apply our abstraction approach to several configurations ($N = 7, 11, 19, 21$) of the protocol. Note that as the number of processes increases, the state space becomes very large and makes the verification quite heavy even using simulation-based methods such as SMC. We use AAlergia for learning and show that we are able to reduce the state space while still accurate for several properties. We consider the bounded properties $\varphi^L = Pr(true\ U^L\ stable)$ and $\psi_N^L = Pr(tokenN\ U^L\ stable)$ where N is the number of processes in the network and L is a bound. The first property states that the protocol reaches the *stable* state in L steps whatever the intermediate ones are. The second specifies in addition that the protocol directly moves from N tokens to the *stable* state (1 token), that is, all the states before *stable* are *tokenN*. We first apply the projection on the traces generated from the different configurations using the properties supports $V_{\varphi^L} = \{stable\}$ and $V_{\psi_N^L} = \{tokenN, stable\}$. Then, we use AAlergia to learn the corresponding models shown in Figure 4. The models for $N = 19, 21$ are similar to $N = 11$ and are omitted for space constraints.

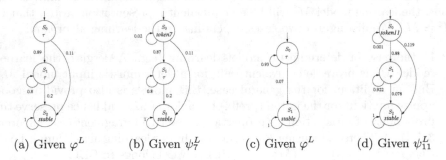

(a) Given φ^L (b) Given ψ_7^L (c) Given φ^L (d) Given ψ_{11}^L

Fig. 4. Learned (AAlergia) Herman's models for $N = 7$ (a,b) and $N = 11$ (c,d)

Table 2 summarizes the learned models characteristics, AAlergia performance when combined with projection, and properties verification results using PRISM [16]. In this table, the first two columns list the used configurations and their corresponding sizes. The third column depicts the properties under consideration. Information about the learning process are then detailed: α_A is the AAlergia compatibility criterion parameter, *Size* is the learned model size, and *Time* is the learning time in seconds. The last part concerns the comparison of the original and the learned model in term of properties probabilities and verification time. The verification part relies on the PESTIM algorithm which is parametrized by two confidence parameters δ and α.

The results in Table 2 point out two important facts. The first is the drastic reduction of the learned models sizes and SMC time compared to the original Herman's Self Stabilizing protocol. Figure 5 summarizes the SMC time of φ^{10} for the learned and the original models when increasing N. The figure and the table allow us to see how big is the SMC time of the original model with respect to the learned one. Figure 5 shows in addition the learning time which is also far below the SMC time of the original model for $N > 11$. Moreover, one can see that the time to learn plus SMC the learned model is below the SMC time of the original model for $N > 11$ which confirms the pertinence of our approach for big models. For instance, for $N = 19$, the learning took about 83 seconds and SMC the learned model about 0.307 seconds while SMC the original one took about 13 hours. Furthermore, since the sampling step is done only once in our approach, its time impact is reduced when considering many properties. The second fact is that, besides this reduction, the models are quite accurate in terms of probability measures as clearly shown in the table and Figures 6a,6b and 6c. These figures show the verification results of φ^L (for different L) on the original protocol versus the learned model for all the considered configurations.

Table 2. Abstraction and verification results of φ^{10} and ψ^{30} using PESTIM

	Size	Prop.	Learning			SMC				
			α_A	Size	Time(s)	δ,α	Learned Model		Original Model	
							Pr	Time(s)	Pr	Time
$N=7$	2^7	φ^{10}	$[2^{-9},2^0]$	3	69.70	$10^{-2},10^{-1}$	0.874	0.180	0.874	3.40 s
						$10^{-2},10^{-2}$	0.880	0.320	0.873	5.44 s
		ψ^{30}	$[2^{-6},2^6]$	3	45.98	$10^{-2},10^{-1}$	0.112	0.050	0.112	0.93 s
						$10^{-2},10^{-2}$	0.109	0.111	0.111	1.51 s
		ϕ	$[2^{-8},2^0]$	4	167.50	$-$	0.160	0.005	0.167	0.02 s
						Sample Size = 5000				
$N=11$	2^{11}	φ^{10}	$[2^{-4},2^6]$	2	54.67	$10^{-2},10^{-1}$	0.517	0.250	0.543	33.1 s
						$10^{-2},10^{-2}$	0.518	0.440	0.543	58.3 s
		ψ^{30}	$[2^{-6},2^6]$	3	60.22	$10^{-2},10^{-1}$	0.011	0.039	0.012	12.1 s
						$10^{-2},10^{-2}$	0.012	0.070	0.011	21.7 s
						Sample Size = 5000				
$N=19$	2^{19}	φ^{10}	$[2^{-4},2^6]$	2	82.95	$10^{-2},10^{-1}$	0.197	0.180	0.148	8.1 h
						$10^{-2},10^{-2}$	0.191	0.307	0.151	13.3 h
		ψ^{30}	$[2^{-6},2^6]$	3	172.58	$10^{-2},10^{-1}$	0.000	0.040	0.0001	5.7 h
						$10^{-2},10^{-2}$	0.000	0.074	0.0008	10.1 h
						Sample Size = 10000				
$N=21$	2^{21}	φ^{10}	$[2^{-10},2^0]$	3	253.71	$10^{-2},10^{-1}$	0.169	0.355	0.172	34 h
						$10^{-2},10^{-2}$	0.163	0.616	$-$	>5 d
						Sample Size = 10000				

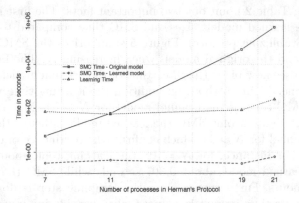

Fig. 5. PESTIM $(10^{-2}, 10^{-2})$ time: original vs. learned Herman's model for φ^{10}

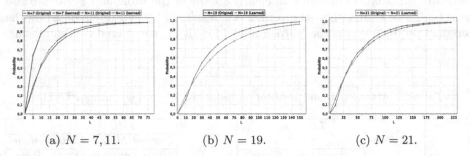

(a) $N = 7, 11$.   (b) $N = 19$.   (c) $N = 21$.

Fig. 6. φ^L verification results using PESTIM for $N = 7, 11, 19$, and 21. The results for $N = 21$ are obtained with PESTIM $(5.10^{-2}, 5.10^{-3})$.

Table 3. SPRT $(10^{-3}, 10^{-3})$ of ψ_N^L on the original and the learned models

	L	Original Model			Learned Model		
		θ	Traces	Time(s)	θ	Traces	Time(s)
	$L = 1$	$[0.109, 0.110[$	622018	25.643	$[0.107, 0.108[$	588357	1.363
$N = 7$	$L = 30$	$[0.111, 0.112[$	622834	25.749	$[0.108, 0.109[$	533885	1.282
	$L = 65$	$[0.111, 0.112[$	651434	26.756	$[0.108, 0.109[$	476883	1.118
	$L = 1$	$[0.011, 0.012[$	147178	85.135	$[0.012, 0.013[$	163600	0.411
$N = 11$	$L = 30$	$[0.011, 0.012[$	105362	60.206	$[0.013, 0.014[$	098493	0.262
	$L = 65$	$[0.011, 0.012[$	137469	80.648	$[0.013, 0.014[$	248300	0.564

In addition to PESTIM, we used the SPRT technique to validate with more confidence the results of the property $\psi_N^L = Pr(tokenN \ U^L \ token1) >= \theta$ for $N = 7, 11$. We fixed the confidence parameters to $\alpha = \beta = 10^{-3}$ and $\delta = 10^{-3}$. Table 3 shows the verification results and performance (verification time and number of traces) for different L values. Note that for this experiment, we used the same model learned previously. In this table, θ is the probability range to satisfy ψ_N^L, *Traces* is the number of traces used by SPRT, and *Time* is the SMC time. This table confirms the observation made in the previous experiment, that

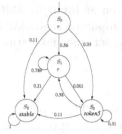

Fig. 7. Learned Herman's protocol model ($N = 7$) using AAlergia given ϕ

is, the reduction of the SMC time when using the abstract model while the probability estimation still accurate.

We did an additional property $\phi = Pr(X(token5\ U\ stable))$ for Herman's protocol with $N = 7$ in order to investigate the usability of this instance of the approach for unbounded properties (all the considered properties so far where bounded). The corresponding learned model is shown in Figure 7 and the verification results are depicted in Table 2. The obtained results show that the probability of satisfying ϕ is almost the same for the learned and the original protocol. This is possible (to check unbounded LTL properties on a learned model with a good accuracy) because, in this case, there exist an equivalent deterministic model to the original Herman's protocol that AAlergia succeed to learn. Since ϕ is unbounded, we rely on classical probabilistic model checking using PRISM.

5 Related Work

We first review some applications of learning techniques for systems verification. For more details, we refer the reader to the literature survey from Martin Leucker [18]. Pena et al. propose to use learning for the purpose of state reduction in incompletely specified finite state machines [21]. Based on Angluin's L* algorithm, which computes the minimal DFA in polynomial time, the authors propose a learning technique that produces an equivalent, reduced finite state machine. In contrast, our work relies on the AAlergia algorithm and assumes that the input data is generated from an LMC. Peled et al. propose to combine model checking, testing, and learning to automatically check properties of systems whose structure is unknown [20]. This paper motivates black-box checking where a user performs acceptance tests and does not have access to the design, nor to the internal structure of the system. The authors, however, conclude that the complexity of their algorithms could be reduced if an abstract model of the system would be available. Additionally, the authors pointed out the need to take into account the property of interest to tackle verification complexity.

Among the works aiming to improve SMC applicability, we mention Sen et al. SMC algorithm for black-box systems [24]. In this work, systems are assumed to be uncontrolled, that is, traces can not be generated on demand. Hence, the approach cannot guarantee a correct answer within required error bounds. It computes instead a p-value as a confidence measure. While our approach is not making such an assumption, it also uses a pre-generated set of traces to learn an abstract model which is given as input to SMC. In contrast, [24] uses the pre-generated traces as direct input to their SMC algorithm. This raises the confidence issue but makes it faster since no learning is performed.

6   Conclusion

Reducing the SMC time of a given LTL property on a large stochastic system is the primary benefit of our abstraction approach. This gain is achieved through the combined use of projection on traces and learning. Projection is performed by considering the support of the property of interest, that is, the set of symbols explicitly appearing in that property. The approach could be instantiated with any learning algorithm. Although, this must respect the conditions discussed earlier to produce accurate models preserving the probability of the property under verification. Experimental results show that (1) verifying the properties of interest on the abstract model is faster than the original one, and that (2) the estimation of the probability of satisfying these properties is accurate with respect to the one obtained on the original system.

The proposed projection definition is currently quite simple. It allowed us to instantiate our methodology and to implement it for validation. As future work, we plan to improve it such that to obtain coarser abstractions, yet preserving the probability of the underlying property (as opposed to a class of properties currently). This could be potentially achieved by taking into account the LTL operators semantics. We shall also apply the approach to other real-life systems and consider using other algorithms able to learn non-deterministic models. Furthermore, our proposed approach is applicable to discrete stochastic systems. An interesting direction to investigate is its extension to continuous systems, such as continuous time Markov chains [23] or probabilistic timed automata.

References

1. Baier, C., Katoen, J.-P.: Principles of Model Checking (Representation and Mind Series). The MIT Press (2008)
2. Basu, A., Bensalem, S., Bozga, M., Bourgos, P., Maheshwari, M., Sifakis, J.: Component assemblies in the context of manycore. In: Beckert, B., Bonsangue, M.M. (eds.) FMCO 2011. LNCS, vol. 7542, pp. 314–333. Springer, Heidelberg (2012)
3. Bensalem, S., Bozga, M., Delahaye, B., Jegourel, C., Legay, A., Nouri, A.: Statistical Model Checking QoS Properties of Systems with SBIP. In: Margaria, T., Steffen, B. (eds.) ISoLA 2012, Part I. LNCS, vol. 7609, pp. 327–341. Springer, Heidelberg (2012)
4. Legay, A., Delahaye, B., Bensalem, S.: Statistical model checking: An overview. In: Barringer, H., Falcone, Y., Finkbeiner, B., Havelund, K., Lee, I., Pace, G., Roşu, G., Sokolsky, O., Tillmann, N. (eds.) RV 2010. LNCS, vol. 6418, pp. 122–135. Springer, Heidelberg (2010)
5. Bulychev, P.E., David, A., Larsen, K.G., Mikucionis, M., Poulsen, D.B., Legay, A., Wang, Z.: Uppaal-smc: Statistical model checking for priced timed automata. In: QAPL 2012, pp. 1–16 (2012)
6. Carrasco, R.C., Oncina, J.: Learning Stochastic Regular Grammars by Means of a State Merging Method. In: Carrasco, R.C., Oncina, J. (eds.) ICGI 1994. LNCS, vol. 862, pp. 139–152. Springer, Heidelberg (1994)

7. de la Higuera, C.: Grammatical Inference: Learning Automata and Grammars. Cambridge University Press, New York (2010)
8. de la Higuera, C., Oncina, J.: Identification with Probability One of Stochastic Deterministic Linear Languages. In: Gavaldá, R., Jantke, K.P., Takimoto, E. (eds.) ALT 2003. LNCS (LNAI), vol. 2842, pp. 247–258. Springer, Heidelberg (2003)
9. de la Higuera, C., Oncina, J., Vidal, E.: Identification of DFA: data-dependent vs data-independent algorithms. In: Miclet, L., de la Higuera, C. (eds.) ICGI 1996. LNCS, vol. 1147, pp. 313–325. Springer, Heidelberg (1996)
10. Denis, F., Esposito, Y., Habrard, A.: Learning rational stochastic languages. In: Lugosi, G., Simon, H.U. (eds.) COLT 2006. LNCS (LNAI), vol. 4005, pp. 274–288. Springer, Heidelberg (2006)
11. Grosu, R., Smolka, S.A.: Monte carlo model checking. In: Halbwachs, N., Zuck, L.D. (eds.) TACAS 2005. LNCS, vol. 3440, pp. 271–286. Springer, Heidelberg (2005)
12. Hérault, T., Lassaigne, R., Magniette, F., Peyronnet, S.: Approximate Probabilistic Model Checking. In: Steffen, B., Levi, G. (eds.) VMCAI 2004. LNCS, vol. 2937, pp. 73–84. Springer, Heidelberg (2004)
13. Herman, T.: Probabilistic self-stabilization. Information Processing Letters 35(2), 63–67 (1990)
14. Hoeffding, W.: Probability inequalities. Journal of the American Statistical Association 58, 13–30 (1963)
15. Jegourel, C., Legay, A., Sedwards, S.: A platform for high performance statistical model checking - plasma. In: Flanagan, C., König, B. (eds.) TACAS 2012. LNCS, vol. 7214, pp. 498–503. Springer, Heidelberg (2012)
16. Kwiatkowska, M., Norman, G., Parker, D.: Prism 4.0: verification of probabilistic real-time systems. In: Gopalakrishnan, G., Qadeer, S. (eds.) CAV 2011. LNCS, vol. 6806, pp. 585–591. Springer, Heidelberg (2011)
17. Laplante, S., Lassaigne, R., Magniez, F., Peyronnet, S., de Rougemont, M.: Probabilistic abstraction for model checking: An approach based on property testing. ACM TCS 8(4) (2007)
18. Leucker, M.: Learning Meets Verification. In: de Boer, F.S., Bonsangue, M.M., Graf, S., de Roever, W.-P. (eds.) FMCO 2006. LNCS, vol. 4709, pp. 127–151. Springer, Heidelberg (2007)
19. Mao, H., Chen, Y., Jaeger, M., Nielsen, T.D., Larsen, K.G., Nielsen, B.: Learning Probabilistic Automata for Model Checking. In: QEST, pp. 111–120 (2011)
20. Peled, D., Vardi, M.Y., Yannakakis, M.: Black box checking. J. Autom. Lang. Comb. 7(2), 225–246 (2001)
21. Pena, J.M., Oliveira, A.L.: A new algorithm for exact reduction of incompletely specified finite state machines. TCAD 18(11), 1619–1632 (2006)
22. Ron, D., Singer, Y., Tishby, N.: On the learnability and usage of acyclic probabilistic finite automata. In: COLT, pp. 31–40 (1995)
23. Sen, K., Viswanathan, M., Agha, G.: Learning continuous time markov chains from sample executions. In: QEST, pp. 146–155 (2004)
24. Sen, K., Viswanathan, M., Agha, G.: Statistical model checking of black-box probabilistic systems. In: Alur, R., Peled, D.A. (eds.) CAV 2004. LNCS, vol. 3114, pp. 202–215. Springer, Heidelberg (2004)
25. Stolcke, A.: Bayesian Learning of Probabilistic Language Models. PhD thesis, Berkeley, CA, USA, UMI Order No. GAX95-29515 (1994)
26. Verwer, S., Eyraud, R., de la Higuera, C.: Results of the pautomac probabilistic automaton learning competition. In: ICGI, pp. 243–248 (2012)
27. Younes, H.L.S.: Verification and Planning for Stochastic Processes with Asynchronous Events. PhD thesis, Carnegie Mellon (2005)

Author Index